SOUTH OF PICO

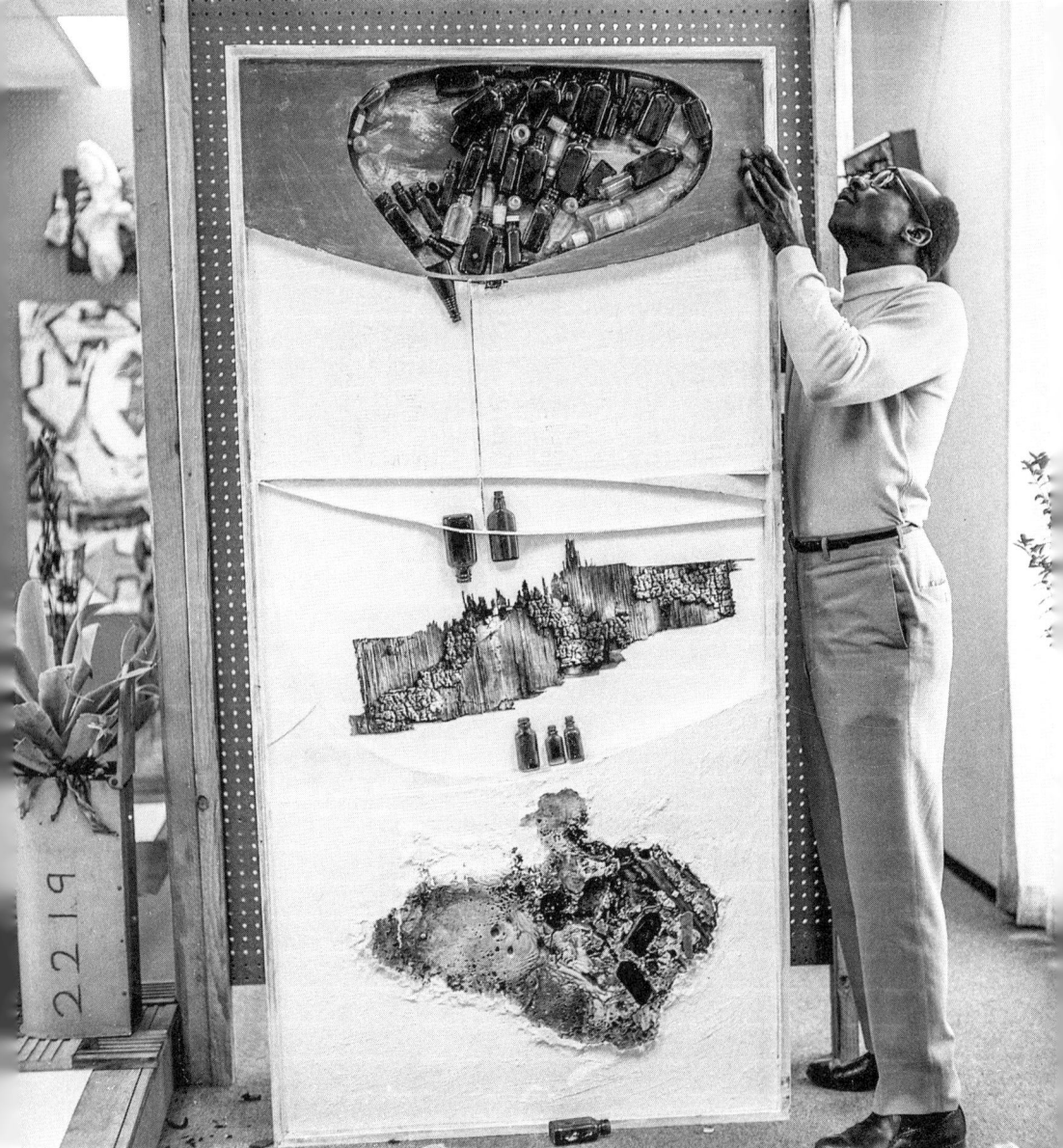

KELLIE JONES

SOUTH OF PICO

African American Artists in
Los Angeles in the 1960s and 1970s

Duke University Press · Durham and London · 2017

© 2017 Duke University Press
All rights reserved
Printed in the United States of America on acid-free paper ∞
Designed by Heather Hensley
Typeset in Minion Pro and Helvetica Neue by Tseng Information Systems, Inc.

Library of Congress Cataloging-in-Publication Data
Names: Jones, Kellie, [date] author.
Title: South of Pico : African American artists in Los Angeles in the 1960s and 1970s / Kellie Jones.
Description: Durham : Duke University Press, 2017. | Includes bibliographical references and index.
Identifiers: LCCN 2016040906 (print) | LCCN 2016041331 (ebook)
ISBN 9780822361459 (hardcover : alk. paper)
ISBN 9780822361640 (pbk. : alk. paper)
ISBN 9780822374169 (e-book)
Subjects: LCSH: African American artists—California—Los Angeles. | African American arts—Social aspects—California—Los Angeles—History—20th century. | Artists and community—California—Los Angeles—History—20th century. | African Americans—California—Los Angeles—History—20th century. | Los Angeles (Calif.)—Race relations—History—20th century.
Classification: LCC N6538.N5 J668 2017 (print) | LCC N6538.N5 (ebook) | DDC 700.89/96073—dc23
LC record available at https://lccn.loc.gov/2016040906

COVER ART: Senga Nengudi setting up for a performance with *R.S.V.P. #X* in her Los Angeles studio, 1976. Just Above Midtown Gallery Archives. Courtesy the artist and Thomas Erben Gallery, New York.

FRONTISPIECE: Noah Purifoy installing *66 Signs of Neon* exhibition at University of Southern California, Los Angeles, c. 1966. Photograph by Harry Drinkwater. Courtesy Jafiel Drinkwater.

Duke University Press gratefully acknowledges the support of the Columbia University Institute for Research in African American Studies, and Department of Art History and Archaeology, which provided funds toward the publication of this book.

Publication of this book has been aided by a grant from the Wyeth Foundation for American Art Publication Fund of the College Art Association.

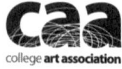

FOR GUTHRIE
whose name means freedom

CONTENTS

ix	List of Illustrations
xiii	Acknowledgments

INTRODUCTION
1   **South of Pico:** Migration, Art, and Black Los Angeles

CHAPTER ONE
23   **Emerge:** Putting Southern California on the Art World Map

CHAPTER TWO
67   **Claim:** Assemblage and Self-Possession

CHAPTER THREE
139   **Organize:** Building an Exhibitionary Complex

CHAPTER FOUR
185   **In Motion:** The Performative Impulse

CONCLUSION
265   **Noshun:** Black Los Angeles and the Global Imagination

277	Notes
359	Selected Bibliography
379	Index

ILLUSTRATIONS

FIGURES

I.1 Curator Beate Inaya and artists Daniel LaRue Johnson, Charles White, and Betye Saar at the Negro and Creative Arts Exhibit, August 12, 1962   7
I.2 Group exhibition at the Altadena, CA, home of Alvin and Jeffalyn Johnson, June 1962   10
I.3 David Hammons, *Hair and Wire, Venice Beach, California, 1977*; photograph by Bruce Talamon   19
I.4 Adam Avila, *Maren Hassinger in front of* Twelve Trees, 1978   21
1.1 Sidney Poitier, Charles White, Ivan Dixon, and Tony Curtis on the set of the film *The Defiant Ones*, 1958   26
1.2 Charles White, *Birmingham Totem*, 1964   34
1.3 Charles White, *Wanted Poster #6*, 1969   47
1.4 Betye Saar (née Brown) and Curtis Tann in the office space of their decorative arts business, Brown and Tann, 1951   52
1.5 Betye Saar, *House of Tarot*, 1966   54
1.6 Melvin Edwards, *Installation view of* Five Younger Los Angeles Artists, *1965*, 1965   58
1.7 Melvin Edwards, *The Fourth Circle*, 1966   59
1.8 Melvin Edwards, *Mojo for 1404*, 1964   61
1.9 Melvin Edwards, *August the Squared Fire*, 1965   63
2.1 Noah Purifoy's interior design work featuring two of his collages, 1950s   74
2.2 Operation Teacup (Tower Easter Week Clean-Up) at Watts Towers Art Center and 107th Street, 1965   75
2.3 Art class with Judson Powell at Watts Towers Art Center, 1960s   77
2.4 Noah Purifoy and Judson Powell at *66 Signs of Neon* exhibition, 1966   80
2.5 Noah Purifoy's *Sir Watts* featured on a poster for the Watts Summer Festival, 1970   83

2.6   Noah Purifoy, *Watts Remains*, c. 1965/1966   85
2.7   Robert A. Nakamura, *John Outterbridge in his studio*, 1970   94
2.8   Poster for Compton Communicative Arts Academy, 1970s   96
2.9   John Outterbridge, *Jive Ass Bird, Rag Man* series, 1971   102
2.10   Betye Saar, *Let Me Entertain You*, 1972   111
2.11   Betye Saar, *The Liberation of Aunt Jemima*, 1972   112
2.12   Robert A. Nakamura, *Betye Saar in her studio*, 1970   117
2.13   Flyer for *Black Mirror* exhibition at Womanspace Gallery, 1973   121
2.14   Sheila Levrant de Bretteville and Betye Saar, *Chrysalis*, no. 4, 1977   122
3.1   Brockman Gallery at 4334 Degnan Boulevard in the Leimert Park neighborhood, Los Angeles, 1970s   145
3.2   Ruth Waddy at a Brockman Gallery opening, 1970s   148
3.3   Alonzo Davis with his work outside Brockman Gallery, 1970s   149
3.4   Dale Brockman Davis in his studio next door to Brockman Gallery, 1970s   149
3.5   Bob Heliton, *Timothy Washington with one of his pieces outside Gallery 32*, 1969   153
3.6   Emory Douglas, *Poster for Emory Douglas exhibition at Gallery 32*, 1969   155
3.7   Announcement for Suzanne Jackson's solo exhibition at Ankrum Gallery, 1974   157
3.8   Exhibition catalogue for *Los Angeles, 1972: A Panorama of Black Artists* at the Los Angeles County Museum of Art, 1972   165
3.9   Gary Friedman, *Cecil Fergerson, at home with his collection*, date unknown   167
3.10   David C. Driskell, Alonzo Davis, and Mayor Tom Bradley, probably at the exhibition *Two Centuries of Black American Art*, curated by Driskell, 1976   171
3.11   *Black Art: An International Quarterly* 1, no. 1, 1976   176
3.12   Advertisement in *Black Art: An International Quarterly* 1, no. 1, 1976   177
4.1   Senga Nengudi, *Swing Low*, 1977   188
4.2   Ken Peterson, *Senga Nengudi with R.S.V.P. #X in her Los Angeles studio*, 1976   194
4.3   Harmon Outlaw, *Maren Hassinger performing in a Senga Nengudi work*, 1977   195
4.4   Senga Nengudi, *Costume Study for Mesh Mirage*, 1977; photograph by Adam Avila   196
4.5   Roderick "Quaku" Young, *Performance space for Senga Nengudi's* Ceremony for Freeway Fets, 1978   198
4.6   Roderick "Quaku" Young, *Performance band for Senga Nengudi's* Ceremony for Freeway Fets, 1978   198

4.7 Roderick "Quaku" Young, *RoHo in the performance band for Senga Nengudi's* Ceremony for Freeway Fets, 1978   199

4.8 Roderick "Quaku" Young, *Senga Nengudi and David Hammons performing in Senga Nengudi's* Ceremony for Freeway Fets, 1978   200

4.9 Roderick "Quaku" Young, *Senga Nengudi and David Hammons performing in Senga Nengudi's* Ceremony for Freeway Fets, 1978   200

4.10 Photographer unknown, *Atsuko Tanaka wearing the Electric Dress suspended from the ceiling at the Second Gutai Art Exhibition at Ohara Hall in Tokyo*, 1956   209

4.11 Houston Conwill petrigraph works on exhibit at ARCO Center for Visual Art, 1970s   215

4.12 Brochure for Houston Conwill's exhibition *JuJu* at Samella Lewis's space, The Gallery, with text by Betye Saar, 1976   218

4.13 Announcement for David Hammons exhibition at Brockman Gallery, 1970   225

4.14 David Hammons, *Three Spades*, 1971   231

4.15 Chris Burden, *Dead Man*, 1972   235

4.16 Asco, *Decoy Gang War Victim*, 1974   237

4.17 Maren Hassinger, *Beach*, 1980   245

4.18 Maren Hassinger, *Whirling, 10 Elements in a Circle*, 1978   256

4.19 Flyer from *Flying* performance, 1982   258

4.20 Maren Hassinger and Senga Nengudi, *Flying*, 1982   259

4.21 Maren Hassinger and Senga Nengudi, *Flying*, 1982   259

4.22 Maren Hassinger and Senga Nengudi, *Flying*, 1982   261

PLATES (FOLLOWING PAGE 144)

1. Charles White, *General Moses (Harriet Tubman)*, 1965
2. David Hammons, *Boy with Flag*, 1968
3. *For Love of Ivy* (film still), 1968
4. Charles White, *Eartha Kitt* from *Anna Lucasta*, 1958
5. Charles White, *Harriet*, 1972
6. Betye Saar, *To Catch a Unicorn*, 1960
7. Noah Purifoy, *Unknown*, 1967
8. Watts Summer Festival, 1969
9. Walter Hopps and Noah Purifoy, probably at the Watts Summer Festival, 1969
10. John Outterbridge, *Let Us Tie Down Loose Ends, Containment* series, c. 1968
11. John Outterbridge, *Case in Point, Rag Man* series, 1970
12. Betye Saar, *Black Girl's Window*, 1969
13. Betye Saar, *Mti*, 1973

14 Betye Saar, *Record for Hattie*, 1975
15 William Pajaud, *Holy Family*, 1965
16 Alonzo Davis, *Pyramid #7* from the *Mental Space* series, 1978–79
17 Dale Brockman Davis, *Viet Nam War Games*, 1969
18 Poster for *The Sapphire Show* at Gallery 32, 1970
19 Suzanne Jackson, *Animal*, 1978
20 Samella S. Lewis and Ruth G. Waddy, *Black Artists on Art*, vols. 1 (1969) and 2 (1971)
21 Samella S. Lewis, *Art: African American* (1978)
22 Suzanne Jackson, *Sundown*, 1974
23 Roderick "Quaku" Young, *Senga Nengudi setting up for her performance Ceremony for Freeway Fets*, 1978
24 Roderick "Quaku" Young, *Senga Nengudi*, Ceremony for Freeway Fets, 1978
25 Houston Conwill, *JuJu*, 1975–78
26 David Hammons, *Murder Mystery (Spade Run Over by a Volkswagen)*, 1972
27 David Hammons, *Murder Mystery (Spade Run Over by a Volkswagen)*, 1972
28 David Hammons, *Bird*, 1973
29 Maren Hassinger, *Forest*, 1980
30 Adam Avila, *Installation view of Maren Hassinger exhibition at ARCO Center for Visual Art*, Los Angeles, 1976
31 Maren Hassinger (*left*) and Senga Nengudi (*right*), *Flying*, 1982
32 Sanford Biggers, Constellation II, *Installation and Performance at Memorial Hall, Harvard University*, 2009

ACKNOWLEDGMENTS

Working on this project over the years has only heightened my appreciation for the treasure troves housed in libraries and archives all over the world. I am forever thankful to Columbia University Libraries, in particular Avery Architectural and Fine Arts Library; libraries at the University of Pennsylvania; Yale University Art and Architecture Library; the Getty Research Institute, Research Library, Special Collections and Visual Resources; New York University, Bobst Library and The Fales Library & Special Collections; Archives of American Art, Smithsonian Institution; New York Public Library, Schomburg Center for Research in Black Culture, and the librarian Sharon Howard; Manuscripts, Archives, and Rare Book Library, Emory University, and Randall Burkett, curator; the libraries at the Whitney Museum of American Art, the Museum of Modern Art, New York, and the Balch Art Research Library, Los Angeles County Museum of Art; and especially University of California, Los Angeles, Department of Special Collections, Charles E. Young Research Library, and particularly the librarians Jeffrey Rankin and Octavio Olvera. Interview excerpts with Kinshasha Holman Conwill, Alonzo Davis, Cecil Fergerson, Marvin Harden, Suzanne Jackson, Samella Lewis, John Outterbridge, William Pajaud, Noah Purifoy, John Riddle, Betye Saar, Curtis Tann, and Ruth Waddy were conducted by the UCLA Oral History Program, Department of Special Collections, Charles E. Young Research Library. I thank them for their assistance.

My writing benefited from several residencies and fellowships: from the Rockefeller Foundation, Bellagio Study and Conference Center, Italy; Terra Foundation for American Art in Europe, Giverny, France; McColl Center for Visual Art, Charlotte, NC; and Columbia University. Thanks to all for believing in this book.

While I have lectured on this project in academic institutions around the country, one of the largest engagements with it came from the five years (2008–13) when I served as curator of the exhibition *Now Dig This! Art and Black Los Angeles, 1960–1980* at the Hammer Museum, UCLA. The show was based on this book in progress, but the book itself also benefited from further involvements with artists, the recovery of individual archives, and the photographing of works that were thought lost or were unknown. I have been fortunate to be in dialogue with most of the artists in the exhibition, and I will always be grateful for their generosity. Dale Brockman Davis and Alonzo Davis and C. Ian White deserve special mention, along with Samella Lewis and Senga Nengudi, whose predilections for the archive have contributed to this project in many ways. I regret that Houston Conwill and William Pajaud along with curators Cecil Fergerson and Karen Higa are not here to see this book come to fruition.

At the Hammer I would like to thank visionary director Ann Philbin along with the myriad museum staff who contributed to such a well-received exhibition. Special thanks goes to Gary Garrels, then senior curator at the Hammer, who after our chance meeting put the exhibition in motion. Naima Keith was the curatorial research assistant for *Now Dig This!* Her insight, focus, and intimate knowledge of things Los Angeles contributed to the show's power. She developed the title for the exhibition and schooled me in the nuances of "south of Pico," which led me to the title for this book. *Now Dig This!* was part of the Getty Foundation's Pacific Standard Time initiative—a wide-ranging, regionwide undertaking documenting Southern California's contributions to artistic movements in the postwar period. I enjoyed the dialogue with other wonderful projects highlighting Art West.

Now Dig This! traveled to MoMA PS1 in New York and the Williams College Museum of Art in Williamstown, MA. I would like to thank all the wonderful people at each venue for making it look stellar. Another highlight was having a symposium dedicated to the exhibition at the Museum of Modern Art. *Now Dig This!* was an award-winning exhibition: it received accolades from the International Association of Art Critics U.S. (Best Thematic Exhibition in the U.S. for 2012–13); and *Artforum* celebrated it as one of the best exhibitions of 2011 and 2012.

I am thrilled to have the opportunity to continue to work with Duke University Press. Its institutional culture around authors, "the visual," and the art of the African Diaspora is unparalleled, and I am so pleased that *South of Pico* has found a home here. Much appreciation goes to my editor, Ken Wissoker, who has created a welcoming and supportive environment; I cherish his patience and friendship. Thanks also to Jade Brooks for graciously keeping me attuned to details and deadlines. Many entities have been generous with images and permissions; special thanks goes to the African American Performance Art Archive and John Bowles at the University of North Carolina at Chapel Hill; Archives of American Art, Smithsonian Institution, and Wendy Hurlock Baker and Elizabeth Willson Christopher; Brockman Gallery Archives; Thomas Erben Gallery; Emily Gonzalez at the Hammer Museum; Alexander Gray Associates; Maren Hassinger; Just Above Midtown Gallery Archives and Linda Goode Bryant; Nasher Sculpture Center and Catherine Craft; Michael Rosenfeld Gallery; Jack Tilton, Connie Rogers Tilton, and Lauren Hudgins at Tilton Gallery; Charles White Archives; and White Cube. At Columbia University, the Institute for Research in African American Studies and the Department of Art History and Archaeology have also provided for the book's visual production. Gabe Rodriguez and Emily Shaw in the Media Center for Art History make sure that all things media are impeccable; I am infinitely grateful for all their aid with this project as well as others.

I have benefited from the support of wonderful colleagues and departmental homes in the academy. In my early years as an assistant professor at Yale University in the History of Art and African American Studies departments, I was fortunate to work and share with a dynamic group of people who provided an atmosphere charged with strong ideas and enthusiasm. As a New Yorker, it has been a dream to teach art history in my hometown. I am grateful to Columbia University and the Department of Art History and Archaeology, including eminent faculty from the Barnard College side. I have an amazing array of colleagues who have encouraged my work and with whom I also share stellar students and great ideas. I would be bereft as a intellectual without the exciting community I have found at Columbia's Institute for Research in African American Studies. Colleagues at the Institute for Research on Women, Gender, and Sexuality; the Jazz Studies Group; and at Barnard, Africana Studies and the Barnard Center for Research on Women have also been important to my life at Columbia. The students in the various iterations of my Black West course continually encouraged me to consider these materials through new frames. Others' assistance with research have helped shape this project too: Louisa Boiman, Drew Bucilla, Dawn Chan, Dasha Chapman, Danielle Elliott, Brandi Hughes, Jerlina Love, Courtney Martin, Debra Singleton, and Irene Small. Martha Scott Burton has been exquisite in pulling together all the final details. The aid of Jane Lusaka and Camille O'Garro has been unparalleled.

Over the arc of writing this book I have been sustained in all sorts of ways by friends and family, including, among many others, Elizabeth Alexander, Saritha Clements, Alicia Loving Cortes, Cheryl Finley, Henry Louis Gates Jr., Thelma Golden, Farah Jasmine Griffin, the Hightowers, the Jones/Dudley clan, Maurine Knighton, Alicia Hall Moran and Jason Moran, Donna Mungen, Alondra Nelson, Fatimah Tobing Rony, Lorna Simpson, Franklin Sirmans, Jacqueline Stewart, Roberto Tejada, Patricia Welcome, and Deborah Willis. My Brooklyn neighbors from Bedford-Stuyvesant and beyond including the Hattie Carthan Community Garden and Market have been crucial to my well-being. My family of origin was my first intellectual community and continues to keep me energized as a writer and curator. My mother, Hettie Jones, and my late father, Amiri Baraka, never gave up on art as the key to our life as humans on this planet. This is the path I continue to follow. The Browns of Harlem—my sister Lisa, her husband Ken, and my niece Zoe—the amazing Hurricane Brown, writer, musician, actor, humanitarian; the Harvests of New Jersey—Keith, Gary, and Deborah and their families—are the coolest cousins ever; the extended Baraka family and the Enoch Archie clan are an inspiration. The family I was gifted in marriage continues to amaze and inspire. My mother-in-love, Celia Ramsey Wynn, together with the Ramseys and the Rosses, have embraced me from the moment I met them. And the younger generations always teach me something new about the world. I am so proud to call Guthrie P. Ramsey Jr. my life partner. His companionship and conversation continue to bring me motivation, comfort, and joy.

INTRODUCTION   South of Pico:
Migration, Art, and
Black Los Angeles

IN 1966 MIRIAM MATTHEWS, a collector and former librarian, wrote to artist Charles White to commission an image of Biddy Mason, the nineteenth-century black pioneer and former slave who had challenged California's shifting black codes.[1] White had always been captivated by the ways the visual could annotate history, and throughout his career he was sought out by all manner of people to illuminate missing or overlooked aspects of the human narrative.[2] What did change for White in the 1960s was the way he approached his craft, as he further complicated the pictorial surface *and* the understanding of history itself.

White's Biddy Mason project follows another important picture of a nineteenth-century figure commissioned by the Golden State Mutual Life Insurance Company. Made from Chinese ink on illustration board, Charles White's *General Moses (Harriet Tubman)*, 1965 (plate 1), is a portrait of this important slave absconder, conductor on the Underground Railroad, abolitionist, and Union spy during the Civil War. In White's almost six-foot drawing, Tubman, the composition's center of gravity, sits on a boulder, as if she is taking a brief rest from the task at hand. She stares out at us with a direct, relentless gaze. The artist takes on history—American, African American, and also diasporic—in a commentary on transatlantic slavery. As in many of White's later works, the landscape is elusive—a small patch of grass and a large craggy stone—more schematic and metaphoric than composed in detail. He uses alternating pools of ink and cross-hatching to create the appearance of a highly textured surface and portray a jagged, rough-hewn, and heavy form. In sitting on the rock, Harriet is rendered part of it, her skirt all but indistinguishable from the craggy plane, her feet blending into the grassy ground.

White was one of a handful of African American artists, like Jacob Lawrence and Elizabeth Catlett, who had made their mark in the 1930s and 1940s with social-realist styles and themes that revolved around black history and politics. In the early 1960s, their work received renewed interest from a younger group who were grappling with their own social and political obligations as artists against the landscape of the civil rights and nascent Black Power movements. For David Hammons, White's presence in Los Angeles was a revelation; as he mused in 1970, "I never knew there were 'black' painters, or artists, or anything until I found out about him—which was maybe three years ago. There's no way I could have got the information in my art history classes. It's like I just found out a couple of years ago about Negro cowboys, and I was shocked about that."[3]

In 1963, so the story goes, David Hammons had set out from Springfield, Illinois, in his not-so-new car. When it broke down just outside of town, he repaired it but didn't return the few short miles back home. Instead he kept going, determined at all costs to keep traveling west and to his destination, Los Angeles.[4] Like many artists heading from the countryside or the small town to the sprawling metropolis, Hammons was drawn as much to the adventures of the big city itself as to the locale of culture and avant-garde activity. In the mid-twentieth century, others of his generation also journeyed west from the midregions of the United States: Bruce Nauman (born Fort Wayne, Indiana), Ed Ruscha (born Omaha, Nebraska), and Judy Chicago (born in Chicago) all sought to stake a claim in the Los Angeles art game. They studied art and began showing their work there in the early 1960s as the city came into its own as a major cultural capital.

What differentiates Hammons's story from these others to a certain degree is its imbrication in another narrative. It is a tale, to be sure, of a larger African American community in Los Angeles in the same period, one that brought us cultural nationalism, the Watts Rebellion, the syndicated TV dance show *Soul Train*, and the films of Charles Burnett as well as a major community of visual artists. Like Hammons, most of the artists discussed in this book—including Charles White (born Chicago), John Outterbridge (born Greenville, North Carolina), Noah Purifoy (born Snow Hill, Alabama), and Senga Nengudi (born Chicago), among others—made their way to California as adults or as children. Those born in Los Angeles, like Betye Saar, were the children of people who had made that same journey. What is significant about this seemingly simple, almost unnoticeable fact is its tie to the much larger, two-century-long narrative of black migration.

African American migration in the nineteenth and twentieth centuries was nothing less than black people willing into existence their presence in modern American life. It represents their resolve to make a new world in the aftermath of human bondage and stake their claim in the United States. It is a narrative that stretches out one hundred years from the moment of freedom, a tale with a genesis in southern climes that then moved north and west. And it is a tale of the role of place in that claim, particularly the role of the West as a site of possibility, peace, and utopia. Artists such as White and Saar, Purifoy and Outterbridge, Hammons and Nengudi, like most African Americans in the twentieth century, were part of this massive relocation of people in some way. My goal here is to understand and demonstrate how their work speaks to the dislocations and cultural reinvention of migration, its materials of loss and of possibility, and sense of reinscription of the new in style and practice.

CRISSCROSSING THE WORLD

While nineteenth- and twentieth-century African American migrations provide a material and intellectual basis for the artwork discussed in this book, the human relocation actually began centuries earlier. The migration of people from Africa all across the globe is historic and legendary, codified now in academic investigations and a field of study that focuses on the African Diaspora. The forced migrations associated with the transatlantic slave trade that began five hundred years ago have been well researched by others and will not be discussed in detail here.[5]

Other migration was voluntary. For example, between the sixteenth and nineteenth centuries, scores of people migrated from Central Mexico to the northern border. Indeed, some of the first people of African descent in the land that eventually would become the western United States spoke Spanish. In 1781, Spanish colonial officials established the legendary Nuestra Señora la Reina de Los Angeles de Porciuncula between the San Gabriel Mission and Santa Barbara's Presidio. Mexico's Sinaloa province had a substantial population of people of African descent; twenty-six of the forty-six people who completed the five-hundred-mile journey overland and by sea from Sinaloa to Alta California were black. The pioneers who settled the cities of San Antonio and Laredo in Texas had a similar racial makeup.[6] Less than a century later, black sailors from the West Indies and other places would jump ship in San Francisco to take part in the gold rush.

Yet such movement, even when self-propelled, is often not just a one-time or permanent thing. There is the notion of crisscrossing, as historian Darlene Clark Hine has posited—forward and backward, but not relentless and linear due to factors such as the scrutiny of black movement, lack of capital, the need to care for relatives left behind, and keeping in touch with "home." In the notion of crisscross we find as well Michel de Certeau's notion of ellipsis, the "gap in spatial continuum," a journey whose synecdochic movements nevertheless compose the semblance of a whole. Voluntary migrations encompassed where people could go and where they could get to, on the physical plane and in the metaphysical cosmic order. And their movement, their quest, was ongoing.[7]

Between 1910 and 1970 more than 6.5 million African Americans left the southern United States for points north and west in what has been called the Great Migration, one of the largest and fastest internal migrations in history.[8] This massive shift of black Americans can be thought of in two phases. The first was one centered around World War I, when some 1.8 million people made the journey. The second phase, which drew women and men to the industries of World War II, took 5 million African Americans out of the South. (In 1940, 78 percent of African Americans lived in the southern United States; by 1970 the number had dropped to 53 percent.) The journey north may have begun with interstate relocation, then accelerated in a trek from farm to town, and from there to the city, the (cultural) capital. Furthermore, in what historian Shirley Ann Moore has characterized as "ever-widening circles of secondary migration," people travelled in stages, even in the late nineteenth century: from the rural South to its cities, from southern cities to those of the North and Midwest, and finally to the West Coast.[9] By the putative end of the Great Migration, the word "urban" had become interchangeable with "black." And there were the classic "push" and "pull" factors of migration: the "push" of the decline in agricultural livelihood, the specter of forced labor (a fear that slavery would reassert itself in the coming future), political and state repression, and the unrelenting violence against persons of African descent; and the "pull" of industrial work and wages, greater access to education, land, and autonomy.[10]

PROMISED LANDS

Railroad porters and peripatetic church choirs were among the scouts for new locations, bringing back information with each trip. Those traveling by train or bus might be forced to stand until they crossed the Mason-Dixon line. Other journeys, like those of David Hammons and John Outterbridge, were made by car, "with their 'mementos, histories, and hope, all tied to the top.'"[11] For African Americans, moving west represented a relocation toward the openness of possibilities, a place without the same sedimented authority. It was a move toward nonfixity and flexibility, the no-place of utopia. In this sense, the West became interchangeable with other locales that African Americans imagined offered prosperity and freedom from brutality and second-class citizenship. Was it a space in this country or a space in the world? Was it California, Africa, or Kansas?

Africa had loomed large as a place of promise in African American minds throughout the nineteenth century. In 1877, facing the abrogation of their political rights under the threat of death and bodily harm, as many as ninety-eight thousand people in New Orleans put their names on emigration lists for Liberia.[12] Emigration Clubs and Liberia Clubs abounded in the Reconstruction period, as did the conversation about places where black people might live a life of untrammeled citizenship. Other locations in the Diaspora, such as the West Indies and even Cyprus, were suggested as sites for peaceful settlement by blacks and whites alike.[13] But for people without access to vast amounts of capital and one step removed from enslavement, traveling within the United States was challenge enough.

Kansas Clubs were also founded in places like Mississippi, Tennessee, and Louisiana. Kansas had entered the union as a free state in 1861; it was a storied stop on the Underground Railroad and home of the radical abolitionist John Brown as well as other "jayhawkers," slave absconders who went into Missouri and led the enslaved across state lines to freedom. After slavery ended, Kansas, and in many respects the West, took Canada's place as the promised land in African American imaginations. Homestead acts that encouraged settlement and land ownership in western states and territories added to the optimistic outlook.[14] Well into the twentieth century, black towns with names like Blackdom (New Mexico); Booktee, Canadian Colored, and Liberty (Oklahoma); Independence Heights (Texas); and, perhaps the most famous, Nicodemus (Kansas) were established. The founders sought sites of self-determination and humanity that these expressive acts of naming gestured toward, where their families could flourish and live as equals under the law. But when these places and others in the western United States were also characterized by unequal treatment, Africa persisted in the imagination as a haven. More than one migrant arrived in Kansas from the South and, impatient with continuing restrictions to the exercise of freedom, then made plans to head to Africa, only to run out of money in Chicago and decide to stay.[15]

Farah Jasmine Griffin, Dana Cuff, and Katherine McKittrick have all explored the uneasy and conflicted notion of "safe space" with regard to migration. For Griffin these are material and discursive sites that evoke the ancestral; they are devices used to negotiate the migrants' new terrain. The ancestral safe space is informed by either the acceptance or rejection of the South as the ancestor and either the rejection of heritage as provincial custom or the acceptance of it in the invocation of music, ritual, language, or food that "takes one home" in memory. It is a reference to the real locales of the American South and, by extension, cultural formations of the African Diaspora but also to psychic space, the home one carries within. For Cuff safe space is understood as a version of homeplace, which is provisional: it is a site of comfort that may also be filled with myriad insecurities for those without access to power. In the words of McKittrick, homeplace is created from a "usable paradoxical space," one that is self-actualizing yet is also to a certain degree informed by compromise.[16]

The creation of art and culture also evokes safe spaces as ancestral forms and forces, whether as actual material inheritance, physical object structures and style, or the power of intellectual meaning—intention made visible. Charles White's portraits of heroines such as Harriet Tubman and depictions of southern workers and migrants, Betye Saar's dreamscapes, Noah Purifoy's assemblages of urban transformation, John Outterbridge's notions of a material homeplace, and Houston Conwill's installations and performative sites do not necessarily long for the South, Africa, or the diaspora (fig. I.1). But they do create safe spaces for contemplation, peace, beauty, the articulation of love, aesthetics, and resistance. These works are antagonistic to traditional geographies and create a notion of security and home, which in turn defines the discursive notion of ancestor.

In the twentieth century, African Americans headed west via car, train, or bus. But in the nineteenth century, they had walked. As Hine reminds us, "Blacks challenged with their feet the boundaries of freedom."[17] Similarly, theorist Michel de Certeau engages the figure of the walker, the person on the ground who rearticulates, and reinscribes, the city/state in her own image, a "migrational" force all but invisible on the city plan, outside the "panoptic power" of the grid. For de Certeau, walking implies the rhetoric of the "pedes-

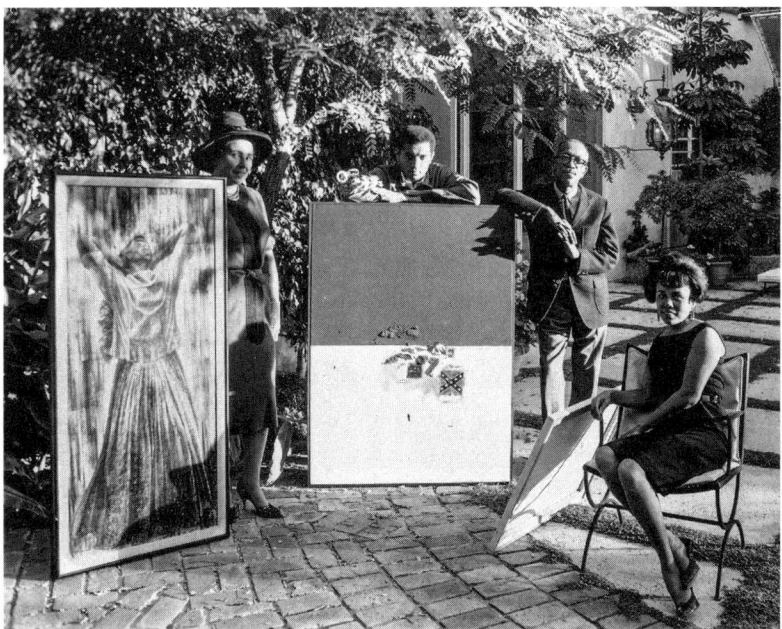

FIG. I.1 Curator Beate Inaya and artists Daniel LaRue Johnson, Charles White, and Betye Saar at the Negro and Creative Arts Exhibit, August 12, 1962. Courtesy Betye Saar and Michael Rosenfeld Gallery LLC, New York, NY.

trian speech act," which appropriates the topographical and offers a language of alternate social relations, connecting positions on the map that are unexpected in the dominant cartographic imagination. The walker is the dreamer, in search of her own true and proper form. The walker exits from the proscribed geographic plan, and in doing so reconfigures it, improvising, inventing something new. Black migrations were spatial movements, bodies creating new paths to selfhood and enfranchisement.[18]

THINKING SPACE

Migrations, then, are motion and action, the articulation of new routes away from a feudal past and toward a modern future. As initiated by African Americans, these activities look to find places where people thrive; they are gestures that inscribe a world for emergence, growth, a renovation of selfhood, and a revision of citizenship. These are assertions of space—cultural or political, as land or property—that create place, whether actual sites in the world or positions in the global imagination. Yet such affirmative declarations of location are also matched by their inversions: the negative valences of apartness, constriction, refusal. As much as migration was spatial claim, segregation was the denial of space, both intellectual and physical, its compression and constriction. While the West did not have the same histories of black enslavement as the South did, the African American westerner remained an ambivalent figure to a certain degree; she was not so much an individual as a representative of the masses, a notion that unleashed the white supremacist fear of a black planet. The public sphere, locations of labor, educational settings, and housing were some of the arenas that continued as nodes of friction to full engagement of black citizenry, even in California and the paradise of black Los Angeles. Such examples show us how the uneven, asymmetrical, or patently malicious and unjust application of spatial logic informed experience and expression.

Numerous writers have described southern migrant pleasures in public places in Chicago, Los Angeles, and other cities—shopping, movies, theaters, concert halls, promenades, and public parks, even the ability to sleep on the beach on hot nights. In Los Angeles, performance venues—such as Club Alabam, Elks Hall, and the Jungle Room along Central Avenue—were legendary, and cafés, clubs, and music halls were among the few places that were consistently integrated.[19] In other areas, access was still circumscribed socially even after legal barriers were dismantled. For example, the California Supreme Court ruled against segregation of public pools in 1932, but the practice continued into the 1940s, with African Americans sometimes allowed to enter only the day before the facility was cleaned. While African Americans could spend their money at the Santa Monica Pier Amusement concessions, they were restricted to only a sliver of beach below it; this area was known as the Inkwell. The black-owned Bruce's Beach, a section of Manhattan Beach, provided African Americans with a resort area until it was demolished through eminent domain in the 1920s. Indeed, as Eric Avila has noted, as municipalities were required to more thoroughly integrate public amenities and amusements throughout the country, these spaces were often increasingly abandoned by whites, resulting at times in eventual closure.[20]

Industrial labor was another major factor drawing African Americans north and west and represented the proletarianization of the black workforce, a chance to leave the agricultural work and sharecropping that seemed so much like "warmed over slavery."[21] In terms of industrial production, Los Angeles was second only to Chicago by the early 1960s, and its productivity lasted into the 1970s, part of what Avila describes as the westward drift of capital in the post–World War II period. Much of this economic growth was in the aircraft/aerospace industry, which became the largest manufacturing area in the United States with expansion into electronic equipment as well as space technologies; by 1957, it employed as much as one-third of the region's workforce.

Most African American migrants in this period were young, married women, a fact that would affect civil rights, Black Power, and arts activism in the latter half of the century. Yet even as early as 1900, most of the black population of Los Angeles was female, evidence of the fact that women had been on the move early in the century.[22] When artist and activist Ruth Waddy (born Lincoln, Nebraska) was denied a job at Lockheed Industries in Chicago, she headed to Los Angeles and found work with Douglas Aircraft.[23] Growth in public sector jobs (transportation) and those in government (health, education, and housing) opened more opportunities to African Americans. John Outterbridge found employment as a bus driver in Chicago. He made a good wage and could choose a schedule that enabled him to continue working as an artist, similar to a number of the musicians who eventually became a part of Chicago's avant-garde. While Outterbridge knew such professional experience could easily translate into a career on the West Coast, when he arrived in Los Angeles in 1963 he was determined to be employed in the arts.[24]

Although Executive Order 8802 barred discrimination in the defense industries after 1941, unions in these fields were allowed to continue discriminatory policies in exchange for "labor stability and productivity." African Americans, barred from general union membership, paid dues to separate auxiliary unions, which not surprisingly offered fewer protections. They received lower wages, were restricted in the types of positions they could hold and the promotions they could win; they also could not head racially mixed crews.[25] Entertainment was another strong industry in Los Angeles, and musicians found employment in the booming nightclub scene along Central Avenue as well as in the film industry. Denied membership in the local branch of the American Federation of Musicians, African American musicians founded Local 767 in 1920.[26] Their union facility, Elks Hall, served not only as a location to rehearse and to find jobs but also as a meeting place and cultural center.

There were many similarities in the physical spaces African Americans made for themselves to promote professional advancement and training. For instance, new skills required for welders and burners in the shipping industry were often passed from one recently trained worker to others in de facto "schools" in home garages. A corollary can be made with the art exhibitions— in homes, in garages, and around pools—that were created in Los Angeles of

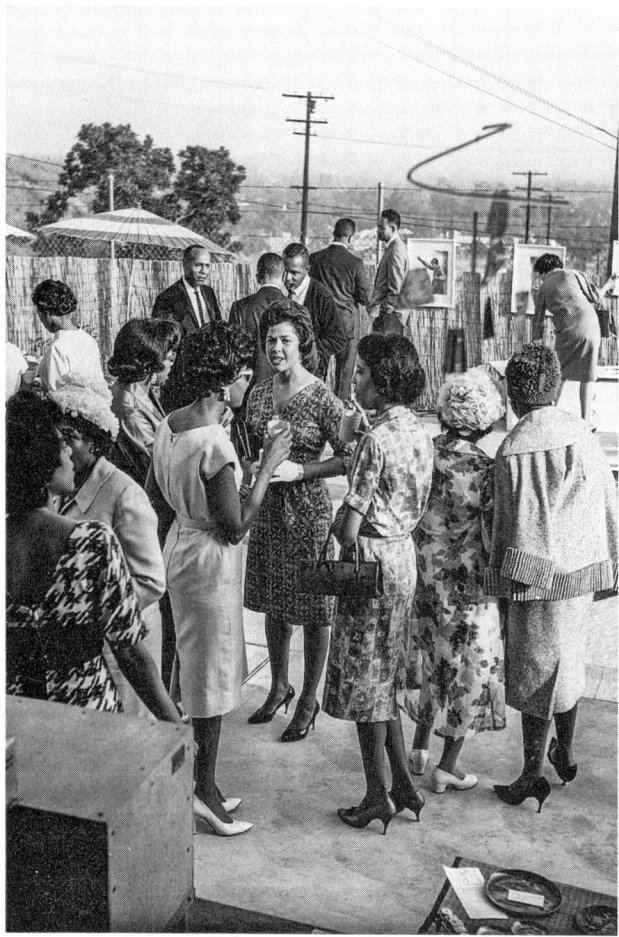

FIG. I.2 Group exhibition at the Altadena, CA, home of Alvin and Jeffalyn Johnson, June 1962. Courtesy Betye Saar and Michael Rosenfeld Gallery LLC, New York, NY.

the 1950s and 1960s (fig. I.2). Just as African Americans carved out their own passageways toward industrial labor, they did the same in the pursuit of their place in the world of contemporary art.

As civil rights activism claimed more and more victories, African Americans integrated the industrial workforce with greater ease. Yet the moment when much headway was made, at the dawn of the 1960s, was the moment of the decline of heavy manufacturing as an economic force. The deindustrialization of urban Los Angeles paralleled a suburbanization of jobs. African Americans found obstacles to suburban employment not only due to difficulties of transportation but because they continued to be barred from living in nearby areas, a scenario played out all over the country during this period. As Avila argues, suburbanization was created in response to the push of racial integration in urban areas. New spatial and economic structures of separation upheld white supremacy and continued the tradition of separate and inequitable resources.[27]

In education's segregated spaces, we can find direct links back to slavery and proscriptions against black literacy. It is another arena in which to identify spatial constructs of difference, as in, for example, the inadequate facilities for black public schools in rented buildings, churches, and barns in nineteenth-century Texas. Responding to a growing African American population in the early part of the twentieth century, Arizona passed a law in which schools with only one black pupil were required to put up a screen around the child's desk to shield her from the rest of the class. In 1950s Chicago, rather than integrate half-empty "white" schools, authorities chose to ease overcrowding in facilities for blacks by bringing in trailers to serve as additional classrooms and having students attend in double shifts.[28]

Many today have heard of *Brown v. Board of Education*, the 1954 case that struck down legal segregation in this country, overturning *Plessy v. Ferguson*, and in which future Supreme Court Justice Thurgood Marshall, then a lawyer with the National Association for the Advancement of Colored People (NAACP), argued for the plaintiffs. Yet what is often forgotten is that the lead case was western: *Oliver L. Brown v. Board of Education of Topeka, Kansas*. While gender and region played a part in the decision to make Brown the lead plaintiff, another reason was that African Americans in Kansas had brought eleven cases to their courts since the nineteenth century, petitioning for equal education on behalf of their children.[29]

Art historian Amy Weisser has quantified in detail the physical inequities of the educational spaces addressed by *Brown v. Board of Education*. Driven certainly by lesser financial resources extended for African American education, items included less acreage; fewer "amenities" such as auditoriums, lunchrooms, playrooms; outhouses rather than indoor plumbing; wood rather than masonry construction; larger class sizes, and so on. Yet, in many cases, those constructing the facilities for African Americans thought they were perfectly adequate, even generous, for the basic education that this servant class warranted. As Weisser notes, "To varying degrees, these buildings internalize[d] disparities in education between the races."[30] Like many of these students, John Outterbridge grew up in North Carolina able to see a school from his home that he was prohibited from attending.

Los Angeles public schools emerged in a multicultural environment, serving Asian, Latino, African American, Native American, and white pupils. In the nineteenth century, however, California law allowed the separation of whites once there were ten or more students of color. This practice continued into the next century, with liberal transfer policies that allowed white students to leave their racially mixed district schools for those where whites were in the majority. Over time, this led to segregated institutions. By the 1970s, Los Angeles was one of the battlegrounds in the ongoing struggle for desegregation and educational equity, reinforcing the view that education continued to be an important emblem of citizenship.[31]

LIVING SPACES

In their quest to (re)make home, black migrants sought places to live, flourish, relax, work, and be happy. Giving perhaps the most substantial definition to Freud's concept of the unhomely, however, their dwellings often became the antitheses of safe spaces. The artists discussed in this book, working in Los Angeles between roughly 1960 and 1980, in some way addressed these ideas. All sought to create sites of a metaphysical home, places of the dream, wellsprings of the creative, even when the notion of homeplace, like the real space of housing, was a significant arena of contention.

Architectural historian Bradford C. Grant has spoken of the roots of residential segregation in slavery, with slave quarters of vast plantations as the beginnings of black ghettos. It is a theory supported by an event that preceded Martin Luther King Jr.'s inauguration of the 1968 Poor People's Campaign: his visit to a road lined with decrepit shacks on Cotton Street in the Delta town of Marks, Mississippi. McKittrick has also addressed the topography of southern plantations. While analyzing the organization of these places as city structures in microcosm, she focuses specifically on the location of the auction block in their planning, a fragment insignificant in terms of architectural beauty and structure but one that was the very fulcrum of slavery's economic engine.[32]

Could the needs and desires of African Americans ever be represented in the modern residential spaces that emerged from such roots? In this light, the infamous kitchenette apartment is emblematic. The first homes of many migrants when they arrived in cities like Chicago and Los Angeles, kitchenettes were typically older apartments that had been subdivided into one- or two-room units. Each floor of five or six kitchenettes might share one bathroom.

For writers such as Richard Wright and Gwendolyn Brooks, the kitchenette represented the overcrowding of urban ghettos and was a metaphor for the restrictions on African American life as well as a symbol of community.[33]

In Los Angeles, such dwellings could be found in the neighborhoods of Bunker Hill and Little Tokyo. During the World War II internment of Japanese Americans, speculators bought property in neighborhoods where they'd lived and created kitchenette apartments for African American migrants, who were arriving in large numbers. For a time, in fact, Little Tokyo was known as Bronzeville, a reference to the renowned black neighborhood in Chicago. As historian Daniel Widener comments, "Little Tokyos became Bronzevilles all along the [West] coast, as blacks moved into vacant houses and storefronts."[34]

Little Tokyo in Los Angeles was seemingly well situated to receive migrants, located just south of Union Station where the Southern Pacific Railroad ended its route from Houston and New Orleans. Indeed, some of the first substantial African American communities in Los Angeles and Oakland had sprung up in the nineteenth century around the termini of westbound rail lines and were inhabited by African American Pullman porters and their families. It was the squalor of substandard housing and confined and restricted living represented by kitchenette apartments that Noah Purifoy mined in his controversial environment *Niggers Ain't Never Ever Gonna Be Nothin'—All They Want to Do Is Drink and Fuck*, which appeared at the Brockman Gallery in March 1971.

Racially restrictive covenants—delineating who could buy, sell, and live in specific parts of the city—had first appeared in late nineteenth-century Los Angeles, but were in frequent use by the 1920s. Such legal proscriptions were reinforced with extralegal reminders like Ku Klux Klan activity. People of color were seen as antithetical to the "Anglo" profile the city took pains to develop, with nostalgic images of archetypal cowboys and the western frontier such as those found in dime-store novels and Wild West shows, and increasingly manufactured by the budding Hollywood industry.

Such "possessive investment in whiteness," as scholar George Lipsitz has cogently described it, also extended to the perception of who was entitled to the suburban home. Indeed, as architect Craig L. Wilkins reminds us, the very notion of "possession," and its realization in forms of property, has been constructed as fundamentally antithetical to black life. Historic relational or spatial strategies posited (white) subjectivity against (black) objectification, with whites as owners and blacks as owned. Thus an articulation of home ownership signified a normative whiteness from the start. White ethnicity was gradually made invisible in the suburbs, at a remove from the urban public sphere, and articulated against an increasingly spatially distinctive "other" in ghettos and slums.[35]

Between 1917 and 1948, however, activists in Los Angeles—at times, a mix of African Americans, Jews, Japanese, Chinese, and Mexicans—banded together to fight such residential circumscription. From 1945 to 1948, more suits connected to housing rights were filed in Los Angeles than in the rest of the country combined, culminating in the federal ban against restrictive residential covenants in *Shelley v. Kraemer* (1948).[36]

As African Americans battled for the right to live out their dreams in the seaside paradise of Los Angeles, debates about public housing were added to the mix. The Housing Act of 1949 initiated nationwide programs of urban renewal. Under the guise of massive projects with a utopian veneer—clean, safe, affordable living spaces—public housing went hand in hand with "slum clearance." In effect, the only neighborhoods open to people of color and the poor were labeled as blighted, where aspects of racial diversity were deemed "inharmonious" to future development. The dismantling of the urban neighborhood also represented the destruction of its economic industrial core, and the move from manufacturing to the service industries. In effect, diverse city spaces—from homes to sites of leisure—were targeted for removal, making way for the suburban megalopolis.[37]

This effectively destabilized notions of acceptance and home, and was visited on new arrivals and the politically weak by a government encouraged by powerful real estate interests. For many, such programs amounted to little more than "urban removal," as many of the projects came to be known. Bowing to the "customs" and "traditions" of segregation, federal, state, and local governments continued to allow public housing only in certain areas, while razing existing homes and communities. Watts was one such site, where three major residential projects—Imperial Courts, Jordan Downs, and Nickerson Gardens—were completed by the mid-1950s. The latter two, designed by African American architect Paul Revere Williams with Richard Neutra, were low-rise structures that incorporated landscaping with broad green spaces, courtyards, and personal garden plots, in keeping with the idea of the availability of beauty and modernity for all. While described as transitional spaces, as people eventually were supposed to be able to buy their own homes, in reality these places concentrated poverty and failed to maintain services for such a dense population. More and more, they became spaces of containment and isolation.[38]

ART AND (SOCIAL) SPACE SOUTH OF PICO

There is a saying among black Angelenos that all black folks live south of Pico Boulevard. While this is, of course, an exaggeration, south of Pico we can indeed find major black communities, from the core of Central Avenue to Watts and Compton south, to Leimert Park and Baldwin Hills to the west and north, areas where the more affluent were able to move with the fall of restrictive covenants. "South of Pico" is also a metaphor for African American migrations and the ancestral home of most black Angelenos. Furthermore, Pico Boulevard is named for Pío Pico, a businessman, politician, and the last Mexican governor of California. His life in Los Angeles spanned its reality as both a Mexican and a U.S. city. He was also a person of African descent.[39]

Thinking of Pico both as a demarcation of division and a hidden history of blackness opens the door to the spatial as well. Spatial theory—in the writings of geographers, philosophers, architects, historians, and art historians—helps us see migration and segregation not just as arenas of social and historical movement and juridical challenge but as the articulation of spatial structure, what Henri Lefebvre has called (social) space. Through it, we can see and understand how people shape their worlds through creative force. The question for us here is, how do artists translate the same experiences into form? How do they transform what they find into what they would like it to be? How, in the words of Elizabeth Grosz, do these "things become the measure of life's actions upon them"? And how is the spatial imperative, seen in life's physical peregrinations and diremptions, found in this "compromise between mind and matter, the point of their crossing one into the other" that place represents?[40]

White, Saar, Hammons, Purifoy, and Maren Hassinger lived through segregation in various dimensions, applications, iterations. However, their generations also experienced greater social and spatial freedoms in the American twentieth century. Nevertheless, like African American migrants, they were faced with conscriptions around education, politics, labor, housing, and in the public sphere. How did they respond as artists to the social and spatial world as they found it? If the rise of the civil rights and black power movements reflected the changing nature of social and political activism, how did this affect artistic expression, inflecting not only the artists' intellectual peregrinations but also the material conditions of the artwork itself?

Several authors have offered positions significant to my thinking about how artists and others articulate spatial prerogatives. According to Lefebvre, "(Social) space is a (social) product." It is at once "a field of action" and "a basis of action"; quantitative in its expanses and qualitative as a depth of thought; material in its physical articulation and matériel in the work that it does.⁴¹ Social space is the interpenetration of "real" space as a material thing with space as mental construct and philosophical iteration. Social space is articulated in the mundane actions of daily life, charted by planners and cartographers as well as by artists' imaginings. Bodies produce social space for their gestures; as such, the built environment follows from a biomorphic core or logic, which underpins architectonics to come. Thus the layers of the built environment—buildings, objects, art—house the trace of corporeal sensibilities. If for Lefebvre space is a container of social relationships, art historian Miwon Kwon sees space, in the site specificity of art of the late twentieth century, as constructed of divergent forms, both material and immaterial. For Kwon, site is simultaneously phenomenological—a physical iteration of practice—and social and institutional, in its conscription of bodies and imbrication in structures such as museums. However, it is Kwon's sense of site as discursive formation that is perhaps most intriguing and, like Lefebvre's social space, threads itself through all types of spaces—concrete, ethereal, and those of memory. Here the notion of site shuttles between "a physical location—grounded, fixed, actual" and a "vector" that is "ungrounded, fluid, virtual."⁴²

Geographer Katherine McKittrick offers another significant framing of spatial thought, that of the sociospatial. If "all knowledges are geographic," she argues, then positionality is geography. In other words, what do you know, and from where do you know it? McKittrick thinks about black geographies and bodily ownership. Like Wilkins, she considers the history of black people through the lens of objecthood, demarcated by "discourses of possession and captivity of the flesh" occasioned by its attachment to the material fragment of the auction block. Because the black body historically is an object that is owned rather than a subject that possesses, it is ungeographic; black is, rather, a concept that "is cast as a momentary evidence of the violence of abstract space, an interruption in transparent space, a different (all-body) answer to otherwise undifferentiated geographies." McKittrick's project is the consideration of respatialization of black as body, as form, as geography, and as a site of contestation and complexity rather than dispossession or peripheral schema. It is located within and outside traditional space, elucidates "black social particularities and knowledges," and ultimately offers a new and expanded understanding of the normative.⁴³

These iterations on the spatial demonstrate its broad conceptual thrust and framing for art historical thinking. Notions of the object in space might be what interests art historians most. What is the mass, volume, density, shape, color? What actions does the object want from or require of its beholder? This last point, however, concerning the object of art's relational mode, also indicates art's social framing and networks as well as its dialogue with the body about space, and signals to the larger discursive mode of the spatial that I want to consider here.

Applying spatial theory to the art object helps us consider how African American migrants thought about and named places and spaces, about the importance of place to those who don't have one or are always searching for one—those who are patently ungeographic, as McKittrick indicates. We can consider further the role of the imaginary/expressive/cultural in that search, the need to imagine someplace beautiful and amazing on a daily basis. As Kwon suggests, the persistent "adherence to the actuality of places (in memory, in longing)" is perhaps "a means of survival."[44]

Place, in the work of the artists considered here, signals desire both to think about the future and to reconsider and reframe the past. In effect, these two positions become interchangeable, as Grosz intimates, in "a reciprocal interaction between the virtual and the real, an undecidable reversibility, as if the image could take the place of an object and force the object behind the constraints of the mirror's plane." The real is converted into a different order, transformed through the concept of the virtual, iterations of an "endless openness" or future.[45] Space as real and imagined, as discursive, offers this spectrum of positions and art presents new creative and life-forms that assert "new geographic formulations" and new spatial demands.[46]

ART AND BLACK LOS ANGELES

Between 1960 and 1980, the time period of this study, the art scene in Los Angeles generally, and certainly among African American artists, became a vibrant, engaged, and activist community. Works tied to traditional media—painting, drawing, prints, sculpture—gave way to dematerialized postminimal installation and body-centered performance. Within these styles and formats were spatial ideas that changed how artists accessed and incorporated notions of history and virtuality, the real and the imagined. These ideas were present throughout the period and used to varying degrees, though earlier works, not surprisingly, evidence a greater interest in history and didactic formulas, while later production moves toward the abstract and ephemeral.

Charles White's mode in the twenty years prior to his move to Los Angeles was in the social-realist vein, re-presenting and repositioning African

American figures as subjects of accomplishment rather than the inhuman and unhistorical empty vessels that the label "slave" suggested. Centered on solid rock, Tubman's geographic presence in *General Moses (Harriet Tubman)* belies the attachment to the perch of the auction block. Metaphorical rather than patently documentary in its presentation, its gloss on freedom is also more broadly allegorical. The drawing was created the same year the Voting Rights Act passed, which dismantled impediments to black enfranchisement in many parts of the United States. The 1965 act and White's piece both marked the centennial of the Thirteenth Amendment, which abolished slavery. The didactic and pedagogical nature of the work in this context seems clear.

We see this same instrumental approach to storytelling and meaning in the earliest works of White's pupil David Hammons. He attended art classes at various institutions throughout the city but particularly sought out White at the Otis Art Institute. White's influence can be seen in Hammons's early choice of the graphic medium as well as in his works' political content. In pieces such as *Boy with Flag*, 1968 (plate 2), a young black man stands behind the U.S. standard, emerging from its shadows, yet still seemingly bifurcated by its cutting edges, which appear to slice through the body. Hammons classically embodies the edifying style of the Black Arts Movement in his figurative presentation and commentary on U.S. racism. The piece also refers to history in its implications of unequal treatment under the law, and African Americans as three-quarters human, as suggested by the partial portrait.

Through the figure of Hammons, we can also chart the evolving visual aesthetics of the community of African American artists in California in the 1960s and 1970s as well as the move from didactic formulas to those that rely on abstraction, dematerialized practices, and performance. We can map these changing aesthetics, for example, in Hammons's works from the 1970s that use black hair, such as the "gardens" of hair threaded on flexible wire (fig. I.3) he "planted" in the damp sand along the shores of the southern California beaches. These were intended to be some version of saltwater grasses; somehow the hybrid cattails seem familiar yet out of place, too close to the water's edge, strangely shaped yet bending easily in the cool ocean breeze. Their importance also lay in their temporary and ephemeral nature: they were made of materials and sited in places that assured their disappearance over time. Yet, as Hammons himself would later recount, hair acted as a signifier of the black body: even though nonobjective in form, it remained self-referential: "I got a visual object and medium that was pure [and] nonsexual, which spoke to everything I wanted to say."[47]

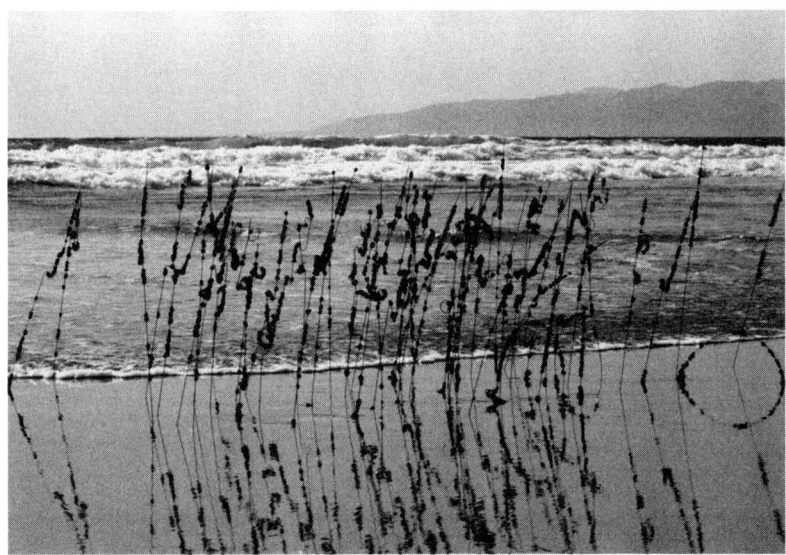

FIG. I.3 David Hammons, *Hair and Wire, Venice Beach, California, 1977*. Site-specific installation. Photograph by Bruce Talamon. Courtesy the artist and Bruce Talamon © All rights reserved.

Similar ephemeral works, structured as installations, by Senga Nengudi and Maren Hassinger are emblematic of the turn to a more freewheeling (in)formal visual play. Examples include gatherings of pantyhose filled with sand draped across spaces and rooms, Nengudi's signature works from the 1970s. Like Hammons, Hassinger planted "gardens" indoors and out from Los Angeles to New York. Yet hers were more massive, formed from towering expanses of unfurled, industrial-grade cable and wire rope. The shift from didactic works to those of greater abstraction by these African American artists of Los Angeles was a move from historical to virtual content—from the consideration of the past, whether distant or immediate, to the imagining of the future. This occurs via a presence that is ancestral, which may appear as a physical trace in style, remains, sound, and spatial technics—a metaphoric hint, a utopic gleam.

This reach across time brings us toward a model of Afro-futurism, which, as scholar Alondra Nelson suggests, uses what is bygone to explain the present *and* prophesize what is yet to come. It glosses time that is not the past but yet not detached from it either; instead, it is "contiguous yet continually transformed."[48] Time and space are not linear; technologies are not always new but lean on earlier and often anachronistic formulas as antennas of the future. This book examines how artists cast an eye toward what came before and think to what lies ahead through modes that are at once historical and futuristic. After Farah Jasmine Griffin I want to think about the art considered here as different kinds of migration narratives, embodying this aspect in their material facture, their intellectual positioning, and their pursuit of African Diaspora cultural form.

In this volume, chapter 1, "Emerge: Putting Southern California on the Art World Map," focuses primarily on Charles White, Betye Saar, and Melvin Edwards as Los Angeles came into its own as a cultural capital in the late 1950s and early 1960s. These artists were part of a generation that willed an African American art community into existence with little traditional art world support. They mounted exhibitions in homes, community centers, churches, and black-owned businesses. Their examples and mentorship were a catalytic force creating and helping to sustain a vibrant black arts scene in the city. White's career took him to Los Angeles in 1956 after he'd made a name for himself in his hometown of Chicago as well as New York. He arrived in the city with an international reputation, one that made him one of the most important African American artists up to that period. Trained as a designer and experimenting with interiors and jewelry while she worked as a social worker, California native Betye Saar emerged as a serious printmaker. Her early works on paper also codify the appearance of feminist themes, which she would build on in the decades to come. Melvin Edwards was one of the West Coast's first black superstar artists, with important shows at the Los Angeles County Museum of Art and the Santa Barbara Museum. White and Saar also represent the twinned concerns with the historical (in the former's interest in singular figures of the black past) and virtual (in the latter's growing focus on spiritual practice and metaphysics), while Edwards's abstract practice seems to combine these two positions.

Chapter 2, "Claim: Assemblage and Self-Possession," focuses on the role of assemblage within the black art-making communities of Los Angeles during the 1960s and 1970s. The West Coast became highly visible with mainstream acceptance of assemblage as an important artistic strategy, particularly with its canonization in the Museum of Modern Art's 1961 *The Art of Assemblage* exhibition. It is often seen as a form of critical practice, laced with such notions in the ruined consumer products of its facture, indicative of both the fraud of 1950s consumer society and its platitudes. Also embedded in the narrative of assemblage is the concept of transformation, the alchemy of taking a thing discarded and changing it into a thing of (re)use.

Assemblage was a clear metaphor for the process of change—the transformation of psyche and social existence—required of art in the rhetoric of

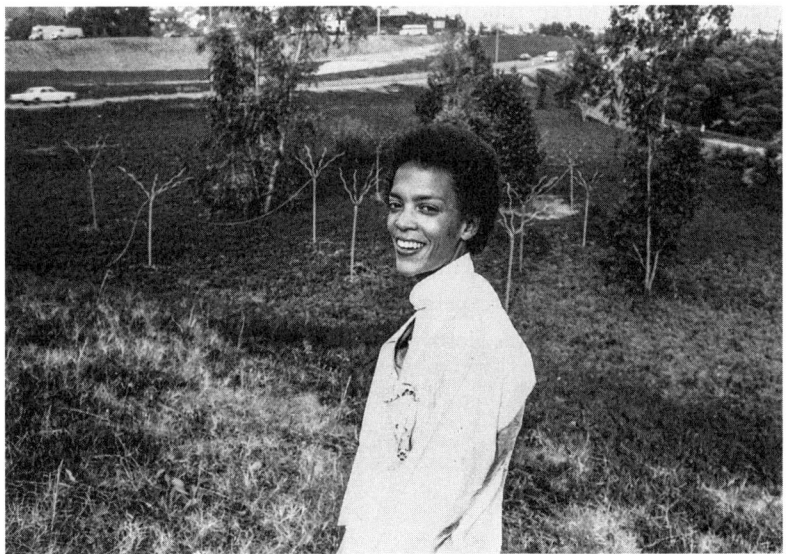

FIG. I.4 Adam Avila, *Maren Hassinger in front of* Twelve Trees, 1978. Site-specific installation, Los Angeles. Courtesy Maren Hassinger.

the Black Arts Movement, art that "advance[d] social consciousness and promote[d] black development."[49] Each artist discussed in this chapter, however, approached the genre from a slightly different direction. Noah Purifoy used assemblage as a system of artistic activism and institutional critique in the period immediately following the Watts Rebellion. John Outterbridge's pieces run more toward a metaphoric narrative that invokes ancestral aesthetics of vernacular art making in black communities as alternate paradigms that intersect with West Coast art practices. Betye Saar, for her part, created temples and altars to spirituality using the fragments of humanity embedded in the discarded.

In chapter 3, "Organize: Building an Exhibitionary Complex," I look at the ways in which African Americans in Los Angeles marshaled the art world in order to disseminate and support their art. Change in the 1960s and 1970s also brought a shift in the traditional museum and gallery scene. Other spaces were brought into existence by artists themselves, including Alonzo Davis and Dale Brockman Davis, Suzanne Jackson, and Samella Lewis. Chapter 4, "In Motion: The Performative Impulse," moves away from the didactic subject matter connected to civil rights and black power and toward greater abstract, dematerialized, and conceptual modes. During the 1970s, artists such as Senga Nengudi, Maren Hassinger (fig. I.4), Houston Conwill, and David

Hammons began to experiment with postminimal ephemerality and performance.

Throughout the 1960s and 1970s, a number of artists who had made Los Angeles an art capital began heading to New York. David Hammons, Maren Hassinger, and Houston Conwill had all relocated there by 1980. Most certainly the presence of these practitioners and others on the East Coast affected New York's expanding discourse of visual and cultural diversity. The concluding chapter, "Noshun: Black Los Angeles and the Global Imagination," considers where their experiences in Los Angeles took them and contextualizes their work in the global continuum, the direction their diasporic turn ultimately led.

CHAPTER ONE   **Emerge:** Putting Southern California on the Art World Map

SO WHAT WERE THE CULTURAL gestures that signaled the emergence of this active and vibrant African American artists community in postwar Los Angeles revealing the life of the black modern? For those deemed "ungeographic" these indicators importantly delineated place, plotting the mind's effects on matter. These spaces of/for creativity, for nurturing burgeoning aesthetics, were hard won. They were safe spaces and homeplaces that remembered the ancestral. But they were also in many ways provisional and negotiated, carved and pried out of the larger American dream.

This chapter focuses on the ways three artists established a strong African American creative presence in Los Angeles in the postwar period. In Charles White, we see how a singular figure coalesced a community as the 1950s became the 1960s. He had commanding East Coast credentials as well as an impressive portfolio and offered an image of professionalism. His presence on the West Coast also points to the role that Hollywood played in the development of black artists. Betye Saar emerged from the solid design background that was the hallmark of many African American artists in midcentury Los Angeles. Accolades for her works on paper in large, all-city shows at the beginning of the 1960s set her on the path to fine arts success.

Melvin Edwards became one of the city's African American art stars in the mid-1960s. His expressive sculptures in welded metal, like the work of

White and Saar, engaged both historical and contemporary time and intuited the architectural. They articulated visions of space and site that visualized a new and exciting yet conflicted future. They outlined the contemporary fight for housing, channeling too the architecturally insignificant yet economic powerhouse of the auction block, its pervasiveness as well as its provisional and fragmentary nature. Edwards opened an adversarial space in found metal sculpture, one whose formal tensions framed historical ones of property ownership and possession against the specter of black objecthood.

These objects made by White, Saar, and Edwards to some degree pursue utopic space through the imagining of diaspora. It is a transhistorical space of solidarity wrought through black expressive culture and signals the importance of the imaginary in making the ground for community. The early careers of these frontrunners took us into the 1960s and cut a path for the emergence of a cadre of professional artists.

"THE ARTIST IS CHARLES WHITE"

Toward the middle of the film *For Love of Ivy* (1968) (plate 3), the owner of a trucking company escorts Ivy Moore, the potential love interest of his colleague Jack Parks (Sidney Poitier), to Parks's swank bachelor pad. As he and Ivy (Abbey Lincoln) enter the stunning duplex, arrayed with books and art, they pause in front of a charcoal drawing. "The artist is Charles White," exclaims the man, Billy Talbot (played by Leon Bibb), as Ivy looks on in awe. The paired tondos of the drawing, smoky heads of a man and a woman, later hover over moments of sensuality and seduction, the first such love scene with black characters in popular film. It also marks perhaps the first time a work by an African American artist is singled out specifically as not only a symbol of status, but of something beautiful *and* coveted for a mass moviegoing audience.[1]

While *For Love of Ivy* introduces the discussion of White's work within the film, allowing it to "perform" as a character, another piece, *Folk Singer*, 1957–58, had appeared a year earlier in the now more famous interracial drama *Guess Who's Coming to Dinner?* (1967). There art asserts itself silently in the study of newspaper man Matt Drayton (Spencer Tracy), future father-in-law of Dr. John Prentice (Poitier). White's print hauntingly symbolizes the irony of white people consuming African American cultural objects and yet continuing to deny equal treatment to black people in American society. But *Folk Singer* also points to the inevitable: black people will become a part of this home and that larger construct called America.

Indeed, 1967 was a banner year for White, a consummate painter, draftsman, and master-printer. He had a solo show at the Palm Springs Desert Museum and another at Howard University, and his work was featured abroad, in exhibitions in Czechoslovakia, Hungary, and Poland.[2] Perhaps even more significant was the release of the book *Images of Dignity: The Drawings of Charles White*, purportedly the first monograph on a living African American artist. The book features commentary by White's dealer, Benjamin Horowitz; the preeminent historian of African American artists, James A. Porter; and popular entertainer Harry Belafonte. Horowitz provides an overview of White's trajectory as an artist, spiced with lively anecdotes outlining his career.[3] Porter describes White as a historian whose murals brought out sublimated African American history even as he was immersed in a cubist formula of overlapping forms, "pauses," and the "discontinuity of shapes."[4]

However, it is Belafonte's foreword that adds something extra to the monograph. The performer calls White's art "tremendously American," and in doing so links the artist to his own focus on folk or historical form, what he identifies as "Negro Americana."[5] Belafonte not only was an inspiration for many of White's pieces about music generally and folk music in particular; he was also a collector of the artist's work and a lifelong friend.[6] Similar to Poitier, he used his star power as a matinee idol — the first American singer to sell more than a million records (*Calypso*, 1956) and the first African American to win an Emmy, for the variety show *Tonight with Belafonte* (1959) — to make things happen for other black artists. Like Dennis Hopper and Dean Stockwell, Hollywood actors who bankrolled the Ferus Gallery crowd, Poitier and Belafonte (and later NFL player turned actor and artist Bernie Casey) played the same role in African American creative communities.[7]

White's engagement with Hollywood began soon after he arrived in Los Angeles in 1956, following more than a decade in New York. He created the title drawings for the film *Anna Lucasta* (1958). A family drama with an all-black cast, it fit well with 1950s films that were more serious, message-oriented, and controversial, shedding the gloss of 1940s black musical fanfare and attempting to channel the changing tide of U.S. society.[8] White created three drawings for the film, one each of principals Eartha Kitt (plate 4) and Sammy Davis Jr., and a third tableau involving the other major figures played by Rex Ingram, Frederick O'Neal, and Georgia Burke. While title drawings ordinarily appeared at the opening of a film, the detailed and consummate nature of White's pieces made producers situate them at the movie's end, where the camera pans over them and the credits roll. White made it very clear that the images were not merely illustrations and that they were

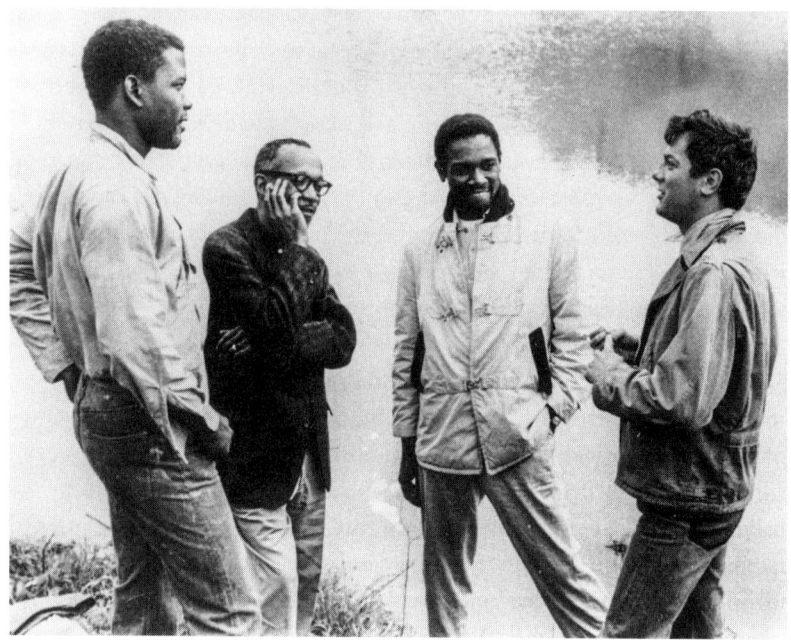

FIG. 1.1 Sidney Poitier, Charles White, Ivan Dixon, and Tony Curtis on the set of the film *The Defiant Ones*, 1958. Courtesy Charles White Archives.

not to be used for advertising purposes. His drawings fared better in *Tonight with Belafonte*, where they were used as intertitles, carrying the action from scene to scene, between performances of Odetta, Brownie McGhee, Arthur Mitchell, and others.[9]

Having once considered an acting career, White had close relationships with actors, musicians, as well as writers and enjoyed visiting movie and TV sets whenever friends such as Poitier, Ivan Dixon, and others were in the cast (fig. 1.1). He attended movie premiers, including the July 1969 opening for Gordon Parks's *The Learning Tree*. White and Parks had been friends since their early days as artists in Chicago and the Works Progress Administration (WPA) circles of the 1930s.[10] Black Hollywood and the performance world supported artists in other ways as well. Poitier, Belafonte, Bill Cosby, Eartha Kitt, Nat King Cole, Lorraine Hansberry, Ruby Dee, and Ossie Davis were among White's long list of collectors.[11]

However, the Charles White who arrived on the Hollywood scene in the mid-1950s was already an important artist. He had traveled and shown work around the globe; lived in Mexico, received John Hay Whitney and Rosenwald fellowships, among others; and executed major murals nationwide. He had shown consistently with American Contemporary Artists (ACA) Galleries in New York since 1947 and had been celebrated in the U.S. and foreign press. Such an artist of international acclaim was heralded by the African American weekly the *Los Angeles Sentinel*, which noted his arrival on the train known as the "Super Chief from New York" in the early fall of 1956.[12]

Indeed, White's renown in this period was matched only by that of Jacob Lawrence and, to a certain degree, Elizabeth Catlett. Yet until his first solo show at Heritage Gallery in 1964, some eight years after he hit the West Coast, White's support from the traditional art sector was scant. Between 1957 and 1967, a major art scene emerged in Los Angeles with the rise of the Ferus, Dwan, Huysman, and other galleries and *Artforum*'s relocation from San Francisco to Los Angeles in 1965. However, the representation of African Americans in these traditional venues was negligible.

White's first solo exhibition in Los Angeles is emblematic of the cultural climate facing African American artists at the time and the role black Hollywood and black communities played in bringing the work of prominent and unknown artists into view. The weeklong show at the University of Southern California (USC) in April 1958 presented thirteen drawings and prints on the theme of spirituals. Three of these came from Belafonte's collection. The presentation was sponsored by the State Association of Colored Women's Clubs and the Southwest Symphony Association, a collective of black classical musicians. A few years later, Judson Powell would emerge from the latter organization to collaborate with Noah Purifoy on art-making activities at the Watts Towers Arts Center.[13]

Another significant exhibition of White's work was held in September 1959 at the Pacific Town Club (PTC), a private social club of black professional men. It lasted only two days, from September 12 to 13, and proceeds from the opening event raised funds for a student art scholarship. Established in the mid-1930s, PTC was one of the few such associations with a permanent clubhouse. In 1952, the group built a new building, a midcentury modern facility designed by architect and PTC member (and in 1947, its president) Paul Revere Williams. The following year, biannual art shows of similar length and purpose as White's were being held at the site.[14] Williams designed buildings in the 1930s and 1960s for PTC member John Lamar Hill, owner of the Angelus Funeral Home. Other clients included club members Norman O. Houston and George A. Beavers Jr., principals of Golden State Mutual Life Insurance, whose flagship building at 4332 W. Adams Boulevard (at Western) was located blocks away from the PTC structure at 1999 W. Adams (corner of Montclair). One of Williams's earliest commissions was a redesign of the

Twenty-Eighth Street YMCA, where he added, among other things, exterior tondos featuring portraits of Frederick Douglass and Booker T. Washington. These decorative touches were meant to visualize and celebrate the African American community served by the facility. Like other YMCAs throughout the country in the 1920s and 1930s, it was a meeting place for those making and interested in African American arts and culture.[15]

Williams's buildings were prominent structures in Los Angeles. They signify the black community's engagement with and ability to commission major arts projects and how an artist like White could be supported, no matter his reception by the larger art community at the time. However, Williams is best known for the homes he designed for Hollywood stars—among many others, Frank Sinatra, Lucille Ball and Desi Arnaz, and Lon Chaney. As with Belafonte, and Poitier, Williams's productive relationship with Hollywood allowed him to take part in creative projects with black communities.

Articles in *Negro Digest* and *Ebony* in June and July 1967, respectively, demonstrate how White's images, story, and reputation were disseminated in black literary and popular networks and outside strict mainstream art world circles. *Negro Digest* was an intellectual journal with probing thought pieces on art and culture. Originally patterned after *Reader's Digest*, it changed its name to *Black World* in 1970, reflecting the climate of Black Power. *Ebony*, of course, was the flagship monthly of African American life; it began publication in 1945 in the era of pictorial magazines and chronicled movers and shakers and current affairs in glossy print. Both magazines were published by Chicago-based media titan John Johnson and Johnson Publishing. The articles on White appeared with the release of his monograph *Images of Dignity*. While the *Negro Digest* essay keenly focused on that event, *Ebony* used the occasion to provide a wide-ranging and lavishly illustrated spread. And there was clearly a dialogue between the two on White's "everyman" imagery and the contours of his artistic career and life.[16]

The responses to the *Ebony* article demonstrate White's popular appeal. He received letters of admiration from all over the country as well as inquiries about purchasing the work. Correspondence came from as far away as Ghana, where Alex Amofa Kophi of Kumasi sent photographs of his own paintings and sought advice on a budding artistic career.[17] The African letters demonstrate the wide circulation of the Johnson Publishing empire as well as *Ebony*'s interest in stories about Africa's independence movements, political figures, and new heads of state, who appeared on its covers during this period. White's drawing, *Two Brothers I Have Had on Earth—One of Spirit, One of Sod*, 1965, is prominently displayed in the *Ebony* piece. It is listed as owned by Sékou

Touré, the president of Guinea, creating a direct connection between the artist and an African audience and revealing White's dialogue with Africa's independence movements.[18]

Still, White sought greater representation in the established West Coast art scene. In 1958, the same year as his solo at USC, he was included in a sprawling group show, *Arts of Southern California V: Prints*, at the Long Beach Museum.[19] But that certainly wasn't enough. Just as Hollywood served as an alternative support system for his practice, another growing community of friends worked with White to invent new art networks. For instance, the recently named postmaster of Los Angeles, Leslie Shaw, and his wife, Ann, hosted an exhibition at their home. Other exhibitions held at places of worship were associated with activist contexts. White exhibited at the First Unitarian Church as early as 1961, a relationship initiated by Charlotta Bass, former publisher of the *California Eagle* (the longest-running black periodical in Los Angeles), and an important figure in West Coast leftist networks. During a one-day exhibit at Lincoln Avenue Methodist Church, the artist showed nine original works, listened to ideas for commissions, and took orders for a recent print portfolio from the audience of three hundred.[20]

An exhibition at First Christian Church in Whittier in 1962 was tied to a program with James Farmer, director of the Congress of Racial Equality (CORE).[21] It was part of a decade of annual shows sponsored by the American Friends Service Committee (AFSC), a Quaker organization dedicated to peace and social justice. These shows, eventually held in the AFSC headquarters in Pasadena, were consciously multiracial, promoting a position of racial understanding. This was the context in which much art by African Americans appeared earlier in the twentieth century, marking it with a certain utility as an engine of social progress. White was embedded in such progressive and leftist networks throughout his life. They were where his politics lay, and they also provided a web of support for his career as an artist. In Los Angeles, the AFSC and similar exhibits became avenues for the wider circulation of the work of African American artists, including painters William Pajaud and Wilbur Haynie and sculptor John Riddle. Betye Saar and her husband, white ceramicist Richard Saar, also participated.[22]

During the early 1960s Beata Inaya's interest in art and architecture as well as politics led her to organize house tours and art auctions to raise funds for local races and initiatives of California's Democratic Party. In 1960, she led major fund-raising activities for the restoration of Simon Rodia's Watts Towers; at that moment, her endeavors begin to intersect with African American communities. In 1962 Inaya acted as the coordinator for the AFSC exhibition at First Christian Church in Whittier, and a program called *The Negro in the Creative Arts*. The latter, held in August 1962, was an event to benefit Thomas M. Rees, an assemblyman running for the state senate who would go on to represent the Beverly Hills area in Congress. The weekend program featured an exhibition as well as, amazingly, a tour of homes designed by black architects. A group of young artists including Melvin Edwards, Camille Billops, and Daniel LaRue Johnson took part, as did Curtis Tann, an enamellist and painter who became director of the Watts Towers Arts Center later in the decade. Charles White was featured prominently on the invitation and also was listed as a sponsoring committee member, as were architects John Lautner, A. Quincy Jones, and Richard Neutra. Painter and printmaker Ruth Waddy, who formed her Art West Associated group of African American artists that same year, was given "special credit." A photo of the event shows Inaya with White, Saar, Daniel LaRue Johnson, and their works in a lush LA patio (fig. I.1).[23] Inaya's name surfaced again at the end of the decade in connection with fund-raising efforts for the Watts Summer Festival.[24]

As in the case of Beata Inaya (a Holocaust survivor), the city's progressive Jewish community also figured importantly in opportunities for African American artists in the 1960s. Jewish Community Centers like Valley Cities in Van Nuys and the Hollywood Los Feliz branch hosted exhibitions and panels. The Westside center on Olympic Boulevard was particularly dynamic. In addition to sponsoring shows with African American artists, the center hired White to teach its life drawing class in 1964. Integral to this connection was Edward Biberman. Like White, Biberman was a painter of murals, had participated in the WPA, admired the Mexican muralists, and was active in progressive creative circles in New York before he moved to California in 1936. According to White's second wife, Frances Barrett White, Biberman recommended the artist for the job at the Westside center and also introduced him to Benjamin Horowitz. It was at Horowitz's Heritage Gallery that Charles White finally had a solo show in a commercial space in Los Angeles, eight years after moving to town. Heritage represented the artist exclusively for the rest of his life.[25]

White's 1964 Heritage show was a hit. Two *Los Angeles Times* reviewers were complimentary, though amazed that there were waiting lists for the pictures. Henry Seldis was a bit cooler toward the exhibition, yet still found White's realism convincing and not in any way faddish. The figures in the twenty-four drawings on view were archetypal, embodying spiritual strength. Art Seidenbaum not only got White's point but was captivated by it. The pictures, he concluded, were about hope and responding to horrible situations with compassion; they were not saturated with violence even as they commented on it, even as the artist himself experienced brutality as a black man in America. The critic understood White's aim to craft a figure that was optimistic, idealistic, black, *and* universal.²⁶

In his article, Seidenbaum set up a contrast between the black artist named White and white artist G. Ray Kerciu, whose works were showing concurrently, and around the corner, at Comara Gallery on Melrose. (Heritage was located on La Cienega.) Kerciu's louder and angrier paintings resulted from the frustration and violence he experienced the previous year while teaching at the University of Mississippi (Ole Miss), which was integrated in 1962. In the photograph illustrating the article, White's work seems to have been brought into Comara—Kerciu's painting is hanging, White's piece is being held by Horowitz—so that they can be positioned side by side. Both refer to black freedom struggles: Kerciu splashes "Freedom Now" across his canvas. The central draped figure in White's drawing confronts us directly as her arms fly free. It is titled *Uhuru*, 1964—"freedom" in Swahili, another connection to the African Diaspora.²⁷

Seidenbaum labeled Kerciu a New Realist, bringing to mind the French circle then showing work at Dwan Gallery, such as Arman, Martial Raysse, and Niki de Saint Phalle. A critic writing in *Time* described Kerciu as following the mode of Jasper Johns and Larry Rivers, artists identified with iconic images, such as flags and words/lettering. To express the current moment, Kerciu, "normally a quiet, representational landscapist," began to identify with Neo-Dada and emerging pop styles.²⁸ In mid-1960s Los Angeles, pop, Neo-Dada, and New Realism were the au courant art languages. This type of work was being shown at Dwan Gallery and at Ferus, where Andy Warhol's soup cans made a splash in 1962, and in the show *New Paintings of Common Objects*, curated by Walter Hopps for the Pasadena Art Museum the same year.

If Charles White's drawings seem vastly different, more romantic and lyrical, there is at least one thing that they share with Kerciu's paintings: they trade on the recognizable. What White's oeuvre shares with pop is realism and a rejection of the nonobjective. And the rise of pop, the enshrining of recognizable subject matter, finally permits the mainstream visibility of White's work on the West Coast in the early 1960s.

White's commitment to realism was unwavering. To him, it presented an art language that was understandable worldwide. Above all, the "communicability" of the representational was key, "how it reflects the great experience of life and singles out that which is most significant and meaningful to its process"; these are portrayals of the subtle and daily human struggles for peace and freedom.²⁹ Like most African American artists throughout the twentieth century, he shied away from debilitating caricature and abject violence. The great effort for African Americans even to be able to be recognized as artists meant that this space was in some ways sacred. It could be a place for protest, yes, but most of all it was reserved for reflections on beauty that were often otherwise misrecognized or unseen.

White's realist focus was shaped by the contemporary leftist and social-realist roots of his practice. However, we can also think about the generation of this work in the seeds of nineteenth-century realism. As Linda Nochlin points out, realism encompassed a similar objectivity about present-day life—depictions of ordinary people stimulated by democratic ideals. The commonplace, marginal, and "socially dispossessed" were linked to the public issues of the day. Realist art envisioned the laboring classes, the brutalization and injustice that they endured, but also insisted on their heroism. According to Nochlin, the aspects of civic concern and activist thrust, the "radical utopian political fervor," as well as the visual availability of the imagery associated with realism emerged in the twentieth century in social realism (and in murals in Mexico and the United States). Later, everyday life also would inspire the work of New Realist and pop artists.³⁰

White's figures share these qualities, imaging black people as the labor that built the country and as its ultimate dispossessed population. These were, of course, timely themes in the United States at midcentury, during the struggles for desegregation. His pieces prized a more truthful (rather than caricatured) depiction that stresses the heroic figure. But there are also differences. While, as Nochlin has argued, Gustave Courbet saw a "coarse" interpretation of peasantry as "true," White shied away from such roughness. Among his artistic models was Francisco Goya, who, a generation earlier than Courbet, valued romantic expressions of the "eternal and recurrent, human situation"—what White prized in his own work as universal.³¹ If we consider definitions of romantic style, we can find White's investment in some of its tenets as well. As outlined by Cordula Grewe, an emphasis on "mystery, magic, and beauty" is very much a part of White's pictures, particularly the work he completed after arriving in California.³² In drawings such as *C'est l'amour*, 1959, an underlying romantic sensibility is evident in the artist's "fragmentary, arabesque form of story-telling, its symbolic richness and its affirmation of the aestheticization of life."³³

If one Los Angeles critic saw the works on view in White's 1964 Heritage Gallery show as "highly romanticized and . . . overly sentimental," perhaps this is what was needed to counteract centuries of portrayals to the contrary.[34] As White mused: "My whole purpose in art is to make a positive statement about mankind, all mankind, an affirmation of humanity. . . . All my life, I have been painting one single painting. This doesn't mean that I'm a man without angers—I've had my work in museums where I wasn't allowed to see it—but what I pour into my work is the challenge of how beautiful life can be."[35]

The countless letters White received are testament to the fact that other people agreed. One from Mrs. Ina Brown Scott of Gallion, Alabama, was addressed to "Mr. Charles White, Somewhere in the World." In it, she described visiting the West Coast for the first time, seeing White's images in a calendar advertising Golden State Mutual Life Insurance, and making "a great sacrifice" to order one of White's portfolios because "I could visualize those prints offering up new avenues for some of the young people I work with." On receiving her package, Scott had been dismayed to find that her two favorite prints, *Awaken from the Unknowing* and *Nocturne*, belonged to a previous (and no longer available) portfolio. "Can't you make some more?" she wrote.[36]

The same year as the Heritage show, 1964, White completed the large ink and charcoal drawing *Birmingham Totem* (fig. 1.2). This six-foot-high work on paper is an homage to martyrs of the contemporary civil rights struggle, particularly the four girls killed the previous year in the bombing of the Sixteenth Street Baptist Church in Birmingham, Alabama. As Andrea Barnwell has pointed out, a "totem" usually venerates the family, clan, the ancestral, but in White's work it is instead a "visual record of destruction, violence, and immeasurable loss."[37] The picture is a reminder of America's self-immolation of her citizenry, the country's fissures, not its union. The totemic structure in the drawing is a mound composed from an exploded building. Planks, beams, the remnants of altars and pews give us the church context. A youthful male figure sits atop the heaping destruction, shrouded, and with downcast eyes surveying the devastation beneath him. But his hands are engaged, as if he is caressing the ruins. From his right hand dangles a plumb line, marking him as a builder and creator, symbolic of those who reconstruct and renew, removed from such despicable acts of racial hatred and intolerance; his generation will build a new house and get it in order, and create a lasting structure for peace, rather than just an illusory edifice of safety.[38] Here White displays his skill as a draftsman. We are struck by the dense versus open spaces of the picture plane, the angular broken planks set against the organic undulations of the body above. There is the intertwining of the allegorical with the spe-

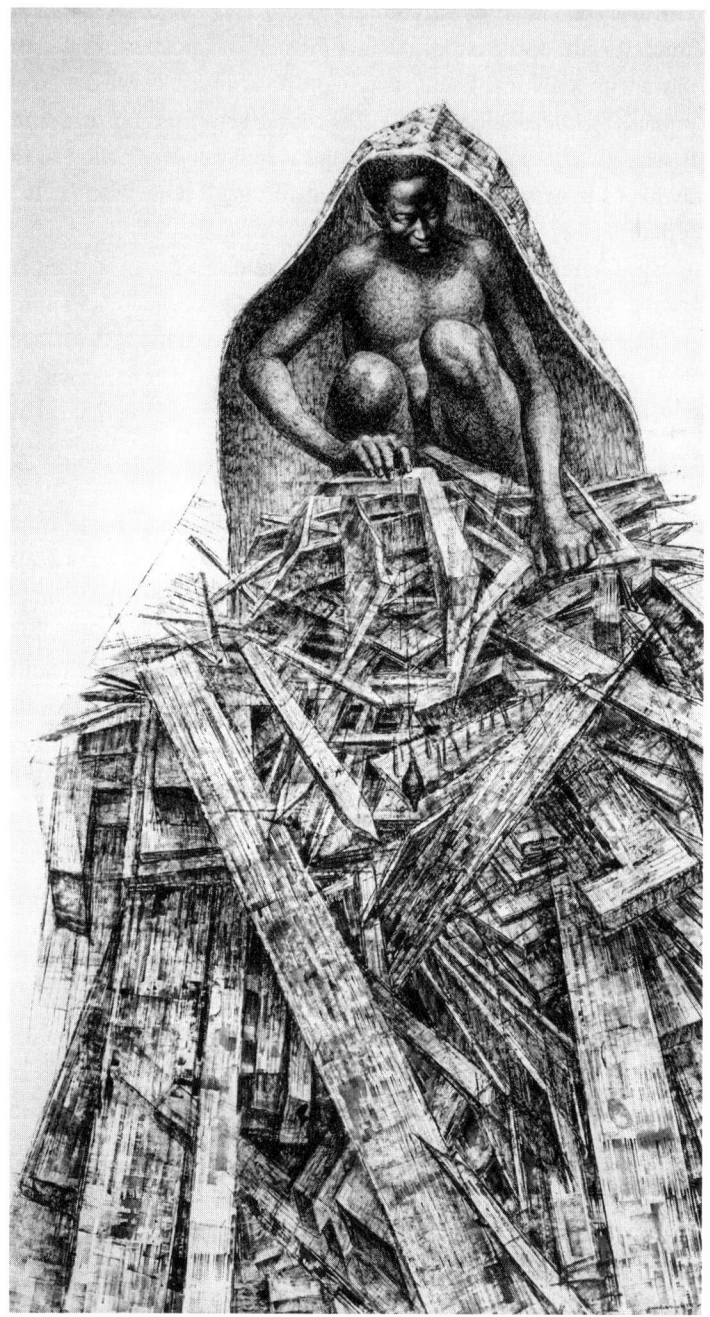

FIG. 1.2 Charles White, *Birmingham Totem*, 1964. Ink and charcoal on paper. The High Museum of Art, Atlanta, with funds from Edith G. and Philip A. Rhodes and the National Endowment for the Arts, 1978.3. Courtesy © 1964 Charles White Archives.

cific, unmistakable protest in the midst of unrelenting beauty. *Birmingham Totem* somehow summons up the past but comments forthrightly on the here and now.

Similarly, the *J'Accuse!* series (some eighteen drawings in charcoal and ink), which White worked on throughout 1966, is a paean to contemporary black struggles. Single figures or groups emerge out of surfaces, deep hued and dense, swirling and primordial, or appointed with the sketchy outlines of place, the intimations of a screened backdrop, or the fine branches of a bending tree. Many of the figures engage and confront the viewer, and in the first person — "I accuse" — indict the United States for its inability to come to terms with its democratic creed and the inequities of society, particularly those based on race. As Barnwell has remarked, the title of White's series recalls the Dreyfus Affair in late nineteenth-century France, where anti-Semitism fueled the court-martial of an artillery officer, Captain Alfred Dreyfus. The scandal and outcry over the case was captured in Emile Zola's 1898 essay "J'Accuse," a public letter to the French president that excoriated the country's military and its racism.[39] Yet White's *J'Accuse* can also be linked semantically to the terms of another antiracist call in the artist's lifetime: a petition brought before the United Nations in 1951 by the Civil Rights Congress on behalf of African Americans, indicting the United States for systematic ethnic slaughter or genocide. The accusation circulated further in a document produced in Paris titled "We Charge Genocide." A drawing by White accompanied a 1952 article on the petition in Paul Robeson's magazine *Freedom*.[40]

J'Accuse! No. 11 presides over Jack Parks's sumptuous living space in the film *For Love of Ivy* (see plate 3). Its paired tondos forecast the intimacy of Parks and Ivy Moore, in what Bogle has referred to as a "Doris Day–Rock Hudson romantic comedy done in blackface."[41] But discussions of Black Power, the NAACP, and Sidney Poitier as Parks, a no-nonsense and cosmopolitan black businessman in a white world, give the film another kind of depth. It is the story line of Abbey Lincoln's character Ivy Moore and her desire to escape domestic service in the suburbs for a more independent and full life in the city, her "liberation," that drives the film. *J'Accuse! No. 11*'s signature presence in the film also embodied such ideas and mirrors Poitier's relationship to the production of the motion picture, demonstrating his star power; he wrote the story and engaged musician Quincy Jones to compose the score, including music by Shirley Horn, B. B. King, and Maya Angelou. *J'Accuse! No. 11* is part of the actor's own art collection as well.[42]

A younger generation of artists connected with White's technical mastery and his activist voice when he began teaching at Otis Art Institute in spring

1965, just months before the Watts Rebellion.[43] In 1977 White became chair of the drawing department at Otis and held the position until his death two years later. Among his many students over the years were David Hammons, Suzanne Jackson, Alonzo Davis, Dan Concholar, Timothy Washington, and Kent Twitchell. Kerry James Marshall and Richard Wyatt began working with White as young teens. Both were part of the Tutor/Art Program sponsored by Golden State Mutual Life Insurance that provided Saturday art classes at Otis for gifted, underprivileged high school students. According to Wyatt, White's teachings went beyond the rubrics of technique and style. He taught that art should be invested with emotion, a tool for expressing injustice, and should have meaning for people in the world.[44]

White's influence on a new generation of artists was neither restricted to those who studied with him formally nor simply in terms of craftsmanship. This is particularly true in the case of young African American artists, and especially the community that was forming itself in California. He recommended them for commissions: for example, ceramicist Doyle Lane completed a mural-scale mosaic for the International Children's School, where White was a board member. He attended studio sales, as a late 1970s invite from painter and writer Yvonne Cole Meo suggests.

Lane, Cole Meo, and White were part of a broad circle in Los Angeles, but others from the Bay Area were also part of the crowd. Larry Walker wrote from Stockton, letting White know about a show he was organizing with local collections that included several of the elder artist's prints. He mused about finding more time for his own painting. Walker was not only a working artist who taught at the university level but also the father of a precocious eight-year-old, the young Kara Walker.[45] Multimedia artist Marie Johnson Calloway was incredibly active in the Bay Area, teaching, curating, organizing, and exhibiting throughout the state. A note from May 1970 reveals the climate on college campuses during this time and the role artists like Johnson Calloway and White played in mentoring new artists/activists. A planned program with White at San Jose State (where Johnson Calloway was chair of the art department) had to be postponed due to student strikes and antiwar protests; he eventually made it there the following spring.[46]

Many artists working in educational settings across the state asked White to present to their classes and programs. Printmaker Margo Humphrey invited the artist to the lithography workshop she had just set up at University of California, Santa Cruz, in 1977. White was not only a master of print method; he had immersed himself for decades in the philosophy behind multiples and graphics. He lectured for Gloria Bohanon's "Black Culture Week" program at Los Angeles Community College (LACC) in February 1974. A painter, Bohanon would go on to teach in all areas at LACC—design, drawing, painting, printmaking—as well as chair the art department during her three-decade career. LACC represented the type of program that attracted White in that it provided affordable education to the working class and people of color. David Hammons and John Riddle both went there. In this spirit, White and other African American artists participated in the exhibition *Black Art in L.A.*, 1970, a collaboration between the school's DaVinci Gallery (run by artist and art historian Kazuo Higa) and the Brockman Gallery in Leimert Park. Younger artists in Los Angeles also got to know White by volunteering to take this nondriver to his various appointments.[47]

White's engagement with emerging African American artists helped catalyze the burgeoning art scene. He lent his support to institutions of all kinds, beginning as early as 1960. He participated in juries for high school art competitions sponsored by groups such as Compton's Allied Arts Committee or by businesses such as Safety Savings and Loan, and made presentations to these groups and at public schools throughout the city. His friendship with William Pajaud, a painter who also worked for the publicity division at Golden State Mutual Life Insurance, led to number of collaborations. White's images featured in a calendar given away to policyholders. The company also commissioned the drawing *General Moses (Harriet Tubman)*, 1965, which jumpstarted its art collecting in earnest, in effect benefiting local and national artists. That same year Golden State began supporting the Tutor/Art Program for high school students at Otis, around the time that White began teaching there. White's commitment to budding black cultural organizations was no less focused. He corresponded with Brockman Gallery, run by the artists and brothers, Alonzo Davis and Dale Brockman Davis, from its inception in 1967. His interactions with the gallery lasted throughout his lifetime. He had a similar dedication to organizations such as the Inner City Cultural Center and the Black Arts Council.[48]

One might posit that White's tireless engagement with artists and the art scene was simply part and parcel of the times—the type of collaborative ethos that one imagines of an American activist art world of the 1960s and 1970s. Yet by the time White arrived in Los Angeles, his reputation was more than secure; he was already a star in the art world. Why did he participate in high school juries and local auctions, one-day shows at churches and black businesses, or group efforts in spaces that were just starting out? White's cultural activism at the grassroots level was part of his profile; for him it was part of what constituted *being* an artist. It was the social and communicative contours of the creative act, learned in his travels throughout the world, particularly in his training grounds of Chicago, Mexico, and New York. And it was part of the progressive ethos that he took to California in the 1950s and that profoundly affected the art landscape of the postwar period.

Progressive New York and Mexico

Charles White called New York home from roughly 1942 until 1956, when he left for Los Angeles. While his initial introduction to progressive and leftist art-making ideals was certainly formed in his hometown of Chicago, the time he spent in the major American art center had a profound effect on his career, creative ideas, and social politics.

Arriving in New York in 1942, Charles White and his first wife Elizabeth Catlett secured summer jobs codirecting the art program for the Workers Children's Camp (known as Wo-Chi-Ca) in Hunterdon County, New Jersey. Founded in 1934 by the Furrier's Union, Wo-Chi-Ca was among the summer camps supported by the labor movement and part of leftist networks that welcomed African Americans from the 1920s into the 1950s.[49] In New York, White was a member of groups such as Artists Union and American Artists' Congress. During the 1940s he was a contributing editor of *New Masses* magazine, and he and Catlett both taught at the George Washington Carver School, an independent institution in Harlem run by the Communist Party (CPUSA).[50] White's long-running representation by American Contemporary Artists (ACA) Galleries also involved him with a leftist cohort. Opening in 1932, ACA was one of the few galleries to showcase American art; its roster was also incredibly diverse, featuring women, Asian, African American, and Jewish artists and others, most demonstrating a radical if figurative bent.[51]

Other groups in Harlem had a similar progressive agenda. The Vanguard, run by cultural activist Louise Thompson Patterson and sculptor Augusta Savage, presented political forums and artistic activities and served as a Marxist study group. Charles Alston and Henry Bannarn's studio at 306 W. 141st Street—called 306—was also a place where a progressive cultural contingent found a home.[52] Indeed, White's imbrication in the New York art scene at midcentury exemplifies James Smethurst's contention that "African American artists and intellectuals were at the center of the cultural conversations and the shaping of the poetics of the Popular Front in the United States," or radical and leftist art networks.[53]

White was drawn, as many American artists were, to the epic walls and radical content of the Mexican mural painters. He finally made the sojourn to Mexico in 1946 when Catlett won a Rosenwald Fellowship to produce her print series *The Negro Woman*, 1946–47, there. They met Diego Rivera, José Clemente Orozco, and Pablo O'Higgins; they even stayed at the home of David Alfaro Siqueiros for a time. White took classes at the Escuela de Pintura y Escultura de la Secretaría de Educación Pública, the famed art school better known as La Esmeralda. He joined the Taller de Gráfica Popular and worked with Leopoldo Méndez, expanding the reach of his print technique. The Taller's grounding in art as a fundamentally democratic practice and interest in making it available to all through multiples deeply appealed to White.[54] He had published prints with the Graphic Workshop in New York earlier in the 1940s and would go on to publish several of his own print portfolios, including through the leftist publication *Masses and Mainstream* in 1953.

White's involvement in progressive and left-leaning art circles in the United States and Mexico provided a firm basis for the style and content of his art. These networks also gave him a sense of what constituted an art community, what it was, what it did, and what it could accomplish.

More Than Migration Narratives

White's fascination with black migration, the American South, and issues of African American as well as African diasporic histories were ideas that captivated many African American artists of his generation, including his Chicago colleague Eldzier Cortor, Elizabeth Catlett, and his lifelong correspondent Jacob Lawrence.[55]

Aided by a Rosenwald Fellowship, which encouraged artists in all areas to chronicle the South in the service of improving "education, health, and opportunity for blacks in the United States," White spent 1942–43 traveling in the region.[56] He aimed to observe and record real people—laborers and farmers—as subjects of future easel paintings and murals. He wanted to create images that could banish and replace "the plague of distortions, stereotyped and superficial caricatures of 'uncles,' 'mammies,' and 'pickaninnies' that were used to portray black subjects in Hollywood and in art."[57] In the fall of 1942, White traveled through Louisiana, Georgia, Virginia, and his family home in Mississippi, experiencing personal violence on two occasions.[58] The artist stayed at Hampton University in Virginia for six months in 1943 completing the fresco-secco mural *The Contribution of the Negro to Democracy in America* for the Wainwright Auditorium in Clarke Hall, which was unveiled on June 25.[59]

Both White and Lawrence were struck by the black visual culture of the South, working-class culture mostly referred to as "folk art" if referred to at all. How homes were decorated with posters, newspaper, flowers, quilts. Both artists recognized in these traditions the fount of their own visual thinking. And they were not alone. Others of their generation, like Horace Pippin, Haywood Bill Rivers, and Romare Bearden, celebrated such principles in their work. Eldzier Cortor's paintings of the 1940s—particularly his focus on interiors, as in *Room No. 5*, 1948—clearly reveal the aesthetics of this push toward decoration, the willing of the beautiful into view. Later, in the 1960s, a younger cohort of black painters (some originally from the South), including Sam Gilliam, Al Loving, and William T. Williams, would see black vernacular visual strategies as a touchstone for abstract works.[60]

Both Guthrie P. Ramsey Jr. and Henry Louis Gates Jr. have written of the development of African American culture in the early twentieth century as a space of cross-pollination and synthesis affected by the motions of migration itself. The outlined polarities of the pastoral South and the industrial North, as "mythic sites of cultural memory" on the one hand and "cultural production" on the other, should instead be seen as a dialogue around modernism and as a conversation that also produces it.[61] As artists like White, Lawrence, Cortor, and others (born and working in the North) realized, and as their work demonstrates too, the environs of their cultural world were still resolutely marked by the South. Indeed, they are examples of the hybridity and contestation that brought the modern into view.

As Ramsey tells us, we can designate this emergent bricolage of northern/southern African American cultures, formed through the processes of early twentieth-century migration, as Afro-modernism. Yet, as film scholar Jacqueline Stewart reminds us, migration also transformed aesthetic systems of the dominant culture in this period, enforcing changes in cinematic codes and filmic languages. Migration and the black modern irrevocably altered American public life, through black urbanization, mobility, and visibility. This is registered in early film with the misrecognition of blackness, at the very moment of migration, which literally and physically challenged prescribed roles in society. In some filmic narratives, blackness is constructed as an entity that is not always immediately recognizable and thus must be policed/contained as sign. As Stewart argues, leisure, pleasure, and the presence of the black body are issues that are worked through in a contested public sphere—on the streetcar and "the stroll" but also in the movie theater and the dancehall. We can also consider "fine art" through this lens, where proscriptions against leisure are also proscriptions against art making. White's example of being denied art training repeatedly in his early years and his determination and success in creating his own opportunities in this regard suggests how emerging black fine artists conquered these hurdles.[62]

Artists of White's generation were obsessed by African and African diasporic histories. In one way, we can even look at them as historians, at the very least autodidacts, since information about African diasporic life was hardly accessible, and they had to uncover and dig for it themselves. Public libraries were key sites for this work. White's relationship with the library began when he was five years old, when his mother (Ethelene Gary Marsh), lacking the resources to afford child care, dropped him there with his lunch on her way to work. He would stay all day, watched over by librarians (who gave him picture books) until his mother came for him at the end of her shift. Books and magazines were his earliest friends. The relationship with the library continued throughout his life, as he read collection after collection as a way to educate himself. His discovery of Alain Locke's *New Negro* (1925) in high school was a revelation, and from then on African diasporic history "became a secret life."[63] His challenges to teachers and other students to see this side of history were summarily dismissed and even caused him to take an extra year to finish high school.

White's original plan of work for the Rosenwald Fellowship had him traveling through the southern United States and to Mexico to study mural technique, but wartime travel regulations curtailed the Mexican portion of his trip. Instead he stayed in New York, enrolling in the Art Students League and conducting research at the Schomburg Center for Research in Black Culture.[64] The Schomburg was, of course, the place where Lawrence gathered the information for his earliest multipanel series; he even commemorated the library with a quasi-portrait of the collection's founder, Arturo Schomburg (*The Curator*, 1937). Scholar Deborah Willis, a former curator there, has elucidated the impact that the Schomburg and other libraries had on African American artists and communities in the early twentieth century. She has written about the multiple ways that these institutions served their neighborhoods, not only with books and manuscripts but also by hosting plays, poetry readings, lectures, and art classes. These places were activist sites, with librarians who saw them as central to the "community's intellectual life."[65] One Schomburg librarian, seeing the impact of street-corner orators, decided to hire a few to promote the library on Harlem streets, a neighborhood now transformed by the presence of black migrants.

According to Willis, the library became a "creative partner" for artists: because books and art were displayed together, one could get the sense that stories had visual aesthetics too.[66] It is interesting to think about an artist like White going to the library before he picked up a brush and making paintings that claim their origins there. Certainly, it was not only artists who made use of libraries, and not only in New York but around the country. The comments of Jean Blackwell Hutson, curator of the Schomburg Collection from 1948 to 1980, are emblematic of African Americans' hunger for knowledge of their origins, to know that which was suppressed. Hutson "observed that Harlem residents had such a 'relentless intellectual thirst' for black and African history that 'rare and out-of-print books could not be replaced when they were worn to shreds, and books still in print could not be replaced fast enough with the money available.'"[67] White addressed this quest in some of his first mature works—*Five Great American Negroes*, 1939–40; *A History of the Negro Press*, 1940; and *The Contribution of the Negro to Democracy in America*, 1943—murals (monumental history paintings) meant to fill the caesuras of American and global histories by illuminating the black past.

The keen study of the African American and African diasporic history by artists and others was done in the service of refuting the images of "subservience, ignorance, and inferiority" that continued to be manufactured and consumed by the dominant white culture.[68] Jacqueline Stewart has discussed this through an emerging African American film culture, where black entrepreneurs of the 1910s, like Nobel Johnson and Oscar Micheaux, responded to the growth of a black moviegoing public "with disposable income and race-conscious views."[69] Such black-owned companies sought to deliver more progressive images. They produced dramas almost exclusively, setting them up as "high art" against the lower end of comedy and the black stereotype. Indeed, we can compare the serious drama of such films to White's initial focus on history painting as an equally critical endeavor to transform the black public image. With their settings in the North, South, and West, these films reflected in art the visibility of black mobility, the centrality of travel and migration. The space of the West in these films is also one of opportunity, the optimal place for black advancement and self-improvement. In this way the western mythos of such early black-produced films mirrors that of their mainstream white counterparts.

Stewart's elucidation of the reconstruction of the black image at this time—a period known more widely as the New Negro Movement—highlights the construction of the black heroic to dispel and transform negative imagery. We find the protagonists of these films—the waiters, railroad porters, and so on—drawn from the life of migration, the heroes of the transformation and construction of black modern life. The other heroic figure in early black film was the soldier. Using government documentary footage from World War I and in fictional narratives, filmmakers described the ultimate African American patriot. White too would use the figure of the black military to similar ends in works created around World War II. He sketched the contours of valiance and bravery in prints such as *Our War*, c. 1947, in which black patriotism abroad was also met by refutation of African American humanity at home.[70]

Left to California

When Charles White wrote in the early 1940s that he wanted to challenge and dismiss "the plague of distortions, stereotyped and superficial caricatures," he was referring not just to fine art but also to the mass culture of Hollywood.[71] It seems only fitting that he himself would end up living in the U.S. capital for the production of such images in the post–World War II period. It is also apropos in the ways in which White brings the West some of the ethos of Popular Front aesthetics. We see this in his creation of work that was available to audiences through realist frameworks yet steeped in a deep understanding of history and form. The work remained available or popular while offering a critique of mass culture.[72]

As scholar Andrew Hemingway sees it, White was one of the most important "Communist" artists of the 1950s; that is, he brought the agenda of the socially engaged art of the 1930s and 1940s into the future. After White's extensive trip to Europe (particularly Eastern Europe) and the USSR in 1951, Hemingway notes that there was a shift toward a seraphic naturalism, where the focus turned to an ideal figure emanating "beauty and optimism," which also marked that phase of Communist culture.[73] Yet White was part of a cadre of American artists, including Jacob Lawrence and Elizabeth Catlett, whose commitment to the figure did not wane during this period. For these artists and others like Jack Levine, Alice Neel, Leon Golub, and José Luis Cuevas in Mexico, an assertion of humanism was what mattered most. "Pictures of people," Neel concluded, affirmed humanity and battled the body's dehumanization and reification.[74]

However, as James Smethurst argues, a leftist black culture was also responsible for bringing these ideas forward. White was a contributor to Paul Robeson's magazine *Freedom*. When it ceased publication in 1954, its ideas and content were continued in *Freedomways* (1961–85), whose managing editor, Esther Cooper Jackson, was a black feminist who not only had been part of the *Freedom* staff, but was also active on the Left and in the CPUSA for decades.⁷⁵ Another such organization was the Committee for the Negro in the Arts. As Frances Barrett White records, "The Committee for the Negro in the Arts (CNA) began in earnest with the nation's obsession with television."⁷⁶ Realizing that TV broadcasts continued the bombardment by images that furthered black artists' sublimation and invisibility, White and others established CNA around 1949; it was dedicated to diversifying the arts both in terms of content and with an eye toward the impact that jobs in industries such as film, television, and theater could have on African American communities. Members such as Ruby Dee and Ossie Davis, Lorraine Hansberry, and Langston Hughes were all part of the black Left at midcentury, attesting to the group's radical stance.⁷⁷ What is also important here is how this organization demonstrates the fundamental critique of stock characterizations of African Americans. It was this problematizing of the black image that White offered to the young artists with whom he engaged in California.

Black revolutionary movements of the 1960s and 1970s had an "open engagement" with Marxist-Leninism as well as the politics of Mao Zedong; they also continued leftist/Communist positions and struggles that had marked the United States from the 1930s through the 1950s.⁷⁸ The concept of a black folk culture—one that was alternative, nonconformist, and outside commercial mass culture—as the basis of an emerging avant-garde in the 1960s and 1970s was again a model drawn from earlier in the century, a facet of both the Harlem Renaissance and the Popular Front.⁷⁹

The West Coast, Smethurst insists, was most influential in terms of the early dissemination of ideas and practices that came to be known as the Black Arts Movement. This was engendered during the early 1960s by local college culture and study groups on African American and African history and Marxism in places like Merritt College in Oakland; San Francisco State College; University of California, Berkeley; Los Angeles City College; and UCLA, and which produced activists such as Huey Newton, Bobby Seale, and Ron Karenga.⁸⁰ Smethurst focuses heavily on the influence of Bay Area print culture in independent magazines like *Soulbook* and *Black Dialogue*; experimental theater produced by Ed Bullins and Marvin X, and the poetry of Bob Kaufman. He also describes as revelatory the Los Angeles activities of poets Jayne Cortez and Quincy Troupe; experimental music groups run by Horace Tapscott, including the Pan Afrikan Peoples Arkestra; the early anthologies *From the Ashes* (1967) and *Watts Poets* (1968); and multimedia works at Studio Watts. Yet Smethurst's reliance on the flow of print culture as the most consistent method for the dissemination of radical black art making leads him to see Los Angeles as never quite living up to its importance as a national artistic center in the 1960s and 1970s.⁸¹

Through the figure of Charles White, we can understand the impact of a visual avant-garde in black postwar culture. Certainly we can see this institutionally in his effects on Ruth Waddy and her organization Art West Associated, on Dale Brockman Davis and Alonzo Davis and the workings of Brockman Gallery, and in the creations of students like David Hammons, Suzanne Jackson, and Timothy Washington, whose work would define this period. In White we also can trace the flow of radical art from the East Coast and a Popular Front context to the postwar West.

We can consider White's impact on West Coast art making and on the younger generation that was a part of the Black Arts Movement through three broad frameworks: a tradition that privileged the figure or representational body; a fascination with visual narratives of history, particularly those of the African Diaspora; and a commitment to making art available to a wide audience, accomplished through visual and political legibility and through medium, that is, his dedication to the print portfolio and to exhibiting in many types of locations, from the church to the museum. In these ways, White's work coalesced a community.

In the late 1960s White came across a cache of nineteenth-century posters that led him to create his well-known *Wanted Poster* series.⁸² These century-old objects are generally found in two categories, those promoting auctions of human chattel and others announcing those who had escaped. These placards' detailed description of the subject in text—in the case of runaways listing things like height, complexion, marks, or scars (from punishment), and in auction posters assuring buyers that the "goods" were disease-free—exist in tension with the illustrations that sometimes accompany them: black silhouettes of stock figures, some on the run. White's series give physical presence and individuality to these vintage generic bodies, envisioning in paint identities and personalities that bring them to life on the page. While the figures remain anonymous, they become paradigmatic, larger than life.⁸³

In the *Wanted Poster* series, White concentrates on the idea of the slave auction. He sets up a series of oppositions, evoked in the friction between showing a detailed and carefully rendered portrait and letting us know that this person, whether adult or child, was for sale. These bodies—at times fulsome (in the case of nude women offered as "healthy") or emaciated (many of the children)—float in planes of oil wash along with other recurring archetypal images, transparent icons of the U.S. nation: flags disembodied into hovering stars and stripes and moribund eagles. In *Wanted Poster Series #17*, the "stars and bars" of the flag transmogrify into vertical shafts that suggest a jail cell. The "Southern Cross" of the Confederate standard is placed across a woman's body in *Wanted Poster Series #6* (fig. 1.3), marking her as a target.

The ground of these paintings recalls the faceted space introduced in *General Moses (Harriet Tubman)*. A sepia tone evokes the feel of crumpled and weathered paper and the vintage posters that were White's models. As with the original placards, text is important in White's paintings. Much of it reflects the language of commerce in the original objects: "sold," "valuable," "dollars," "insured," "negroes." The words are painted to appear stenciled, their florid serifs another indicator of bygone days. But what is notable is how the embedded words also echo the way other American artists were handling language at this time. While its use as art form has been ascribed to conceptualists such as Sol LeWitt, Lawrence Wiener, or Joseph Kosuth, the radical graphic tradition among California-based Chicano artists like Rupert García, Malaquias Montoya, and Andrew Zermeño arrayed language with image in flyers, posters, calendars, prints, and other equally available forms to bring art to a wider public. *The Wall of Respect*, 1967, a mural painted by the African American artists collective Organization of Black American Culture (OBAC) on an abandoned building in the South Side of Chicago, included images and poems and was created at times as actual readings or music performances were taking place.[84]

This imbrication with language that characterizes the *Wanted Poster* series expands the conceptual readings and sensibilities of these works. At the same time, the breaks, folds, cracks, tears, and washes that White inscribed onto the surface are indicative of the problems of painting. These marks show more than a passing connection to what so many others were trying to work out at this time as they grappled with the medium's very validity.[85] White's use of such a faceted effect had its roots in the cubist picture. He had started out professionally as a muralist who used space and perspective in ways that allowed for the constantly changing and almost never straight-on orientation of the viewer. The captive figures in the *Wanted Poster* series are seen from above and below and straight ahead. Yet they are adrift in a primordial scene suffused with Americana that disintegrates before our eyes. This is not perspective but transhistorical space, one where the past and present collide, shift, pass each other by, and coexist at once. These are not the history paintings that White was known for at the beginning of his career—featuring heroes from an earlier moment with much to tell us about our own time—but works where the past and present inform each other on the physical plane of the picture itself.

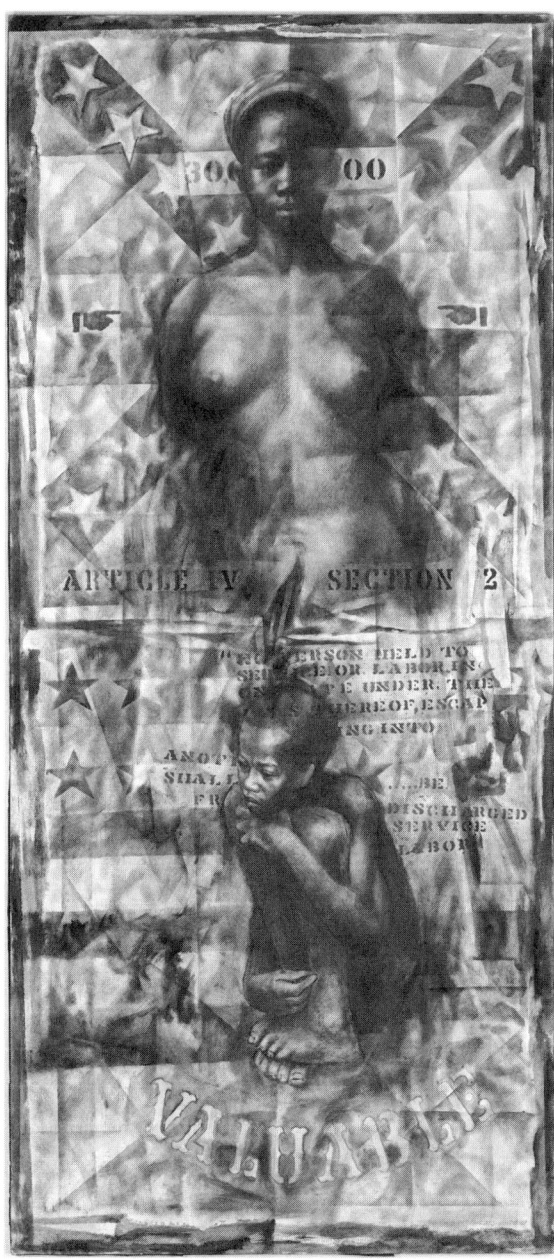

FIG. 1.3 Charles White, *Wanted Poster #6*, 1969. Oil wash on board. Blanton Museum of Art, University of Texas at Austin, The Susan G. and Edmund W. Gordon Family Collection, 2014. Photo Credit: Milli Apelgren. Courtesy © 1969 Charles White Archives.

Scholars Salamishah Tillet and Huey Copeland have both remarked on slavery's reappearance in late twentieth-century art, a lens through which African American artists have refracted the "ongoing effects" of the peculiar institution and glossed an experience of democracy that continues to be conflicted, in what Tillet calls "civic estrangement."[86] These artistic endeavors are interested in how slavery has extended its ghostly presence into the modern day. Such creative forays are more metaphoric than realistic, "sites of slavery" that revisit specific places but engage and explode the aporias of memory and reconfigure symbols and understandings of Americanness. Unlike later artists such as Renee Green or Glenn Ligon, White did not reject the frame of black portraiture or move toward the fully nonobjective, but his development of faceted surfaces and minimalist planes in the *Wanted Poster* series speaks to the lure of abstraction's freeing ambivalence. The simultaneously backward and forward pull of the transhistorical is also a sign of what some call Afro-futurism.

White's work also addresses what Copeland finds a significant aspect of these turns to such fraught global histories: the reckoning with African diasporic subjects as property and how such "economies of slavery" continue to haunt the present.[87] Black people become the ultimate commodities, the slave modernism's ultimate readymade.[88]

Names were also an important textual aspect of the nineteenth-century posters White would have encountered. On the one hand, there was the potential for individuality that could come through in such identifications; on the other, appearing in print in these documents, they functioned much more as an extension of their labor or task, as in "Harry 27 an excellent fisherman." Such lists of names, ages, and professions read as the manifests they were.

Ironically, perhaps, it is this type of commercial/clinical/pseudoscientific language that marked the conceptualism of the period. In *Wanted Poster Series #17*, 1971, a mother and child are framed by a column of names to the left and corresponding ages to the right. "Earl speaks French," while Nancy's skill cannot be made out as it disappears into the picture surface. Toward the end of the grouping, we see "Harriet." By this time, we know her as a recurring personage in the artist's oeuvre, the manifestation of the slave absconder, who chooses freedom for herself and also makes it possible for others. Next to Harriet is "Hastie," which might not hold any special meaning for us unless we know that Hastie and Harriet are the names of the artist's great-aunts.

The manufacture of transhistorical space in the *Wanted Poster* series thus allows White to insert the personal as it relates to the larger arc of history and meaning. Two other paintings, made a year after *Wanted Poster Series #17* and visually very different, continue these ideas. In *Harriet* and *Mississippi*, both from 1972, White substitutes the active faceted space with one that is more stark and minimalist. Both center on a single shrouded figure above whose head hovers a bloody form. In *Harriet* (plate 5), a violent red splatter interrupts the stillness and symmetry of the body in black on the white ground. The figure in the other painting becomes the center of a compass; a crimson handprint and the word "Mississippi" substitute for the South. These pictures bring to mind civil rights struggles and black migrations as well as the self-liberation of the enslaved. However, they also commemorate White's family: the Mississippi where his grandmother was born a slave, the Mississippi in which his aunts Harriet and Hastie stayed, the Mississippi that his mother left, the Mississippi where four relatives were lynched.[89]

From *General Moses (Harriet Tubman)* to *Mississippi*, White's heroic visual narrative was dominated by women during the 1960s. But women had been asserting themselves in his oeuvre for years. In 1951, for his third solo show at ACA Galleries, for instance, he centered his presentation on such images. Critics saw in the paintings, drawings, and "oversized linoleum prints" the monumentality and social message that he had been developing since his mural work. The figures radiated the colossal, the undaunted, with large "strong hands" signaling epic labor and a boundless creativity.[90] Included was an early print version of *General Moses (Harriet Tubman)*, along with a drawing of the artist's mother. Through these works on paper, White not only celebrated women generally but paid homage to people like his mother, whose intrepidness was the untold story of the modern United States.

White's overwhelming turn to images of women beginning in the midcentury, however, was not necessarily random. In fact, this focus seems to have coincided with theoretical positions advanced by some in his New York circle, including activist Esther Cooper Jackson, journalist Marvel Cooke, and artist Elizabeth Catlett. Scholars Farah Jasmine Griffin, Mary Helen Washington, and Erik S. McDuffie have unpacked the discourse of "black left feminism" that developed from the 1930s forward. Linked to the aims of the Popular Front, it was a stand that placed working-class black women at the center of social struggle in ways that spoke to the intersection of race, class, gender, and ultimately transnational discourse.[91]

In these critical ideas that center on black working women as vanguard, and particularly domestics, White would have seen his aunts Harriet and Hastie, but particularly his mother, who similarly made her way from the South to the streets of Chicago, alone, to a (continuing) life of domestic service. For White, women were the ultimate figures whose bodies signified the makings of the modern. They were emblems of migration and of the exigencies of labor. In the complexities of the intersectionality of race and gender he understood an oppositional consciousness. Their struggles with domination and subordination pointed to a topography of resistance. White dedicated his work to the travails of such women but celebrated the forward-looking "utopian content" of their own visions, which he visualized through their beauty.[92]

White's influence on LA's community of African American artists from the 1950s onward is legendary. It emanated from an eloquently crafted and exquisitely detailed representational style that privileged the black body as a cipher both historical and magnificent. Reception was key: art was to be available as an object that could be appreciated *and* purchased by a larger public; art was to coalesce community. These ideas were joined with a keen focus on the female form as a sign of the African American modern. This latter stream was taken up by the young Betye Saar, whose early concentration on female subjectivity would blossom in the coming decades.

BETYE SAAR: DESIGNER TO ARTIST

In 1960 Betye Saar created *To Catch a Unicorn* (plate 6). The color etching was among her first prints, and in it, she hints at the imagery she would mine for years to come. The sun and the moon, elements of the cosmos, hover over a dark sky. They shine above a forest scene in which a woman grasps a unicorn; both tilt their heads skyward. In Western mythology, the unicorn is a force for good, though it is wild and able to be tamed only by a virginal maiden. In Saar's work, the virgin stands against the unicorn's traditional whiteness—shapely, nude, and black.

The activities of artists like Saar, Charles White, and Melvin Edwards helped bring an art community into existence. Some initially continued to work commercially while pursuing fine arts.

Curtis Tann and William Pajaud, who both migrated to California in the 1940s, are emblematic. Originally from New Orleans, Pajaud arrived in Los Angeles in 1948. He eventually found employment as a designer of neckties for the Countess Mara Company and then as an art director for Los Angeles County Air Pollution Control before moving on to a similar position at Golden State Mutual Life insurance. During the 1940s and 1950s, he sold his watercolor paintings at department stores, such as Hartfield's in downtown Los Angeles and Robinson's in Pasadena, where they were displayed in the store windows. Part of Curtis Tann's design background was in creating sets for theater. He and his wife, actress Ethel Mae Henderson, were involved with Cleveland's Karamu House—a settlement house and cultural center whose emphasis on theater attracted significant African American creators, including Langston Hughes——before landing in Los Angeles in 1946. Although Tann was also interested in printmaking and painting, he remained more resolutely within the decorative arts, as they provided him with a stable living. He too worked in textile design, producing neckties for Allen of California and Palm of California between 1946 and 1952. Thereafter, he focused on enamelware at Renoir-Matisse, Sasha Brastaff Industries, and Hanley Corporation, and took on private commissions. Pajaud and Tann were among the first black professional artists Saar would meet. Their example showed her she could pursue a life as an artist. She too would begin in the commercial realm, and early on she created a business with Curtis Tann.[93]

Ebony's "Speaking of People" column offered brief snapshots of African Americans with interesting vocations. Featured in the October 1951 issue were Curtis Tann and Betye Brown (soon to be Saar), who created jewelry and other fine crafts from enamel under the name "Brown and Tann" (fig. 1.4). The piece explains how enamelware is made and how the work is marketed and distributed "in gift shops and interior decorator studios." These outlets, in addition to state fairs, local competitions, and exhibitions in homes and churches, served Brown and Tann and other African American artists throughout the 1950s. The *Ebony* article confirms such working methods and informal networks: "[The] couple uses Tann's garage as a workshop, and his living room as a display room for prospective buyers."[94] With the expansion of the African American population in Los Angeles after World War II, there was a growth in the community of artists and creation of structures to support their work. Saar recalls a variety of black social groups holding events to display art. Tann remembers that Brown and Tann exhibitions were extremely popular, particularly those held in homes: they would clear out all the furniture and set the place up like a gallery, and often sold out. There were also backyard exhibitions around one pool or another. All this activity points to the vibrancy of the developing artists' community and the enthusiasts who supported it.[95]

Unlike New York, Southern California had space—the beach, the desert, the sky, but also homes, backyards, and garages that were easily converted into studios and temporary exhibition spaces for artists. This space of the home is interesting, not so much because of the possibilities that size seems to suggest, but because it was identified with "hobbyists," "amateurs," and "homemakers": labels attached to black women and men struggling to make a living and to support their predilection for art making. If they were lucky, they found work as graphic or window designers. As Judith Wilson points

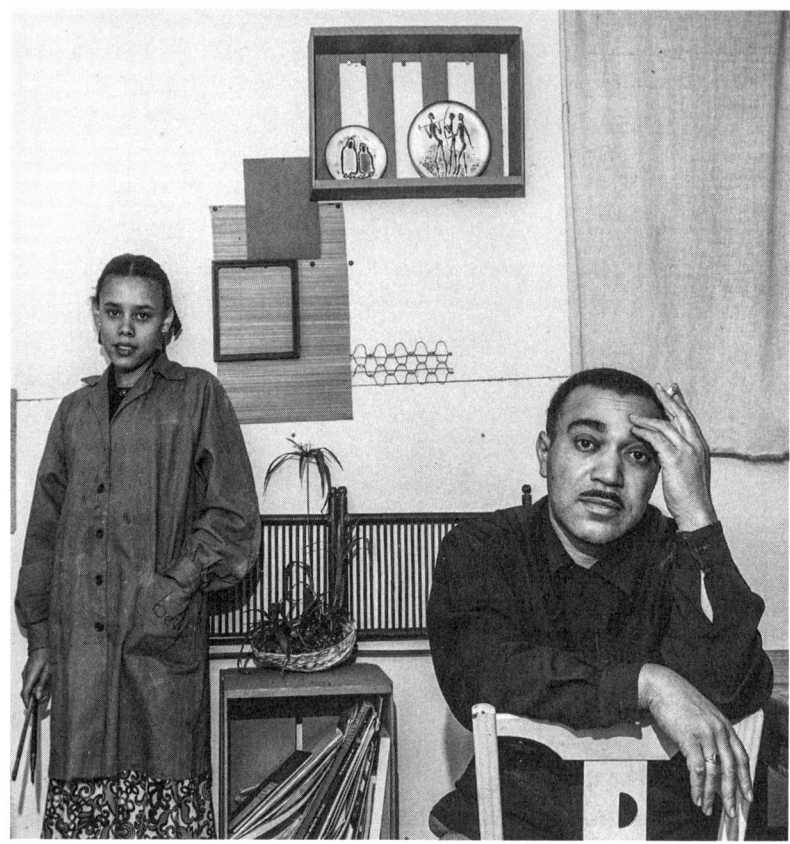

FIG. 1.4 Betye Saar (née Brown) and Curtis Tann in the office space of their decorative arts business, Brown and Tann, 1951. Courtesy Betye Saar and Michael Rosenfeld Gallery LLC, New York, NY.

out, women thrived in the craft, applied, or functional arts, particularly in homes or clubs; they were the antithesis of the male "fine" artist brooding in a garret. However, African American women *and* men usually flourished in the crafts as well. Certainly this goes back to the "usefulness" that such functional art had under slavery and in the postbellum period for people trying to survive economically.[96] Wilson also cites modernism's predilection for incorporating traditions from outside the trajectory of the Western fine art canon, whether these were the arts of Africa, Asia, or Latin America or the artifacts of the functional world. In California, the line between fine and applied art was more permeable, and not only, it seems, for African Americans. Certainly this was evident in the 1950s and 1960s with the huge popularity of Peter Voulkos and John Mason, artists who worked with ceramics on a monumental scale.[97]

In the 1950s, what did it take for a woman to become an artist, especially in a postwar environment in which more women than ever before were trained in the profession, yet were denied access to careers and professorships?[98] Betye Brown (Saar) was born in Watts in 1926, the same year that independent town was annexed to the city of Los Angeles. She spent her early years there, raised by her father, Jefferson Maze Brown—who had come there from Louisiana earlier in the century as a child with his mother—and her mother, Beatrice Parson Brown of Iowa, who had followed an aunt to Los Angeles. Later the family moved to Pasadena, another nurturing space for black communities, especially creative ones. Saar attended Pasadena City College from 1945 to 1947, taking a variety of classes in art, craft, and design. In 1947 she transferred to UCLA, graduating in 1949. She recalled that at both institutions African American students were guided away from the fine arts toward craft and design and were blocked from campus art clubs.[99]

After college, Saar moved from Pasadena to Los Angeles, supporting herself as a social worker while further developing her creative profile. She did small interior design jobs and graphic work for community businesses and, after connecting with Tann and his crowd and learning the enamel process, created her own jewelry and decorative objects. As part of Brown and Tann, Saar showed at regional holiday gift fairs at hotels such as the Biltmore, the Alexander, and the Ambassador. It was at one of these venues that she first met ceramist Richard Saar, who also had pieces on display. A graduate of Jepson School of Art and Chouinard, Saar had his own ceramic business. Betye and Richard were married in 1952.[100]

With the birth of their first daughter Lezley in 1953, Saar resigned from her job as a social worker. While her creative life was compromised to a certain degree, she began making a line of greeting cards. Known as "Studio Cards," they were based on the artist's individual sketches, and then sold by agents to small boutiques. In 1956 the Saars' second daughter, Alison, was born. As Betye later recalled, "In 1956 I had two children, so it wasn't as easy to work as an artist, but I still did my greeting cards."[101] By the late 1950s Saar felt herself being pulled increasingly toward the fine arts—she returned to college to get a teaching credential and study printmaking. Works on paper and the duplication and experimentation possibilities of the print format provided both technological innovation and the creative forms she could manage more easily as a mother.

In interviews that later came her way in the wake of the women's movement, Saar addressed many of the issues raised by women's art making. Creating amid the swirl of activity of three daughters (now older) and sundry

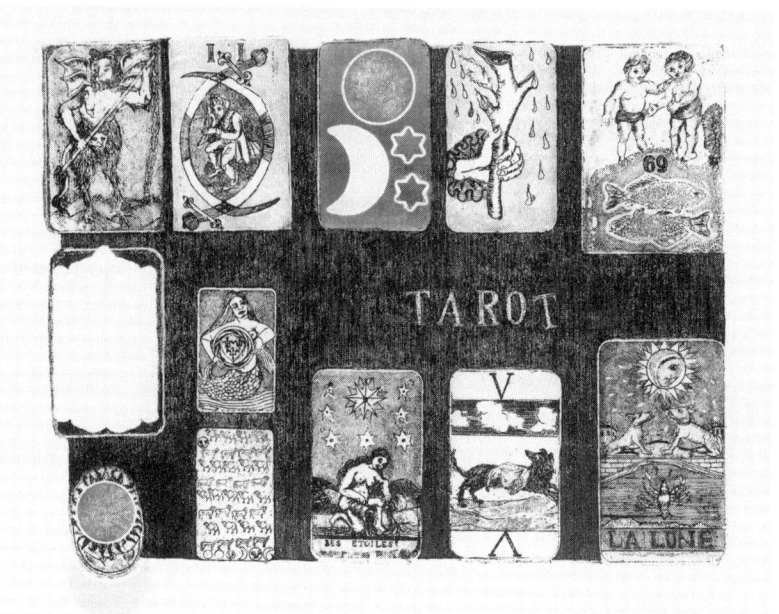

FIG. 1.5 Betye Saar, *House of Tarot*, 1966. Color etching. Courtesy the artist and Michael Rosenfeld Gallery LLC, New York, NY.

pets, when she was asked, "How do you handle being a mother and an artist?" she answered, "What's the difference? It's just dividing the time."[102] Like Faith Ringgold in New York, Saar stressed the importance of motherhood and did not retreat from that gendered role. Rather, she sought to make a better place for the next generation, for her own daughters.[103]

Saar began to focus primarily on printmaking around 1958, the year she returned to school to study those techniques at California State University, Long Beach. Visible are a number of thematic threads and art-making strategies that she would continue to explore throughout her career, including the centrality of images of women, alternative spiritual practices and cosmologies, and the collision of textures. Saar experimented with a wide variety of graphic techniques but favored etchings and serigraphs because she could do them more easily from home. These early prints also manifested the influence of her design training and drew on her work in graphics. Even Saar's interest in texture can be considered evidence of her more three-dimensional thinking (with interiors, for instance) that was manifest later in her assemblages and installations.[104]

Prints such as *To Catch a Unicorn* and *House of Tarot*, 1966 (fig. 1.5), involve themes of palmistry, astrology, and the tarot. These unconventional framings of spirituality were linked in some ways to Saar's own wide-ranging experience of religion as a child—from her parents' more alternative interests in nondenominational, Unity, and Christian Science teachings to the traditional Baptist and Episcopalian churches of her grandmother, aunt, and uncle to the African Methodist Episcopal (AME) traditions of her stepfather. Such a wide variety of possibilities for and freedom of worship was another factor that drew African Americans to California between the wars.[105] The notion of spirituality in Saar's early prints was also related to the national craze for alternate belief systems of the era, and was linked to the life she lived then, connected to the artist communities in the LA canyons. After staying in Hermosa Beach and Redondo Beach, the Saars moved to Laurel Canyon, where Betye was surrounded by creators such as Gabi and Klaus Brill, whose small printing press she would borrow; Edward Kienholz lived there as well. Topanga Canyon is where Saar's contemporaries George Herms and Wallace Berman resided, who were known for similar mystic explorations during this period.[106]

Saar's early works on paper codify the emergence of feminist themes, which she would build on in the decades to come. This is revealed, for instance, in *To Catch a Unicorn*'s curvaceous black maiden, along with the natural world, celestial bodies in the forms of the sun and moon, and the verdant background embracing woman and beast. She repeated these themes in pieces such as *Anticipation*, 1961, in which a woman, full with child and grasping a flower, looks meditatively into the distance, perhaps thinking of what is to come in both of their lives. This layered and textured serigraph anticipates her move into three dimensions. Saar's focus on the female body, a full decade before the preeminence of feminist art making in the 1970s, speaks to her force as a member of the vanguard and is similar to the groundbreaking work of Carolee Schneemann, who also shifted from painting to multimedia practice in the early 1960s.[107]

Saar began submitting her prints to large annual art shows and won accolades. She shared the top prize in the second annual Alondra Park Art Show in Lawndale for 1961. She won a cash award in the 1964 All-City Outdoor Art Festival at Barnsdale Park. In the 1965 Miracle Mile of Art along Wilshire Boulevard, she handily won top honors for graphics with her etching *The Beastie Parade*, 1964. These shows had hundreds of artists' entries and were seen by thousands of visitors. Such distinction surely boosted the profile as well as the self-assurance of the mother of three in her thirties who was pushing herself as an artist. As Saar would later comment, "It took a long time for me to say, 'I am an artist.' I would say, 'I am a designer or an artisan or a craft person.' To say I was an artist took a lot."[108]

In the mid-1960s, commercial galleries began to pick up Betye Saar's prints. Beverly Gleaves, owner of Kozlow Gallery in Encino, saw the work at the 1964 Barnsdale All-City show and offered Saar a solo exhibition that same year. Two years later, Saar had a solo at Ankrum Gallery, which was located on La Cienega Boulevard in LA's gallery row. Archives from Ankrum reveal swift sales in the months following the opening on June 6, 1966. The majority of prints featured animal or mystic subjects. These were not unrelated themes. Jane Carpenter has pointed out the place of animals in mythical iconography, and particularly their role in the tarot, which showed up consistently in Saar's oeuvre over the years.[109]

By late 1966, Saar was affixing her prints to found window frames, effectively moving into the assemblage practice for which she would become known. There is a consistent focus on alternative spiritual systems in these first three-dimensional pieces, including *View from the Palmist's Window*, *View from the Sorcerer's Window*, and *Mystic Window for Leo*, all from 1966. These structures provided a new kind of support for Saar's graphics but also set up a fresh narrative organization that, like a film storyboard, allowed the action of the picture plane to unfold incrementally. In works from this period, the hand becomes the marker of identity, whether the schematic of the palm reader's trade or an impression of the artist's own. These alternate with images of lions for the zodiac sign of Leo, Saar's birth sign, as in *Mystic Window for Leo*. The feline also represents the artist's own powers of vision, as suggested by tarot symbolism. And as has been argued elsewhere, the mystical arena evoked by Saar—and others like Sun Ra—during this period represented a surrogate space of liberation.[110]

Saar's *To Catch a Unicorn* is emblematic of her emergence as a fine artist and her early exploration of print technique. It is also an allegory of a changing cultural landscape. The rising strength of the black community in Los Angeles was representative of the new political, social, and economic power of African Americans across the nation between 1960 and 1980. A growing black majority laid hold to the mystical utopia that Los Angeles symbolized. They worked to tame institutional discrimination, white repression, and racism through the collective power of civil rights and Black Power activism. In the process, it changed the sense of what constituted African American identity *and* American culture.

MELVIN EDWARDS: MEANING IN METAL

Melvin Edwards was another key figure in the evolution of African American artistic communities in Los Angeles in the postwar period. He arrived in Los Angeles from Texas in 1955 to pursue his college degree, living first with an aunt and uncle, Clive and Modie Huddleston. Edwards's example represents a classic black western migration pattern and the importance of region in this regard. Most migrants to the West came from Texas and Louisiana. Those who made it to the Midwest were often from Georgia and Mississippi. The Carolinas sent their folks to the East Coast. Both of the artist's grandfathers worked on the railroad, valiant figures in narratives of African American migration. He remembered them years later as he walked along railroad tracks collecting scrap metal for his sculpture.[111]

Edwards's educational path is indicative of the increased presence of African Americans in BFA and MFA programs at midcentury, fueled by disintegrating barriers to both de jure and de facto segregation. Similar to other artists in this study, like Betye Saar, John Outterbridge, and Noah Purifoy, Edwards's creative world started as a child when he made things for his own entertainment. He was so drawn to art as a youth that his father, Melvin Edwards Sr., and family friend and amateur painter George Gilbert built an easel for him, showing both the creativity and the will of self-creation in the black South(west) at the time. Edwards eventually sought instruction at the Museum of Fine Arts, Houston.

Between 1955 and 1965 Edwards pursued training as an artist in California, in formal institutional settings as well as on his own. He started out, as many others did, at Los Angeles Community College, then moved on to the University of Southern California (USC), where he studied art and played football. There he met another artist/athlete, painter Marvin Harden. He also took classes at the Los Angeles County Art Institute (later the Otis Art Institute) and connected with Daniel LaRue Johnson, Ron Miyashiro, and Edmund Bereal, who were at Chouinard Art Institute (later California Institute of Arts). Edwards graduated from USC in 1965; for the last several years he attended at night, by then being married, with three children.[112]

By the time Edwards left Los Angeles for New York in 1967, he was one of the West Coast's hottest African American artists. In the late 1950s, he had started participating in the large group shows for which Los Angeles was known—the All-City Outdoor Art Festival at Barnsdale Park, 1959, and the Artists of Los Angeles and Vicinity exhibition at Los Angeles County Museum of Art, 1960. He also took part in the La Jolla Museum of Art Annual of

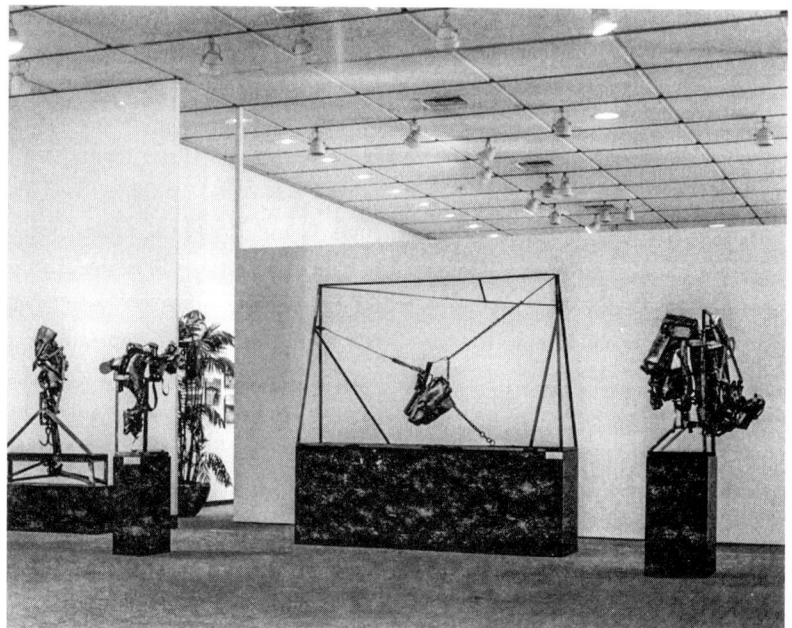

FIG. 1.6 Melvin Edwards, *Installation view of* Five Younger Los Angeles Artists, *1965*, 1965. Courtesy © Melvin Edwards / Artists Rights Society (ARS).

1962. But 1965 was Edwards's year. He was hired to teach at Chouinard, had a solo exhibition at the Santa Barbara Museum of Art, and was included in *Five Younger Los Angeles Artists* (fig. 1.6) at the new home of the Los Angeles County Museum of Art (LACMA) on Wilshire Boulevard. He was twenty-eight years old.

The 1965 show in Santa Barbara, though not particularly large, had a huge impact. Photos depict a well-attended opening. But the review of the exhibition in *Artforum* was also significant, particularly in the climate of a rapidly emerging African American arts scene. Rarely had an African American artist been singled out for a "sophisticated and highly urbane selection of sculpture," something exquisite in workmanship and form. And in the 1960s, perhaps only Romare Bearden in New York—specifically his collage work beginning in 1964—had the same overwhelmingly affirmative critical reception.[113]

Yet the group show at LACMA later that year was similarly, perhaps even more, intriguing. The museum included Edwards in the roster of new talent as an equal with other young artists (or rather young men) of his generation—Tony Berlant, Llyn Foulkes, Lloyd Hamrol, and Philip Rich. The result-

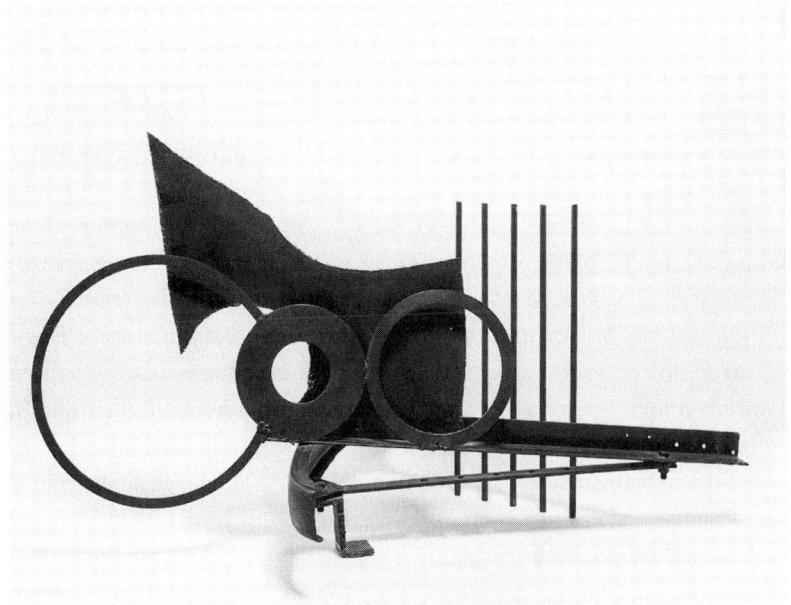

FIG. 1.7 Melvin Edwards, *The Fourth Circle*, 1966. Painted steel. Los Angeles County Museum of Art, Contemporary Art Council, New Talent Purchase Award (M.67.12). Courtesy © Melvin Edwards / Artists Rights Society (ARS), New York; Digital Image © 2015 Museum Associates / LACMA. Licensed by Art Resource, New York.

ing show was curated by its newly hired senior curator of twentieth-century art, Maurice Tuchman, who would go on to put the institution on the map for contemporary art. In such an orbit, Edwards became a hot artist in a sizzling Los Angeles scene.

Five Younger Los Angeles Artists also recognized those selected for New Talent Purchase awards, supporting the acquisition of one work for LACMA's permanent collection. The following year *The Fourth Circle*, 1966 (fig. 1.7), by Edwards was added. The program also provided a stipend each artist could put toward living and working expenses for one year. The wonderful grant, exhibition, and recognition in one of LA's venerated and newly reconfigured institutions was certainly an important step for Melvin Edwards and for the African American artist community in Los Angeles.[114]

Only two of the works shown in Edward's solo in Santa Barbara seem to have been featured in LACMA's presentation, *Standing Hang-Up #1* and *The Lifted X*, both from 1965. These were large works in metal, "welded steel and found-object sculptures," where, as critic Don Factor suggested, "there are extreme and evocative tensions drawn from the play between heavy masses,

EMERGE • 59

suspended tortuously within steel frameworks, and a finely articulated accumulation of curvilinear forms."[115] Welding, in some ways, brought art and life together for Edwards. As he commented, "Once you start to weld, you get as much influence from walking down a street that has welded railings and grids. It's a funny thing. You don't know the world is welded until you weld."[116]

In the early 1960s, Edwards established a studio on Van Ness Avenue, where he completed his first important smaller sculptures: the *Lynch Fragment* series. Begun in 1963, its first phase ended when the artist left for New York in 1967. Critic Michael Brenson has noted an "economy of form and clarity of arrangement" in these early pieces, a compression of the tension between solid mass and gleaming steel details that Don Factor identified in the larger pieces.[117]

The popularity of Edwards's sculpture was tied to its vocabulary of abstract expressionism and its links to the modernist sculptural practice of artists like Julio González and David Smith. In some ways, the *Lynch Fragments* place Edwards in the space of pop art: each compact metal mass is composed from found industrial culture—locks, chains, tools, gears—whole, rearranged but intact. They are found objects of a certain type, yet without the ephemerality of assemblage. They have more in common with John Chamberlain's car parts or Mark di Suvero's I-beams from that period.

The African Diaspora is also felt in these works, and that too was a reason for their popularity. We see it, to a certain extent, in early titles like *Afro-Phoenix #2* and *Mojo for 1404* (fig. 1.8), both from 1964, and *Mamba*, 1965.[118] It was their correlation with African masks, as well as sculptural icons of fertility and ritual from the continent, that were compelling to art audiences. Intimations of migration were part of Edwards's sculptures as well, in the found metal he utilized: what *were* the things that people could and did take with them on such journeys, and what did they have to leave behind?[119]

Many of his welded sculptural abstractions were forged from things that connoted labor as well as violence. In this way they also signified the history of brutality against the black body. As Edwards told Tuchman, "I use chains—as in *Chaino* and *Hang-up*—both as a dynamic and symbolic thing."[120] In this sense, the *Lynch Fragments* grew out of his increasing political awareness and activism. He participated in protests against housing discrimination. At one march in nearby Torrance sponsored by the Congress of Racial Equality (CORE) around 1962, he and painter Marvin Harden were met by white homeowners who "just happened to be watering their lawns that day, standing out on their lawns with hoses to shoot water on us, of course, as we went by."[121]

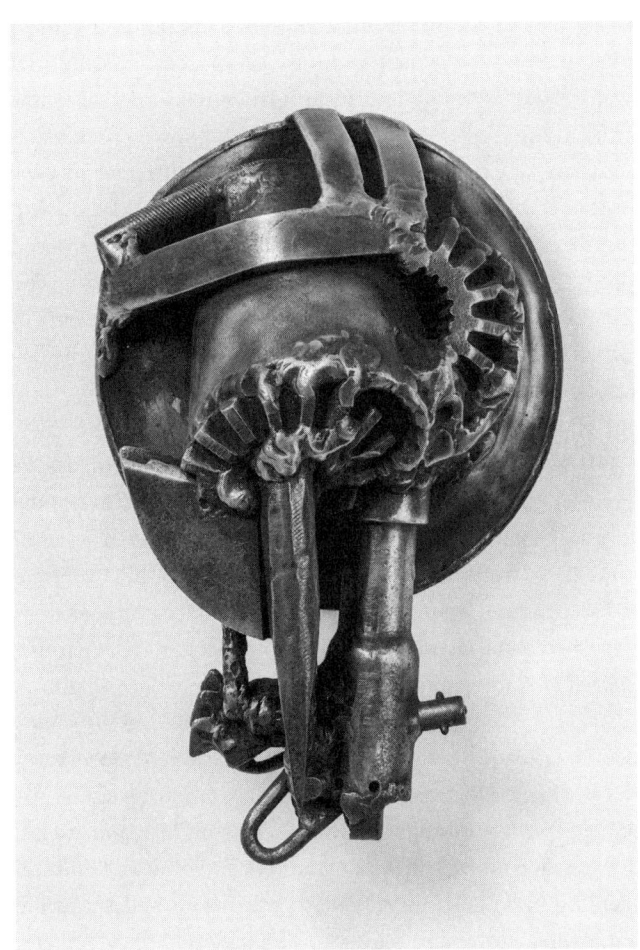

FIG. 1.8 Melvin Edwards, *Mojo for 1404*, 1964. Welded steel. Courtesy © Melvin Edwards / Artists Rights Society (ARS), New York, and Alexander Gray Associates.

There was also police brutality. "Police harassment was real," even for someone like the law-abiding Edwards, a former member of the naval reserve.[122] Vivid in his mind was the attack on the Nation of Islam's Los Angeles mosque in 1962, in which seven black men were shot, one fatally. For Edwards, these events connected with the long history of African American abuse, particularly lynching.[123]

The compact and tough profile of the *Lynch Fragments*, both formally and emotionally, was expanded in larger works from the same period. As painter and critic Frank Bowling suggests, the works moved toward the architectural, not just in terms of scale but also in the attention to the distribution of mass and volume, similar to the ways in which Anthony Caro pushed his sculptural direction.[124] Edwards would develop these ideas further in his 1968 solo show of polychrome work at the Walker Art Center in Minneapolis and in his first large-scale commission for Cornell University, *Homage to My Father and the Spirit*, 1969. The support the artist received—a John Hay Whitney Fellowship in 1964 and the year-long grant from LACMA in 1965—seem to have allowed him to expand both the scale and the formal complexity of his work. The more ambitious suspended elements in *Chaino* evolved into experiments in suspension in *Cotton Hang-Up*, 1966, and other works at the end of the decade, amplifying Edwards's sculptural voice.

In the tensions of their striking juxtapositions and captivating intricacy, other large works in the LACMA show—such as *The Lifted X* and *August the Squared Fire* (fig. 1.9), both from 1965—evoked for critic Don Factor not the allusions to historical brutality in the *Lynch Fragments* but rather "a series of destructive, painfully contemporary images."[125] Written six months after the Watts Rebellion, Factor's review references that Los Angeles event, as does Edwards, whose crushed metal elements seem to dangle from a skeletal frame in *August the Squared Fire*, named for the month in which the uprising took place. Malcolm X was assassinated while Edwards was at work on the sculpture that became *The Lifted X*. Its title and vertical orientation allows us to imagine the leader as a martyr to African American freedom struggles; its upward thrust also suggests the promulgation and elevation of Malcolm's ideas, which would have a major impact on African American social and cultural thought in the coming period. Three years earlier, Edwards had heard the activist speak in the city, addressing the LAPD's attack on the Los Angeles mosque. Historian Gerald Horne argues that Malcolm's immersion in Los Angeles, with its jagged contours of police brutality, spurred him to further develop his engagement with social justice outside the spiritual realm and the bonds of the Nation of Islam. After hearing Malcolm, Edwards began his *Lynch Fragments* series. For the artist, embedded in politics were also principles that could have aesthetic outcomes.[126]

In the wake of Edwards's solo show at the Santa Barbara Museum of Art, he was picked up by the Esther Bear Gallery in that city. Edwards's relationship with the gallery scene of Los Angeles, though, as was the case of most African American artists of the time, did not necessarily translate into exhibiting on a regular basis. With his skills in welding, he was called upon to repair Jean Tinguely's kinetic sculptures for the Dwan Gallery. He also helped install some large public works by Mark di Suvero, one of the gallery's artists.

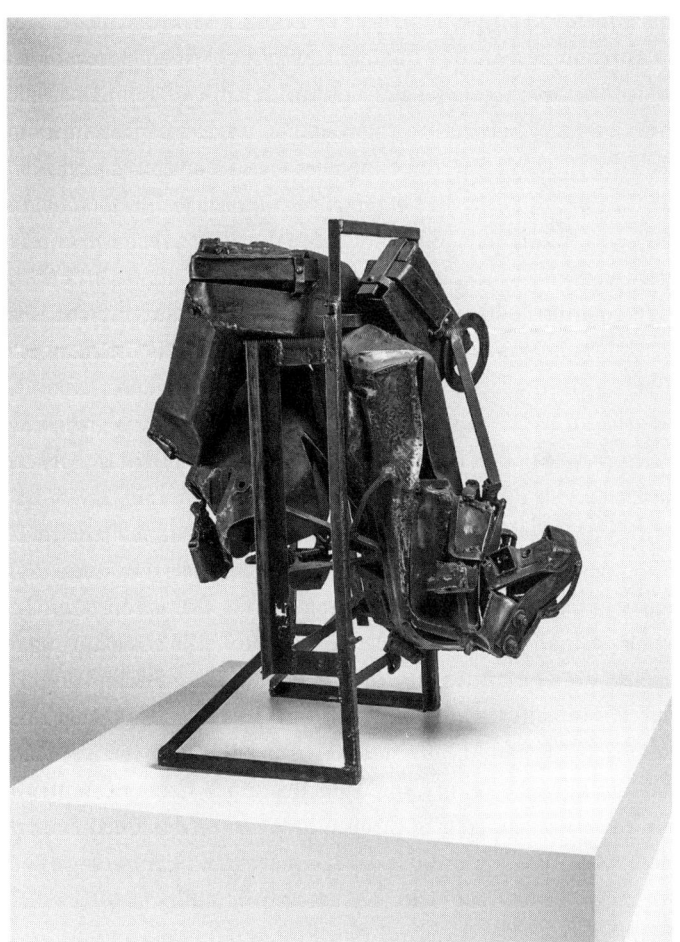

FIG. 1.9 Melvin Edwards, *August the Squared Fire*, 1965. Steel. San Francisco Museum of Modern Art, Purchase, by exchange, through a fractional gift of Shirley Ross Davis. Courtesy © Melvin Edwards / Artists Rights Society (ARS), New York; photo: Katherine Du Tiel.

This led to the collaboration with di Suvero on the construction of the massive steel armature for the Artists' Tower of Protest, also known as the Peace Tower, a public antiwar sculpture in Los Angeles, in 1966.[127]

While Edwards's work might not have been particularly well represented by the Los Angeles galleries, there was one occasion where it was seen by millions of viewers. A group of sculptures appeared on the television show *Bob Hope Presents the Chrysler Theatre* during the fall 1966 season on NBC. Sponsored by the Chrysler Corporation and hosted by the comedian between

1963 and 1967, it included programs of varying genres from comedy to music and drama. Fourteen pieces, a mix of large and smaller works, appeared on a dramatic episode titled "Crazier Than Cotton." It featured actor Bradford Dillman as an "artist torn between creativity and materialism."[128] Needless to say, Edwards himself wasn't featured on the broadcast. Nevertheless, it is an instance, as with Charles White and others, where we see the imbrication of African American artists in the West Coast entertainment industry, even if in a sporadic fashion.[129]

After a dozen years in Southern California, Melvin Edwards moved to New York in 1967. By 1975 he was married to poet Jayne Cortez, who had also developed her early artistic voice in Los Angeles.[130] On the West Coast, Edwards and Cortez did not travel in the same creative circles. However, comparing a profile of her practice to that of Edwards reveals the breadth of activity by African American artists during this time.

Jayne Cortez was raised in Watts, and at eighteen she married jazz innovator Ornette Coleman.[131] She linked the avant-garde black music scene of the 1950s to early creativity in a black nationalist vein that emerged in the next decade. She helped start the Los Angeles chapter of the Student Nonviolent Coordinating Committee (SNCC) and also founded Studio Watts, a space that offered students training in visual, performing, and language arts beginning in 1964. Cortez ran the drama and writing programs, which eventually evolved into a separate entity, the Watts Repertory Theater Company. Between 1964 and 1966, she created projects that can be described as performance pieces, combining literature, jazz, visual art, and politics. Cortez is best known, however, as a poet with a keen sense of orality, noted for her ability to "chant" her words and deliver "evocative, jazz-influenced vocalizations."[132]

It wasn't until 1969 and in New York that Cortez brought out her first book of poems, *Pisstained Stairs and the Monkey Man's Wares*, which was self-published. The volume featured eleven drawings by Melvin Edwards and in many ways represents his growing participation in the Black Arts Movement as it developed on the East Coast. The ink drawings created for the 1969 volume are fairly representational: Edwards focuses primarily on mask-like heads. The poet and artist collaborated again on a second project in 1971, *Festivals and Funerals*. This time Edwards's contributions on paper were made with a felt-tip marker and present themselves as linear adaptations of his small sculptures. Poet and scholar Roberto Tejada has unpacked the dialogue between the two artists in shared leitmotifs that signal both the partial and the surplus, flesh and "ritual geography," and where viciousness always erupts. The visual and verbal offer us transmutations; there are affinities but not unequivocal "one-to-one relationship[s]," even in a poem called "Lynch Fragment."[133] In *Pisstained Stairs and the Monkey Man's Wares* a comparable set of shifting vocabularies circulate the sexual and the scatological, in a way that Tejada likens to "a strand of surrealism that saw picture and word as indivisible, the abject is a pageantry not of things that degrade but of all that we treasure."[134] Edwards's cover drawing of a figure composed of geometries—all squares, triangles, cylinders—makes prominent display of its corresponding genitals, "the monkey man's wares." Writing later in the 1970s, Studio Museum in Harlem director Mary Schmidt Campbell, extending Edwards's own intimations of fecundity in the pieces, would find many of the *Lynch Fragments* "aggressively erotic."[135]

Edwards continued to accumulate accolades in the late 1960s. He did a number of projects with the city of Minneapolis in 1968. While his solo show of polychrome outdoor work for the Walker Art Center offered the most visibility in art world networks, he also spent the summer as an artist-in-residence at the Sabathany Baptist Church and signed on to the group show *Thirty Contemporary Black Artists* at the Minneapolis Institute of Arts.

In 1971, Edwards penned a statement that lays out the geographic or spatial imperative that African American artists carried with them as they carved out new landscapes in American art. Using the au courant (if conflicted) term "Black Art," he suggests that these objects "made by Black people . . . are in some way functional in dealing with our lives here in America." The psychological function of art Edwards alludes to can be activated through symbols ancestral and diasporic found from rural Texas to Guyana to Tanzania that offer "ideas, subjects and symbols for radical change." These signs open psychic spaces of self and community actualization. However, it is not only symbolic space that black art can alter. From another perspective it has an architectonic valance, interceding as a tangible object in the world. "The works can be of such large physical scale, and in the right places, as to make real change," Edwards notes. "It should always be known that these works are our methods of changing things."[136]

As Melvin Edwards, Betye Saar, and Charles White insinuated themselves into the Los Angeles art scene, they opened up trajectories for African American artists that redefined the place of the ungeographic. Not only did they expand the African American reach into the art world; they also imagined through their works new and different roles for art.

CHAPTER TWO   **Claim:** Assemblage
and Self-Possession

WHEN PICASSO AND BRAQUE "invented" assemblage and collage in 1912, these ways of making art had already been around for hundreds of years. We can look to Asian traditions with pasted paper going back to the eighth century, mixed-media works in Germany and the creation of Valentine's Day cards by European nuns in the eighteenth century, early photomontages by Lewis Carroll and O. G. Rejlander in the nineteenth century, and amateur and folk art traditions by naive artists and housewives in the United States for evidence of the way people have used mixed-media techniques over centuries.[1]

Collage and assemblage among some early modern artists in the United States, such as Arthur Dove, were also spurred by nineteenth-century practices of folk and Victorian art and an early twentieth-century craze for Americana. Even Joseph Cornell, who made assemblage his own in the 1930s, could be seen as partaking of the same spirit of an American folk aesthetic.[2] And the term "assemblage" itself seems to have cropped up first in an American context, when mixed-media works by Dove were described as multifarious "assemblages" of materials creating unclassifiable "things" that were works of art.[3]

The adoption, incorporation, and interpellation of what Harold Rosenberg called this "way of making" into high art paralleled Western modernism's taste for non-Western, functional, and folk art forms.[4] The use of found materials injected anecdotal and popular qualities into the fine art object. What all these new elements had in common was an apparent weak authorship and the sense that intellectual ownership was in the public domain, not the property of the non-Western, the nonmale, or the untrained. Those were not "proper" authors, and there was a sense that the "real" Western (usually white male) genius could transform these underutilized raw materials of creativity into something sublime.

The incorporation of common and even shoddy materials put artists in a new and unknown place from which to work, an off-balance space of experimentation. As Picasso would comment, "We sought to express reality with materials that we did not know how to handle and which we prized precisely because we knew that their help was not indispensable to us, and that they were neither the best nor the most adequate."[5] Years later Jean Dubuffet continued this line of thinking in comments to William Seitz for the 1961 exhibition *The Art of Assemblage*: "I have always loved—it is a sort of vice—to employ only the most common materials in my work, those that one does not dream of at first because they are too crude and close at hand and seem unsuitable for anything whatsoever. I like to proclaim that my art is an enterprise to rehabilitate discredited values."[6]

The crude and unsuitability of the place from which to work, as the apogee of making, inverts the notion of artist as solitary and exceptional genius, putting him on the plane with everyday people who themselves use these materials adequately or inadequately, making do. In championing discredited and maligned values, Dubuffet seemingly supports those who work in this way, cobbling things together, relying on what Michel de Certeau would call a tactic, participating and intervening in the systems of power by using what is at hand. In California assemblage of the 1950s, scavenged, found, and makeshift materials made over into art also became a way of transforming art making. Found matter elicited a certain detachment from the object itself. It could be sold for a song, traded, or given away but also could be returned to the streets, to the land, or to the junk pile. Sometimes it was left to ripen, and sometimes it was just left.

In their treatise on the formless, Yve-Alain Bois and Rosalind Krauss use the writings of Georges Bataille to interrogate notions of modernism and representation as a shifting field of parameters and operations, finding clues in the marginal, the scatological, and heterology, at once nondifferentiated and nonideal. In one passage, dust becomes Bataille's emblem of overproduction and inescapable waste, which provides the fecund culture for the formless. Emphasizing the inundation of modern form and categories, as well as our inability to stem this tide, Bataille muses, "Dust will probably begin to gain the upper hand over the servants."⁷

But dust *is* the servants. On the scale of representability, servants may be only one notch above the lumpen aspects of society that become abandoned waste products. Indeed, "servant" as category implies not necessarily a human figure but the body as machine, as the discrete "parts" that render service. As one southern scion noted, the full representation of such people was nonexistent; they were invisible except as "a pair of hands offering a drink on a silver tray."⁸ This comment attests to a sublimation of representation as defined by class and power. The nonimage is not a fixed category but an alteration of that which is allowed to be represented. It is enforced by a willful definition of what is representable and what is outside that frame.

For Krauss and Bois, the unrepresentability of the formless leads back to "minor" works and artists, which is certainly useful for our arguments regarding the underknown California artists featured in this book. But Bataille's dust-laden servants get us there with a vengeance. African Americans suffered de jure and then de facto servitude; they built the United States but then were given the leftovers, the shoddy, for themselves, along with the partial remains of representation. African American life in the United States has been an ongoing battle for the fulfillment of the contract of citizenship: to be full, not partial, human beings; to be given full, not partial, access to justice, education, housing, and income. And black artists in the last three centuries have strived for the same rights when it comes to the ability to represent themselves.

Indeed, black people wanted to get away from the specter of the shoddy, the inadequate, those things that had followed and defined them in the larger world. Noah Purifoy's genius in the 1960s was to exploit these very ideas: jumping into the tension between the striving for excellence and perfection and the inadequateness of the tools given; transforming this notion of lack into something useful, aesthetic, and in the service of good; altering trash and shoddiness into that from which beauty flowed.

On the West Coast, the profile of assemblage acknowledged its debt to the art of the non-Western, primarily in Asia and Africa, particularly in strategies of accumulation and surface patterning. The profile of vernacular or quotidian aesthetics—in car customizing, for instance—came to the fore as artistic models.⁹ Both of these examples in a sense provided an avenue or rationale for people of color to lay claim to assemblage techniques, as heirs to non-Western traditions, on the one hand, and to the mundane strategies of making beauty that were allowed to people on society's margins, on the other. In critic Clement Greenberg's articulation of collage in "The Pasted Paper Revolution" (1958), the protagonists are characterized as "intrusions" that complicate the illusion and smooth surface of the picture plane.[10] What Thomas Crow further defines as "intruder objects" take the form of low-class, nonart materials introduced into high art's seamless and controlled depictions of itself, much like Krauss and Bois's formless interloper.[11] In each of these accounts, material difference also articulates a representational otherness, a formless intruder, that at once marks the excitement of the representational unknown as well as its boundaries.

The adoption of found and discarded materials also could be translated as the embrace of the outcasts who inhabited society's margins. In the post–World War II era and during the rise of the civil rights movement in the 1950s, black Americans fit the bill. And black bebop, hard bop, and jazz generally became the soundtrack of alternative aesthetics and visions for an American future. Even Clement Greenberg was a jazz fan. The aesthetic profile of assemblage during this period, as Rebecca Solnit relates, "challenged conventional ideas of workmanship, originality, value, and purity."[12] The found, the random, the accidental, the ruined became key partners in authorship.

JEWELS: WATTS AND NOAH PURIFOY

> In essence Art and Creativity
> are eons apart.
> Creativity
> is the act of doing
> void of the idea of productivity.
> Art is what people
> say about Creativity.
> —Noah Purifoy

Noah Purifoy composed these words in 1967.[13] It was one of his more poetic missives, which appeared in the various catalogues, newsletters, formal presentations, and personal letters in which he set out his views on creativity and art production. They reflected his training as an educator, social worker, and artist; this preparation led him to seek out art whose meaning had a purpose and reflected expanded human creativity and connection, something that led to a better life for both artists and audience. In a self-published newsletter called *One to One: Quarterly Report on Aspects of Creativity*, the same publication where the words above appeared, Purifoy further elucidated how assemblage in particular—and its very notion of connecting, assembling, joining, and linking objects and ultimately people across myriad divides—would become his method and battle cry:

> We wish to establish at the outset that there must be more inside of Art than the creative act; more than the sensation of beauty, ugliness, color, form, light, sound, darkness, intrigue, wonderment, uncanniness, bitter, sweet, black, white, life, and death. There must also be a ME who is affected permanently.
>
> Assuming that the assemblage puts together two or more unrelated inanimate objects, transpose the concept thus: two or more seemingly unrelated inanimate objects assembled constitutes the possibility of communication. Here ART becomes something other than—other than as many opinions as there are people. Art can become a new thing when and if it is virtually and willfully used as a symbol through which someone becomes better.
>
> Art of itself is of little or no value if in its relatedness it does not effect a change. We do not mean a change in appearance of physical things but a change in the behavior of human beings.[14]

The very notion of linkage and connection that assemblage represented, the assemblage aesthetic if you will, became a trope that described and defined Purifoy's practice as an artist and more broadly as a cultural worker and philosopher. It helped him join the disparate parts of his own life together into a related whole. True to the form itself, these elements—the creative and social-purpose sides of his life—did not always reside in easy proximity or harmony. When art and life were playing well together, the result was art's ability to act as catalyst, as change, not necessarily as "art" in the Western sense but dissolved into a more general and less elitist notion of creativity.

Purifoy's concept of art-as-change was informed by his interest in existentialist philosophy. Writings by Sartre, Merleau-Ponty, De Beauvoir, and others popularized in the United States during the 1950s and 1960s were birthed in the French Resistance of World War II and immersed in ideas of freedom, political action, and the absurd aspects of reality. They also affirmed existence, focusing on individuality in the face of mass standardization. This trajectory of thought connected with the Beat Generation and the civil rights movement that was emerging at midcentury.[15] The artist also absorbed the writings of Edmund Husserl and Martin Heidegger and ideas advanced by Freud.

Analyzing the artist's statements and projects in a variety of contexts, conceptions of phenomenology seem particularly useful in their engagement with the study of being, the "lived experience of inhabiting a body," and how these could be applied to the contexts of a new subject, one born in rebellion.[16] One got at the "living experience of meaning" by bringing focus to the human encounter of the world through objects that were "reachable," grasped in the "bodily horizon."[17] However, Purifoy's line of thought also relates to the emergence of African American modernist art practice during the twentieth century and philosophies of art making that were linked to self-expression, imbricated with cultural nationalism and antiracism. In particular, his concept of art-as-change relates to the notion of black cultural accomplishment as the key to ending prejudice found in ideas developed during the Harlem Renaissance / New Negro Movement of the 1920s. For example, Alma Thomas, a painter who came of age during the earlier period but whose recognition arrived in the mid-1960s, understood that art had the power to dispel ignorance and racism because people with a "sensitivity to beauty" and culture were superior, moving on an elevated plane. "A cultured person is the highest stage of the human being," Thomas said. "If everyone were cultured we would have no wars or disturbance. There would be peace in the world."[18]

Purifoy's art-as-change loses much of the language and framework of elitism, the baggage that comes with high culture, with which Thomas had no problem. Still, in Purifoy's mind, art had to be "willfully used as a symbol through which someone becomes better," casting art's active use similar to Thomas's Harlem Renaissance thinking. Art's progressive force, its capacity to cause someone to be a "better" person, also demonstrates its connections to social science, its ability to address and eradicate social inequity. The target of art is not only the elite viewer who would be transformed by the work—Thomas's "cultured person"—but also the psyche of the maker. In a sense, Purifoy's dream was informed by his experience with social work, a relationship to social science / philosophical discourses generally, and perhaps black social science schemas specifically. In a coded way, art-as-change addressed racism and the so-called "Negro problem" by being a catalyst to transform and eradicate the thoughts and behaviors that accompanied them.[19]

There is no doubt that Purifoy saw sociological theory and concepts of social work as ways to address and change African American existence. Likewise, art played a similar role in his decisions and focus. Building and creating things had always been a part of his life. For Purifoy, the other artists in this study, and the majority of black people living in poverty at the time, making art was part of making do. Born in 1917 in the small rural town of Snow Hill, Alabama, he was the eleventh of thirteen children of farmers and sharecroppers. Like people with limited means everywhere, they made things, recycled, improvised something out of nothing. Purifoy, for instance, created things to play with, like a scooter from discarded roller skates.[20]

Purifoy was able to attend college in the Depression era South, graduating from Alabama State Teachers College in 1939 with a BS in education. As he tells it, he forced the issue, hanging around the campus in Montgomery after he was rejected, until he eventually was admitted. He worked his way through college as a janitor. With his degree in hand, like so many of his African American peers, the best job Purifoy could find was teaching industrial arts at the high school level, so he became a shop teacher.[21] After three years of teaching in various schools in Montgomery, Purifoy volunteered to serve in World War II, as a way to change his life. His degree and experience translated into a position as a carpenter's mate first class with the Navy Seabees. He was assigned to the construction battalion, building airfields and Quonset huts and preparing military camps. After the war, he headed to Atlanta University, getting a master's in social work in 1948, then working in social services in Cleveland and the Los Angeles County Hospital. By the mid-1950s, however, he'd left social work behind, and he dedicated himself to art and art-related jobs for much of the rest of his life.

Purifoy attended Chouinard Art Institute, focusing first on industrial design and, when that was discontinued, changing to fine arts. He took a night shift at Douglas Aircraft, cutting templates on a shearing machine. He eventually switched from the strenuous work at Douglas to occupations closer to what he was being trained for—interior and furniture design, supporting his art making through the commercial art sector (fig. 2.1). Purifoy created furniture for the Angelus Furniture Warehouse and served as a window trimmer for Cannel and Schaffen Interior Designs on Wilshire Boulevard and the Broadway department stores, a gig he held for almost a decade. He also had his own company for a time with partner John H. Smith, another black art student at Chouinard (whose other job was mail carrier). But by the early 1960s Purifoy had moved away from the commercial sector as well, unable to pierce the glass ceiling as a black interior designer, even with his own company. He returned to the night shift, working as a janitor.[22]

After leaving the commercial art sector Purifoy "came home, and just sat around for a year thinking about doing art.... I had a studio clean enough to eat off the table. I never did a lick of work there. I had a beret and all. I ate cheese and drank wine, but I wasn't an artist yet until Watts. That made me an artist."[23] While much of this is true, particularly as it reveals Purifoy's ambivalence to a career as artist, in fact he did make things in the 1950s and early

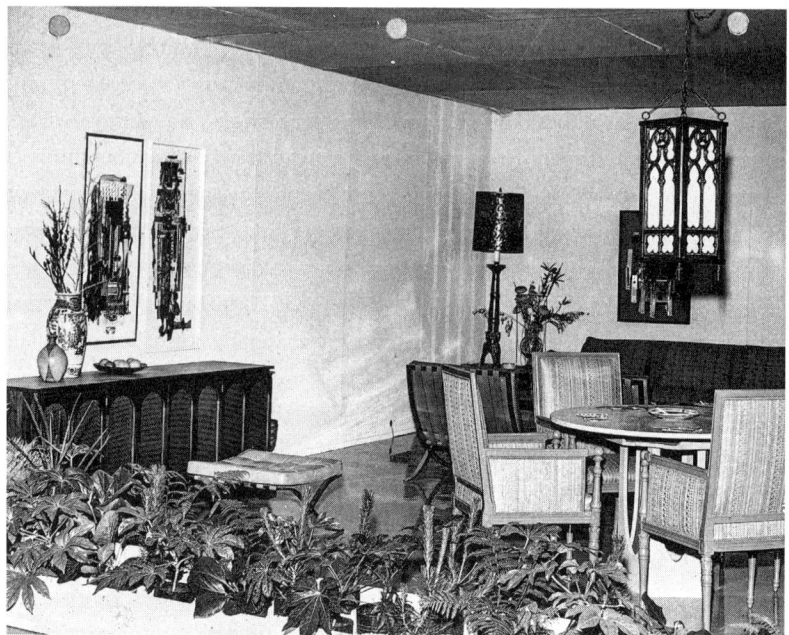

FIG. 2.1 Noah Purifoy's interior design work featuring two of his collages (*upper left*), 1950s. Noah Purifoy Papers, 1935–1998, Archives of American Art, Smithsonian Institution.

1960s, collages inflected with Asian and African overtones as well as furniture. His apartment became the hangout, the place where people gathered for a certain kind of community and to "wrassle" with notions of art and aesthetics. "I wasn't even an artist, but they flocked around me anyhow because I pretended to be an artist," he said. "I'd graduated from art school, and I had ten years of experience vaguely with artists. So I was accepted as an artist. In fact, I didn't have anything to show for it."[24]

What he did have was an elaborate hand-built sound system. People came from all over to experience his nine feet of speakers and to listen to his thoughts about art. Purifoy's theories and philosophies would have an impact on generations of artists in Los Angeles—from John Outterbridge and John Riddle, who both came to understand art as tool for change, to David Hammons. In walking the line between artist and nonartist, taking a vow of poverty, and using found materials, Hammons paid homage to the older artist.

The work that really put Noah Purifoy on the map came in the mid-1960s: his connection with the Watts neighborhood and his interest in creating an

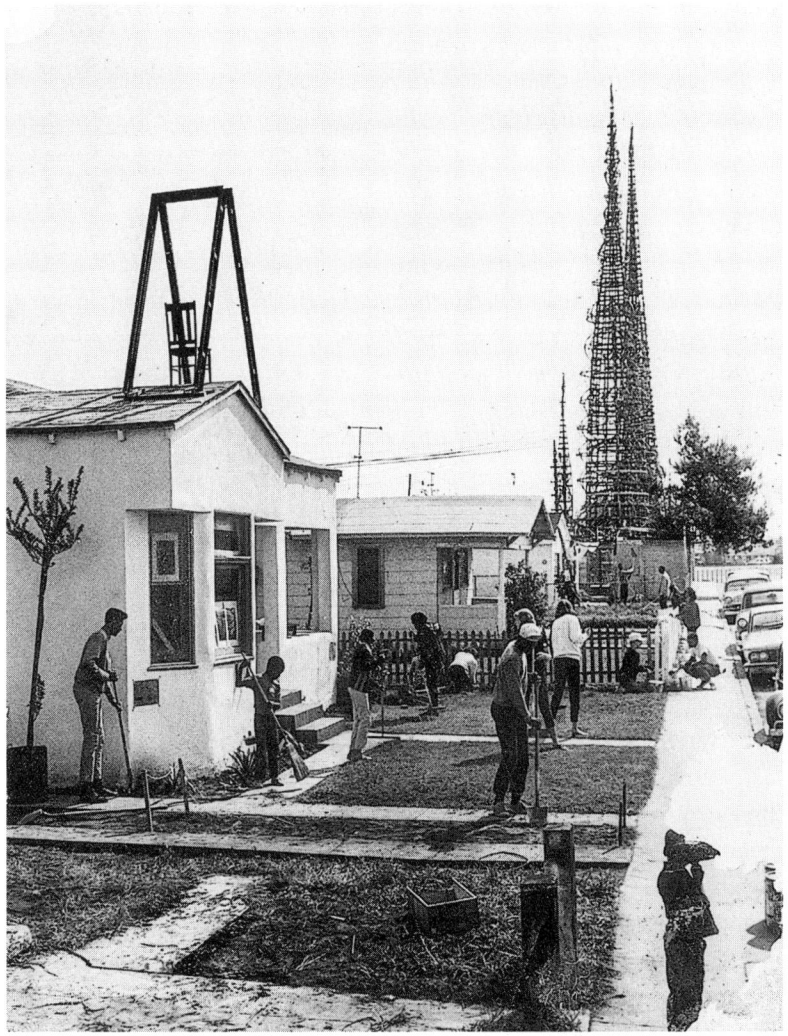

FIG. 2.2 Operation Teacup (Tower Easter Week Clean-Up) at Watts Towers Art Center and 107th Street, 1965. Courtesy the Noah Purifoy Foundation.

urban environment where art could mobilize and energize black people. In 1964, he was asked by Eve Echelman of the Committee for Simon Rodia's Towers in Watts to look after the Towers and the small school that operated there. He is credited as the founding director of what would become the Watts Towers Arts Center (WTAC) (fig. 2.2), a site for classes in visual and performing arts, primarily for young people, as well as exhibitions and concerts. It also became a place where artists found employment. Eventually Senga Nengudi, John Riddle, Suzanne Jackson, Curtis Tann, and John Outterbridge, among others, would offer their talents at WTAC.

The famed Towers, which have marked that site for most of the twentieth century, are among the earliest as well as the longest-lasting evidence of Watts as a cultural hub. Created by Italian immigrant and laborer Simon Rodia between 1921 and 1954, they are composed of a series of interconnected spires of steel rods and concrete, embedded with shells, stones, broken glass, and all manner of refuse, brought together in a mosaic-style surface. The structures, including fountains and birdbaths, reach almost one hundred feet at their highest point. After Rodia abandoned the property in the mid-1950s, the Towers began to deteriorate from lack of upkeep. During the age of urban renewal, the city cast its eye on the Towers as a site for removal. Because they were located in what had become the African American neighborhood of Watts—seen as unclean and dangerous—it was a likely site for reform. The Committee for Simon Rodia's Towers was formed in the late 1950s to protect this amazing landmark.

The committee pushed to preserve a structure that would come to represent the city of Los Angeles, but it also had to deal with the now African American neighborhood that surrounded the locale. As Cecile Whiting points out, to engage the community and attract attention and support the preservation project, the committee began to conceptualize the area as a site for cultural activity.[25] In 1961, it began offering summer workshops for children. In 1963, the year the Towers were designated a Cultural Heritage Monument, the committee sought to expand its offerings to teenagers and professionalize these classes through the development of a community arts center. Its mission would be to address "problem" youth by using the arts as a tool of cultural uplift, which at once demonstrated art's value and the good works that Watts Towers could perform. Such strategies had been used in the United States since the late nineteenth century and were standard practice during the New Deal.[26] To attract neighborhood investment in the site, the committee looked for a qualified African American to take on a leadership role. Trained in both the arts and the social sciences, Purifoy had the perfect credentials for the job. It was not only, as Whiting details, that both the committee and Purifoy were interested in notions of "uplift"—it was that such notions had been part of African American creative and social culture throughout the twentieth century.[27] They found resonance with Purifoy on a number of important levels, not least of which was the way he could combine his interests in art and social work.

Early on, Purifoy created art programs with a team that included musi-

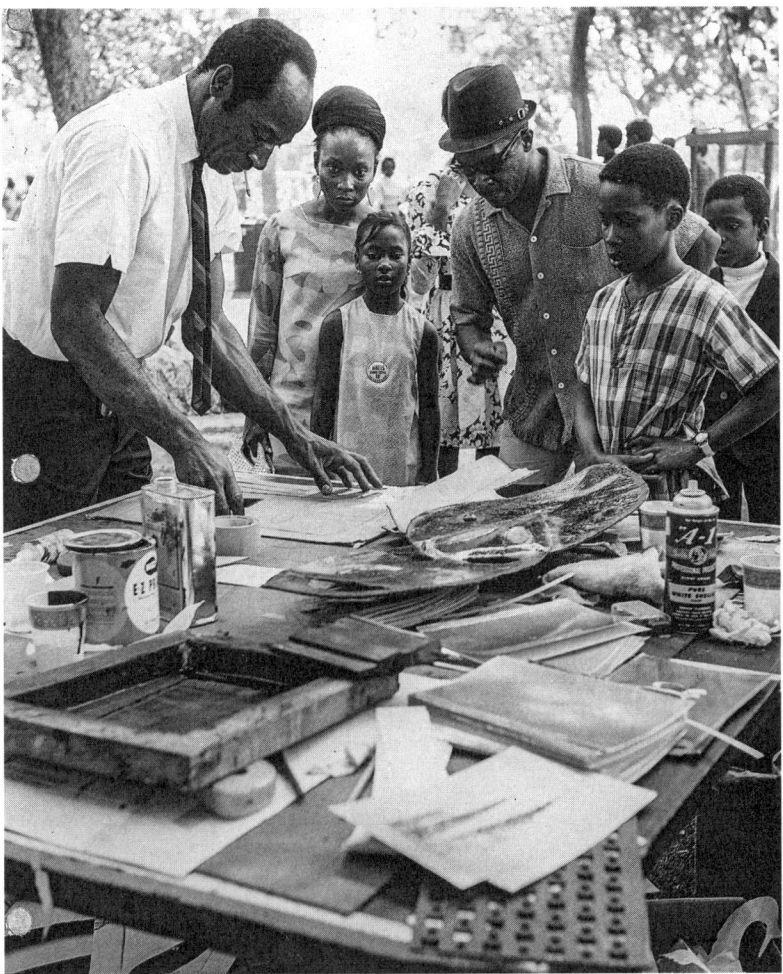

FIG. 2.3 Art class with Judson Powell at Watts Towers Art Center, 1960s. Courtesy the Noah Purifoy Foundation.

cian Judson Powell (fig. 2.3), artist Debbie Brewer, and teachers Sue Welsh and Lucille Krasne, a member of the committee who taught the first summer workshops in a small, abandoned house next to the Towers. Purifoy's visions were wide-ranging, and he sought to develop the community through the development of self: "It is through . . . the creative endeavor that the self is arrived at and affirmed."[28] This was achieved through traditional art activities such as painting, dance, and instrument making.[29] But there were also larger, grander projects: street theater that engaged the locale, or when he and the kids painted all the houses on 107th Street, the block where WTAC was located. Local stores donated the paint. They concluded by washing the street and having a nighttime "open house" party.³⁰ Purifoy was among the first to elaborate on this kind of creative development and civic engagement in African American neighborhoods in Los Angeles during the 1960s.

WTAC was at the forefront of a growing movement of local centers that sprang up to assert control and cultural enrichment of neighborhoods. Some, like WTAC and Studio Watts, came into existence before the 1965 Watts Rebellion. Many others were born in its wake.³¹ This was part of a national antipoverty effort that poured services and jobs into ethnic communities to stem the flow of protest and rebellion. For Purifoy, the local art center opened the door to culture as broad, antielitist, and connected to the wider world.³²

The Watts Rebellion occurred a year into Purifoy's tenure as director of WTAC and some four blocks away. The rebellion "made [him] an artist" and allowed him to find meaning for himself and for African American populations through art making.³³ As Purifoy remembered, he experienced the rebellion, the destruction, the looting, from the "backdoor" of the center. "While the debris was still smoldering," he and Judson Powell "ventured into the rubble like other junkers of the community, digging and searching, but unlike others, obsessed without quite knowing why. By September, working during lunchtime and after teaching hours, we had collected three tons of charred wood and fire-moulded [sic] debris."³⁴

While Purifoy recorded some of his own earliest work as collage, he was eventually drawn to assemblage because of the accessibility and availability of materials, because it was made from discarded things. In his eyes, such junk was democratic; it didn't discriminate against those with fewer advantages (or access to art materials) because it was free. Assemblage also had a relationship to narratives of poverty; it reflected communities ravaged by a social system that cared little for them. The rebellion and its remnants could be turned into not only something of beauty but also something of African American life — art created by the people themselves who were not only the drivers of American aesthetics but makers too.

Whiting has noted the contrast between Purifoy and Edward Kienholz, the best-known of the LA-based artists working with assemblage. Kienholz related the excitement of cruising municipal dumps and secondhand shops, hunting for materials. Purifoy talked about finding stuff on the streets of one's own neighborhood.³⁵ His practice was transformative, a way to transfigure the perception of one's living space, use what was available, and create something meaningful and beautiful. In his classes with kids, he used organized "junk hunts" to turn the *finding* into part of the *making*.³⁶

The terms "junk art" and "assemblage" were used interchangeably at the time to describe art made with found objects. Whiting argues that Purifoy's use of the term "junk" over "assemblage" emphasized materials rather than facture.[37] But "junk" also was much more user-friendly for young people and others in Purifoy's locality. In fact, he was most interested in the notion of the process, the way things and people are transformed by the art experience, which fit well with his belief that culture was a therapeutic force. For Purifoy, found-object art represented a useful tool in mental health practices. It was a method for working with black trauma, a simple solution that black or poor people could employ. He was a voracious reader, and while working as a social worker in Cleveland in the early 1950s, he'd tried using what he called "bibliotherapy"—giving books to the mentally disturbed as a tool in their healing. With art he found more success as a way to reintegrate the mind and body.[38]

With the materials gathered in the months after the Watts Rebellion, Purifoy and Judson Powell eventually landed on the idea of creating a sculpture garden in the neighborhood. When they were informed that the money for their positions would expire in the spring of 1966, their plans changed to creating an exhibition.[39] Purifoy and Powell joined up with two local high school teachers, Leslie Aisenman and Paul Tanzawa, who were planning the first Simon Rodia Commemorative Watts Renaissance of the Arts Festival (discussed further below). Their goals were to take advantage of the growing focus on the Watts Towers as a national heritage site and modern art monument, to bring positive attention to the neighborhood and change its outlaw status, and to get others thinking the same way. At the festival's core was an exhibition of found-object art called *66 Signs of Neon* (fig. 2.4), featuring works by Purifoy, Powell, and other artists working in this style. Their collaborative goal was to communicate the human potential of Watts to the neighborhood itself and the world. As Purifoy explained: "'66 Signs of Neon' entered the Watts Festival as a single entry. Its purpose was to reflect the August 11 event on a symbolic level and to demonstrate to the community an existing fact: If the community of Watts found itself in the midst of something—something like junk—value could be placed on it to far exceed the few cents paid at the junk stores on Monday morning."[40]

Like the message of this celebration and Watts itself, *66 Signs of Neon* was an exhibition that kept regenerating. After opening at the festival, the show traveled for three years nationally and internationally, an envoy from the streets of South Central Los Angeles. It was initially composed of sixty-six separate works; as pieces were sold (or fell apart), new ones joined the display.

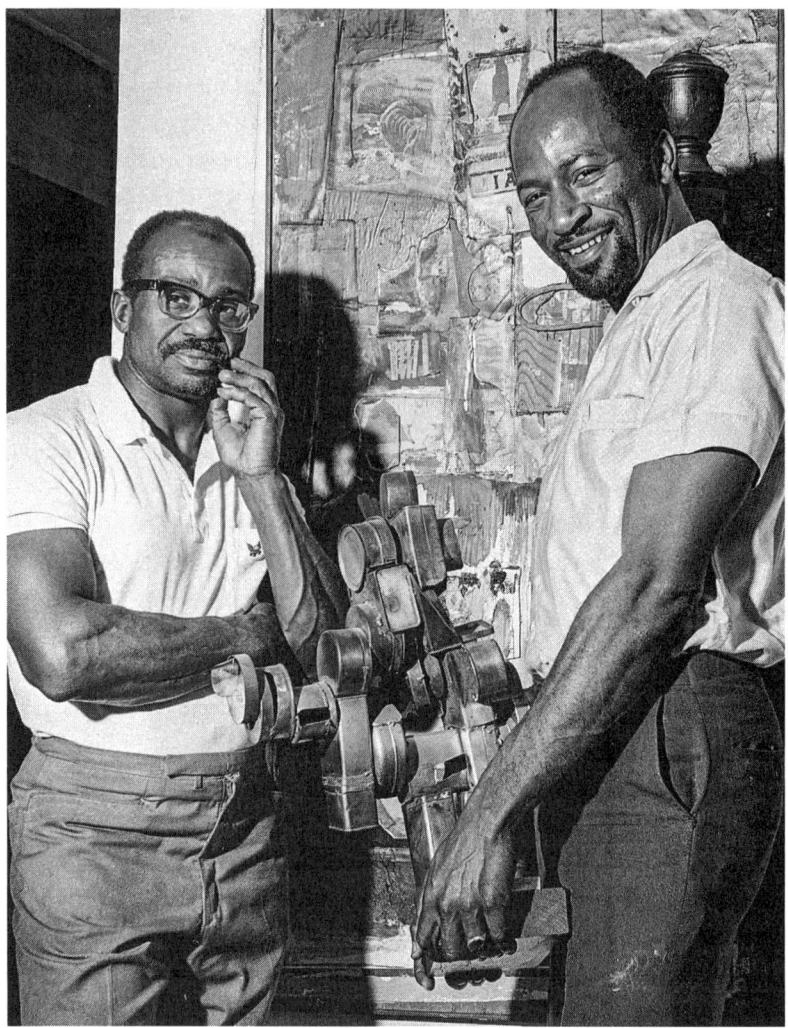

FIG. 2.4 Noah Purifoy and Judson Powell at *66 Signs of Neon* exhibition, 1966. Noah Purifoy Papers, 1935–1998, Archives of American Art, Smithsonian Institution.

That was the case with the participating artists as well. Composed of a diverse group from the beginning, the tour was joined over time by additional artists and their works.[41]

In the late 1960s, Whiting argues, the Towers "acquired a split identity." On the one hand, they came to embody a homegrown modernist aesthetic based in assemblage; on the other, they put Watts on the map and increasingly became a symbol of African American place and pride. *66 Signs of Neon*, she continues, also "became closely identified with a black cultural renaissance in Watts even though the participating artists represented various ethnic and racial heritages and lived all over the city."[42] Indeed. But the point was that the project was directed by Purifoy and Powell, two black men. In 1965–66, this was extremely important, even more so because of the rebellion. Purifoy and Powell invited others to collaborate. It was entered into the festival as a "single entry" composed by the Watts community under their direction. Purifoy and Powell's aesthetic control and shepherding of *66 Signs of Neon* was in line with the role of new black subjectivity and power that were among the demands and self-possession associated with the rebellion. In a sense, this stance was a rejoinder to narratives of assemblage whose sources came from black culture, whether it was jazz, the neighborhoods destroyed in urban renewal, or unnamed folk artists. In the narrative of *66 Signs of Neon*, African Americans were not just natural resources used by white artists; rather, they wielded artistic control.

Phenomenology's "turn toward objects" was a way to unpack individual consciousness.[43] But what of an object's "conditions of arrival"?[44] As with assemblage generally, these were things not intact, so-called failed objects. Instead, the "reachable" things of Watts—its "junk"—were those that must be transformed, first in the throes of rebellion and then through the processes of art making or re-creation. In applying such philosophical precepts, Purifoy set his sights on the idea of "commodity" as simply "one moment in the 'life history' or career of an object."[45] At their base, the materials of *66 Signs of Neon* were formed by black agency, energy, discontent, and vision into "hunks of melted neon signs, medicine bottles embedded in the molten remains of colorful plastic raincoats, twisted bits of metal, charred wood, pieces of smashed automobiles."[46] These were then reconfigured, if you will, by artists. As Purifoy would emphasize in the press, "We uncovered them and we thought they were little jewels. Nobody had ever seen shapes and forms quite like this."[47] For Purifoy, this junk was a sign of black efficacy or control, creativity, and, fundamentally, humanity. The material retained and revealed the life force and power of its "maker," which was then manifest in the work of art. The materials of the aftermath retained the power envisioned in the rebellion's force of disruption and resistance.[48]

In the spring of 1966, Purifoy created an entity called Joined for the Arts, which in the coming three years would travel *66 Signs of Neon*, generate a catalogue for the show, and produce a newsletter (*One to One*), a book of art and poetry (*Untitled*), and a local arts festival. With this independent organization, Purifoy attempted to take on the functions of a cultural center.[49] As its name suggests, Joined for the Arts represented the spirit of collaboration and community focus that Purifoy wanted. It also mirrored the foundational concept and action of junk art or assemblage: bringing together disparate entities to create something entirely new.

Between 1966 and 1969, the exhibition was shown in at least six venues, including the first and second Watts arts festivals.[50] The University of California system provided a number of sites. The show was hosted by student unions, imbricating Purifoy in the youth activism of the time. In 1966, the exhibition appeared at the University of California, Los Angeles (UCLA), in June; at University of California, Berkeley, in December; and at the San Francisco campus the following year. Its presentation at Berkeley coincided with a boycott of classes and protests that marked the continuation of the 1964 Free Speech Movement.[51] In addition, in the fall of 1966 the show traveled to a trade show at the Los Angeles Sports Arena.[52]

The assemblage that became a signature piece for the traveling show was Purifoy's *Sir Watts*, 1966 (fig. 2.5). One of his more figurative works, as the title suggests, it is modeled after medieval armor. What we see, however, is a partial torso molded out of metal, with abbreviated arms and head. Where a face might have been, a small purse of metal mesh was affixed, which in some photographs is open and gaping like a hungry mouth. The belly was a series of wooden drawers, while the chest cavity was covered with a scarred piece of glass, revealing a complicated agglomeration of small personal objects (hair pins, a fork, buttons). The heart was an open hole through which poured hundreds of tangled safety pins, dripping down the front of the sculpture. The image of violence, of the warrior—the knight of Watts as a sign for "people in battle"—would have growing resonance with the wounded body of the Vietnam War veteran and activism against that conflict.[53]

In 1968 and 1969, *66 Signs of Neon* expanded its tour nationally. It landed first at the Washington Gallery of Modern Art in May 1968. Shown on the heels of uprising in Washington, DC, after the assassination of Martin Luther King Jr., the exhibition extended the context of urban rebellion, with photos of the Washington conflict shown in an adjacent gallery. It received a fervent, page-long review from art critic Paul Richard, who spoke of the show's nuances (its uses of figuration and abstraction) and inspiration from the Watts Rebellion (even though it was not protest art).[54]

The Washington, DC, showing was organized by Walter Hopps, the final director of this short-lived space, dedicated to bringing contemporary art to the capital city.[55] The show seemed to be perfect for the art and policy angle that Hopps had pursued at the Institute of Policy Studies in the shadow of

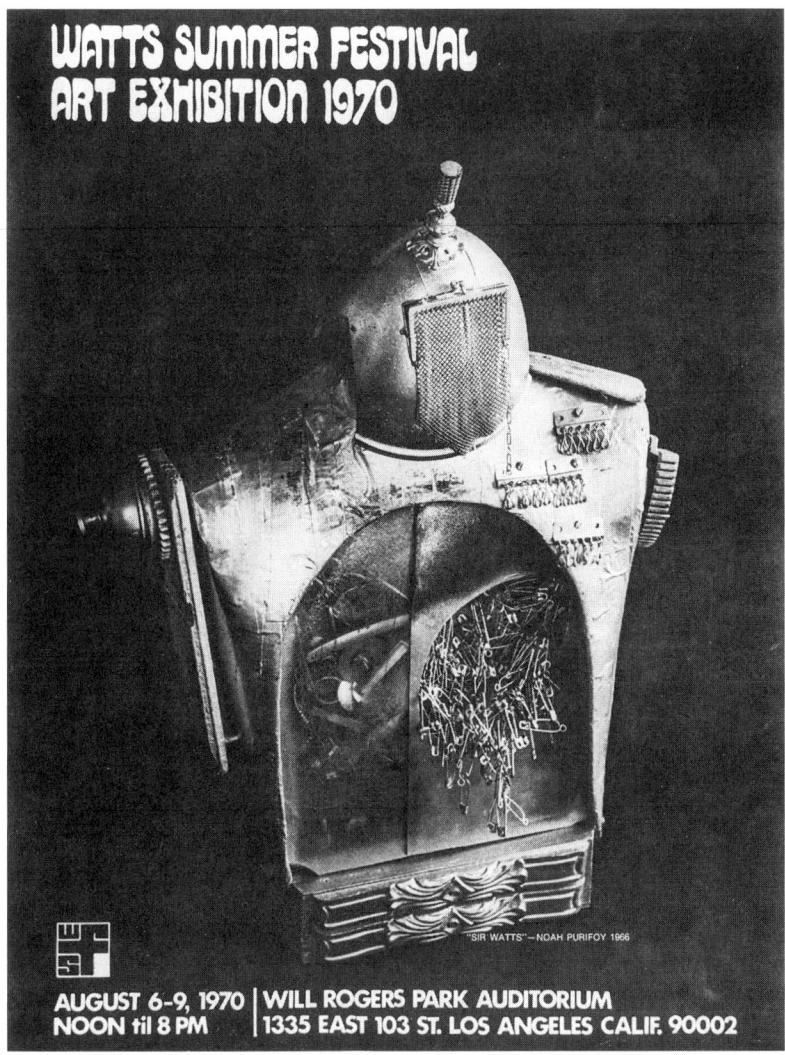

FIG. 2.5 Noah Purifoy's *Sir Watts* featured on a poster for the Watts Summer Festival, 1970. Courtesy Charles White Archives.

Lyndon Johnson's Great Society programs. In 1967, Hopps had left Los Angeles to become part of this Washington-based think tank to explore interactions of art, culture, and public policy with the likes of Herbert Marcuse and Stokely Carmichael. Almost immediately Hopps was drawn into the art world again, taking over the helm of the upstart Washington Gallery of Modern Art, which then merged with the Corcoran Gallery of Art, where he was curator, then director, between 1967 and 1972. The relationship between

Hopps and Purifoy in Los Angeles during the curator's early years there remains unclear. However, one photograph in Purifoy's archive—a snapshot of the two men at the 1969 Watts Summer Festival (plate 9)—reveals at least some interaction, though it was after the traveling exhibition.[56]

During the spring of 1969 *66 Signs of Neon* traveled to the Hunter Gallery in Chattanooga, Tennessee, perhaps its southernmost venue. The complete multiartist exhibition of *66 Signs of Neon* seems to have run its course by the end of that year, going back to its original state of junk, like many other pieces of West Coast assemblage in this era. A fragment of the idea lived on in an international context when Purifoy exhibited at the Berlin Industries Fair in September 1972 in a show that later traveled to Poland. The exhibition, *Garbage Is Beautiful*, whose theme was environmentalism, also included Edward Kienholz and was circulated by the United States Information Agency. By this time, the creative energy that Purifoy had found and nurtured in Watts had been thoroughly co-opted.[57]

Most of the pieces from *66 Signs of Neon* were eventually sold, lost, or destroyed; the current locations of many of them remain unknown. Of late some of Purifoy's own work from the period has begun to resurface. Several bring us back to the Watts uprising and are made in its immediate aftermath. These include *Pressure*, c. 1966, a bulbous metal form that has been compressed by the force of change, the heaviness of the rebellion. *Watts Remains*, c. 1965/66 (fig. 2.6), is not so compacted by the dynamics of history but appears molded by flames, melted and ashen. Its form is book-like, recalling Purifoy's prior experiments with bibliotherapy as a tool in individual psychic transformation. *Watts Riot*, 1966, is a painting with relief elements rather than a freestanding assemblage, its lower half bulky with dark hues and charred disks lining the bottom edge. This weightiness gives way to lightness at the top, yet the overall sense is one of smoldering tones that underscore the burning of the neighborhood. All of these evoke the idea of evidencing that phenomenology describes: art as objects and situations experienced by the subject, made not so much by Purifoy himself as by the people of Watts. Here meaning is uncovered through acts, truth is made by communities and validated there, as advanced in the later writings of Husserl. These fragments are also noematic: things of thought, scraps remembered and transcendental.[58]

Yael Lipschutz has written about Purifoy's oeuvre from this time as reflecting roots in Western avant-garde practices of the early twentieth century: his *Sudden Impact*, c. 1965/66, for example, a gloss on Marcel Duchamp's *The Bride Stripped Bare by Her Bachelors, Even*, 1915–23, or other works that recall the accumulations of Kurt Schwitters. Purifoy would have had the oppor-

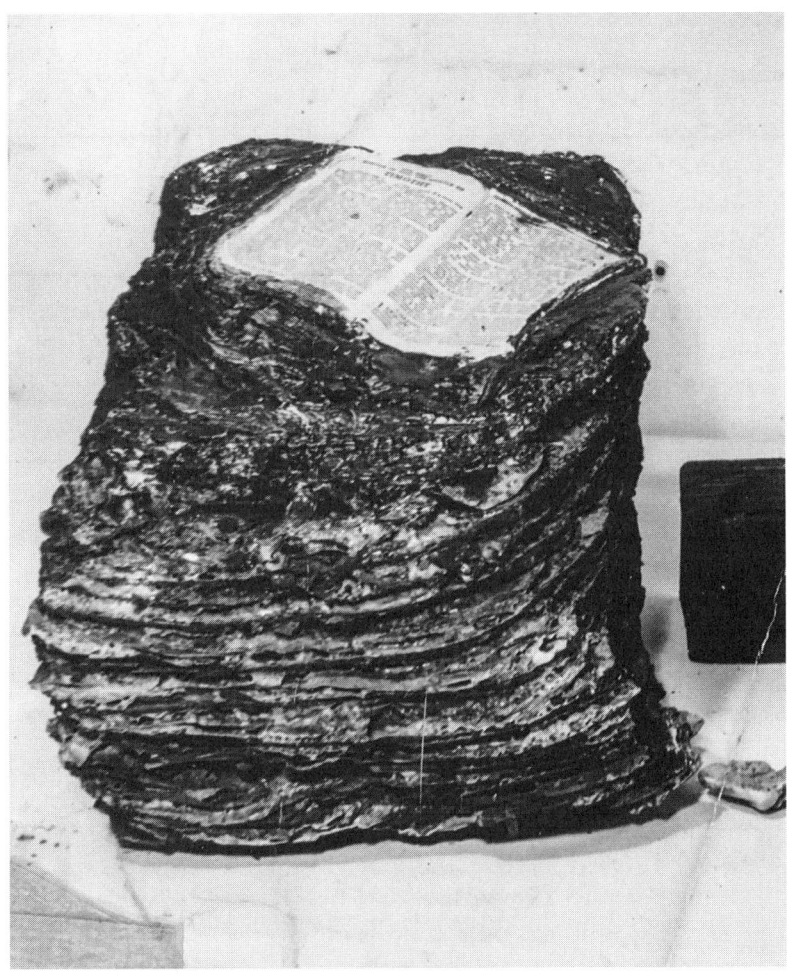

FIG. 2.6 Noah Purifoy, *Watts Remains*, c. 1965/1966. Found-object assemblage. Noah Purifoy Papers, 1935–1998, Archives of American Art, Smithsonian Institution.

tunity to see both of these artists at the Pasadena Art Museum in the early 1960s.[59] To these I would add *Unknown*, 1967 (plate 7), whose combination of the remnants of a parasol, umbrella, birdcage, and gaming chips against a color-laden ground recalls the eccentric juxtapositions of the Dada artists who were much admired by Purifoy.

66 Signs of Neon was an important undertaking for an independent-minded African American artist in the 1960s, particularly as it was achieved with little institutional support. Purifoy's independent organization, Joined for the Arts, mirrored others—like Weusi in New York and AfriCOBRA in Chicago (and later Washington, DC)—that took the dissemination of art and education of black people about that art into their own hands. The show trod a thin line between African American producers and a shifting body of multicultural artists, representing the largest urban uprising of the decade in one of the most populous African American places. It was junk art, sang of protest, and as a theme could enter into dialogues emerging around "black art." Purifoy's figurative pieces, such as *Sir Watts*, worked well with emerging black nationalist consciousness, but other more abstract things had a more tenuous connection, as with many African American artists working nonobjectively at this time.

However, the 1966 festival had a longer lifespan than *66 Signs of Neon* and so continued to mark the creativity of Watts as place. Purifoy was involved from the outset and his participation lasted from its heyday in the mid-1960s through the early 1970s, although the festival continued into the mid-1980s. In its first four years, Purifoy helped transform a local celebration focusing on neighborhood revitalization through the arts into a major arts festival.

The first Watts arts festival that Purifoy was involved with was known as the Simon Rodia Commemorative Watts Renaissance of the Arts Festival and took place at Markham Junior High School on 104th Street during Easter week of 1966. The organizers featured dance, music, and theater but did not shy away from showing photographs of the catalyst for the festival—the rebellion itself.[60] The visual arts section, coordinated by Purifoy and Powell, included a purported fifteen hundred entries from amateurs and professionals, children and adults.

The initial impetus seems to have come from art teachers connected with area schools, such as Paul Tanzawa, who taught at Jordan High. Also involved were Leslie Aisenman and Linda Flaherty, both connected with the committee to save the Towers. Their profile seems to match the one Sarah Schrank used to describe those who rallied to save the Towers from destruction in the late 1950s: largely "white, middle-class art students, artists, architects, and engineers."[61] Purifoy acknowledged that he and Powell added their concept of a show of junk art from Watts to a festival effort already in progress.

Historian Gerald Horne tells of another reason why this first festival may have come about: in November 1965 students from the Markham and Jordan schools (and others at the elementary level) staged a protest, four hundred kids strong, at the local Giant market. The chain had been a target during the Watts Rebellion, besieged for its subpar services and products. As Horne reports, during the throes of the August uprising, cashiers at that store had even brandished guns. The business continued to be unrepentant about what it chose to offer people in Watts, patrons who management pointedly described as not worthy of healthy or prime fare. This mirrored the services offered to segregated and poor communities across the country. Though describing 1940s Harlem, writer Ann Petry's words capture the landscape of castoffs that black people made do with: "All of them—the butcher shops, the notion stores, the vegetable stands—all of them sold the leavings, the sweepings, the impossible unsalable merchandise, the dregs and dross that were reserved especially for Harlem."[62]

Thus it was not surprising that the material remains of the Watts uprising were reused and reanimated into something else and into the centerpiece of the festival that would capture the imagination of many constituencies. The festival was a great success, attracting perhaps as many as ten thousand people to *66 Signs of Neon* and other exhibits, as well as theater, dance, and music performances at Markham Junior High.[63] It was repeated in spring 1967, with Purifoy's Joined for the Arts listed as a sponsor, and adding the Watts Happening Coffee House as another site.[64]

This public acknowledgment of neighborhood and community also attracted another independent celebration. Known as the Watts Summer Festival, it drew more attention than its predecessor—bigger names, performances, celebrities, crowds, and financing—and would continue into the mid-1980s. It was so popular in the early 1970s that the performances were moved out of Watts to the Los Angeles Memorial Coliseum, where the Wattstax concert, immortalized in sound recording and film, would attest to its national and international success.

The Watts Summer Festival became one of the best-known cultural institutions in the community (see fig. 2.5). It embodied ideas of rebirth and celebration, as did its predecessor, but also commemoration, as it was held one year after the 1965 uprising. In early 1966, a group began planning activities to mark the anniversary under the auspices of the Jordan High Alumni Association, among them graduates Billy Tidwell and Stan Sanders, a Rhodes scholar and Yale law school student who worked for the Westminster Neighborhood Association. Other festival organizers included Booker Griffin, radio host and journalist with the *Los Angeles Sentinel*, and Ron Karenga, an instructor in Swahili and head of the recently formed US Organization. Indeed, that group's cultural nationalist profile was identified with the event from the outset.[65] Starting with its own members, the US Organization set out to educate African Americans about African history, language, and traditions and "construct a new black culture."[66] A key aspect of Karenga's program was the creation of rituals that focused on contemporary milestones in African American life: Uhuru (Freedom) Day, celebrated on August 11, marked the Watts Rebellion.

From the beginning, then, the Watts Summer Festival, more than its predecessor, was a place to celebrate black culture, emerging black nationalism, and Black Power activism. Pageantry and culture were on view in the form of parades, beauty contests, black cowboys and a rodeo, and exhibition sports as well as theater, music, and art. Civil rights activist James Meredith attended the 1966 festival. The following year, the parade's grand marshal was Muhammad Ali, who was then appealing his conviction for refusing to enlist in the army. The theme "Black Is Beautiful" was borne out in the proliferation of natural hairstyles and natural beauty and the celebration of African arts, particularly that of South Africa, represented by dancers, singer Letta Mbulu, and trumpeter Hugh Masekela. This also reveals Karenga's hand in the proceedings.[67] In 1968, two women were the grand marshals, although Betty Shabazz and Myrlie Evers were chosen as living reminders of their husbands' assassinations and the need to continue the struggle.

The Watts Summer Festival committee sought to replace the destruction of the uprising with constructive deeds, with the event serving as the starting point for "positive community action," nurturing hope and ambition.[68] It presented a chance for black people to be "seen in a different light. They [were] first of all human beings with anxieties, with values, with hopes, with a reason to be treated like all other citizens of this city."[69] In these and other statements, there was also clarity about and an insistence on the fact that the uprising was not random but a rebellion against substandard life and treatment, a method of community action that disturbed existing structures of power. There was a recognition that municipal, state, and federal governments had to be held accountable for the state of Watts and had to take measures to rebuild the infrastructure, provide services, and combat brutality against citizens.

In the aftermath of the Watts uprising, the image of beauty and power rising from the ashes was vivid; out of destruction, life arose. Though made literal by the devastation of the cityscape, Watts became a discursive space, a metaphor for the rise of black consciousness and power, indicative of people's changing expectations and the way they looked at the world, from Los Angeles to Harlem to the South Side of Chicago to the newly independent African nations of Ghana, Nigeria, and so on. From ugliness, from the junk of citizens cast away by their country, came exquisiteness and transformation.

Performance and pageantry was of great importance to the Watts Summer Festival; in addition, however, visual art was always an integral part. The first festival, in 1966, included displays of paintings, sculpture, and crafts by African American and Caribbean artists. There were no mentions in the press of *66 Signs of Neon* or the junk art program associated with Purifoy and the earlier festival. Yet one article did speak of fifteen hundred works on view by "local artists," parlance used to describe the art presentation at the Rodia festival in March, leading one to speculate about how easy it might have been to re-present some of those works a few months later in pretty much the same arena.[70]

By the 1969 summer festival (plate 8), the focus on visual art finally garnered a major appearance in the press and reflected a defining cohort who were demanding to be seen and heard. This showing was one Purifoy helped bring into existence. As the press narrative reveals, first there was a multicultural band of artists, with *66 Signs of Neon* and Purifoy standing in for them. By 1967, Purifoy was pictured out front, though obscured, making way for "local artists" like Ruth Waddy and John Riddle, who stand almost tentatively behind him. In 1969, Betye Saar and Alonzo Davis take center stage as professional black artists. While Purifoy was clearly identified as the director of the art exhibit, the appearance of so many others—not only artists but black arts professionals—in 1969 is impressive. It included not only local artists, amateurs, and students but also those who were beginning to take their place in national and international arenas. Along with Saar and Davis, there were Riddle, Dan Concholar, John Outterbridge, John Stinson, Marion Epting, Charles Dickson, and others who would appear in exhibitions and publications that marked and defined this period in the LA art world. A prize competition at the 1969 festival included jurors such as collector Dr. Leon Banks; Curtis Tann, an artist and the WTAC's new director; and William Pajaud, a painter and by that time an adviser for the black-owned Golden State Mutual Life Insurance collection.[71] Noah Purifoy's activities in the 1960s gave West Coast black visual arts a national stage. If the Watts uprising made him an artist, as he mused, he also molded others—from children to those who later dedicated their lives to art.

Around 1974, Purifoy ended his relationship with the Watts Summer Festival and purportedly with art making itself. He returned to his job as a social worker at the Central City Community Health Facility of Los Angeles, where he continued to think about art and its role in mental health services. As antipoverty funds dried up and the goals for Watts and black communities everywhere remained unfulfilled, Purifoy was reflective about and disappointed in art's inability to catalyze the massive infrastructural changes needed to combat inequities in U.S. society. Instead he witnessed the continuing school dropout rate and the increase in gang violence and crime. Sadly, exposure to the arts, community-based or otherwise, didn't ensure "a better life for the culturally deprived." Instead, Purifoy reminisced, "we harbored other unfulfilled dreams as we struggled with our conviction that Art was an effective tool for change. We learned since then, given the right circumstances, baseball will do the same."[72]

In an undated letter to "Sue," most probably WTAC art teacher Sue Welsh, Purifoy described dichotomies and conflicts between art and the realities of African American life, now seen close up and focused through the eyes of the social worker.[73] He had just returned from site visits to Chicago and Cleveland on behalf of the health facility to study urban gang activity with an eye toward solutions for LA. Instead, he felt moved to join the gangs, since nothing had changed for poor black people: "The reality is that since the riot nothing has been restored, nothing has been improved, socially or economically." Although he once thought "art was the only problem-solving mechanism left for poor people," he now was skeptical and unconvinced, thinking rather that his dreams had ensconced him in an ivory tower, isolated from the realities of people's lives. He felt that the art world and the world of the black poor were two separate and irreconcilable realms. Only his community of artists and cultural workers kept him believing and confident that art as a catalyst for change was still somehow possible.

At that moment Purifoy was rightly conflicted as he faced the overwhelming structural inequities still in place in America and the understanding that creativity alone cannot change decades, indeed centuries, of institutionalized discrimination. By all accounts he remained inactive as an artist in the late 1970s and into the 1980s. There was one exception, however. In 1976, he became one of the inaugural members of the California Arts Council, which provided state monies for the arts in various categories. It replaced the California Art Commission, which had funded Purifoy's initial activities at the Simon Rodia Commemorative Watts Renaissance of the Arts Festival in 1966. Purifoy designed programs and set guidelines for arts in education, covering artists working in communities, schools, social institutions (such as prisons), and alternative grassroots-initiated sites. He was finally able to help others implement structural changes on a larger, statewide scale. Much of the work that he did in his eleven years on the council continued the things he'd tried in Watts.[74] After retiring from the council, he once again committed himself to art making, this time in the semiabandoned landscape of the California desert.

JOHN OUTTERBRIDGE: HOME GROUND

> I have always felt that assemblage was a way of life, in that you assemble your own directives. Assemblage, for me, means more than the manipulation of objects. It has a great deal to do with the piecing together of possibilities.
> —John Outterbridge

He got it honest. John Outterbridge's assembled aesthetic, as he has recounted on numerous occasions, was learned at his home in the Greenville, North Carolina, landscape of his birth.[75] His parents, John Ivery and Olivia Northern Outterbridge, were creators in their own right. They were musical, wrote poetry, made toys and clothes, and crafted other things. But they were not necessarily unique. These were the skills expected of black people in the first half of the twentieth century, not just for surviving in segregated and poor communities, but for thriving: making new clothes from castoffs or flour sacks, creating new toys from old, repurposing newspaper as wallpaper. Some of Outterbridge's earliest explorations were paintings on window shades.

The senior Outterbridge was what his son called a hauler or "junkster," but above all a businessman. With his trusty truck, he carted away trash for the well-to-do, always finding great treasures in the mix. He hauled garbage from markets many times in exchange for food. He set up a transportation service to get black workers to their jobs in war industry plants during World War II. He served as a volunteer firefighter in his community and, when the circus came to town, delivered the needed sawdust to the large tent, giving John and his siblings a sneak preview of the excitement. One man, one truck, and a world of possibilities.[76]

Yet it was clear that segregation and poverty still defined and constricted opportunity. While loving the warmth of his community and marveling at the magic and beauty of its creativity, John Outterbridge realized at a certain point that he would have to leave. As much as he might like to, he knew he wouldn't be allowed to go to East Carolina Teachers College, a mere seven-minute walk from home. Instead, in 1952 he made his way to the historically black North Carolina Agricultural and Technical State University in Greensboro. Later in the decade that school would be among the sites of the first civil rights actions.

Like many young people, then or now, Outterbridge signed up for the Reserve Officers Training Corps and later for the military as a way to pay for his education. After one year in college, he shipped out as part of the armed forces operating during the Korean War. Stationed on alert in West Germany, he trained as a munitions and weapons specialist, eventually rising to the rank of corporal. Later he would muse, "When I was discharged in 1955, if I wanted to assist the [Black] Panthers in blowing some things right, it would have been so easy!"[77]

Inspired by the German countryside, Outterbridge continued to paint. When his commanding officer discovered his talent, he gave the young soldier a studio, a jeep, money for materials, and assignments to decorate the officers' club and military-connected schools. He continued this work along with his munitions assignments throughout his tour of duty.

Outterbridge returned to the United States the year after the historic *Brown v. Board of Education* ruling of 1954 struck down "separate but equal" facilities across the country. In its wake, the civil rights movement went into high gear, with marches, protests, and boycotts. Like other African American military personnel throughout the twentieth century who returned from conflicts overseas, he found himself changed by his experience and refused to accept that one could fight for democracy abroad but be expected to slip back into a life of diminished opportunities and inequality without blinking an eye: "I remember, as an ex-military person — who came back after the Korean conflict in 1955, a few months after the Civil Rights movement started — being in uniform and getting on a segregated bus. It was not an easy thing to swallow. Two days back in the country and you go to the back and sit down. You hurt with that."[78] He knew he could no longer live in the South. And while he thought briefly of pursuing art school in France, his ties to home kept him on U.S. soil. He headed instead for Chicago, where he attended the American Academy of Art, his tuition paid for by the GI bill. In the Midwest, he found a greater sense of personal freedom and access as well as a supportive and nurturing artistic population.

It was during his Chicago period (roughly 1956 to 1963) that Outterbridge began to develop his collective ethos as a creator, as both a musician and a visual artist, through organizations on the city's South Side. He sang in the choir at Saint Anselm, a Catholic church that at times collaborated with the Chicago Symphony Orchestra and the Chicago Lyric Opera; he also started a jazz quartet, Opus de Four.[79] Along with others, he formed an artist's co-op called the Seventy-Ninth Street Collective. They showed and sold works out of a space they called Gallery 79, located at Seventy-Ninth Street and Cottage Grove.[80] Outterbridge found an audience (and a collector base) at Gayle Galleries, which also handled the paintings of Archibald Motley.[81] Soirées at the home of artist, poet, and organizer Margaret Burroughs were an inspiration, where his thoughts on black consciousness and culture were further nurtured. He developed a practice driven by painting, but on a variety of surfaces and with an array of materials in mixed-media combinations.

After eight years, Outterbridge and his new wife, Beverly McKissick Outterbridge, left Chicago and headed to Los Angeles in late 1963. They were lured by the more forgiving and familiar weather and environment as well as the greater possibility of actually supporting oneself through creative endeavors.[82] For most of his years in Chicago, Outterbridge had worked as a bus driver for the transit authority. It was a job that offered financial security as well as the flexible hours that could support his creative lifestyle.[83] He could have easily slid into a similar position in Los Angeles because of his strong record as an operator in a large municipal transit system. But Outterbridge held out for a job in the arts.

In LA he initially found work with Tony Hill, an African American ceramicist and internationally celebrated designer whose modernist pieces were coveted for Southern California interiors. Hill employed other artists as well and at times allowed them to experiment with their own designs. Through Hill, Outterbridge began to be exposed to the Los Angeles art world. Melvin Edwards worked for Hill for a time.[84] Outterbridge's eventual foray into welded steel may have owed something to Edwards's model, though perhaps not stylistically. From Tony Hill's studio, Outterbridge moved on to another creative post at Artcraft, a division of TRIAD Corporation, which supplied cameras and equipment to the aerospace industry and the military. He joined an artist's division with a varied portfolio, including the film industry. Outterbridge befriended TRIAD colleague Vertis Hayes, who was known for his WPA murals in the 1930s—particularly those at New York's Harlem Hospital—and who had arrived in Los Angeles in 1951.[85] Working on a larger scale and with access to an array of industrial tools, paints, and color, alongside creative colleagues from around the world, moved Outterbridge to think bigger in terms of his own art. The downside was that after working all day with painting applications, the personal joy was drained from such efforts; painting became a job. He began to apply the quick painting techniques and skills he used in his day job to his own pieces. Not comfortable with this development, he turned his focus to sculpture.[86]

His sculptural practice began to blossom when he left TRIAD. He worked methodically with stone, metal, and wood, going back to what was at hand and what he could get into for very little money. To support himself and his family, he cobbled together a series of part-time jobs. From roughly 1968 to 1975, he held numerous positions in the Los Angeles art world: he signed on

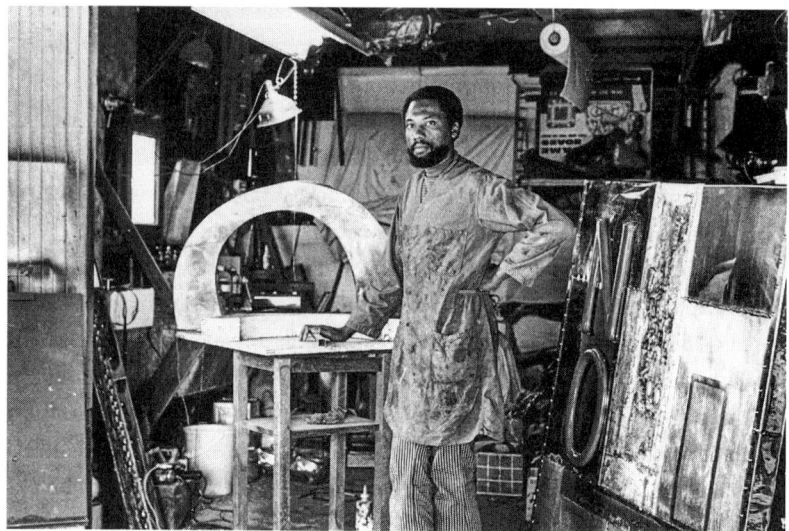

FIG. 2.7 Robert A. Nakamura, *John Outterbridge in his studio*, 1970. *No Time for Jiving*, 1969, is at right. Courtesy Robert A. Nakamura.

as a preparator and art instructor at the Pasadena Art Museum; taught at California State University, Dominguez Hills, and Pasadena City College; and directed programs at Compton Communicative Arts Academy (CCAA).

The camaraderie of the art scene in Southern California had an impact on Outterbridge (fig. 2.7). There he discovered the language for creativity, protest, and expression. True, he had found a similar community in Chicago, through music, art school, and the homegrown gallery scene. But things were bigger and more expansive in California; there were different notions of space, more artists in general, and an informality in dress and style that signaled a comfort zone of being, speaking, communicating. Similarly, Outterbridge learned that the boundaries of form in art were equally expansive, and he felt a greater sense of creative license. Part of this he also ascribed to the changes in the social and political life of the country itself.

A key place for meeting with other artists was the Watts Towers Art Center (WTAC). In early 1964 Outterbridge ambled over to that "tiny house on 107th Street." He fell in immediately with Noah Purifoy and Judson Powell and whatever project they were working on that day. And the conversations began. This was the beginning of Outterbridge's creative community, his "homeplace." Through them, he connected with the growing population of Los Angeles artists. And thus began the talk, or "verbiage," as Outterbridge framed it—informal summits at Purifoy's house: "We'd go and get into big fights at times, almost physical fights, and drink good wine and solve the problems of the world and then critique our work, you see. It was during a period, too, when things were alive in the streets, not just for African Americans, but the civil rights era was a period when the adrenaline of the American society was flowing, and everybody tried to be as open and honest as they could be."[87] Outterbridge's growing consideration of art's instrumentality and social function was encouraged by Purifoy's rhetoric and example. He began to think "how art and culture could effectively participate to help build a community, break existing moulds [sic] and create an interest in social change.... Artists were challenged to think in new ways."[88] For Outterbridge, art with social commentary also evolved naturally in the climate of the times. It was indeed part of the aesthetic of assemblage, "how you use whatever is available to you, and what is available to you is not mere material but the material and the essence of the political climate, the material in the debris of social issues."[89] Catalyzed by the times, Outterbridge came to think of himself as an "activist-artist" whose "studio was everywhere."[90]

Besides the WTAC, he also found a place in the larger local exhibition scene that began to emerge with Alonzo Davis and Dale Brockman Davis's Brockman Gallery in the Leimert Park neighborhood; Suzanne Jackson's Gallery 32, near the art schools Otis and Chouinard; the various spaces run by Samella Lewis, including The Gallery; as well as Studio Watts, the Black Arts Council, and Mafundi. And there were more personal interactions: driving Charles White to his various appointments; early morning field trips to scavenge for materials with John Riddle; and meeting Greg Edwards (Melvin's brother) at the Watts Summer Festival.

In this environment emerged Outterbridge's method of collectivity, an understanding of art and community that was both inclusive of adult working artists and focused on youth and positive futures. The work that Outterbridge did, following in the footsteps of Purifoy and Powell, established a space for creativity and motivation in a broader setting.

"I'd always been very confused as to what art was. I think it can be a thousand things," Outterbridge told an interviewer in 1973.[91] This prismatic notion of art emerged at CCAA between 1969 and 1975 (fig. 2.8). Outterbridge was initially approached by Powell to help create an arts center in a small house donated by the Salvation Army to the Compton Willowbrook Community Action Council, an antipoverty agency. Collaborating with some willing high school students, Outterbridge cleaned up the place, painting walls and floors, weeding and planting flowers, in effect allowing people to create their own cultural center with donated materials, sweat equity, and creativity. Other

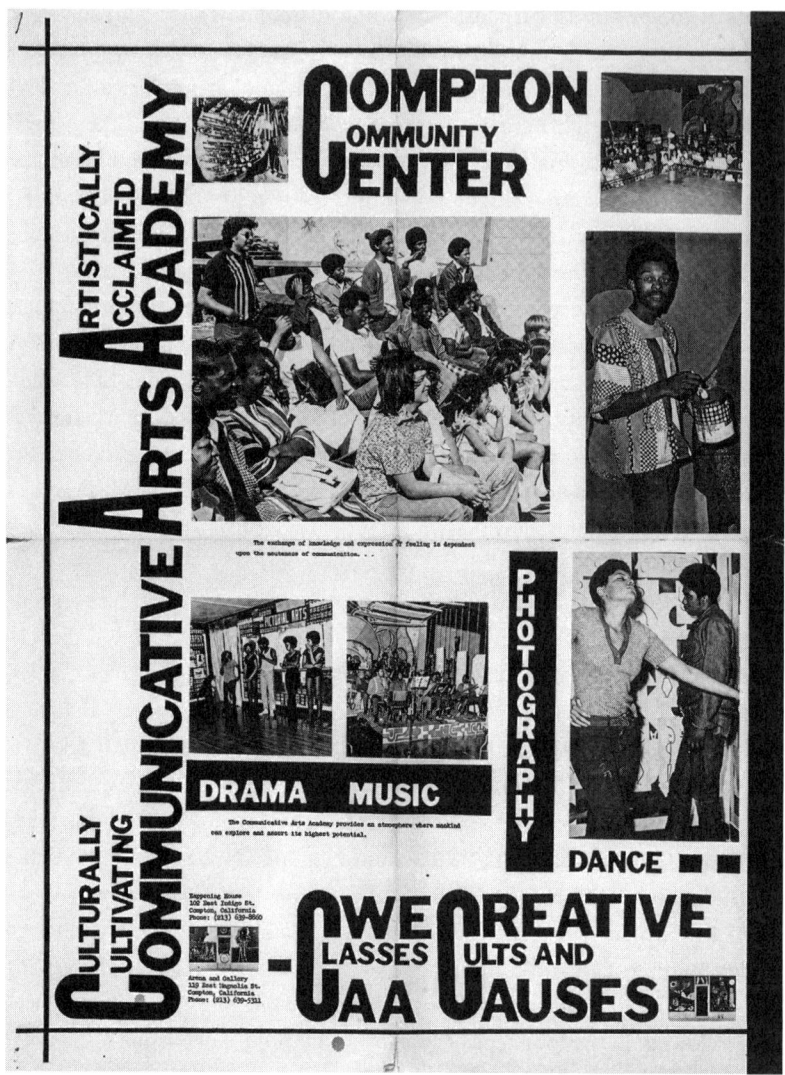

FIG. 2.8 Poster for Compton Communicative Arts Academy, 1970s. Courtesy John Outterbridge and Tilton Gallery, New York.

spaces were added, including a large, domed, abandoned skating rink, which became the centerpiece of CCAA action.

In late 1960s and early 1970s, CCAA captured the imagination of many professional artists besides Outterbridge, including sculptor Charles Dickson, muralist Elliott Pinkney, and painter Yvonne Cole Meo. They gave their time and skills for very little monetary return. Others, like Gloria Bohanon, brought classes of students to participate in activities there. Young artists, such as Kinshasa Holman Conwill and Houston Conwill, helped with the construction or painted murals. There were sculpture, painting, cinematography, and jewelry classes. Poetry and plays were produced; neighbors used the space for meetings. There were music classes and a jazz orchestra headed by saxophonist Troy Robinson; as a founding member of the Association for the Advancement of Creative Musicians (AACM), Robinson had been part of the experimental music scene in early 1960s Chicago before heading west.[92]

Two decades later, Outterbridge acknowledged that CCAA itself became his environment, installation, and process; his work as an artist was in a sense creating a situation for others to grow creatively, motivating people to establish their own cultural and creative centers, where aesthetics and beauty would not be dictated by an elite and estranged art establishment.

Outterbridge, in effect, was creating a safe and affirming space for the Compton community. It was a version of homeplace, embedded with ideas of nurturance and the domestic yet a wholly public locale. Built using repurposed materials, Outterbridge's CCAA also embodies the tenuousness of homeplace, its provisional nature as outlined by Dana Cuff, and its paradoxical complexity as cast by Katherine McKittrick. For bell hooks it is a place both fragile (and gendered) available to those on society's margins—but made over by culture into a location of validation and defiance, what she calls "homeplace: a site of resistance."[93]

Still, Outterbridge conceived of some projects as his own constructed environments, a form of living sculpture, as a few of the structures within CCAA were created from some of the same materials and in the same manner that the artist used in his individual but smaller-scaled work. For instance, an exhibition gallery in the space was made from foraged wood. Another was used for performances and meetings and housed a restaurant and coffeehouse. Outterbridge's inspiration was the magic made from little in many black communities both in the South of his youth and in neighborhoods like Compton and Watts.[94] In this environmental work, Outterbridge brought in fantastical elements. The walls were not just made from scrounged wood: elements like a piano harp, which could be played, were embedded in them; there was a diaphanous ceiling that filtered colored light. As a concept, how different was this from environments created by Allan Kaprow, Claes Oldenburg, or Jim Dine? The main difference it seemed was the constant use and the intention that lay behind this "work," the intention to marshal artistic forces in the creation of beauty and social capital.[95]

We find a similar ethos in Chicano and Asian American art-making practices in Los Angeles of this period, collective work and projects that explored the idea of art as a wide-ranging rather than elitist practice. Chicano groups such as Self-Help Graphics and Mechicano Art Center focused on the creation of prints, posters, and murals to produce a body of work that was engaging and easily distributed and could provide hands-on access. Visual Communications was an Asian American activist media group that took photography and film production into community settings.[96]

This type of camaraderie and the creativity in social forces drove Outterbridge's practice; the intermingling, intersection, and intermedia of the arts at CCAA provided a way to think through a creative process that was his own. His first mature artwork reflecting his Los Angeles reality emerged in 1967. The *Containment* series, 1967–69 (plate 10), sets the pace for works through the early 1980s, with the use of salvaged and inexpensive materials as a conscious and aesthetic choice. In these sculptures, metallic skins are applied over wooden armatures, some affixed to the wall, others freestanding. While the metal occasionally came in sheets, some of the first pieces were formed from cans that had been flattened and refashioned. Critics have seen in these works a "controlled and gentle hand" whose focus is never the "pathos" of the discarded.[97] Instead, Outterbridge presented classical still lifes of an urban variety, poised, gemlike.[98] Perhaps it was the sensibility located in the found and weathered elements joined with old chrome or surfaces polished to brilliance. Perhaps, as Robert Farris Thompson would tell us, it was in the "flash," the signal of motility, and the spiritual force that was revealed. In Outterbridge's hands, these materials came together as an homage, not a screed, as meditations on "re-invention."[99] In their tenuous materiality they inscribe perseverance, the homeplace of the re-membered subject. They flicker with the flash of life over death.

Lizzetta Lefalle-Collins has compared Outterbridge's *Containment* series to Warhol's *Campbell's Soup Cans*, 1962, which render a mundane three-dimensional object on a flat, printed surface. Outterbridge's works are similarly compressed and reengineered in an art context, making visible the proximity of assemblage and pop art practices. The move from three dimensions to two also inscribes acts of transmutation, of radical boundary breaking, into their surfaces. Belts, straps, and other fasteners and compressed metals embody the restraints as well as bonds of boundaries. By continually rethinking wall-to-floor orientation and discarding frames, canvases, and paintings, Outterbridge questioned the parameters of traditional form, as did many other artists during this era.[100]

The *Containment* series embodied a reach across boundaries in other ways. In part, it held the memory of an early friendship with the white sculptor Mark di Suvero. In the second half of the 1960s di Suvero spent a lot of time in California. He moved to Northern California in 1964 and began building large-scale and kinetic pieces such as *Nora Albion* and *PreColumbian* (both 1965), which were shown at LA's Dwan Gallery in September 1965. Between 1968 and 1970 di Suvero lived in Pasadena installing the work *Victor's Lament*, 1970, on the grounds of the Pasadena Art Museum, where Outterbridge worked in various capacities.

Outterbridge was impressed by di Suvero's process; his use of a full-scale crane as a tool expanded Outterbridge's notions about art practice. In turn, di Suvero was engaged by what Outterbridge was doing but also amazed that he was cutting metal by hand. Leaving for another commission, di Suvero loaned his tools to Outterbridge for a year, including a pair of electric power shears. It was during that period that the artist completed the more than fifty sculptures that made up the *Containment* series.[101]

These works, along with others, were presented in Outterbridge's solo show at Brockman Gallery in October 1969. It was the first exhibition featuring one artist that the gallery had presented in its two years of existence, and it received a review from *Los Angeles Times* resident critic William Wilson, another gallery milestone.[102] Grudgingly complimentary of the objects, Wilson nonetheless rejected Outterbridge's direct and written statements on the purpose and meaning of the work, considering them unnecessary. This was a pattern of many critics at mainstream publications at the time, who rejected black artists' directions and parameters for their intellectual and aesthetic output. It was a position, repeated in art criticism throughout the country, that revealed a fundamental lack of understanding and familiarity with art by African Americans and an unwillingness to accept the possibility of other aesthetic formations and notions of beauty.[103]

Works from the *Containment* series weren't the only pieces on view in the solo show at Brockman. Others were hybrid, often garment-like constructions of metal and fabric. These were transitional things that led to the following *Rag Man* series, 1970–78. Like those in the *Containment* series, these objects offered a critique of the strictures of traditional categories of art making. While the *Containment* series may have spoken to the breakdown of boundaries between painting and sculpture, *Rag Man* addressed the divide between high and low forms, the difference between working with paint on canvas and forming clothes and other things from pieces of fabric; canvas, at the end of the day, was little more than a rag.

Outterbridge's practice reflected the blurred boundaries between media in works that were conceptual and postminimalist. Even more specifically, Outterbridge's *Rag Man* series was in dialogue with pieces by African American artists on both the East and West Coasts: Al Loving's dyed and shredded canvases, Sam Gilliam's enormous billowing forms, Joe Overstreet's architectural panels fastened with rope. These artworks not only demolished accepted paradigms of form but also returned to and incorporated something that was known and vernacular. In creating such works, Loving, Gilliam, and Outterbridge recalled sewing, tailoring, and quilting traditions that were part of their early years and homeplace.[104]

Claiming these alternate inheritances for art making addressed the specter of marginality both racially and materially. Along with writings by Frank Bowling, Robert Farris Thompson, David Driskell, Samella Lewis, James Porter, and the like, such assertions effected the dismantling of dominant monologic histories of making and mastery. There were other ways of creating beyond classic fine arts conventions; there were also other makers of value outside canonical narratives. In other words, to be a practicing black artist one need not make oneself new from whole cloth, cast aside all that one had been; one need not forget. As bell hooks points out, it was a "politicization of memory that distinguishes nostalgia, that longing for something to be as once it was, a kind of useless act, from that remembering that serves to illuminate and transform the present."[105] Such artists practices then speak to Tillet's notion of civic estrangement, the American intolerance that instantiates a distancing and disaffection. Yet here the periphery's remove offers possibility over deprivation; it is a place from which radicalism can be launched.

For Outterbridge, the *Rag Man* series was also inspired by another aspect of personal and African American history, a figure from his youth in the South and later years in the "up south" Midwest, who would come by to collect cast-off clothes for reuse and resale.

> I knew people as a kid who sold rags and collected rags. In Chicago it was very exciting to hear the ragmen move in and out of the alleys calling up for rags. People sometimes two or three stories up would throw bags of rags down to the ragman, things that they wanted to get rid of. Sometimes they received a few pennies for those rags, but a lot of people would just get rid of things and the ragman would just take them and run. On the South Side there was a ragman who had a conga player on the back of his wagon, and they'd have all these call-outs that became very familiar songs, really, on a bright spring morning or in the summer early in the morning. ... I used to look at these wagons and how colorful they were with all the

rag mixtures on them and just the whole aura of one who picks rags for a living.[106]

In part, the *Rag Man* series was composed of fabric portraits of various individuals, constructed and at times stuffed figures, some affixed to walls. Others, such as *Case in Point*, c. 1970 (plate 11), had different profiles. *Case in Point* was shown at CCAA and is one of the few extant pieces from the series. Built from seven leather lozenges, it is filled with rags held together with leather straps similar to those in the *Containment* series. A handle rises from the top, and an enlarged tag hangs from the side with the legend "Packages Travel Like People"; here the specter of the black commodity hovers nearby. Yet it also suggests that Outterbridge's thinking about the rag man was an investment in the African American migration narrative: people and packages moving out of the South and, in this case, to the Midwest, where southern traditions were transposed. For the migrants, the notion of home becomes mobile. New positionalities become part of the new perspectives on the world. But nothing is forgotten. Thus if African American populations of the twentieth century were built in motion, they were also built on memory.[107]

While *Case in Point* appears representational, other pieces are more ambivalent. *Jive Ass Bird*, 1971 (fig. 2.9), is a study in white, a jumble of pillows, pouches, and straps topped by a bulbous and monochromatic slice of an American flag. Though its overstuffed appendages recall Faith Ringgold's soft sculptural dolls or Claus Oldenburg's pneumatic pieces of the same era, in its raggedness, Outterbridge's sculpture leans toward the nonobjective and away from the cartoonish tableaux of these colleagues. *Jive Ass Bird* speaks to another sense of such outlying aesthetics, what hooks thinks about as a profound edge, a radical openness that nourishes, and that for Huey Copeland remains unrecognizable, unconfigured, and unmarked yet equally potent.[108]

Outterbridge's *Ethnic Heritage* series, 1976–82, continued some of the ideas of the *Rag Man* series, primarily in the emphasis on fabrics, cloth, and leather—found, recycled, reconfigured—and how these could be made to conjure and visualize the figure. What was somewhat more subtle in the *Rag Man* series—the notion that African American and African tradition are a basis of fine art practice—is spoken more directly in these pieces, as the artist thinks through ancestral legacies and aesthetic strategies. In the 1970s, familiarity with African objects, particularly those from West and Central Africa or Egypt, was a given; some knowledge of African aesthetic practices had been absorbed intellectually by African American artists as a comfort zone, as a promise, as a way to describe meaning in their own work.

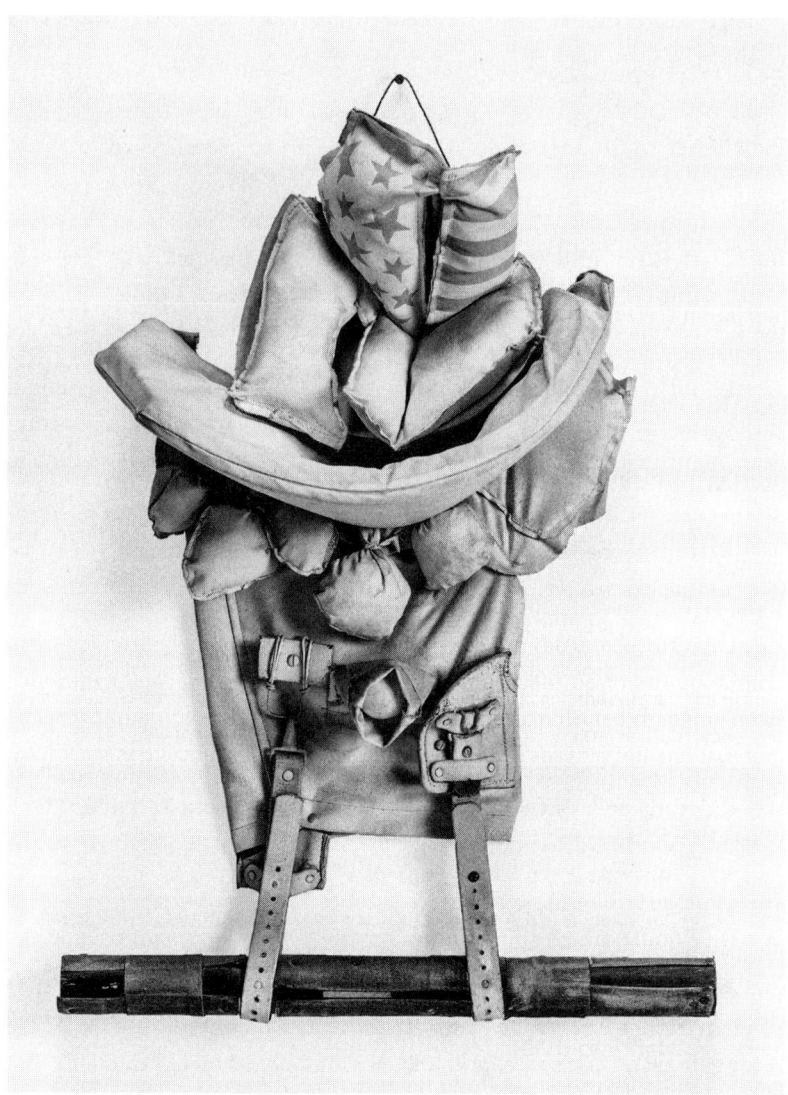

FIG. 2.9 John Outterbridge, *Jive Ass Bird*, *Rag Man* series, 1971. Mixed media. The Greg and Diane Pitts Family Collection. Courtesy the artist and Tilton Gallery, New York.

To some extent, Outterbridge mimed these practices in these small sculptures from the late 1970s. Identified at times as "tribal figures" or "elders," these are iconic images. This is particularly the case in the *Ethnic Heritage* series, whose figures have a vertical upright orientation, angular limbs held close to the body, and masklike spirit features. The sculptures are "dressed" in clothing that may be fabric or paint, stylized and elegantly arrayed garments that emphasize the body's carriage, grace, and spiritual power. These garments are also embellished: accents of beads and medicines are arrayed like jewels around the form, calling attention to the figure's aesthetic pleasure and extrabodily power.

Another group of works within the *Ethnic Heritage* series takes us in a distinctly different direction, although some of the same elements and aesthetics are in play. Qualified by the phrase *Captive Image*, these figural pieces are more exaggerated and fragmented. Body coverings are ripped and torn, with ragged and uneven edges. Ideas of binding and constraint that appear in the *Containment* series are often continued on human forms. In one work, a figure is laid out across a small cart, held down with straps while one leg attempts to kick free. The notion of "captive image" as the enslaved is literal here. Yet many of these pieces are more abstracted, distorted, and larger, with metal introducing ideas of restriction. For the most part, facial features disappear; heads come to a point, crowned with helmets of metal. Hips and thighs expand. Yet all the pieces in the *Ethnic Heritage* series use the body as a focal point. Outterbridge's *Ethnic Heritage* series, with its focus on tribal and captive images, brings us through the 1970s in much the same way that other African American artists in Los Angeles do, with some emphasis on Africa and the ancestral. But while many would focus on royal roots, Outterbridge did not forget slavery's inheritance. Outterbridge's memories of the South, and the slave economies haunting that life, allowed him to honor the traditions passed down through struggle and strife.

Such an aesthetic of making do was a sacred heritage for Outterbridge, exemplified by his father, who created worlds with a shovel and a truck. It was part of a "life mode," a philosophy, much more than art in the Western sense. Part of it was also "craft," the magic of making something from almost nothing. But it was also not just the ability to make things. African Americans had built the United States, made the nails and boards to put it together, created Monticello and the White House, and provided the factory for presidents like Jefferson, men who were broke after leaving high office. They made the clothes, raised the foodstuffs, and cooked and served them too. They were carpenters, blacksmiths, seamstresses, potters, who worked with wood, fabric, metals, and earth. Black people knew craft; they knew making. This long history of making went into Outterbridge's works.

However, he also drew on another level of creating that paralleled these realities. Aesthetic actions from slavery to freedom were about making space and creating place, preparing the land, gardening, decorating and improving space as an act of community, working the land as a moral force and critique, approaching the earth in ways that parallel what Grey Gundaker and Judith McWillie have called "yard work." This labor was about beautification *and* control. These practices marked and designated homeplace, demonstrating attention and love but also encircling the land with protection. Gundaker and McWillie have documented a distinct lexicon showing that these outdoor spaces reveal surfaces that flash and things that are tied, thrones for sitting and wheels for moving, broken and "experienced" objects, water and the vessels to contain it.[109] These traditions are southern, African American, and creolized, yet all demonstrate strong West and Central African roots.

Such activity in the domestic spaces of African American families was noted by early twentieth-century writers like James Weldon Johnson and Zora Neale Hurston as well as white commentators in the South. They described yards that were immaculately swept and details of whitewashing and bottles driven into the ground and hanging from trees. The persistence of and the need and desire for these traditions is found too in the work of authors such as Alice Walker and bell hooks, who muse on the tradition of intellectual and creative labor that they inherited. In their essays, gardens and quilting are activities through which their mothers and grandmothers can rise above the hardscrabble everyday; leave the corporeality of the body and free their minds and spirits; find a space for contemplation and creation that is personal, spiritual, and self-nurturing, a space in time where, as hooks's grandmother would say, she could "come back to herself."[110] Through these acts, both women keep the notion of creativity alive and in forward motion.

Walker's mother, like Outterbridge's, made all the family clothing as well the sheets and quilts. In her garden, her mind stretched and blossomed; with flowers and plantings she engaged the "work her soul must have."[111] It is not surprising that this vegetation was also placed inside the house, where sunflowers covered the wall in places. It was a decorative action that wrapped the house with fecundity, color, life.[112] As with quilts, where each scrap and the larger whole hold a story of a moment, context, and conditions of use, flora placed just so wrapped a tale in place.

It was this kind of cultural practice, one that marshals spatial form as both a haptic and an ocular experience, that Outterbridge also recognized, celebrated, and wanted to embed and remember in his own actions. As he has pointed out, one can make something defined as sculpture or mixed-media installation, "but there is also a little old lady who has the greatest flower garden in the world, and if you could steal it away from her and take it to an art museum, it would be a hit."[113] While he knew he could not live again in the

South, it remained a homeplace and spiritual center, one of sustenance and creative effluence even after he moved to Los Angeles. As Gundaker and McWillie recognize, a worked yard could become a "promised land," a site of unrestricted autonomy and exponential possibility, a space of transformation and movement that signaled ownership and home. The tradition of yard work radiated out from the South to Detroit, New Haven, Los Angeles, and other points north and west. In these actual and symbolic landscapes, "things [were] thoughts"; they gave intellectual and spiritual concepts visibility and corporeality.[114]

Yards were protected spaces, cared for, looked after, cultivated, guarded. In the social landscape of the twentieth century, ripe with the inequities of segregation, discrimination, and racial power, these domestic sites ascribed a certain personal control to their owners. They turned the lurking uncertainties of dispossession into something mutable and contained, and converted them into something of beauty and bounty. The ground, the plantings, and decorative pieces were fixed to inform those who passed by that they modeled their keeper's desire and will to improve the surroundings. The upkeep of these locales decreed that they were shelters and areas of respite. However, the other modality of yard work was as a protective force, where vigilance was encoded in objects and surfaces, where tied fences and things installed at thresholds admonish, where materials arranged in and around homes shield the physical body from harm and secure property against theft and confidence schemes alike. They were aesthetic in their presentation and defensive in their logic. These installations at home ground were, according to Robert Farris Thompson, one vast *nkisi*, wrapping the dwelling with avatars of power, virtuosity, and fortification.[115]

Outterbridge recalled similar practices in and around his North Carolina childhood home: an interior wallpapered with newspaper, his father's French horn given pride of place on a wall when it was not in use, window shades adorned with paintings. Then there were the things "hung on the door, on fences," groups of dried gourds lifted on poles topped with a bit of rag, placed in gardens to scare away predators.[116] His father's accumulations of "old stuff" were found in all manner of places and kept "around the house and in the backyard."[117] Indeed, the son nominated his father a "junkster" because his livelihood was hauling away, and often recycling and transforming, "old stuff." The terms "old stuff" or "junk," as Gundaker points out, can be read both as a reason for the dismissal of these actions, as based in poverty and lack, and as the phrases of indirection and multivalence taken up by African

American yard workers. Like the word "antique," these expressions also suggests ancientness, a time of ancestors (as in that "old slave-time junk"), and a certain marginality.[118]

In Outterbridge's mind, the worked home ground of his youth was part of a continuum of traditional practices that organized his world: necklaces of fabrics embedded with medicines that changed color as a sign of their efficacy (asafetida bags); red clay used not just for vessels but also for body plasters; local herbs and long-standing rituals to heal maladies common and uncommon.[119] Into the Western sense of art, he poured all these notions of family creativity and the value of objects and practices that he inherited from his North Carolina home ground. These were very personal and intimate practices that attested to the staying power of an African American aesthetic vision of ancient modalities. As he recalled: "I ended up doing art simply because I felt good about the things that influenced me: the things that I saw, the things that I heard, the things that I felt, the images that you wanted to hold onto. So art became that—it wasn't a business. It wasn't something that you knew would create salaries. I never thought about it in that way. It was a way of saying what I felt to other people. It was also a way for me to keep a journal about the things that were close."[120]

In California, his practice was more solidly sculptural, took a greater spatial tone, and rejected the frame as a corral, fence, or deterrent; he thought through and reanimated the traditions of homeplace on Los Angeles soil. Using things that were inexpensive but not inexperienced, rags or surfaces that glinted and gleamed, Outterbridge re-created sites of refuge, where one could "come back to oneself," but which equally and unquestionably asserted themselves in the visual landscape. These were spaces of familiarity and intimacy that insisted on their power to make things happen. Such ideas of intentionality, purpose, ambition, and the efficacy of the art object bring us again to the "antiques," "junk," and yard work that Gundaker and McWillie describe. They also help us see the actions embedded in Outterbridge's sculptural works from another vantage point.

He has suggested that his use of belts, fasteners, and bindings in the *Containment* series and other pieces as well as his rejection of any painted surface for metal were refutations of certain formulas of art making as well as a commentary on the larger social constraints faced by African Americans historically. Perhaps his work is not really too far from the tying and wrapping that Gundaker and McWillie describe, an action that seals intentions and that they trace back to Kongo practices in Central Africa.[121] Applied to objects, thresholds, and fences, tying and wrapping secured the area, the charm, and the power, and activated these things in the home and the very landscape itself. In a work such as *Let Us Tie Down Loose Ends* (plate 10), Outterbridge thus not only stated his position formally as an artist and socially as an African American but bound and locked in their power; by sealing the piece with leather straps, he ensured the effectiveness and value of this object in the world. His narrative—in which binding also inscribes its opposite, the will to break down boundaries—mirrored the ambivalence or oscillation of power that can be used for healing as well as harmful ends as seen in his artworks' southern and African predecessors.

When Outterbridge put together *Case in Point*, c. 1970 (plate 11), part of his *Rag Man* series, its valise-like shape, leather casing, and legend—"Packages Travel Like People"—evoked African American migration narratives and the varying dematerialized forms of 1960s western art practice. However, the leather straps have specific aesthetic value too: the wrapping and tying of intention, a pledge of safety en route and in one's new world.

Yet migration's impact on the work of artists in general is not only about how specific aesthetic precepts travel but the artistic responses to dislocation and resettlement as well as the transmutation of home. While the works he made were unquestionably art objects, Outterbridge, like Purifoy in particular and Saar to some extent, thought of his concatenations as having an even larger portfolio: "When I use the term art, I always think of it as whatever I need it to be. You're lucky when you can do selfish things that have relevancy to someone else. Who needs a little box that I build out of my anguish? Who needs it? Maybe I do for the moment."[122]

Over and over, Outterbridge has described both the will to creativity and the barriers to the same in his southern milieu as well as among his peers in Chicago and Los Angeles. In North Carolina, he cited, among other nodes of ingenuity and vision, the constructive and entrepreneurial skill of his father, the sewing abilities of his mother, the musical pulse of the local Pentecostal church, the expert reworkings of the local shoemaker (Mr. Black), and the philosophizing of the itinerant minister (Reverend Highsmith). Yet there was also his Uncle Buddy, trained as a concert pianist, who suffered because he was unable to find an outlet for his gift. In Los Angeles, Noah Purifoy and Troy Robinson reaped a certain success from the their visual art and musical dexterity alike but experienced a negative impact as well due to the lack of consistent institutional and infrastructural frameworks that allowed them to develop their creative propensities to the fullest extent. Taking stock of such situations, in the quote above, Outterbridge described a task for art that was much more expansive than its role as a precious object for a leisured class or a curio for display in a museum. More important, it filled a psychic space. As Alice Walker, Gundaker, and McWillie have also advocated, art in these modalities offered a place for expansiveness of the soul, a freedom, release, and a control of space, body, and mind.

HOODOO YOU LOVE: BETYE SAAR
Constructing Counterculture

Betye Saar's art star had been shining brightly since the early 1960s, when she began to win awards on the professional level. However, it was a series of works on African American subject matter later in that decade and into the 1970s that brought her widespread attention and landed her on the national stage. *Black Girl's Window*, 1969 (plate 12), a significant piece of this period, is also marked by a subtle change in technique. Saar worked primarily with prints in the first part of the 1960s and eventually began employing window frames, pasting the prints to the back of the glass and using the panes effectively as linear and relief elements of the collage. In *Black Girl's Window*, the collage elements migrated to the front, and Saar created small compositions within each pane. Though each is linked to the larger narrative of the whole, they can stand alone and in this way prefigure her sculptures composed from boxes.[123]

The title figure of the work fills the entire bottom half of the frame. Parted diaphanous curtains sit behind her as she presses her raised hands and face against the invisible glass of the windowpane. She seems to look out at viewers, addressing and confronting them with the narrative arrayed in the panes around her; zodiac and celestial signs abound, some inscribed on her palms. But Saar has insisted on several occasions that her girl is looking into or through the window, seeing what is to come in her own life, peering "into her future."[124] Indeed, Saar felt the autobiographical nature of the piece even at the time—its narrative of her new independence in light of divorce from ceramicist Richard Saar a year earlier, her growing focus on black struggle with the Watts Rebellion and the death of Martin Luther King Jr.[125] We can see the development of her feminist consciousness as well: she was turning her back on the domesticity that the curtains represent as she looked into the space beyond.

On a formal plane, *Black Girl's Window* did presage what was to come: the artist's move toward fully three-dimensional sculpture and the centralizing of the black figure. It was at this moment that Saar began to work not only with boxes but also with what Patricia A. Turner has nominated "contemptible collectibles," stereotypical figurines of African Americans whose bodies were usually serving or performing. While many of the images themselves had their origin in the nineteenth century and were tied to minstrelsy and later the backlash against Reconstruction, they had become a cottage industry of sorts. Many continued to be produced well into the twentieth century. These derogatory images of black people, in object form, as well as sheet music and postcards, were ubiquitous at the swap meets and other places Saar haunted for her sources.[126]

Expanding on Clement Greenberg's understanding of kitsch as failed seriousness, performance scholar Tavia Nyong'o has theorized the imagery that Saar began working with at this moment as racist kitsch, a type of failed humor. Such materials in attempting "to say something banal" and be "unobtrusive" actually point up the opposite, their being "laden with meaning."[127] But such things are also surplus or waste and as such are seen as impervious to the violence that is continually heaped upon them. While a site of disgust or distancing, there is also a mode of reassigning such images, what Nyong'o calls curating, that is seen as modifying their hatefulness, that then recasts these media as oppositional.

Compelled by the notion of black representation, as it surfaced in secondhand markets and as it burgeoned in the general consciousness, Saar indeed mused on how to use and recycle these images. Similar to those who take something that's been cast off and incorporate it into something altogether new, Saar sought to reimagine such caustic visions, to redeploy them as their opposite.[128] In considering this style of artwork and its engagement with ideas of black liberation and the protocols of the Black Arts Movement, Mary Schmidt Campbell has identified art that dismantled "icons of racism" and thus fulfilled their role as "weapons" of the black cultural revolution.[129] Saar's recycling and Campbell's mapping the dismantling of meaning in racist kitsch are both ways to think about such oppositional curating or positioning. Other African American artists, like Joe Overstreet and Murray DePillars, also revisualized stereotypes in this era. What set Saar apart from her peers was her incorporation of actual materials, from figurines to graphics.[130] Such repositioning emerges in an assemblage such as *Whitey's Way*, 1970, which has the central motif of an alligator in pursuit of a black child or "pickaninny," a recurring trope of vintage imagery. Saar extended it from the old-fashioned chromolith into a three-dimensional mirrored box, where a phalanx of now-white gators flank a black skeleton, highlighting the violence that had been implicit and also contemporizing the image.

A separate series on men and women focused on the implications of gender, both in the objects and in African American history. In *Sambo's Banjo*, 1971–72, and *I've Got Rhythm*, 1972, black men's dancing and music-making bodies are paired with the specter of their doppelgangers: lifeless, lynched men hanging from trees. Saar used an actual banjo case in the former, with a dangling puppet ready to perform, mirroring the photo of the lynched figure just above its head. In the latter work, a body attached to the hand of a working metronome swings along, keeping time; inside the case, images of lynchings provide a background setting. Also significant is Saar's use of printing processes and the repetition of images to create a graphic ground while calling attention to the central figure. This would become an artistic signature of sorts.

The stereotype of the performing black figure, Sylvia Wynter reminds us, embodies lack. The minstrel is a sambo: irresponsible, childlike, intellectually challenged. He is a dependent phantasm created to stabilize the force of white paternalism. During slavery, Wynter writes, "The plantation order which made it illegal for a slave to learn to read and become educated, which exhausted the black with relentless work, then produced empirical evidence of the Negro's 'lack of intellectual faculties.'"[131] In this way lack is assigned to the minstrel. But the song-and-dance man is emblematic not only of black culture but of popular culture, and opposed to middle-class norms. He fills his apparent deficiency with dynamic and subversive cultural forms—practices that will energize Western culture in the modern period.

Similarly, in *Sambo's Banjo* and *I've Got Rhythm* Saar suggests that legendary black performance is the key to survival, whether it be the tradition of black minstrels, the vaudevillian antics of Bert Williams and George Walker, or the later roles of Stepin Fechit. Or I might suggest an earlier inception: in the disguises and actions black people used to escape from slavery.[132] *Let Me Entertain You*, 1972 (fig. 2.10), uses the artist's window-framing device to set up a parallel narrative. Here the minstrel is compared to the contemporary black revolutionary. Posed in front of the red, black, and green colors of black liberation, the latter has replaced the banjo with a rifle, the ultimate tool of survival. Yet as Saar's title implies, the radical too remained a figure of diversion.

Saar's series featuring Aunt Jemima appealed to feminist art circles. The artist created a group of images, again mostly sculptural, that narrated women's power and independence. The mammy and ultimate caregiver, Aunt Jemima, became emblematic of a woman's function in much of the globe. But she also represented what historian Darlene Clark Hine has identified as a "culture of dissemblance," one mobilized to "protect the sanctity of inner

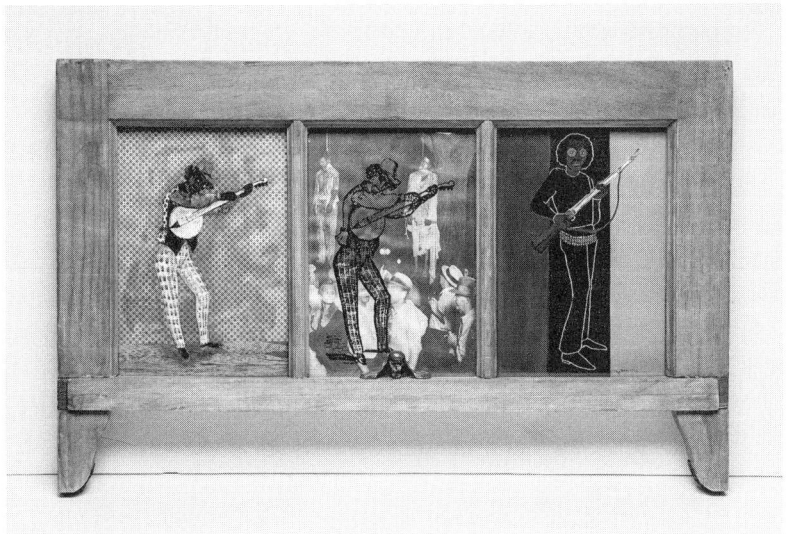

FIG. 2.10 Betye Saar, *Let Me Entertain You*, 1972. Mixed-media assemblage. The National Afro-American Museum and Cultural Center, Wilberforce, Ohio. Courtesy the artist and Michael Rosenfeld Gallery LLC, New York, NY.

aspects of their lives," and masking other roles and revolutionary power.[133] There was performance here too, the portrayal of obedience and service with a smile.

The first in the series, the now iconic *The Liberation of Aunt Jemima*, 1972 (fig. 2.11), was originally made for a group exhibition, *Black Heroes*, at Rainbow Sign Cultural Center, an African American community gallery in Berkeley, where E. J. Montgomery was then curator.[134] The central element, formerly a vessel for stationery and pens, becomes a gun-toting mammy; the center of her body is a Black Power fist. The figure is reflected literally in a mirrored container but also, as were the male figures in *Sambo's Banjo* and *Let Me Entertain You*, in the replication of graphics, in this case from a pancake box and a postcard. Though not particularly large in scale, its imagery was incredibly strident, promoting the threat of violence. Of the African American artists working in Los Angeles during this time, only David Hammons and perhaps sculptor and printmaker John Riddle seem to have come close to Saar's direct message. Other works in the series showed Aunt Jemima ready to rumble with volatile materials. In *Measure for Measure*, 1973, a cup of flour to her left is balanced by a cup of dynamite to her right. In *The Liberation of Aunt Jemima: Cocktails*, 1973, her "brand" is affixed to a Molotov cocktail.

Deborah Willis understands Saar's pieces as "reinterpreting the working-

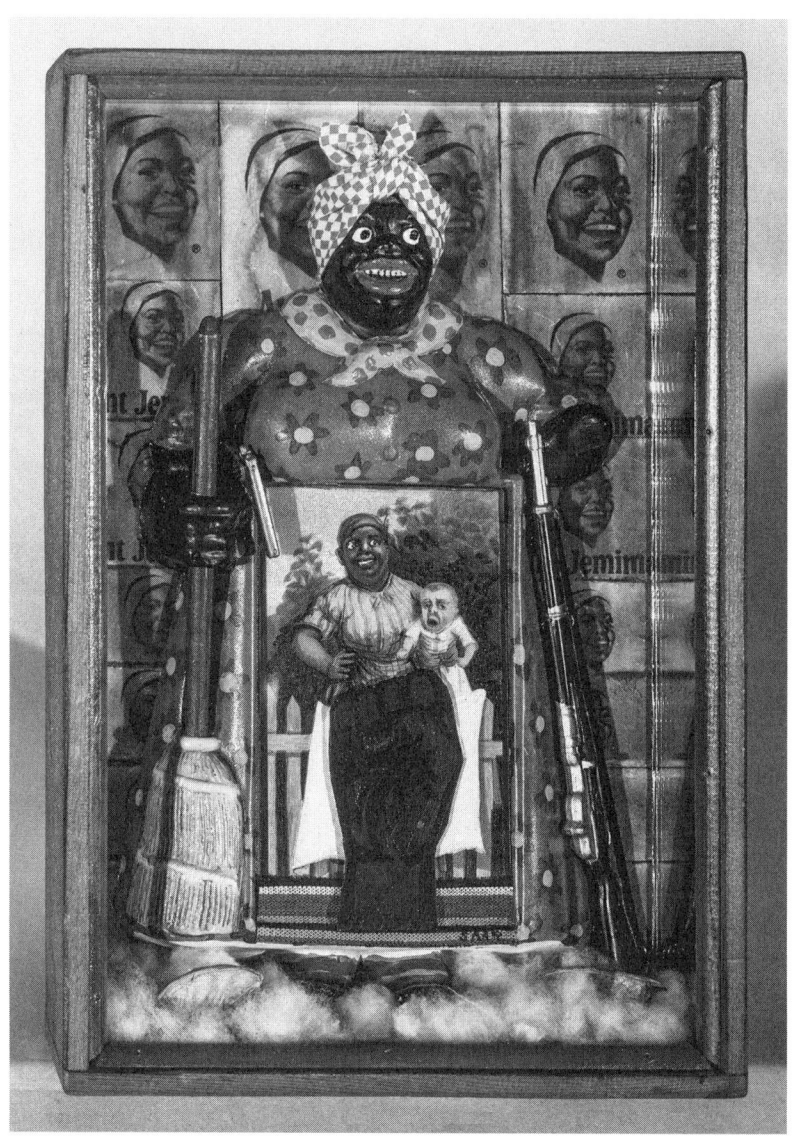

FIG. 2.11 Betye Saar, *The Liberation of Aunt Jemima*, 1972. Mixed-media assemblage. Collection of University of California, Berkeley Art Museum; purchased with the aid of funds from the National Endowment for the Arts (selected by the Committee for the Acquisition of Afro-American Art). Courtesy the artist and Michael Rosenfeld Gallery LLC, New York, NY.

class woman."¹³⁵ The wide circulation of derogatory images in advertising and popular culture established Aunt Jemima as the personification of the "cook, servant, mammy" of hospitality that are redolent of southern climes. Her joy of serving bespeaks love and devotion to the old South and its masters and is emblematic of nostalgia and fantasy for a status quo where the black servant signifies white luxury and power. Saar confronted these debased ideals with her own graphic and constructed repetitions that upended the "romanticized images of . . . black servitude."¹³⁶ Yet we can also consider Saar's recycling and reinvention of contemptible collectibles as part of a broader act of wide-ranging cultural restructuring and redefinition.

Around the same time that Saar began composing sculpture from derogatory objects, she started another series of nonprint works, with wall-based orientations but in a completely different style. The central element was a freeform scrap of leather festooned with various small sculptural items that had appeared in early boxes like *Omen*, 1967, or *Africa*, 1968. They were not man-made, however, but constructed from natural materials such as shells, feathers, and bones. Some were quite large and suspended from the ceiling. One of the most interesting things about these works is their titles and where they take us. In *Gelede* and *Eshu (The Trickster)*, both 1971, Africa is the source, particularly the Yoruba culture of modern-day Nigeria; *Gelede* is a masquerade, and Eshu is the deity of the crossroads. Several years later Saar visited Nigeria, first in 1974 and later to attend FESTAC (Second World African Festival of Arts and Culture) in 1977. In the fall of 1968, however, the exhibition *Sculpture of Black Africa: The Paul Tishman Collection* was held with much fanfare at the Los Angeles County Museum of Art. The show's strength was in three-dimensional art objects. The appearance of Saar's box *Africa* in the same year suggests her inspiration there.

Yet some of the first pieces in this series in leather, *Mojo Bag*, 1970, and *John the Conqueror*, 1971, are not focused so much on tracing routes back to Africa as on what happened when such spiritual and cultural systems touched down in the Americas. These two works referenced the world of hoodoo in the United States. Hoodoo is related to similar African-descended spiritual systems throughout the Americas, like Santería and Candomblé, and also has roots in West and Central Africa, particularly through language and aspects of material culture.¹³⁷ In *Mojo Bag* and *John the Conqueror*, Saar remembered African Americans' relationship to Africa but placed its cultural eruption in American forms.

John the Conqueror, thought to be among the most powerful charms in the hoodoo pantheon, takes the shape of a twisted root. It is a plant form seen in the yard shows described by Gundaker and McWillie and of Central African Kongo derivation.[138] "Mojo," a term known from American blues songs, meaning an amulet or charm, is derived from the Kikongo word *mooyo*, referring to a spirit that caused these effects. Yet the title *Mojo Bag* takes us to something even more specific: large leather bags carried by Mandingo healers in the Mande areas of West Africa. These carried materials of the trade but also were seen as healing pouches. The term used by eighteenth-century Europeans was Gregory bag, an anglicizing of the Mande word *gris-gris*.[139] The expression *gris-gris* itself also made its way to the Americas, where it came to mean "charm." Saar continued these themes in pieces such as *Gris-Gris Box*, 1972, and *Ten Mojo Secrets*, 1972.

For Saar the 1970s were also a period when she was in prodigious contact with Northern California, exhibiting frequently. It was at that moment that she met writer Ishmael Reed. Their creative conversation was potent and tangible. One gets a sense of a vibrant dialogue around globalism and multiculturalism as it was manifest on the West Coast. Reed began his literary career in New York as part of Umbra, a group of early black nationalist poets, but moved to the Bay Area during 1960s. He began to push an American aesthetic, which he labeled Neo-HooDoo, using sympathetic magic as a point of departure. Neo-HooDoo destroyed Western monologic thinking and in its place offered a multicultural landscape of cultures and traditions in dialogue.[140]

Reed's aesthetic inquiries also dealt with art and architecture. In his collected volume of essays, *Shrovetide in Old New Orleans* (1978), he writes about architect J. Max Bond and artists Doyle Foreman, Joe Overstreet, and Betye Saar. Saar appears in no less than three pieces in *Shrovetide*; these date from 1973 and include an interview in which the artist muses on her sources and practice of the moment. She also illustrated his book of poems *A Secretary to the Spirits* (1978), returning to her graphic roots. It is clear that Reed was fascinated by her art, which seems to conjure in material form so many things that he divined in print.[141]

Clearly African-descended cultures were potent sources for both Saar and Reed. They both focused on American folk practice and systems as African diasporic schema within an expanded context that was global and yet reflected the locality of the California context. Thus, Saar leaned toward Asia in altars such as *Sadhana*, 1976, and *Samhadi*, 1977. She thought about the Latino history of California as well as the contemporary moment, as evinced by the assemblage *Fiesta of the Dead*, 1969; the plethora of Mexican milagros in her pieces; or even the use of the Spanish language in earlier prints such as *El Gato*, 1960.[142]

Saar's assemblages featuring contemptible collectibles caught critics' eyes in shows at Los Angeles's Multi-Cul Gallery and Berkeley's Rainbow Sign Cultural Center in 1972 as well as a large survey of her art at California State University, Los Angeles, in 1973. A good portion of the work on view at these shows, however, was the artist's leather charms. Her hanging leather amulets, festooned with the stuff of nature, seem antithetical—in their materials, focus, and presentation—to the discarded and rejected thinking of humanity from print and material culture seen in works such as *Sambo's Banjo*. The streams began to come together in works that combined both commercially manufactured and environmental objects in boxes, such as *Gris-Gris Box*. Here, hair, bones, snakeskin, and feathers enmesh a central black female figure in a red headscarf, a mammy doll who has become the central source of amuletic power.[143] In *The Liberation of Aunt Jemima*, also made in 1972, the centralized figure's talismanic force is the gun, a source of revolutionary activation rather than the spiritual kind. Both works are amulets, yet at the same time demonstrate art's role as weapon by enacting the destruction of negative imagery. By incorporating these problematic figures in their work, artists sought to consume their power, enact physical and artistic cannibalization, and thus drain their negative magic. Following Wynter, we can see Saar in most of her series as laying claim to "stigmatized cultures" of the black working classes, offering alternative definitions and planting seeds of cultural transformation.[144] In each case Saar constructed a counterculture.

An altar like *Mti*, 1973, enshrines such action by setting up a site of participation.[145] The central element in *Mti* is a small palm-frond table on top of which are affixed a series of boxes that seem to flow more directly from pieces Saar was known for at that time. Paired candles frame the work at the upper and lower levels, adding to the ceremonial feel. Layers of wax melted over time add texture and patina in line with the use and reuse of the logic of assemblage. When it first appeared its title was *Shrine: Mti*, marking it as a devotional object. By 1977, when it surfaced again at the Baum-Silverman Gallery in Los Angeles, the title was simply *Mti* (plate 13).[146] In the intervening years, Saar had created a number of similar objects and so the specific designation "shrine" was no longer necessary. Rather, the new understanding and use of this object simply demonstrated that choice. On view at Baum-Silverman, it was sequestered in its own alcove and raised on a plinth. A simple sign invited people to add an offering. Instantly, Saar created a participatory art installation as friends and strangers left money, toys, jewelry, art, and other items, along with notes and requests, draping them on and around the piece. At the end of the show, people could retrieve the things they brought or exchange them for others with the idea that the collective spirit and force amassed over the month would be transferred back to each participant. Saar acknowledged Arnold Rubin's article "Accumulation: Power and Display in African Sculpture," which appeared in *Artforum* in 1975, as the impetus for her move in this direction and her subsequent fascination with mounting energies—ancestral in the form of experienced materials and contemporary in form of contributions from participant/viewers—that would infuse her works with a certain power.[147]

Increasingly in this period Saar's works explored Africa and its diaspora as well as the globe. Like *Mti, Indigo Mercy*, 1975, is emblematic of works that feature small tables at their core with boxes mounted on top. They share commonalities with Haitian Vodou altars, which often rise in shelf-like tiers and are piled with sanctified objects.[148] *Damballa*, 1975, is adorned with a variety of reptilian parts. Snakeskins and imagery predominate in recognition of the sculpture's namesake, the supreme god of the Haitian Vodou pantheon, which manifests itself as a sacred serpent.[149] Its diasporic roots are found in the omnipotent earth god Da, a divine python of Fon origin, from the kingdom of Dahomey (modern-day Benin). In *The Jewel of Ogun*, 1977, Saar's boxy altar form is transmuted into metal in recognition of the Yoruba deity of iron and war.[150]

Like other African American artists, Saar thought anew about her ancestry and her relationship to Africa.[151] Her fascination with the culture and traditions of Louisiana, where such African-derived traditions thrived perhaps most visibly, was linked to the fact that her paternal relatives came from there, specifically the city of Lake Charles. Missouri, the home of Saar's mother and the great-aunt who helped raise her, was another stronghold of these traditions and a place where one could find Mande-derived Gregory bags. Yet Saar's interest in African ritual and spiritual systems and their workings in the Americas also corresponded to her interest in alternate cosmologies generally—from the tarot and palmistry that had pride of place in her earlier prints and windows to the altars.

Black Mirror

Between 1975 and 1981, Saar was the subject of a spate of interviews that brought her greater visibility within feminist art arenas and solidified her presence as an artist of significance within *those* contexts. The feminist mission of these interviews is clear. Women's art was seen as a common project; whether in sculpture, painting, or alternative practices, these artists shared a collective story. They were self-created women whose struggles and passions

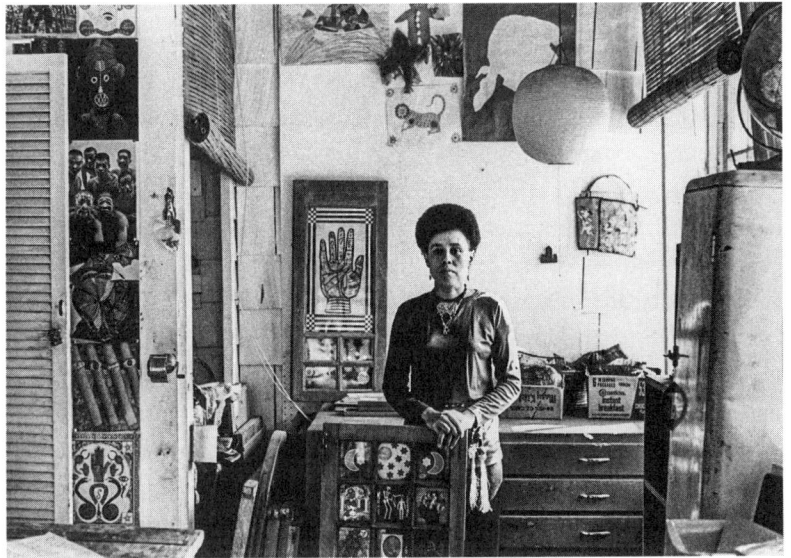

FIG. 2.12 Robert A. Nakamura, *Betye Saar in her studio*, 1970. *View from the Palmist Window*, 1966, is behind her at left; she is holding *Black Girl's Window*, 1969. Courtesy Robert A. Nakamura.

were poured into and visible within their work, bespeaking self-invention and self-fashioning. Women artists of the 1970s willed themselves into the art world despite being unwelcome in its boys' club and separated from the banter and fruitful connections, aesthetic and otherwise, made in the culture of bars and other public locales. Instead, women made art many times in solitary, in back rooms, hidden away, in acts that were sometimes furtive and often undesirable in the society at large.[152]

Feminist writing during this period recalls the place, both physical and intellectual, that women artists inhabited. "I thought serious artists had to have big, professional looking spaces," wrote Lucy Lippard. "I found women in corners of men's studios, in bedrooms and children's rooms, even in kitchens, working away" (fig. 2.12).[153] Isolation was not only a working process that was hidden and undisclosed but also marked by a distance from critical discourse. The word "woman" put next to "art" or "artist" was something that everyone up to the 1970s, including women themselves, turned from, causing Lippard to ask, "Why are we all still so afraid of being *other* than men? Women are still in hiding."[154] Her statement reminds us of the importance of feminist criticism as well as art-making strategies that privileged "non-high art forms" and the questioning of standard Western categories, such as "genius" and "universality." In other ways, the focus on figuration, portraiture, and decorative arts pushed arguments for an "expanded definition of modernism."[155] Women, like African Americans, were similarly intruding subjects in canonical art fictions, causing problems for the smooth surface and natural order of white male privilege.

In interviews from the period, Saar performed her intersectionality. She explained African American culture to new audiences, specifically ideas about black pride, African art, and the diaspora. The artist's *Aunt Jemima* series, in particular, allowed white feminist writers to engage her "poignant ... statements of black feminist protest."[156] She also defined a black trajectory on feminism, what Alice Walker would later call "womanism." Saar brought into focus alternative "Third World" notions of female liberation, where race and gender were not compartmentalized but "inextricably linked," with commitments to a broader construction of community, where homeplace was a site for nurturing creativity, subjectivity, and resistance; it was a population that understood the expansion of an oppositional consciousness "functioning beyond the demands of dominant ideology."[157] Saar also did not shy away from speaking about the discord and tensions between the feminist and Black Arts movements.[158]

The influence of civil rights and Black Power on other late twentieth-century U.S. liberation movements, including the women's movement, has long been acknowledged. Black women were integral to both the struggles for black freedom and women's liberation. But as a number of writers have concluded, black women were expected to disregard the racism and class privilege of white feminism and also turn a blind eye to the misogyny of Black Power. The effluence of black women's creativity in the late 1970s is often seen as the end point of the Black Arts Movement, which conveniently ignores the extent to which the voices of women were heard throughout the period.[159] Indeed, the women's movement and the Black Power Movement are generally seen as antithetical and at odds with each other to the extent that they both squeeze out black women, who shift uneasily from one foot to the other, each planted securely in the other world.

However, some writers, including Harryette Mullen and art historian Lisa Gail Collins, instead consider intersections and parallels between feminist and black arts, and through this we can see what women like Betye Saar negotiated from each in a practice that was mobile and multipositional and did not accept the elision of either race or gender. Both movements imagined and vigorously worked toward a world where people could thrive and find "value and legitimacy," where art was also "cultural work" for "social and political change," a place to redistribute the wealth and power of calcified and discriminatory cultural formations.[160] As mentioned above, this practice occurred outside the shiny spaces of power, with homes and streets as important sites, both nonelite and liberating. There were also notions of shared imagery and aesthetics that followed from communal identity, and the sense of uncovering a hidden past, undiscovered or underexplored histories that could influence the present and future.

Still, there were connections between women of color and whites in the women's movement. And Saar continued to avail herself of the opportunities that presented themselves and offered another kind of visibility. She built friendships and relationships that would last a lifetime and would have an impact on the feminist art movement as well.[161]

As early as 1968, Saar was included in *25 California Women of Art* at Lytton Center for Visual Arts, which also featured a young Vija Celmins's early gray figurations of violence and Helen Pashgian's resin objects in the West Coast minimalist style. The exhibition was among the first large projects in Southern California to present women artists. *Los Angeles Times* critic William Wilson's visible grappling with the show in print gives us insight into the uneasy reception of art by women as a growing movement, and the battle fought by the status quo to maintain categories that ensured its own aesthetic order. According to Wilson, the work was by turns romantic, decorative, and sensuous, leaning toward a personal statement and away from the "stringent" aesthetic that was au courant. Yet he was also compelled by its freedom, interest, and attraction. Wilson wrote that the exhibition needed the participation of minimalist Judy Gerowitz, whose plastic domes and acrylic paintings had gained her entry into the larger national scene as long as "working like a man" was her greatest goal.[162] Around the time of the Lytton show, Gerowitz was sending up smoking clouds, signaling her move from minimalism to postminimalist and feminist practice, announcing her imminent name change from Gerowitz to Chicago. By 1970, Judy Chicago was at Fresno State College, inaugurating the now historic Feminist Art Program.[163]

25 California Women of Art was organized by Josine Ianco-Kline (later Josine Ianco-Starrels). A curator who consistently supported a diverse vision of the Los Angeles art world, she was another significant figure linking African American and feminist art practices during this period. She began her career at Lytton Center and moved to the Fine Arts Galleries at California State University, Los Angeles, where she mounted important early solo shows by Betye Saar (1973) and David Hammons (1974). Between 1975 and 1984, Ianco-Starrels was director of the Municipal Art Gallery at Barnsdall Park.

She also contributed to the Calendar section of the *Los Angeles Times* during part of this period. As a result of her efforts, African American artists, both women and men, and numerous unsung others received visibility, in exhibitions as well as in print.[164]

Saar made other feminist connections in Southern California as well. She served, for instance, on the inaugural board of Womanspace Gallery, which opened in 1973. Although it was active for only eighteen months, Womanspace hosted numerous exhibitions and programs and produced a journal. It eventually became part of the Woman's Building, the better-known and longer-lived entity that advanced women's creativity and feminist work. Documents and articles reveal the Womanspace program's attempt to create a space that was open to the diversity of women's lives and experiences and how Betye Saar figured into and advanced that goal.

As a board member, Saar participated in numerous activities at the organization, including contributing art to a fund-raising auction, publishing in its journal, and organizing an exhibition on its premises at 11007 Venice Boulevard.[165] In the second issue of *Womanspace Journal*, Saar wrote a brief article on the show *Black Mirror* (fig. 2.13), which she and Samella Lewis had curated for the gallery. On view between March 31 and April 22, 1973, it included art by five women: Gloria Bohanon, Marie Johnson (Calloway), and Suzanne Jackson, along with Lewis and Saar. Saar explained that the paintings and mixed-media pieces presented were different from what one might expect from the feminist art scene at that moment. The goal was for African American women to offer their "own mirror image," apart from dominant feminist narratives and also from the male-dominated Black Arts Movement.[166]

Not only were the artists on hand to discuss their work at points during the run of the show, but numerous events offered a wide array of perspectives on African American cultures, from dance and theater to film and poetry. Saar and Lewis staged other activities that explored black women's creativity in a broader context. They invited women to showcase culinary artistry; for example, New Orleans native Harriet Craft Pajaud (then married to painter William Pajaud) made creole dishes in the gallery. There were sessions of hair braiding and jewelry production. For Saar, who had emerged from the world of design and craft, this was an important framing that fit within the context of feminist art making. A lecture by Lewis advanced the idea of the manufactured gap between art and craft. This angle on contemporary practice meshed easily with West Coast rubrics in which work in ceramics was also pushing against the craft / fine art divide.[167]

In 1971, Judy Chicago had brought the idea of women-only art education

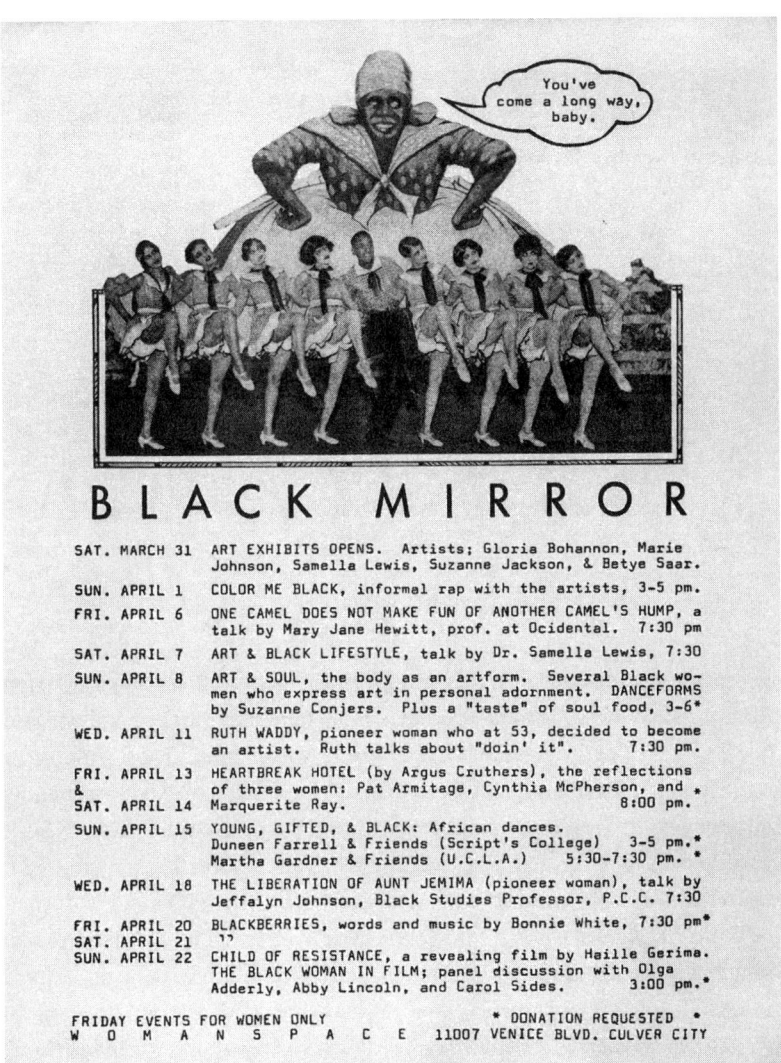

FIG. 2.13 Flyer for *Black Mirror* exhibition at Womanspace Gallery, 1973. Ankrum Gallery Records, 1960–1990, Archives of American Art, Smithsonian Institution.

from Fresno to Los Angeles, moving the Feminist Art Program to California Institute of Arts (CalArts). She was joined there by other artists, designers, and educators, including Miriam Shapiro, Sheila Levrant de Bretteville, and Arlene Raven. Several years later, they developed the Woman's Building to promote women's creativity and feminist work, a "public center for women's culture."[168]

Through these networks, Saar met and developed a friendship with Sheila

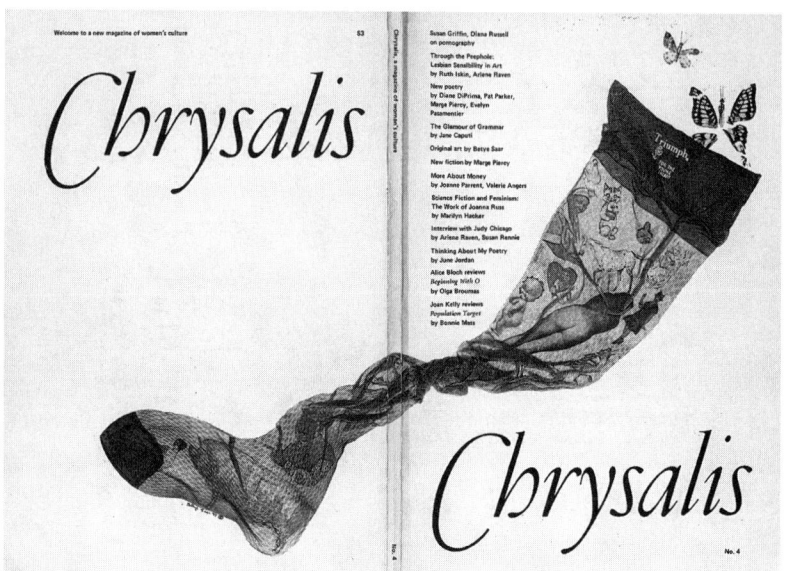

FIG. 2.14 Sheila Levrant de Bretteville and Betye Saar, *Chrysalis*, no. 4, 1977.

de Bretteville, a graphic designer and the power behind the Women's Design program at CalArts. Born in Brooklyn, and trained at Barnard College and Yale University, de Bretteville had spent time working in Europe. Influenced by the youth-movement protests of the day, she looked for ways to channel both that energy and those democratic ideals into the graphic plane.[169] Educated as a designer herself, Saar shared that common creative language with de Bretteville. They would collaborate for years to come. Saar's work adorned the cover of *Chrysalis*, no. 4, 1977 (fig. 2.14), a Woman's Building publication designed by de Bretteville, who would also shape a number of Saar's exhibition catalogues.[170] Saar participated in the Power of Place initiative begun by Dolores Hayden and de Bretteville in 1984 to create sites for the remembrance of ethnic and women's history in public art and spaces. Both Saar and de Bretteville contributed to the commemoration of Biddy Mason's home at Broadway and South Spring Street in downtown Los Angeles.

In a 1978 interview Saar recounted that one of the things that stimulated her to become an artist and to push herself into a successful career was thinking about her female relatives and their dissatisfaction with their lives simmering just below the surface. Yet their "dissatisfaction" had less to do with being bored suburban housewives — they were women who worked — and much more to do with the limitations that race and gender afforded them, even in the relatively progressive city of Los Angeles. The series Saar began in the early 1970s exploring her matriarchal roots was in dialogue with any number of feminist productions from the time.

Certainly, pieces like *The Liberation of Aunt Jemima* rejected historical gender roles. However, Saar also created a parallel body of work that revealed a more human and humane side of black portraiture. This emerged from her collecting of vintage photographs, which asserted itself in the early 1970s. *Bittersweet (Bessie's Song)*, 1973, is emblematic in its central photograph of two African American women, whose sassy clothes are mirrored in the plumes, velvet, and jewels that surround them as well as in the elegant attire of blues singer Bessie Smith, who smiles in a handbill. This piece uses photographs to re-create an ancestral past imbricating and intertwining a historical figure (Smith) as well as unknown and found family. Here Saar fills in the historical record in an action that numerous artists of her generation, like Charles White, would also perform. In doing so, they created expanded families and larger diasporic histories. Scholar Marianne Hirsch has explored such actions in the manipulation of family photos, which become eloquent sutures of memory and collective history, recasting the circulation of meaning through the configurations of family.[171] It is a process that Saar, in particular, enacted through her collages and assemblages, many of which incorporate photographic documents.

In 1975, Saar's great-aunt Hattie Parson Keys passed away. Keys had been more like a grandmother to Saar, and she was given the job of going through her great-aunt's home and effects. There she discovered a treasure she was excited to convert into her next series. Rather than paying money for stuff from strangers—photos, letters, dance cards—she kept her aunt's things, delving deeper into her own personal history in the process but weaving it into her larger intellectual project as well. Though often described simply as autobiographical, the power of these works is their dialogue with larger histories as archetypes and avatars of U.S. and diasporic worlds.[172]

By 1977, the series centralizing material from Aunt Hattie was well under way. When describing the works in an interview, Saar singled out *Record for Hattie*, 1975 (plate 14), a container of blushing pinks and deep reds that "has all the things I remember her using: a pincushion she had on her bureau, with pins and rings still on it. Her girlhood autobiography book. An egg timer."[173] In *Last Dance*, 1975, the artist gathered items Hattie might have assembled on her dressing table before heading to a party: a fan, compact, silk flower, and ribbons for her hair. Saar's genius is in her compression of materials, ideas, and feelings; the intermingling of delicate, turn-of-the-century trappings, seamlessly arranged, subtly painted in a contemporary construction;

the aura of romance that the composition exudes. It is "a funereal box that simultaneously suggests a makeup kit, jewel casket, and reliquary." A program listing the order of dances and the names of participating partners is paired with "an engraved response to a sympathy card."[174] Black netting radiates elegance but inserts a layer that distances viewers. With their inky hue, these accoutrements of vanity oscillate between the formal attire of a ball and symbols of Hattie's death that year.

Other female relatives emerge in Saar's collages and assemblages around this time. In *Veil of Tears*, 1975, an image of her maternal grandmother, Emma Kelley Parson, leans toward the center of the box, staring out from behind a diaphanous wedding veil held down by three white gloves, stand-ins for her grandmother's Irish heritage. A framed butterfly to the right signals death and rebirth in Saar's developing iconography. Because she didn't want to use the actual images, Saar began to experiment extensively with color photocopy technology, what one critic called "that new invention halfway between gimmick and ghost," which also gave the artist's graphic sensibilities free rein at a relatively low cost.[175] *Grandma Draugh*, 1977, made using this technique, is sewn to a small square of fabric. A portrait of Saar's paternal grandmother, she is shown smartly dressed and floats above ladies in nursing uniforms, sisters in her trade.

The fabric collage *Frances Parson White*, 1977, is an image of Saar's maternal great-grandmother. Like *Grandma Draugh*, it uses a pocket square stiffened with gel medium that approximates its use as a heavily starched and ironed piece of clothing. Saar made many of these handkerchief collages from her aunt's belongings. Their fabric bases and sewn details are part of the heritage of feminist art-making techniques that took what had been denigrated as lesser crafts or "women's work" and raised them to the status of high art form. Indeed, these pieces, created throughout the 1970s, elevated female imagery and women's history well in advance of Judy Chicago's massive *Dinner Party*, unveiled in 1979. Chicago's dialogue with the "lady arts" of china painting and embroidery in the porcelain and napery of *Dinner Party* is contextualized as modern art because it merged "surface image and color," an argument we can make for Saar's handkerchief collages as well.[176] As Saar related, Frances Parson White was prolific in these arenas too—as lace maker, china painter, and creator of embroidery. Saar's own hand-stitching in that collage appears as delicate flowers and crosses, framing the colored image of her great-grandmother.[177]

Another discrete group of works emerged from Hattie Parson Keys's bequest to her grandniece. Under the rubric *Night Letters* or *Letters from Home*, these collages incorporate actual letters sent to or by Aunt Hattie. Many were love notes mailed between Hattie and her second husband, Robert Keys, who was employed for a time on the railroad. Large and deep hued, with sensuous surfaces, some of these pieces evoke the solitude and loneliness of the traveler on the road or the ache of family/friends/lovers left behind. In *Night Letter: Special Delivery*, 1977, Hattie's knowing smile suggests that she anticipates more than a letter.[178] As with other pieces in this series, including *Wish You Were Here*, 1976, paper and photographic fragments float in layers of netting, gel medium, and latex in somber tones. Handmade paper adds to the painterly texture. These works also avail themselves of conceptual-art strategies using language and grid-like torn squares and could be grouped with the Mail Art movement that was current in the 1970s. In fact, Saar taught those very techniques at the Woman's Building.[179]

In boxes such as *Grandma's House* and *Grandma's Garden*, both 1972, Saar incorporated pieces of glass and beads, things she might have found digging in Grandma Draugh's yard in Watts as a child, as well as her grandmother's eyeglasses and cameo. The difference with the family-oriented assemblages and collages is that Saar uses actual materials that were theirs. This is particularly true in the *Aunt Hattie* series, and it does make a difference.

All assemblage, as we know, is about recycling and reuse. It involves taking old narratives and transforming them into new ones while allowing latent readings of the past to shift subtly through and forward. It is an action in which Saar is particularly interested, utilizing energies of earlier times to inflect the aura of her current work. Part of this certainly is the desire to reconnect with history, both personal and in broader African American and diasporic frameworks. Yet this also is part of the practices, as Gundaker and McWillie argue, used by self-taught artists and in yard shows: the incorporation of an object that is seen as "experienced" rather than "used," particularly things belonging to loved ones who are "deceased or absent" and those in which the autobiographical connections are strong. This was linked to practices of grave decoration, where the last thing the dearly departed had touched, slightly altered and placed on a grave, became the trousseau of personal items that he or she carried to the realm of ancestors. Through this metalanguage of objects, family lives and struggles are recalled.[180]

The pieces that remember Saar's Aunt Hattie are important, not simply because of their numbers or because they tell stories of women's strength—particularly Hattie's personal power as the tough pioneer woman—through the artist's gathering of life's flotsam and jetsam. Aunt Hattie was also a migrant. And, in effect, these works narrate black migration through its material evidence and physical remains.

Aunt Hattie and Saar's maternal relatives lived in Saint Louis, Missouri, in the late nineteenth century. They could have arrived with many others from Mississippi, Tennessee, Louisiana, and Texas around the time of the Kansas Fever exodus of the 1870s, since Saint Louis was the first destination one reached on the way. Hattie was a schoolteacher there before she headed to Los Angeles after the death of her first husband. A number of Saar's works speak to her Saint Louis roots. In the collage *Letters from Home: Mash Note (Schoolboy Crush)*, 1976, a love note sent to Hattie by one of her students in the segregated Saint Louis school is a focal point, as is a picture of her third-grade class. The note is extended in grid-like form on either side, similar to the technique in *Wish You Were Here*, from the same year, where pieces of a torn letter extend a cobblestone street walked on by a pair of high heels, moving toward Los Angeles. In the center plane of the latter collage, a group portrait peaks out from inside an envelope, pushing a letter addressed to Hattie to the top of the frame. The address is in Hollywood, perhaps a Christmas greeting from a friend, as the date stamp is "Dec. 18 1925, Kansas City, Missouri."

A piece of material culture, this letter resonates with the story of African American migration. Hattie Parson Haynes arrived in Los Angeles in the very early part of the twentieth century, widowed and reinventing herself, exemplifying a multitude of female migrants. Although she was a teacher in Saint Louis, in California she experienced what Shirley Ann Moore has described as the "downward thrust" of migrant labor. In other words, she could not work as a teacher in Los Angeles but did find jobs as a maid. The Hollywood address in *Wish You Were Here* is that of the actor whom she worked for, also signaling the growing prosperity of the culture industry.[181] When Hattie married Robert Keys, they both worked "out," he as a cook and she as a maid in Flintridge. Keys was originally from Kentucky. He had worked on the railroad and owned the Harlem Renaissance dining establishment New Libya (c. 1910–20) in New York, before heading to Pasadena, where he and Hattie bought a house.

Saar's mother, Beatrice Parson, was nine when her own mother died. Beatrice's parents, the Irish Emma Kelley Parson and Albert Loden Parson, had lived around Des Moines, Iowa, for a time. After the death of his wife, Parson sent Beatrice to be raised by his sister Hattie and his mother, Frances Parson White, in Saint Louis. When Hattie moved to Los Angeles, Beatrice eventually followed, working as a laundress, attending UCLA, and through those associations meeting Saar's father, Jefferson Maze Brown. In 1931, when Saar's father passed away, Beatrice and her three children moved in with Hattie and Robert Keys. Thus Hattie was not only an aunt but a mother and grandmother figure to Saar's family and exemplary of the kinship ties that held people together and helped them thrive in the burgeoning Los Angeles community. Beatrice and her children lived in the house that Hattie and Robert owned but only visited on Thursdays and Sundays, their days off. They were also very social and their activities were emblematic of the church, clubs, and networks that migrants built and for whom Betye and her sister Jeffalyn would dance and perform as children.

Jefferson Maze Brown was no less a part of this African American story. He was born in Lake Charles, Louisiana, and with his mother, Irene, as a small child traveled to Southern California, where they settled in Watts. Irene, the sassy figure of *Grandma Draugh*, had been married to a Mr. Estorage in Louisiana and most probably arrived in California as a single mother after 1909, marrying Horace Brown, who adopted Saar's father. Like John Outterbridge's father, Horace Brown (originally from Saint Louis) was an entrepreneur with a truck.

Jefferson Brown's life in early twentieth-century Los Angeles exemplified what African Americans sought in the West. He graduated from an integrated Jefferson High School in 1921, went on to UCLA, where he received a BA, and was working toward an MA there when he died. Brown met Saar's mother at UCLA where she was also enrolled. For much of his short life, he worked at the Twenty-Eighth Street YMCA near Central Avenue, a focus in the 1920s of literary activities that were part of the Harlem Renaissance cultural movement, the same locale renovated with black culture in mind by architect Paul Revere Williams. Brown was last employed by Golden State Mutual Life Insurance, where Beatrice Brown also held a secretarial position for a short time. Around 1937 Saar's mother married again; her new husband was Emmette Trowell, a navy veteran of World War I from Galveston, Texas, whom she might have met at one of her favorite places to socialize: Elks Hall, the famed Central Avenue jazz spot. Beatrice and her family then moved out of Aunt Hattie's house to another in Pasadena.

When Saar told an interviewer in 1990 that her family was very matriarchal, with many strong women, she was not just repeating the homilies of the feminist movement. She was instead acknowledging the past and the role of migration. Beatrice Parson Brown Trowell, Hattie Parson Haynes Keys, Irene Maze Estorage Brown Draugh—these names are links not only to various husbands they outlived but also to the places and spaces they traversed to get to Los Angeles and make themselves in the world. The gloves, brooches, plumes, lush fabrics, and dried flowers that signify finery and beauty in many of Saar's two- and three-dimensional works present a foil to the derogatory archetype of the servant found in the specter of Aunt Jemima. Such pieces celebrate these women, many of them indeed domestics. Saar recalls their struggles in twentieth-century America, but also remembers the amazing and radical worlds they created in the changing landscapes they called home and in the affirming spaces where community was created. In this series of works Saar instead resists the black stereotype, containing black women in a world of splendor. In *Mama's Flowers*, 1973, a boxed photograph of Saar's mother is surrounded by floral wallpaper and silk buds, speaking to her feminine charms. Additional family images allude to loss, first of a mother, which would "set her flowing" west, and then a husband, whose death would change her life again. A handkerchief collage like *Grandma Draugh*, with all of her names neatly penned at the bottom next to the word "grandmother" and the confident smile on the figures above, is a reminder of women like her (and Hattie), who challenged the strictures of old lives—leaving, moving, migrating—and embraced the new.

CONVERSATIONS WITH CORNELL

Even before Betye Saar became involved with the feminist art movement in Los Angeles, she had made inroads into the New York art world. She captivated New York with no less than three shows at the Whitney Museum of American Art between 1970 and 1975, including her first-ever solo show in the city.

Like the other artists in the 1970 Whitney Sculpture Annual, Saar sent just one piece to the show. *Omen*, 1967, is an assemblage measuring a little over a foot high and among the first of her constructions in the format of a box. On the bottom left, a vintage astrology chart floats above block letters in wood, proclaiming the work's title, reversed and upside-down characters emphasizing the uncanny and supernatural alluded to in the sculpture's title. A formal photographic portrait of a white family sits in one compartment, while in another, a collection of rocks and glass supplies a natural feel, extending the largely wooden elements' palette of warm colors. A significant portion of the surface is covered by a glass panel on which a hand is printed hovering over the composition, extending the otherworldly sensibility.

In *Omen*, we can see the emerging skill she demonstrated with such fragments: the fine juxtapositions, clever and subtle transformations, and painted altered elements that add patina and time. Intimacy became the key to their language. And it became Saar's forte. The scale of this and other pieces—some sized to fit in one's hand—seem anathema to the largeness of sculpture in this moment, including signs carved out in western deserts, like Robert Smithson's *Spiral Jetty*, or Richard Serra's steel curves rising in the Bronx, works that were part of the Sculpture Annual but were too vast to fit within the Whitney itself. With Saar's pieces, one is forced to lean in, look closer, and in places consider stereotype, one's investment in such recognition, and U.S. (global) problems of race. As Manthia Diawara points out, they function as surrogates of activism couched in the language of mass imagery.[182] Saar's rearticulation of these images channels the black politics of the day but in a way that is stylish and captivating. We see this most clearly in her handling of the oscillation between photographic and derogatory images. The antique photos reveal a more complete, specific, or "real" view of things, while the chromoliths and figurines occlude.[183]

The notion of presaging or foretelling future in the title of *Omen* continues topics of alternate spirituality and fantasy that Saar had been working with for several years. They are themes shared by Saar's contemporaries George Herms and Wallace Berman. Herms's work can be seen as "nurtured in the psychedelic ferment of the early 1960s," an angle from which we should consider Betye Saar's contribution as well.[184] Like Saar, Herms has been characterized as a "celebrant of secret mysteries" and one whose "forgiving cosmology" of assemblage would later include the type of personal homage—such as *Berman Piece*, 1986, a large-scale, tableau tribute to his friend Wallace Berman—that had captivated Saar at an earlier time.[185] His work also resonated between "found objects and images."[186] There was a moment when Herms found himself heavily into the science of astrology, exemplified by the *Zodiac behind Glass* series of the mid-1960s: relatively smaller boxes covered with protective glass sheets.[187]

The glass-fronted container resonates formally with the work of Joseph Cornell, whose famed boxes were on view in Los Angeles with increasing regularity in the postwar period; there were solo shows at the Ferus Gallery in 1962 and at the Pasadena Art Museum from late 1966.[188]

Through her creative conversations with the work of the older American artist Saar was encouraged to move out of the two-dimensional window frame and into the three-dimensional world of the box and beyond.[189] This encounter led to the emergence of her own voice within the language of found objects.

The scale of both Saar's and Cornell's work underscores the issue of intimacy. These small-scale works beckon one to come close in order to know them. In her book *On Longing*, Susan Stewart describes the miniature as one that reconstructs the space of the interior, providing an experience of an inner, private, personal life distinct from that of the public (what she calls the gigantic) sphere. Historical time is seen through the lens of nostalgia and display. The object "[moves] from event to memory and desire," from the public or the exterior, to the private, the interior, and toward art. The collection or tableau of disparate elements/souvenirs offer a "particularization . . . of the moment" and occasion for the development of narrative.[190]

For Saar and Cornell, intimacy is invited by scale but also revolves around the notion of gift, art as a "social transaction" that joins people in "mutual desire."[191] Cornell's works are often about artists and historical figures but also at times are presents to them. Embedded in the idea of the gift is the idea of the haptic, a notion just below the surface in so many pieces by Saar and Cornell.

Scholars over the years have been afraid of the sentiment in Cornell's oeuvre, labeling its affective nature and antiquarianism "queer." More generally, there is also the feminized nature of assemblage as practice; it represents the world of the consumer, over the producer, a certain retreat from authorial control. The open negotiating of identity through the consumer object was rebuffed by East Coast assemblagists and Neo-Dada artists working more than a generation after Cornell. They rejected the poetic, the metaphoric, and the narrative. As in pop art, nostalgia was nemesis. Instead, artists such as Robert Rauschenberg and Jasper Johns located meaning in the boundary between public and private.[192]

After Eve K. Sedgwick, I want to argue that the art of Joseph Cornell and Betye Saar, along with that of Noah Purifoy and John Outterbridge, is reparative. The "additive" and "accretive" density of surface (or, in Sedgwick's words, "juicy displays") and "fragmentary" or "leftover products," particularly those with a sheen of the antique, signaled an embrace. The marshaling of material as a healing, protective force of repair was a way to address the fear "that the culture surrounding it is inadequate or inimical to its nurture; it wants to assemble and confer plenitude on an object that will then have resources to offer an inchoate self."[193] What we might also think about as patina as love, an over-the-top display and coating that wraps an object and suggests "loving attachments as inevitably private and ephemeral," as Susan Larsen has proposed in the assemblages of George Herms.[194]

The way this is effected is with objects as evocations of experience. While this is evident in works of Purifoy and Outterbridge, Saar favored figural and representational structures over abstraction. Her works are souvenirs, reportable fragments, their metonymic value expanded through the narrative of the assemblage, which offers back the missing experience of the life or event. The souvenir is allusive; it moves from public to private realms. In this way, Saar was emblematic of West Coast artists who reveled in the quality of objects as a way of chronicling life. In many ways, their work was different from that made by their East Coast counterparts. Indeed, as Branden Joseph points out, Rauschenberg endeavored to sublimate nostalgia and "kill the souvenir quality" in his early autobiographical constructions.[195]

For artists like Saar, Purifoy, and Outterbridge, the situation was different. They were people whose history was denied, whose generation was the first to have exact birth dates or birth certificates. In their families were women whose accumulation (and shedding) of names had left the past behind. Their four-hundred-year history as Americans was said to amount to very little; vestiges, even through the lens of nostalgia, proved their very existence. Souvenirs were something they would not easily relinquish. Narrative became "a structure of desire" for the reparation of history.[196]

Betye Saar's conversation with Joseph Cornell is also the conversation that African American artists have had with modernism. It is an exchange that generally excluded them as creators of fine art, except perhaps as producers of raw experience and performative culture that became grist for the modernist mill. As such it is a contestatory dialogue, what Lowery Stokes Sims has presciently called the "challenge of the modern," the struggle for the African American visual artist's self-expression to be seen as intellectual history, their imaginings as agents of creative change or transformation.[197] Instead of advancing a model for understanding the work of African American artists that continues such received patterns of servility and sublimation, Sims wants us to imagine a modern aesthetic made by African Americans that conjures different kinds of ruptures with the art historical past and that also inflected and reflected both their social conditions and concerns and their patently unequal access to American life and liberty.

That Saar's conversation with modernism took place at the Pasadena Art Museum in the 1960s was no accident. That was where curator Walter Hopps was creating important and influential exhibitions that expanded these ideas in Southern California between roughly 1960 and 1967. These included important historical shows of artists such as Kurt Schwitters (1962), Marcel Duchamp (1963), and Joseph Cornell (1966). Hopps's take on modernism was not necessarily seen as canonical at that point; it focused on collage, assemblage, and Dada roots in a way that opened out to installation, performance, and conceptualism. To this notable profile, he added new artists and trends. The now legendary *New Painting of Common Objects*, 1962, advanced the emerging pop art and careers of Andy Warhol, Roy Lichtenstein, and Edward Ruscha, among others. A solo show of works by Edward Kienholz (1961) preceded by half a decade the artist's controversial exhibition at LACMA in 1966. The latter would put the discourse around "appropriate images" (particularly of sexuality) front and center; it is also the same year Saar's three-dimensional pieces began to make themselves known. If Saar's dialogue with art history through Cornell is quite clear, one is also made visible with her contemporary, Kienholz.[198]

Saar and others confronted modernism and its legacy in part through shows at the Pasadena Art Museum. The exhibitions and atmosphere there were organized by Hopps and grew from the activities that had their germination at the Ferus Gallery, which he also founded. However, another question we should ask is, how did Hopps and others, in return, confront or "converse with" the modern black subject? One way into this topic is to look at the place of women as artists within this constellation. Though early shows featured Jay DeFeo and Sonia Gechtoff—both from the Bay Area—Ferus was known primarily as a "boys' club." Women were marginalized and "put up with [the men] and cheered and cried and cooked," as Shirley Neilsen recalled.[199] African American artists were even less a part of the Ferus scene, with perhaps the exception of sculptor Edmund Bereal, a classmate of a number of these artists from Chouinard and a preparator at Ferus as well as for Hopps personally.[200] The closing of the gallery in 1967 marked a change in the LA art world. The model of the white male artist as stud that the artists connected with Ferus represented came to an end; the scene was no longer about them or that. The year that saw the demise of Ferus also was the inaugural one for the African American–owned, –operated, and –focused Brockman Gallery.[201]

However, Hopps was like so many of the white artists and cultural workers of this period: although their relationship with black visual artists was nonexistent, they were not totally estranged from African American culture. Hopps and Shirley Neilsen were famously married in 1955 at the Watts Towers. In the early 1950s, prior to becoming a curator, Hopps and his college friend James Newman began Concert Hall Workshop, which booked jazz shows at colleges around the country. Hopps had developed his passion for jazz as a teenager in the 1940s, like many who were raised in Southern California on the sumptuous diet of music and the classic scene of Los Angeles' Central Avenue. His early show on the Santa Monica Pier carousel, *Action 1*, revolved to a soundtrack that was largely jazz.²⁰² As we have seen, it was not in Los Angeles but in Washington, DC, the next stop on Hopps's curatorial journey, that he truly interacted with African American artists.

Hopps certainly wasn't the only one in conversation with the black modern, even if that conversation was a sublimated one. Closer analysis of some assemblages by Bruce Conner and Edward Kienholz reveals the substrate of black content and context with which they were in dialogue. Though based in San Francisco, Conner had a solo exhibition at Ferus in 1962. Beginning in late 1950s, his imagery bespeaks a classic California assemblage that was more clearly composed of the detritus of contemporary life than what would emerge later as California Funk, which had a cleaner edge and was more aligned with the Finish Fetish style of minimalism.

Rebecca Solnit sees Conner's sculpture as heavily invested in the critique of militarism and human exploitation, where women's bodies are used to signal such ravaging and degradation; different writers have simply found it haunting. Conner and his compatriots, then, were influenced by the alienation in American society, as seen in the San Francisco neighborhoods where they lived and worked—diverse communities like Fillmore and Haight-Ashbury, mixed neighborhoods, but particularly the Western Addition, an African American enclave that had been attacked by the ravages of urban renewal. Like many urban neighborhoods across the country, including Watts, it was left to disintegrate and then summarily destroyed. Conner and others frequently went to the Western Addition to procure materials from the demolition. A work called *Bomb* by Conner addresses this idea directly. The neighborhood in distress, junk shops, and vernacular installations: these were the very same things that inspired Noah Purifoy, John Outterbridge, and Betye Saar. Even David Hammons was called a "hip junk dealer."²⁰³ Yet the challenge for African American artists was to be seen as modern, as contributing to prevailing art discourse rather than simply supplying its fuel, its raison d'être.

Edward Kienholz is another artist whose name is irrevocably attached to assemblage in California. Like Conner's, his works critiqued American society's obsession with sex and violence. His interest in the spectacle of American life led him to a style that would reproduce it materially in sprawling, narrative tableaux.

The first of these was *Roxy's*, 1961–62, a warren of rooms imaging a brothel of monstrous female bodies / distressed cyborgs in a rundown domestic interior with worn furnishings. Initially presented at Ferus, it was a breakthrough for Kienholz and represented the expansion of assemblage into room-scale multimedia productions, the move from discrete objects to environments. But a key element for us here is that many of the constituent parts of *Roxy's* had been scavenged from a condemned theater on Central Avenue, a place where jazz and black people had thrived.[204] As with Conner, we see the same substrata of actual black lived experience and material as the infrastructure to build this work. George Lipsitz tells us that in the 1950s and 1960s African Americans nationally lost 20 percent of their housing stock to urban renewal, which led to the loss of neighborhoods, businesses, and social structures. In reality, "urban renewal in inner cities produced very little actual renewal but a lot of vacant lots."[205] And a lot of destroyed and condemned buildings and other materials were left ready for the picking and for reimagining as art. Following Lipsitz, the "hidden history" of the rise of assemblage and other mixed-media forms is the availability of the materials in the form of destroyed neighborhoods, largely inhabited by people of color.

Then there was jazz, the music of African Americans. Central Avenue in Los Angeles was, of course, a storied home of black musical and performative cultures where at midcentury bebop embodied the sounds of change. These artists presented a new aesthetic fierceness seen in the intellectual aura surrounding the sound, down to the titles the musicians bestowed upon their songs. For many, this revolution in American music reflected changing times and rising activism; it signaled a counterculture. Transgression and freedom were also seen in the hip, cool stance of practitioners, exemplified by Miles Davis's *The Birth of the Cool* (1957).[206] This new black self-possession would only be carried further in the 1960s.

As the 1950s gave way to the 1960s, African American culture became more widespread than ever before, with a growing influence on national life and international visibility. The British rock band the Rolling Stones named themselves after a song by bluesman Muddy Waters, and the Students for Democratic Society learned their techniques from southern civil rights workers. Likewise, the relationship between white West Coast artists and African American culture is an effortless conclusion to reach about art in this time period, particularly with a generation who shared black disappointment at the national enterprise and the status quo around the world.[207]

If collage and assemblage were marked with an urban profile that came from cubism or the Merz works of Kurt Schwitters, these forms also forecast the importance of place. This was not landscape as it was traditionally conceived but the texture of the topographic, spaces of the city that were traversed and scoured. Surrealism, Thomas Crow has argued, discovered the "material unconscious of the city."[208] If that was the case, then it wasn't just the delectations of thrift stores that excited artists like Herms, Conner, and Kienholz, but the neighborhoods that had been left to crumble and the rampant destruction of urban renewal. In a number of his artist's books, including *Real Estate Opportunities*, 1970, Ed Ruscha focused on desolate urban spaces in Los Angeles. Gordon Matta-Clark on the East Coast also dealt with the built environment and urban waste, streets without economic value, and buildings whose physical condition made them dangerous in areas whose zip codes reinforced that profile.

Black people, then, are identified in the language of post–World War II assemblage practices in the United States in several ways: in the use of "poor" materials that could be identified with those on the margins of society, that were not part of the fine art tradition and which "intruded" into the space of fine art and as such performed a "transgression of form"; in the materials taken from black neighborhoods, particularly those facing the wrecking ball of urban removal; in cultural forms like jazz, associated with African American creativity that provided inspiration to artists of the era; in the political and social climate of the country generally where the inequities of a society built on slave labor were again being questioned and repudiated in the growing activities of the civil rights movement.[209]

As Katherine McKittrick has argued, the idea of marginality as a place of black enunciation in the world at large does not make it less important. Rather, she demonstrates how notions of center and periphery are locked in a reciprocal dance for the articulation of meaning. Her demonstration of how cultural articulation works spatially finds analogues in Toni Morrison's arguments for similar interlocked pairings of the raced and nonraced in the language of fiction. McKittrick's theory also shares similarities with Branden Joseph's description of the continual oscillation of forces, forms, language, and visuality in play in our readings of the assemblage combines of Robert Rauschenberg, forces considered both outside and resident in the interstices of accepted narrative strategies and formulations, "an indeterminate form of difference that evades."[210] In all cases, the concept of a singular and predominant grand narrative is replaced by the multinarrative, or the scavenged, found, pieced narrative, made from and through creative joining of partialities and remnants.

The layering and oscillation of assemblage takes its energy from materials found and reconfigured, repositioned and recontextualized. It represents not only the rejection of purity and fixity in materials but also the singularity and fixity of address. In the juxtaposition of myriad things formerly subjected to a variety of uses and materials plucked from the topography of streets of the world, artists like Purifoy created things that held these original significations and context and yet in the act of making art freed them, releasing signification back into the cycle and play of meaning between object and viewer. This continual action, in effect, led one to always having to "settle certain questions each time you look at an assemblage," as critic Lawrence Alloway noted, in an ongoing reconceptualization of art and meaning.[211]

The transformational action that Purifoy found in the creation of assemblage refuted the negative spin found in the materials themselves and in the places they came from. It was the difference between "Watts knows about junk" and "Watts is junk," the difference between shoddy materials and shoddy people. Assemblage as a site for actions of transformation and reconceptualization was also tied to the postmodern actions of Rauschenberg and John Cage, whose critiques of totality and subjectivity, Joseph tells us, presented themselves as positive openings and interrogations. For Purifoy and his peers, the oscillation of meaning in assemblage allowed one to evade the fixity of blackness—its looks, meanings, materiality, and form. These works never provided the singular didactic message of most painting and sculpture created outside California and in the throes of the Black Arts Movement.

Perhaps most important in thinking about African American artists working with assemblage in Los Angeles in the 1960s and 1970s, meaning might have been conditional, affected by dynamic interactions of materials, time, place, and audience, but it was not forever evaded and undetermined. For African American artists in the twentieth century, the conceptualization, and manipulation of meaning was paramount. It was the prize. It was the reward of living through past centuries and present days, of continually struggling against the will of the United States and the world to define and debase, render inadequate and ignorant, ugly and worthless. The power to have and control the methods of representation and keys to signification was grasped firmly and fiercely.

In a post–World War II and postmodern period, one finds the evacuation of holistic notions of history, subjectivity, and power. Positioned in this era, Rauschenberg's first combines in the early 1950s, Joseph argues, incorporated bits and pieces of the artist's personal history.[212] But by the end of the decade, this apparent nostalgic glance had been cast aside, leading to an archival focus severed from individual experience. In the use of materials that signal the everyday, the mundane, society's debris, there is a democratic indeterminacy; in this mountain of materials was a heap of shifting signs. For Rauschenberg, the collections of elements that comprise the combines are not archival in the historical sense. Instead, they are things collected by an objective hoarder, one who does not discriminate in a narrow, highly structured and defined way but piles it on without regard to singular message, position, viewpoint. The combines do not embody and promote history; instead these accumulations simply provide a physical perch from which to launch the next craft.

But this notion of history as a lifeless and musty archive, whose concerns are stagnant, frozen, and no longer ours, was not one that African American artists in this moment ascribed to. Indeed, it was the opposite; they were in some ways obsessed with history. African Americans lived in a society that, though slavery had been outlawed one hundred years prior, until recently had been denied personhood by physically separating black from white bodies in public spaces. Segregation in housing, transportation, schooling, and constraints in many places against legal marriage were matched by intellectual, pedagogic, and political constraints. There was no notion of real African American history represented in the everyday. For the most part, only stereotypes, aspects of fear and violence, ignorance and inadequacy were depicted. History and narrative from an African American perspective and concomitant meaning was prized and precious. And as Tillet and Copeland have both noted, art and its metaphoric maneuverings continued to have an important role to play. It could both fill in the lost and unknown aspects of history, and unpack the ongoing effects of legacies of inequality, in moves that spoke to the past and present, in objects that mined transhistorical space.

Cheryl Finley has posited a visual theory regarding artists of the African Diaspora, which she calls "the tradition of remembrance." Here remembrance is a duty and a responsibility to guard against historical and visual erasure, and "memory is used as an aesthetic tool and organizing principle," emphasizing recurrent themes such as "the Middle Passage, plantation slavery, the quest for Africa, and racial violence directed at the black body" as well as, I would add, more local histories, threaded through with personal vantage points and narratives.[213]

All these sources are brought to bear and used as a way to interject meaning and connect artists and black people to the motion of history interrupted, severed, lost, sublimated. At the same time that artists such as Purifoy, Outterbridge, and Saar were incorporating history and personal, political, and quotidian elements into their works, the assemblage format kept these notions from alighting on one frame or message and kept the ideas in a swirl of movement that led to activation, not a settling in. Patricia Leighten has discussed the political messages in certain of Picasso's early collages, works that held their abstract and formal qualities.[214] Certainly this sense of a political meaning that floats in and among these fine art aggregations is not new.

The circulation of politics and political meaning is paralleled by other apparent incursions into the traditional picture plane: mundane substances; materials that perform other kinds of labor; paper, metal, wood, rope, used to think, build, construct. Such things not only offer aesthetic solutions but also link us in certain way to the very people who wield them: carpenters, printers, and so on. Picasso and Braque's use of "decorator materials" ultimately leads us to Purifoy, a "real decorator" who brought these ideas of construction to bear on the work of art. He was a creative person who was able to successfully transform himself into an artist by using these very methods to his own ends.

Purifoy demonstrates that sensibilities thought of as marginal to the construction of Western artistic discourse are in fact central to its progression, reinvention, and advancement. If the place of the marginal in modernist discourse is to continually energize the center, as McKittrick and Morrison have shown, it is only remote in theory, while being interlocked and close at hand. As Joseph has written, "This outside is not so much apart from a reified society as present, virtually, within its interstices."[215]

During the 1950s and 1960s in the United States (and for our purposes with regard to the development of assemblage on the West Coast), this outside collection of forms and forces many times went black. In their use of distressed materials from vulnerable places, in popular musical beats and the country's political seams, African Americans were always present in the interstices as an alternative subjectivity, an outsider within, separated spatially by law. But as the society that condoned and perpetuated this formation began to rupture, in the remnants of these increasingly old histories, newly activated intelligences were born.

CHAPTER THREE   **Organize:** Building an Exhibitionary Complex

IF AFRICAN AMERICAN ARTISTS in Los Angeles were dismantling old forms and reimagining and reconfiguring them in unexpected ways, they were also seeking alternative institutional structures that could nurture and support them. Historically, most African American artists were not welcomed with open arms, if at all, within most museums and galleries in Los Angeles or the rest of the country. The post–World War II period began to see a slow shift in African American relations to the art world structure, a trend that picked up momentum in the 1960s. We can consider these changes in terms of different types of activity, actions that were more integrationist in focus (e.g., penetrating preexisting institutions) paired with those creating autochthonous formations (e.g., new galleries and periodicals).

In some ways, this advance was driven by growing African American attendance in BFA and MFA programs, fueled by disintegrating barriers to de jure segregation as well as the GI Bill. John Riddle, Noah Purifoy, and John Outterbridge were all veterans who used their educational benefits to attend art school. Each of them also ended up working in new institutional settings that supported the work of African American artists. Riddle moved to Atlanta in the mid-1970s, becoming the head of the Neighborhood Arts Center that gave David Hammons one of his first solo shows. Outterbridge assumed the directorship of the Watts Towers Arts Center in 1975, the year it officially became a municipal art space. Purifoy, the first director of Watts Towers between 1964 and 1966, eventually joined the newly created California Arts Council, where he remained for eleven years. However, African Americans had been concerned with marshaling the forces of art and exhibition for much of the prior century. Indeed, black investment in what Tony Bennett has called the "exhibitionary complex" had a storied history long before the 1960s.[1]

BLACK AMERICANS AND THE EXHIBITIONARY COMPLEX

In Bennett's concept of the exhibitionary complex, modern museums present immense arenas for the work of representation. If their predecessors in cabinets of curiosities were sites of momentary wonder, modern settings of display presented space for the contemplation of epochs. The representational potential embedded in the visible was "significant not for its own sake but because it afford[ed] a glimpse of something beyond itself," invoking the arc of history.[2] As such, museums were highly flexible fields of learning, advancing a common knowledge base and goals that inscribed the viewer as a subject, not an object, of knowledge. These institutional structures additionally enforced a type of self-observation and regulation by molding behavior through the peregrination of space (and ultimately of time, metaphorically speaking).

Beginning with the Centennial International Exhibition in 1876, black Americans had debated the value of such displays and attempted to engage themselves in them with varying degrees of success. The world of fairs and later museums and galleries and their representational potential held out a promise for creating new societal accounts of the African American citizen. Through exhibitions, African Americans crafted "public narratives of who they were and wanted to become."[3] Though these visual tales changed over time, as Mabel Wilson argues, they were fundamentally stories of black progress, constituting a black counterpublic sphere.[4]

Though the era of grand expositions would wane, African Americans continued to invest in the exhibitionary complex, exposing the life of mind, the black interior, and using it as a forum to advance social justice and civil rights.

MIRIAM MATTHEWS AND EARLY EXHIBITIONS IN LOS ANGELES

The social and political efficacy of exhibitions in the hands of black Americans in the nineteenth century set the stage for activities in the twentieth century. Miriam Matthews was one individual who energized pre–World War II

African American communities in Los Angeles by engaging the exhibitionary complex.

Born in Pensacola, Florida, in 1905, Matthews moved with her family to the city in 1907, when her parents decided to make a better life outside the strictures of southern segregation.[5] After studying at UCLA and the University of California, Berkeley, and armed with degrees in Spanish and librarianship, Matthews became LA's first black librarian in 1927, despite pressure to take up teaching, a more typical profession for black women at that time. In a more than thirty-year career spent primarily in Los Angeles, Matthews served as the head of the Helen Hunt Jackson, Vernon, Watts, and Vermont Square branches, then worked as a regional librarian overseeing twelve libraries.

From the beginning of her career, Matthews's library work was imbricated with exhibitionary modes, in ways that we have come to know primarily through the example of Arturo Schomburg's collection and eventually programming of literature, art, and African American culture at New York's 135th Street library from 1926 onward. Matthews built collections of African American literature and history; created displays of rare books and papers as well as art; and sponsored book clubs and lectures. In 1934–35, she invited writer Arna Bontemps—an Angeleno who moved to New York in the 1920s, during the Harlem Renaissance—to the library for readings and to be a mentor to a theater group. Before becoming the first African American to exhibit at the Los Angeles County Museum in 1935, Beulah Woodard had shows at the Vernon (her neighborhood facility) and Central library branches that were organized by Matthews. Over the years, the librarian hosted exhibitions by African American as well as other artists.[6]

Matthews's endeavors eventually moved beyond library frameworks. With Beulah Woodard, she began the Los Angeles Negro Art Association (LANAA) in 1937. As Matthews recounts, it was "the first of its kind in the city ... to help promote local Negro artists."[7] One of the group's first documented events was a show of Woodard's masks at the Mayan Theater on Eleventh and Hill Streets. That fall, LANAA presented another major public event, the *Negro Art Exhibit*, at the Stendahl Art Galleries on Wilshire Boulevard. In keeping with the excitement about such shows (then or now), in the mere week the exhibition was on view, attendance reached twenty-five hundred.[8]

In 1950, Matthews and Woodard formed another black art collective, Eleven Associated. The cooperative gallery, located at 1046 South Hill Street in downtown Los Angeles, held juried shows with an interracial roster.[9] The artists donated a portion of their sales for the upkeep and rental of the space, seeking to gain visibility for their practice and greater control over their creative market. Growing out of her work with the library and LANAA, Matthews began to "sponsor" artists: that is, she served as an unpaid agent, promoting, selling, and buying work. She arranged painter Alice Taylor Gafford's first solo show in 1941 and worked with her until 1975.[10] Matthews's work with artists over the years enabled her to start her own collection. When she retired from the library in 1960, she made collecting her focus, amassing some five hundred objects by the time she died in 2003 at the age of ninety-eight.[11]

ART, BLACK CORPORATE POWER, AND THE GOLDEN STATE

In 1967, when Alice Taylor Gafford was commissioned to make twelve pictures of African Americans for the black-owned Family Savings and Loan, it was not the beginning of such engagement but the continuation of a tradition. As Mabel Wilson has demonstrated, black businessmen had been involved with the world of fairs and exhibitions since the nineteenth century. By 1940 displays of black businesses dominated the space of fairs, edging out exhibits dedicated to accomplishments of black colleges. Banks and insurance companies were particularly active in this regard, both nationally and in Los Angeles. They offered not only financial support but also space, providing sites for meetings, offices, and even exhibitions.[12]

Gafford, for instance, had also exhibited at Safety Savings and Loan in 1962. This Christmas presentation included paintings, prints, jewelry, ceramics, and enamels, which were on view at the bank's street-level community room at 2638 S. Western Avenue; they were also for sale. Exhibiting with her was Yvonne Cole Meo, a younger multimedia artist who would exhibit with and write about Nengudi, Hammons, Conwill, and other artists of their generation.[13] Safety's art program dated from at least 1961, when it began hosting high school art competitions. The financial institution aimed to serve its community by familiarizing people with the work of local artists and providing a space for them to show consistently.[14] When Ruth Waddy organized Art West Associated, one of the first artists' groups in the 1960s to take up Woodard and Matthews's mantle, she held meetings, and eventually exhibitions, at Safety Savings and Loan.

Ruth Waddy (who left the Midwest for Los Angeles in 1942) became an artist late in life, and in the early 1960s, art was her preferred method of organizing civic action. For Waddy art had another "social value"—it made people think. She founded the artists' group Art West Associated in 1962 to press for greater African American representation in mainstream arts institutions in Southern California. One of Art West Associated's initial "civic projects" was to petition for a juried exhibition of African American artists at the Los Angeles County Museum to commemorate the centenary of emancipation in 1963. Such tributes had been observed by African Americans since the nineteenth century. In promoting this Waddy joined a list of curator/activists—from Booker T. Washington to W. E. B. Du Bois to Alain Locke—who had highlighted emancipation in their displays and who over the century had also seen art and culture as having a key role in the political landscape.[15] Though the Los Angeles County Museum rebuffed Waddy's early efforts, several years and protests later (and under its new identity as the Los Angeles County Museum of Art), it began to include more African American artists in its programming.

Art West Associated was very active in the early 1960s, presenting as a group at the All City Outdoor Festival, Security First National Bank in Compton, the Slauson branch of the YWCA, and various sites in the black vacation community of Val Verde.[16] For Negro History Week (and its successor, Black History Month) it focused on books and authors in addition to exhibitions.[17] In related projects during this time Waddy traveled throughout the United States by bus collecting original prints from artists for T. V. Roelof-Lanner's book *Prints by American Negro Artists*, published by the Cultural Exchange Center of Los Angeles in 1965; the following year she traveled to the Soviet Union to take art by African Americans there.[18] On the top of Art West Associated's agenda was the development of a permanent cultural center that celebrated African American artists and also offered art instruction. These ideas of a dedicated space were heard around the country and eventually bore fruit, but not without struggle.[19]

Arguably, the black corporate entity that had one of the greatest impacts on LA's African American art scene was Golden State Mutual Life Insurance. Established in 1925, it was one of the earliest significant black businesses in the city; by the 1950s, it had some eight hundred employees and hosted operations in fourteen states. From the start, Golden State committed itself to supporting black creativity. Three years after its founding, the company constructed a signature building on Central Avenue, in the heart of the city's bustling black business district. To celebrate twenty years in business, Golden State commissioned a new building from famed architect Paul Revere Williams. Opening in 1948 at 1999 W. Adams Boulevard, the building featured two murals—Charles Alston's *The Negro in California History: Exploitation and Colonization* and Hale Woodruff's *The Negro in California History: Settlement and Development*. Miriam Matthews spoke at the building's dedication, describing the paintings' historical scenes (she had also advised the artists about their content).[20]

It was painter William Pajaud (plate 15) who moved Golden State to a new level of support for artists. Pajaud landed a position as an art director at Golden State in 1957; he would also serve as director of public relations and eventually vice president in a career that spanned thirty years. He struck upon the idea for a corporate art collection several years into his tenure. The inspiration came from Beulah Woodard—her life and legacy, but also the lack of attention to such work after her death in 1955. While Pajaud was unable to convince Golden State to acquire the Woodard estate, the idea of the corporate collection eventually took hold in 1965 as a way to celebrate the company's fortieth anniversary. Newly commissioned portraits of founders Norman O. Houston and George A. Beavers Jr. by painter Hughie Lee Smith joined a bronze of founder William Nickerson Jr. created by sculptor Richmond Barthé in the 1940s and the two murals. Charles White's *General Moses (Harriet Tubman)* was acquired that year, and a small show, which included works from Woodard's collection that had been loaned by Matthews, was held in the offices.[21]

With encouragement and direction from Pajaud, the company began building an art collection in earnest during the 1960s, eventually acquiring more than two hundred works. The collection featured pieces by African American artists from throughout the nation—for example, Henry Ossawa Tanner, Romare Bearden, and Elizabeth Catlett—as well as those by artists who defined Los Angeles in this era, including Woodard, White, Saar, David Hammons, Daniel Larue Johnson, and John Riddle. The company also purchased African art, including masks and sculpture from the Ivory Coast and Gabon. Art was hung in the Williams Building and other local district offices, initially for the pleasure and edification of employees. Later Golden State made its art holdings more widely accessible by offering tours to the general public, primarily to elementary schools; employees in uniforms served as tour guides. The artwork of the collection was reproduced in annual calendars and catalogues.[22]

Pajaud was also behind the Tutor/Art Program, which provided art instruction to underserved communities. Golden State launched the program in Watts in the wake of the rebellion, eventually partnering with Otis Art Institute. Some of this activity must also be ascribed to Norman O. Houston, one of the company's owners; as leader of the local NAACP branch, he offered a more progressive perspective on the uprising in Watts and the climate of dissent than many others in the black business community.[23]

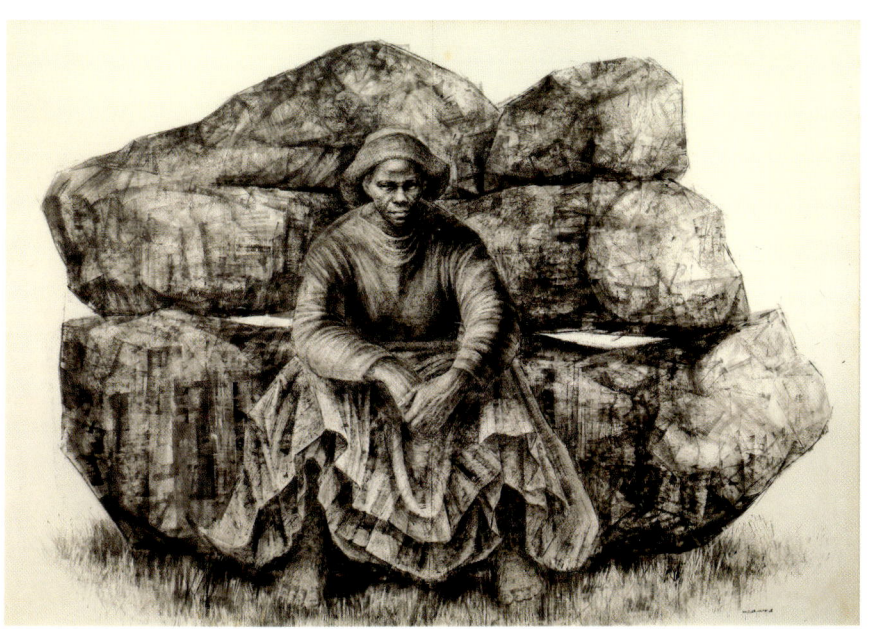

PLATE 1 Charles White, *General Moses (Harriet Tubman)*, 1965. Chinese ink on two joined sheets of illustration board. Courtesy Swann Galleries © 1965 Charles White Archives.

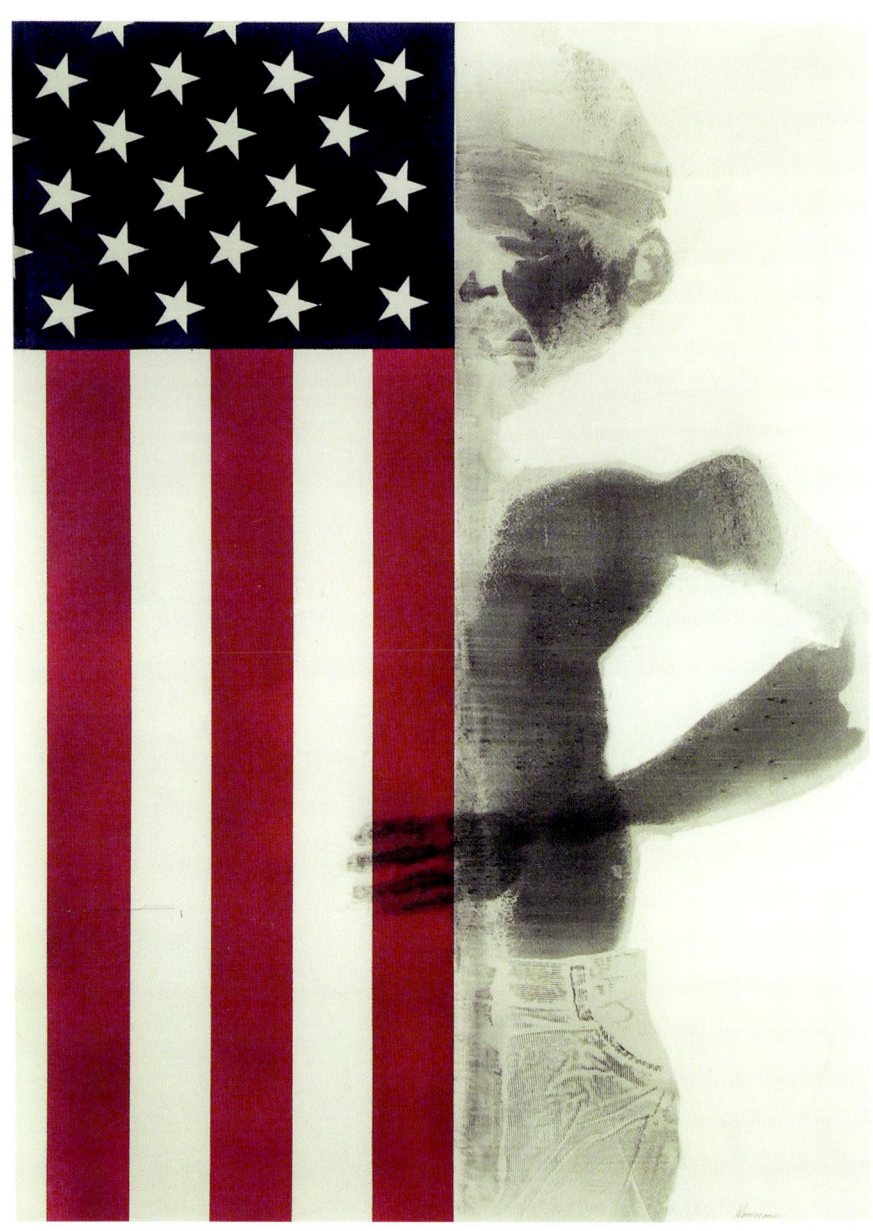

PLATE 2   David Hammons, *Boy with Flag*, 1968. Body print and silkscreen. Courtesy the artist and Tilton Gallery, New York.

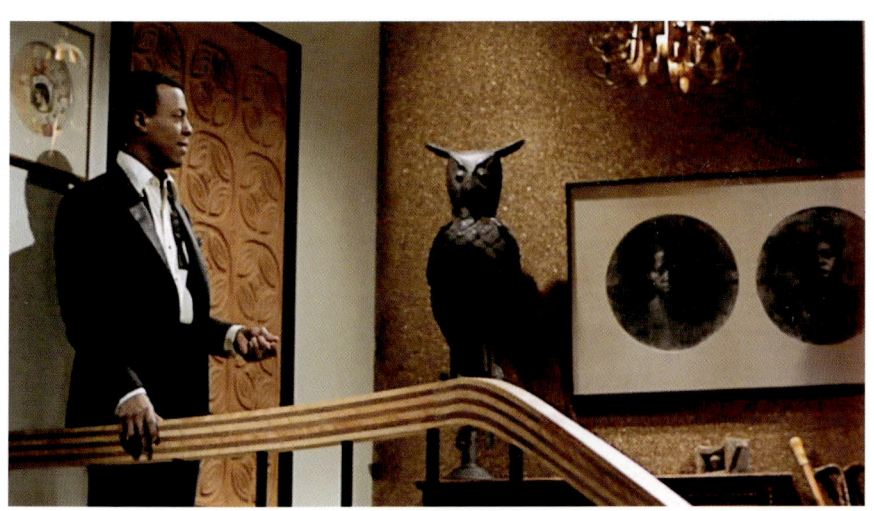

PLATE 3 *For Love of Ivy* (film still), 1968.

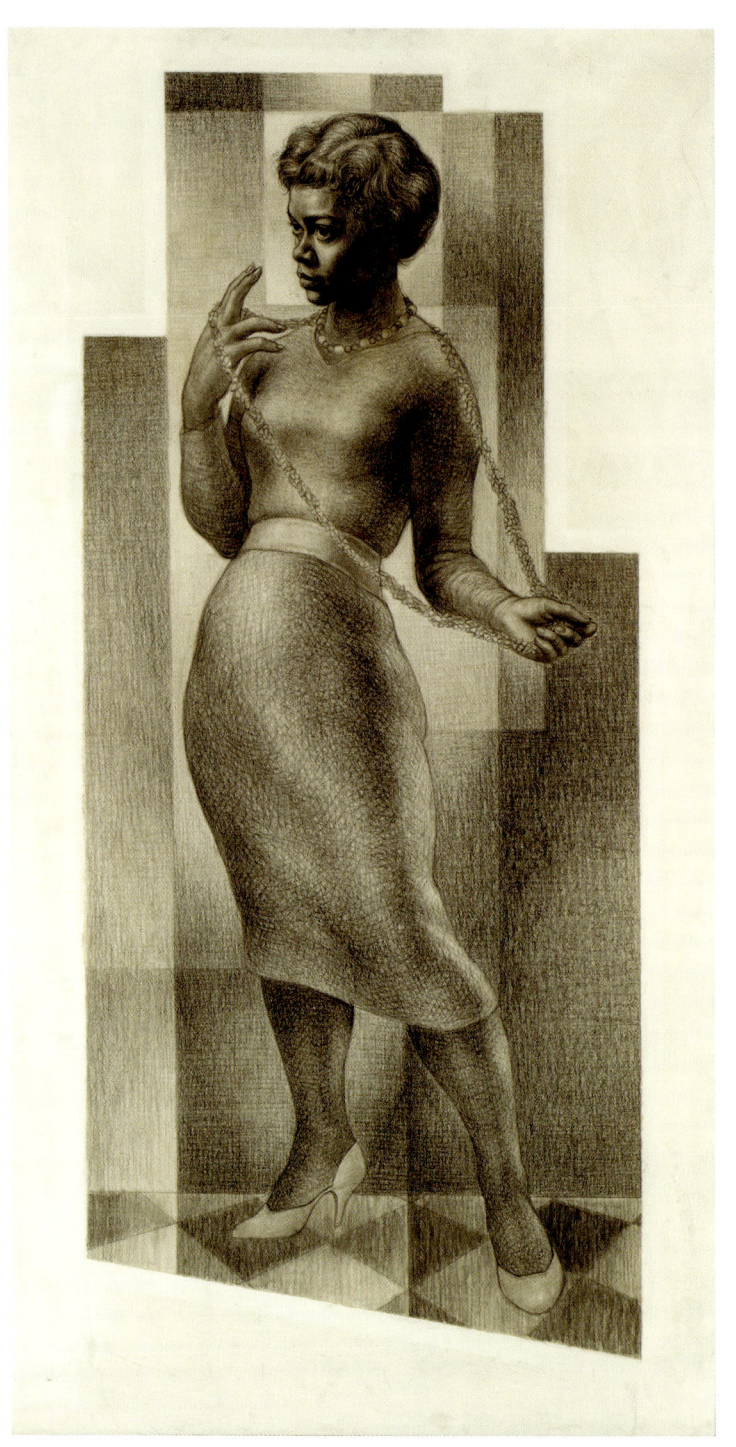

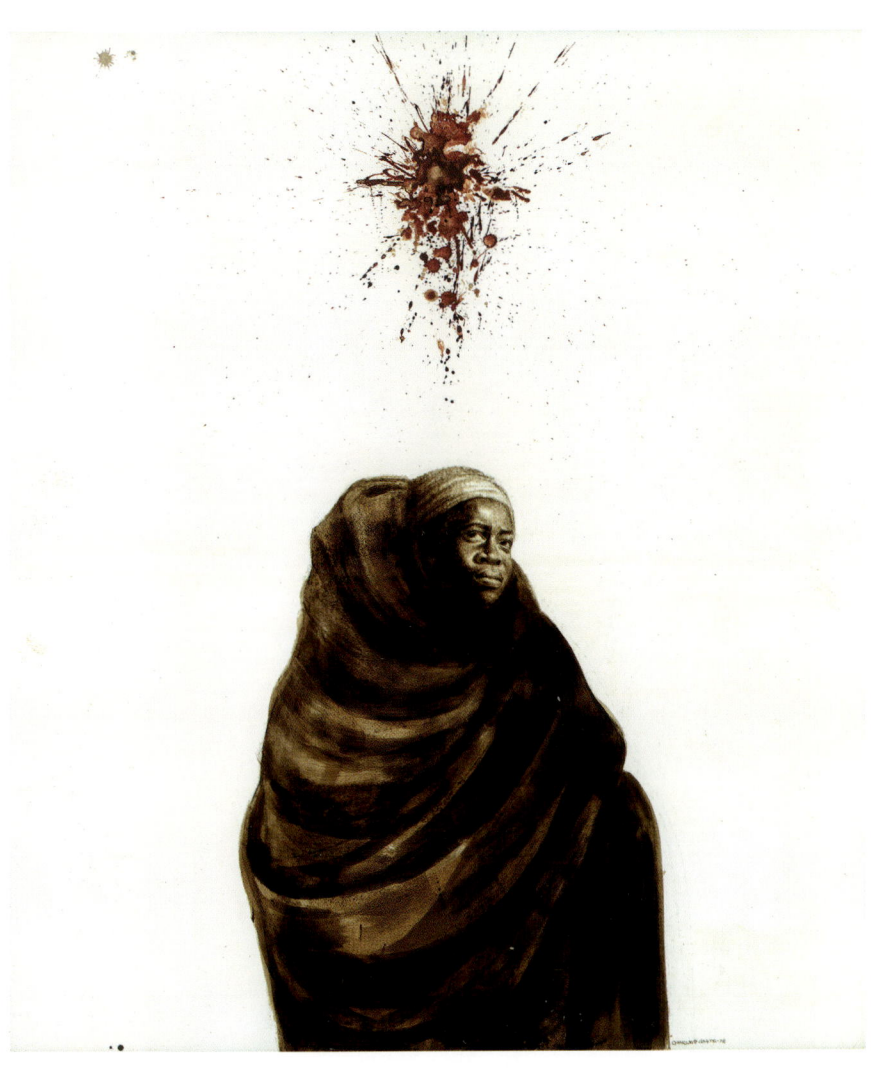

PLATE 4 (FACING PAGE) Charles White, *Eartha Kitt* from *Anna Lucasta*, 1958. Wolff crayon on board. Courtesy © 1958 Charles White Archives.

PLATE 5 Charles White, *Harriet*, 1972. Oil wash on board. Courtesy © 1972 Charles White Archives.

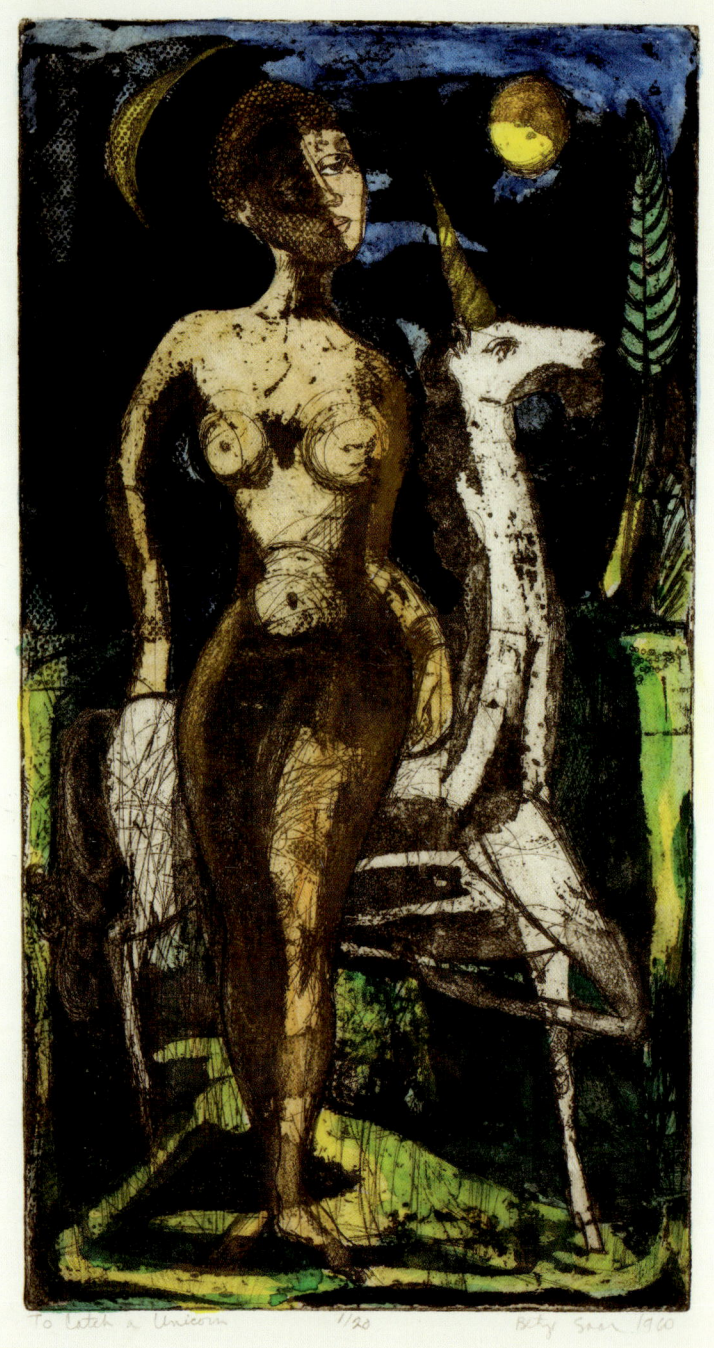

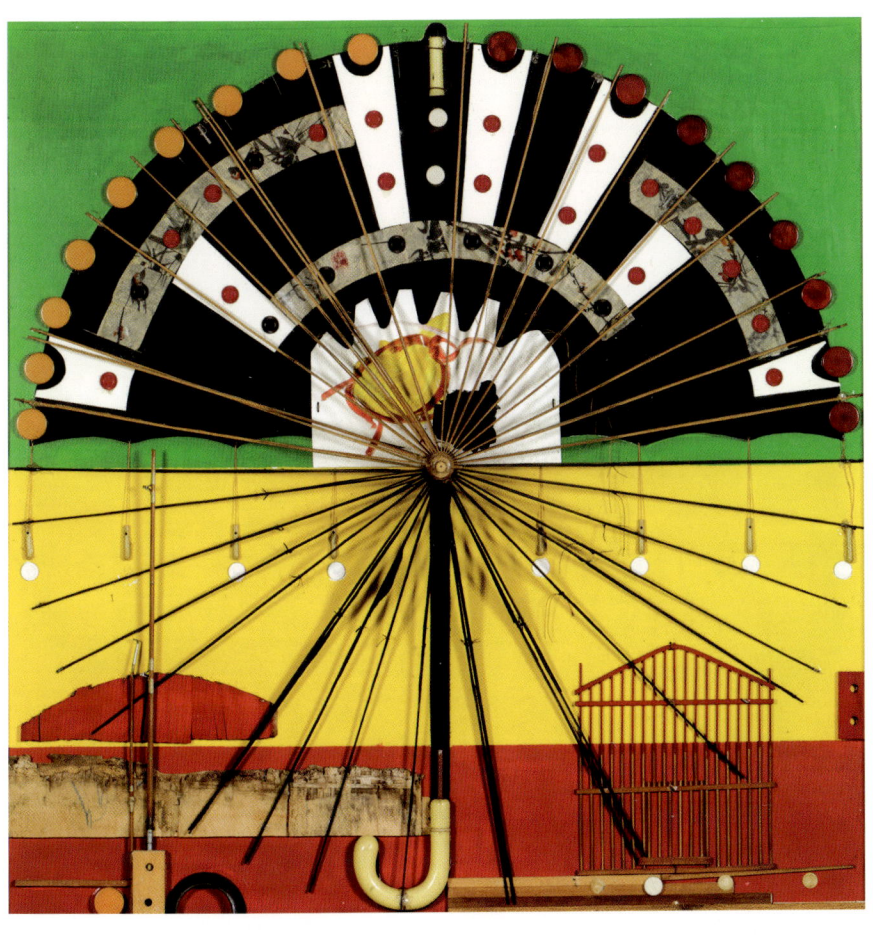

PLATE 6 (FACING PAGE) Betye Saar, *To Catch a Unicorn*, 1960. Color etching. Courtesy the artist and Michael Rosenfeld Gallery LLC, New York, NY.

PLATE 7 Noah Purifoy, *Unknown*, 1967. Mixed media. Collection John Outterbridge. Courtesy the Noah Purifoy Foundation.

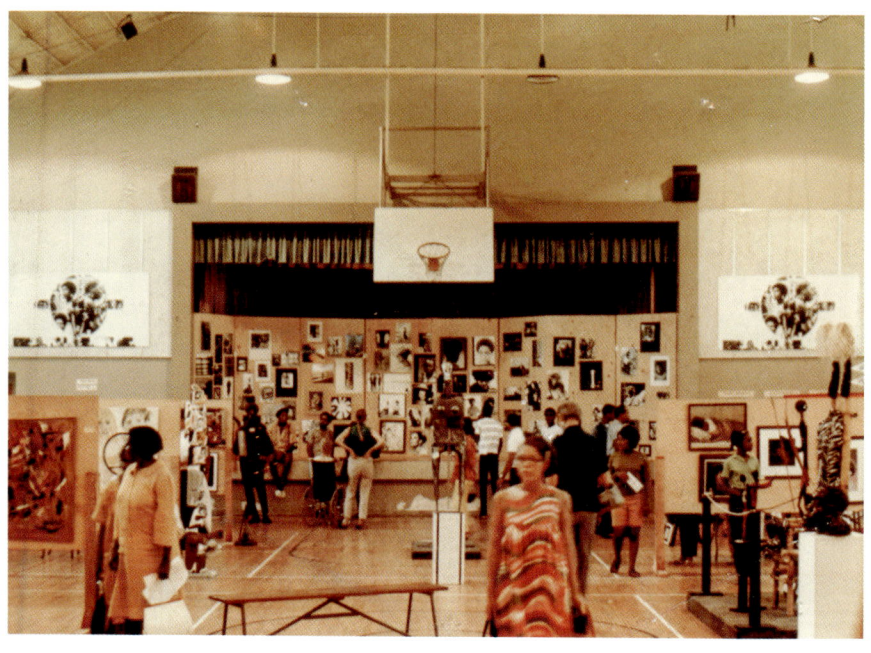

PLATE 8 Watts Summer Festival, 1969. Noah Purifoy Papers, 1935–1998, Archives of American Art, Smithsonian Institution.

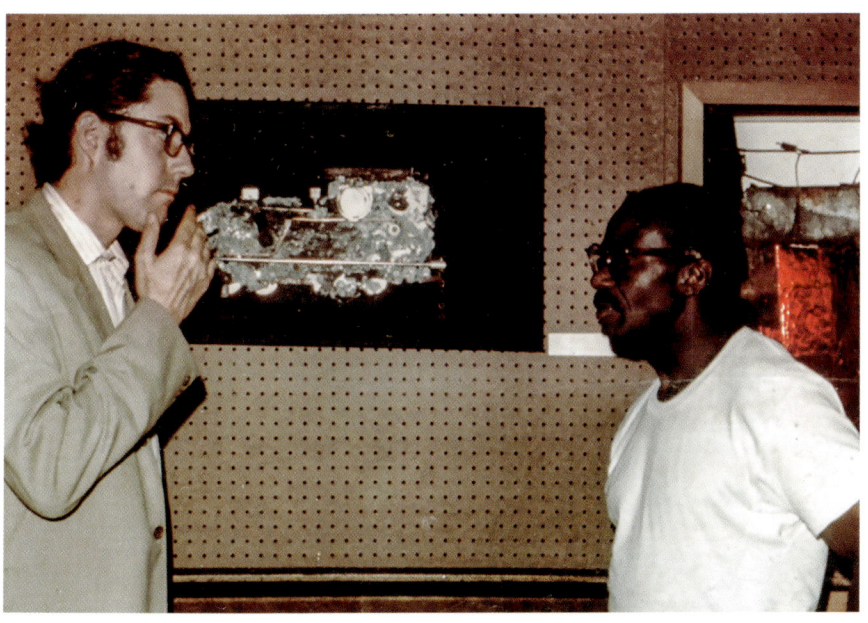

PLATE 9 Walter Hopps and Noah Purifoy, probably at the Watts Summer Festival, 1969. Noah Purifoy Papers, 1935–1998, Archives of American Art, Smithsonian Institution.

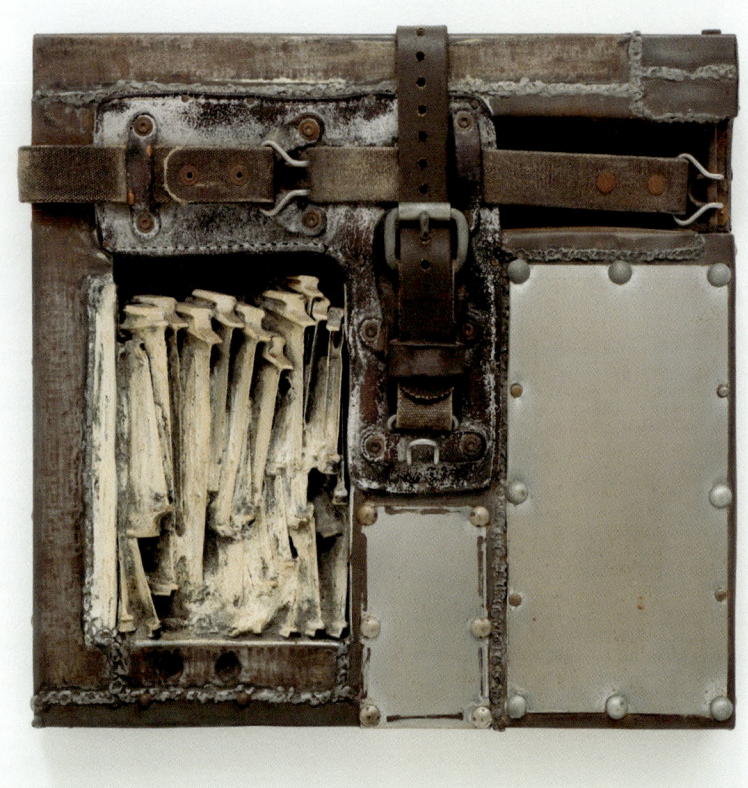

PLATE 10 John Outterbridge, *Let Us Tie Down Loose Ends*, *Containment* series, c. 1968. Mixed media. Collection Andrew Zermeño. Courtesy the artist and Tilton Gallery, New York.

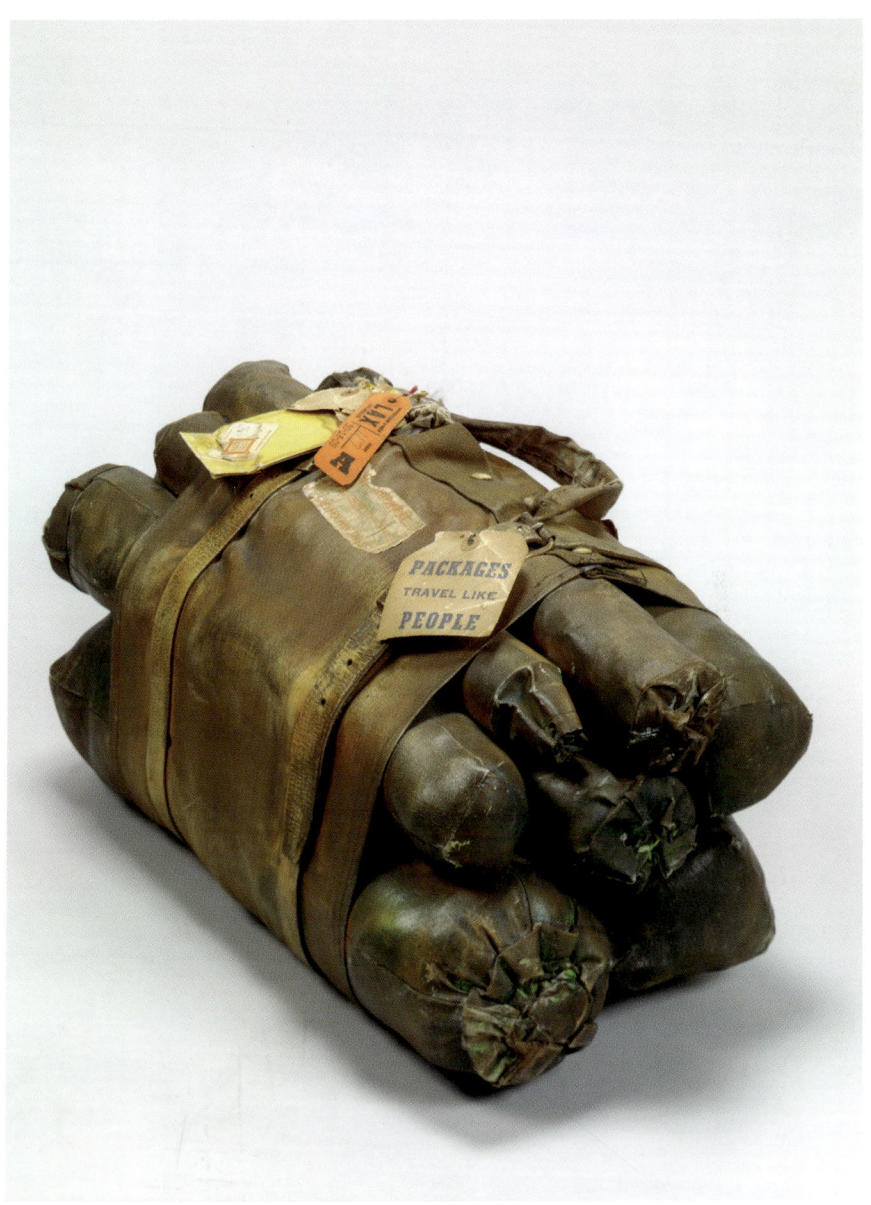

PLATE 11 John Outterbridge, *Case in Point*, *Rag Man* series, 1970. Mixed media. Hammer Museum, Los Angeles. Purchase. Courtesy the artist and Tilton Gallery, New York.

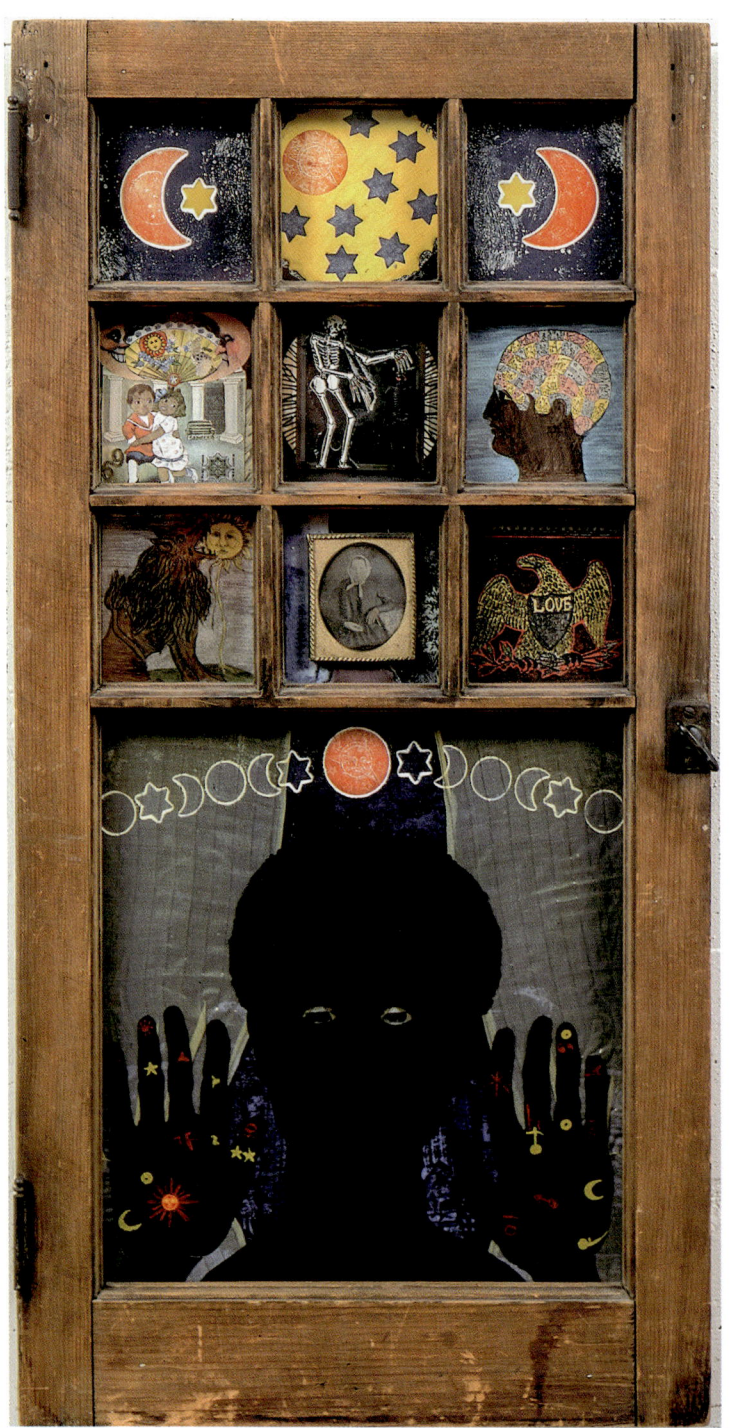

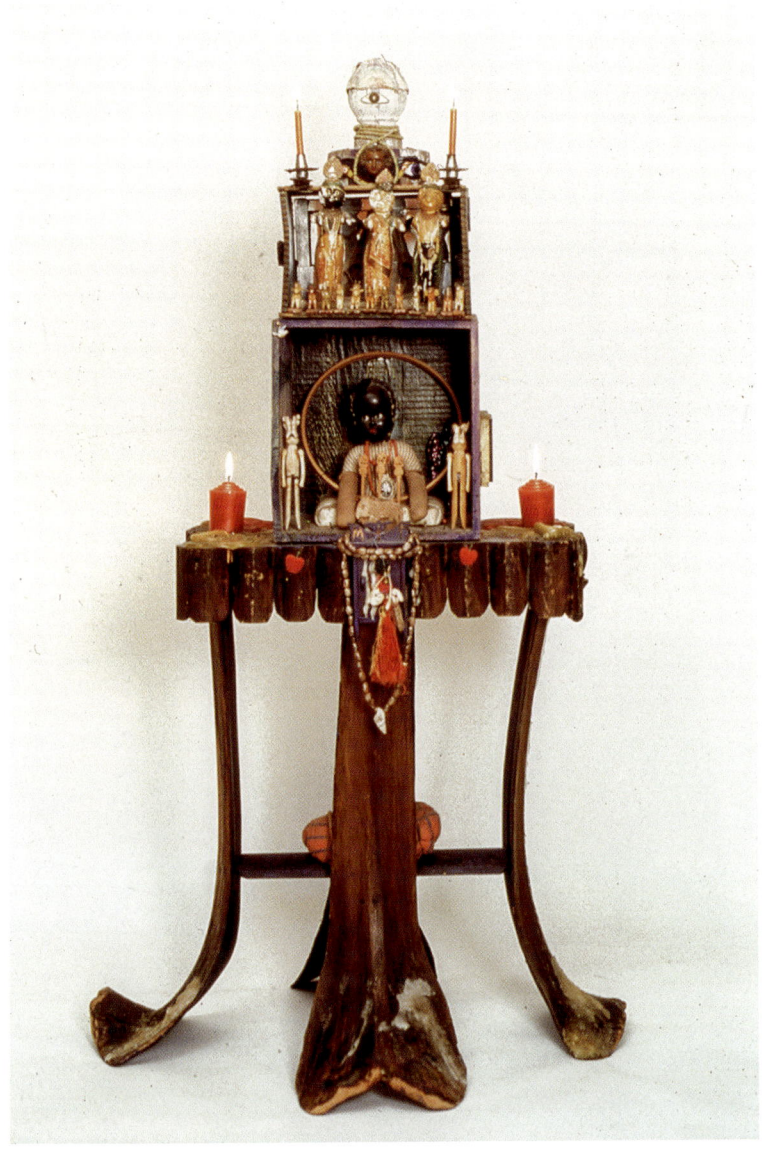

PLATE 12 (FACING PAGE) Betye Saar, *Black Girl's Window*, 1969. Mixed-media assemblage. Collection of the Museum of Modern Art, New York, The Modern Women's Fund and Committee on Painting and Sculpture Funds. Courtesy the artist and Michael Rosenfeld Gallery LLC, New York, NY.

PLATE 13 Betye Saar, *Mti*, 1973. Mixed-media assemblage. Courtesy the artist and Michael Rosenfeld Gallery LLC, New York, NY.

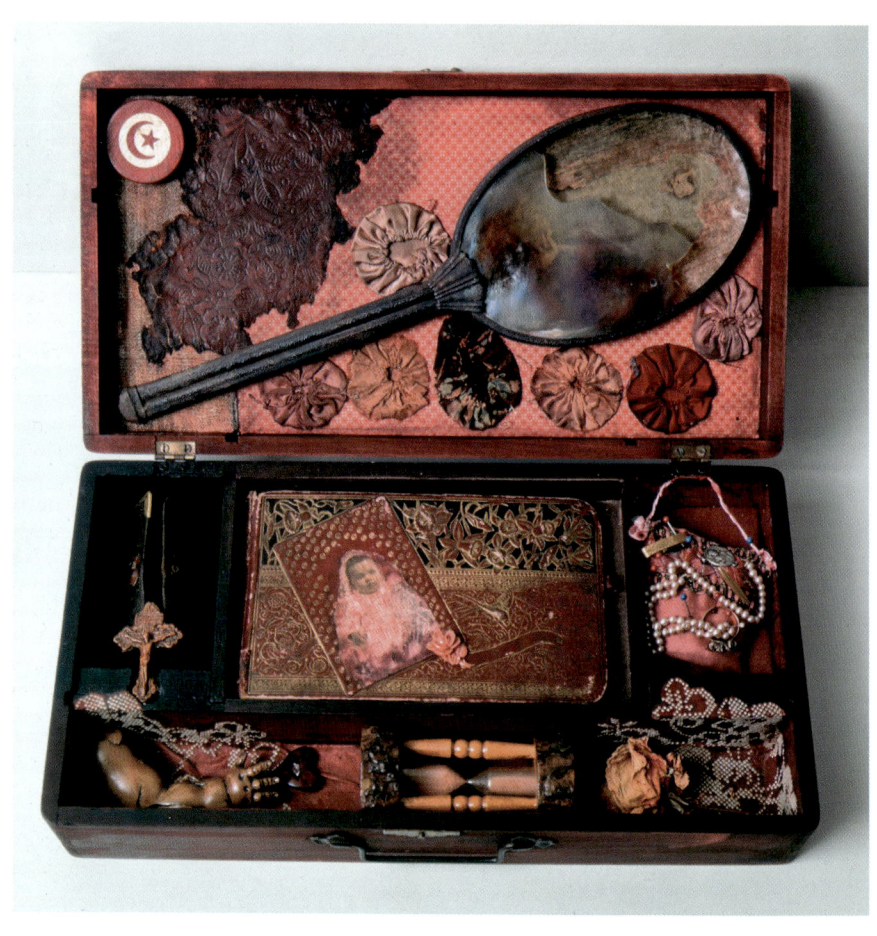

PLATE 14 Betye Saar, *Record for Hattie*, 1975. Mixed-media assemblage. Courtesy the artist and Michael Rosenfeld Gallery LLC, New York, NY.

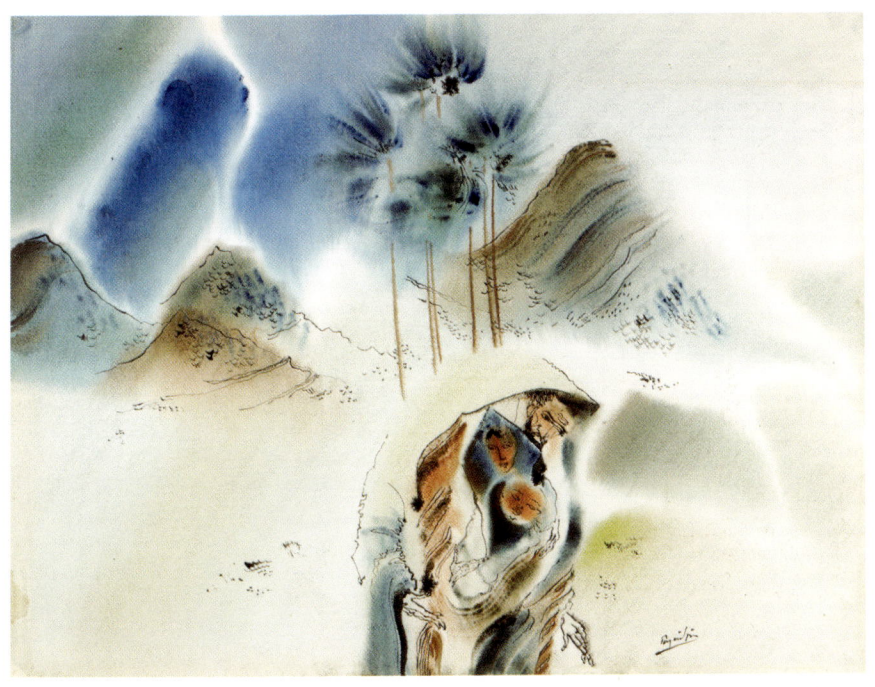

PLATE 15 William Pajaud, *Holy Family*, 1965. Watercolor, pen and ink on paper. Welton Jones, WAJ Collectibles. Courtesy the estate of William Pajaud.

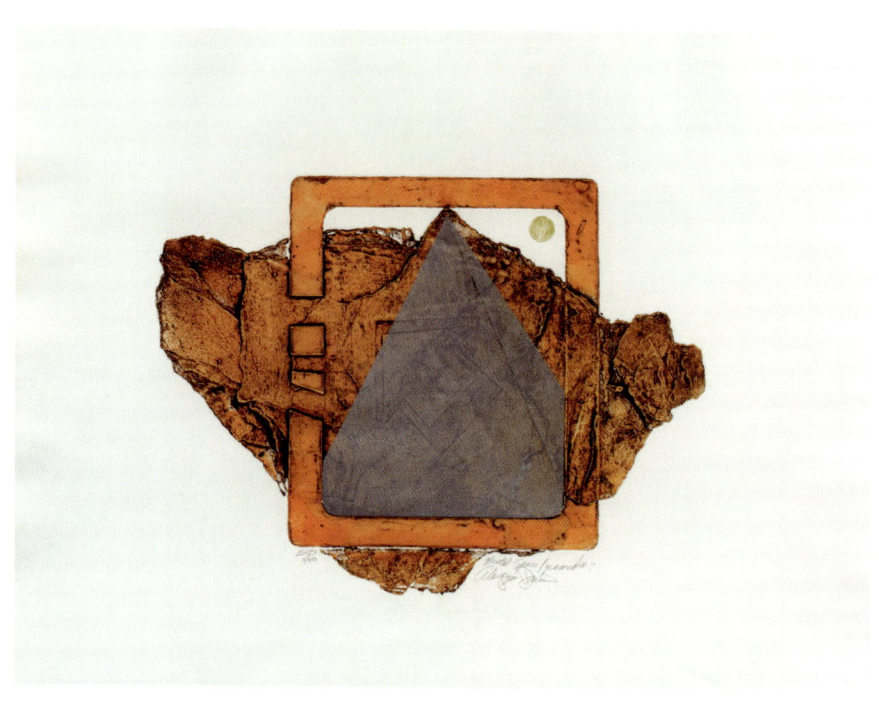

PLATE 16 Alonzo Davis, *Pyramid #7* from the *Mental Space* series, 1978–79. Color collograph. Courtesy the artist and Brockman Gallery Archives.

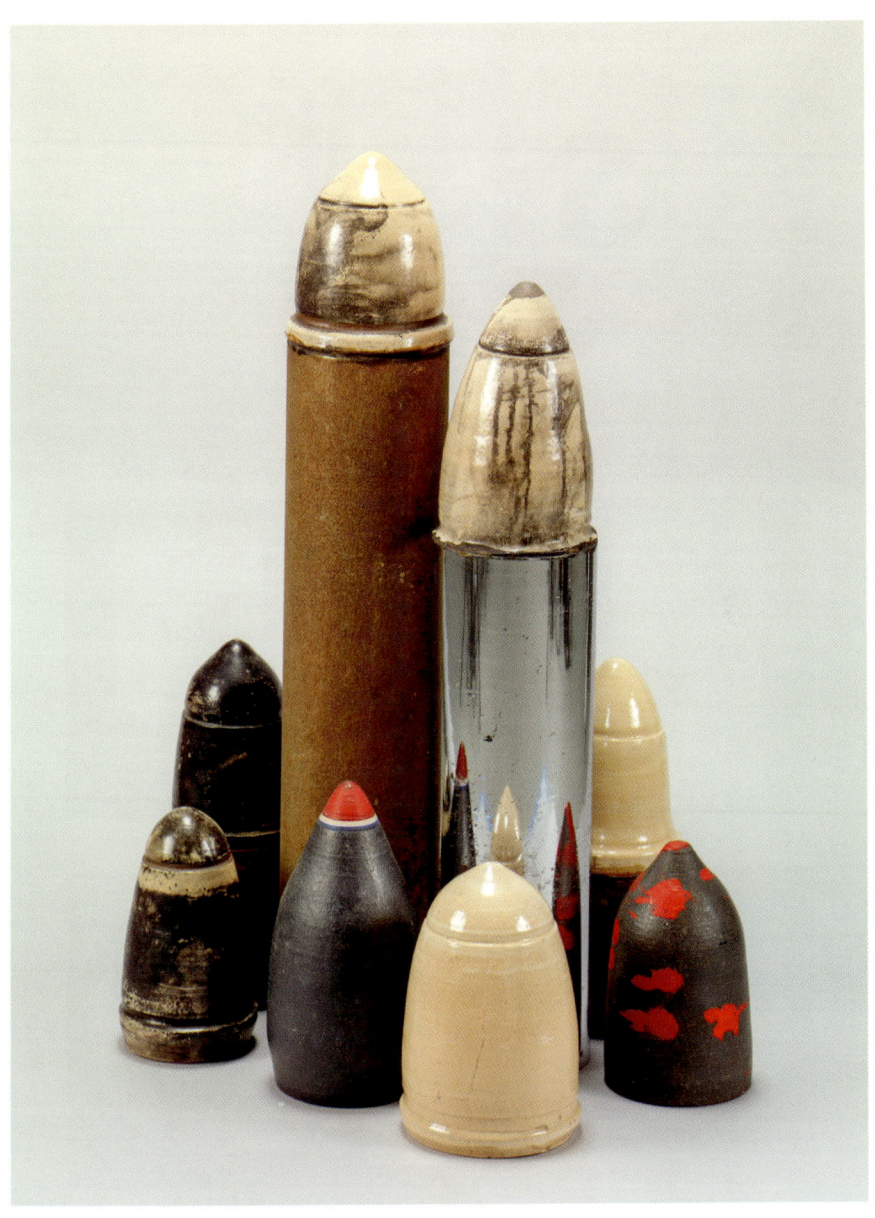

PLATE 17 Dale Brockman Davis, *Viet Nam War Games*, 1969. Clay and metal. Courtesy the artist and Brockman Gallery Archives.

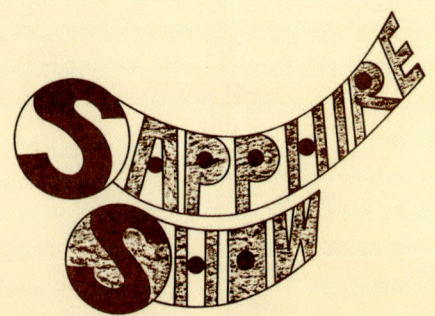

PLATE 18 Poster for *The Sapphire Show* at Gallery 32, 1970. Ankrum Gallery Records, 1960–1990, Archives of American Art, Smithsonian Institution.

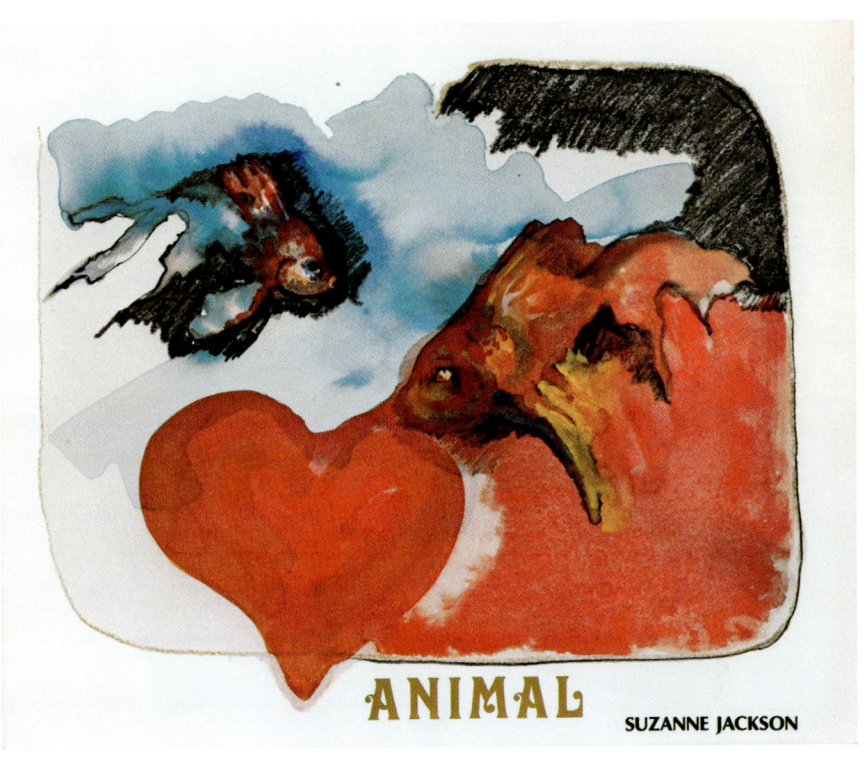

PLATE 19 Suzanne Jackson, *Animal*, 1978. Artist's book.

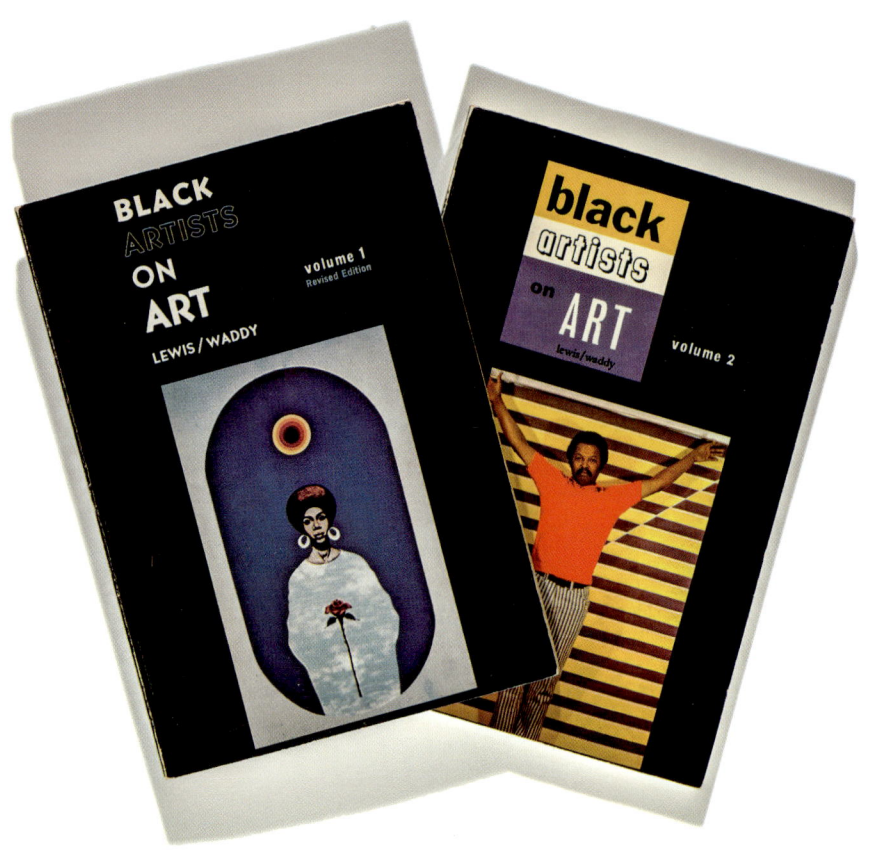

PLATE 20 Samella S. Lewis and Ruth G. Waddy, *Black Artists on Art*, vols. 1 (1969) and 2 (1971).

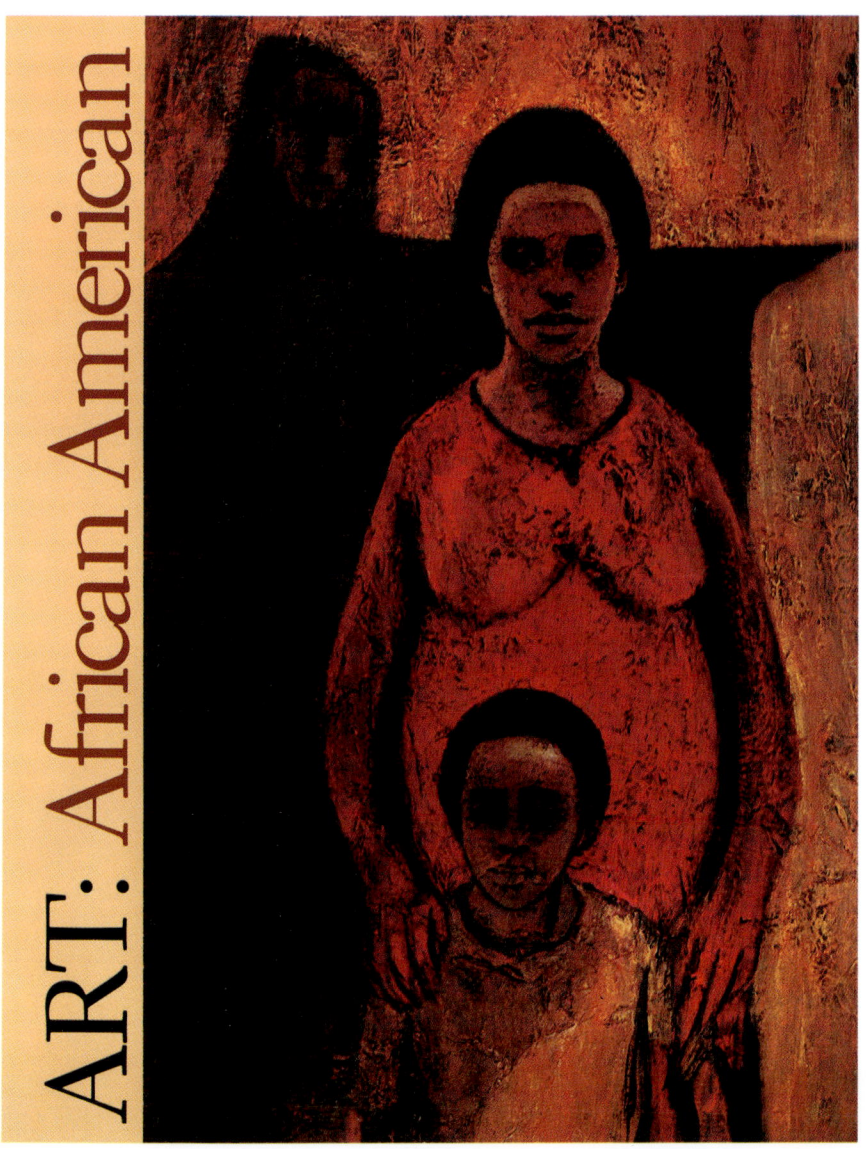

PLATE 21 Samella S. Lewis, *Art: African American* (1978).

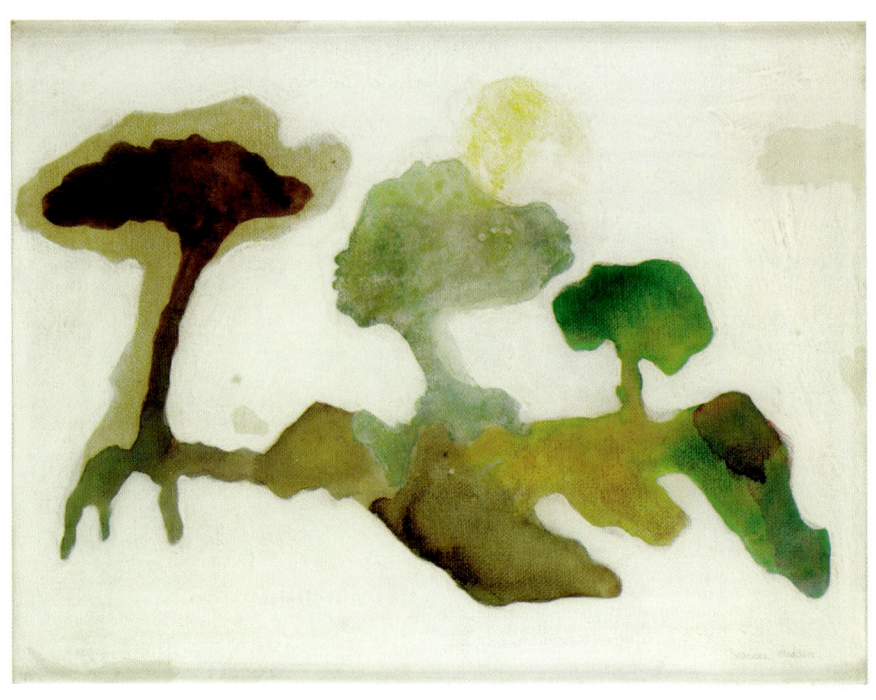

PLATE 22 Suzanne Jackson, *Sundown*, 1974. Acrylic wash on canvas. Collection Marguerite Ray. Courtesy the artist.

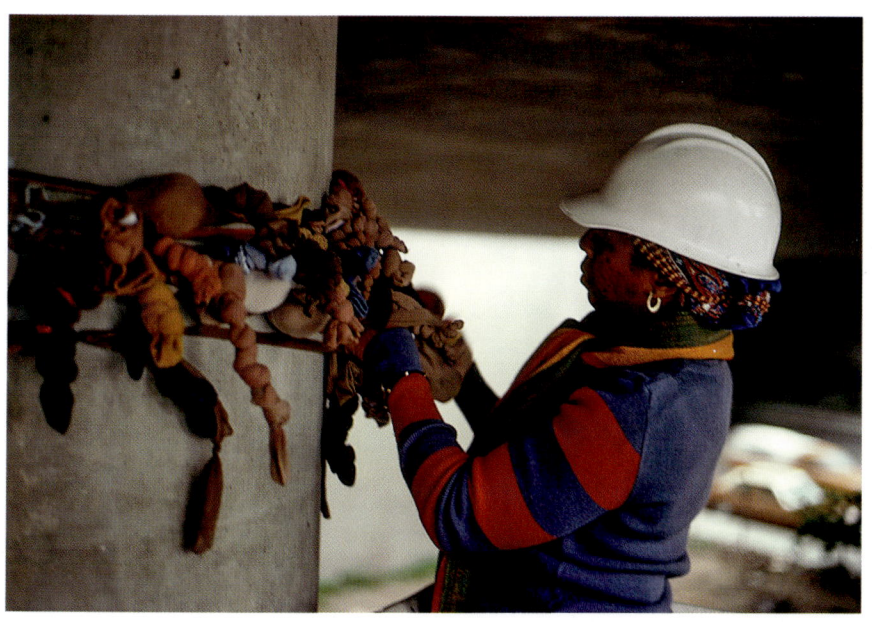

PLATE 23 Roderick "Quaku" Young, *Senga Nengudi setting up for her performance* Ceremony for Freeway Fets, 1978. Performance, Los Angeles. Courtesy the artist; Thomas Erben Gallery, New York; and the African American Performance Art Archive, University of North Carolina, Chapel Hill.

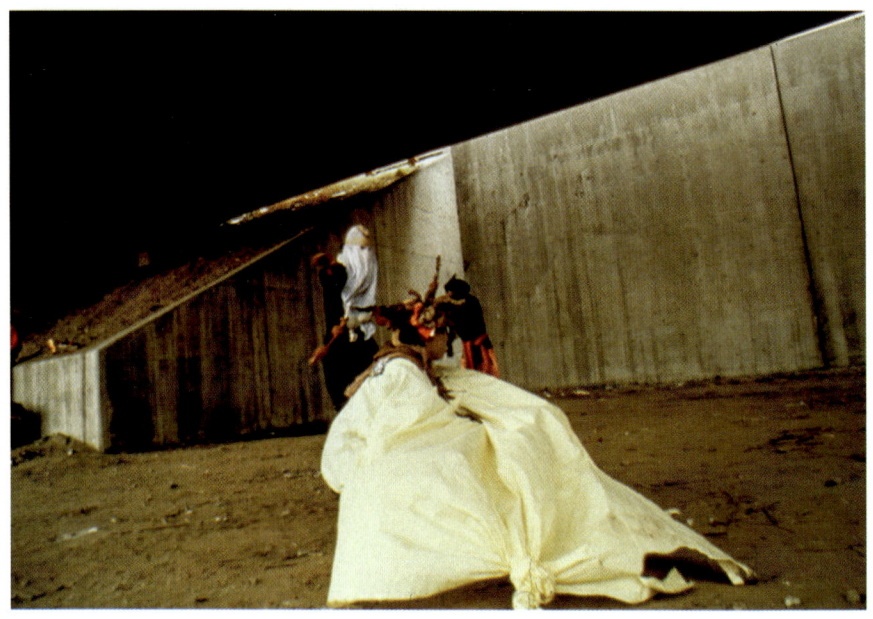

PLATE 24 Roderick "Quaku" Young, *Senga Nengudi*, Ceremony for Freeway Fets, 1978. Featuring (*from left to right*) Maren Hassinger, Nengudi, and David Hammons. Performance, Los Angeles. Courtesy the artist; Thomas Erben Gallery, New York; and the African American Performance Art Archive, University of North Carolina, Chapel Hill.

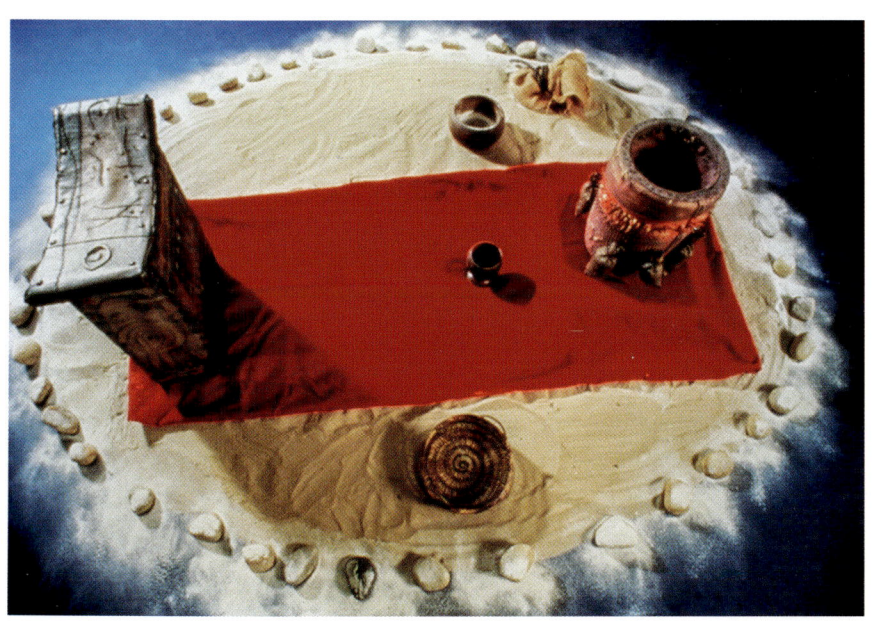

PLATE 25 Houston Conwill, *JuJu*, 1975–78. Mixed-media installation. Courtesy the artist; photograph by Stanley Gainsforth.

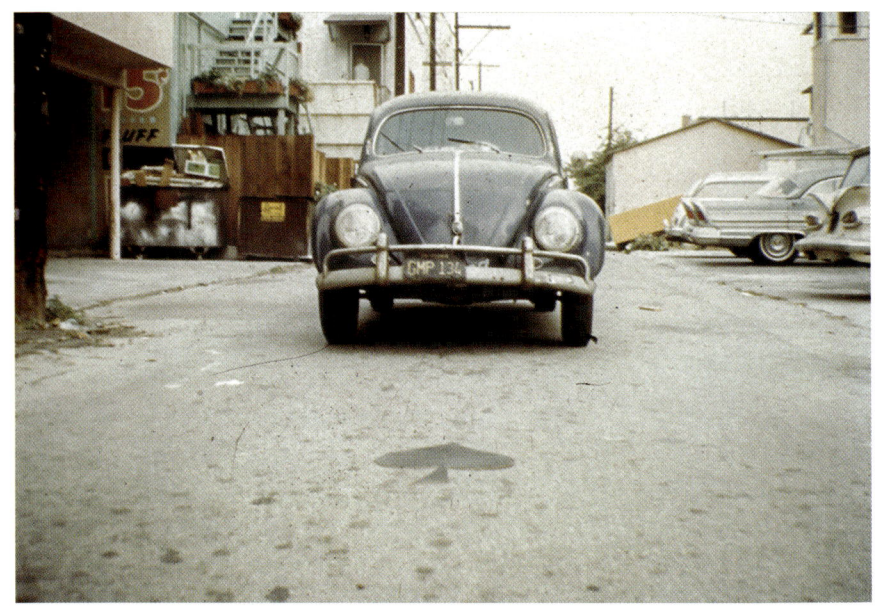

PLATE 26 David Hammons, *Murder Mystery (Spade Run Over by a Volkswagen)*, 1972. Performance, Los Angeles. Just Above Midtown Gallery Archives. Courtesy the artist and Tilton Gallery, New York.

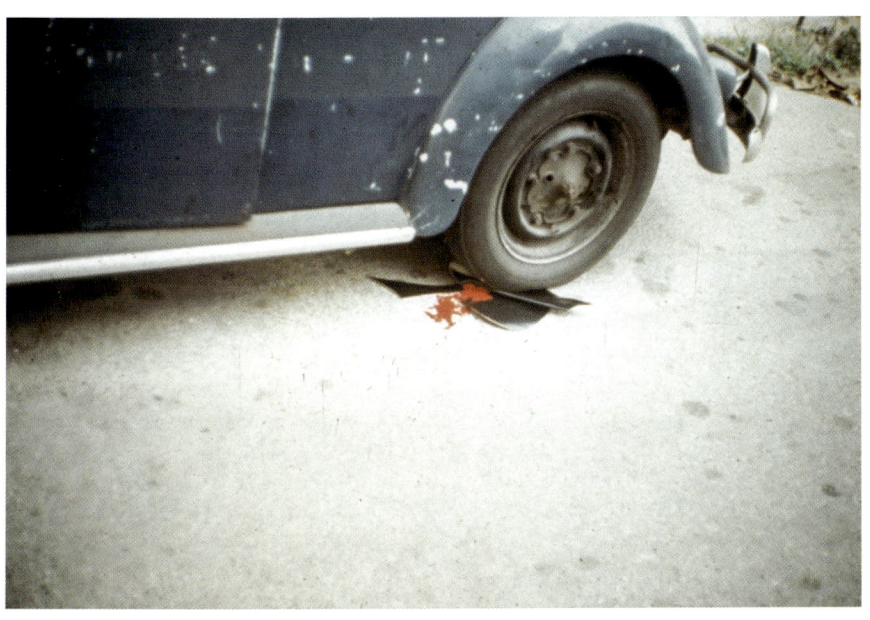

PLATE 27 David Hammons, *Murder Mystery (Spade Run Over by a Volkswagen)*, 1972. Performance, Los Angeles. Just Above Midtown Gallery Archives. Courtesy the artist and Tilton Gallery, New York.

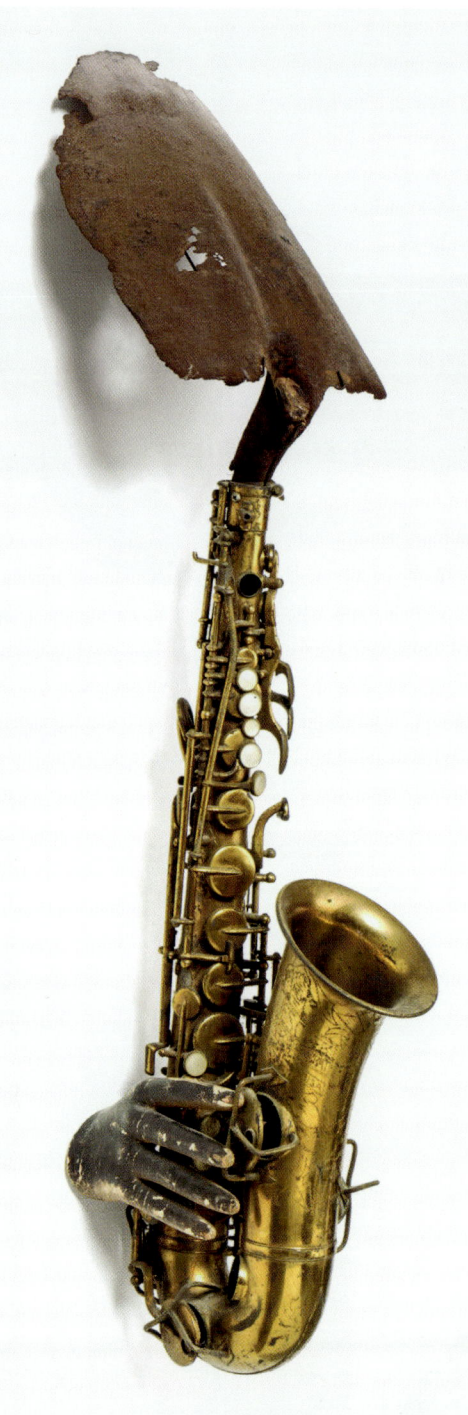

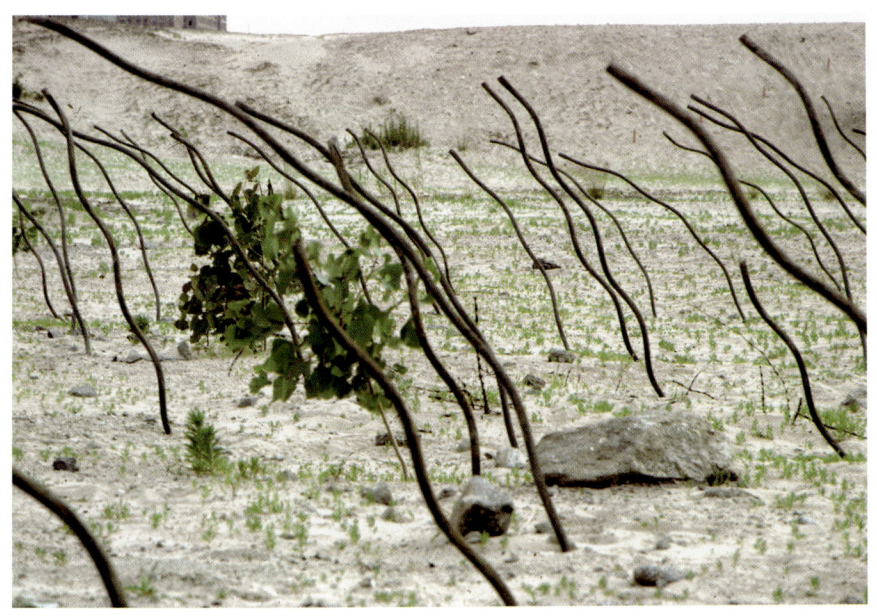

PLATE 28 (FACING PAGE) David Hammons, *Bird*, 1973. Mixed-media assemblage. Courtesy the artist and Tilton Gallery, New York.

PLATE 29 Maren Hassinger, *Forest*, 1980. Site-specific installation, Battery Park, New York. Courtesy the artist.

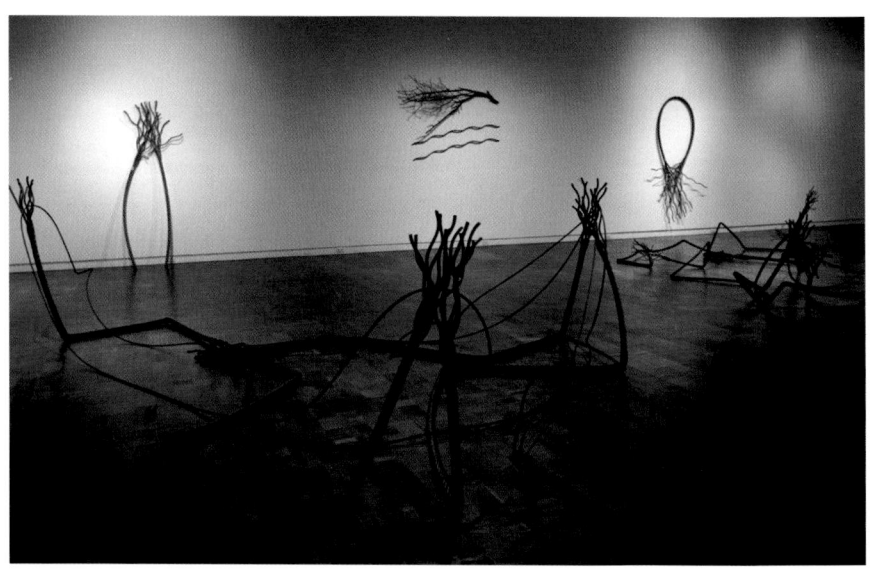

PLATE 30 Adam Avila, *Installation view of Maren Hassinger exhibition at ARCO Center for Visual Art*, Los Angeles, 1976. ARCO Center for Visual Art Records, 1976–1984, Archives of American Art, Smithsonian Institution.

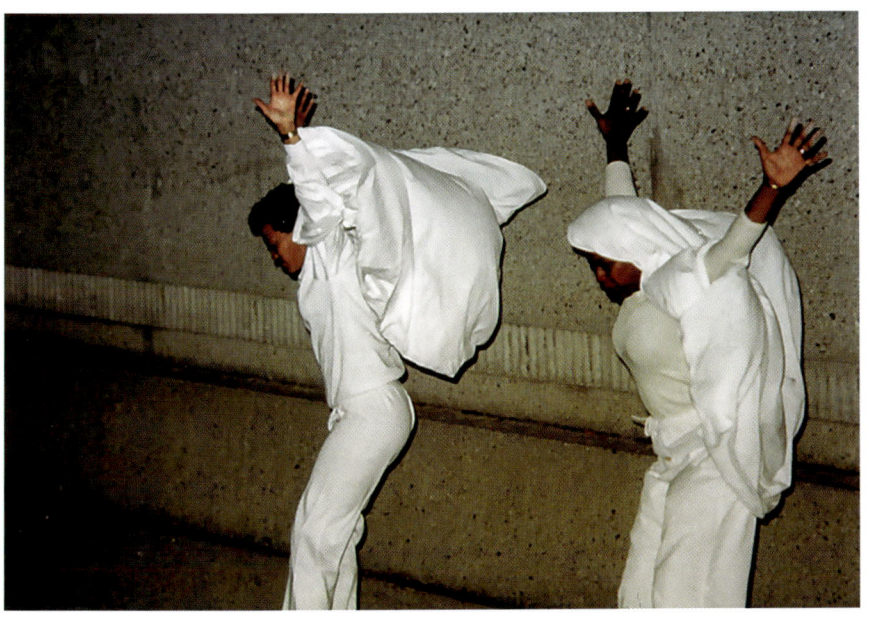

PLATE 31 Maren Hassinger (*left*) and Senga Nengudi (*right*), *Flying*, 1982. Performance, Los Angeles. Courtesy Maren Hassinger; Thomas Erben Gallery, New York; and the African American Performance Art Archive, University of North Carolina, Chapel Hill.

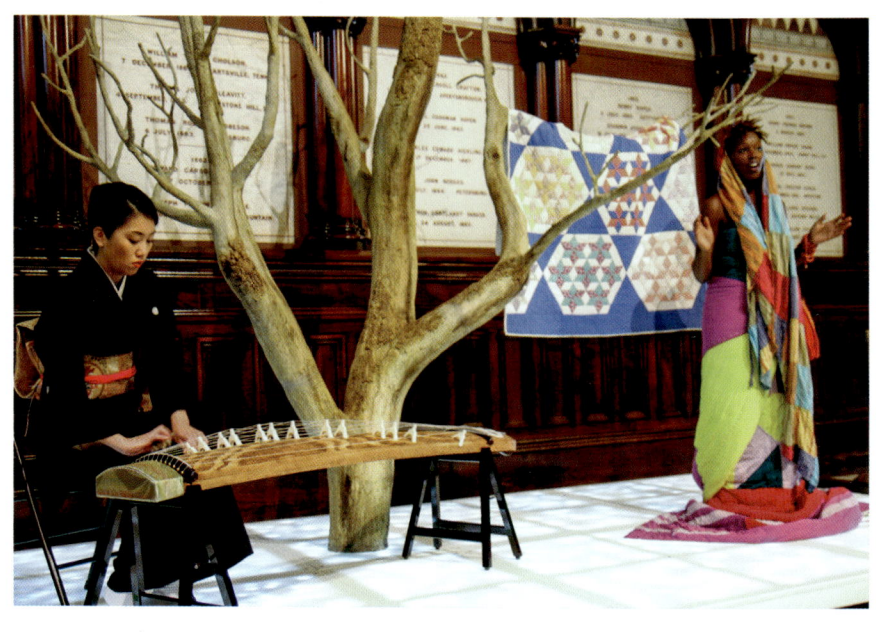

PLATE 32 Sanford Biggers, Constellation II, *Installation and Performance at Memorial Hall, Harvard University*, 2009. Courtesy the artist; photograph by Anita Kan.

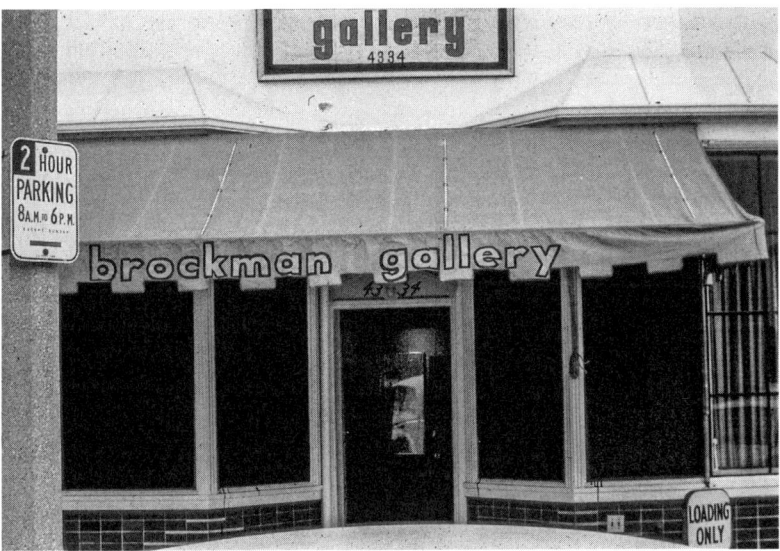

FIG. 3.1 Brockman Gallery at 4334 Degnan Boulevard in the Leimert Park neighborhood, Los Angeles, 1970s. Courtesy Brockman Gallery Archives.

BROCKMAN GALLERY AND BROCKMAN GALLERY PRODUCTIONS

The late 1960s saw the formation of several nonmunicipal, independent art establishments. Brockman Gallery (fig. 3.1), Gallery 32, and The Gallery were all venues run by and largely for African American artists. While Brockman Gallery had the longest life span of the three—1967 to 1990—the other two enterprises were very active in the first half of the 1970s. At their core, these were spaces run by artists for artists. This critical cultural activity, however, was also motivated by the radical actions of the time.

In August 1965, the image of Los Angeles changed in the black American imagination. The Watts Rebellion was a beacon of sorts that validated uprising as an effective tool of social change, which was replicated in countless cities in the 1960s. As Gerald Horne and others have pointed out, Watts was not an isolated frontrunner in this regard but indicative of a more widespread feeling in the country.[24] Many cultural institutions were born in California in the wake of the Watts Rebellion, including the Inner City Cultural Center and Watts Happening Coffee House, where antipoverty funds were pumped into the community to dispel further destruction. The independent institutions described below filled themselves up with the energy of change to effect their own transformations of the cultural environment.

ORGANIZE • 145

In the summer of 1966, young artists and brothers Alonzo Davis and Dale Brockman Davis set out on a road trip. They clocked thousands of miles in a Volkswagen Beetle, perhaps the hippest car of the era. They alternated, one sleeping on the ground, one sleeping in the car, and once in a while they even got a hotel room. They traveled across the United States in what Alonzo has called a "word-of-mouth" tour, rambling across the country, meeting creative people, and seeing "artists of color, that they were out there, that they were doing it, they were making a significant statement."[25] In Detroit, "Motown was hot," but they also experienced a city full of "muscle and energy."[26] There were murals in Chicago, and jazz there and in Kansas City. In Washington, DC, they met the Howard University contingent. They moved through Philadelphia and on to New York, where they connected with members of the Spiral artists' group, including Hale Woodruff, Norman Lewis, Merton Simpson, and Ernest Crichlow. They were struck by Romare Bearden's generosity. From there, Alonzo and Dale drove up the East Coast through Connecticut and Maine, all the way to Quebec.

One might find parallels with Sal Paradise and his comrades in Jack Kerouac's *On the Road* (1957), the now-classic novel of youthful experience, coming to consciousness, and the Beat Generation. The novel lays out the growing awareness of the breadth of the American landscape—physically, racially, and sexually—imagining its place in a larger, global circuit. If Kerouac found the essence of new America in the musical cultures and general textures of black America, the Davis brothers were seeking something much more specific: African American artists who validated their own vision of themselves.

In *On the Road*, black music was emblematic of radical newness in American culture of the early 1950s, but it was replaced by an even more visible and widespread militancy in the 1960s, in the narrative of the Davises' trip. Both Dale and Alonzo have acknowledged that part of the impetus for their journey was to participate in the June 1966 March Against Fear. This civil rights march between Memphis, Tennessee, and Jackson, Mississippi, was organized by James Meredith, the first black student admitted to the University of Mississippi (Ole Miss) in 1962. The march became known not only for the violence visited upon protesters—Meredith was shot shortly after it began on June 6—but also as the moment that SNCC's Stokely Carmichael first proclaimed "Black Power," nudging the African American freedom struggle away from the narratives of civil rights.[27] The context of their trip was the Watts Rebellion: an energy and fire that sent them across the country from the reaches of the West.

The story of Alonzo Davis and Dale Brockman Davis on the roads of

America in 1966 is also part of the larger migration narrative. They headed to the Southwest, to Arizona and Texas, and to the South—to Mississippi, North Carolina, and their birthplace, Alabama. The brothers had been born in the 1940s and raised on the campus of Tuskegee Institute. Their father, Alonzo Sr., taught psychology and education and at one point was the school's dean of education. Their mother, Agnes Moses Davis, was a former schoolteacher who worked in Tuskegee's library; the brothers also came from a long line of college graduates and educators.[28] Their life on campus was a zone of relative privilege in the South; they had access to great facilities, their own elementary and secondary school, and businesses that served them. Downtown, however, was a foreign and segregated world.[29]

Alonzo Sr. and Agnes separated in 1956, and the brothers headed to Los Angeles with their mother. There was extended family there, and they moved again to a college community, near the University of Southern California, where Agnes pursued a degree in library science.[30]

The Davis brothers' 1966 trip put them back in touch with family. Darlene Clark Hine has written about kinship networks that drew folks back to the South, crisscrossing the country. Alonzo and Dale connected with their father, who by then was teaching at North Carolina Central University in Durham. They caught up with a cousin in Detroit. And indeed, this wasn't their first time back in Alabama since heading to California in 1956. In fact, their road trip was familiar in that they often found themselves heading to the South to visit relatives.[31]

Somewhere on their 1966 journey, as they were remarking on the beauty of Utah or dreaming among the expanses of corn in Iowa, the Davis brothers mused in an "off-the-cuff" way about opening a gallery in Los Angeles that would be a platform for art by African Americans. At that time, the city did not have a regular space for showcasing the visual culture of black people. The idea entered their minds after they encountered the New Breed art space in Washington, DC, run by Topper Carew. Inspired by the Watts uprising, they also talked about community control and how they could effect the redistribution of power.

The following year the Davises started Brockman Gallery (fig. 3.2). Named for their maternal grandmother who had been a slave, they dedicated Brockman primarily to the work of African American artists. They found a great location in a former frame shop at 4334 Degnan Boulevard, situated in Leimert Park on the west side of Los Angeles, an area that had been open to African Americans for a decade. It was one of the wealthiest black enclaves, and the Davises chose a site there in a bid to attract that clientele. Such space

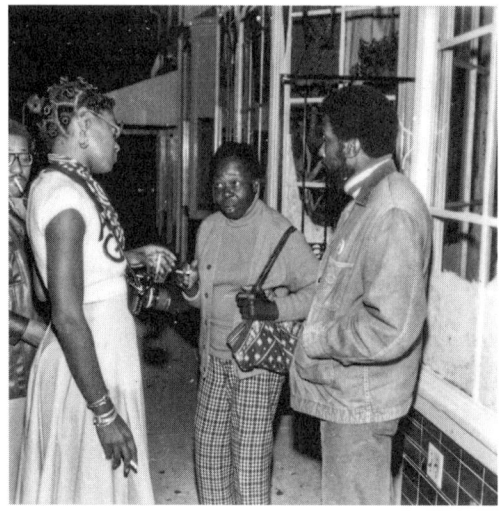

FIG. 3.2 Ruth Waddy at a Brockman Gallery opening, 1970s. Courtesy Brockman Gallery Archives.

became accessible in the wake of the Watts Rebellion as longtime (generally white) shopkeepers vacated, leaving more commercial real estate available.[32]

The Davises opened their gallery in January 1967 with shows of their own work (fig. 3.3), a testament to how their trip also advanced their practice as artists. During the cross-country drive, they located African American artists and absorbed lessons about the African Diaspora and the America around them. Alonzo's focus on paintings and prints retained a spiritual core, as in his series of color collographs, *Mental Space*, 1978–79 (plate 16), which feature metaphysical symbols and take inspiration from Egyptian imagery. Dale's ceramics (fig. 3.4) connected him to California artists, blurring the line between craft and art in the postwar period, as seen in works in clay by Peter Voulkos, Ken Price, and John Mason but also looking back historically to those like Sargent Johnson. A piece such as *Arabian Nights #2*, 1969–70, meditates on North African or Arab cultures in the African Diaspora constellation, while *Viet Nam War Games*, 1969 (plate 17), is an antiwar installation.[33] It is a testament to how the art world—indeed, the whole world—had begun to shift that Brockman Gallery was established the same year that Ferus, perhaps the most storied gallery in LA during this period, shut its doors.

In its more than two decades of existence, Brockman presented a huge number of African American practitioners active in Southern California. The Davis brothers committed themselves to group shows in the first two years. By 1969 solo presentations began to appear, with artists such as John Riddle and John Outterbridge. A two-person show with Noah Purifoy and David Hammons that same year was extended by popular demand.[34]

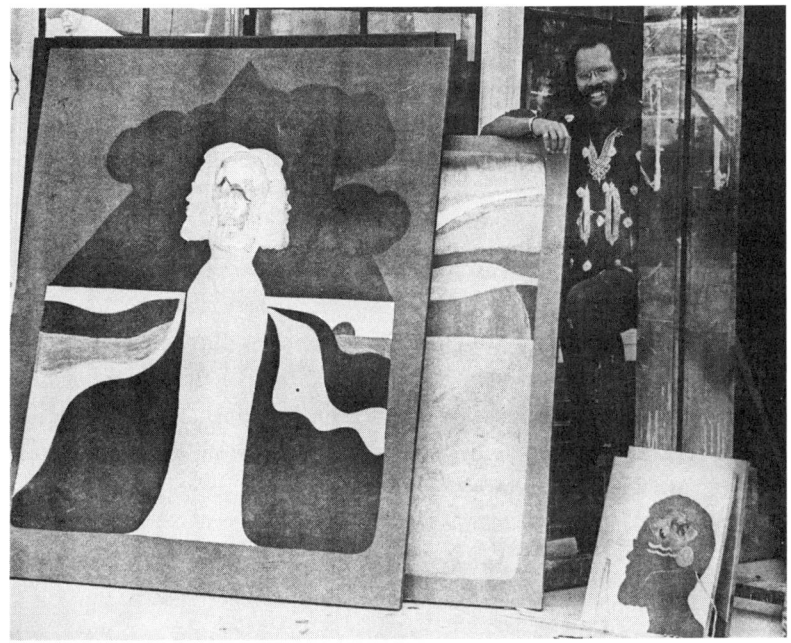

FIG. 3.3 Alonzo Davis with his work outside Brockman Gallery, 1970s. Courtesy Brockman Gallery Archives.

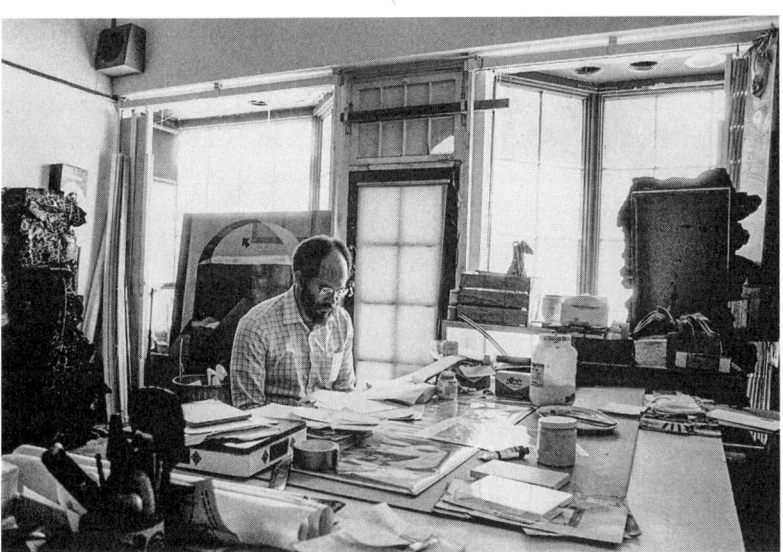

FIG. 3.4 Dale Brockman Davis in his studio next door to Brockman Gallery, 1970s. Courtesy Brockman Gallery Archives.

Noah Purifoy's solo show in March 1971 was among Brockman Gallery's most visible and perhaps most controversial. An environmental installation that encompassed the entire gallery, Purifoy's *Niggers Ain't Never Ever Gonna Be Nothin'—All They Want to Do Is Drink and Fuck* re-created the interior of a poverty-stricken home. The scene confronted viewers on all sensory levels—the grimy dishes, clothes, and furniture around the room; a refrigerator emitting a foul odor; a fetid bathroom; overflowing ashtrays; and evidence of roaches and rats. The walls were created from torn wallpaper and newspapers, with a chromolith of Jesus surveying the scene. Ten mannequins lay on pallets on the floor, "shrouded" in blankets, as one viewer wrote, and "sleeping fitfully in the cold glow of the TV."[35] In one corner, a couple of these figures screwed mechanically, liquor bottles on the nightstand at their side. A radio also emitted urban sounds, from fighting to a ringing telephone to Purifoy singing hymns. At the opening, the artist served cornbread and black-eyed peas.[36]

Purifoy's intent was to re-create what he had seen during his days as a social worker, to capture "the very essence of poverty."[37] It was emblematic of the conditions of privation, discrimination, and inequity that had led to the insurrection in Watts and around the country, a protest against the exigencies of ghetto existence and the decay of America's urban life.[38] Critics agreed, finding the piece effective, "psychologically unsettling," and moving.[39] Purifoy had doubts, though. Recapitulating reality, he thought, meant that imagination had to take a backseat. "It was probably more gratifying than anything else I've ever done, and also the least creative."[40] He imagined redoing *Niggers Ain't Never Ever Gonna Be Nothin'—All They Want to Do Is Drink and Fuck* sometime in the future accompanied by a piece he called *Extreme Object D-E-D*, a room decorated in French provincial style, with a white couple seated on opposite ends of the bed staring into space and a Rolls Royce parked outside.[41]

Brockman Gallery also exhibited the work of artists with more established reputations, like Jacob Lawrence. Elizabeth Catlett, who had lived in Mexico since the mid-1940s, had her first U.S. solo show in many years at the gallery in 1971; it featured both prints and sculpture. Alonzo Davis recalls driving to Tijuana, loading his van with art, and dealing with the complications of getting the work across the border. This reminds us not only of the proximity of Mexico but of its significance in African American history, as a place of refuge and imagination and as part of an important transnational network.[42] Indeed, the Davis brothers were quite committed to an inclusive vision for the gallery, one that reflected the plentitude of artists and visions that mirrored the realities of Los Angeles and the nation. Brockman featured pieces by Chicano, Asian, and white artists. As early as 1969, for instance, they presented a group show of Asian and Asian American artists titled *Oriental America*.[43]

They always envisioned Brockman Gallery as a commercial venture. And they certainly had some high-profile clients, including Bill Cosby.[44] Yet Alonzo and Dale were also very active in the community, helping with other exhibitions and events. To handle their expanding community-focused activities, in 1973 they set up Brockman Gallery Productions, a nonprofit entity that was eligible for public funding. By 1976, Alonzo was able to quit all the other jobs he'd held to keep the gallery afloat and concentrate on running these enterprises.[45]

As a nonprofit, Brockman expanded its reach exponentially. Spurred by Alonzo's interest in public art, the gallery became a base for a street art and mural movement in the early 1970s. One development was the Los Angeles Street Graphics Committee, a group of muralists that included Houston and Kinshasha Holman Conwill, Ulysses Jenkins, Tony Riddle (one of John Riddle's sons), and others. Certainly this was part of the urban mural renaissance of this period, beginning with projects such as the city of Chicago's *Wall of Respect*, 1967; it was energized by protest and vitality in the street, forces just outside the studio.[46] Public projects expanded from "street graphics" to site-specific installations and performances through funds infused by the Comprehensive Education and Training Act (CETA). CETA functioned as a WPA-like program during the economic downturn of the 1970s. Through it, Brockman funded projects by Maren Hassinger, Dan Concholar, and Senga Nengudi, among others; painter Suzanne Jackson worked as Brockman's CETA coordinator.[47]

During the decade between the mid-1970s and mid-1980s, Brockman Gallery Productions cast itself more broadly as a production company and presenting organization. It put on film festivals and hosted concerts in the village center known as Leimert Park, with the likes of pianist Horace Tapscott and his Pan-Afrikan Peoples Arkestra, and initiated the Watts Towers Jazz Festival. The Davis brothers helped Japanese American jazz-fusion band Hiroshima land its first commercial recording contract. Through Brockman Gallery Productions, they were able to support more artists than ever before because commercial viability was no longer an issue.[48]

Due to his involvement and innovation in public art, Alonzo was tapped to head a freeway mural program in Los Angeles as part of the 1984 Olympics.[49] During this period, Alonzo developed his theory of the "color bath," a philosophy of murals and freeway culture in which an image emerges in space and time, with viewers comprehending more with each diremption of the painted expanse.⁵⁰ After the Olympic murals project, Alonzo eased out of his position at the helm of Brockman Gallery and Brockman Gallery Productions. He began pursing artist-residency programs nationally and internationally. After handing over operations to a series of business managers, Brockman closed its doors in 1990, the end of an amazing twenty-three-year run.⁵¹

GALLERY 32

Searching for a new studio space in MacArthur Park in the vicinity of both Otis Art Institute and Chouinard Art Institute, painter Suzanne Jackson found a beautiful two-story place on Lafayette Park and was encouraged by friends to turn it into a gallery. In 1968 Gallery 32 opened its doors (fig. 3.5). Jackson had been born in 1944 in Saint Louis, Missouri, an entrepôt of modern black migratory culture since at least the nineteenth century. Her family had relatives in San Francisco and moved there before Suzanne was one, and then eight years later to Fairbanks, Alaska. Like John Outterbridge's dad, Jackson's father, Roy, was entrepreneurial. He went to Fairbanks ahead of his family, purchasing property for a minimal amount and then homesteading. Alaska at that time was a territory, not a state, and Roy Jackson's actions recalled that of blacks and others who had carved out homes in the West in the nineteenth and early twentieth centuries. Fairbanks was home to a military base and the local university, and Jackson's father worked in sales serving those communities, eventually taking up real estate. It was black soldiers who introduced Jackson to black music, evidence that Alaska too was part of the diaspora.⁵²

As an adult Jackson moved to San Francisco, as much to be a part of the creative culture of the Beat scene as to pursue college, which she did at San Francisco State College (later San Francisco State University). She studied art and dance at what even in 1961 was a commuter school, whose visual arts faculty were almost all working artists experimenting with abstract expressionism, pop art, and new forms. A job in college pulling slides for art history classes exposed her to a range of historical works from a variety of cultures; this was part of her inspiration for Gallery 32.⁵³ Jackson also was involved in many dance communities, studying with Rod Strong, who worked at the Pacific Ballet alongside experimental dancer Anna Halprin, and dancing with Lynwood Morris, a choreographer trained by Katherine Dunham. During this time, she performed in the San Francisco staging of the groundbreaking

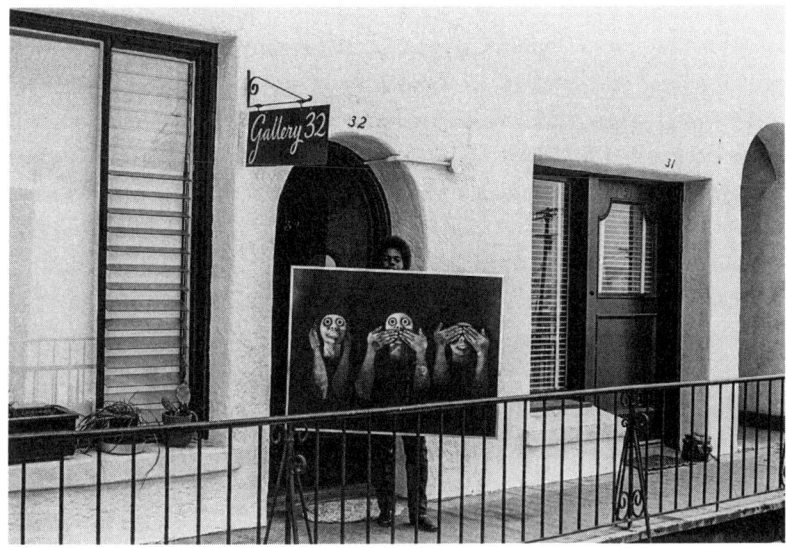

FIG. 3.5 Bob Heliton, *Timothy Washington with one of his pieces outside Gallery 32*, 1969. Courtesy the Bob Heliton Archive.

musical *Fly Blackbird* (1959). Written by C. Bernard Jackson and James Hatch, it was a play about the civil rights movement with a significant multiracial cast, which had an Off Broadway premiere in 1961 and won an Obie award the following year.[54]

In 1966, after she'd graduated from college, Jackson danced with the Sacramento and Fresno Light Operas Music Circus and toured Latin America with Music Theater USA. The State Department–sponsored circuit was mandated to be integrated, so the shows that went on the road were *Showboat* and *Carousel*. Jackson believed it was the way she would "see the world" in the absence of money for a grand tour of European museums. Around 1968, she moved to Los Angeles.[55]

Like so many artists, Jackson supported herself with a variety of jobs in the process building her own creative community. She worked at the post office and concurrently for the Los Angeles Unified School District as an elementary school art instructor; then she taught dance and visual art at Watts Towers Arts Center. She was a model in art classes at Watts Towers and for Charles White's courses at Otis Art Institute. She also sat in as a student in some of White's sessions, which is how she first met David Hammons, Dan Concholar, Alonzo Davis, and Timothy Washington. In response to finding this larger creative community Jackson decided to dedicate part of her new two-story live/work space to those who lacked consistent opportunities to exhibit. Gallery 32 was located neither in the traditional La Cienega gallery district nor in the black commercial precinct of Leimert Park, but it lay in close proximity to LA's important art schools.[56]

By 1970, Gallery 32 was visible, progressive, and full of energy. It was not necessarily a "black gallery," although its proprietor and the majority of its artists were African American. In fact, the inaugural show featured a mixed group, two white artists—David Swanson (an art school friend from San Francisco) and Gordon Dipple (a painter and jeweler from Santa Barbara)—and LA artist Timothy Washington. There was a healthy competition between Brockman Gallery and Gallery 32, though they often shared opening weekends—Brockman debuted shows on Friday, and Gallery 32 on Saturday—and some artists (Hammons, Washington, Concholar). However, Brockman exhibited more established practitioners, while Gallery 32 specialized in a younger, eclectic, and, in some ways, more political group.[57]

Jackson considered her effort an alternative, a space for artists who weren't really showing elsewhere. She did not necessarily make a serious effort at commercial viability; part of the idea behind Gallery 32 was to get communities—particularly communities of color—to support younger artists and in the process develop something wonderful.[58] The invitation for John Stinson's exhibition of photographs—showing him standing in the doorway of his mail truck—drew crowds of politicos as well as everyday folk.[59] Women also had great visibility, including Yvonne Cole Meo and Eileen Abdulrashid; Elizabeth Leigh-Taylor's first exhibition in 1969 focused on the Greek resistance.[60] *The Sapphire Show*, 1970 (plate 18), presented black women artists—Betye Saar, Yvonne Cole Meo, Gloria Bohanon, Senga Nengudi, and Jackson herself—a full three years before Saar and Samella Lewis curated almost the same group for the Woman's Building in *Black Mirror*.[61]

Arguably, the best-attended of all Gallery 32 exhibitions was a 1969 solo by Emory Douglas (fig. 3.6), minister of culture of the Black Panther Party and principal illustrator of the *Black Panther* newspaper. Along with the original drawings that became illustrations for the newspaper, Douglas showed his pastels, what Jackson described as "soft, lovely, sort of traditional portraits of all the Panther leaders."[62] Jackson had been contacted by Panther leadership about the project, which she saw as providing a safe space for presenting the full spectrum of the organization's agenda and supporting their social programs, such as free breakfasts for children. The exhibition opening highlighted the political work that even art could do; police posted nearby dissuaded people from entering the gallery, and curious observers, their necks heavy with cameras, snapped shots everywhere. Like many artists during this

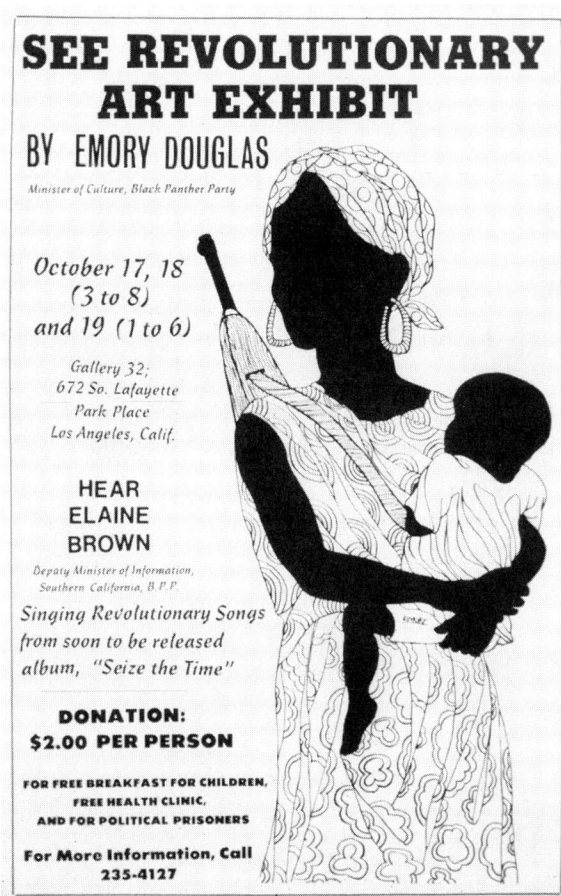

FIG. 3.6 Emory Douglas, *Poster for Emory Douglas exhibition at Gallery 32*, 1969. Center for the Study of Political Graphics. © 2015 Emory Douglas / Artists Rights Society (ARS), New York.

period, Jackson was harassed and seen as subversive; the exhibition arena as a meeting place, as a place to debate the artist's relevance to the black community, came under scrutiny. The gallery's continuing work in the face of such provocation established it as a place of resistance. Spaces like Gallery 32 encouraged cultural invention but also challenged coercion and generated social power. They were counterhegemonic sites that set up new networks of belonging.[63]

There were also fund-raisers. A Christmas show benefited the Black Arts Council, a group that, like Gallery 32 and Brockman, was dedicated to supporting the work of African American artists and spreading the word to a larger community about their existence. Another project exhibited art made by children at the Watts Towers Art Center. Like other African American gallerists, including the Davis brothers and Samella Lewis, everyone had supplementary jobs to keep afloat not only their own art but also their commitment to showing others.[64]

Some of Gallery 32's most faithful patrons were from the film and theater worlds, including football player–turned–actor and artist Bernie Casey, and actress Marguerite Ray. Interestingly, Jackson's credentials as a professional dancer never led her down the road of performance art pursued by her contemporaries David Hammons, Senga Nengudi, or Maren Hassinger, with one exception: her wedding to Pete Mhunzi was a happening of sorts, a creative celebration held in Mococahuenga Canyon in Griffith Park. At the conclusion of the ceremony, on August 30, 1970, the bride and groom rode away on a motorcycle. Shortly afterward, Gallery 32 closed for good.[65]

However, throughout the 1970s, Suzanne Jackson in her role as an arts administrator made inroads in the visual arts. After Gallery 32, she spent several years in San Francisco. She was appointed to the California Arts Commission (later the California Arts Council) by Governor Jerry Brown, serving from 1975 to 1978 with Noah Purifoy. At the San Francisco Civic Center, she organized the art and dance aspects of Black Expo '72, a grand exposition–style undertaking that explored the spectrum of African American cultural production, including literature, music, and drama.[66]

Later in the 1970s, Jackson moved back to Los Angeles, serving as the artist-coordinator for Brockman Gallery's CETA-funded program during 1977–78. While she held that position, she also was able to create her own pieces, including two murals, *Wind*, at Crenshaw and Fiftieth Street, and *Spirit* at Twenty-Fourth and Western.[67] The 1970s, in the period after the closure of Gallery 32, also marked Jackson's development and productivity as a painter.

Some of her first solo shows, in both Northern and Southern California, were in 1972. A spring show at the University of the Pacific in Stockton was organized by Larry Walker. Recommended to Ankrum Gallery in Los Angeles by another of its artists, Bernie Casey, Jackson began showing at the gallery in 1969 with her first solo show in the fall of 1972. She became a significant presence, with additional solos there in 1974 (fig. 3.7), 1976, and 1978. Her growing list of collectors included Vincent Price and Johnny Mathis, and as with others in this Los Angeles cohort, her work was featured in film—in Jackson's case, the Diane Keaton vehicle *Looking for Mr. Goodbar* (1977). Her paintings were frequently seen on the East Coast at the Studio Museum in Harlem, Just Above Midtown Gallery, the New York Cultural Center, and the Herbert F. Johnson Museum at Cornell University.[68]

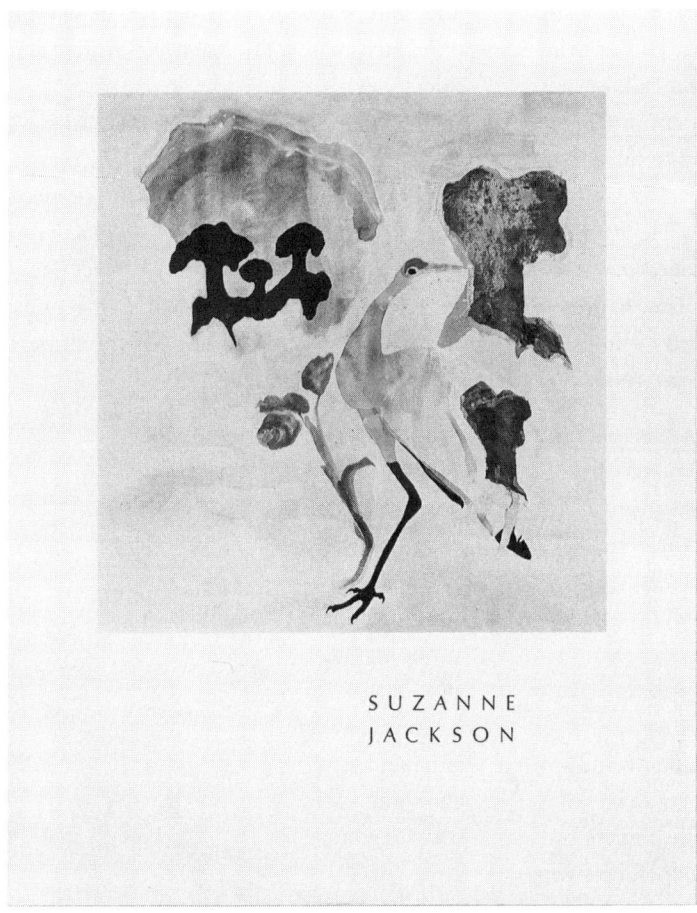

FIG. 3.7 Announcement for Suzanne Jackson's solo exhibition at Ankrum Gallery, 1974. Ankrum Gallery Records, 1960–1990, Archives of American Art, Smithsonian Institution.

The artist's layering of acrylics in luminous washes was something she consciously worked on, experimenting with various products. Her glazing techniques were more associated with oils, in which the process is slowed down by adding gels to create a series of coats that are independent, interactive, vibrant, and translucent.[69] Jackson's mix of figures and amorphous and organic patches of color in spaces of whimsy and fantasy in the paintings from the 1970s were in many ways mysterious to critics, who often remained confused by their lack of protest and seemingly open-ended and inconclusive narratives and grounds. A similar art world reception accompanied her two amazing and ethereal artist's books, which combined her paintings, drawings, and poetry, *What I Love*, 1972, and *Animal*, 1978 (plate 19); these were self-produced and evidence again of Jackson's will to make her creative and cultural vision known.⁷⁰

It was not just the mainstream art world, however, that found Jackson's work hard to categorize. Her experience working with the Black Panthers on the Emory Douglas show at Gallery 32 also brought such tangled questions into relief. The Panthers directly challenged her work, its lack of didacticism and so-called purpose, and the reach and aim of her gallery project. Jackson's response to these and other creative and cultural tests to the structures, figures, and forms of her painting as well as to her own cultural commitment was addressed head on in her first book *What I Love*, 1972:

STATEMENT: 1971

In answer
to panther
rhetoric about
art: they
say in order
to relate to
the people—
for people
to understand—
it's got to have
all the fingers
and toes. i say you
intimidate
the people
you say that
the people have
no minds for
dreams for
making some
kind of pleasant
fantasy within
their own realm
of wishful need.
you say
the people have
no capacity
for filling in
or for making
new images
within their own
minds when
they look at
art—or at most
what you say
is that the
people should
not be allowed
to delve
into fantasies
which might relate
to their own
reality, more
than to yours.

Jackson's Gallery 32 was seen perhaps as a political outpost based on its activities—whether she was showing art by Emory Douglas or Elizabeth Leigh-Taylor—and because it served as a home for an eclectic mix of people. Yet her paintings garnered the opposite response; they were dreamy, colorful landscapes, lyrical and surreal, with no clear agenda that could be labeled "political" beyond the use of the black figure itself. However, the above poem strikes a very pointed tone, pushing back against the will to categorize, define, and judge her approach to representation, realism, and the progressive life. Her writing is a defense of the breadth and freedom of the human capacity for dreams. In creating an arena for public discourse, Jackson marshaled public space, making a place for her own and her community's oppositional, counterhegemonic voice. In the tradition of black migrant women before her, she also remade the West in her own image. It was a specter of freedom, evincing "female self-invention,"[71] whose independence and mobility on many levels was a threat to the patriarchal order.[72]

It is significant to recall Jackson's upbringing in Alaska, which was unquestionably rural. Natural phenomena abounded in her world, which explains in part why she was drawn to images of nature; "I grew up listening to the wind and water and animals and leaves," she has commented.[73] She even joined the Audubon Society as a child, hoping to bring the natural world and an understanding of its creation closer to her. She was amazed to learn years later, during her curatorial research, that John James Audubon had African heritage. Her images were also inspired by native cultures, by things Inuit, Athpascan, and Tlingit. Her life in the territory of Alaska also remained a significant factor in her thoughts and imagination. Although she was born and spent her early childhood in the continental United States, her return as a young adult marked a significant change, a desire to be part of the San Francisco youth culture. But her arrival "in the United States" also represented a move not only to a profoundly urban understanding of blackness but also to a life of activism, civil rights, and freedom struggle, contextualizing her parents' own independence.[74] In Jackson's attachment to and feeling for land, she found she had more in common with rural black southerners and their shared sense of being "able to step out and know that something is growing out there."[75] Her art, like the cultural life of many migrants, was a way to re-create aspects of "home" in a new place and form.

The pervasive white grounds of Jackson's paintings in the 1970s also recall Alaskan geography. In these white expanses, one can locate the hyperblack North—freedom, a space depicted by African American artists since the nineteenth century and in the Canadian paintings of Grafton Tyler Brown and Robert Scott Duncanson. Jackson's Alaska signals the continuation of this idea and its extrapolation by artists of African descent in the twentieth and twenty-first centuries. In these instances, the black explorer Matthew Henson's reaching the North Pole is an indicator not only of accomplishment—as in the celebratory busts by Henry Bannarn in the 1930s—but also of a command of Western culture and a spectrum of possibilities for the black imagination in works by contemporary artists as diverse as Terry Adkins, Isaac Julien, and Tavares Strachan.[76]

In the example of Suzanne Jackson in 1960s and 1970s, in both her gallery and art practices, we can trace the archetypal openness that the West Coast represented. Through Jackson's connections to the LA-based Ankrum Gallery, we can also locate the continuing relationship of African Americans to the mainstream exhibitionary complex in the United States.

COMMERCIAL AND NONPROFIT LOS ANGELES

Suzanne Jackson was a major presence at Ankrum Gallery in the 1970s. But she was not the only African American artist showcased there. Of the commercial galleries on the important La Cienega strip during this period, Ankrum truly extended itself to African American artists. Established in 1960 by Joan Ankrum and in business for thirty years, the gallery began showing black artists almost immediately.[77] Ankrum's records from the 1960s reveal a vigorous market for the early prints of Betye Saar and John Riddle. Bernie Casey was another gallery mainstay. Dan Concholar exhibited there, as did Bay Area artist Joe Overstreet and a young Portland-based Robert Colescott. Samella Lewis presented her work at Ankrum and was also involved with the gallery on the curatorial side. *The Art of African Peoples*, on view in February and March 1973, featured sculptures and masks from West and Central Africa. Drawn from local private collections, the show was a collaboration between Ankrum and one of Lewis's many publishing entities, Multi-Cultural Productions, which produced the accompanying catalogue.[78]

Other Los Angeles galleries began to add African Americans to their rosters in the 1960s: the painter Marvin Harden at Ceeje, Daniel LaRue Johnson at Rolf Nelson, Charles White at Heritage.[79] Only Ankrum Gallery made the commitment to show more than a token presence. Neither of the two major galleries that were part of Los Angeles's rise as an art center—Ferus and Dwan—paid much attention to African American artists. While Ferus included women in its roster, which was fairly revolutionary for the time, it seems not to have considered African Americans. Dwan, on the other hand, did open its roster, if minimally, to artists of color.

Virginia Dwan started her gallery in 1960, the same year Joan Ankrum opened hers. Like Ferus, Dwan Gallery initially focused on mixed-media work but had a more international focus, showing French New Realists, such as Arman, Niki de Saint Phalle, and Yves Klein, as well as Robert Rauschenberg and Larry Rivers, and eventually New York minimalism in the practice of Carl Andre, Robert Grosvenor, and Sol LeWitt.[80] In the gallery's first year, it presented works by Japanese American painter Matsumi Kanemitsu and a few years later Arakawa (1964). The sprawling *Boxes* show of 1964 featured thirty-five artists, including usual suspects Lucas Samaras and Larry Bell but also adding Edmund Bereal, Daniel LaRue Johnson, and Ron Miyashiro. The last three had all attended Chouinard Art Institute. Bereal in particular was associated with the "boys' club" that emerged from Chouinard and came to represent this Los Angeles era, including Ed Ruscha, Joe Goode, Larry Bell, and Llyn Foulkes.[81]

Johnson and Bereal, in particular, were identified in general discussions of West Coast assemblage. Johnson's work appeared in *Directions in Collage: Artists in California* (1962) at the Pasadena Art Museum, and in the California Annual of 1963 he was singled out as a significant talent to watch—as were Richard Pettibone and Dennis Hopper—for his black-box works.[82] Incorporating fragmented doll parts and other black-lacquered objects on a black ground, these assemblages, such as *Untitled*, 1961, also examined the violence against civil rights activists that was becoming increasingly visible in the national and international media. Such pieces also take on the complexities of black as both color and social signifier explored by others, including the Bay Area's Raymond Saunders, in particular his polemical pamphlet *Black Is a Color*, 1967, and later Fred Eversley, as in his large resin disk *Untitled*, 1976.

Both Bereal and Miyashiro appear in the infamous poster for the *War Babies* show at Henry Hopkins's Huysman Gallery in 1961. Each of four figures—and exhibiting artists—holds an item stereotypically emblematic of his ethnicity or religion: Bereal, a slice of watermelon; Miyashiro, a bowl and chopsticks; the Jewish artist Larry Bell, a bagel; and Catholic artist Joe Goode, a can of herring. The outcry against this show and its censorship caused the gallery to close after a year in operation. Huysman had made an overture to artists of color only to be shuttered for its efforts. Nevertheless, Hopkins rebounded as a curator at the new Los Angeles County Museum of Art, which opened in 1965.

In the museum and nonprofit world of Los Angeles, African American artists began to do a bit better in the 1960s. As institutions expanded their representational profiles, they opened themselves up to new democratic vistas and identities, in the process producing space for citizens who had been previously overlooked.

While the Pasadena Art Museum (PAM) played a significant role in the lives of black artists, once again they were primarily workers, not practitioners. This was *not*, however, during the golden years of Walter Hopps's association with the institution—first as an informal adviser, then as curator and later director from 1960 to 1967. Instead, John Outterbridge worked at PAM in the late 1960s as a preparator and museum educator. It was there in 1970 that Outterbridge met Mark di Suvero, who was installing a site piece. PAM had been established in 1924, and an important bequest of German avant-garde paintings in 1953 marked the museum as a home for the modern. Its other programs were also remarkable: a junior museum, established in 1947, that offered classes in visual and performing arts for children; an experimental music series; and a place for performance art in the 1960s and 1970s. PAM employed Senga Nengudi in its famed youth program, and during that tenure she soaked up performance art.[83] In the early 1960s when African American artists were hardly seen or heard, Melvin Edwards's exhibitions at the Los Angeles County Museum of Art and the Santa Barbara Museum (both in 1965) were phenomenal accomplishments. Other LA museums began to follow suit.

The Dickson Art Center at UCLA opened its 1966–67 season in a new building and to much acclaim, with the exhibition *The Negro in American Art*. It began with Robert Scott Duncanson's *Blue Hole, Flood Waters, Little Miami River*, 1851, an example of Hudson River School sublime, and ended with the immense canvas panel of Sam Gilliam's nonobjective *Urge*, 1966. The show was national in scope, yet highlighted LA artists, opening as it did a year after the vivid rebellion in Watts. Fruitful collaboration with the university's extension program brought a roster of exciting speakers and performers to the campus, including poet Gwendolyn Brooks, composer Duke Ellington, art historian James Porter (also the exhibition catalogue essayist), and musician Randy Weston.[84] *The Negro in American Art* represented perhaps the first such artistic framing on the UCLA campus, demonstrating the use value of black artists for American museums in this era. While local cultural spaces such as the Watts Towers Art Center pumped resources and dollars into neighborhoods, mainstream museums produced exhibition spaces that connected citizens to broader narratives of national belonging and achievement. Objects were used to win hearts and minds and ultimately to envision a civic order, mobilizing a vision of a progressive American culture.[85]

However, it was arguably the Los Angeles County Museum of Art (LACMA) that made the most inroads in presentations with African and African American content. As with many cultural (and other) institutions across the country, this was certainly a response to the social climate and to African Americans' greater demands for full access.

The first exhibition that can be considered a part of this constellation of projects was *Sculpture of Black Africa: The Paul Tishman Collection*, which opened in the fall of 1968. The show featured almost two hundred selections of stunning objects hailing from Mali to Madagascar. The substantial catalogue was written by Roy Sieber and Arnold Rubin, scholars at the forefront of changing Western understanding of African art. Nevertheless, the initial reception to the presentation was apparently tepid, something that did not thrill lender Paul Tishman, a New York real estate developer. Evidently displeased that not enough black people were attending, Tishman requested that LACMA take some action. The museum went to its largely African American security detail, who were given a budget and took up the charge to create programming; they knew how to connect with this audience, what radio, periodical and other media outlets would reach black Los Angeles. The result was a massive one-day Black Culture Festival held during the December holiday season, a gala with live music, dance, and a fashion show of African designs. The evening's emcee was Hollywood star Ivan Dixon; he was joined by a number of college homecoming queens (styled in African dress) who circulated throughout the museum as additional hosts for the affair. Tours of the Tishman Collection, led by the security guards, took place throughout the night. In the end, a staggering four thousand people were thought to have visited LACMA that day.[86]

Paul Tishman initially "arranged a private showing and lecture for the museum's black personnel" of the exhibition "because of the cultural significance he felt the collection" offered, encouraging them to get black communities through LACMA's doors.[87] Yet as longtime LACMA employee and cultural activist Cecil Fergerson surmised, this was only because the exhibition did not initially attract much attention from visitors or press. As Fergerson remarked, "I think that, had white people flooded to the exhibit, Tishman wouldn't have cared less about whether the black people came to see it or not."[88]

In the 1970s African American artists finally got a second showing at LACMA; the first had been some thirty-five years earlier with the weeklong exhibit of sculpture by Beulah Woodard at its earlier incarnation as the Los Angeles County Museum. *Three Graphic Artists* (1971) brought art world legend Charles White together with up-and-comers David Hammons and Timothy Washington. Organized by Ebria Feinblatt, head of the department of prints and drawings, and departmental assistant Joseph E. Young, this was the only one of four black-themed LACMA shows that relied on in-house curators.[89]

Three Graphic Artists offered an expansive take on the idea of medium—

"new ways of gravure," as Feinblatt defined it—moving from White's traditional processes of linocut and drawings in ink and charcoal to Hammons's seminal body prints and Washington's engravings on aluminum.[90] The pithy catalogue is illuminating in its revelation of each artist's technique within the graphic form: White's scrubbing into his paper surface with various tools; the detailed articulation of Hammons's body-print method; the constructedness of Washington's aluminum plates. Besides situating their works solidly within the centuries-long history of Western printmaking, interviews with each artist interspersed throughout the text gave the show a contemporary edge. Washington, for instance, explained why he worked directly with the "cold and hard" metal of the aluminum rather than print from it: it was a result of his learning that he had been "reclassified" for Selective Service (the draft) as 1-A, or unrestricted; these, then, were antiwar pieces.[91] LACMA purchased at least one work from each of the artists for its collection, in the process benefiting local galleries like Brockman and Heritage.[92]

The following year the museum presented *Los Angeles, 1972: A Panorama of Black Artists* (fig. 3.8), a group show of some fifty contemporary practitioners. *Panorama* was an invitational exhibition, open to all whose work fit the advertised parameters and who carried their pieces into LACMA for consideration in November 1971.[93] The sole juror was African American art historian Carroll Greene Jr., a highly accomplished curator and scholar who had worked for the Smithsonian organizing *The Art of Henry O. Tanner* (1969), and for the Museum of Modern Art, putting together *Romare Bearden: The Prevalence of Ritual* (1971).[94] Given such experience, Greene was certainly poised to present African American artists at another hallowed American art institution. In his brief catalogue introduction, he defined his project, in part, as introducing new artists and representations to the museumgoing public and addressing the problem of "obscurity" for a range of African American creators. His selections, he maintained, reflected a current in American art that had national and historical precedent: "Black Americans today are insisting on the 'black image' in art (the way Americans insisted on portraiture during the seventeenth and eighteenth centuries) because this image has so obviously been absent in any, other than disparaging, forms."[95]

The last very visible project that LACMA undertook in the 1970s involving African American artists was the large historical exhibition *Two Centuries of Black American Art* (1976). It was groundbreaking, providing a thorough, scholarly, and much-needed context for the contemporary art scene, moving from an eighteenth-century crafts and decorative arts heritage to twentieth-century abstractions in painting and sculpture. It reminded the public that

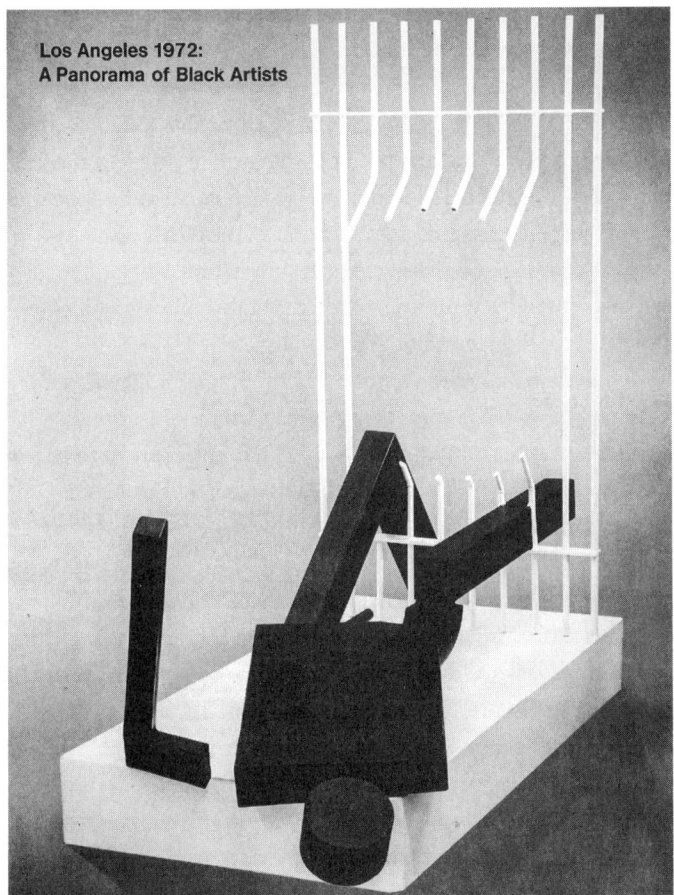

FIG. 3.8 Exhibition catalogue for *Los Angeles, 1972: A Panorama of Black Artists* at the Los Angeles County Museum of Art, 1972. On the cover: *There's More at Stake Here Than Just Attica*, c. 1971, by John Riddle. Courtesy Brockman Gallery Archives.

people of African descent in the United States had been around and creative for hundreds of years and that amazingly, given their circumstances for much of that time, they had made some beautiful things. Again, LACMA asked an outside expert to put the show together: the renowned professor, artist, and curator David C. Driskell, then chair of the art department at Fisk University. The show traveled extensively and was a huge success; its catalogue often served as a key text in courses on African American artists that were beginning to be taught at this time.[96]

There had been endeavors earlier to create black art historical overviews at world's fairs as well as other venues, but never before by a major American museum.[97] UCLA's *The Negro in American Art*, a decade prior, had presented several nineteenth-century works while focusing primarily on contemporary Los Angeles artists. In that instance, Dickson Art Center director and exhibition curator Frederick Wight had made a bold decision to privilege the current scene, especially those artists identified with Noah Purifoy and the Watts Towers Art Center who had reclaimed the remains of the rebellion as art. The context for *Two Centuries*—and the sweep of its project from 1750 to 1950—was American history itself, coming as it did during the country's bicentennial and Americans' contemplation of their own legacy.

While Driskell drew criticism for, among other reasons, ending his survey just shy of the contemporary period, the show nevertheless drew praise for uncovering an African American art history that had previously been barely discernible.[98] More than a few critics were captivated by the nineteenth-century works of Edmonia Lewis, Robert Scott Duncanson, and Henry O. Tanner.[99]

In a stunning interview for the *New York Times* just after the exhibition opened in Brooklyn, Driskell said his concept revealed "a body of work which showed first of all that blacks had been stable participants in American visual culture for more than 200 years" and, in fact, "had been the backbone" of U.S. creative cultures.[100] At the same time, he framed the term "black art" itself as primarily utilitarian. In doing so, Driskell responded to numerous critics who disparaged African American artists for not demonstrating some palpable, perceivable, cogent aesthetic sign that was identifiable as racial: "I have no dislike for the term black art. . . . I think it's a sociological concept. I don't think it's anything stylistic. We don't go around saying white art, but I think it's very important for us to keep saying black art until it becomes recognized as American art."[101]

Though these four exhibitions at LACMA between 1968 and 1976 had their drawbacks, they did move the dialogue forward on what constituted art and art history, who had access to cultural institutions and culture generally, and who had the right to frame cultural narratives. Of course, museums like LACMA did not just arrive effortlessly at such changes in policy and intellectual culture. Similar to comparable East Coast institutions—the Whitney Museum of American Art and the Museum of Modern Art, most prominently—they were forced to make such radical shifts.[102]

Like the LA-based Art West Associated before it and the Black Emergency Cultural Coalition in New York, the Black Arts Council (BAC, 1968–74) served in part as a watchdog organization, the thorn in the side of major art insti-

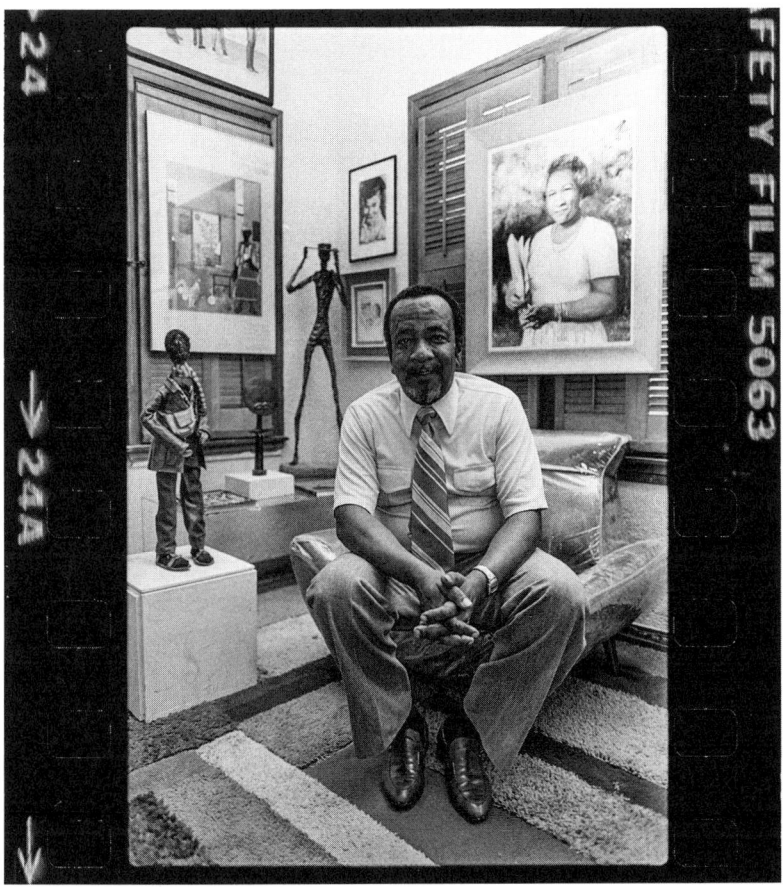

FIG. 3.9 Gary Friedman, *Cecil Fergerson, at home with his collection*, date unknown. Los Angeles Times Photographic Archives (Collection 1429). UCLA Library Special Collections, Charles E. Young Research Library, UCLA.

tutions, demanding that they be more fully representative of the city they served. Cecil Fergerson (fig. 3.9), one of the BAC's founding members, had begun working at the Los Angeles County Museum as a janitor in 1948. By the mid-1960s he had risen through the ranks to the position of preparator. With the climate of social change alive in the United States, the rising prominence of the Black Arts Movement, and growing consciousness about the importance of culture, Fergerson and BAC cofounder Claude Booker, another LACMA preparator, "both realized how important arts were to people. Up until that point, I just looked at art as a [nice club] for the rich. Because you have no point of reference—right?—being black. No black museums. No black people in the collection."[103]

In an extensive oral history, Fergerson explained how LACMA's labor hierarchy functioned during his thirty-eight-year career.[104] On his first day as a janitor, he was given some rules to live by if he wanted to hold on to his job: "No. 1: keep a broom in your hands at all times and walk fast. No. 2: always keep a white man white. Meaning—always make a white man feel superior."[105] Fergerson outlined the way the largely black workforce of janitors was able to slowly slide into the position of "museum helper," a purportedly lower-skilled (and lower-paid) classification of preparator, who until the 1960s donned white jackets and acted as servers at openings. His narrative demonstrates the labor inequity and growing impoverishment that led to Watts and other uprisings, and the role of these events to disrupt and resist. As Kimberlé Crenshaw and Gary Peller report, "The language of insurrection conceives of the uprising as a communal response to a much larger set of issues of social power."[106]

As a preparator, Fergerson was the "arms and legs" of museum curators, but he also gained much information about art that came his way, because "being black, they never thought I wanted to use that [information]. I was like a stool sitting beside the door, right? They had no qualms about saying certain things in front of me."[107] While white preparators made the leap to curatorial assistants, Fergerson eventually had to sue LACMA to bring about his own promotion in 1972.[108] However, he also acknowledged that the institutional culture began to change in the 1960s as a generation of cultural workers and artists more aligned with "beatniks, hippies, and flower children" and appreciative of black culture through their love of jazz began to take control.[109] Edward Kienholz, whose 1966 solo show at LACMA caused such controversy, attests to the same camaraderie within the museum at that moment, acknowledging the importance of the black preparators and security guards.[110]

The BAC was formed in the wake of LACMA's 1968 presentation of the Tishman Collection and the successful programs that introduced thousands to the museum. From that point on, Fergerson, Booker, and a growing list of BAC members continued to lobby LACMA for change.[111] With the success of the Black Culture Festival in December 1968, the BAC started pushing for a museum lecture series, which came to fruition in fall 1969. They included presentations by prominent area artists such as Charles White, Bernie Casey, and John Riddle. Another panel considered the relationship between art and music. Artists Arenzo Smith, John Outterbridge, Dan Concholar, and Gloria Bohanon were joined by a live performance from the Curtis Amy–George Bohanon Sextet. One program purportedly broke museum attendance records with 750 attendees. Samella Lewis also gave a talk, titled "The Relationship of the Black Artist in Our Society," after which she was hired by LACMA's education department.[112]

The BAC's efforts led to additional exhibitions involving African American artists at LACMA in the 1970s. This was clearly evidence of Watts-era activism and cultural workers' imbrication in an expansive climate of political action. But initial attempts to represent African American artists encountered problems. Like similar projects on the East Coast—for example, *Harlem on My Mind* (1969) at the Metropolitan Museum of Art and *Contemporary Black Artists in America* (1971) at the Whitney Museum of American Art—black cultural workers and activists who had been pressuring for change, and in some cases had been (mostly informally) consulting on these projects, finally had their fill of institutional inertia and cultural supremacy and rejected these faulty partnerships. They picketed, and in the Whitney case, artists withdrew from the exhibition.

At LACMA, BAC members—whose direct activism had made *Three Graphic Artists* happen—protested once the show was open, because Charles White had been paired with the younger David Hammons and Timothy Washington. White, they insisted, was of such stature that he deserved a solo show at the institution and one in a larger space.[113]

Space was the contested issue with *Los Angeles, 1972: A Panorama of Black Artists*. It was held in LACMA's rental gallery, which was not only small but also located in the basement. It raised the specter of liminality, an inheritance that went back to the Negro Buildings at world's fairs and shows in the children's wings and foyers of American museums. The Whitney Museum's exhibitions of African American artists during this period—amazingly, some of the first ever at this museum dedicated to American art—were almost exclusively in its smallest first-floor gallery, off its lobby. Such placement raised the specter of segregation on the one hand, but even more visibly the notion of inequality. Artists grumbled. At least one put her feelings down on paper. Suzanne Jackson, then based in San Francisco, wrote to Samella Lewis, "I am still not interested in any basement shows for black artists. It is insulting for any artist. If the entire Museum was a basement that would surely be a different story—if the politics were straight. There are always so many 'ifs.' Anyway not one of us is too old to have to begin to make compromises at this point. Life is really more beautiful if we stand up consistently for our ideals."[114]

The BAC, acknowledged as a copartner for the project even by LACMA itself, generally stood behind *Panorama*, however, even responding to William Wilson's caustic review in a letter to the *Los Angeles Times*.[115] In the black press, the concept of the rental gallery was not seen negatively but rather as an opportunity, a space where unknown artists could gain greater visibility and where those who wanted to purchase or even rent works could do so and try art out.[116]

By the time of *Two Centuries of Black American Art*, Claude Booker had died and the BAC had disbanded. Interestingly, Booker (and thus the BAC) was given a fond remembrance in the exhibition catalogue acknowledgments and credited with the initial idea for the show. Fergerson, however, who was alive and well and a LACMA curatorial assistant, was shut out from any role on the organizing team.[117]

Scholar Bridget R. Cooks's research on *Two Centuries* reveals other institutional discomforts with the show. Contemporary art curator Maurice Tuchman refused to attend David Driskell's initial presentation of his ideas in 1974. The following year two curators actually resigned (from the areas of American art and education, respectively) rather than participate in this form of bicentennial celebration. Then there was the controversy surrounding the nineteenth-century painter and naturalist John James Audubon. Driskell's research revealed that Audubon, born in Haiti, was of African descent; the curator thus included his print *Virginian Partridge*, 1830, in the show. That persuaded an Audubon descendant to threaten legal action against Driskell and the Brooklyn Museum. Yet, as Cooks recounts, the family member, "Walter Audubon, John James's great-great-great-grandson," later ceased his intimidation, admitting in private correspondence with Driskell "that he knew the Audubons had black ancestry, but was afraid his pregnant wife would leave him for fear that their child might look black."[118]

Like many of the exhibitions focusing on the creations of African American artists discussed in this chapter, *Two Centuries of Black American Art* drew some of the largest crowds LACMA had ever seen. The exhibition's official opening date, September 30, 1976, was proclaimed "Two Centuries of Black American Art Day" by Los Angeles mayor Tom Bradley (fig. 3.10), the first black man to lead the city.[119]

While there were problems with aspects of each of these exhibitions at LACMA between 1968 and 1976, the institution did some things differently, and correctly, compared to its East Coast counterparts. In some cases it found and hired outside scholars and curators known for their expertise in the art of African America. That Carroll Greene and David Driskell were African Americans themselves was also crucial, an approach that the Whitney and Metropolitan refused to take with similar projects. LACMA also added African Americans to its board of trustees in the 1970s, a move that supported such issues on other institutional levels.[120]

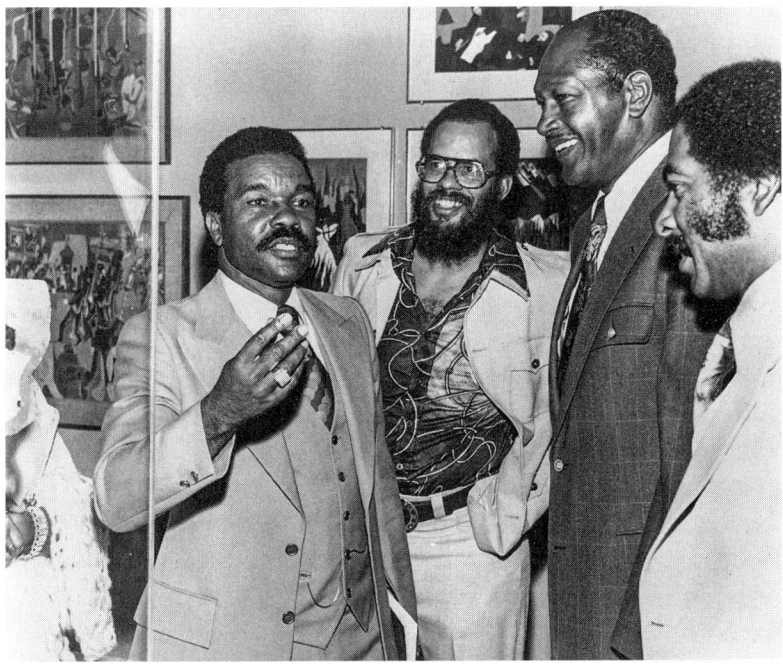

FIG. 3.10 David C. Driskell, Alonzo Davis, and Mayor Tom Bradley, probably at the exhibition *Two Centuries of Black American Art*, curated by Driskell, 1976. Courtesy Brockman Gallery Archives.

However, it remains true that grassroots efforts by the museum workforce kindled and kept the idea of African American representation at LACMA alive. This was also a change from the East Coast, where pressure came from groups of artists and cultural workers *outside* the institutional structure. LACMA is a city institution, and the security guards and preparators there were municipal workers. This gave them greater job protection, as evinced by Cecil Fergerson suing, and winning, his case for promotion. Government and municipal jobs were also what opened up to southern migrants after those of the war industry in the first part of the century began to dry up. Claude Booker (born San Antonio, Texas) and Cecil Fergerson (born Boley, Oklahoma, a storied black town) were both part of that generation whose impact was felt nationwide.

While much of the BAC's focus was on correcting LACMA's oversights, the group also involved itself in the larger community. Fergerson and Booker lent their installation skills to a full gamut of organizations and projects throughout the city. In doing so they offered people tools that would effect a broader sense of aesthetic ownership and control.

With materials (and overtime) donated by LACMA and the Junior Chamber of Commerce, the two preparators created modular structures that could be assembled to host exhibitions almost anywhere. The BAC installed the visual arts portion of the Watts Summer Festival between 1970 and 1974, although Fergerson had helped out since the event's inception in 1966. They put on exhibitions at tennis courts, worked with prisons, and created shows that traveled to financial institutions. Black student unions also engaged the BAC's services to create a black visual presence on college and university campuses. The group helped hang shows at emerging black-owned galleries such as Gallery 32. The gallery in turn opened its space for the organization's meetings and at least once for a fund-raising exhibition.[121]

Booker and Fergerson, the energy behind the BAC, also each pursued other work as art consultants. Before his death Booker advised and provided artwork for *Black Omnibus*, a WNET television series hosted by actor James Earl Jones. Taped in 1972 but airing in 1973, it interspersed interviews and live performances, including a number of musicians who performed at LA's Wattstax Festival.[122] Fergerson took his curatorial skills to community arts institutions beginning in the late 1970s, while he was still employed by LACMA, creating shows for the William Grant Still Community Arts Center and Watts Tower Arts Center. He retired from LACMA in 1985 and became director of the art gallery at Los Angeles Southwest College in 1989.

SAMELLA LEWIS INK

Artist and academic Samella Sanders Lewis arrived in Southern California in the mid-1960s with a PhD from Ohio State University and more than fifteen years of teaching under her belt. Born in New Orleans, she trained first at Dillard University and then at Hampton Institute (later Hampton University) with Elizabeth Catlett in the 1940s.[123] After receiving her doctorate in 1951, she went to work at two historically black universities, Morgan State University in Baltimore, and then Florida Agricultural & Mechanical University (FAMU) in Tallahassee. Her academic career in the South lasted for much of the 1950s.[124] As chair of the fine arts department at FAMU she put the wheels in motion for the creation of the National Conference of Artists, an organization of African American creators. Her participation in civil rights activities during her time in Florida eventually brought harassment, including from the Ku Klux Klan. Concerned for the safety of her family, Lewis accepted a position at State University of New York, Plattsburg, in 1958; she remained on its faculty for a decade.[125]

After traveling to Southern California for research, Lewis eventually ended up taking positions at California State University, Long Beach, and then California State University, Dominguez Hills. By 1968 she had joined LACMA as coordinator of education. Her hiring was the result of agitation by groups such as Art West Associated and the BAC, which sought greater visibility for African Americans in this large municipal art center that their tax dollars went to fund but that provided them with little access and even less inspiration.[126]

Lewis was hired by LACMA to address such issues. In the fall of 1969, along with the BAC, she hosted a series of highly successful public events at the museum.[127] In addition, Lewis made LACMA's children's programs more diverse in terms of their curriculum and student body.[128]

Frustration with the pace of change at the museum led her to resign in fall 1970. In this era of activism and protest, Lewis did not leave LACMA rapidly or quietly. Instead a cycle of negotiations—similar to those staged in New York between groups such as the Black Emergency Cultural Coalition (BECC) and the Whitney Museum of American Art—pressured LACMA and attempted to come to some agreement about a more diverse cultural profile. Similar to the Museum of Modern Art, the Metropolitan Museum of Art, and the Whitney, LACMA was hit with protests following Lewis's resignation, actions that continued into the following year.[129] In 1971, the museum began to address the gaps in its exhibition programs with such shows as *Three Graphic Artists*.

Lewis's disenchantment with museum institutional culture led her to develop groundbreaking projects, which would distinguish her as a major force in African American art in the twentieth century. As one reporter noted, "She got tired of picketing and carrying signs, trying to make museums open up" and decided to create her own opportunities.[130] These projects—several galleries, books and films, a magazine, and a museum—all came to fruition in the decade between 1969 and 1978 and flowered in the California landscape. Lewis was emblematic of the power of the woman and migrant in the city, inheriting that force from those who came before her. The metropolis was made over in the image of the black female migrant as women changed the geography of the nation and left an imprint on urban public spaces.[131]

Lewis opened her first independent commercial space around 1972, partnering with Bernie Casey. Originally called Multi-Cul, it was located at 1019 Redondo Boulevard near Olympic; Betye Saar had an early solo show there featuring her sculptural boxes.[132] Later Lewis moved to a location on 5271 W. Pico Boulevard and changed the name to The Gallery; this was the place where Houston Conwill performed one version of his JuJu project. Lewis eventually turned her attention to building a collecting institution, forming the Museum of African American Art in 1975. For a while the gallery and museum shared the same building. Ultimately Lewis relinquished the gallery to focus on the museum, leaving what was by then known as Gallery Tanner in the care of Joyce Thigpen.[133]

In its initial phase, as Lewis drummed up support, the Museum of African American Art primarily presented exhibitions off-site. The parks, libraries, airports, banks, senior citizens' residences, and colleges mirrored the spaces carved out by self-made curators earlier in the twentieth century.[134] Scholar Mary Jane Hewitt eventually joined Lewis in this endeavor. In their quest to move out of a commercial storefront and into a building that could truly house a museum and collecting institution, Lewis and Hewitt pressed municipal authorities and local politicians for support and space for years. In the early 1980s, the May Department Stores Company offered up the third floor of its branch on Crenshaw Boulevard. The proposal was enthusiastically supported by Councilwoman Pat Russell, who believed that the museum could be part of the cultural and economic revitalization of her district. In its eighth year of existence, the museum moved to the May Company (now Macy's), where it is still located.[135]

In addition to running galleries and a museum, working with artists, and organizing exhibitions in Los Angeles and elsewhere, Lewis published books and related material. She also produced several films and made her own art. The entrepreneurial spirit that allowed her to balance all this was aided by her investment in collaboration.

The first of the two *Black Artists on Art* volumes (plate 20) was published in 1969; it had been hatched somewhat earlier by Lewis, Ruth Waddy, and E. J. Montgomery in the latter's Bay Area living room.[136] It featured introductory texts by Lewis and Waddy that reflected the rhetoric of the Black Arts Movement and attested to the unique vision of African American artists and the need for the mainstream to expand notions of aesthetic beauty. Each artist was represented by a brief statement and at least one image. Many of the contributors were from California; in effect, the book reproduced their networks from the 1950s to the contemporary moment. In Lewis's eyes, the publication legitimized their work, demonstrating that they were worthy of exhibitions, jobs, and general support by the larger culture. A second volume of *Black Artists on Art* appeared in 1971. Both were self-published under Lewis's Contemporary Crafts imprint. Together they highlighted the work of almost 150 contemporary African American artists, an amazing number given Lewis's resources and the one or two figures often showcased in mainstream contexts (even today).¹³⁷

To keep the ideas in the books up to date, Lewis, Val Spaulding, and Jan Jemison launched the magazine *Black Art: An International Quarterly* in 1975. This first periodical devoted to African American artists and those from African Diaspora changed its name to *International Review of African American Art* in 1984; it is still in print.¹³⁸ In an opening statement from the first issue produced in the fall of 1976, the editors provide a window onto their motivating ideas, colored certainly by Black Arts Movement semantics around renovation in its radical reconsideration of visuality and aesthetics. "Black peoples," they insisted, are possessed of "a living art." These modalities do not simply register "technique" or formal style; rather, they provide "a matrix of joy and sorrow and pain and fulfillment expressed through myriad paths of feeling and visualization." Such global "historical and cultural experiences" become "resources for human development."¹³⁹ The editors' use of a plural form of address reveals that they embraced the African Diaspora from the outset, a notion signaled by the moniker "International Quarterly" in the periodical's title. Indeed, articles in the premiere issue—including "African Influences on Black American Art," by scholar Floyd Coleman, and "Afro-Brazilian Art: A Liberating Spirit," by artist Abdias do Nascimento—easily make the case. Elizabeth Catlett, mentor and enthusiastic supporter of *Black Art*, contributed her *Mother and Child*, 1971, to the cover (fig. 3.11). Inside, a section that focused on her work included a foldout offset print, suitable for framing.¹⁴⁰ Presenting essays on music and theater as well, this inaugural issue offered a broad sweep on the landscape of black arts. Such topics would continue to be addressed, but the journal's emphasis remained on the visual arts.

Spaulding (the editor-in-chief), Jemison (the managing editor), and Lewis (the art editor) used their own funds to launch *Black Art*, soliciting backing from friends across the country. Gallerist Merton Simpson contributed, and archivist and artist Camille Billops held a fund-raiser. Along with grants from the National Endowment for the Arts and assorted corporations, they received in-kind support from printers in the form of paper and other materials. Any unsold copies were often donated to public schools and prisons.¹⁴¹ The journal also promoted Lewis's other ventures, such as her note cards, print projects, and galleries (fig. 3.12). Others, like Brockman Gallery, took out ads as well.¹⁴²

In 1978, Lewis transformed her various lectures on African American artists into a book called *Art: African American*. This survey joined only a few

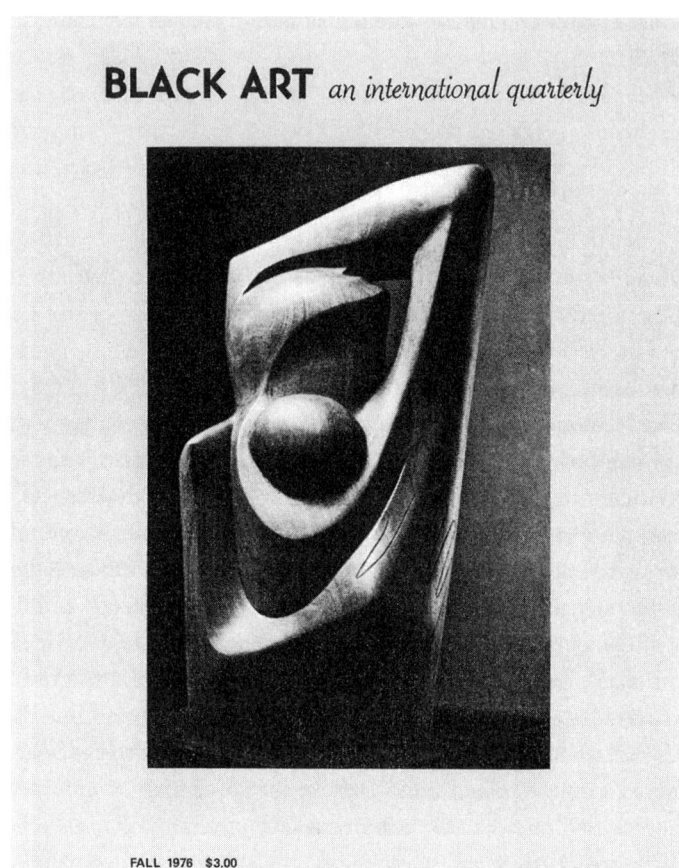

FIG. 3.11 *Black Art: An International Quarterly* 1, no. 1, 1976. On the cover: *Mother and Child*, 1971, by Elizabeth Catlett.

others: James Porter's *Modern Negro Art* (1943), Cedric Dover's *American Negro Art* (1960), and Elsa Honig Fine's *The Afro-American Artist: A Search for Identity* (1973). Until the mid-1990s Lewis's book was the standard academic text for introducing new students of all ages to the field.[143]

Art: African American begins with African American craft heritage of the seventeenth century and ends with street art of the 1970s. Graced by a foreword from Lewis's friend Jacob Lawrence, it is a compensatory history, meant to fill art historical caesuras. Publishing the book a scant two years after the launch of *Black Art*, Lewis continued the militant narrative of the Black Arts Movement in her introduction: "Today African-American artists are energetic participants in a cultural revolution. Driven by needs that are both so-

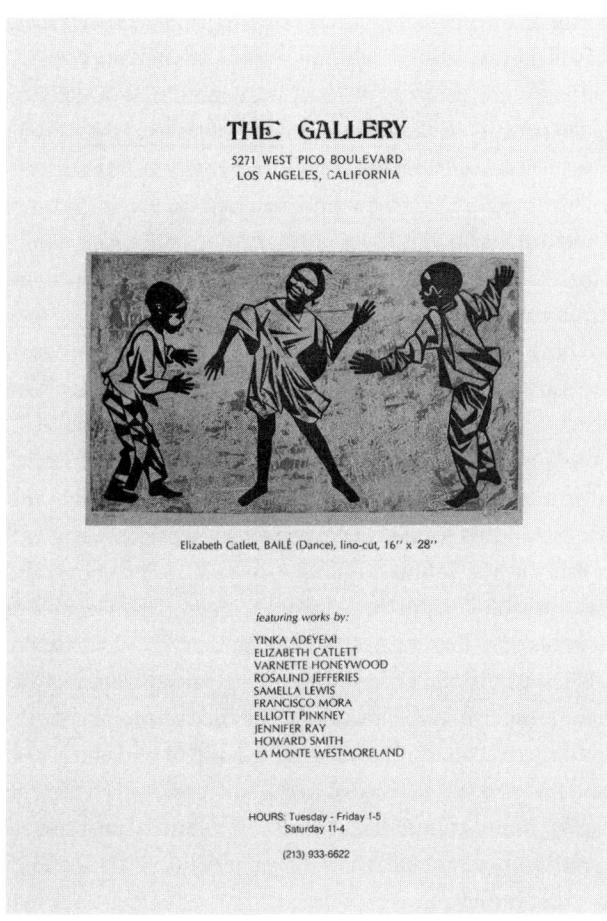

FIG. 3.12 Advertisement in *Black Art: An International Quarterly* 1, no. 1, 1976.

cial and aesthetic, the African-American artist searches for cultural identity, for self-discovery, and for self-understanding."[144]

These artists, Lewis insisted, had their own standards, interests, and aesthetics; they were "responding to their own" lives.[145] In effect, this was a liberatory narrative of insurrection and self-determination. For artists to stay relevant, however, they had to understand their importance as community resources and their responsibility to enhance the quality of the black environment. At the same time, Lewis argued, there must be a diversity of approaches to art making, opening a broader discussion about more varied practices, including abstraction, conceptualism, and performance. In subsequent years, Lewis brought out other important books—*The Art of Elizabeth*

Catlett (1984), published under her Hancraft Studios imprint, and *Barthé: His Life in Art* (2009), issued by another independent press, Unity Works.

Contemporary Crafts and Hancraft Studios were more than just book-publishing outfits. These were entities that encompassed Lewis's larger vision of disseminating imagery centered on black life and by artists of African descent worldwide. This included printed matter, such as books, magazines, prints, portfolios, and note cards, but also a wider array of media, such as film and slides. In this manner Lewis wielded all aspects of the exhibitionary complex, controlling the array of representational power at her disposal.

Contemporary Crafts was born in 1969 with the publication of *Black Artists on Art* and had offices at 5616 San Vicente Boulevard. (Later, with the opening of Multi-Cul Gallery, its base of operations moved to Redondo Boulevard.) Lewis saw this not as a typical retail operation but as a method of distribution for things she produced. Ever the collaborator, Lewis was joined in this endeavor by her sister, Mildred Sanders, who served as business manager.[146] An early brochure lists the first volume of *Black Artists on Art*, two films, and several slide sets as available for purchase through mail order. The sets of slides had titles like "Black Artists on Art," "Contemporary Black Artists of California," and "Black Craftsmen of California" and ranged from forty to one hundred images. From this, it is evident that the slide sets were conceptualized from Lewis's own research and extended the reach of her scholarship in different ways and through various media. In the late 1980s, after letting go of her roles as gallerist, museum founder, and academic, Lewis ran a similar multimedia enterprise out of her home under the name Sanders Art Media.[147]

As a practicing artist herself, Lewis was attuned to the many ways that ideas and images could propagate. With the launch of Contemporary Crafts, Lewis began to make her own films. She produced three between 1969 and 1971 while she was also at work on the two volumes of *Black Artists on Art*. These were documentary shorts, about a half hour in length and shot in 16 mm. Each one follows artists in the studio, showing them at work, interviewing them within the filmic frame, and adding nondiegetic commentary (perhaps read from preexisting artist statements) about their philosophical approaches to art and art making and the role of "black art" and artists. The first project, *The Black Artists* (1969; also known as *Three Black Artists*), includes Lewis at work as a painter, along with William Pajaud and John Riddle. It is perhaps not so extraordinary that this film was released the same year as the first volume of *Black Artists on Art*. It extended the ideas of the book in a Hollywood-friendly medium and was another example of Lewis's efforts to control the full spectrum of representational options and outlets. It is also not a surprise that Lewis worked collaboratively with Paul E. Hickman, who is listed as the producer.

With the next two films Lewis took full control and is credited as the sole producer. *Bernie Casey, Black Artist* (1970), sheds light on the creative process of this multitalented and popular figure, an initial partner in Lewis's gallery endeavors. During the first four minutes of *John Outterbridge, Black Artist* (1971), the artist speaks to us from the stunning shores of a beautiful beach, where pieces of his sculpture are placed strategically in the sand. This is Los Angeles, we are reminded, with its surf, sand, sun, and stylish black artists. The film moves on to Outterbridge's outdoor studio, where he is at work on his *Containment* series, pieces both wall-bound and freestanding, sheet metal over wood. His incessant burring, sanding, welding, incising, and general obsession about the perfect surface demonstrates perhaps an unexpected link to California's Finish Fetish approach to minimalism.[148]

Though her 1969 film debut shows her creating an abstract canvas, Samella Lewis the painter is known primarily for her figurative work. She began drawing as a child to express feelings that were inexpressible in a segregated society: anger, rebellion, pain.[149] At times celebrated and encouraged as a young person for her talents, she found ways to gain more skills. As an undergraduate at Dillard University, she pursued a path of consistent professional art training with Elizabeth Catlett, which she continued at Hampton Institute and in her graduate studies at Ohio State University.[150] A linocut from the 1960s demonstrates how Lewis was able to link issues from her early life to late twentieth-century concerns. In *Field*, 1968, a powerful figure centered in a cultivated landscape raises a fist to a darkened sky, clearly connecting the work to contemporary revolution. The title *Field* and the setting are reminiscent of the South, whether the depiction is of sharecropping or earlier plantation slavery. Surely the reverberation between previous histories and her current context was not lost on Lewis. The figures in another linocut, *Migrants*, 1968, seem to be resting, stopping at a roadside clearing. The piece celebrates those who made the journey from the South during the Great Migration but also those who created new cultures in places like Los Angeles.

Lewis continued to be active as an artist in the 1960s and 1970s, locally and nationally.[151] Perhaps one of her best-known paintings is *Royal Sacrifice*, 1969, which appeared on the first edition of *Art: African American* (plate 21). It demonstrates similar tropes of moving across time. While the title recalls ancient eras and customs, the mother and child depicted have contemporary clothing and Afro hairstyles. A third figure is the grim reaper, who embraces the two others with a shrouded arm. The young mother holds her son by his shoulders, trying to keep him from his fate, yet her expression is one of resignation. This sentiment, of course, was widespread in the 1960s and 1970s, when young black people were being killed in their quest for social freedoms.

Incredibly, during this period Lewis continued to work full-time in academia. In 1970, she was hired as a professor of art history and humanities by Scripps College, part of the Claremont University Center (CUC), a consortium of colleges. There she focused not on African American artists but on the arts of Asia, Africa, and Native America. Such an academic concentration was typical of study earlier in the century, when these fields (along with pre-Columbian cultures) were joined together under the rubric of primitive art. As a member of CUC's black studies program, Lewis lectured on African American art and mentored students.[152] Additionally, CUC provided support for several of Lewis's projects, particularly the museum, magazine, and media programs.[153]

COLLECTING AND THE BLACK MUSEUM MOVEMENT

Samella Lewis, as we have seen, tried to make art available to black audiences in a variety of ways. She created opportunities for people to experience art and encouraged purchases by offering images in different formats, from inexpensive prints and note cards to original objects. Controlling representation and making culture available were core aspects of the Black Arts Movement, which touted the positive psychological effects associated with the consumption of black images. The key was not only for galleries and eventually African American museums to support black artists but to develop in individuals the desire and ability to collect art.

Yet it was hard to sustain a for-profit business this way; Lewis continued to work full-time as a college professor. In the Western tradition, monarchs and popes were the original patrons and collectors, followed by bankers and mercantile interests, and only much later by a middle-class clientele. For the most part, African Americans' economic position—and legal status—precluded such positions as supporters of the arts. Other galleries also struggled with profitability and sustainability. As discussed above, Brockman Gallery eventually established a nonprofit and grant-ready entity, Brockman Gallery Productions. Lewis's establishment of the Museum of African American Art was a different approach to the same problem. Just Above Midtown Gallery, which showed West Coast artists and similar work in New York, turned wholly nonprofit.

Yet black (and white) patrons did emerge. On the West Coast, black Hollywood stars were natural supporters of African American artists. As creative people, who may have made visual art themselves, they had grown creatively in the company of artists or at the very least understood the artistic process. In the 1960s, as the market for their performances in film and television grew, so did their incomes. Thus we see Harry Belafonte, Sidney Poitier, and Sammy Davis Jr. approaching art collecting wholeheartedly.[154] Bill Cosby, now known for his extensive art collection, started acquiring objects during this time. He had a keen eye for art by black practitioners, buying pieces from Brockman Gallery and Heritage Gallery, among others. As early as 1968 the actor boasted upward of a dozen pieces by Charles White alone. Over the years, some of Cosby's holdings appeared on his television sitcom *The Cosby Show*, 1984–92, including paintings by West Coast painter Varnette Honeywood.[155]

Even those without such global recognition bought art and maintained beautiful collections (plate 22). Marguerite Ray was a star of stage and screen beginning in the 1960s. She appeared in soap operas such as *Days of Our Lives*, detective dramas like *Ironside*, and the cult classic *Dynasty*. Perhaps her most high-profile turn on the small screen was on *Sanford* in the early 1980s. She played a wealthy Beverly Hills widow and Redd Foxx's love interest on this revival of *Sanford and Son*, the successful mid-1970s show about an LA junk dealer and his family. She was also a regular on the theater circuit, performing often at the Inner City Cultural Center, where she met Betye Saar, who designed for that organization in the 1970s. Ray participated in *Black Mirror*, the exhibition Saar and Samella Lewis curated for the Woman's Building in 1973, offering her views on the world of acting in one of the accompanying programs.[156]

The social and political environment of black consciousness in Los Angeles in this era produced other interesting collectors too. One was Stan Sanders. Born and raised in Watts, Sanders won national recognition when, in 1963, he became one of the earliest African American Rhodes Scholars.[157] From the largely white Whittier College, where he was student body president and majored in political science, he headed to Oxford University, earning a degree in English before returning to the United States and Yale Law School, bypassing offers from the National Football League and the Chicago Bears.[158] After two years in Europe, Sanders had arrived home to find a neighborhood that seemed unchanged by all the civil rights activity he had been reading about.[159] A week later the Watts Rebellion occurred, propelling him to join the Westminster Neighborhood Association in Watts, directing summer programs focused on employment, college readiness, and voter registration. He was active with the newly formed Police Malpractice Complaint Office, which investigated civilian charges of police brutality.[160] He became known for his legal activism, winning a case that challenged the University of California's unfair application of NCAA eligibility rules to black athletes and organizing a standing human rights forum for the Los Angeles County Bar Association.[161]

A Jordan High School alum, Sanders developed the first Watts Summer Festival in 1966. While the visual arts would become the "main attraction" at the festival, Sanders became even more involved after joining the Black Arts Council, brought in as the group's legal representative by Watts neighbor Cecil Fergerson.[162] In exchange for his pro bono support, Sanders asked that art be displayed in his offices, which Fergerson and Booker were happy to provide. Immersing himself in art activism and working directly with artists through the BAC, it was natural for Sanders's interests to expand to collecting.[163]

As journalist Kevin West points out, unlike the profiles of extreme wealth exhibited by prominent white West Coast collectors of a similar generation—the Norton Simons and Eli Broads—black collectors were solidly middle class. They included a segment of black LA professionals who perhaps could be considered a more traditional collector class: physicians. Among these was pediatrician Leon Banks, who grew up in Washington, DC, with the nation's public museums and began collecting while he was stationed in Europe in the air force. Moving to Los Angeles in the 1950s, he eventually bought work by local artists such as John Altoon and others with growing national reputations such as Robert Rauschenberg and Sam Francis. Banks was also active at LACMA and in the Black Arts Council. In some instances, he and others would trade medical services for art, which was useful for artists with young families, like Daniel LaRue Johnson, Melvin Edwards, and David Hammons. Of particular interest is how Banks and certain African American physicians in Los Angeles, such as radiologist Vaughn C. Payne Jr., inspired the next generation of art collectors. Another radiologist, V. Joy Simmons, was excited by LACMA's *Two Centuries of Black American Art* while she was in medical school. She considers Banks and Payne professional mentors but also supporters of her passion for art and the idea of black ownership of black culture; for them, collecting was part of what you did as a doctor.[164]

Banks was also active in the founding of the California African American Museum (CAAM) in the late 1970s. Together with Samella Lewis's Museum of African American Art, CAAM was part of what can be considered a black museum movement in the late twentieth century. Mabel Wilson has discussed the growing quest for institutional stability among champions of black artists. She sees such activity as building on activism from the 1940s (and even earlier) and a desire for permanent displays that could narrate racial progress and accomplishment. The ultimate goal was to marshal the exhibitionary complex in the service of the African American pride and psyche but also to proclaim the cultural gifts of black people far and wide and in perpetuity. Most of these institutions were founded and developed in African American communities, not necessarily by museum professionals. Margaret Burroughs's investment in documentation and exhibitions of black artists beginning in the 1940s led to the founding of Chicago's DuSable Museum of African American History in 1961. In 1963 the American Negro History Museum was established on Boston's Beacon Hill, and in 1965 Charles Wright held the first meeting to launch the International Afro-American Museum in Detroit. Wright, an activist and gynecologist, had participated in the Selma to Montgomery march with Martin Luther King Jr., administering to the injured. He eventually began the museum in his former home and office on Detroit's west side.[165]

While the earliest black museums highlighted the importance of African American and African diasporic history, art objects were a critical part of their curatorial narratives. In the late 1960s, art museums dedicated to the work of African Americans began to appear, such as the Studio Museum in Harlem and the Museum of the National Center of Afro-American Artists in Boston, both of which opened in 1968. As with the history-focused institutions, the art museums' goals included illuminating lost histories, changing the perception of African Americans among both local residents and the larger culture, and expanding the black public sphere into a permanent realm, all things that were the legacy of the earliest nineteenth-century black fair organizers, and what they pursued so fervently in the role of the exhibitionary complex.

When Golden State Life Insurance decided to expand its corporate headquarters, public relations director William Pajaud became even more ambitious about collecting art: "That's when somebody looked around and said, 'Hey fellow, we're in the life insurance business.' . . . I wanted [Golden State] to be the L.A. County Museum for Black Art, you know."[166] For Cecil Fergerson, places like Golden State, Watts Towers Art Center, and the William Grant Still Community Arts Center functioned as "museum-type" spaces by default, offering places not only to see works of art but to experience them in a historical, intellectual, and greater cultural context.[167]

A few months after the Watts Rebellion, Stan Sanders wrote an analysis for *The Nation*. The uprising, he opined, should be seen not as a local event but as one that foretold a change in black people and in America itself. No longer willing to be what Sanders considered passive figures, African Americans wielded revolt as one "weapon," albeit a violent one, in its arsenal against second-class citizenship. At the same time, Sanders argued, rebellion should be considered a sort of communication or language, an aspect of expression. It cleared a space for the something new that his generation desired, demanded, and worked tirelessly to achieve in the wake of the uprising. But that confidence and optimism about profound and lasting change was slowly eroded over the years as significant transformations in job availability and access to services, housing, and decent infrastructure did not come through for the community. Ultimately, for every dollar spent on education in Watts, two more were spent on policing. The brutality of the LAPD remained legendary even after the Watts Rebellion, when counterinsurgency became a "growth industry."[168] Frustrated, Sanders eventually left his position as a posh Beverly Hills lawyer and started his own firm focused on black businesses.[169]

Over the century a black counterpublic sphere wielded the exhibitionary complex with greater and sometimes lesser success, but moving ever forward with representational goals that could help achieve greater equality and freedom; it imagined a blueprint for a utopian future. When asked (the perennial question) why a "black show" was still needed in 1977, David Driskell, the curator of *Two Centuries of Black American Art*, responded: "Because you have propagated the notion that blacks are not part of the system. So until such time as you free your thinking enough to see that they've always been a part of it, and should rightly be included in the history books and what have you, we'll have to keep having black shows."[170]

CHAPTER FOUR   **In Motion:** The Performative Impulse

IN 1966, CRITIC LUCY LIPPARD wrote about an "eccentric abstraction" that presented a new vision of the sculptural, with neither the expressive, monumental roots of modern sculpture nor the ties to the solid geometries of minimalism. Formal structure joined with sensuousness, the visceral profile of sensate materials.[1] Lippard noted a fluctuation between two and three dimensions, an integration of the pictorial within the sculptural, that engaged gesture and invested in a scale concomitant with the human body. At the same time, such works were unconnected to allegory, expressionism, and the anthropomorphic inclinations of the past. Lippard found these objects to be "funereal"—not in the same sense as sculptural memorials or monuments, but in an inert, dumb, deconstructed gesture that was "inactive," responding both to the availability of new technologies and to materials like rubber, vinyl, resins, and electronics.[2]

While these new formations were seen on both coasts beginning in 1963, Lippard was clear that they were not assemblage, with its smaller scale, its "additive, conglomerate" pose, its "recognizable objects" and anecdotes. In 1968, she and John Chandler called this changing notion of sculpture (and art in general) "dematerialization." Over the next decade, this shifting terrain was identified as "process art" and "postminimalism," encompassing a broader conceptualization of method and meaning.³ Critic Robert Pincus-Witten later mused that Eva Hesse, Keith Sonnier, Alan Saret, and Linda Benglis had a willful drive to distinguish themselves from an earlier generation. But he also noted that their work bore the mark of the politics and "utopianism" of its time, particularly by the end of the 1960s. Such an assessment paralleled dance scholar Sally Banes's discussions of postmodern dance, which moved from an ascetic practice in dialogue with minimalism during the first half of the decade to one that freely incorporated ritual and narrative after 1968. The changing profile of concert dance during this period was marked by audience and political engagement and dialogue with Third World activism and non-Western aesthetics.⁴

At this same moment, African American artists were turning their attention to ancestral Africa. On the one hand, we can ascribe this to the growing visibility and subsequent influence of independent African countries over the decade and the expanding influence of black cultural nationalism expounded by Los Angeles–based Ron Karenga and the US Organization. On the other hand, as Paul Gilroy has noted, after 1969, as the violent backlash against Black Power took its toll in human lives, direct discussions of radical social activism in the arts were replaced by the search for an African spiritual home.⁵

This period saw a renewed interest in the American South and its folk cultures. The trope of ritual was important, particularly in the fiction of African American women writers. In Gloria Naylor's *The Women of Brewster Place* (1982), sacred and metaphysical time and space are at the core of healing modern-day ills; for Toni Morrison in *Song of Solomon* (1977), ancestral bones/remains have the same effect. Similar actions were performed by artists Senga Nengudi, Houston Conwill, and David Hammons as a way to create safe spaces of memory and meditation on African diasporic aesthetics and its futures.⁶

In its destruction of categories—the dismantling of the lines drawn between two and three dimensions, painting and sculpture, landscape and monument—the new fine arts suggested new visualizations and technologies as well as the "force of change."⁷ In Europe, similar experiments were gathered under the rubric of Arte Povera. As Richard J. Williams explains, the European style was politically marked: it was "poor art's" attack on the excesses of the rich. Only later was art subsumed into a larger universe where those same elements read simply as matter and form.⁸

In Europe pieces by Michael Heizer, Richard Serra, and Robert Morris became "newly legible as anti-institutional acts."⁹ The work reproduced skepticism of authority and opposition to war in Southeast Asia and became empowered by civil rights struggles. As Pincus-Witten later pointed out, "In their own day, these eccentric forms were enhanced by the social agitations and advancements made by hitherto grandly disenfranchised sectors of the community—blacks, gays, women."[10] Thus after 1968, the inert, mute object began again to speak. And the visual image of others, "the disenfranchised," became the lens through which these processes were read; they became the method and "cipher for the looking self" of the Western patriarchal art establishment.[11]

In 1979, Rosalind Krauss published "Sculpture in the Expanded Field," an article that famously used a mathematical formula (known as the Klein group) to diagram the complexities of new sculpture that had emerged over the previous decade. Around the same time, two other publications charted the evolution of similar practices in other locales. Writing in the Mexican journal *Plural*, critic Rita Eder discussed contemporary modes of ephemeral art making throughout Latin America, which dispersed quite effortlessly into the flow of everyday life as "spectacle or political act."[12] A year earlier, in their 1978 book *Contextures*, Linda Goode Bryant and Marcy S. Philips had charted the activities of a group of primarily African American artists, some of whom, like David Hammons, had been showing with Goode Bryant's Just Above Midtown Gallery since it opened in 1974.[13]

In *Contextures*, Goode Bryant and Philips define what they see in these artists' work as a "contextural" method, that is, one in which these increasingly indeterminate formulations derive signification not so much from their materiality or composition but from their place. Art was defined not by what was inside its borders but by its siting, its margins, its frame, and its location. Integral to the contextural practice was the use of "remains," elements "leftover from a primary action."[14] Often linked to readymades and discards, remains were nonetheless different: "Unlike a discard, which had a function or a purpose that ceased to perform, or a ready-made, which has an intended purpose and function it still performs, the remain has no particular purpose or function, or a definition clarifying itself."[15] Because of this indeterminate posture, the site of the work becomes key to its ability to speak.

It is the work's indeterminacy, and particularly as "black art," that both vexes and frees artists such as David Hammons, Houston Conwill, Maren Hassinger, and Senga Nengudi (fig. 4.1). As Pincus-Witten noted, this was not the "propagandistic representationalism of putatively insurgent and rebellious anecdote" that described much of the work collected under the Black

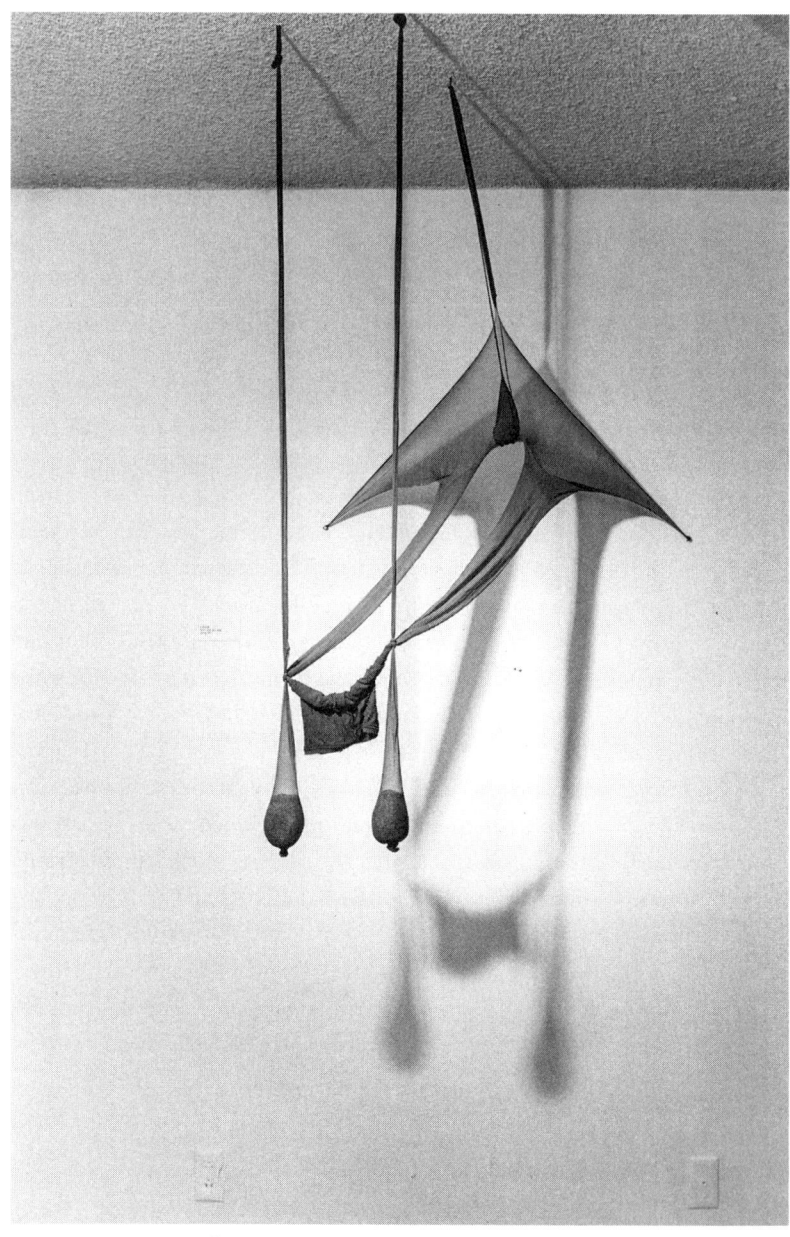

FIG. 4.1 Senga Nengudi, *Swing Low*, 1977. Mixed-media installation. Just Above Midtown Gallery Archives. Courtesy the artist and Thomas Erben Gallery, New York.

Arts Movement in the 1960s and 1970s.[16] As Nengudi later remembered, for the most part neither mainstream nor ethnic-oriented institutions knew what to do with the art made by these practitioners, who kept making it anyway.[17]

The indeterminacy of practice marked these artists, in a fashion similar to one identified by Lippard a decade earlier, as those who had been trained as painters but chose to work sculpturally. That formula applied to only one artist in this group, Houston Conwill. The others traveled to sculpture along different paths: Hammons was a draftsman and commercial artist; Nengudi and Hassinger were dancers. This trend toward sculptural and three-dimensional form from somewhere else implied movement, something "between kinesthetic and kinetic," as Lippard declared.[18] For all these artists based in Los Angeles, sculpture led to and from bodily movement, viewer participation, and performance.

The image of remains, theorized by Goode Bryant and Philips in the late 1970s, also takes us toward the performative. Remains are leftover from a primary action; they are extra, additional, things that seem to have no place. Remains are surplus. If we think about these artists and the work they produced from the 1960s to the 1970s, we can see that the problem with recognition was that it was in excess, unrecognizable because it did not follow easily understood formulas for "black art." Performance art also trafficked in such excesses, where the body as flesh revealed, as Amelia Jones has posited, its "subjectivities and identities," its contingency, its context, in the way that classic modernist objects never did.[19] Performance art, in which the body became the work, tangibly exposed the fallacy of patented formalist, disinterested approaches to the object and revealed its inherent meaning. As understood through poststructuralist and feminist thought, the body presented a new visual product, a new subject, and new connotations and values for art. Performance art, as it erupted as part of visual arts practices of the 1960s and 1970s, marked the indeterminacy and "dispersal of the modernist subject ... [and the] splitting, decentering, dislocation, or fragmentation of the self."[20]

The story of modernism was disrupted and decentered by the multiple histories of other bodies, speaking subjects. As Stuart Hall famously intoned, "Now that, in the postmodern age, you all feel so dispersed, I become centered. What I've thought of as dispersed and fragmented comes, paradoxically, to be the representative modern experience!"[21] W. E. B. Du Bois's "veil" is another trope that reminds us not just of the self as fragmented but also of the notion of "parallel" histories living side by side.[22] This diversity of experience is excess too, extra to the standard-issue Western narrative, where African cultures are made in darkness and their descendants in the Americas lose everything in a boat trip along the way.

It is these notions of fragmentation, multiplicity, and layering that inform the work of artists such as Hammons, Conwill, Nengudi, and Hassinger. The objects they created and the performances they made were a surfeit, in this sense, to the roles prescribed. In many ways, these artists mirrored some of the strategies that Daphne Brooks has revealed about African American creators at the turn of the twentieth century, who "clearly traffic in cultural excesses, layering aliases and costumes, devices and genres atop one another, . . . demonstrat[ing] the insurgent power of imaging cultural identity in grand and polyvalent terms which might outsize the narrow representational frames bestowed on them."[23] Figures such as Henry Box Brown, Adah Isaacs Menken, Pauline Hopkins, Bert Williams, George Walker, and Aida Overton Walker problematized or gave movement to what Brooks calls the "stillness" of black stereotype, the immobile black grotesque.[24]

Poet Elizabeth Alexander has also mapped the black body's slide between the real and the metaphoric as a creative figure and form, the difference between experience lived daily in an imperfect world and experience willfully, consciously (re)constructed and (re)imagined. Alexander's observation supports art historian Kathy O'Dell's notion that the body cannot "be known 'purely' as a totalizable, fleshy whole that rests outside of the arena of the symbolic."[25] If we muse again about the concept that "other" bodies become the cipher for looking/vision in the West, then we can more fully grasp this idea of the slide or oscillation between the actual and the symbolic uncovered by Alexander, manifest in the realm of the visual as the shift between the poles of hypervisibility and invisibility.[26] Here the hypervisible transmogrifies into the black grotesque, a figure that becomes ever more monstrous because of its fixity, as the location of unchanging horror. The power of invisibility, what Peggy Phelan calls being "unmarked," is the force and energy of something that doesn't announce itself, finds strength outside the "surveillance of the object," and "willfully [fails] to appear."[27] The unmarked bears similarities to the concept of maroonage advanced by Houston Baker, where figures evade signification, and which takes its logic from the flight from enslavement in the Americas.[28]

Within an African American context, concepts of performance have always been tied up with the means of survival. As scholars have suggested, during slavery, subsistence within the domain of white supremacy enforced the continual enactment of happy subjugation, the performing of healthiness on the display of the auction block by dancing, jumping, and other bodily movement, along with the continuing trope of the jovial and contented slave. Liberation from enslavement often involved theatrical dissimulation, including cross-dressing and "passing" (for white), to say nothing of the coded songs and language that alerted potential escapees to the moment or place of departure.[29]

Not that things ended there. Nicholas Lemann describes the dissimulations in the twentieth-century sharecropping cultures of Mississippi, a virtual continuation of the social hierarchies and economies of the plantation South. Black dissent was "kept hidden under a mask of slightly uncomprehending servility that black people knew fit whites' basic picture of them." Also common were acts of rebellion that were barely visible, with workers chopping off the roots of cotton plants to destroy crops, or switching shirts with one another so that they could go through the queue for payment multiple times, since they were unrecognizable as individuals.[30]

In the body of the self-liberated slave, we can plot notions of hypervisibility and invisibility nestled closely side by side. From one perspective, the escapee was a lawbreaker and criminal, violent, desperate, and savage, a figure whose monstrousness was visible and incarnate in the desperate moves for freedom embodied in the membrane of black skin. However, seen from the opposing point of view, the escapee was self-liberated and invisible, blending not only with the black population at large but at times even (imagine!) with the white populace as well. The figure was invisible in his or her ability to fade into the crowd but highly layered, too, with disguises, affects, and dissimulations. Brooks defines this as "spectacular opacity," a way of hiding in plain sight that resists the ostensible "transparency" of the black body, its seeming access to a raw literalness, the mark of transgression carried on the skin, the "real" stripped of any possibilities of metaphor or imagination.[31] Indeed, she imagines this alterity of an earlier century as "transformed into specific strategies for expressions and performance." Described by Brooks as "Afro-alienation acts," these strategies render the stillness of stereotype into strangeness, oddness, things in motion and off-center that resist timelessness as well as narrow realism and also "signify on the social, cultural, and ideological machinery that circumscribes African Americans."[32] This was the world and practice that artists in late twentieth-century Los Angeles would inherit.

SENGA NENGUDI: TAMING THE FREEWAY

> She used to put colored water in plastic bags and sit them on pedestals. This was the Sixties. No one would even speak to her because we were all doing political art. She couldn't relate. She wouldn't even show around other Black artists, her work was so "outrageously" abstract. [She] came to New York and still no one would deal with her because she wasn't doing "Black Art."
> —David Hammons

Here David Hammons describes the early work of Sue Irons (later Senga Nengudi), his friend and sometime studio mate.[33] According to Hammons, Irons was rejected by the then-burgeoning West Coast Black Arts Movement because of her nonrepresentational tendencies, confirming how certain types of stylistic experimentation created issues of comprehension for her and other artists.

Sue Irons was born in Chicago in 1943. Her maternal grandparents had come there from Festus, Missouri, in 1922, with their one-year-old daughter, Elois Lillian Jackson (Irons), the artist's mother. After visiting cousins in Berkeley, California, one summer, Elois decided that was the place for her "to be and dream." She arrived in Pasadena with seven-year-old Sue in 1951.[34]

Irons attended California State University, Los Angeles, receiving both a BA and an MA, which she was awarded in 1971, the same year she participated in the exhibition *8 Artistes Afro-Américains* at the Musée Rath in Geneva, Switzerland, touted as Europe's most extensive showing of African American artists.[35] During her graduate and undergraduate training, she worked in the dance and art departments at the Pasadena Art Museum (PAM). In the 1960s, the museum was a prime location for Happenings, where many artists—including Jim Dine, Claes Oldenburg, and Allan Kaprow—were allowed to work right onsite. Irons was also employed at another fairly new cultural organization, the Watts Towers Arts Center (WTAC), where she came in contact with Noah Purifoy, John Outterbridge, and, of course, the amazing architectural tour de force by Simon Rodia that defined the site. For Irons, these were distinct wellsprings of information and contexts for art making that nurtured her own practice.

Irons originally considered a dance major when she began college in 1961 but decided to pursue art, retaining dance as her minor field.[36] As she later recalled: "I never had a 'dance body' or anything like that. I always felt as though I could not do it, although that's been proven wrong by many people. I personally had a hang-up about that. I continued to dance but never really did it full force because of that. And basically, even with dance, I preferred the creative side of it, choreography or developing concepts for movement."[37]

Irons did not fit the mode of concert dance she found as a student in the 1960s, though she was nonetheless compelled by the kinesthesia of the body. Exposure to happenings and alternate and dematerialized visual art practices that she encountered at PAM and the WTAC opened other arenas that encouraged her to think about corporealness as form in a way that concert dance would not allow.

Between 1971 and 1974, Irons lived in New York, working on new ideas. She replaced her vinyl—*Water Compositions*, the "plastic bags" filled with liquids Hammons referred to—with fabric and began making works from flag material. These hung outside, and the unpredictable force of the wind shaped and changed each piece. With the transformation in style and material concerns came a transformation in identity: by 1974, Sue Irons had become Senga Nengudi.

She began to create what would become her signature works, freeform sculptures constructed primarily of nylon mesh (pantyhose) and sand. Their "skin-like forms . . . stretched and pulled," and "linear extensions and appendages"[38] were tied and knotted, shaped, twisted, and suspended from walls and ceilings. Their material and anthropomorphic form certainly suggested the body in motion. However, their pliant nature was not just part of an antisculptural, environmental orientation, or feminist bearing. They were supposed to be interacted with: caressed, fondled, and stroked by artist and viewers. It was through participatory three-dimensional works that movement and finally performance (re)entered Nengudi's oeuvre as an important creative force.

A photograph from fall 1976 shows Nengudi experimenting with the intersection of materials, three-dimensionality, and the living body. The artist poses with *R.S.V.P. #X*, 1976 (fig. 4.2), in her Los Angeles studio, one piece in a series that would be part of her first New York solo exhibition, at Linda Goode Bryant's Just Above Midtown Gallery in March 1977. *R.S.V.P. #X*, in part, suggests a human body with rail-like nylon legs weighted securely to the floor by feet that are pouches of sand. The legs meet at a pantyhose crotch whose looser fabric conjures alternately a loincloth, a skirt, or genitals. If the legs are readily identifiable, as we move up the sculptural form, distinct mimetic allusions fall away. An inverted pair of taut hose suggests arms, but the central area between the two sections is articulated by the nylon mesh simply drawing in space to hint at the possibility of a torso. One upper limb is attached to

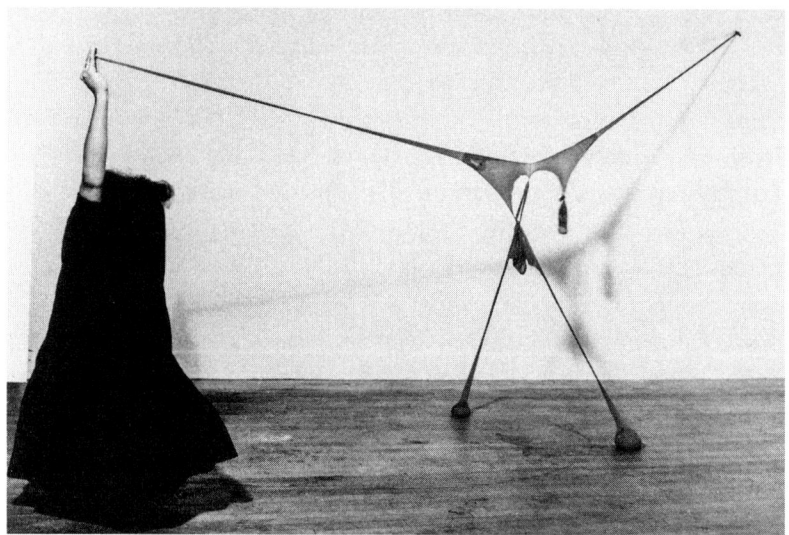

FIG. 4.2 Ken Peterson, *Senga Nengudi with R.S.V.P. #X in her Los Angeles studio*, 1976. Courtesy the artist and Thomas Erben Gallery, New York.

the wall. The other is held by Nengudi, who is draped in black, squatting and pulling another appendage of *R.S.V.P. #X* above her head.

The public coming together of Nengudi's performative and sculptural interests can be seen more fully in photographs of her next solo exhibition, at the Pearl C. Woods Gallery in Los Angeles in May 1977. In line with her professed choreographic bent, her pantyhose contraptions enmesh fellow artist Maren Hassinger (fig. 4.3). Lengths of dark nylon fiber radiate out from the kneeling Hassinger's torso, mooring her in place. Properties of mass and volume, tension, and the articulation of space as well as transparency that Nengudi had explored in the vinyl *Water Compositions* are transferred to materials that even more fully incarnate and embody human form.

However, it was in another example from 1977, *Costume Study for Mesh Mirage* (fig. 4.4), that Nengudi finally made the decision to let her sculpture leave the secure anchor of the wall—not just freestanding, but liberated, movable, and kinetic, and attached to the human body itself. In contrast to the simple black throw that barely disguised the artist as a puppet master in *R.S.V.P. #X*, Nengudi shrouded herself in a skein of brown paper with evidence of splattered paint, something peeled from the studio workspace. Her neck was festooned with a collar of paper in various stages of shredding, dipping in some places almost to the floor. In this piece in particular the aesthetics of assemblage were refashioned into a looser, more performative situation,

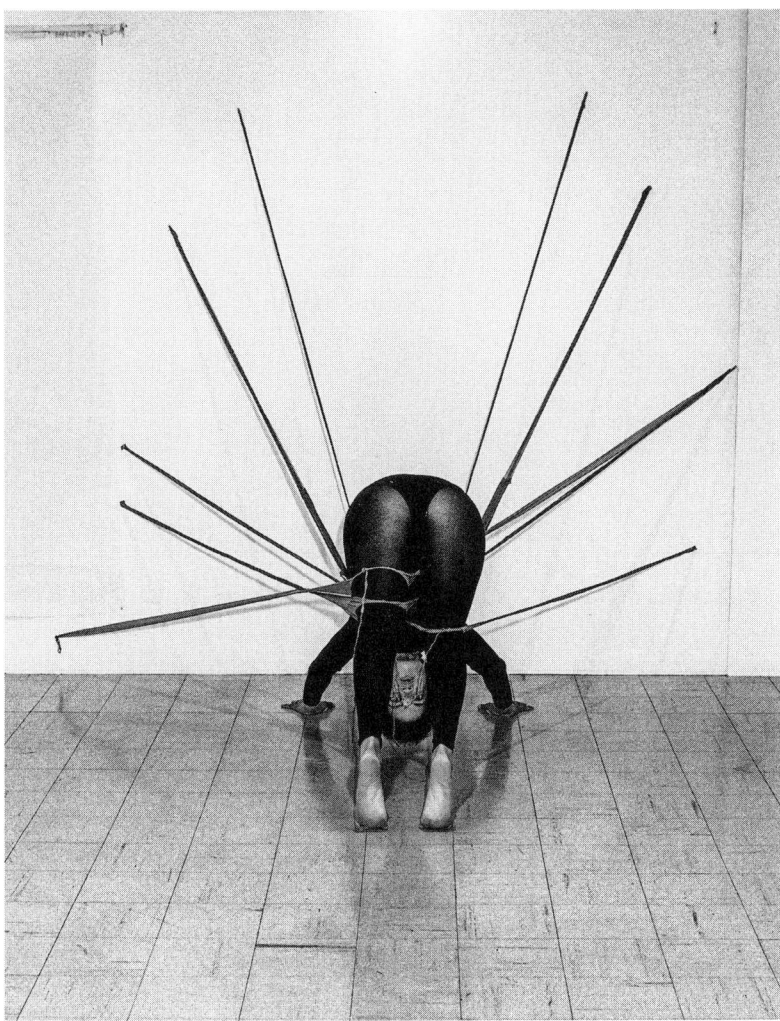

FIG. 4.3 Harmon Outlaw, *Maren Hassinger performing in a Senga Nengudi work*, 1977. Los Angeles. Courtesy the artist and Thomas Erben Gallery, New York.

into the postminimal. Finally Nengudi's head was covered in a pantyhose mask, her nose peeking through a vagina-like opening, with truncated mesh thighs for eyes.

Nengudi's first full-length work of performance took place in April 1978. *Ceremony for Freeway Fets* (fig. 4.5) (plate 23) was a public art project supported by a Comprehensive Educational Training Act (CETA) grant and sponsored by Alonzo and Dale Davis's Brockman Gallery Productions and Caltrans (LA's transportation system).[39] A one-time event, it took place under a

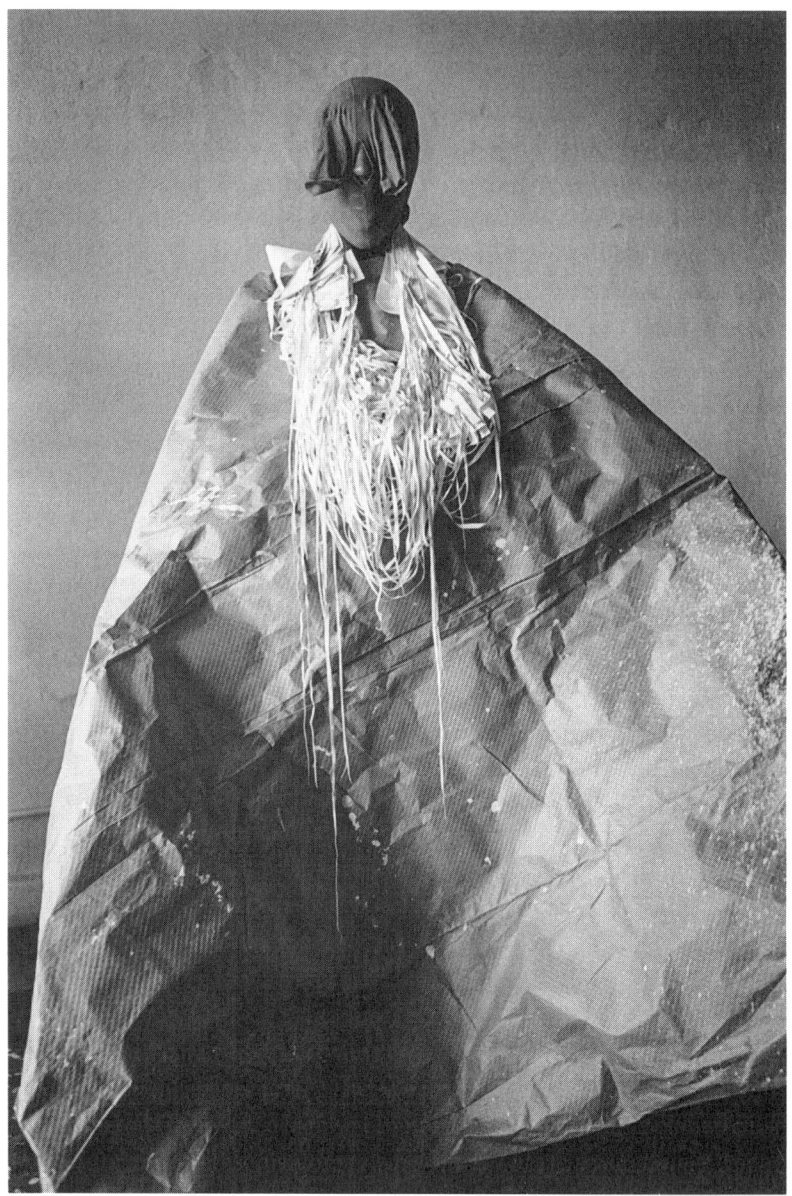

FIG. 4.4 Senga Nengudi, *Costume Study for Mesh Mirage*, 1977. Courtesy the artist and Thomas Erben Gallery, New York; photograph by Adam Avila.

section of the freeway near the Convention Center at a point of confluence of various routes.

It was outdoors yet sheltered, located in the downtown hub of a major metropolis yet cut off from the energy of the city. As Nengudi recalled: "I really liked the space because there were little tiny palm trees and a lot of dirt. It wasn't as extreme as it is now, but even at that time there were a lot of transients who slept there; so there were little campfires and stuff. For me, it had the feel of what I imagined an African village to be. Because it was under the freeway it was kind of cloistered in a sense. You could have this rural atmosphere in the midst of an urban setting."[40]

Ceremony for Freeway Fets began in the morning and lasted for perhaps an hour. A small orchestra composed of students and artists played saxophone, flute, drums, and other less traditional instruments (figs. 4.6 and 4.7). Nearly everyone was equipped with a form of Nengudi's sculpture, from Frank Parker's knotted and twisted headdress to RoHo's full mask. Nengudi, Hassinger, and David Hammons provided the work's major movement. Hassinger's larger role in the piece had been confirmed only that day. Hammons was already familiar with the work and used his own prop, a decorated staff.

Hassinger wore a military-style jacket with epaulets, unbuttoned and festooned with pantyhose sculpture. She sported a simple headpiece, her face covered by a gauzy white veil (fig. 4.6). In performance, Hassinger spun wildly as if she were some centrifugal force.[41] Nengudi and Hammons's figures were designed more elaborately. Hammons's face was covered with black pantyhose, whose unused legs became sort of antennae. He wore a black sweater and shiny, persimmon-colored pants, a wide woven belt tied at his waist. His staff was ever present. Measuring about five and half feet tall, this object was topped with shells, colored bits of cloth, and accentuated with a microcosm of other found objects (figs. 4.8 and 4.9).

However, it was Nengudi who seemed to truly embody and "bring to life" her sculptural practice. What was seen in *Costume Study for Mesh Mirage*—the shift from objects as anthropomorphic form to those that are attached to live bodies—became fully animated in *Ceremony for Freeway Fets*. The tent-like structure that she moved inside brought together earlier ideas of fabric and movement that she'd explored in New York. With each step, her performative silhouette changed radically. She was crowned by a gathering of stuffed and knotted pantyhose and cloth scraps, some of which hung almost halfway down the tented costume. On one side, where a hand might have been, similar nylon forms cascaded forth, punctuating the air frequently and emphatically. As Hassinger noted: "As I look back on it, there was something

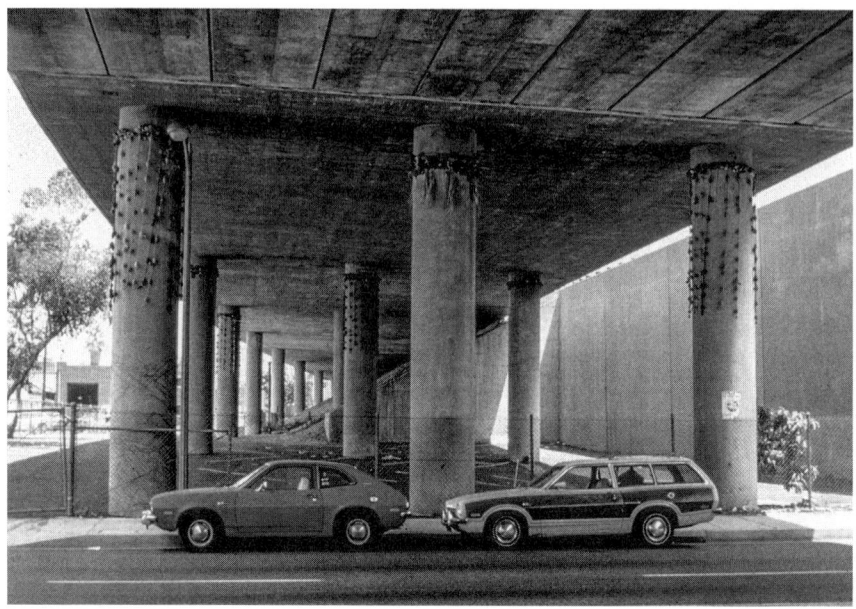

FIG. 4.5 Roderick "Quaku" Young, *Performance space for Senga Nengudi's* Ceremony for Freeway Fets, 1978, featuring pylons dressed with the artist's pantyhose sculpture. Performance, Los Angeles. Courtesy the artist; Thomas Erben Gallery, New York; and the African American Performance Art Archive, University of North Carolina, Chapel Hill.

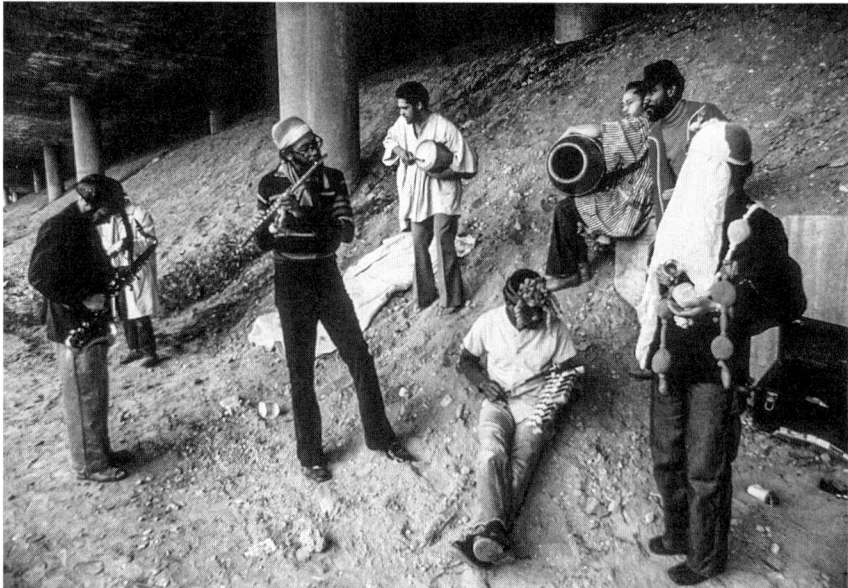

FIG. 4.6 Roderick "Quaku" Young, *Performance band for Senga Nengudi's* Ceremony for Freeway Fets, 1978. Maren Hassinger stands far right. Seated on the ground at her left is Frank Parker. Performance, Los Angeles. Courtesy the artist; Thomas Erben Gallery, New York; and the African American Performance Art Archive, University of North Carolina, Chapel Hill.

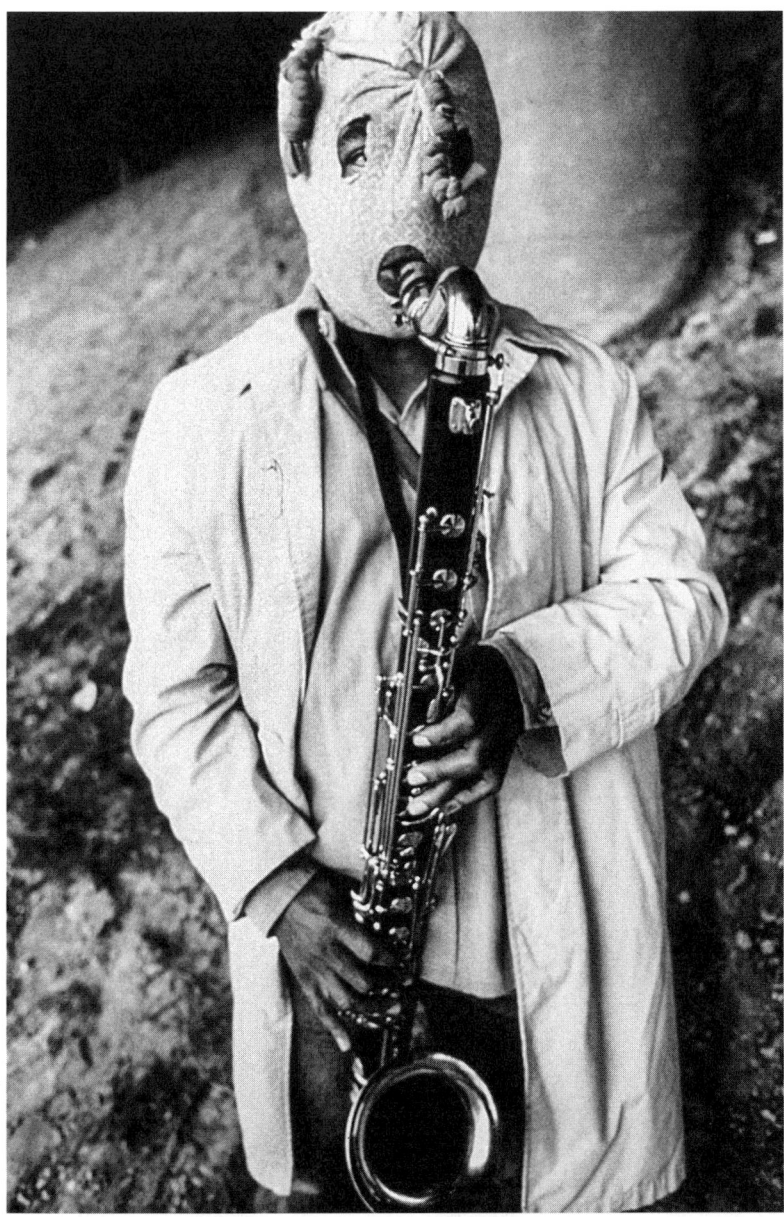

FIG. 4.7 Roderick "Quaku" Young, *RoHo in the performance band for Senga Nengudi's Ceremony for Freeway Fets*, 1978. Performance, Los Angeles. Courtesy the artist; Thomas Erben Gallery, New York; and the African American Performance Art Archive, University of North Carolina, Chapel Hill.

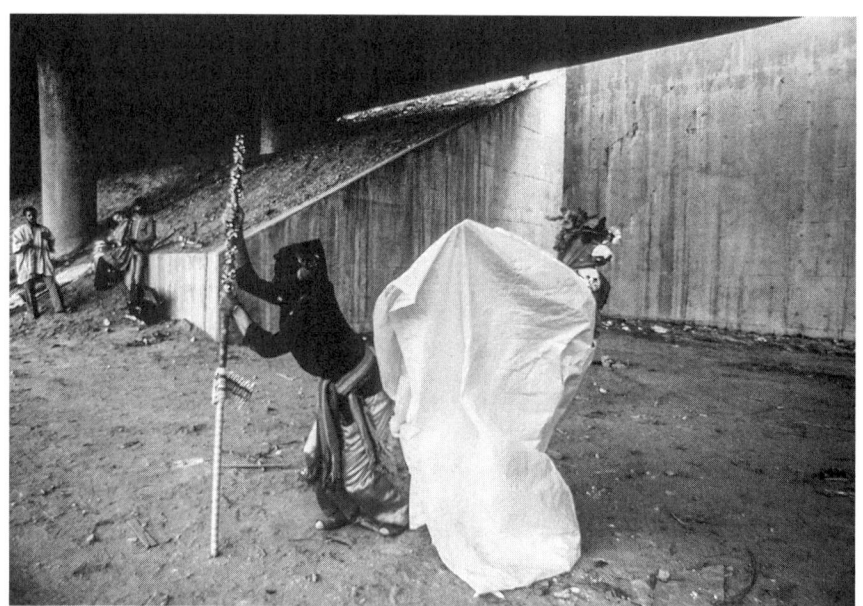

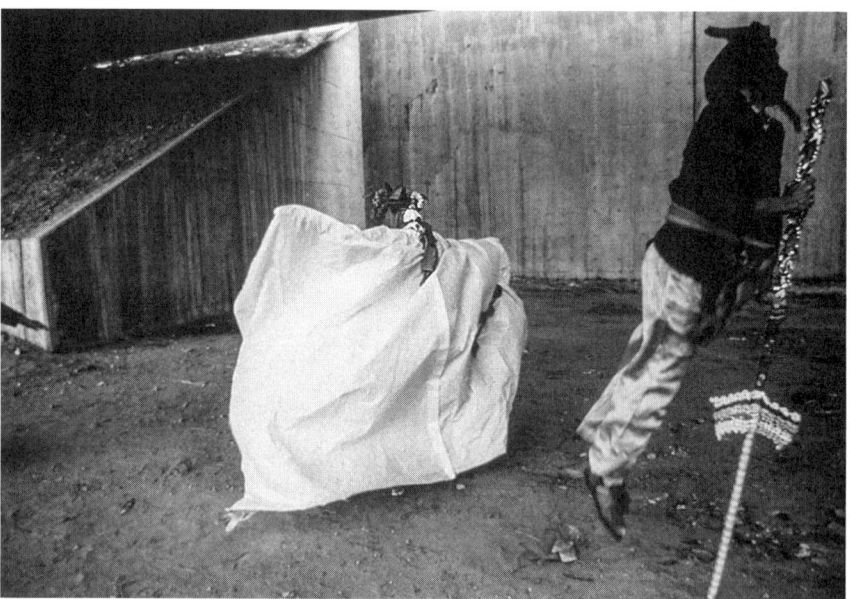

FIGS. 4.8 AND 4.9 Roderick "Quaku" Young, *Senga Nengudi and David Hammons performing in Senga Nengudi's* Ceremony for Freeway Fets, 1978. Performance, Los Angeles. Courtesy the artist; Thomas Erben Gallery, New York; and the African American Performance Art Archive, University of North Carolina, Chapel Hill.

incredibly African about it. If you have seen a kind of traditional performance, there might be some talking, then there might be this burst of insane energy. And that's what that twirling around was for me. It was this burst of insane, from nowhere, kind of energy.... I associate that kind of timing, that kind of surprise punch with African theatrical tradition."[42]

In Hassinger's description, we see a confluence with certain modalities of African dance. During this time, Robert Farris Thompson was describing virtuosic solos that combined youthful energy and flexibility in dances from Africa, including iconic gestures such as a crouching "get down" position, "high affect combinations," and "off-beat phrasing," which had been documented over centuries. All matched Hassinger's account of "wild" spinning and darting, dramatic movement.[43]

African dance idioms, notes dance scholar Brenda Dixon Gottschild, value polycentric and polyrhythmic bodies. They demonstrate "a democratic equality of body parts," with one "played against another" in movement that is simultaneous and originating "from more than one focal point," meaning that limbs may move independently and differently to layered rhythms. By contrast, classical European dance privileges the torso and an erect spine, which generates all other movement.[44] Indeed, as Dixon Gottschild argues, what is "American" about modern dance is African: torso articulation and pelvic contraction, "the barefoot dancers reifying contact with the earth, touching it, rolling or lying on it, giving in to it" (a signature of Martha Graham).[45] These movements, "traits [of] African and African American dance," enter the modern canon through the kinesthetic "wisdom" of "Africanist-inspired American vernacular and pop culture," since there are "no coordinates in European concert or folk dance traditions."[46] We should not be surprised, then, that Nengudi struggled with these conflicting visions of dance and the body in motion.

Ceremony for Freeway Fets shares similarities with the larger aesthetic systems of West and Central African masquerades. By the 1960s and 1970s, there was a growing holistic understanding, spurred by Thompson and Herbert M. Cole, among others, who saw performative totality as the driving aesthetic force.[47] African art was not just a sculptural tour de force of utilitarian or figural icons or masks in wood. As Cole suggests, translation of these aesthetics should be tripartite and include mask, masking, and masquerade. There was not only the carved and polychrome headpiece, the mask, but the rest of the costume, made from fabric, grasses, beads, and other natural and man-made items. The legions of "fully costumed characters," the rules of display, covering not only the head but the entire body—all this was masking. The concept of masquerade filled a larger universe, articulated through days of events with "dancers, musicians, and their audiences."[48]

Western scholars began to comprehend that the masquerade form presented the "interplay of the social, religious, and aesthetic" in ways that were difficult to separate.[49] Masks were engines of transformation that allowed cosmic intersession into human affairs; judges and mediators; divine links between the living and the dead; guides and teachers; and forms of entertainment. Marked by events that were transient in nature, they were cultural systems for "ordering experience and experiencing order."[50] Or, as Babatunde Lawal has posited, they combined "art and ritual dance in order to amuse, educate and inspire to worship, all at the same time."[51] The headdress was an extension of that grand theatrical "stage," projecting ideals "in sculptural metaphors."[52]

In Nengudi's *Ceremony for Freeway Fets*, the crew of performers and musicians wear special clothing; some are masked and some are in full-body gear. This contemporary ritual clothing is what Pamela Franco calls "dressing up and looking good," a type of vestment that is distinctive from the everyday, signaling the transformation that marks the beginning of the masquerade and displays the pleasing or correct aesthetic affect.[53] Nengudi's wearable sculpture culminates in a crown that seems to be placed on top of the head, calling to mind the elaborate wooden superstructures found in many masquerades. The object that spins in her hand finds a comfortable analogy in the horsetail whisks and other items often carried by African masqueraders. But much of the artist's interest revolves around fabric, from full-body sheaths to retrofitted pantyhose (plate 24). And in this focus we find an intriguing connection to Yoruba masking arts in southwestern Nigeria.[54]

Egungun masquerades among the Yoruba celebrate the ancestors and regulate relations between the living and the dead. Most intriguing is the physical nature of Egungun masking, whose costumes center attention on cloth and the sway of fabric and bodies to the almost total exclusion of a wooden carapace. The faces of performers are covered with mesh or folds of fabric, comparable to Hammons's pantyhose-clad headpiece (fig. 4.9) in *Ceremony for Freeway Fets*. As Thompson insisted, "The cloths have the power *in themselves*.... They make and bring back the spirit."[55] The costumes in Egungun run the gamut from tight-fitting numbers in which a performer is given what amounts to a new cloth "skin," to impressive, towering columns of intricate appliqué, whose swirling masses encode in fabric each articulation of the dance, "abstract textile compositions which strike the eye as autonomous sculptures."[56]

The Nigerian masquerade known as Gèlèdé provides another compelling framework for unpacking the stylization of Nengudi's first major performance work in Los Angeles. Gèlèdé masquerades pay homage to and appease female power. Traditional Yoruba societies are patrilineal, yet women have great metaphysical authority, on a par with or sometimes even greater than that of deities. As with many African masking practices, Gèlèdé maintains harmony in the society's social dynamics or village structure; it promotes good gender relations by advocating respect for mothers and women. It is danced by men performing as women in their idealized state, and the ubiquitous cloth becomes an important signifier. Known for its elaborately carved headpieces, the Gèlèdé costume has a body primarily composed from rich layers of women's head ties and baby wrappers or sashes. These fabrics remind the audience (and wearer) of women's vital force and intelligence and the importance of women in the continuity of community.[57]

Created in the 1970s, Senga Nengudi's free-form sculptures can be placed in many categories. Engineered from found and used objects, they brought assemblage aesthetics to new places. Bruce Conner had experimented with nylon hose in Northern California in the 1950s and 1960s, but his wrapped and bound solid and clunky objects, with torn and scarred layers, presented a very different vision. Nengudi's emphasis on the material's elasticity and flexibility seemed to articulate promise and possibility rather than defeat. If the limp vinyl of *Water Compositions* took heed of the deflated contours of Oldenburg's pop objects, Nengudi's work from the 1970s appeared cognizant of such explorations. In *Costume Study for Mesh Mirage*, 1977, Nengudi seems both aware of her relationship to modern art history and comfortable with her engagement in it. If Picasso saw the clue to *Guitar*, 1912, and the engines of assemblage in a Ivorian/Liberian Grebo mask, Nengudi, thinking about Picasso, modernism, Africa, and diasporic traditions, created a mask in skin-hugging fiber whose very detumescence, in the face of these histories, took into account contemporary modes of postminimalist expression.

However, perhaps the most common reading of Nengudi's sculptural inventions in the 1970s, at least in public discourse, was a feminist one. At the level of materiality they made use of an item that alluded to the female body but was also stylistically linked to fiber and decorative arts, crafts that were identified with traditional (Western) notions of women's creativity. Like the head ties on Nigerian Gèlèdé masks, pantyhose metaphorically referenced "woman" within the boundaries of the performance. And like Gèlèdé, these practices were rituals of respectful celebration of the body: not only its metaphysical power, but also its awesome splendor.

Feminist art in the 1970s celebrated the female body with pieces that emphasized processes, physical attributes, and genitalia. And Judy Chicago and Miriam Shapiro's Feminist Art Program, as well as other groundbreaking projects such as Womanhouse and the Woman's Building, were all located in Southern California. Nengudi was, of course, aware of this burgeoning mode of art making and would become active with the Woman's Building in the 1980s.[58] But if a piece such as Chicago's *Menstruation Bathroom*, 1972, conjured menses as installation art, it offered a different understanding of embodiment than that sought by Nengudi. Hers instead was more subtle, not "explicit" in the way that Rebecca Schneider has used the term, describing work that intercedes into fantasy constructs as excess and inappropriate, flaunting "a ribald refusal to vanish," whose factualness "collapse[s] symbolic space."[59]

Ceremony for Freeway Fets also can be seen as part of the history of diasporic reinscriptions of African traditions. Pamela R. Franco has commented that New World performances recalibrated ancestral forms. Now part of an oppressed minority, performers of African descent "turned to participation in European-based celebrations in which their masquerades' primary concerns were self-representation and symbolic repositioning."[60] In doing so, they also often reversed African mores of secrecy, transformation, ritual obligation, and men as primary keepers, aestheticians, and performers because their situation as subjugated populations necessitated alternate creative responses (i.e., in slave societies, black people were not allowed to conceal their identities). Reborn in these new performative structures of carnival, they envisioned and indeed staged "self-rule," encoding a black aesthetic and social order.[61]

We see this same action of refashioning experience in the calls for and will to self-determination by African American artists in the 1960s and 1970s under the aegis of the Black Arts Movement. In a sense, the events of the late twentieth century took the will to self-rule out of the coded space of masquerade theater and applied it to the larger social world, with the arts as a reinforcement of political and social motivation. If the civil rights and Black Power movements pressed for radical changes to American societal structures, art organically reflected the transformations in society with its destructuring and restructuring and new approaches to materials, possibilities of form, and vision. Nengudi thus worked with inherited structures of diasporic aesthetically coded "self-rule," but in her conscious privileging of African modes of production, layered, reinforced, and added sumptuousness to cultural traditions that were already in place. Many of these diasporic practices were subtle and presented themselves differently, not in the mode of Western "fine arts." They were attached to what Cuban scholar Gerardo Mosquera has referred to as "religious-cultural complexes," including Santería, Vodou, Candomblé, Shango, and Hoodoo; they were carried by a plethora of African civilizations arriving on American shores in continuous waves (as well as over them) from the seventeenth through the nineteenth centuries as well as through folktales, gesture, performance, and aspects of attendant material-culture production.[62]

From one perspective, the focus on African traditions by African American artists during the 1960s and 1970s was a way to celebrate the ancestral, link the present with the past, and provide a "social unifier" in the living community and with the community's dead, as we would find for instance in Yoruba Egungun or other masquerade forms.[63] Nengudi based *Ceremony for Freeway Fets* loosely on the theme of the relationship between African American women and men. Hassinger represented the female presence, and Hammons the male; Nengudi was the spiritual bond between them, linking the polarities in a positive way. This certainly ties in with African concepts of masquerade as forces for social good and the reinforcing of the "sense of community and common purpose," with dancing as a warming, strengthening activity that keeps death at bay.[64] In Nengudi's approach to the communal, why not enlist the vitality of the Yoruba goddess Oya, ruler of the wind (and connected to the energetic whirling of the Egungun), especially since it is a force she had already tried to marshal within her own creative practice? In a performance in 1977 in Los Angeles affirming relations between genders, why shouldn't Nengudi drape herself in yards of yellow, the color of Oshun, patron saint of love among the Yoruba? A conscious choice, yes, but one that again avails itself of diasporic tenets, for, as Judith Bettelheim argues, historically color-coded costumes may have covertly communicated meaning, functioning in this way as a mask.[65]

In fact, Los Angeles had become a locus for the study of the arts of Africa with the establishment of the African Studies Center at the University of California in 1959, an institute dedicated to teaching, scholarship, and bringing a larger public focus to the continent. The center was certainly an important force behind the establishment at UCLA of the Museum and Laboratories of Ethnic Arts and Technology (later the Museum of Cultural History and currently the Fowler Museum), which opened in 1963, focusing on art and material cultural from Africa, the Americas, Asia, and the Pacific. This institution and the Frederick S. Wight Art Gallery (now the Hammer Museum) were important venues for the significant exhibitions of African art, including *Black Gods and Kings* (1971) and *African Art in Motion* (1974), curated by Robert Farris Thompson, and *Arts of Ghana* (1977), organized by Herbert Cole and Doran Ross. The Los Angeles County Museum of Art also contributed to the strength of African arts on the West Coast with some significant shows, such as the exhibition of the Paul Tishman Collection in 1968.

Nengudi has acknowledged the importance of the UCLA's African exhibitions for her during this period.[66] However, her interest in things African was also planted during her time in New York in the early 1970s. She understood that her work might not fit within a dogmatic Afrocentric or Black Arts Movement rhetoric, but she sought this space out nonetheless, associating with institutions such as the Studio Museum in Harlem and Nyuumba Ya Sanaa Academy, run by the Weusi artists' collective. Her experiences in New York further layered her connection to African culture through art and spirituality and her contact with those "religious-cultural complexes" to which Mosquera referred. An important figure in the Weusi group was Ademola Olugebefola (born Bedwick Loyola Thomas in St. Thomas, Virgin Islands), who was initiated into Santería in the early 1960s and took a Yoruba name. Nengudi also met the artist Charles Abramson, who became a dear friend and an important artistic and spiritual influence; he was a priest in the religion.

Nengudi had no official shows during her four years in New York. Instead, she hung the lithe flag works from her windows in East Harlem, as evanescent spirits.[67] Not surprisingly, East Harlem (also known as Spanish Harlem and El Barrio) was one of the first neighborhoods where Puerto Rican migrants to New York settled.[68] Some of them certainly were *santeros* or practitioners of Santería. And Nengudi probably encountered *botánicas*, stores for ritual objects, that could be found in the area.

There is no doubt that Africa was on Senga Nengudi's mind when she created *Ceremony for Freeway Fets* in 1978. She considered the space where she performed the African village of her mind's eye. Her collaborator Maren Hassinger characterized their dance movements as miming certain aspects of African dance. The performers' clothing was evocative of West African masquerade dress. We see this in Nengudi's title for the work too: "fets" is short for "fetishes"; although perhaps *retardaire*, it was a nod to Africa just the same.[69]

But it was the site itself, under the freeway, that evoked not only Africa but also its diasporic double, perhaps even more powerfully. While ceremonies of closed societies and initiations are hidden in private locales, the West and Central African masquerades to which I have referred take place in public spaces, marketplaces, and town squares, where they find the crucial audience component that completes their rationale. We find these logics of place in the

Americas too, where similar aspects of the cityscape exert what Joseph Roach defines as a "gravitational pull" (he adds boulevards, theater districts, and cemeteries to the list), drawing performers and audiences to sites of "commerce and pleasure."[70] The location of Nengudi's performance was not accidental, then, but incredibly strategic. It evoked not only Esu's domain, the crossroads—Esu is the deity practicing Yorubas must first acknowledge before petitioning all others—but also the New Orleans carnival of black Mardi Gras Indians, who, according to Roach, "parade on unannounced routes . . . around the public housing projects and *under highway overpasses*" and transform these spaces into "places of embodied memory."[71] Such spaces attract "vortices of behavior" that constitute performance for Roach.[72] These physical places are also among Pierre Nora's *lieux de mémoire*, or sites of memory, remains or indicators of ritual where objects or spaces stand in place of bodily knowledge, marking "the intention to remember."[73] In the logic of the diaspora that is not a direct and pure channel from Africa, Nengudi's performance, like that of the black Mardi Gras Indians, is both public—outside, using the major routes of transportation—and liminal, following alternate paths, in the dust and dirt beneath the freeway itself. It is the incarnation of Renato Rosaldo's explanation of ritual as a "busy intersection."[74]

The growing Los Angeles freeway system was the site of increasing protests by citizens. Many of them were people of color whose neighborhoods and homes were being dismantled by government-organized programs of urban renewal to make way for the "refurbishing" of the city's downtown core. Often these were diverse neighborhoods, targeted because their "incomprehensible" demographics labeled them "blighted," which did not replicate themselves in new locales. The most probable location of Nengudi's *Ceremonies for Freeway Fets* was at the intersection of the Harbor (I-110) and Santa Monica (I-10) freeways. Both corridors were sites of extensive protest by African Americans because of the destruction and displacement the freeway system visited on their neighborhoods.[75]

However, just as art in the diaspora is not a strict duplication of African form but a reinvention and redeployment for new and different situations, we can imagine that Senga Nengudi has something else in her hip pocket. Her understanding of Africa is gleaned in part from Latino New York, for instance. In fact, in its imagination and facture her work celebrates notions of modernity signified by trade routes, the "new archetypes, people, communities, and cultures" that develop in "modernity as a circulatory system of exchange and site of translation"; it centralizes "diasporic histories of Africa and the Americas" in the making of the world we know as modern.[76] But in looking west, Nengudi eventually arrived in the East. And then there was Japan.

Curiosity about Asian art and philosophy eventually led Nengudi to Japan.[77] She spent 1966 to 1967 in Tokyo, where she studied at Waseda University during the interval between her undergraduate and graduate years at California State University, Los Angeles. She was particularly fascinated by the unorthodox objects and exhibitions of the Gutai Art Association. Formed in 1954 in the Kansei region (Osaka, Kobe, Kyoto) around the figure of Jiro Yoshihara, during the mid- to late 1950s Gutai experimented with mud, water, fabric, and air as well as the incorporation of time in exhibitions that were held outdoors, in theaters, and in traditional spaces. *Gutai* generally is translated into English as "embodiment," and this sense of the work is what attracted Nengudi. Gutai members often involved their bodies in art making, framing these actions as methods for generating painting and not as creative forms in and of themselves.[78] Nengudi and others were transfixed by their poetry and considered them archetypal because they suggested the incorporation of movement and performance.[79]

Kazuo Shiraga's and Saburo Murakami's works were the most iconic in the West, but the formal structure of pieces by Sadasa Montonaga and Atsuko Tanaka may have had an even greater impact on Nengudi. In 1955–56, Montonaga created shapes from vinyl and colored water, which he installed in landscape and gallery spaces. Light played an integral role, passing through the clear vinyl and illuminating the water's jewel-like tones. In galleries, these appeared as delicate pouches affixed to the windows. Nengudi's *Water Compositions* seem to owe much to Montonaga's experimentations in the 1950s, in the confluence of water and plastic in pouch- and pendant-like enclosures and the concern over weight and suspension. Tanaka's *Electric Dress* (fig. 4.10), however, haunted Nengudi's more performative works, such as her 1976 piece encasing Hassinger and mooring her to the wall's surface. Worn by Tanaka, *Electric Dress* seems an encumbrance, with her literally wired up and stationed at the power source.

In Japan, Nengudi broadened her knowledge of Japanese theatrical traditions, becoming more familiar with Noh, Kabuki, and Butoh and taking private art and dance classes.[80] In the Japanese performative arts, the artist encountered ancient customs going back some fifteen centuries. At the root of these forms was a shamanic tradition that predated Buddhism and Shinto religious practices and was Pan-Asian in reach. Shamanic trance was performative and public and provided dramatic structure. The *miko* or shaman (usually female) conjured the *kami* (deity) through "dancing, rhythmic

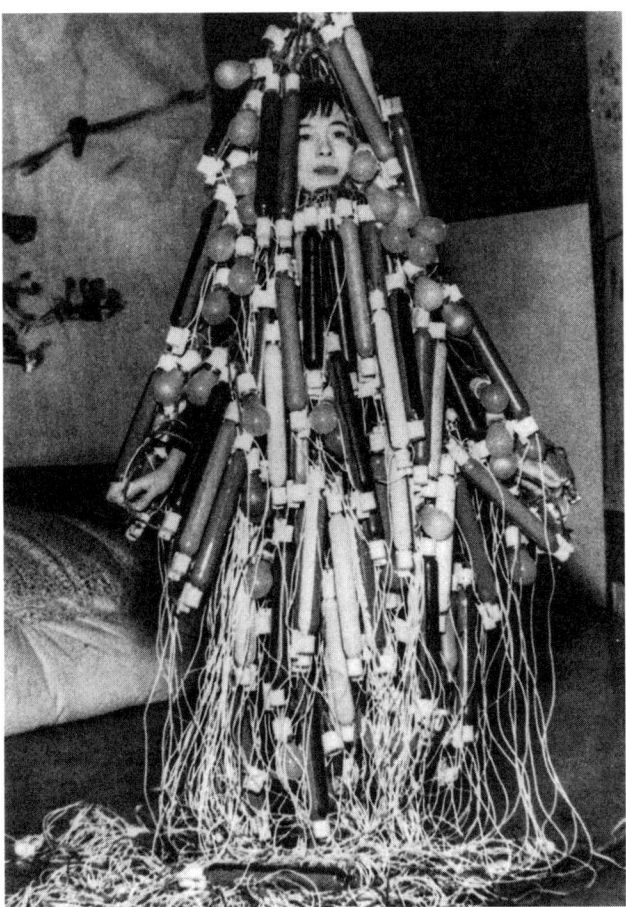

FIG. 4.10 Photographer unknown, *Atsuko Tanaka wearing the Electric Dress suspended from the ceiling at the Second Gutai Art Exhibition at Ohara Hall in Tokyo*, 1956. Sculpture. Courtesy © Kanayama Akira and Tanaka Atsuko Association.

stamping, [and] singing."[81] From the late nineteenth century to the 1950s, these forms of traditional Japanese theater were out of favor, discarded for Western practices, which encouraged the development of protest theater, reintroduction of women as actresses, and realism. In the late 1950s, however, Japanese artists turned to historical performative arts as a way to critique the West in the postwar period. In addition, avant-garde Western artists began to be fascinated by these traditions. Japanese cinema, and directors such as Akira Kurosawa and Yasujirō Ozu, also embraced historic theatrical stylization and helped to circulate these aesthetics more widely.

Other clues to Nengudi's work can be found in later forms of Japanese performance. Low dancing, with crouching positions and the orientation of the hips to the ground, is valued in Noh performance as well as in much traditional Japanese dance, a characteristic shared with African custom.[82] Noh's use of masks is also significant; while these shows have no directors, a mask will suggest "how the role should be enacted."[83] The rest of the costume follows, and of great importance here is an elongated sleeve that accentuates the expression of the dance; we can certainly connect this with the flowing robe Nengudi used to cover herself. Another fascinating correlation is the structure of the performance space itself, which is traditionally bounded by four pillars. In *Ceremony for Freeway Fets*, Nengudi clearly incorporates the freeway's pylons (fig. 4.5), dressing them with pantyhose sculpture. Though the artist casts the site as an African village, one wonders how much the staging, particularly the active incorporation of the freeway's supports, owes to Japanese theater. In Kabuki, Nengudi encountered a musical theater with musicians and singers positioned off- or onstage and music performed throughout the show. Again, this was similar to *Ceremony for Freeway Fets*, with its fairly large accompanying band of musicians. Perhaps the most fascinating link between Nengudi's performance in late twentieth-century Los Angeles and ancient Japan was the act of performing while holding objects in one's hand, seen in Nengudi's grasp of her pantyhose sculpture as well as Hammons wielding his staff. The fan is an omnipresent prop in traditional Japanese theater arts because of its link to shamanic tradition. As an object, it replaced the sacred branch or spear, the place the deity inhabited during ritual trance.

Not only ancient knowledge but also the example of contemporary theater and dance in Butoh and other avant-garde styles are clearly felt in Nengudi's 1978 piece. In the refutation of modern Japanese theater (*shigeki*), early 1960s avant-garde artists also placed value on antiart aesthetics—that is, on things that were not pristine, or performance that demonstrated its rejection by the mainstream through its use of "cramped, dirty venues, outdoor and tent performances, ragged costumes and poor props."[84] Juro Kara's Situation Theater of the mid-1960s was staged "in disused corners of the urban night," at construction sites and the perimeters of parks, with the performance space signaled by a red tent.[85] The importance of fabric to Kara brings us back to Nengudi's fascination with it as a medium and connects us as well to Kabuki, not only in the extravagant costuming but also in aspects such as dressing-room curtains, a series of elegant hanging panels that often were emblazoned with the actor's name and family crest and the name of the donor. This was another potential source for Nengudi's flag works in the early 1970s.

On closer inspection, Nengudi's oeuvre certainly seems to have blossomed from its contact with Japanese theatrical and visual arts. Yet Nengudi claimed that she never managed to meet any of the avant-garde visual artists in Japan. While her work suggests a dialogue, clearly that could take place without the artists' presence. The pieces by the Gutai Art Association that attracted Nengudi (and other U.S. artists) were largely created in the 1950s. After 1960, individuals and groups such as Matsuzawa Yutaka, Yoko Ono, Zero Dimension, and Hi Red Center used conceptual and performative practices for much more political and confrontational ends. The change was spurred in part by growing anti-American sentiment; young people's opposition to the continuation of the U.S.-Japan Security Treaty, which legitimatized the American military presence in Japan; and America's increasing engagement in the war in Vietnam. Radical artists in Japan were loath to have any contact with Americans, especially those lacking full command of the Japanese language. Nengudi also mentioned that Waseda University was a site of daily protests at the time.[86]

Nengudi's Afro-Asian experimentations seemed more possible on the West Coast. With its Pacific coast facing the whole of Asia, California has a substantial history of embracing Asian aesthetics, certainly in ceramics and paintings by Sargent Johnson, Ken Price, and John McLaughlin. Nengudi thus followed a West Coast tradition of sorts. For this reason, it is also not surprising that these works did not read as "black art" on the East Coast and did not fit into the requirements promoted by the Black Arts Movement. California represented that kind of embrace, the prospect of encompassing more. Sue Irons became Senga Nengudi when she returned to California. That sense of possibility drew Houston Conwill there as well.

HOUSTON CONWILL: RITUAL SPACE AND TIME

Houston Conwill was born in 1947 in Louisville, Kentucky, a place with its own interesting tradition of black visual art in the figures of Bob Thompson and Sam Gilliam. Conwill joined the Howard University student body in fall 1970, transferring from the University of Texas, Austin, after three years in the military. In the early 1970s, Howard University was fighting a battle to banish its profile as a finishing school for middle-class Negroes and transform itself into a bastion of radical, black-focused politics.[87] Howard's art and design students encountered such thinking in the person of painter Jeff Donaldson.

Donaldson's ideas were a major force behind the collective AfriCOBRA

(African Commune of Bad Relevant Artists), whose theories perhaps most defined visual arts in the Black Arts Movement. It began in Chicago in 1967 when, as part of the Organization of Black Culture (OBAC), Donaldson and others produced *The Wall of Respect*, the famous mural on an abandoned building on Chicago's Southside that was a catalyst for a late twentieth-century mural movement among African Americans.[88] Following that success, AfriCOBRA, a group composed solely of visual artists, was formed in 1968. An instructor at Northwestern University from 1968 to 1970, Donaldson came to Howard University with a mission and a manifesto.[89] His article "Ten in Search of a Nation," published in the fall 1970 issue of *Black World*, offered some guidelines for art making through a set of aesthetic principles: representational imagery, fragmented planes combined with organic form (called free symmetry and rhythm), bright colors (augmented by "shine"), and embedded words that clarified message and content. Thematically, the works should define the past, through a consideration of African heritage; identify the present, in the exploits of contemporary black heroes; and offer direction for the future, with images of black families. As AfriCOBRA was overwhelmingly composed of painters, these tenets, not surprisingly, were more focused on qualities of two-dimensional art.[90]

Beginning with Donaldson's arrival in 1970, the aesthetics of AfriCOBRA dominated visual instruction at Howard. Generally, color-laden and figurative work was encouraged, total abstraction frowned upon.[91]

As his wife, Kinshasha Holman Conwill, recalled, "Houston himself actually painted a lot of abstract art at Howard. It was not totally embraced."[92] It made sense, then, that in 1973, his last year in college, the same year as Sam Gilliam's solo show at the university, Conwill signed on as the senior artist's studio assistant. Gilliam, who moved to Washington, DC, in 1962, had dedicated himself to abstraction by 1964; however, it was his experiments, several years later, with staining and folding canvas that exploded into the draped works for which he is perhaps best known: huge skeins that pushed the Washington Color School into new dimensions.[93] The paintings Conwill made during the year he worked with Gilliam were pyramidal canvases washed with color, retaining his abstract orientation, with a nod to symbolism that apparently spoke to the aesthetics of Africa.[94] Yet the energy at Howard was not completely anathema to the direction that Conwill seemed to be going. He was stimulated by Donaldson's (and AfriCOBRA's) "democratic approaches to art ... creating posters to make art accessible to a wider audience, the creation of positive imagery to inspire the people." These things engaged his own sense of commitment to the social and political aspects of art.[95]

While the majority of Conwill's work during his undergraduate years was nonrepresentational, symbolic imagery did make its way into his paintings. According to scholar Rosalind Jeffries, during that time he returned often to the pyramid in both two- and three-dimensional forms. He was also captivated by Egyptian hieroglyphs, sometimes incising scripts from the Egyptian *Book of the Dead* into his canvases while wet.[96] The practices of two other Howard faculty members were also significant. The Ethiopian painter Skunder Boghossian offered alternative structure and color sensibility. His pictures of muted tones with organic and figural elements in a mythic vein were part of Africa's own revitalization of traditions and developing modernism. Lois Mailou Jones had been interested in Haitian spiritual scripts since the 1950s. Another source for a sacred language in art was Romare Bearden's 1971 solo show, *The Prevalence of Ritual*, at New York's Museum of Modern Art. Viewing the exhibition, Conwill felt challenged to locate the spiritual core in his own practice.[97] But the constructedness of Bearden's collages also rang true, as did the work he did with Gilliam on pieces that pushed at the formal boundaries of painting and sculpture.[98]

Conwill and Kinshasha bonded as workaholic young artists who stayed in the Howard art studios until the wee hours. They married in December 1971 in what the *Chicago Defender* described as "ceremonies in the African tradition," which nonetheless took place at the New Bethel Baptist Church in Washington, DC.[99] At this moment, numerous African Americans around the United States were patterning lifestyles after traditional African examples. Nigeria's Yoruba culture held particular influence, as seen in practices at Washington's Zaro House, New York's Yoruba Temple, and Oyotunji Village in South Carolina.[100] The rites the two created colored their performances together in Los Angeles in the 1970s and formed part of Conwill's later collaborative work as well.[101]

Conwill did not head directly to Southern California on graduating from Howard University in 1973. Instead he and Kinshasha stopped off in his hometown of Louisville for a year, where they took up a commission to do murals and stained-glass windows for the Saint Augustine Catholic Church.[102] From Louisville, the artists continued west to Los Angeles, where Houston entered the MFA program at the University of Southern California (USC) in the fall of 1974.

Between 1975 and 1978 Conwill created an artistic vocabulary for objects and performances that adopted a ceremonial structure and referenced both African and African American visual and ritual heritage. Performances often took place within different solo exhibitions of objects. These included the shows *JuJu Funk* (1975), at the Lindhurst Gallery of the University of Southern California; *JuJu III* (1976), at the Pearl C. Woods Gallery; and *JuJu* (1976), at The Gallery, the space on Pico Boulevard run by Samella Lewis. *Notes of a Griot* was first performed at Space Gallery in 1978 as part of a group exhibition. Conwill re-created the performance in a solo exhibition in New York later that year at the Just Above Midtown Gallery.[103]

Like Senga Nengudi's use of the term "fets" to suggest spiritual substances or "African fetishes," Conwill used *juju* to signal African-based devotional practices. His use of the word was in line with general definitions of *juju* as both object—a charm or amulet—and the supernatural power ascribed to it.[104] In Conwill's *JuJu* installations hybrid painted/sculpted elements hung from the walls and were laid out on the floor; he also invented two specialized items that became recurring ingredients in his performances. The "juju bags" were constructed from cast latex, later combined with Rhoplex, plastic media that could be poured out in sheets, painted, and incised, and which dried to a rubbery consistency. The resulting "fabric" was then sewn together to form bags, sometimes measuring three to five feet high or taller. Conwill "was fascinated by the physicality of the stuffed image"; the bags seemed to take on lives of their own, resembling human or animal forms.[105] The earth-toned pouches were embossed with a variety of emblems, symbolic writings, and blues lyrics. Inside, they held crosses, shells, rosary beads, and other avatars of healing, as might be found, for instance, in *nkisi* figures from the Congo/Angola region of Central Africa or Gregory (*gris-gris*) bags in the African American conjuring tradition as well as the medicinal asafetida pouches celebrated by John Outterbridge.[106] In designating the interior (and largely unseen) space of the juju bags as an "internal collage," artist and writer Yvonne Cole Meo also made Conwill's link to Romare Bearden more palpable and in doing so cast ritual as something that was material as well as experiential.[107]

Conwill gave the name "petrigraphs" to his latex sheets (fig. 4.11), which eventually replaced the large juju bags and his more traditional paintings on canvas. Their surfaces extended the symbolism he had begun developing in Washington; their planes evolved into new age fossils and cosmic maps. Cole Meo and Jeffries have compared these pieces to records and texts written on the body, whether as spiritual cicatrisation or as brands. His facility with intaglio printmaking processes was also evident.[108] Canvases immediately preceding the petrigraphs demonstrate a collage sensibility as Conwill moved toward a full multimedia expression; latex strips were added intermittently, as were bones, between 1974 and 1975. His change in materials, particularly

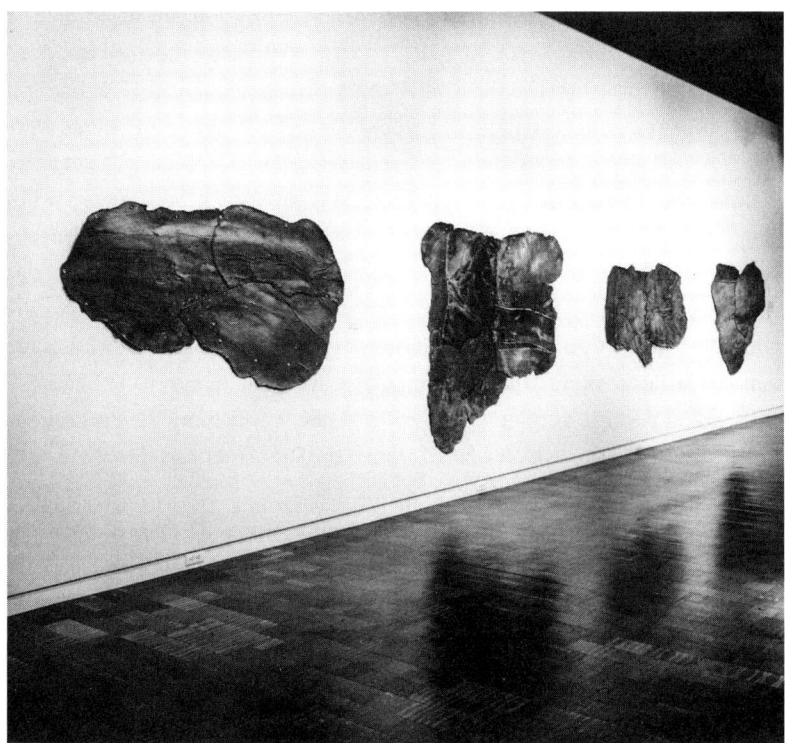

FIG. 4.11 Houston Conwill petrigraph works on exhibit at ARCO Center for Visual Art, 1970s. ARCO Center for Visual Art Records, 1976–1984, Archives of American Art, Smithsonian Institution.

his growing experimentation with latex and Rhoplex, also reflect changes in painting that were taking place throughout the country.[109]

The juju bags first suggested the idea of performative rites. As Yvonne Cole Meo notes, at a certain point "Conwill became aware that he was constructing . . . ritual object[s]." The artist's initial performance at the Lindhurst Gallery was a relatively modest interaction with the medicinal sacks he had created. At every subsequent performance, elements were added—dance and invocations, montages of chants and sounds—and more performers were included. They played music, danced, or traced the petrigraphs with their hands, "reading" the information held there.

In each instance, the focus came back to "the ceremonial space at the center of the room" (plate 25).[110] The action revolved around a central sculptural tableau. One or two circular fields of sand, approximately sixty inches

IN MOTION • 215

in diameter and surrounded by stones, formed a base. One of these circular environments held a narrow strip of red carpet ("a rich requiem-type red," according to the artist) linking a petrigraph-covered stool or chair at one end and a juju bag-ringed pail at the other.[111] Seemingly mundane items were transformed into ceremonial tools. The pail became a "gutbucket"—an antebellum container of "the food remains given [to] slaves."[112] Here Conwill's allusion to African American foodways celebrated heritage but also vernacular practice; the creation of delicacies (such as chitterlings) from discards was yet another approach to and commentary on the practice of assemblage. The gutbucket was a sign of a core "emotion or experience," an inspiration for that down-home blues, and fundamentally symbolic of survival.[113] The circular arena became a mnemonic device, visibly confirming the cyclical nature of Conwill's rite, which moved from Africa to American slavery time to bicentennial-era LA and its future and back.

Perched on the stool during the performance, Conwill's painted body became a medium, calling his forebears with an evocative litany. This base held the seated energy of the African ancestors in much the same way they do in the Akan traditions of Ghana, where stools are the absolute possession of the owners and are thought to be the seats of the soul. Most visibly, the stool is a symbol of state power. The rise and fall of political leaders is marked by the terms "enstooled" and "destooled," respectively. To rule is to "sit upon the stool," and when a leader dies, "the stool has fallen."[114] The Golden Stool symbolizes the unity and sovereignty of the Asante nation and is seen as embodying its essence. Gilded and festooned with ornaments and with amulets shaped like powerful animals (leopards, elephants) or covered with their skins, it is "treated like a living person, with its own set of regalia, musicians, and retainers."[115] Stools also can be sacred objects through which ancestors are venerated, mediums through which one contacts the dead, who watch over and secure the success of the society of the living.

In his extended *JuJu* project, 1975–78, Conwill reiterated such forms in a new, late twentieth-century, postmodern fashion, through performance and multimedia installation and in exciting, and surely diasporic ways. While the title suggests Nigerian roots and routes, the importance of seating in this work owes its logic to Akan traditions of Ghana. African Americans have been criticized for such cultural neologisms, seen as the result of misinformation about the continent, rather than admired for the creative reconceptualization of ritual and visual traditions. Yet the fact that African countries in the throes of independence in the 1950s and 1960s revisited traditions that had been suppressed and reconceptualized them gives us another contemporary context for such actions.[116]

Journeys of diasporic return, known as "roots tourism," emerged during the era of African independence as Americans and others fueled by the excitement of the postcolonial future made pilgrimages to try to make sense of their past. In castles and forts along the West African coast—like Gorée in Senegal and Cape Coast and Elmina in Ghana—peoples of the African Diaspora found "places where material evidence of the legacy of slavery still stands before their eyes and is available to be touched, walked through, and experienced with all of their senses and with the movement of their bodies through the space."[117]

Conwill's performance (at times referred to as *JuJu Ritual*) evoked this type of travel on a performative and metaphysical plane. It addressed what Saidiya Hartman has thought about as a kind of a leaky slavery, and what Salamishah Tillet sees as the conflicted feel of contemporary democracy—the experience of continuing unfreedom in the present—with the figure of bodily ownership instantiated through performance.[118] Here the artist substituted historical chronology for time that is nonlinear, synchronic, and syncretic, respatializing these geographies through bodies and objects. In doing so he evoked what Rebecca Schneider and others have referred to as tangled temporalities: a sense of time that is syncopated, where "then and now" punctuate each other;[119] what José Muñoz thinks of as "not-quite-here" and "no-longer-there," where bygone moments remain in the present and the present modulates the age-old.[120] This sense of seeing the past "from its future" inflects the everyday, signaling the new availability of past signs as modalities for action rather than simply shadows of style.[121]

As Schneider remarks, the moment of the cross-temporal is the space of performance, in which the question of "when" is vexed: "The undoing of linear time is part of the nervousness or queasiness of theatricality, contributing to the uncertainty of where and how time takes place: today's agendas necessarily contain, recompose, recite, and touch 1678, and vice versa."[122] In his performance Conwill evoked the body reliving and reconstructing the cycle of African diasporic history through ritual and through a constructed environment whose abstracted material culture did not strictly mime things in African tradition but, like contemporary Africans on the continent, created a modernist object/space that signaled a future of freedom.

The 1976 shows and performances took place in black-owned spaces: *JuJu III* at the Pearl C. Wood Gallery, run by Greg Pitts, and *JuJu* at The Gallery,

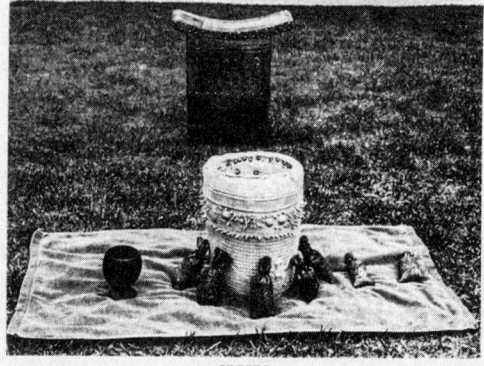

FIG. 4.12 Brochure for Houston Conwill's exhibition *JuJu* at Samella Lewis's space, The Gallery, with text by Betye Saar, 1976. ARCO Center for Visual Art Records, 1976–1984, Archives of American Art, Smithsonian Institution.

run by Samella Lewis (fig. 4.12).[123] At the latter site Kinshasha Holman Conwill renewed her collaborations with her husband, moving from wall-based, mural projects to live action. It was around this time that she ceased to make her own objects altogether.[124] The more elaborate costuming and makeup in Conwill's work surely owed something to Kinshasha's interest in body ornamentation and dress. Another influential source may have been *African Art in Motion*, the exhibition organized by Robert Farris Thompson and on view at the Wight Art Gallery at UCLA in 1975. A video displayed there showed a Basinjom masquerade from the Ejagham of Nigeria and Cameroon, with an initiate using a knife to ritually cleanse his eyes and vision. This footage probably provided the inspiration for *JuJu Ritual*'s knife dance around the perimeters of the circular floor motif, symbolic of exorcising negative spirits.[125]

These first three *JuJu* performances by Conwill coincided with the end of his graduate school career at USC. It was also the time of the bicentennial celebrations surrounding the founding of the United States, which evoked for a number of African American artists (including David Hammons, Faith Ringgold, and Benny Andrews) an opportunity to reflect on black citizenship, its partial, inadequate, and incomplete project. Octavia Butler's novel *Kindred* (1979) similarly engages this moment and, like Conwill's piece, evokes time travel between a slave past and contemporary Los Angeles.[126] Both Conwill's and Butler's works are manifestations of African American artists' mobilization of aspects of a collective past, specifically a slave past, in commentaries on present-day life. As such they are emblematic of Hartman's, Copeland's, and Tillet's discussions of the uses of enslaved histories to narrate aspects of unfreedom in the twentieth century (or slavery's future). Pondering marginalized temporalities, Elizabeth Freeman's writing on "queer time" is particularly useful, especially her notion of "temporal drag": ideas of delay, retrogression, and the "pull of the past on the present" at moments when historical situations can be more fully comprehended, exerting a "necessary pressure on the present tense."[127] It is a deployment of "'drag,' so central to theorizing the mobility of gender identification . . . as an excess . . . of the signifier 'history.'"[128] These and other objects and artists recounted in this book manifest a parallel "queer desire for history," one that does not simply inhabit "temporal and historical difference" against a chrononormativity that sublimated such histories and cultural practices.[129] Instead, these are people who have had to seek out and rebuild that which came before using "whatever heuristic is at hand: conjecture, fantasy, overreading, revision."[130] They create things mindful of a temporal transitivity that does not abandon anachronism but remobilizes it.

Conwill's two 1978 performances demonstrate a further evolution of the *JuJu* performance concept along these lines. The Los Angeles version at Space Gallery was still embedded in an exhibition context but as a three-person (rather than solo) show that probably offered a more limited access to space, possibly a contributing factor to the growth of the live component.[131] It also presented another moment for the Conwills to collaborate. The stool or chair, the gutbucket, red carpet, petriglyphs, juju bags, and floor-based circles made from stones and sand remain consistent from earlier iterations.[132] There was a sound collage of music (spirituals, blues), and the artists' own chanting, but they were also accompanied by live musicians on flute and congas.[133]

Wine, water, ethereal dust, and liturgical drama were added.[134] "They bow, kneel and wash their hands," one viewer observed. "After lighting candles and incense, they apply ceremonial markings to their bodies and call on their ancestors to witness the celebration."[135] After the knife dance, Kinshasha placed a petrigraph inside one of the circular fields. Conwill anointed the ears of the audience with oil to receive the litany, and circumnavigated the other circle, sprinkling dust and chanting while Kinshasha traced his tale on the petrigraph as he spoke. The piece ended when the artists shared a chalice of wine, then distributed figs from a basket to the audience.[136]

Later that year, the full performance was returned to the solo-exhibition format—in this case, Conwill's New York debut at Linda Goode Bryant's Just Above Midtown Gallery (JAM), the only black-owned space on the city's exclusive commercial gallery row. It followed the same pattern as the Los Angeles piece. While Kinshasha didn't participate, her part was expanded. David Hammons performed the knife dance, taking his wild spinning movements (accentuated by arcing dreadlocks) from his role in Nengudi's *Ceremony for Freeway Fets*. Singer/composer Diana Wharton delivered a chant or "ritual litany"; Ed Fletcher and Al Jackson played congas and flute, respectively.[137] Baskets of mulberries and dates constituted the final offering to the audience, replacing the California figs.

Notes of a Griot, 1978, had an alternative title, *Imani's Tale*, which was taken from a petrigraph of the same name. For the first time, the performance concentrated primarily on a specific account of an individual archetypal character: a young woman who becomes the guiding force of her family on the death of her mother and older brother. Imani is pregnant, so the stage is set for a cycle of communication between the living, the dead, and the unborn. In his move from more schematic and intuitive actions to interactions with objects, Conwill revealed the larger story he was, perhaps unconsciously, trying to tell. It was a chronicle replayed and resounding throughout the globe, across the routes and way stations of the diaspora. It was not so much that *Imani's Tale* was more traditionally narrative, but that it was more "representational"; indeed, many of the visual components here certainly remained fairly abstract. But the symbolic impact seems evident. Conwill's "ritual setting" used items that that were in continuous conversation. The thick latex wall hangings, the floor-based field of installation, and live action that became ritual were symbolic equivalents on different planes. Together, they sketched out a place that became an avatar of time; place became time physically remembered.

Imani's Tale speaks to both the time and place of diaspora. By creating modern rituals that look to Africa for their cultural logic, Conwill and friends, like Nengudi, perform "transatlantic identification." As Saidiya Hartman reminds us, Africa becomes a mirror, a territory where African Americans work out notions of home, identity, and kinship. However, "the journey 'home' is always a journey back, that is, back in time, since the identification with Africa as an originary site occurs by way of the experience of enslavement."[138]

Imani's Tale not only gives us the trope of past, present, future in which we can imagine these histories—of Africa and enslavement, the Afro-futuristic tomorrow, and the contemporary artist as shaman bringing them together—conversing and colliding. Here temporal crossing is not only between the old and new but with the historical imbricated with the ritual. As Freeman posits, ritual/theatrical/performative time is outward, public facing and as such embraces the allegorical. These contemporary narratives that compound new stories with old are never simply personal: a dissident past becomes the fuel to "detonate... a transformative future."[139] In Conwill's performance, gesture—suggested rather than coherent movement—is, Muñoz tells us, an "idealist manifestation," the "not-quite-here" that has hope in and faithfully anticipates another future.[140]

Also important here is the specter of kinship that pervades and structures the piece. *Imani's Tale* centers the notion of the protagonist's biological family; yet in effect these positions—child, mother, brother—that offer the structure of the cycle are abstractions that appeal to deep-seated desires. Indeed, as Hartman notes, "slavery denied the captive all claims of kin and community; this loss of natal affiliation and the enduring pain of ancestors who remain anonymous still haunt the descendants of the enslaved." This is what Toni Morrison has seen as constructing the world through remains and through memory.[141]

It is this longing that drives the push for Pan-African unity between Africa and its diaspora. The return to the native land often is impossible and taboo; this is understood as loss and dealt with through mourning.[142] In *Notes of a Griot / Imani's Tale*, Conwill's rite, with its fixation on ancestors, acknowledged this loss and sought to exorcise the accompanying pain with the knife dance. But the focus was also on what came next: moving into the future, survival. In the alternate title, the name Imani spoke to this too: the word means "faith" in Swahili. It is the seventh and final principle of the Nguzo Saba (Swahili for Seven Principles), which forms the basis of the Kwanzaa celebration, another African American ritual of kinship started in Los Angeles about a decade before. By this time, Conwill had nominated himself a griot, a West African storyteller, historian, and praise singer. Through ritual, the artist invented a realm of healing that was cognizant of antecedents in "slave music, slave religion, slave folk beliefs [which] created the necessary space between the slaves and their owners and were means of preventing legal slavery from becoming spiritual slavery."[143]

In one sense the context of the diaspora may be one of mourning and loss: the state of ensuing slavery and contemporary unfreedom offer up pain. However, as curator and critic Gerardo Mosquera reminds us, we should not see the resulting culture as struggling "survivals"; on the contrary, African culture "on the other side of the Atlantic" is flexible, appropriative, transformational, and dynamic, in the process inflecting and shaping modernist cultural dynamics and the space of imagination.[144] Loss is countered by creation and reinvention, the exuberance of the retelling, and the retelling as its own success and victory. In these performances and installations between 1975 and 1978 Houston Conwill created ceremonial settings, using his body to address, confront, and ultimately transcend "remnants of transatlantic slavery," through ritual.[145]

Rather than thinking of Conwill's art practices at the moment as simply a neo or faux African rearticulation in contemporary form, we should also consider the possibility of its continuities with praxes throughout the diaspora and over time. Conwill's flexibility of approach allowed him to alter and change elements. The substituting of the stool for the chair in the central ceremonial space brings us right up against other diasporic modes. Consider Cuban modernist Wifredo Lam's *The Chair*, 1943, a seemingly straightforward painting of a piece of furniture in the midst of a garden scene. But the centralization of the chair makes it the painting's singular interest, its protagonist, and rather than a person a vase of flowers is seated there. Made when Lam returned to Cuba from France during World War II, the painting is an articulation of a type of Santería altar and is accompanied by additional sketches Lam made of ceremonial spaces.[146] This portrait of ritual reconnected Lam with his cultural heritage. In his formidable treatise *Face of the Gods: Art and Altars of Africa and the African Americas*, Robert Farris Thompson reveals a panoply of devotional objects and sites that anchor women and men "at life's deepest moments. . . . They back up crisis or transition with the immortal presence of the divine."[147] Their defining and collective tropes were the "additive, eclectic, non-exclusivistic" properties that allowed their existence, hidden in plain view of dominant and suppressive powers.[148] Their objects were mundane, apparent discards or simple everyday things. Like the slave church, they were ephemeral, existing "where two or three . . . gathered together" in the name of the Lord, furtively and quickly, and then dissolving into the day or night.[149] As Thompson recounts, in traditions all over the world, an altar is the word of god raised on high and celebrated. In some West African (Akan) and Latin American (Surinam, Haiti) examples, these altars can be made of fabric, flags consecrated to the divine and emblazoned with ideographic writing.

Conwill, in effect, did the same; his petrigraphs were latex wall hangings, mounted on the wall. They were embedded with "texts" revealed by the artist/shaman/reader. Conwill made it very clear that his juju bags had medicinal and metaphysical powers of healing and were patterned after African prototypes.[150] Indeed, we can see this very specifically in Kongo *nkisi* sculptures, which include pouches of medicinal and ideographic avatars of healing. In Haiti, these became *pacquets congo*, fabric sacks topped with feathers invested with the same properties. Similarly, Conwill's circles in stone and sand were improvised Kongo ideograms that can be drawn on the floor to create an altar and are re-created in liturgical rites in Haiti as *veve* and in Brazil as *pontos riscados*. Yet Thompson concludes that African and African American altars are both fixed (that is, invested in objects) and mobile (evoked in "happening and motion, climaxed by possession").[151] And indeed, "all altars overthrow time"; they are concentrations of devotion, spirituality, divine power, and energy.[152] Conwill was making an altar without making an altar.[153]

Los Angeles critic Suzanne Muchnic noted that "the physical closeness of an overflow audience seated on the floor and the performers' convincing involvement with their narrative gave *JuJu Ritual* an impact of religious or community experience quite different from most contemporary performance."[154] Richard J. Powell, reviewing the New York presentation for *Neworld* magazine, agreed; he found the piece to be "a curious mélange of Dadist [sic] soap-boxing, Yoruba ceremony and Revivalist soul-stirring."[155] Conwill and the other performers were "celebrants," much more a description of New World religious ritual than what may have constituted contemporary performative forms elsewhere. Indeed, Powell continues, *Notes of a Griot* was without the "vacuous mystification" that seemed to characterize trends of the period where the body was considered an object to be manipulated, in works by artists such as Chris Burden, Vito Acconci, Carolee Schneemann, or even Adrian Piper.[156]

Performance in this period was enacted by a skeptical body, according to Peter Gorsen; it detailed the "perversion of progress" that was the postmodern experience and thus was transfixed by tropes of crisis (such as alienation, madness, illness, the exigencies of identity).[157] Written on the performer's body, the boundaries between real and theatrically manufactured pain were often blurred. A thin line was drawn between the *reinterpretation* of life's plights and their wholesale *repetition*. Under the rubric of "ritual" some artists breached social boundaries, transforming gender, performing acts of systematic self-mutilation, and interacting with bodily fluids and wastes.[158] Perhaps the most infamous artists subscribing to this type of performance were the Viennese Actionists active during the 1960s.[159] Casting themselves as shamans performing sacrificial acts, they sought to emancipate the body from a regulated socialization and the mechanisms of technology, in a critique that was directed more at the state than at narrowly defined art audiences.

These models of what Philip Ursprung calls "hurting and healing" were also present in pieces by other European and American artists, like Gina Pane, Linda Montano, and Paul McCarthy; but they seem to be absent from the work of Conwill or the other Los Angeles–based artists discussed here.[160] Yet certainly the black body as sacrifice was much more visible and, in one sense, had much more social currency. Within the American historical context, the image of the violated black body held a long-standing and powerful symbolism: from the moment of capture and shipment in Africa (immortalized by the slave-ship schematic) to punishment and torture under a system of forced labor to the lynching process that constituted a type of spectacle and entertainment for whites. Given this history of the black body in pain, it has been hard for some audiences, black audiences in particular, to see similar images reinscribed as "art." For some, the horror is best banished altogether, since to put those reflections out there, even to deconstruct them, fixes them once again in our memory.

The visualization of the abject black body is largely absent in the various versions of Conwill's *JuJu* project from 1975 to 1978. This was the case for much fine art produced by African Americans throughout the twentieth century; in Jacob Lawrence's *Migration* series, for instance, lynching is represented by an empty noose rather than a hanging body. However, like earlier artists, Conwill relies on metaphorical evocations, particularly in the first exhibition in the series, *JuJu Funk*, which features life-size juju bags. Conwill discussed the anthropomorphic cast of one particular piece, a six-foot sack suspended inside a frame of stretcher bars that referenced violent death, lynching, and crucifixion.[161] Some African American artists did access the potent authority of the highly charged figural presence of the black body. David Hammons was one of them.

DAVID HAMMONS: IN SPADES

"Ritual is an action word," declares David Hammons (fig. 4.13) as he moves methodically between one unassuming pile of rubble and another. Back and

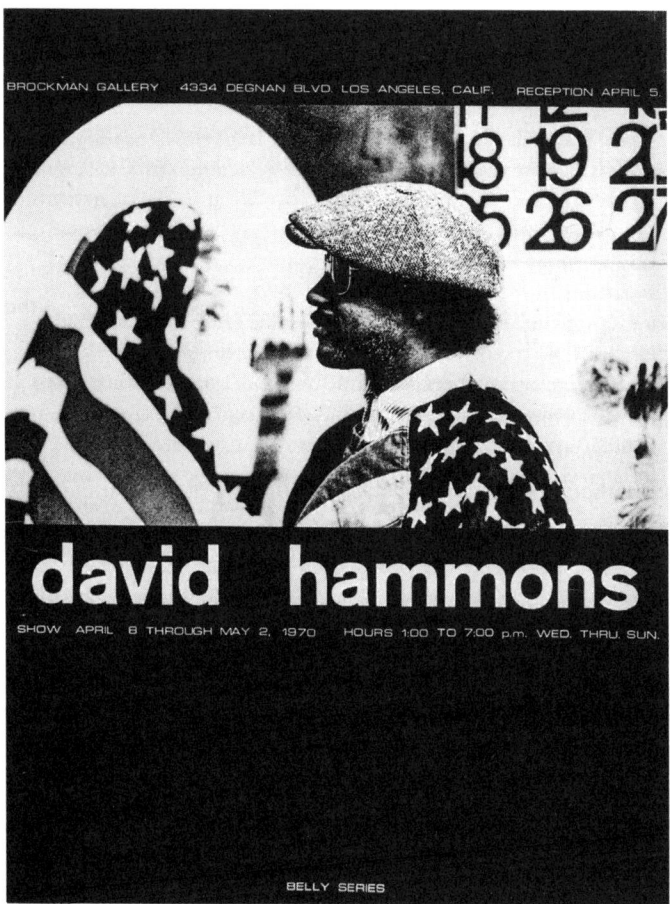

FIG. 4.13 Announcement for David Hammons exhibition at Brockman Gallery, 1970. Courtesy Brockman Gallery Archives.

forth he paces, trying to hide the long cord of the otherwise well-hidden microphone that snakes subtly behind him. Hammons is addressing interviewer and director Barbara McCullough in the latter's compelling film *Shopping Bag Spirits and Freeway Fetishes: Reflections on Ritual Space* (1979). Conceived as a meditation on African American art and ritual, McCullough looks at the production of poets and musicians but dedicates most of the film to visual artists. In his ruminations, Hammons refers again and again to the art of Betye Saar. What captivates him in particular is the notion of her works as sites for gathering, recycling, and recirculating energy, whether creative or spiritual. No matter the physical manifestation, these become altars or "spirit catchers," places that motivate performative rites.

Saar's dialogue with David Hammons began in the 1960s. A pair of works—Hammons's *Black Boy's Window*, 1968, and Saar's *Black Girl's Window*, 1969—tell the tale. In Hammons's piece, the conjunction of a window frame and his body print take us to the space of separate but equal or even to jail, as the bar-like structure of the window grill placed over the figure accentuates both exclusion and containment. The boy's hands are raised, either banging for entry or held high in a posture of surrender ("No, I don't have a gun"). Saar's work also uses a window frame to organize compositional structure. *Black Girl's Window*, however, represents the reinscription of the recognizable black self after its disappearance for a number of years. Saar's girl holds her hands against an invisible windowpane, seeming to peer out at what is to come. Her palms are covered with mystical symbols, some of which are reiterated in smaller panes above. Saar's piece is more otherworldly and elusive, a meditation on black biography and autobiography that is not as forthright and didactic as Hammons's take. Her assemblage is delicately polychromed, while his emphasizes the contrasting black and white of the print and the bars and weathered wooden surface of the window. Hammons's *Black Boy's Window* also retained a window shade with a pull, as if one could just as easily shut out what was going on with African America in 1968. The implied motion pointed toward the performance practice the artist would soon develop.[162] The dialogue between Saar and Hammons here is quite clear—from their titles to the central figurative/autobiographical form to the found frame. Both are mixed-media assemblages. Yet Saar made more use of painting and collage, while Hammons's two-dimensional component is one of the intriguing "body prints" that first catapulted him into the public eye.

The body prints captured the public imagination with their subtle textures and figural and sensual presence. However, it was his development of the printing process itself that was most compelling. He used himself as the printable "plate," greasing up (usually with margarine), leaning or lying on a piece of paper or board, then sprinkling the grease-infused areas with powdered pigment to create a positive reproduction. They are fundamentally monoprints, although Hammons, at times, added silkscreen elements to these emblematic indexes. The fulcrum of signification, however, revolved around the performative body. In these graphic images, as in much of his art in the ensuing ten-year period, Hammons employed the African American figure as active signifier rather than simply seeking to fix a likeness.

The body prints share some similarities with the *Anthropometries* of Yves Klein. And indeed, Hammons had witnessed this technique as it was taught at Chouinard Art Institute, where he studied after getting fed up with both Los

Angeles Trade Technical College and Otis Art Institute.[163] Rather than using a woman as a titillating paintbrush (one that was further objectified as her limp form was pulled around a surface), Hammons was the dynamic agent, collapsing the position of auteur with those of signifier *and* signified. Or, as Richard J. Powell put it, with this work he began his "contextual 'slow dragging' with the visual/sensorial 'self.'"[164]

Particularly with the earliest body prints, between 1968 and 1970, the tales Hammons weaves are social, ethical, political; as he commented in Samella Lewis and Ruth Waddy's *Black Artists on Art* (1969), "I feel it my moral obligation as a black artist, to try to graphically document what I feel socially."[165] Pieces such as *Black Boy's Window*, 1968, and *The Door (Admissions Office)*, 1969, commented on African American exclusion from opportunity; in *Injustice Case*, 1970, persecution by the American system was the theme. Another group of works used the American flag as a symbol of black disenfranchisement (e.g., *Boy with Flag*, 1968) and fit within work by artists nationwide who used the flag to represent the failure of the American dream.[166] However, like Charles White, Hammons produced other pieces that caressed the black body, emphasizing the beauty and sensuality of women and men (e.g., *Untitled Couple*, no date) and that still fall under the rubric of Black Arts Movement celebration of black corporeality.

Hammons's prints were connected to assemblage through the materials of facture, though their deconstruction signals postminimalism: oil or grease, smoothed over the body; pigment (often chalk ground to dust); scraps of fabric, yarn, and other items used to create the compositional image; and even the body itself. The surfaces themselves were unique: paper and wallpaper in a variety of weights and colors, collaged and fragmented, keep us in the realm of found materials. In some pieces, such as *Black Boy's Window* and *Admissions Office*, assemblage is even more evident in the printing on windows and doors.[167] *Injustice Case*, 1970, fits this profile as well. A large print measuring five by three feet, its border is an actual American flag. The piece was originally enclosed in a display case (later destroyed accidentally in transit), which added to its substantial presence.

However, *Injustice Case* also signaled the direction in which Hammons was heading. He would create a series of works highlighting the specter of American and diasporic violence, pieces that revealed the black body caught in a historical cycle of brutality perpetrated by a world that based its own wealth on traffic in the flesh. The gift of these works, though, is that the element of violence is seen not as an immobilizing force but as one in which black language can intervene. *Injustice Case* is an image of a black man gagged and bound to a chair, Hammons's vision of Bobby Seale, cofounder and chairman of the Black Panther Party. Seale was forcibly restrained for four days in the courtroom during the trial of the Chicago Eight, who were charged with inciting a riot at the Democratic National Convention in 1968. Refusing to allow Seale to serve as his own lawyer, the judge had Seale contained, in a spectacle of authoritarian cruelty. In Hammons's multimedia print, fabric is transmuted not only into the material of restraint but into rope, making tangible the conflation between brutality perpetrated against the black body in the late twentieth century and the specter of the past in slavery and lynching.

As Kristine Stiles observes, body-centered art not only represents but continually reinscribes survival, taking as its object the body's ability to emerge and thrive even in the midst of annihilation, laying out a recuperative function for Hammons's piece.[168] Saidiya Hartman might cast the artist's actions here as a counternarrative or countermemory, "as if the location of the wound was itself a cure."[169] In this case, the wound was slavery but more expansively the panoply of violence, both historical and present-day, perpetrated against the black body. Even Hammons's use of materials—including black bodies—can be seen as a type of "mourning" that "makes visible the lost object."[170] According to Hartman, the "lost object" becomes concepts of home, kin, belonging, stripped away by the Middle Passage and by brutality. But that turn of phrase is a boon for our art historical narrative, as it embraces and honors the types of elements that Hammons and others were working with at this time.

Injustice Case also reveals the centrality of language to Hammons. The piece first appeared in a solo exhibition at the Brockman Gallery in April 1970, not hung on the wall but in a seven-foot-high glass case with locked doors. This enclosure was lit and lined with black velvet like a fixture used for displaying jewelry or precious museum objects. Inside, "on a slightly elevated section, directly in front of the print, rested a gavel, presumably the sort a judge would use to call a court of law to order."[171] The metaphor of black unfreedom, delivered in the printed vision of the bound and gagged figure, framed by the Stars and Stripes, was finally brought home by the artwork itself being contained "in justice's case."

In Hammons's work, the possessive form of the noun "justice" was implied but not used, which certainly made the pun more effective. But it also approximated a vernacular approach to syntax found in African American communities. Hammons would continue to be inspired by the everyday speech of black people. In this sense, his fascination with the word as an identifying force, as method of defining self and space, was parallel to and in dialogue with poets of the Black Arts Movement. This affection for language would be a key aspect throughout the artist's career and would ultimately mark him as a conceptualist. He captured this spirit more fully in his next group of works.

With his *Spade* series, c. 1971–74, Hammons moved further into a multimedia and performance practice and pushed the manipulation of language. Its basis was the concept of a "spade," not just as shovel or symbol from a deck of cards but as a derogatory attribution for African Americans. By showing the spade in so many permutations—as two- and three-dimensional objects and as theater—he sought to empty it of charged symbolism, reverse and open up its meaning, deconstruct the image, and divest it of its power. The spade became something recognizable yet unknown, "an instrument to pry apart the structures of habit."[172] As the artist recounted:

> I was trying to figure out why black people were called spades as opposed to clubs. Because I remember being called a spade once, and I didn't know what it meant; nigger I knew but spade I still don't. So, I just took the shape, and started painting it. I started dealing with the spade the way Jim Dine was using the heart . . . then I started getting shovels and made masks out of them. It was just like a chain reaction. . . . I was running my car over these spades and then photographing them. I was hanging them from trees. Some were made out of leather (they were skins).[173]

Jim Dine's practice, like Hammons's, was shaped by a multimedia sensibility. Primarily a painter, he began to bring bits of the world—a shoe, a tie, a lawnmower—into his canvases in the late 1950s, either as assemblage or in painted form. Similar in spirit to Jasper Johns and Robert Rauschenberg, Dine was nevertheless linked more closely to pop art because it was not the emotional register of painting but the aura of objects that took center stage in his pieces. The things he focused on were pervasive and proved to be open and flexible vehicles that could shoulder a wide variety of connotations. Opposed to the restrictive label "pop," Dine felt the items he chose were invested with more symbolic meaning and autobiographical weight; he was concerned with the life of objects as allegorical vessels for human existence.[174]

Dine's emblematic use of the body attracted Hammons. Corporeality was a text in a broader context and a larger world—if not the body itself, then clothing, tools, and things that embodied its trace. Dine began working with hearts in the late 1960s and, like Hammons's spades, they were articulated in a variety of media, from painting to assemblage to prints. Clothing and other articles traced bodily gesture and as such suggested a crystallization of the pathway between the conscious and unconscious, ultimately intimating the connection between object and body. Things became vessels for people and ideas. However, Dine's project was more openly an individualized self-portrait, while Hammons spoke with a stronger collective voice.

The body print *Three Spades*, 1971 (fig. 4.14), shows a black man (the artist "in print") holding two familiar (if enlarged) emblems taken from a deck of playing cards. The conflation between symbol, slur, and human being continues the tradition of straightforward social commentary practiced by artists like White. In sculptural pieces such as *Laughing Magic* and *Bird* (plate 28), both 1973, Hammons took a more celebratory stance. Each paid homage to respective African and African American legacies, one through the use of the mask form, the other as a quiet monument to the musical genius of alto saxophonist Charlie "Yardbird" Parker. In his interaction with spade objects, Hammons created some of his earliest performance works. Using the spade as a performative device, however, gave his concept a more violent edge. Shapes cut from cardboard or leather served as his props, but they also became stand-ins for black bodies.

These early performances, easy interactions with objects, became known as *Spade Mysteries*. According to Linda Goode Bryant and Marcy S. Philips, Hammons invented a "series of social and psychological dramas," putting the spade in situations where it was "cut, tied, and chained."[175] Given the violent repression of African Americans and Africans who were agitating against injustice and colonialism, it would not be a stretch to see Hammons's spade performances as a coded response to the times. Despite their ephemeral form, these pieces traced the mutilated and secreted bodies of Emmett Till and Medgar Evers, the brutal assassinations of Martin Luther King Jr. and Malcolm X, the targeted extermination of the Black Panthers and other casualties of the African American struggle for equity in the latter half of the twentieth century. Hammons's actions also accessed more historical events—the viciousness of antebellum slavery as well as the lynching of countless African Americans, known and unknown, male and female, going back to the nineteenth century. As Jacqueline Goldsby has argued, lynching was both a spectacle in its marshaling of technologies of modernity and secret in the way the racial violence was discounted, justified, or never acknowledged.[176]

Hammons no doubt experienced some forms of hostility and coercion in his daily life in Los Angeles and earlier in his upbringing in Springfield.[177] In this sense we can think of him and his family as "witnesses" to Springfield's history of violence in the ways that Elizabeth Alexander has constructed the term. Looking at texts, from slave narratives to the televised accounts of the

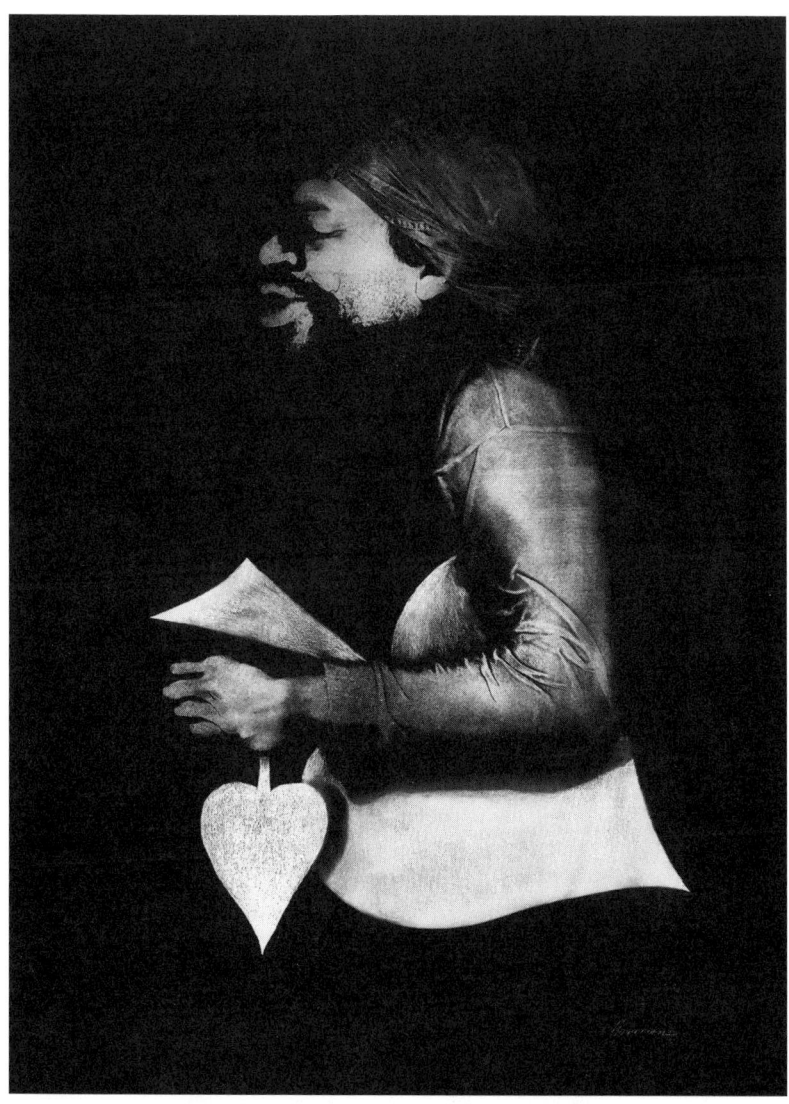

FIG. 4.14 David Hammons, *Three Spades*, 1971. Body print. Glenstone Museum, Potomac, Maryland. Courtesy the artist; photograph by Alex Jamison © 2015 David Hammons.

Rodney King beating in Los Angeles a century later, Alexander dissects what it means to witness. Writers of slave narratives, like Frederick Douglass and Linda Brent / Harriet Jacobs, see or hear brutality perpetrated against others and feel it, knowing they will be next (that being the purpose of the spectacle of cruelty, after all). As Alexander explains, people "who receive [these] stories" are made witnesses as well, although at a distance.[178] This becomes particularly clear if we think of the "audience" for the Rodney King video and the reaction it compelled in the form of urban rebellion in Los Angeles: people who felt the pain of the decision in their bodies and put them on the line in responsive protest. Witnesses and the stories they engender become forms of knowledge that can be carried and recorded in the body. Such storied violence, notes Alexander, is "passed along so that everyone knows the parameters in which their bodies move."[179] These are tales at once apocryphal and instructive, filled with horror so that one might live. Alexander's notion of witness is at home with other examinations of the flows of temporalities—Schneider's tangle, Freeman's drag—that think about history's availability in the present, particularly occluded, secreted, sublimated histories and intelligence passed down as bodily knowing. It is the potentiality that lives in gesture for Muñoz and which challenges chrononormativity and pushes a dissident and hoped-for future.

In this light, how might David Hammons and his family have metaphorically "lived" or "experienced" Springfield's race riot of 1908, where people died at the hands of mob violence and black homes and businesses were burned to the ground.[180] How might this incident, early in the century, have charged the terrain and colored the landscape that the young Hammons moved through in the 1940s and 1950s? In 1955, at a sweltering summer funeral in nearby Chicago, a casket was left open, revealing the mutilated body of the teenage Emmett Till—a body purposefully left unprettified by the mortician's hand—so that "all the world [would] *witness* the atrocity."[181] Not quite forty years later, Hammons created an installation in northwestern Massachusetts titled *Yardbird Suite*, an homage to Charlie Parker and the tune he penned in the 1940s after being beaten and jailed in Jackson, Mississippi, for violating a nightly curfew for African Americans.[182] It is clear, then, that *Bird*, Hammons's 1973 (plate 28) homage to Parker—with its tender application of a painted mannequin's hand to the keys of a sax and a corroded spade where the mouthpiece should be—conflated image and slur in a way that accessed this same history of abuse.

The tropes of absence and presence in Hammons's *Spade Mysteries* access such occlusions of history, what Goldsby refers to as the "spectacular secret," things that make a highly visual and violent imprint on the mind but remain unaccounted for in the national record or the nation's memory. Communities of people thus are compelled to remember, retain, and recalibrate this violence as litany, tale, and art. Hammons captured this sensibility in works from the early 1970s in which the black body was at once absent and present. The artist has referred to one piece from the series, *Spade Covered with Sand* or *Buried Spade*, no date, as an "earth work," the action being what the titles/descriptions suggest: Hammons dug a hole and entombed the form in the ground.[183]

Documentation of *Murder Mystery* (also known as *Spade Run Over by a Volkswagen*), 1972 (plates 26 and 27), shows a cardboard spade "crushed" under the wheel of a Volkswagen Beetle, with painted blood pouring forth. Cars formed a very active palette for art making at this moment; examples include Chamberlain's crushed metal sculptures; Dine's *Car Crash* performance, 1960; or any number of pieces by California artists, like Edward Keinholz's infamous *Back Seat Dodge '38*, 1964, or Suzanne Lacy's *Pink Jalopy*, 1972.[184] But perhaps the most useful comparisons to *Murder Mystery* are a few early performances by Chris Burden, which share a Southern California context, a private aspect in which the public viewing is very limited, and a fascination with violence. There is symmetry between *Murder Mystery* and Burden's *Transfixed*, 1974; both seem to employ the car as machine confronting the living body. Burden, like Hammons, uses a Volkswagen Beetle as a central protagonist.[185] In Burden's piece, the artist had his hands nailed to the roof of the car in the posture of a crucifixion. The process of nailing took place in a small garage in Venice; the car backed out of the structure, revealing Burden's body affixed to the vehicle, and moments later rolled back inside. In one photograph of *Murder Mystery*, we see the Volkswagen Beetle on the road. In the next image, the spade is caught under the wheels with blood oozing from the cardboard character.

As in the rest of the spade actions discussed here, Hammons's own body is absent, but the outsize shape stands in its place. These are protoactions, almost nonactions, in which the spades assume the posture of bodies, signaling activity and presence. In one sense, they demonstrate Hammons's refusal of the figure, with the spade as a tool to free him from the tyranny of the body as form, as he shifted away from the prints that both represented and captured the human index. In the context of the Black Arts Movement, Hammons's move toward performance was a rejection of simplified notions of representation, which made visible the previously invisible and thus remained tied to the corporeal form. In the *Spade* series, he grappled with decoupling the body from artistic signification. But these activities also evince his will to represent processes ensnaring the individual: to effect, capture, invade, mark, and articulate it through the mechanics of pain; to enunciate the body not as the perennial "Negro problem" but as a site for the perpetration of violence, experienced daily by people of color around the globe.

Perhaps Chris Burden's most sensational piece is the performance *Shoot*, 1971. For all its publicity, it was a very private affair with a few friends as audience/witnesses, including the marksman who grazed Burden's arm with a bullet. "How do you know what it feels like to be shot if you don't get shot?" he rationalized.[186] Here the empiricism and literalism of minimalism and the specter of war were conflated to pose ethical questions: if this is what we are doing to others, we must experience it for ourselves. However, with the body itself positioned as the site of empirical investigation, we are led to post-minimalism and performance. To Burden, being shot was very "American," from movie myths—cowboy shoot-'em-ups to space chases—to the context of the war itself. But as scholar Frazer Ward emphasizes, *Shoot* reinscribed the "colonial asymmetry" of Burden's action; it was not specifically an antiwar protest. There was nothing at stake for the artist himself (as there was for the "friend" who fired the shot or the witnesses who could be cast as accessories to a crime). And while the artist acknowledged that his action didn't compare to the vicissitudes and vagaries of war, it was one he had elected to do to understand such aggression.[187] As Ward argues, though Burden's deeds were private, they nevertheless were addressed to the public sphere. However, there was an ambiguity in Burden's acts, whose vagaries and occluded nature permitted a variety of readings.

In an interview with the artist in 1973, Peter Plagens raised the notion that Burden's—for all intents and purposes—self-inflicted wound mirrored not only those of soldiers in Vietnam but also those of "street gang" members.[188] In this regional context, the word "gang" also immediately and silently evoked the apparition of race, of black and Latino gang bangers, the figures of the urban rebellions, the old wine of the "Negro Problem" in an updated bottle, coloring Los Angeles in the process as a violent landscape.[189]

Maybe this is where Chris Burden and David Hammons found real common ground: with their images of the violated body, private acts addressed to a larger public via remnants or relics, small objects, and unassuming photos or video documentation. While Burden in some ways was *privileged* to be able to use his own body in such self-inflicted acts of violence, Hammons chose as

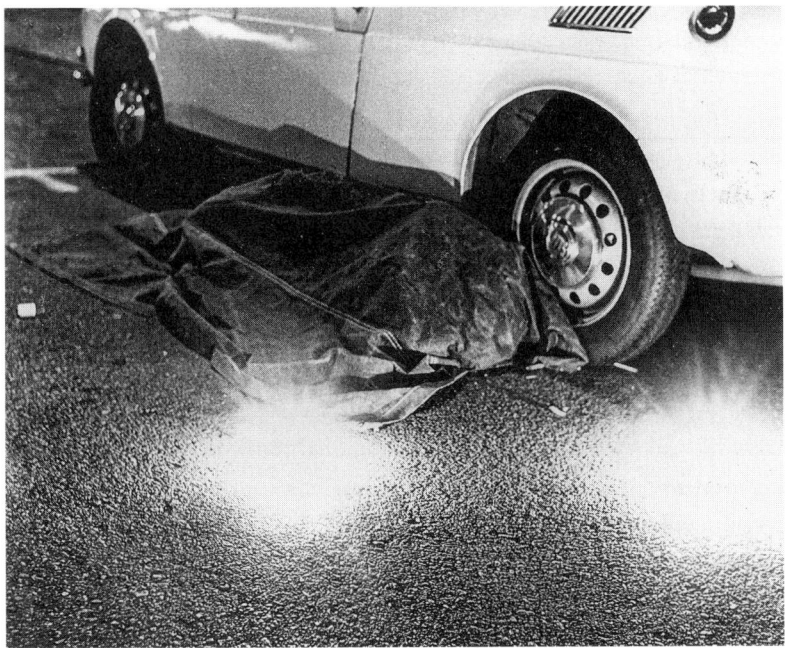

At 8 p.m. I lay down on La Cienega Boulevard and was covered completely with a canvas tarpolin. Two fifteen-minute flares were placed near me to alert cars. Just before the flares extinguished, a police car arrived. I was arrested and booked for causing a false emergency to be reported. Trial took place in Beverly Hills. After three days of deliberation, the jury failed to reach a decision, and the judge dismissed the case.

FIG. 4.15 Chris Burden, *Dead Man*, 1972. Performance, Los Angeles. Courtesy the Chris Burden Studio and Gagosian Gallery, New York © Chris Burden.

corporeal replicas flimsy cardboard that mimed the photos and documentation used by conceptually focused artists in this moment.

What was unremarkable in the context of life, war, and urban violence became something remarkable and unique in the world of art. Both Hammons and Burden used art to call attention to brutality afflicting the body and the body politic. But Hammons declined to put himself in harm's way for the next action, while Burden took that leap. Was this because Hammons knew that, beginning at birth, the black body was under attack in the United States? For Hammons, to be shot was indeed unremarkable and imminently possible, while it pushed Burden into a new realm of experience. Even closer to Hammons's *Murder Mystery* is Burden's *Dead Man* (fig. 4.15), both created in 1972. Burden lay down on La Cienega Boulevard covered by a tarpaulin; he was next to and almost underneath a car, his figure outlined by two flares. Com-

IN MOTION • 235

positionally, there are many similarities between the two tableaux, starting with the relationship of Hammons's spade and Burden's body to the cars and their tires. Hammons's action, however, took place during daylight hours, while Burden's *Dead Man* was performed at night. But the outcomes of *Murder Mystery* and *Dead Man* point to the real divergences between these two pieces. In 1972, Burden was arrested for his action and "booked for causing a false emergency to be reported." As the artist recalled, "[The trial] took place in Beverly Hills. After three days of deliberation, the jury failed to reach a decision, and the judge dismissed the case."[190]

However, Hammons's real body was a magnet that marked him as someone to be stopped and potentially arrested for just walking down the street or having alternating sides of his head and face shaved.[191] Lying down in the street or having oneself shot were elements of the everyday for Hammons and were not so far outside the realm of possibility to approach the symbolic, a vision differentiated enough from the violence of real time to be art. Like Houston Conwill's *JuJu Ritual*, allegory opened a mythical space from which to see and create the stuff of art. Elizabeth Alexander's analysis of corporeality and the tension between reality and invention seems spot on here: "'Black' is always a metaphor, and 'black' is always real" because "metaphor fills in where logic cannot."[192] Art helps us rethink what we know and how we know it. Through art history we may be able to fill some of the gaps in our understanding and knowledge of the historical record. And art can help us imagine things about violence against the black body that "we cannot admit we need to know."[193]

If we compare *Murder Mystery* to Burden's *Dead Man*, we must include a third comparison, *Decoy Gang War Victim*, 1974, by Asco (fig. 4.16), the Chicano art collective based in Los Angeles. Asco ("nausea" in Spanish) was formed in the late 1960s and created art with a changing band of members until 1987. The original four participants—Gronk, Willie Herrón, Patssi Valdez, and Harry Gamboa Jr.—met in high school. Their practice was a reaction to both the contemporary art world and the world of ethnic and community arts, particularly the nationalism of Movimiento Chicano, the original organization of politicized Mexican Americans (established around 1965). For the members of Movimiento Chicano, murals featuring themes of an ancestral Mexican legacy (Aztec warriors, corn goddesses, etc.) were the template of progressive aesthetics. Through performance and other forms of conceptual practice, Asco provided a critique of Chicanos' relationship to the urban environment of Los Angeles and the politics of erasure from the American dream. Early projects included walking murals, performances in which each mem-

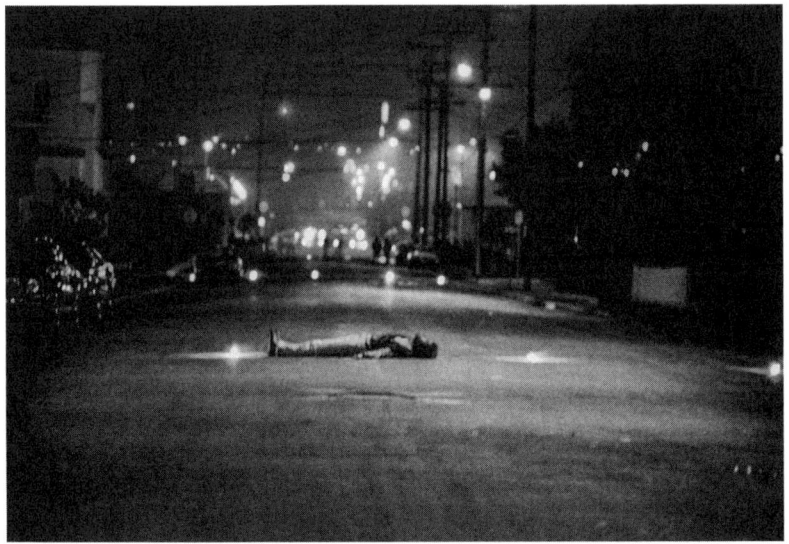

FIG. 4.16 Asco, *Decoy Gang War Victim*, 1974. Performance, Los Angeles. Whitney Museum of American Art, New York; purchase, with funds from the Photography Committee 2014.46. Courtesy the Whitney Museum of American Art, New York © 1974, Harry Gamboa Jr.

ber transformed himself or herself into three-dimensional and satirical versions of what might be found on a wall. But Asco's placement of these pieces was highly strategic. A walking mural from Christmas 1971—*Stations of the Cross*—ended at the Marine Recruitment Center, where the group anointed the scene with popcorn and a large cross, acknowledging the overrepresentation of Chicanos in the Vietnam conflict. A year later, they staged a similar performance in East Los Angeles, where the annual Christmas parade had been canceled by the city as a precaution against urban uprising. At Asco's substitute event, the artists simultaneously became "the participants and the floats."[194] After Asco was told by curators at the Los Angeles County Museum of Art in 1972 that Chicano artists were only folk artists or members of gangs, not people capable of creating contemporary art, its members threw up graffiti tags on the outside of the museum building, documenting it as "the first conceptual work of Chicano art to be exhibited at LACMA": *Spraypaint LACMA (or Project Pie in De/Face)*, 1972.[195]

Decoy Gang War Victim, 1974, addressed gang violence in a way that was both confrontational and controversial. The piece was repeated on a number of occasions in locales of potential unrest. Asco would close off a city block with flares. One member would lie in the street covered in ketchup, posing as a victim of urban violence. Asco then extended this action by documenting the "dead body" and sending photos to television stations and newspapers, highlighting how easy it was to manipulate the media with certain kinds of stories and questioning the objective stance of the press.

Hammons's *Murder Mystery*, Burden's *Dead Man*, and Asco's *Decoy Gang War Victim* all formed part of a dialogue about a national body framed by violence in an urban space and the use of creative endeavors to comment on and intervene in the situation. Each work could also be viewed within a broad global context—Burden's with the specter of Vietnam, Asco in the potential circulation of their "documents," and Hammons with extrapolations to the diaspora. Still, all three actions are connected to the landscape of Southern California. Asco and Burden include real bodies, in a way leaving Hammons as an outsider, a pretender, not bold enough to engage the live body in real time. However, other elements linked Asco and Hammons and set them apart from Burden. In the actions by Asco and Hammons, the heavy hand of law enforcement was postponed. Hammons's performance was private; there seemed to be no witnesses or audience outside the camera lens. The artist was not seen, and the event was known only retrospectively in documentation. Someone seemed to roll a car over what looks like garbage; because the "body" remained a fictive construct, there was no apparent infraction of the law. In *Decoy Gang War Victim*, the artists blocked off an entire street. This actually kept police at bay, preventing them from immediately confronting the art action, and potentially arresting the collective. Though they used live bodies, the artists did not seek the attention of authorities; they were not looking to be wards of the state, which had already perpetrated violence on Chicanos and their neighborhoods. Only later, by sending images to the press, did they reveal themselves as potential vandals rather than artists. But even that interpretation depended on the recipient's recognition that the action was false and then passing that information on to the authorities.

Hammons moved from painting to printing to performing as a way to understand the term "spade." He wanted to shed light on and ultimately release or at least comprehend its offensive associations. The last spades were not made from cardboard but from leather, the artist identifying them as skins, making a direct correlation with human beings. As was the case in the work of Jim Dine, a symbol took the place of the body. Yet in Hammons's case, language changed this simple act, turning it into something much more charged because of the implications carried by the word "spade."

Hammons's performed spades were buried, run over, and hung from trees—reproducing in effect the methods of racial violence visited upon the

African American body over centuries. As Goldsby reminds us, by the end of the nineteenth century, lynching had become a catchall term for a wide variety of racially motivated murders: "black people were 'lynched' in any number of ways (hanging, shooting, stabbing, burning, dragging, bludgeoning, drowning, and dismembering)."[196] Goode Bryant and Philips have argued that Hammons's actions work as sympathetic magic to dispel pain and break the cycle of violence, making them similar in intent to Conwill's *JuJu Rituals*.[197] This analysis underlines the serial nature of Hammons's action, its commitment to repetition. The artist described the context of his work with spades as a "chain reaction," starting with painting and moving through a variety of methods, materials, and techniques. These were Hammons's mechanisms for producing knowledge and understanding, and in their ritual reiteration revealed the mechanics of exorcizing pain. Through repetition and reproducibility—the multiple in action and materials, the repeated gesture, found objects, and prints and cardboard that mimic the methods of reproduction that characterize conceptual practice—Hammons also reproduced the seriality of violence, centuries of unending and often unmitigated cruelty, meant to exact control.

Both Jacqueline Goldsby and Paul Gilroy have argued that racial oppression and brutality was the shadow side of modernity's progress.[198] This authority resided not so much in its omnipresence or omnipotence but in a force that was modern and could be reproduced and repeated. Such repetition extended the scope and reach of violence, making it pervasive. Because it was everywhere, it created a situation that Michael Rogin calls "motivated forgetting" in which things that were "insistently represented become, by being normalized to invisibility, absent and disappeared."[199] Hammons's spade performances played out these situations of violent modernity that existed as hidden force. His actions are occluded, the live body disappeared; the gestures were repeated, serialized not in identical ways but taking many forms just as racial violence and murder do.

In his continual rearticulation of the spade as motif, Hammons was inspired not only by Jim Dine but by sculptor Melvin Edwards as he moved toward a more metaphorical and conceptual practice. Hammons's lynched spades seem to be a homage to Edwards's *Lynch Fragments*, even though the latter left Los Angeles in 1967 and Hammons's spade pieces begin around 1971. But the shovel was, after all, a sign of labor, like the many tools that formed the basis of Edwards's series.[200] It was the *Lynch Fragment* as concept, however, rather than the solid metal construction of the spades, that proved most meaningful. Another relatively unknown and more transitional aspect of Edwards's oeuvre provided more of a material and compositional roadmap for Hammons:

> I was influenced in a way by Mel Edwards's work. He had a show at the Whitney in the 1970s where he used a lot of chains and wires. That was the first abstract piece of art that I saw that had cultural value in it for Black people. I couldn't believe that piece when I saw it because I didn't think you could make abstract art with a message. I saw the symbols in Mel's work. Then I met Mel's brother and we talked all day about symbols, Egypt and stuff. How a symbol, a shape has meaning. After that I started using the symbol of the spade.[201]

Here Hammons refers to Melvin Edwards's solo show at the Whitney Museum of American Art in March 1970. A room-scale installation, it had two components. *Curtain for William and Peter*, 1969–70, was a thirty-foot-long sheer drape of barbed wire edged with links of heavy gauge chain. In the room's corners, Edwards created two pyramids of barbed wire (one inverted) that climbed the walls from floor to ceiling. These pieces used the dematerialized language of postminimalism while still clearly (at least for Hammons) keeping notions of the politics of violence (and the body) front and center.[202]

As the 1970s moved on, Hammons's performances became less secretive and, in some cases, more spontaneous. Their unplanned nature made them more playful; they were something the artist did to keep from being bored and from making art only for the wall. Mostly they documented ideas. Many times, these performances focused on mundane interactions between artist, objects, and street audiences, with, as Robert Storr has suggested, the street becoming Hammons's "workplace."[203] There was a sense of openness and vulnerability that Hammons cultivated when facing the unknown factor that a street audience might bring. By interacting consistently with the "real" as opposed to the "art" world, the artist felt he could "cleanse" himself of narrow-minded ideas about what constituted aesthetics.[204]

Photographs of two such street interventions from around 1977–78 show Hammons acting out in Los Angeles. Both actions were staged in front of a wall of his graffitied text with the artist carrying the signature staff that had been part of Nengudi's *Ceremony for Freeway Fets*. One took place at a bus stop near Nengudi's storefront studio, and the backdrop verse—"T.V. IS FAKE"—foreshadows Hammons's later and more pointed critiques of consumerism through sales of snowballs and doll shoes in the 1980s or his more recent commentary about the fur industry.[205] Nengudi recalled of the bus stop performance: "David just sat there and just kind of waited for response from people. He'd sit next to people who were waiting to catch the bus and then get up. So that was the piece, just sitting there with the staff."[206]

The other documented event depicts Hammons, dreadlocks concealing his face, leaning heavily on his staff in front of two-foot-high letters that spelled out "ZAIRE," a reference to the conflict in which the Congolese National Liberation Front tried to destabilize and end the thirteen-year dictatorship of Mobutu Sese Seko in what is now the Democratic Republic of Congo.[207] In the last frame Hammons lay face down on the concrete, one arm pointing stiffly at the written word. Concern with and communication about Africa, the diaspora, and politics continued to play an important role in the work that Hammons and others created in Los Angeles in this period.

Hammons's impromptu street acts were usually performed in African American neighborhoods. By soliciting response and interaction in this context, he pressed for recognition of the artist as part of an African American community. But this also revealed his penchant early on for what Franklin Sirmans has described as "social sculpture," events that involved everyday people—often unwitting, nonart "audiences"—in the creation of the work and its meaning, through their stories, tales, and observations as well as the artist's exchanges with them.[208] Art was something else that people could run across (or into) in their environment; as Hammons mused early on, "Then they don't have to pay. It's in the neighborhood. It's just there like clouds and things."[209] Certainly this predilection was inspired by the Black Arts Movement, with its emphasis on aesthetics that communicate with a larger black public. This inclination was part of the public focus of Nengudi, Maren Hassinger, Conwill, and Hammons and was a coalescing factor among this group of Southern California–based artists.[210]

Hammons also performed prodigiously in the works of these other artists, many times in gallery contexts. As we have seen, he participated in Nengudi's *Ceremony for Freeway Fets*, 1978, and Houston Conwill's *Notes of a Griot*, 1978. At the 1980 opening for *Beach*, Hassinger's solo exhibition at Just Above Midtown Gallery, he ambled through her sculptural "dune" while playing the flute.[211] These artists formed the core of a loose collective called Studio Z. This informal group came together at Hammons's studio on Slauson Avenue, sometimes weekly, to engage in spontaneous actions, which also were performed in the streets of LA. Studio Z had a changing membership (if one could call it that) and included at various times Frank Parker, Ulysses Jenkins, and RoHo in addition to the artists listed above. Hammons's space, a huge old dance hall with a wooden floor, was a perfect place to work out ideas; at least once the artists held an exhibition of companion art objects there.[212] With

Studio Z, Hammons found the safe space of the collective to push and try things in public. As with Asco, there was safety in numbers, which allowed him to anticipate the harassment that was inevitable. Studio Z also shared an aesthetic of multimedia art making that at once led to and issued from performance.

In his early art life, Hammons moved from traditional art materials to untraditional found materials, on a trajectory that evolved from silkscreen to body prints and from spades to greasy bags and barbecue bones. Hammons's found-object assemblage art was inspired by artists like Noah Purifoy and John Riddle, not just in the manner in which they manipulated materials but also in their uncompromising stance as black men and creative beings.[213] Like them, Hammons saw the poetry in things "at the end of their personal and household usefulness"—old clothes and rags, discarded shovels, chains, instruments—which could become "active agents of memory."[214] These were elements for constructing countersystems and narratives reflecting people and things discarded by an inequitable social system that were nevertheless filled with accounts of race, ingenuity, "dedication, and empty pockets," offering the "power of black self-recognition."[215] From these artists, Hammons learned to take the "need of money" out of the art-making equation.[216] However, he moved further, taking on garbage, debris, bones, hair, and dirty, oily bags—degraded, dematerialized organic materials that once had been a fundamental part of life and essentials of the body.[217]

The centrality of the body remained clear whether in materials or performance. And it was an idiom shared by the members of Studio Z. Hammons has described exchanging methods and approaches with Nengudi, trading ways of being abstract and figurative (or body-oriented) artists.[218] Houston Conwill's petrigraphs also had bones hanging from their rubbery panels. This shared language was also one of ritual and signs. Conwill became enamored of pyramids around 1971, and they appeared off and on in his work thereafter. Hammons had an epiphany about that image when he saw Melvin Edwards's show at the Whitney in 1970; pyramids made of hair would surface in his work some years later. Such free-form, dematerialized practices also recall the powerful presence of Betye Saar.

Like the performances, the more dematerialized and postminimal works from the 1970s rebelled against being bought and sold. In rejecting salable artwork, particularly through the body prints, Hammons moved away from selling the image of the black body itself or placing it on the auction block. The words of critic Greg Tate are instructive here: "The specimens were framed and then hung. Framed. And then hung. Given our history with those terms of endearment, entrapment, and engagement, consider it a given that we would have a problem with institutions where framing and hanging you is tantamount to saying I love you."[219] The art from refuse, what Goode Bryant and Philips referred to as the "remains," offered another perspective. As Hammons said in 1977, these things that

> no one will buy ... outrageous art ... it will make people think, think about themselves and what that means. You can't sell this ... they won't buy this ... old dirty bags, grease, bones, hair. ... It's about us, it's about me. ... It isn't negative. ... We should look at these images and see how positive they are, how strong, how powerful. ... Our hair is positive ... it's powerful, look what it can do. There's nothing negative about our images, it all depends on who is seeing it and we've been depending on someone else's sight. ... We need to look again and decide.[220]

The talismanic force, the ritual energy, and the performative mapping came back to the body, to the power of seeing and deciding, in Hammons's words, who we were and what we valued. If, as Hammons claimed, "ritual was an action word," such gesture also created a narrative of who we were. The concept of the ceremonial was stretched too. Gesture + action + repetition = ritual. In the work of Maren Hassinger, the trappings of ritual were shorn from the action, leaving simply spare movement and sculpture.

MAREN HASSINGER: SCULPTURE AND DANCE

> I don't see art performance as a form where you necessarily have to entertain an audience or feel compelled to make them laugh or cry or clap their hands, because what it's really about is communication. It's a spiritual endeavor. Hopefully, you would go away having some thought. It's not necessarily narrative; it's not necessarily abstract; it's not necessarily formal. It's not necessarily filled with Baryshnikov-type leaps and bounds. In fact, it doesn't necessarily have anything to do with the traditional experience of going to the theater, Broadway or off Broadway, or of going to a dance concert, even if it was at the Brooklyn Academy of Music. It's not any of that. It's like having your art thoughts and sticking them on the body and having your body move around. It's absolutely an extension of those art thoughts.
> —Maren Hassinger, 1996

Maren Hassinger shares with David Hammons, Houston Conwill, and Senga Nengudi—those artists who made up the core of Studio Z—a notion of creative thoughts moving through a variety of media from prints and sculpture to performance.²²¹ Hassinger and Hammons find common ground in their sense of repetition and seriality, betraying perhaps a minimalist root but producing a postminimalist effect. In sculpture and action, this repeated structure took on an air of ritual.

There was funky, stylized replication in Hassinger's first-ever solo exhibition at New York's Just Above Midtown Gallery (JAM) in winter 1980. Though she had shown in Southern California throughout the 1970s, it is telling that her first solo show took place in New York. It signaled the ultimate dispersal of the group away from the fecund landscapes of Southern California for other beckoning and receptive locales.

Reviewing Hassinger's JAM debut, Judith Wilson was struck by the artist's ability to balance the organic and inorganic, the natural and the manmade, strict formalism and a pliant and visceral materiality.²²² The installation *Beach* (fig. 4.17) consisted of a room full of reedlike elements tilted at an angle, as if enduring a gale-force wind. Closer inspection revealed that these were birchwood dowels, leaning out of three hundred "stones" made by the artist from plaster and sand, the raw shoreline recombined into a facsimile of itself. Creation of this type of "industrial vegetation," as Wilson called it, became Hassinger's mature statement, a comment on nature, its loss, its rebirth.

During an impromptu opening-day performance, David Hammons wended his way through the pathways of *Beach*, a Pied Piper with his flute, enticing people to walk through and experience the piece. Hammons and Hassinger shared the iconography of the shoreline, as exemplified by the black hair that Hammons stuck in the West Coast surf circa 1975–77 and the translation of such "gardens" indoors with rubber bands, wire, and hair. For Hassinger, the garden became a primordial form, symbolic of human community, the basis of civilization, an icon of "our shared beginnings."²²³ For this reason, she has returned to it again and again, seeing, in nature, life, the body, and its compromises.

Though she still lived in Los Angeles, 1980 proved to be a good year for Hassinger in New York. Linda Goode Bryant, director of JAM, put her in a multiartist project in the waiting room of Grand Central Station. She was also part of *Afro-American Abstraction*, an important show at PS 1 Institute for Art and Urban Resources (later MoMA PS 1), which offered major visibility for black artists working nonobjectively, including several of Hassinger's California colleagues. There was also an outdoor project for Creative Time, an organization dedicated to taking art into public and nontraditional sites. Beginning in the mid-1970s, its famous "Art on the Beach" program used unde-

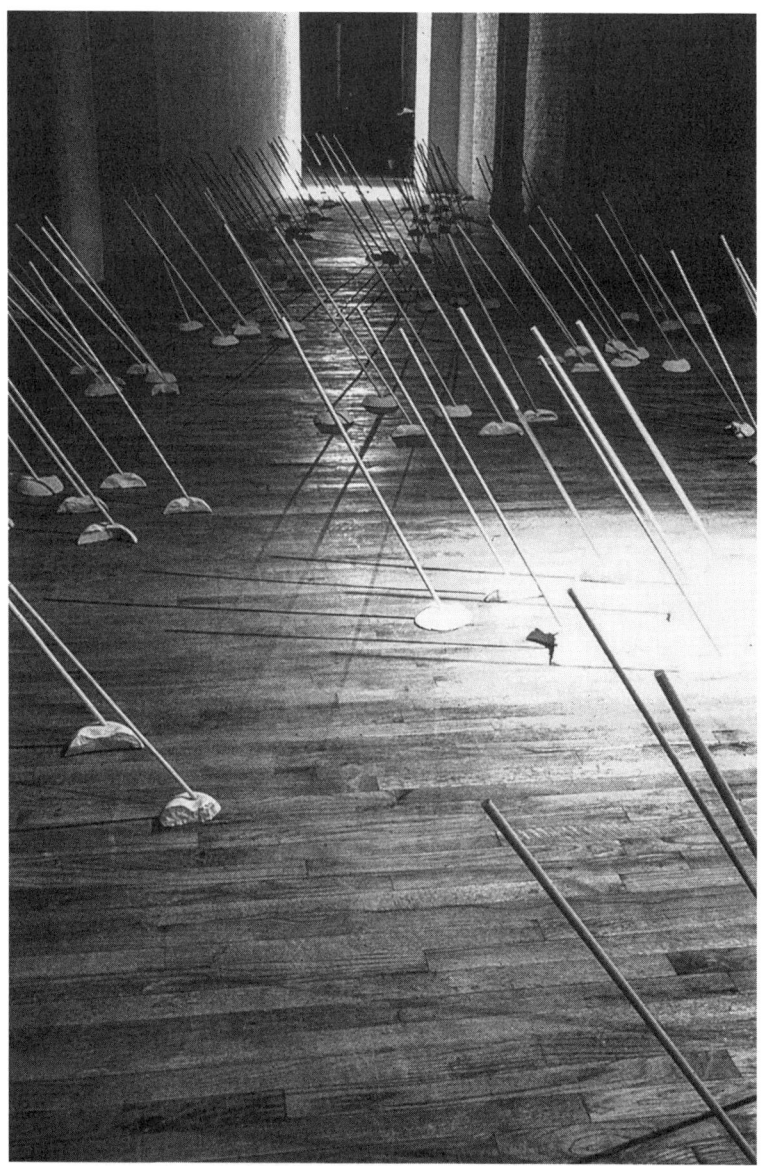

FIG. 4.17 Maren Hassinger, *Beach*, 1980. Mixed-media installation, Just Above Midtown Gallery, New York. Courtesy the artist.

veloped waterfront lands for summertime, largely site-specific art projects, which were eventually discontinued after the construction of the Battery Park City residential community. Hammons's *Delta Spirit*, 1985, an eccentric house complete with clothesline and performances by Sun Ra, was part of the same series. Hassinger's *Forest*, 1980 (plate 29), was a large-scale vision of what she later presented at JAM. Both *Forest* and *Beach* started with a stand of reeds bent by an unseen force, blowing seemingly in unison. *Forest* covered a thirty-by-thirty-foot outdoor plot with galvanized steel cables that "grew" directly out of the sand in undulating waves. These metal vines stood six feet high and reached not toward the water in a bid for nourishment but toward the unused elevated highway at the beach's border and the rising steel and concrete buildings beyond.

Movement in both *Forest* and *Beach* was implied, if frozen, a comment on the ruined nature of the outdoor site and the industrialism of the late twentieth century. However, their seriality also created patterns, paradigms of motion for bodies to follow. If Hammons opened *Beach* with his solo actions and tunes, Hassinger completed the cycle with her performances. In *Still Wind*, 1981, also sponsored by JAM, Hassinger and another dancer performed with the galvanized steel cables of *Forest*, mirroring the angled motion with their bodies and evoking both the burst of force and the icy stasis, limbo as well as balance and calm.[224] The parallel lines of bodies and steel created an impression that the sculpture was also a force of nature.

Born in Los Angeles in 1947, Maren Hassinger (née Jenkins)—like the other artists in this study—has a background that reveals the histories of African American migrations that made modern California and the United States. Her father, Carey Kenneth Jenkins, a successful Los Angeles architect, was born in Saint Louis, but her paternal grandparents hailed from Alexandria, Louisiana. Her mother, Helen Mills Jenkins, was born in Cincinnati, Ohio; her parents were originally from Union Mills, North Carolina. Both of Hassinger's parents migrated to Los Angeles with their families as children and attended local high schools. Thinking expansively about how her life mirrored a larger history, the artist mused, "We *all* came from the South."[225]

Like her colleague and frequent collaborator Senga Nengudi, Hassinger was raised by people who followed their dreams west. Both came to art and performance from dance, and both had been discouraged by their respective colleges from majoring in dance at the undergraduate level. Hassinger attended Bennington College from 1965 to 1969, one of only a handful of black students there at the time.

Bennington, of course, had a storied history related to modern dance.

Shortly after its founding in 1932, as a college for women devoted to the arts, the institution established its dance program. Between 1934 and 1939, the Bennington Summer School of the Dance trained students and educators and disseminated modern dance at the university level throughout the United States. At the core of the curriculum were classes taught by Martha Graham, Doris Humphrey, Charles Weidman, and Hanya Holm. Louis Horst, founding director of the journal *Dance Observer* and music director to Graham, and *New York Times* dance critic John Martin were also part of the faculty. Its legendary status as the birthplace of modern dance was one of the reasons Hassinger was attracted to the school.[226] However, that same history also represented certain calcified behaviors and structured expectations that prevented her from formally studying dance there.

In her book *Modern Dance, Negro Dance: Race in Motion* (2004), Susan Manning charts how the history of African Americans in dance was separated from the canon of modernist development. While black dancers struggled to find support in the 1930s, white practitioners—affiliated with what came to be known as modern dance—were buoyed by a rapidly developing network. Modern dance emerged from the same cauldron as modernist art, that is, by abstracting "primitive" traditions (Native American, Asian, and African), fusing them with European precepts, and creating an avant-garde Western form. Manning terms this process "metaphorical minstrelsy," where white bodies "reference" and take the place of "nonwhite subjects."[227]

African American dance artists began defining what came to be known as Negro Dance (later Black Dance), which was of course its own form of modern expression. They usually had a different take on such sources. The performative mode became historical and political, exploring the transfer of traditions from Africa to the Americas and how they erupted in vernacular performance. Yet black dancers also synthesized their history with European training. Trailblazers of the 1930s, such as Edna Guy and Charles Williams, studied at Denishawn and the Bennington Summer School. Katherine Dunham trained in both ballet and modern dance. Pearl Primus studied with the leftist New Dance Group, Humphrey, Weidman, Horst, and Graham. What gave Dunham and Primus authority was that they were both academically trained scientists. Dunham was an anthropologist from the University of Chicago; Primus had degrees in biology and physical education from New York's Hunter College.[228]

Black dancers found themselves in a predicament that would define African American, Caribbean, and Latin American artists throughout the century. Their talent was pulled between poles, ascribed to either "natural ability" or bad copies of the status quo. The performance of an authentic, visible otherness was the way the West liked its black culture. But black artists who created work outside such parameters and offered a new synthesis of what was modern remained an anathema, unsupported and ignored.

Decades later Hassinger and Nengudi found that being defined as an artist in the world of dance had changed little. Their rebuff by the world of professional dance to a great extent had to do with what was (is?) perceived as the correct body type for concert dance.[229] Bill T. Jones alluded to this issue in a *New York Times* op-ed that contrasted ballet's ideal of the otherworldly sylph with real human bodies on the move.[230] Others have been far more blunt about how body type and body image has been racialized, including Alvin Ailey in his autobiography, *Revelations*: "In the 1940s and 1950s, the American dance world practiced a pervasive racism. For a variety of reasons: our feet weren't shaped right, our butts were too big, our legs wouldn't turn out correctly; blacks simply weren't wanted; and so on. The people who ran the major and minor ballet and modern dance companies coldly rejected, and broke the hearts of, many aspiring young black dancers. In the dance world, at that time, we were not welcome. The white ballet companies didn't want us; neither did the modern dance groups."[231]

Having studied dance from age five, Hassinger went off to Bennington College with the intention of making it her focus. In her first year, she was told her dancing wasn't good enough and that she would not be allowed to pursue it as a major.[232] She found herself pushed into fine arts. She eventually gravitated toward sculpture even though the differences between dance and art initially seemed vast: "Sculpture seemed foreign to me. I couldn't figure out why I was supposed to be so much better at sculpture when I had just picked up a piece of clay. I had never been in a formal, three-dimensional class before."[233]

Both the dance and the visual arts departments at Bennington were dominated by formalist aesthetics, specifically the vision of Clement Greenberg, whose relationship with the college began in 1952 when he organized Jackson Pollock's first museum survey there. Throughout the 1950s, Greenberg brought other shows to Bennington, including works by Hans Hoffman (1955) and Barnett Newman (1958). In the fall of 1962 and again in spring 1971 Bennington invited him to give a series of seminars. Thus he made his imprint on the college over the span of two decades, the period that saw the ascendance of his power and influence as a critic. It was also during this time that his notion of an "involuntary or disinterested" aesthetics, a universalism based on intuition, increasingly became contested.[234]

Hassinger's attendance at Bennington intersected with Greenberg's presence there. She remembers him participating in student critiques in the art department. She made a splash with her senior project when she placed her boxy architectonic constructions in the meadow behind the art department. The formal concerns that pervaded Hassinger's work, even in what would become a postminimalist vein, surely had some root in her experiences at Bennington, where she eventually became fluent in photography, graphics, drawing, and sculpture.[235]

Her time at the college also coincided with the emergence of postmodern dance, which has been called a rebellion against the "myths, heroes, and psychological metaphors" and elegance of ballet.[236] The mid-1960s was a time, notes dance historian Sally Banes, when dances were created from mundane "movements and objects," when choreographers rethought bonds between performers and their audiences and articulated "new experiences of space, time, and the body."[237]

According to Banes, the years 1963 to 1968 were a period when dance was characterized as stripped down, highly formalistic, and analytical, with a rejection of musicality. Scholars such as Maurice Berger, Thomas Crow, Anna Chave, and Carrie Lambert have suggested not only that this dance asceticism had an impact on minimalism, but also that the convergence of the performance and visual arts created a new context for seeing and understanding. As Lambert argues, "If a performance quality—temporality—extends in real time the experience of viewing sculpture, and a sculptural—fixity—counters the fleeting aspect of the dance spectacle, their crossing creates a kind of cultural staging ground at the issue of viewing itself."[238] Yet with all the suggestiveness of gesture and movement that dance brought to minimalism, the body—the personal and personhood—that the dancer represented, as Lambert notes, was still troubling. The dance body led back to the moving, breathing, thinking person.[239]

After 1968, the fascination with formalism in postmodern dance gave way to themes of politics, audience engagement, and non-Western aesthetics, inspired by a growing consciousness of struggles in the "Third World" and a concomitant focus on cultures with different attitudes toward "time and the body."[240] This journey away from the spare, the ascetic, and the minimal was also a move toward the "spiritual, religious, healing, and social functions" that dance conveyed elsewhere.[241]

This opening of Western dance traditions in the late 1960s did not seem to work for Hassinger while she was at Bennington. The school represented a bastion of tradition rather than the new visions of the avant-garde. However, the West Coast offered a different scenario. Dancers like Anna Halprin and the Los Angeles–based Lester Horton had been training and working with black dancers as early as the 1940s. The popular dramatic edge in Horton's work and his choreography for Hollywood helped dancers translate their modern training into paying gigs in movies and popular stage shows. This was certainly true for black dancers along the famous Central Avenue nightclub strip during the 1940s and the 1950s. With her partner Welland Lathrop, Halprin ran her modern dance company from 1946 until the mid-1950s. Alvin Ailey and Maya Angelou studied with her in the 1950s, and Ruth Beckford had a much longer association with her that stretched over decades.

In the late 1950s Halprin made a conscious effort to move beyond the formulas of modern dance; she closed her studio in San Francisco and began exploring new forms of movement on her "dance deck," an outdoor performance platform that extended from her Marin County home into the surrounding landscape. With its built-in viewing area, it was both a spectacle and a revelation: "The dance deck creates theatrical space in the midst of raw nature. Walls are replaced by trees, the ceiling is a canopy of trees and the sky, and the sounds of this space are the muted calls of fluttering leaves, the hum of insects."[242]

Alvin Ailey also performed with Lester Horton's company, leading the Southern California–based group after a short period of time. Perhaps he took some of Halprin's techniques to Horton, or vice versa. Hassinger later studied the Horton technique with Yvonne de Lavallade.[243] Yet Hassinger's performances also seem related to Halprin's dance deck, which united the dancer's body and the natural world. While such convergences can be ascribed to a "West Coast aesthetic," the histories of these artists are more proximate than they first appear.

Brenda Dixon Gottschild and Susan Manning have both made cases for the indelible stamp of black dance (diasporic and local) on modern dance. If that is the case, then Hassinger might have unknowingly had exposure to some of these gestures, without making the "identity-based" work that apparently comprised black creativity, danced or otherwise.

After graduating from college, the artist lived in New York for a year, worked at Harcourt, Brace & World as an art editor, and married writer Peter Hassinger before returning to Los Angeles for graduate school. She was passed over by the sculpture program at UCLA but accepted as a design student with a concentration in fiber structure. Tapestry and weaving were having a renaissance due to the energy of the Women's Movement and works by artists like Magdalena Abakanowicz. Hassinger decided that she "would take what I learned in fiber and then just make sculpture. I wouldn't make tapestries, just sculptures."[244] This concentration would prove to be a fortuitous step in a multidimensional career. For a while, she experimented with welding and made beautifully poetic works using chain and rope (*River*, 1972, and *Untitled*, 1972). Then one day in a junkyard she stumbled upon what would become her pivotal medium: wire rope. In her hands, this material came to embody the changing landscape of American sculpture, from minimal to postminimal. It was a synthetic substance that with subtle intervention could echo organic form.

One of the first exhibitions to put Hassinger on the art world map after she graduated from UCLA in 1973 was a two-person show with painter William Mahan. It was held in 1976 at the newly opened ARCO Center for Visual Art (plate 30), a corporate art space sponsored by the Atlantic Richfield Oil Company, which would support contemporary art for the next eight years.[245] While it is clear she was still experimenting with these materials, the power and beauty of her visual language was exceptional. Sculptural compositions moved from floor to wall in linear motion; in works such as *Loci: This Way Now*, 1976, the lyrical lines of the industrial made the objects seem natural, effortless. The unadorned wire rope became a perfect visual and material statement in and of itself, creating an autonomous and iconic minimalist testimony. There was also the elegance, sheen, and beauty of the flexible metal; the unexpected curves, twists, turns; the poetry and lyricism that moved it to the postminimal. In these works, mass and volume were indicated by their trace, similar in effect to the work of Robert Irwin or Fred Sandback. Hassinger's notion of sculpture as a drawing in a postminimal voice was echoed in the equally graceful wall works of Martin Puryear from this period—*Some Lines for Jim Beckwourth*, 1978, made of twisted rawhide, and *Some Tales*, 1977, a text of saplings for the wall.

For Hassinger herself, real inspiration came from other artists. In 1973, two shows at the Pasadena Art Museum were pivotal: Agnes Martin's paintings of subtle monochrome and textured geometries, and the idiosyncratic and affecting sculpture of Eva Hesse.[246] The working process for both women seemed to be the creation of a whole statement through the accumulations of repeated, if not strictly identical units. This eccentricity thrown into minimalism's assembly-line aesthetics added an excitement and poignancy to the work that riveted Hassinger. As she recalled about the Hesse exhibition: "It was as if I was looking at somebody's spirit made manifest.... It was an absolute gut level, wrenching experience... as if the sculpture were made flesh.... Later when I began to read about her, it was as if she had managed somehow to put all the emotional truth of her life [in these works].... It was a total true expression of life."[247]

Throughout the 1970s, Hassinger's experiments with materials continued to include the interspersing of industrial metallic rope with its apparent opposite, layered branches of wood. In the wall piece *Dry/Flow*, 1976, from the ARCO show, the equation was evident as two wire lines undulated beneath a forked sapling of more or less equal size, whose brushy network of small branches provide a busy counterpoint, the chaotic and pulsing energy of the natural world contrasted with the smooth power of the man-made. For the next several years Hassinger explored such comparisons in works like *Pas de Deux*, 1977, where one is made aware of the coupling and dance of the two material forces, or *Wreath*, 1979, a floor-based circle of branches and wire more than thirteen feet in diameter and so tightly meshed that the disparate elements were almost indistinguishable.

By the end of the decade, she had turned her full attention to the industrial and the constructed and away from materials found in nature, separating organic materials from their inorganic doubles. In the heavy-gauge wire rope and the artist's proliferation of faux rocks, commentators saw both a representation of nature and its defeat. The "bushes," "weeds," and "trees" that Hassinger constructed, whether outdoors or in galleries, were embedded with a sense of loss. There was longing and desire, a coveting of natural space and form in a time when concrete and steel appeared to rule. Her commentary on the growing dichotomy between "nature" and "culture" and her environmental concerns seemed clear. Still, as curator Beryl Wright saw it, Hassinger's wire-rope sculptures were metaphors for both nature's "demise and persistence."[248] In other words, the apparent ossification signaled growth, life, and movement.

Hassinger's fascination with the industrial world's encroachment on nature was inspired, in part, by the writings of Walker Percy. A southerner trained as a medical doctor who also studied philosophy, Percy wrote about the alienated life of the late twentieth century and the banality and paradoxes produced by a society controlled by technology and science. As Maurice Berger has indicated, Hassinger's comments on industrialism were invested in the materials that she chose: the oppression that metal, wire, and plaster could connote. Yet the artist was uncomfortable with "the seeming mutual exclusivity of repressive industrial systems and materials and the sanctity of nature."[249] The result was her creation of art in the space of the paradox, where the material could become a symbol of something entirely different, which was the underlying thread of much of Percy's writing as well. "Ultimately," Berger continues, the artist's "attitude towards materials is transformatory; she permits heretofore repressive industrial materials . . . to also suggest conditions of softness or fragility."[250]

Growing up on the west side of Los Angeles, Hassinger had been a neighbor of Alonzo and Dale Brockman Davis, who later started the Brockman Gallery.[251] However, she never became part of the gallery's permanent roster. Her work, like that of many others experimenting in Los Angeles, proved challenging to sell.[252] Hassinger's pieces also seemed the least concerned with African American or African aesthetics, which may have been difficult for Brockman as well.

However, in the late 1970s, the Davis brothers, under the auspices of Brockman Gallery Productions, did support two public works by Hassinger for the Los Angeles freeway through CETA. Hassinger's project, like Senga Nengudi's, was done in collaboration with Caltrans, the city's transportation system, which provided the land, the required permits, and some technical assistance. Additional aid and supplies came from the Paulsen Wire Rope Company and the California Arts Council. The two pieces were completed a year apart. *Twelve Trees*, 1978 (see fig. I.4), was sited at the Vermont Avenue on-ramp of the southbound Hollywood Freeway; *Twelve Trees #2* stretched for 150 feet beside the northbound San Diego Freeway along the Mulholland Drive off-ramp.[253] These vertical growths of thick steel cable shot ten feet high, both echoing and mocking the natural landscape and the soaring electrical towers along the freeway.[254]

With *Twelve Trees*, Hassinger became more interested in site-specific approaches. These pieces could be seen as part of the earthworks movement but with significant twists. Her projects were never huge undertakings, like Michael Heizer's monumental slices into western landscapes or Robert Smithson's construction of a walkable jetty. On the whole, her works had a more human scale that she could accomplish with a couple of assistants. Unlike Heizer and Smithson, Hassinger formed her sculpture from hard, cold industrial cable rather than natural materials; nevertheless, she managed to imitate, extend, and exaggerate nature.

Her narrative in these industrial pieces became perhaps most evident in her spring 1981 project for the Los Angeles County Museum of Art (LACMA), organized as part of its "Gallery Six" program, which highlighted modern and contemporary artists. Hassinger would become the first African American artist to have a solo show at the museum. Groups like the Black Arts Council had struggled to make African American artists visible at LACMA; this was certainly a quiet and subtle victory, not least because her sculpture eschewed standard features that were linked to art and African American identity.

What captivated Hassinger was the tough, forceful, and menacing aspect of the materials in the installation she titled *Dangerous Ground*, 1981. The narrow, high-ceiling gallery space suggested an enclosure that both produced and reflected a certain anxiety. She created objects "to intimidate, to infringe, to threaten."[255] These were "angry bushes," twenty-one haystack-like formations whose bristling was set off by dramatic lighting that added to the ominous effect.[256] The tight placement of the sculptures indicated a restricted navigation; the sense that they could tear garments or even skin added to the sense of foreboding. This malevolent and haunted atmosphere, as critic and curator Maureen Megerian later pointed out, conflated "the dangers of nature with the urban environment."[257]

As Hassinger noted in the show's brochure, "In a sense, the construction of these bushes (in their dissolution of form and their tumultuous placement) reflects the turmoil of contemporary urban reality where one feels a sense of confusion—a decline in the order of things, a profound sense of loss, vulnerability, and lack of 'centeredness.'"[258]

This statement reflects Walker Percy's beliefs that modern humankind is adrift in a world whose pace is set by a modern industrial machine. Hassinger's words also fit in well with the concurrent discussions of "the postmodern condition," which would be applied even more to art in the 1980s. But Hassinger's words and work also perhaps most clearly identify the postindustrial landscape, especially as it was manifest in Los Angeles, as the war and aerospace industry sputtered to a halt in the 1970s. In a sense, the artist's projects did not just lament the loss of natural landscape but expressed anxiety about declining industrialism; an urban society whose livelihood was being slowly drained, changed, and not necessarily replaced with something new; the construction of more freeways bulldozing through neighborhoods, ripping apart communities in their wake.

Just as trees and bushes change with the seasons and evolve over time, Hassinger's manufactured plants degrade, fall prey to development, and transform; neither nature nor its industrial double is stagnant. In many of these pieces, one gets the sense not only of the living organism but also of other anthropomorphic connotations. As the artist later commented: "After a while, I began to think I was really doing figurative sculpture even though it wasn't figures. They were bushes, but they were figurative, especially in *Walking* and *Whirling* and *Leaning*—where I talk about physical gesture, human physical gesture."²⁵⁹ If the impression of the body in motion is quite explicit here, the allusion to the element of process and obsessive human endeavor is evident as well. Indeed, process-oriented work creates an "event" within its medium of choice, incorporating action and its evidence.²⁶⁰ Thus for Hassinger, solid, industrial, process-driven sculptures became the "initiators of activity," lending themselves to the temporality of performance and encouraging her to return movement to her creative endeavors.²⁶¹

As Hassinger noted above, in her creative mind, art and performance were extensions of one another. And if sculpturally it was important for her "to explore the relationship between static and moving objects," it was not surprising that an early performance, like that of Houston Conwill, took place within one of her three-dimensional installations.²⁶² *High Noon*, 1976, performed at the ARCO Center for Visual Art, attempted to expand sculptural notions into time and motion. One reviewer wrote: "The *appearance* of Maren Hassinger's works connotes sculpture. The *reality* is movement. They are linear leaps and sags, invisible volumes and dramatic gesturings that activate space."²⁶³

Wire rope allowed her to create a form that fluctuated between mass and line, concrete object and oscillating movement. Such shifts enacted in the sculptural installation materialized as the push and pull of performative action in *High Noon*, tapping the energy vibrating around and among its participants. This was made even more visible by articles of clothing suspended between the six players and yanked back and forth in lively confrontation.

Another performance took place on Easter Sunday, 1977, at David Hammons's Slauson Avenue studio with the loose group known as Studio Z. This time Hassinger performed not among her own works but among those of Hammons. A photograph depicts a work from Hammons's series *Greasy Bags and Barbecue Bones*, collages composed of oil-stained brown paper bags with licked-clean spareribs, hair, and glitter. Hanging from the wall on the upper left is a Persian carpet, clearly the seeds of his *Flying Carpet*, 1990, planted years before. Some of the performers were from Hassinger's Horton-based dance class.²⁶⁴ Here again, they (including Senga Nengudi) were linked through the interchange of objects, in this case wood saplings. The performance was tied directly to her sculptural pieces that combined wire rope and wood, like *Pas de Deux* or *Deep Down*, both from 1977. As with *High Noon*, the title of this piece, *Ten Minutes*, is blandly descriptive in the mode of classic, language-driven conceptualism. The spareness of the branches, the performers' light-colored and soft clothing, and their simple actions captured the minimalist edge seen in Hassinger's sculptures as well.

The unpretentious movements of a third work, *Diaries (Part 1 of Lives)*,

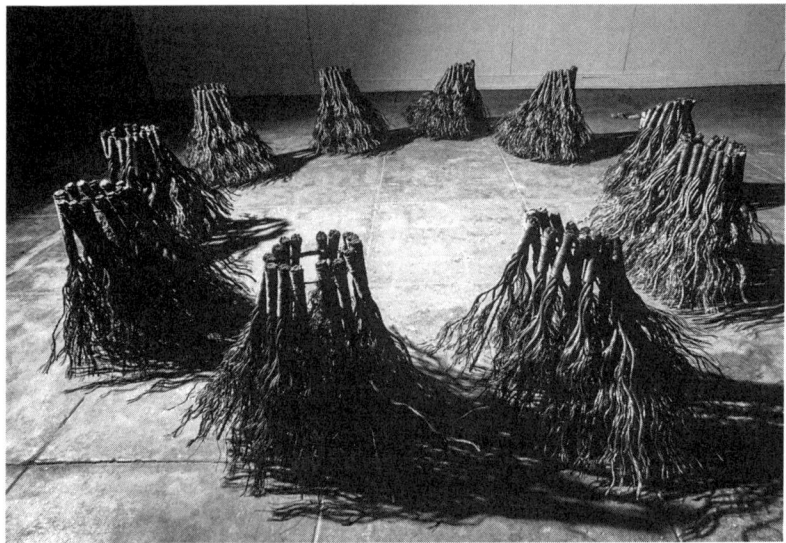

FIG. 4.18 Maren Hassinger, *Whirling, 10 Elements in a Circle*, 1978. Wire-rope installation. Courtesy the artist; photograph by Adam Avila.

1978, found corollaries in her other major sculptures from that year, *Walking, 148 Elements*, and *Whirling, 10 Elements in a Circle* (fig. 4.18). Hassinger's anthropomorphic visions became clear. However, it is also evident that the quotidian or basic indices of human existence—the task base of postmodern performance—found in the simple jumping of the performers also inspired Hassinger's sculptural gesture. *Diaries (Part 1 of Lives)* was performed at the Vanguard Gallery, a newly opened alternative space in downtown Los Angeles. It was part of the trend of postmodern dance finding support in art galleries and artist's lofts and the sharing of media, themes, and practitioners.

Hassinger's sculptures seemed little concerned with the rhetorics of African American culture. However, in retrospect she did feel there was a connection:

> One thing I think I have discovered along the way, after years of feeling compelled to do things and many of those years doing them in collaboration with Senga [Nengudi] and Ulysses [Jenkins] and Frank Parker, and then recently looking at slides from African performances and masquerades and reading ... I realized that in Africa ... time-based movements are not separated from the static work in the same way.... You know, it's the flip side of one coin. And I really do think that it's the impulse that moves through all of our work.... [This gives a context to] my impulse to take the

sculpture and expand it so that the idea exists in time and includes movement and includes people, sound and voices, and things."[265]

This comment recalls Lawal's discussion of the Gèlèdé spectacle combining sculpture and dance, and its role as a vehicle promoting society's spiritual well-being.[266] Indeed, costumes were not secondary to the action, as Margaret Thompson Drewal has indicated about Yoruba performance, but had "visual, kinetic, tactile, and audible attributes that contribute[d] dramatically to the dances' expressive qualities."[267] This sense of a holistic aesthetic, how actions extend from objects, is mirrored by the idea that the divisions between spectator and performer are not fixed. Both complete the performance and are active. It finds a corollary in the continuum between the visible and the invisible. In Yoruba tradition, masquerade has the capacity to manifest the metaphysical, at least temporarily; it is a given that there are "permanent, otherworldly dimensions of reality that, until *revealed* by knowledgeable performers, are inaccessible to human experience."[268] Artists like Hassinger, Conwill, Hammons, and Nengudi pushed their work specifically into the place between the tangible and the intangible, the solid and the formless, where performance became ritual and one thing became another.

In the spring of 1980, April Kingsley curated *Afro-American Abstraction* for New York's PS 1 Institute for Art and Urban Resources. The exhibition organizers were interested in raising the visibility of black artists working nonobjectively but also wanted to provide a broader historical context for their practice. Of the initial twenty artists included, four were part of Studio Z: Hassinger, Houston Conwill, Hammons, and Nengudi. Melvin Edwards, who had left LA more than a decade earlier, also participated. Unlike many exhibitions in the 1960s and 1970s, this show was thematically coherent, bringing together abstract art by African American artists and revealing its relationship to African aesthetics. In a sense, this emphasis provided a view of what was to come in the 1980s, when the focus would be on "identity-based" practices. *Afro-American Abstraction* was well received, though critics were skeptical about the one-to-one relationship between the nonobjective pieces on view and traditional African art. Even Kingsley herself suggested, "I became convinced that the pluralism of the 70s and the growing need for humanistic content and mythic and ritual significance in art offered optimum connections for Afro-American artists," hinting at a more expansive reading of the contextualization of this work.[269]

In the summer of 1982, the show arrived at the Municipal Art Gallery in LA's Barnsdall Park. It provided an opportunity to celebrate the visibility of

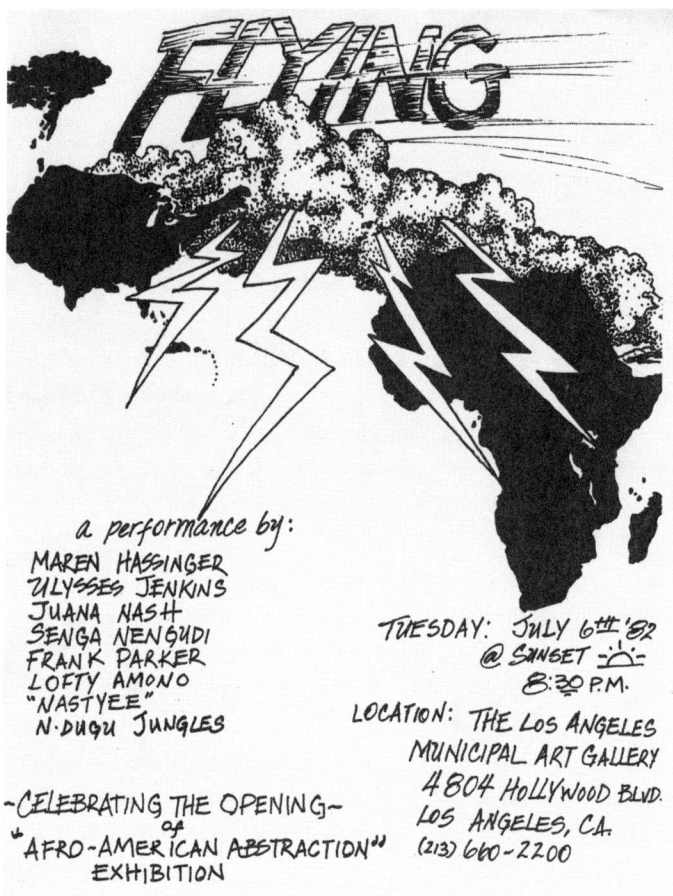

FIG. 4.19 Flyer from *Flying* performance, 1982. Courtesy the African American Performance Art Archive, University of North Carolina, Chapel Hill.

artists based in or connected with Los Angeles, and the African American art presence in the city. In addition, it was a moment for exulting in the growing institutional support of this work not only by the Municipal Art Gallery but in two dedicated museums, the Museum of African American Art, founded by Samella Lewis and then being run by Mary Jane Hewitt, and the California Museum of Afro-American History and Culture (later the California African American Museum).[270]

As part of the opening festivities for *Afro-American Abstraction*, Hassinger and Nengudi created a performance titled *Flying* (figs. 4.19 and 4.20). It suggested a hopeful future for their work and that of their fellow travelers, a

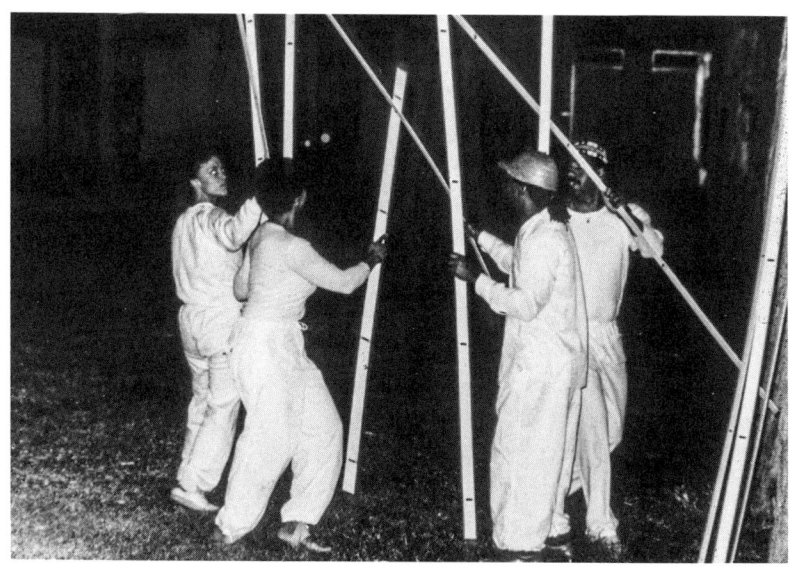

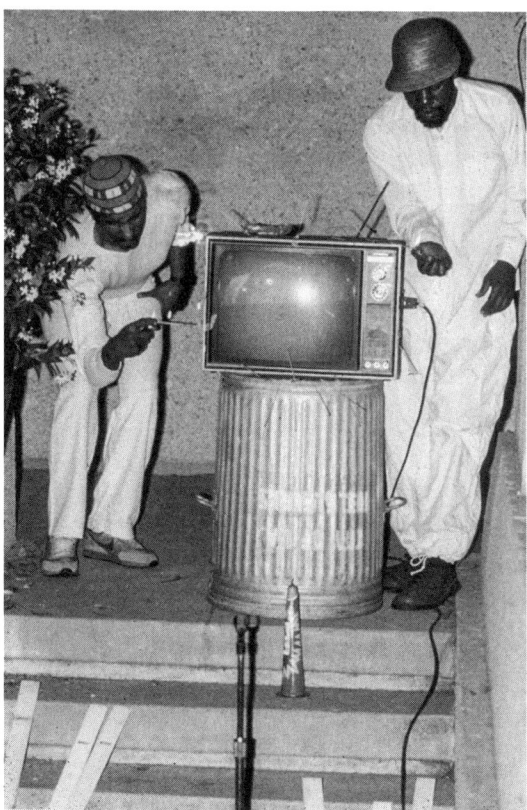

FIGS. 4.20 AND 4.21 Maren Hassinger and Senga Nengudi, *Flying*, 1982. Performance, Los Angeles. Top: (*left to right*) Hassinger, Nengudi, Frank Parker, Ulysses Jenkins. Bottom: Ulysses Jenkins (*left*), Frank Parker (*right*). Courtesy Maren Hassinger; Thomas Erben Gallery, New York; and the African American Performance Art Archive, University of North Carolina, Chapel Hill.

launch into new arenas of acceptance and success. Collaborating with them were Frank Parker, a member of the band in Nengudi's *Ceremony for Freeway Fets*, and Ulysses Jenkins, who was experimenting with video as well as performance. Hassinger's association with Jenkins represented the new face of Studio Z, as Hammons finally had made his relocation to New York permanent and given up his large LA studio.[271] May Sun and Rudy Perez joined their ongoing activities, and Jenkins's place on Vermont Avenue became their new performance space.[272] Hassinger and Parker appeared in Jenkins's video pieces as well. But by 1984, Hassinger too would head east, to become an artist-in-residence at the Studio Museum in Harlem.

Flying reflected its era and the predilections of its collaborators.[273] It evinced Nengudi and Hassinger's fascination with forms in space, whether sculptural or human. To the sounds of drumming and a trumpet, the performers moved from the Municipal Art Gallery into the landscape. Dressed in loose-fitting white clothing, each person held white slats of a venetian blind, the same material that Nengudi used for her sculptural piece that was traveling with the show. Although Nengudi had created performances outdoors, land as activated space pointed back to Hassinger's work, especially in the ways that the performers wove their actions around two eucalyptus trees. As a reviewer noted, "At one point the dancers seemed to draw energy from one of the trees by circling it and using the slats as radii from its trunk to their bodies."[274] Jenkins's contribution was the video portion, which was manifest in several ways. At one point, Jenkins and Parker brought out a movable altar topped by a video monitor; the entire construction was surrounded by the flash of candles and sparklers (fig. 4.21). Alternating images of a large, "all-seeing" eye flickered across the screen as the audience was asked to come forth with offerings. At the end of the performance, all four artists came together, seeming to float in formation. They mimicked the flight of a flock of seagulls simultaneously projected onto their bodies, their white costumes acting as screens (plate 31).

Reviewer D. Francine Farr saw conflict in *Flying*, the modern battle of nature versus culture, with technology as a divisive force.[275] This reading seems to follow from Hassinger's approach to working in the landscape during these years. However, from another perspective, *Flying* seemed to ameliorate the relationship between industrial and natural forces by constantly fluctuating between them. The performance moved from the architectural space into the landscape, the site of both a tower of technology and towering trees (figs. 4.21 and 4.22). It ended with the synchronization between human and animal movement, technology and nature—the incorporation of contemporary

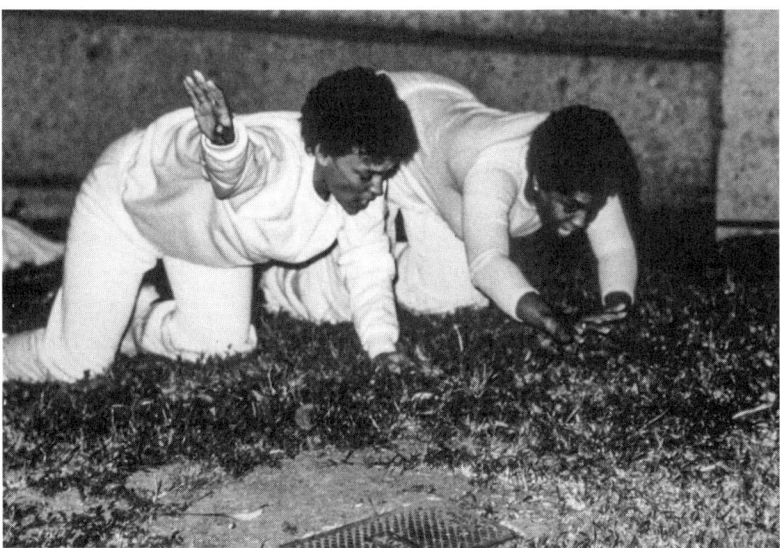

FIG. 4.22 Maren Hassinger (*left*) and Senga Nengudi (*right*), *Flying*, 1982. Performance, Los Angeles. Courtesy Maren Hassinger; Thomas Erben Gallery, New York; and the African American Performance Art Archive, University of North Carolina, Chapel Hill.

modes of expression into more ancient and ritualized structures. The piece offered a broad and mutable vision that described the art of Hassinger and her cohort in Los Angeles.

MEMORY, HISTORY, COMMUNITY, AND THE AFRO-FUTURE

In the works of Senga Nengudi, Houston Conwill, David Hammons, and Maren Hassinger we find a creative commitment to memory, history, and community. The attraction to postminimalist elements and processes was part of a generational shift of practice but also allowed for new kinds of signification. It permitted these artists to flee the body—that is, to escape from being predictable and anticipated, which could be troubling to African American as well as other audiences. To many viewers, black artists were defined by protest in the 1960s and 1970s. They focused on black dissent, which was legible and perhaps easier to manage and understand, rather than configurations that encompassed the abstract and uncategorizable. This was not a new trend. In the 1950s, for example, Norman Lewis's abstract expressionist colleagues thought he should make pictures of lynchings, not nonrepresentational canvases.[276]

Yet the threads of memory, history, and community running through the art of these practitioners gave it another purpose. African American audiences needed to see something recognizable to connect them to the work; likewise, while the artists moved toward the fully nonobjective, they also needed to connect with black observers in their own way. Much of this was through performance, which incorporated a ritualized approach to materials (including sound and music), space, and the body.

In keeping with their generation, these artists used new materials and material newly used as art, employing signification that bordered on apparent incoherence, changing the shape and organization of space. However, their context and purpose differed. As Kimberly Benston reminds us, much of the avant-garde art of the postwar period was "set in opposition to the intricate burdens of history and the sinuous responsibilities of remembrance."[277] Instead, the work of Nengudi, Conwill, Hammons, and Hassinger was posited against real and social death, intervening in these conditions and turning their estrangements into creative device. Certainly, these works fit in with the rising narrative approach in the American visual art and dance context after 1968. Yet it is also clear that the link to memory, history, and community ran throughout the work of these and many other African American artists, no matter how formless they might appear.

Maren Hassinger's cable sculpture from this period involved itself, like Robert Smithson's, in the industrial landscape. But while he was captivated by entropy, Hassinger was concerned with regeneration, not only the regrowth of nature but the reconceptualization of urbanity. David Hammons's *Spade* series and body prints took the African American figure as their subject, conceptual motivation, and means of production. He saw the corporeal as beautiful as well as under siege, although the actual body itself was not subjected to violence, as in Chris Burden's work, because brutality in the black community was a mundane and daily occurrence that did not need to be reenacted in real time to be understood. Similarly, in Houston Conwill's objects and performances the aggression found in actions by the Viennese Actionists was absent. The female body drove the sculptural and performance work of Senga Nengudi. But its feminism was much more subtle, not "explicit" in the way that Rebecca Schneider has used the term to describe work by women in this genre.

Bodies produce social space, Lefebvre tells us, generating area for their gestures. The sociospatial experience, McKittrick concurs, is the generator of new geographies, both contestatory and imaginative. In considering place or site as a discursive mode, Kwon finds that the dematerialization, deconstruction, and expansion of site's meaning in contemporary art transforms it into performance. Artists' use of site to critique institutional spaces of art is transferred to imbrication in social issues, expanding as cultural work/labor.[278]

Memory, history, and community became the context for their oeuvre. Consider the work of Hammons again, this time in comparison to that of Robert Morris. Dirt, grease, felt, plastic, and electric lights were important substances in the latter's *Continuous Project Altered Daily*, 1969, shown in New York. A few years later in California, Hammons created a series using grease, bones, hair, and brown paper bags, similar elements of detritus. But if Hammons's work reads as more "decorative" and more like narrative, this is because it was meant to read that way: a metaphoric mode was embedded there to attract certain readings and audiences. Guthrie P. Ramsey Jr.'s observations on the midcentury musical object through the figure of bebop pianist and innovator Earl "Bud" Powell are useful to recall here. For Ramsey, Bud Powell demonstrated his modernism and jazz manhood through structures of virtuosity, improvisation, and risk, yet the traditional harmonics of any song remained recognizable.[279]

Similarly, Hammons's grease, as Gylbert Coker has suggested, became a signifier of the black body, what she calls a "black object." As a product used to achieve radiant and emollient skin, grease carried a subtext of love, care, beauty: "How many times has your Momma told you to get yourself some grease 'cause your legs were ashy?"[280] Hammons's work did not parry in the same way with destruction (although it was laced with bones); it was not the offal, the annihilation Morris read into his work in the context of the Vietnam War.[281] It did reference the black body under siege, as so much of his work at this time did. However, as with Hassinger's projects, the end point was not the scene of destruction but renewal, reconfiguration, and resurrection, not the seen (the destroyed body) but the unseen (the spirit). As Muñoz has posited of queer futurity, such things did not present the culmination of statements on bodily knowledge; rather, they opened up its horizon.[282]

CONCLUSION **Noshun:** Black Los Angeles and the Global Imagination

IN 1849, JAMES PRESLEY BALL—a former itinerant photographer from Virginia, an African American, and an abolitionist—opened Ball's Great Daguerrean Gallery of the West in Cincinnati. It became one of the most successful photographic outfits in that antebellum city. In the post–Civil War period, Ball moved his business, following a changing U.S. frontier. In the 1870s he opened a shop in Minneapolis, a neighbor of another African American photographer, Harry Shepard of Saint Paul. The following decade found Ball in Helena, Montana, where he launched a third thriving studio before he headed to Seattle. Ball's last place of residence was Honolulu, where he resided in the early twentieth century. While Ball's businesses served a variety of clientele, what all these locations share is that they were important black western communities that thrived from the late nineteenth century into the twentieth.[1]

One such community was Nicodemus, Kansas, the most famous of the black towns that emerged in the period. Like most of the others, it was set up as a utopian place in an otherwise hostile landscape, with the shining possibilities of self-government and self-determination. Survival was made harder when transportation that could be the lifeblood of the town, the transcontinental railroad, was consciously routed away from its precincts. By the 1920s most of these smaller locales had died as people were drawn to larger cities. Later in the twentieth century, some became identified as "ghost towns," while others fought for life.

In 1976, one hundred years after its founding, Nicodemus was designated a historic district by the state. And as researchers would later show, and was perhaps true in other cases, rather than recording a death knell to these towns early in the century, there was instead an ebb and flow in populations in the redistribution from town center to township: as the central town was vacated by entrepreneurs and businesses, the land of the plains was repopulated by its (black) owners. In a sense, outside the township blacks were imperceptible; it was impossible for them to be seen as owners of the land.[2] What is fascinating is the designation of an entire African American town as a landmark in the landscape of the United States. As Amy Weisser reports, public sites dedicated to African American history and memory arose most significantly during the civil rights era. These are locations identified with protest and resistance: "lunch counters, bus depots, parks, highways, schools." They point to the complexity of black civic and national identities, disavowing "the ordinary presence of African Americans in the public landscape and, in effect, writ[ing] large a lack of place that African Americans have long experienced."[3]

On one hand, we can think of public space dedicated to black history as a commercialization, popularization, and thus degradation of sacred and fragile memories. Yet on the other, these represent the expansion of the black presence in civic arenas, recognition rather than disavowal, acknowledgment of spatial realities that chart a move from object to subject. Thus in 1980, one year after Charles White's death, Altadena residents voted to name a municipal space in his honor, a tribute to his support of that community. Charles White Park sits on Mountain View Street, its five-acre verdant expanse now used most often for soccer; it is one of the few parks in this country named for a visual artist.[4]

At the end of the 1980s, Noah Purifoy created his own park of sorts. More than a decade earlier, he had come to the conclusion that his artistic efforts would not change the world. He returned first to work as a social worker and then focused on his duties for the California Arts Council. After retiring from the council, he committed himself once again to art making, this time in the semiabandoned landscape of the desert of Joshua Tree, California. He'd gone there in 1989, moving onto land owned by Debbie Brewer, an artist friend from his days at the Watts Towers Art Center, and devoted himself to art full-time. The resulting outdoor museum stands to this day on seven and a half acres. Purifoy created large tableaux using found objects, motivated by what he described as the "pleasures" of the hunt.[5]

By the late 1990s, Purifoy's star was again on the rise.[6] His 1997 retrospective, *Noah Purifoy: Outside and in the Open*, organized by curator Lizzetta Lefalle-Collins for the California African American Museum in Los Angeles, opened to great acclaim. It showcased large-scale works he'd created since moving to the desert, and Purifoy was heralded in *ArtNews*, *Art in America*, and *Sculpture Magazine*. After his move to Joshua Tree, Purifoy became a mentor to many artists fleeing LA's rising real estate prices for the wide-open spaces farther south. Andrea Zittel thrived there, opening the "live-work compound" she calls A-Z West in 2000, and has sponsored the yearly art festival called High Desert Test Sites.[7]

After Purifoy's death in 2004 the Noah Purifoy Foundation came into existence. Set up to preserve the artist's legacy as well as his sculpture garden as a public park, the effort was spearheaded by Sue Welsh, another friend from Purifoy's days at Watts Towers.[8] Embracing "art, education and environmental concerns," it championed reuse, recycling, and the retooling of beauty, ideas Purifoy had always reinforced. These concepts were exciting and in tune with contemporary environmentalism, showing Purifoy's prescience in such things. This motivation also fit in well with the needs of the isolated desert locale, where objects were "precious" and things were always swapped or resold.[9]

In 2005 in Bar Harbor, Maine, Betye Saar began a lecture at an arts facility with a discussion of art making as seen from her eightieth year. Ever concise and to the point, Saar didn't dwell on her many accomplishments, grants, or the tour of her installation work throughout Asia while in her seventies. Instead, she offered the briefest overview of a career and turned her focus to ideas for new series and shows, her continued excitement at the challenges of making art, and the great things she found in the thrift stores of Maine. Among those in residence during that Maine summer of 2005 were Maren Hassinger and Senga Nengudi, who made the trip to collaborate on a new performance and installation. Nengudi later completed an artist's residency at the Fabric Workshop and Museum, Philadelphia, in 2007. Her video installation *Warp Trance*, 2007, captured the rhythmic pacing and sound of industrial weaving, creating mechanical trance and industrial ritual.

Traveling back and forth between Los Angeles and New York for much of the 1970s, Hammons had claimed New York as his home base by 1980. However, it would be another ten years before the mainstream art world caught up with his genius. In 1990 he was awarded the Prix de Rome, and the following year a MacArthur Fellowship. These prestigious honors were followed by a survey exhibition, organized by Tom Finkelpearl at what was by then called the PS 1 Museum, that subsequently traveled across the country. By the end of the tour, Hammons, for all intents and purposes, was the hottest household name. He was a postminimalist phenomenon, an artist who cared little for artworld conventions, and one of the few African American artists singled out as an international artworld star. In an interesting parallel to Romare Bearden's breakout moment, Hammons was in his late forties, having pursued the muse for almost thirty years when he was "discovered."

Houston Conwill too had made New York his home by 1980. Winning the Prix de Rome in 1985, several years before David Hammons, Conwill continued to create objects and sites for public performances that were often collaborative. Like most artists of his generation, he moved between media.

In New York, Conwill expanded the idea for his petrigraphs, changing materials and translating textured surfaces from rubber to bronze in public sculptures that were often outdoors but were marked as creative spaces for the sacred. These include *Open Secret*, 1986, a bronze relief located in the subway station at 125th Street and Lexington Avenue, the first commission under the city's Arts for Transit program.[10] At the Schomburg Center for Research in Black Culture, Conwill let go of three-dimensional elements and instead concentrated on mapping the wide-open interior floor space, using materials such as terrazzo and brass. There was a commingling of the graphing of waterways with a cosmogram, a floor-based diagram of meditation. Both were routes of travel, one of this world, the other of the cosmos. *Rivers*, 1991, embedded fragments of the 1921 poem "The Negro Speaks of Rivers," by Langston Hughes. The waterways Conwill charted—the Euphrates, Congo, Nile, and Mississippi—are mentioned in the poem, and the poet's ashes are interred in the Harlem ground beneath the artwork. Several years later Conwill completed a project in which the cosmogram format referred more specifically to performance and thus to his creative roots, in a sense transforming it into a dance diagram. *The New Ring Shout*, 1994, was one of several projects in Lower Manhattan that commemorated the unearthing of an eighteenth-century African Burial Ground as the government dug foundations for a new federal building.[11]

Conwill completed such pieces throughout the 1990s with a collaborative team including his sister, the poet Estella Conwill Mojozo, and architect Joseph dePace. They were emblematic of the shift Miwon Kwon charts in notions of site. Although these works were in a sense site-specific in that they did engage place, they were also "community-specific" or "audience-specific" settings that remembered African diasporic histories and were made with those communities in mind. Conwill's collaborative existed, as Kwon suggests, as a design group, a professional managerial class offering artistic services.[12] Yet the intention and the objects themselves brought something into the built environment that marked and commemorated black presence.

In the mid-1990s, Chicago-based painter Kerry James Marshall began his *Garden Project* series, large-scale works that explored the title "Garden" as it was applied to public housing both in Chicago and Los Angeles. Born in Birmingham, Alabama, in 1955, Marshall migrated to Los Angeles with his family eight years later, settling in Nickerson Gardens in Watts; with more than one thousand units on some sixty-nine acres, it had the distinction of being the largest tract of public housing west of the Mississippi River.[13] Marshall's lush surfaces celebrated these spaces as sites of hope and pleasure, even as they engaged the poverty that people endured. Among the last generation of Charles White's students, Marshall began studying with the elder artist while in high school as part of the Tutor/Art Program, eventually receiving his BFA from Otis Art Institute in 1978. His representational, graphic style and sizeable canvases cast him as an heir to White's large-scale, figurative approach. More than anything else, it is Marshall's acceptance of the mantle of the beautiful black figure as a necessity in the visual field that confirms his inheritance of White's way with painting.[14]

Of course, scores of contemporary artists have made it happen in Los Angeles.[15] The critical mass of art schools has played an important role in the expansive artists' community. There are those who stay around the city and those who head out to the New York scene. Among those who continue to send missives from Los Angeles is Mark Bradford, whose oversized mixed-media paintings and collages are sophisticated communiqués. Based in Leimert Park, he has also continued the work of keeping the area visible as a cultural precinct, opening the multiart space Art & Practice there with philanthropist Eileen Harris Norton. Bradford and Harris Norton have thus reenergized the legacy of the Brockman Gallery and its founders, Alonzo Davis and Dale Brockman Davis.[16] Those who have chosen New York over their West Coast hometown include Kira Lynn Harris, with her photo-based, mixed-media practice, and Kehinde Wiley, known for his heroic and sensuous portraits.[17]

Then there is Sanford Biggers, who seems to be the heir both to the peripatetic postminimalist aesthetics of Nengudi and Hammons and to their relentless expression as performance. His works take many shapes and forms; they may appear indoors or out, on walls and floors, as sculpture or video, as drawings, scores, and music. At the center of this interdisciplinary work is a particular evanescence that reflects the spirit of his postwar predecessors. Biggers deflects. He becomes a facilitator, creating an archetypal or paradigmatic space. It is an approach to a kind of absence that, as Toni Morrison reminds us, becomes a form of "ornate" presence.[18] It is a way of escaping categorization.

Biggers was raised in Baldwin Hills, one of the areas African Americans were able to move to with the fall of restrictive covenants in the second half of the twentieth century. It was a neighborhood with one of the best public school systems, there was access to modern conveniences, goods, and services, and fabulous housing, perhaps appearing to many as one prototype of a black utopia.[19] Like West Adams and Leimert Park, it was due north and west of Central Avenue and Watts. But it was still south of Pico Boulevard.

Biggers, born in 1970, is from a family of doctors and medical personnel, the same cohort that gave much support to the artists of an earlier generation. He left Los Angeles, heading to Morehouse College, pursuing graduate studies at the Maryland Institute College of Art and the School of the Art Institute of Chicago before landing in New York. His creative ethos was influenced by the performative cultures of hip-hop—from breakdancing to graffiti—in which he had participated growing up in Los Angeles, writing under the name Midas. Trained as a painter, he eventually moved into sculpture. Yet when he landed in New York, he worked as a musician, performing at CBGB, Spy Bar, and Knitting Factory along with two of his Morehouse classmates, poet Saul Williams and performer Martin Luther, and DJ Jahi Sundance. Over a decade, Biggers has created a body of work that uses a constellation of recurring signs and objects. His is a developing voice that engages notions of syncretism and indirection as ways to think about ideas of violence, desire, and landscape in the performative and cultural traditions of the African Diaspora and in a global world. "Noshun" (a neologism meaning idea or "notion") is one term he has used to designate his neoconceptual practice.

Sanford Biggers has an obsession with trees. They first appeared in a performance in 1998, accompanied, like many of his pieces, by music. Biggers placed a piano in the woods of Skowhegan, Maine, and over a month-long period went out to play it, in the nude. Weather and moisture changed the instrument's sound quality over time. At the end of the month, Biggers destroyed the piano in a roaring bonfire.

Video documentation of this 1998 work led to *Bittersweet Fruit*, 2002. A tree was taken into a gallery, and a small monitor with the video of the earlier piece was embedded in it. Headphones hung from branches so people could hear Biggers playing. But the headphones hung like nooses, and toward the end of the video, Biggers's feet dangled above the piano keys, only just possibly playing the instrument. The centrality of the piano, its alteration and destruction, was in dialogue with contemporary art and performance histories of John Cage, Nam June Paik, and Raphael Montañez Ortiz. But the bonfire took us elsewhere. The 1998 performance was a commemoration of James Byrd, a black man who had been dragged to his death in Texas earlier that year in a late twentieth-century lynching.[20]

Rather than didacticism, one finds in Biggers's allusions to violent acts the aesthetic context of Los Angeles found in Melvin Edwards's *Lynch Fragments* or David Hammons's more performative and ephemeral hanging of leather (skins) from trees. Yet the commentary, the "noshun," still floats there, obliquely, lightly, insistently.[21] Arrayed around the tree in *Bittersweet Fruit* is a collection of empty beer bottles. Are they stand-ins for the perpetrators of the crime, as their arrangement and upright posture seems to suggest (and that we know from the robust genre of lynching photographs and postcards)? Or do the bottles access the vernacular histories of appointing African American landscapes—on trees or in the ground—with the flashing power of protection that the glinting glass suggested? It is these choices and at times their indistinguishable nature, the oscillation and embeddedness of these antithetical positions, with which the artist leaves us.[22]

Such polyvocality was on display in *Blossom*, 2007, a title that as a noun and a verb speaks to the range of Biggers's practice, at once performance- and object-based. A large artificial tree rose from a patch of dirt in the gallery space, exploding through a baby grand player piano. The piano bench lay nearby, overturned and discarded, adding to the violence of the scene. The tree grew through the piano, becoming intertwined with it, as the instrument continued to play; emanating from the piece was Biggers's own arrangement of "Strange Fruit," the jazz (and antilynching) classic made famous by Billie Holiday. As an action word, the title took viewers to the verdant and to revitalization.[23]

In a video called *Cheshire*, 2007, trees, repetition, and restitution are on view. In this single-channel work, black men representing a spectrum of class positions climb trees in different settings and seasons. They repeatedly conquer them, looking out once they are settled into the branches to regard what they have surmounted. Commenting on the ongoing appearance of the tree in his oeuvre, Biggers has noted: "Actually, my hope was to reclaim nature and the African American male's entitlement to be in nature without the fear of torture or death."[24] The video's title is further elucidated by a sculpture with the same name: *Cheshire*, 2008, is an aluminum-and-Plexiglas smile, more than five feet long, whose red lips gleam and pearly white LEDs flash. It is from the Cheshire cat of Lewis Carroll's *Alice in Wonderland*, a character that appears and disappears (often in trees), sometimes leaving only its smirk behind. This grin is also the minstrel mask, a confluence that Biggers intends as well. In works like *Sambo's Banjo*, 1971–72, and *Let Me Entertain You*, 1972, Betye Saar too remarked on the dyad of performance and lynching, with African American singing and dancing as the performance, literally, of survival.

It is Biggers's *Bound*, 2009, however, that resonates in surprising ways with practices of his predecessors in Los Angeles. In this photographic series, we see a black man roped to a tree, the visualization of the act Biggers alluded to but did not directly portray for a decade. The figure is not naked and bloodied but dressed in a fine red, white, and blue suit. His bindings are not rough, abrading or cutting the skin, but delicate silk skeins arranged and knotted just so. In *Bound*, Biggers replaces lynching's brutalizations with *shibari*, the Japanese technique of erotic bondage. Pain opens onto pleasure; the work asks questions about the desire also lurking beneath violent U.S. practice. In African American vernacular landscape traditions, as Grey Gundaker and Judith McWillie remind us, while trees signify the living world and the mundane, their roots are mnemonic devices for the wilderness, the place of the spirit, enlightenment, escape. Lynching's tree of death is also Buddhism's tree of life, the Bodhi Tree, under which Siddhartha (Buddhism's founder) achieved enlightenment.[25]

While not a practicing Buddhist, Biggers learned its tenets and symbolism when he lived in Japan for three years in the mid-1990s. Yet he had been culturally prepared for his experiences there by a childhood in Los Angeles. Certainly the influence of Asian cultures on West Coast art making is substantial and long-standing, from ceramics to painting. However, Asian America as constituted on the West Coast is also part of larger a multiculture, not only locally and nationally but also one that has contributed to the understanding of African American place in a larger international community.

As a number of scholars have shown us, Asia and Asian America have played an important role in the African American understanding of the discursive notions of race. We can point to the parallelisms between the forced labor of African Americans and the indentured servitude of Chinese and Indians in the nineteenth century. In twentieth-century Los Angeles, Japan and Japanese American culture have a similar coefficient profile. Secondary migration has also played an important role: as African American migrants moved to Los Angeles, Japanese people moved to Hawaii and other parts of California before they too headed to LA. African American, Japanese, and eventually Japanese Americans inhabited the inner cities, living in proximity to each other and in overlapping areas.

After the Japanese defeat of Russia in the Russo-Japanese War (1904–5), African Americans saw in Japan a champion, a protector of the "colored races" worldwide. The powerful dream of international links imagined then extended into the Garvey movement and later the Nation of Islam. The South Asian support of anticolonial struggles after 1947 and the Bandung Conference of nonaligned nations in 1955 demonstrated continuing Afro-Asian connections, parallel histories, and mutual support. Along with the emergence of independent African countries, China came into view as a world power.

Vietnam's struggles for self-determination inspired a generation of American citizens, who supported antiwar and Third World liberation movements. Gerald Horne documents the referencing of the Vietnam conflict during the Watts Rebellion, in the modeling of guerrilla tactics and connections to oppressed populations in a place called "Viet-Watts."[26] If Asia was a signpost for African American freedom dreaming in the twentieth century, groups like the Black Panthers (inspired by Chinese Communism) influenced the U.S. multicultural Left and the formation of groups such as the Young Lords, Brown Berets, Red Guard Party, and Students for a Democratic Society. Much was shared in the desire for release from the stranglehold of European social, political, and aesthetic power. In this context, it is not surprising that Asia and Asian America formed an integral part of Biggers's and Senga Nengudi's aesthetic constellation.[27]

Biggers was aware of the Japanese culture in and around his neighborhood in the Crenshaw district. And as we have seen, at midcentury Asian Americans and African Americans fought alongside each other to battle restrictive covenants in housing, and eventually the city's west side opened up. Eleven Associated Gallery, the co-op started by Beulah Woodard and Miriam Matthews around 1950, included one Asian American member, painter Tyrus Wong. From its inception in the 1960s Brockman Gallery showed Asian American artists. Though Samella Lewis's books and curatorial accomplishments have elucidated the artists and traditions of the African Diaspora, she focused on Chinese art for her PhD in art history (Ohio State University, 1951), showing that it was a base for her explorations of world cultures. One wonders, too, about such influences on the work of David Hammons, who mentioned Asia at least once, in the piece *Afro Asian Eclipse (or Black China)*, 1979, a scroll-like object with fabric and hair.[28] Or we might find Asia in the work of Melvin Edwards, who once commented that the sense of "finish" in his early sculpture was inspired by his neighbor and friend, sculptor Ron Miyashiro.[29]

In Japan, Biggers began thinking about pattern and performance through the mandala, a ritual aesthetic element that revolves around a circular form often bound by a square. While overseas he experienced hip-hop culture in new ways, coming to understand it as a formidable global language. During the 1990s, hip-hop artists often were banned from performing in the United States, due to concerns about violence at their concerts. They took their shows abroad, and a huge and initially underground following developed in Japan.[30] In *Mandala of the B-Bodhisattva II*, 2000, the artist created a floor painting that served as the "stage" for a breakdancing "battle," a standard contest where competitors show off their moves. For *Creation/Dissipation*, 2002, the dance space was made from five abutting circles, drawn, in traditional fashion, in sand. As five dancers performed together, the sand drawing dispersed and disappeared. Movement is also suggested in the sculptural work *Bounce, Rock, Skate, Roll*, 2000. Titled after a popular song well known to those who enjoy recreational roller-skating, Biggers uses skate wheels and a fire hose to repeat the mandala's circular form. Other aspects of Japanese ritual and performative cultures come into play as well. *For Hip Hop Ni Sasagu (In Fond Memory of Hip Hop)*, 2004, members of the Joanin Soto Zen Temple in Ibaraki, Japan, performed a Biggers musical composition on bell-like singing bowls. The bowls themselves were created from a collection of silver hip-hop-style jewelry that had been melted down.

It is in some of Biggers's more recent work, however, that his syncretic aspirations seem most realized. During a residence at Harvard University in 2009, the artist installed *Constellation II* (plate 32). It was sited in Memorial Hall, a building dedicated to the memory of Union soldiers who lost their lives in the Civil War. Biggers layered the piece with additional meaning by also honoring African Americans who had been enslaved and those who had resisted in this same moment. An LED platform mapping stars and a barren tree hung with a quilt became a stage. There African American alternative music diva Imani Uzuri sang poems by Rumi, the thirteenth-century Sufi mystic, arranged in the form of Negro spirituals. Uzuri was joined by the campus a cappella group KeyChange and by Sumie Kaneko playing a traditional Japanese string instrument, the koto. Kaneko was dressed in a kimono, while Uzuri's garb was another quilt that pooled on the floor.

Among the conceits of *Constellation II* is the notion of African Americans as stargazers and star travelers, like Harriet Tubman, who used astronomy to navigate to freedom. She becomes, for Biggers, an astronaut. The stars are maps but also cosmic and Afro-futuristic concatenations. Rumi's words "My place is placeless, a trace of the traceless, neither body or soul. I belong to the beloved" connect to Buddhist teaching and also to the necessities of escape, the idea of willful disappearance.[31] The immaterial star maps also evoke charts in more tangible form. Some scholars have argued that African Americans in the antebellum period made quilts not simply as bed coverings but as devices to navigate the roads to freedom. Patterns were created, in fabric and stitching, that offered clues to safe places and areas of danger, times and locations as the "conductor" moved the train north along the Underground Railroad. Quilts hung on fences, washing lines, or even trees displayed these messages that were "hidden in plain view."[32] So Biggers's introduction of the quilt to his recurring tree took on a new role as navigational instrument. Works such as UGRR:US2, 2009, and UGRR:US2.2, 2009, can be seen as companion pieces, vintage quilts that Biggers has overlaid with stitched constellations and dance diagrams alluding to the mapping qualities of their predecessors.

In *Constellation II*, Biggers's conflation of slave self-liberation and space travel sung in real time in African American and Asian harmonies is for the artist an Afro-futuristic modality. As such, it signals heterochrony, the possibility of multiple time frames coexisting. It is the interruption of a type of chronology that regards those who stray from a monologic notion of Western cultural narrative as belated and backward. Instead objects and performances hold different textures of time that create their own histories. As Keith Moxey remarks, "The texture of the past is threaded through an account of the work's reception in the present."[33]

Constellation II's invocation of transhistorical time also imbricates space. It is one that bell hooks understands as a planetary "radical openness," while Edward Soja sees it as common and yet allusional, a "remembrance-rethinking-recovery of spaces lost . . . or never sighted at all," a gesture to futurity in restless and revisionary forms.[34] For Biggers and his African American predecessors on the West Coast, the look to Asia and Asia America can be understood as a gesture of solidarity with a larger, expansive, but equally contestatory notion of what Edward Said sees in the Orient as "not-Europe." An extension of the body not so much through incorporation but intersection. Asia is a way of thinking about futurity by adding new textures to the everyday. As Sara Ahmed posits, "Everyone, one might say, has an east; it is on the horizon, a visible line that marks the beginning of a new day."[35]

In these convergences, too, we need to consider Brent Hayes Edwards's idea of *décalage*—the unhappy, uneasy modality of translation, its gaps—

which describes black internationalism and diaspora thinking and births a new entity. This is what Homi Bhabha calls a third space that "enables other positions to emerge . . . and sets up new structures of authority, new political initiatives, which are inadequately understood through received wisdom."[36] Such intersections speak of proximities which are both ordinary and mundane but not dangerous, yet which engage "queerness, affiliation, and social contingency."[37]

As Brent Edwards argues, anticolonial actors of the interwar generation, spurred by their own global migration and travel, practiced international organizing as a form of "bad nationalism." Making alliances across national, colonial, and racial boundaries was a threat to colonialism and imperialism.[38] The imaginary and experimental, Edwards tells us, go to places and do the "work that labor organizing and more straightforward history are unable to do."[39] It is a necessary supplement, particularly the tentative and investigational, the mixing of a variety of genres to achieve a radical feel, sensibility, and message.

Biggers's interest in absence, deflection, and Buddhist mystical thought, in notions of selflessness and "immaterial essence," has many valences.[40] These are ways of escaping a history of black pain but also transforming it, reimagining such images in other spaces and times. It is a "re-gathering," advancing new claims that point "toward the future and toward a world that we have yet to inhabit."[41] Absence, the invisible, and the visually transformed are also methods of "bad nationalism" and forms of internationalism and collectivism that in their inability to be precisely tracked and marked, in their deflection, are aesthetic markers imagining types of connection and activist practice that lie beyond the gaze of dominant power, yet in plain view.

NOTES

ABBREVIATIONS

AGR   Ankrum Gallery Records, 1960–1990, Archives of American Art, Smithsonian Institution

CWWP   Charles W. White Papers, c. 1930–1982, Archives of American Art, Smithsonian Institution

MARBL   Manuscripts, Archives, and Rare Book Library, Emory University

NPP   Noah Purifoy Papers, 1935–1998, Archives of American Art, Smithsonian Institution

INTRODUCTION

1. Biddy Mason had been an influential figure in nineteenth-century Los Angeles. A midwife and nurse, she was among the founders of the First African Methodist Episcopal Church. She'd started her life as a slave, walking westward from Mississippi to Utah and arriving in San Bernardino County, California, in 1851. There she petitioned for her freedom in a highly visible case, winning it in 1857. This occurred just before the *Dred Scott* decision ruled that slaves who traveled to nonslave territory were not automatically free, one of the incidents that set the stage for the Civil War. Like others inquiring about a commission, Miriam Matthews provided White with a biographical document on Biddy Mason. Miriam Matthews to Charles White, July 13, 1966; Miriam Matthews to Charles White, undated card, c. winter 1966; Miriam Matthews to Charles White, July 30, 1967, reel 3189 microfilm, Charles W. White Papers, c. 1930–1982, Archives of American Art, Smithsonian Institution (hereafter CWWP).

2. In 1955, for instance, White received a letter from a Eugene Feldman of Winston Salem, North Carolina, asking him to create a likeness of one "James T. Rapier, Negro congressman of Alabama 1873–75," providing a detailed biography. See Eugene Feldman to Charles White, July 9, 1955, reel 3189 microfilm, CWWP.

3. David Hammons quoted in Joseph E. Young, "Los Angeles," *Art International* 14, no. 8 (October 20, 1970): 74. Hammons discusses Charles White's impact on him

further in *Three Graphic Artists* (Los Angeles: Los Angeles County Museum of Art, 1971), 7. He studied at Los Angeles Trade Technical College and Otis Art Institute between 1966 and 1968. In early résumés Hammons also lists private studies with White. On the multiracial cowboy population, black cowboys, cattlemen, and vacqueros see Quintard Taylor, *In Search of the Racial Frontier: African Americans in the American West, 1528–1990* (New York: Norton, 1998), 156–63; Nat Love, *The Life and Adventures of Nat Love* (New York: Arno, 1968; first published 1907).

4. Robert Sill, ed., *David Hammons in the Hood* (Springfield: Illinois State Museum, 1994), 8.

5. On concepts of the African Diaspora see Paul Gilroy, *The Black Atlantic: Modernity and Double Consciousness* (London: Verso, 1993); Michael A. Gomez, *Exchanging Our Country Marks: The Transformation of African Identities in the Colonial and Antebellum South* (Chapel Hill: University of North Carolina Press, 1998); Tiffany Ruby Patterson and Robin D. G. Kelley, "Unfinished Migrations: Reflections on the African Diaspora and the Making of the Modern World," *African Studies Review* 43, no. 1 (2000): 11–45; Brent Hayes Edwards, *The Practice of Diaspora: Literature, Translation, and the Rise of Black Internationalism* (Cambridge, MA: Harvard University Press, 2003); Saidiya V. Hartman, *Lose Your Mother: A Journey along the Atlantic Slave Route* (New York: Farrar, Straus and Giroux, 2007).

6. Taylor, *In Search of the Racial Frontier*, chap. 1, 82–84, 196–97.

7. Darlene Clark Hine, "Black Migration to the Urban Midwest, the Gender Dimension, 1915–1945," in Joe William Trotter Jr., ed., *The Great Migration in Historical Perspective: New Dimensions of Race, Class, and Gender* (Bloomington: Indiana University Press, 1991); Michel de Certeau, *The Practice of Everyday Life* (Berkeley: University of California Press, 1984), 101. See also Gretchen Lemke-Santangelo, "'Women Make Community': African American Migrant Women and the Cultural Transformation of the San Francisco East Bay Area," in Quintard Taylor and Shirley Ann Wilson Moore, eds., *African American Women Confront the West, 1600–2000* (Norman: University of Oklahoma Press, 2003). Maya Angelou also chronicles her own such journey, a childhood spent between Stamps, Arkansas, and St. Louis, Missouri, and her eventual move to San Francisco, in her autobiography *I Know Why the Caged Bird Sings* (New York: Bantam, 1971).

8. Nicholas Lemann, *The Promised Land: The Great Black Migration and How It Changed America* (New York: Vintage Books, 1992; first published 1991), 6; Josh Sides, *L.A. City Limits: African American Los Angeles from the Great Depression to the Present* (Berkeley: University of California Press, 2003), 37–38; Taylor, *In Search of the Racial Frontier*; Trotter, *The Great Migration in Historical Perspective*.

9. Shirley Anne Moore, "Getting There, Being There: African American Migration to Richmond, California, 1910–1945," in Trotter, *The Great Migration in Historical Perspective*, 113, 107.

10. Samuel Roberts, introduction to Carter G. Woodson, *A Century of Negro Migration* (Mineola, NY: Dover, 2002; first published 1918); Nell Irvin Painter, *Exodusters: Black Migration to Kansas after Reconstruction* (New York: W. W. Norton, 1992; first published 1977), 191–93.

11. Taylor, *In Search of the Racial Frontier*, 256–57. See also Sides, *L.A. City Limits*, 199.

12. Painter, *Exodusters*, 87.

13. On the West Indies as a safe haven see Woodson, *A Century of Negro Migration*, 69–70; on Cyprus see Painter, *Exodusters*, 124–25.
14. Painter, *Exodusters*, 140–59, 179, 194–95, 215; Taylor, *In Search of the Racial Frontier*, 81, 94, 135–41.
15. Taylor, *In Search of the Racial Frontier*, chap. 5; Kenneth Marvin Hamilton, *Black Towns and Profit: Promotion and Development in the Trans-Appalachian West, 1877–1915* (Urbana: University of Illinois Press, 1991); Hine, "Black Migration," 127; Painter, *Exodusters*, 258; Lemann, *The Promised Land*, 49.
16. Katherine McKittrick, *Demonic Grounds: Black Women and the Cartographies of Struggle* (Minneapolis: University of Minnesota Press, 2006), 42; Farah Jasmine Griffin, *"Who Set You Flowin'?": The African American Migration Narrative* (New York: Oxford University Press, 1995), 9–10, 111; Dana Cuff, *The Provisional City: Los Angeles Stories of Architecture and Urbanism* (Cambridge, MA: MIT Press, 2000), 39–40, 307.
17. Hine, "Black Migration," 127.
18. De Certeau, *The Practice of Everyday Life*, chap. 5.
19. Jacqueline Najuma Stewart, *Migrating to the Movies: Cinema and Black Urban Modernity* (Berkeley: University of California Press, 2005); Davarian L. Baldwin, *Chicago's New Negroes: Modernity, the Great Migration, and Black Urban Life* (Chapel Hill: University of North Carolina Press, 2007); Guthrie P. Ramsey Jr., *Race Music: Black Cultures from Bebop to Hip-Hop* (Berkeley: University of California Press, 2003); Sides, *L.A. City Limits*; Clora Bryant et al., *Central Avenue Sounds: Jazz in Los Angeles* (Berkeley: University of California Press, 1998).
20. Eric Avila, *Popular Culture in the Age of White Flight: Fear and Fantasy in Suburban Los Angeles* (Berkeley: University of California Press, 2004), chap. 1; Sides, *L.A. City Limits*, 21. There is still an Inkwell Beach on Martha's Vineyard, Massachusetts, reminding us of the reaches of such practices. Chicken Bone Beach in Atlantic City, New Jersey, is another example.
21. In Los Angeles prior to World War II, some 87 percent of women and 40 percent of men of African descent held positions as domestic servants. Painter, *Exodusters*, x. See also Taylor, *In Search of the Racial Frontier*, 251.
22. Roughly 53 percent of migrants at midcentury were women. Quintard Taylor and Shirley Ann Wilson Moore, "The West of African American Women, 1600–2000," in Taylor and Moore, *African American Women Confront the West*, 12–13. On women and migration at the turn of twentieth century see Samuel Roberts, introduction to Woodson, *A Century of Negro Migration*.
23. On westward drift of capital see Avila, *Popular Culture in the Age of White Flight*, 9, 33, 149. See also Edward Soja, *Postmodern Geographies: The Reassertion of Space in Critical Social Theory* (New York: Verso, 1989), chaps. 8 and 9; Sides, *L.A. City Limits*, 26, 57–58, 81–93. As Sides notes, in 1960, 8 percent of African American women nationally worked in clerical posts, compared to 16 percent in California. By 1970, 32 percent in California worked in such jobs. Karen Anne Mason, interview with Ruth Waddy (1993), *African American Artists of Los Angeles* (Los Angeles: Oral History Program of the University of California, 1992–2000), 1–30.
24. George Lewis, *A Power Stronger Than Itself: The AACM and American Experimental Music* (Chicago: University of Chicago Press, 2008); Lemann, *The Promised Land*, 201, 252.

25. The U.S. Supreme Court struck down auxiliary unions in 1945. Moore, "Getting There, Being There," 118–20.
26. C. Bryant et al., *Central Avenue Sounds*, 12, 404.
27. Avila, *Popular Culture in the Age of White Flight*, chap. 1; Sides, *L.A. City Limits*, 176–83; Soja, *Postmodern Geographies*. We can find similarities for the suburbanization of employment in the case of Macon, Georgia, for instance. See Walter J. Hood Jr. and Mellissa Erikson, "Storing Memories in the Yard: Remaking Popular Street, the Shifting Black Cultural Landscape," in Craig E. Barton, ed., *Sites of Memory: Perspectives on Architecture and Race* (Princeton, NJ: Princeton Architectural Press, 2001), 178–79.
28. Taylor, *In Search of the Racial Frontier*, 215–19; Lemann, *The Promised Land*, 91. Philanthropist Julius Rosenwald used some of his wealth to address this issue in the South. Between 1912 and 1937 more than five thousand "Rosenwald schools" were constructed to serve African Americans in rural areas. Eric Eckholm, "Black Schools Restored as Landmarks," *New York Times*, January 15, 2010, A16.
29. Cheryl Brown Henderson, "Lucinda Todd and the Invisible Petitioners of *Brown v. Board of Education of Topeka, Kansas*," in Taylor and Moore, *African American Women Confront the West*, 317. Henderson argues that Oliver L. Brown was chosen as the lead plaintiff in the NAACP case because he was a man, and because he was a pastor and not a civil rights activist. As a union member he also had job security. Kansas was also chosen to lead because it gave the case a more national rather than southern tone; the other petitioning states, along with Washington, DC, were Delaware, South Carolina, and Virginia. See also Taylor, *In Search of the Racial Frontier*, 281–83.
30. Amy Weisser, "Making *Brown v. Board of Education*: Memorializing Separate but Unequal Spaces," in Barton, *Sites of Memory*, 103.
31. Taylor, *In Search of the Racial Frontier*, 215–16; Sides, *L.A. City Limits*, 19, 159, 194–95. Looking to the African Diaspora we can see the same problematics with the notion of colonial education, where Western education is both the pinnacle and the elusive goal. South Africa's Soweto Riots of 1976, for instance, were a response to apartheid educational strictures as both spatial and pedagogic. See N. Ola Uduku, "The Colonial Face of Educational Space," in Lesley Naa Norle Lokko, ed., *White Papers, Black Marks: Architecture, Race, Culture* (Minneapolis: University of Minnesota Press, 2000), 44–64.
32. Bradford Grant, "Accommodation, Resistance, and Appropriation in African American Building," in Barton, *Sites of Memory*, 109–18; McKittrick, *Demonic Grounds*, chap. 3. The anecdote on Martin Luther King Jr. is found in Lemann, *The Promised Land*, 216–17. We also find Cotton Street as a booming thoroughfare in pre–World War II Macon, Georgia; see Hood and Erikson, "Storing Memories in the Yard."
33. Griffin, *"Who Set You Flowin'?,"* 75–76, 103–7; Lemann, *The Promised Land*, 52–53; Cuff, *The Provisional City*, 301.
34. Daniel Widener, "'Perhaps the Japanese Are to Be Thanked?': Asia, Asian Americans, and the Construction of Black California," *positions* 11, no. 1 (Spring 2003): 135–81. On blacks in former Asian communities see Taylor, *In Search of the Racial Frontier*, 266–73; Sides, *L.A. City Limits*, 15, 44; Angelou, *I Know Why the Caged Bird Sings*, 177–79.
35. Avila, *Popular Culture in the Age of White Flight*, chaps. 1 and 2; George Lipsitz, *The*

Possessive Investment in Whiteness (Philadelphia: Temple University Press, 1998), chap. 1; Craig L. Wilkins, *The Aesthetics of Equity: Notes on Race, Space, Architecture, and Music* (Minneapolis: University of Minnesota Press, 2007), chap. 1.

36. Sides, *L.A. City Limits*, 17–18, 95–100; Taylor, *In Search of the Racial Frontier*, 269–70. Many of the petitions were filed by Loren Miller, a Los Angeles attorney who was part of the NAACP legal team that, along with Thurgood Marshall, won the battle against restrictive housing covenants; he was also a member of the group that would successfully argue against educational segregation in *Brown v. Board of Education*. Miller, a cousin of Leon H. Washington Jr., owner of the African American newspaper the *Los Angeles Sentinel*, eventually took over as owner of the storied black periodical the *California Eagle*.

37. One of the biggest debacles of this nature involved the clearing of the largely Mexican American neighborhood of Chavez Ravine in the late 1940s and early 1950s. While public housing was promised, manipulation by real estate interests abrogated these guarantees. Instead, a privately owned sports stadium was erected in its place to lure the Dodgers baseball franchise from New York to Los Angeles. As Eric Avila has argued, the battle over home and space in this instance led to increased politicization among Chicanos more evident in the Chicano movement. See Avila, *Popular Culture in the Age of White Flight*, chaps. 5 and 6; Cuff, *The Provisional City*, chap. 7. August Wilson's final stage play, *Radio Golf* (2005), took aim at such practices in Pittsburgh, Pennsylvania.

38. Sides, *L.A. City Limits*, 115–20. It is also important to note that much of the public housing open to African Americans, in Watts for instance, was sited on land originally owned by Japanese Americans that had been confiscated during internment. See Widener, "'Perhaps the Japanese Are to Be Thanked?,'" 167, and Vijay Prashad, *Everybody Was Kung Fu Fighting: Afro-Asian Connections and the Myth of Cultural Purity* (Boston: Beacon, 2001), 116.

39. Pío Pico's grandmother Jacinta de la Cruz Pico was a woman of African descent. Taylor and Moore, *African American Women Confront the West*, 5; Taylor, *In Search of the Racial Frontier*, 45.

40. Elizabeth Grosz, *Architecture from the Outside: Essays on Virtual and Real Space* (Cambridge, MA: MIT Press, 2001), 177, 170.

41. Henri Lefebvre, *The Production of Space* (Oxford: Blackwell, 1991), 26, 191.

42. Miwon Kwon, *One Place after Another: Site-Specific Art and Locational Identity* (Cambridge, MA: MIT Press, 2002), 29–30.

43. McKittrick, *Demonic Grounds*, 15, 74, 19, 7.

44. Kwon, *One Place after Another*, 165.

45. Grosz, *Architecture from the Outside*, 79, 88.

46. McKittrick, *Demonic Grounds*, 143. Both McKittrick and Wilkins have presented cases for the spatial formations of expressive culture through music rather than visual art. See McKittrick, *Demonic Grounds*, 138–41, and Wilkins, *The Aesthetics of Equity*, part II.

47. David Hammons and Louise Neri, "No Wonder," *Parkett* 31 (March 1992): 53. For more on Hammons's hair works see Kellie Jones, "In the Thick of It: David Hammons and Hair Culture in the 1970s," *Third Text* 12, no. 44 (Autumn 1998): 17–24.

48. See Alondra Nelson, "Introduction: Future Texts," in "Afrofuturism," ed. Alondra

Nelson, special issue, *Social Text* 20, no. 2 (Summer 2002): 8. For more on artists and Afrofuturism see Naima J. Keith and Zoé Whitley, *The Shadows Took Shape* (New York: The Studio Museum in Harlem, 2013).

49. Karen Anne Mason, interview with John Riddle (2000), *African American Artists of Los Angeles*, 123.

ONE. EMERGE

1. Film historian Donald Bogle suggests that *For Love of Ivy* presented characters that were all but obsolete by the late 1960s but nevertheless presented the first onscreen romance between black people in a mass-marketed film. Donald Bogle, *Toms, Coons, Mulattoes, Mammies, and Bucks: An Interpretive History of Blacks in American Films*, new exp. ed. (New York: Viking, 1991; first published 1973), 217–19.
2. The Howard University exhibition also traveled to Morgan State University and Fisk University in 1968.
3. Benjamin Horowitz, *Images of Dignity: The Drawings of Charles White*, foreword by Harry Belafonte, introduction by James A. Porter (Los Angeles: Ward Ritchie, 1967). It was Horowitz who brought the publication together, leaning on friend and Los Angeles publisher Ward Ritchie to take a risk and publish an art book on a black artist. After the book went into a second and then a third printing, Horowitz found other publishers interested in producing another book on White. The artist refused. Rather than another monograph focusing on him, he wanted other African American artists to have that opportunity. Benjamin Horowitz, "On the Road with Charlie White," in "Charles White: Art and Soul," special issue, *Freedomways* 20, no. 3 (1980): 163–64.
4. Trained as an artist and art historian, with degrees from Howard University, New York University, and the Sorbonne, Porter was affiliated with Howard University throughout his career and directed the school's art department and art gallery from 1953 to 1970. His book *Modern Negro Art* (1943) was the first comprehensive text on both fine and decorative art making by African Americans. James A. Porter, "The Art of Charles White: An Appreciation," in Horowitz, *Images of Dignity*, 4. See also James A. Porter, *Modern Negro Art* (Washington, DC: Howard University Press, 1992; first published 1943).
5. Harry Belafonte, foreword to Horowitz, *Images of Dignity*, 1–2.
6. See telegrams from White to Belafonte, September 13, 1978, and July 19, 1979, reel 3190 microfilm, Charles W. White Papers, c. 1930–1982, Archives of American Art, Smithsonian Institution (hereafter CWWP); "Oral History Interview with Charles Wilbert White, 1965 March 9," Archives of American Art, Smithsonian Institution; Frances Barrett White with Anne Scott, *Reaches of the Heart: A Loving Look at the Artist Charles White* (New York: Barricade Books, 1994).
7. Kristine McKenna, *The Ferus Gallery: A Place to Begin* (Göttingen, Germany: Steidl, 2009), 157, 280. For more on Harry Belafonte's impact on U.S. culture of the period, see Harry Belafonte with Michael Shnayerson, *My Song: A Memoir of Art, Race, and Defiance* (New York: Alfred A. Knopf, 2011), and the documentary film *Sing Your Song* (dir. Susanne Rostock; S2BN films, 2011).
8. Bogle, *Toms, Coons, Mulattoes, Mammies, and Bucks*, 160. *Anna Lucasta* was also the most famous production of the American Negro Theater in New York, begun by

Abraham Hill and Frederick O'Neal in 1940. Holding rehearsals at the Schomburg Center, it was one more site of progressive African American cultural activity during that era. It would certainly have been one of White's communities while in New York and another place where he gathered with the likes of Ruby Dee, Harry Belafonte, and Ann Petry (who tried her hand at acting for a time and took classes at the Harlem Community Art Center as well). Farah Jasmine Griffin, *Harlem Nocturne: Women Artists and Progressive Politics during World War II* (New York: Basic Books, 2013), 101–3.

9. Charles White's second wife, Frances Barrett White, described the appearance of his drawings on *Tonight with Belafonte* as "full stage backdrops" (White with Scott, *Reaches of the Heart*, 181). White's *Folk Singer*, 1957, a drawing clearly based on Belafonte's image (and in his collection), is prominently displayed in at least one episode. See the documentary film *Sing Your Song*.

While White enjoyed visiting Hollywood (and TV) sets, and did so when friends like Poitier or Ivan Dixon appeared in the cast, he remained conflicted about his paintings and drawings appearing onscreen, because of the ways they could be used, abused, and manipulated there. A similar project for the film adaptation of Lorraine Hansberry's *Raisin in the Sun* (1961)—also starring Sidney Poitier—seems to have fizzled. See Philip Rose and Columbia Pictures Corporation to Charles White, October 4, 1960, reel 3189 microfilm, CWWP. Regarding the Anna Lucasta project see "Anna Lucasta" (probably written by Frances Barrett White) and Charles D. Silverberg, attorney for Longridge Enterprises, Inc., to Charles White, June 27, 1958, reel 3190 microfilm, and Producer Sidney Harmon to Charles White, October 7, 1958, reel 2041 microfilm, CWWP; "Oral History Interview with Charles Wilbert White, 1965 March 9," Archives of American Art, Smithsonian Institution; and White with Scott, *Reaches of the Heart*, 107. For mention of White's work appearing on *Tonight with Belafonte* see Arnold Shaw, *Belafonte: An Unauthorized Biography* (Philadelphia: Chilton, 1960), 317. For an account of the conflicts Belafonte encountered in producing that show see Henry Louis Gates Jr., "Belafonte's Balancing Act," *New Yorker*, August 26, 1996, 140. Belafonte eventually reprised a version of the show in 1968 when he hosted a week of the *Tonight Show* for Johnny Carson.

10. On Charles White's thoughts on an acting career see "Oral History Interview with Charles Wilbert White, 1965 March 9," Archives of American Art, Smithsonian Institution, and Horowitz, "On the Road with Charlie White," 165–66. On the *Learning Tree* premier see telegram from Max Bercutt and Warner Brothers–Seven Arts to Charles White, July 5, 1969, reel 3189 microfilm, CWWP. Basing it on his 1963 autobiographical novel, Gordon Parks wrote the screenplay, scored, and directed the film *Learning Tree*, which introduced him as a significant Hollywood force.

11. A brief and undated note from Ruby Dee on American Airlines stationery remarks, in part, "Dear Charles, What a delight to see you today. Just a line to confirm the work we talked about and to send a slight down payment." See Ruby to Charles, undated letter, reel 3189 microfilm, CWWP. See also Harry Belafonte and Sidney Poitier, "Brothuhs," in "Charles White: Art and Soul," special issue, *Freedomways* 20, no. 3 (1980): 195–96. On driving see White with Scott, *Reaches of the Heart*, 107.

12. The *Sentinel* writer has the date of Charles White and wife Frances's arrival as October 11, 1956. Frances Barrett White, however, lists the date of the couple's arrival in

Pasadena somewhat earlier, on September 15, 1956, after a three-day cross-country journey. Esther Jones, "Artist Charles White Settles in Pasadena," *Los Angeles Sentinel*, November 8, 1956, B4; White with Scott, *Reaches of the Heart*, 89–90.

13. A. M., "Excellent Exhibit Marks Landau Gallery's Birthday," *Los Angeles Times*, April 27, 1958, E12.

14. "PTC to Show White Drawings," *Los Angeles Sentinel*, September 3, 1959, B4; "Invitational Art Exhibit at Town Club," *Los Angeles Sentinel*, May 24, 1956, B2.

15. *Ebony* 8, no. 2 (December 1952): 80–86; "Los Angeles," *Jet*, September 4, 1952, 43; Jesse Mae Brown, "Pacific Town," *California Eagle*, January 30, 1947, 10; Karen E. Hudson and Paul R. Williams, *Paul R. Williams, Architect: A Legacy of Style* (New York: Rizzoli, 1993).

16. "Image of Dignity: The Drawings of Charles White," *Negro Digest* 16 (June 1967): 40–48; Louie Robinson, "Charles White: Portrayer of Black Dignity," *Ebony* 22, no. 9 (July 1967): 25–28, 30, 32, 34–36. *Negro Digest* had also published an earlier story on White: Hoyt Fuller, "Charles White, Artist," *Negro Digest* 12 (July 1963): 40–45; and *Ebony* had commissioned the artist to create a cover for its August 1966 special issue, "The Negro Woman" (*J'Accuse! No. 10*, 1966, collection of John Johnson). However, White's work had appeared in both publications as early as 1945. On *Negro Digest* and *Ebony* see James Edward Smethurst, *The Black Arts Movement: Literary Nationalism in the 1960s and 1970s* (Chapel Hill: University of North Carolina Press, 2005), and Adam Green, *Selling the Race: Culture, Community, and Black Chicago, 1940–1955* (Chicago: University of Chicago Press, 2007), particularly chap. 4.

17. Alex Amofa Kophi to Charles White, June 5, 1968, reel 2041 microfilm, CWWP. Many other letters are found in this reel, including correspondence from Cape Coast and Accra, Ghana.

18. The reproduction of the drawing appeared on page 28 of Louie Robinson, "Charles White: Portrayer of Black Dignity," *Ebony* 22, no. 9 (July 1967). Sékou Touré was the cover story of *Ebony*'s February 1960 issue. See also the documentary film *Sing Your Song*.

19. The show traveled for a year, and at the end of the run White kindly donated the two prints he exhibited to the museum. These were *Solid as a Rock* and *Folk Singer*. Jerome Allan Donson, director, Long Beach Museum of Art, to Charles White, December 2, 1958, and Jerome Allan Donson, director, Long Beach Museum of Art, to Charles White, February 12, 1959, reel 2041 microfilm, CWWP.

20. Esther B. Jones, "Charles White Exhibit Enriching Experience," *Los Angeles Sentinel*, November 9, 1961, C1. The portfolio for sale at this event was probably that released by Pro Artis Publishers of Los Angeles, which included ten lithographs—among them *Go Tell It on the Mountain*, *Southern News*, *Flying Fish*, and *Awaken*—of 17 by 22 inches. The wildly popular *Awaken* was probably a print version of the drawing *Awaken from the Unknowning*, 1961. See also Fuller, "Charles White, Artist," 45, and "Charles White Art Portfolios," reel 2041 microfilm, CWWP.

White's wife, Frances Barrett White, had become friendly with Ann Shaw at her first Los Angeles job at the YWCA in Woodlawn, where both were employed: White with Scott, *Reaches of the Heart*, 106–7. On the relationship between Charlotta Bass and White see White with Scott, *Reaches of the Heart*, 106–7; Charlotta Bass to Charles White, March 7, 1961, reel 3189 microfilm, CWWP; "Art News," *Los Angeles*

Times, March 18, 1962, A27; "Church Group Schedules Festival," *Los Angeles Times*, March 6, 1962, C6.

21. CORE hosted numerous art exhibitions in the 1960s as fund-raising tools. Many were held in New York and at various galleries and featured some of the era's hottest artists, including Frank Stella, Jim Dine, Robert Rauschenberg, Robert Indiana, and Romare Bearden. See Dalila Scruggs, "Chronology," in Teresa A. Carbone and Kellie Jones, eds., *Witness: Art and Civil Rights in the Sixties* (New York: Monacelli Press and the Brooklyn Museum, 2014), 121–60.

22. See letters from American Friends Service Committee, Pasadena, CA, to Charles White for the years 1962, 1966, 1968, and the invitation to "The 980 Art Exhibit," December 1966, reel 3189 microfilm, CWWP; "Friends Service Committee Exhibit Scheduled," *Los Angeles Times*, December 8, 1963, B27; and "980 Show Will Present Major Works," *Los Angeles Times*, December 6, 1964, 34.

23. The "Negro in the Creative Arts" benefit was held August 11 and 12, 1962, at the Beverly Hills home of Mr. and Mrs. Jack Sylvester. Invitation to "The Negro in the Creative Arts," reel 3189 microfilm, CWWP; "Educators Unit Will Meet Here," *Los Angeles Times*, April 4, 1957, E12; "State GOP Leaders to Map Strategy," *Los Angeles Times*, August 4, 1958, 22; "$800 Raised for Watts Towers," *Los Angeles Times*, February 7, 1960, C1; Joan Burnham, "Guild Will Hold Pasadena Dance," *Los Angeles Times*, March 17, 1960, D8; "Democrats Hold Festival, Sale," *Los Angeles Times*, September 25, 1960, WS9. Beata Inaya is listed as coordinator for the 1962 AFSC exhibition in Curt Moody and American Friends Service Committee to Charles White, October 3, 1962, reel 3189 microfilm, CWWP.

24. Maggie Savoy, "Watts Arts Festival," *Los Angeles Times*, August 6, 1969, D5; William Wilson, "Watts Festival Strives for an Afro-American Art Style," *Los Angeles Times*, August 15, 1969, D9.

25. White with Scott, *Reaches of the Heart*, 99; "Jewish Center Adds Two New Art Teachers," *Los Angeles Times*, September 24, 1964, 16; "Jewish Center to Show Art Works," *Los Angeles Times*, July 12, 1964, SF-A7; "Jewish Center Art Exhibit Opens Tonight," *Los Angeles Times*, July 21, 1964, SF8; Hollywood Los Feliz Jewish Community Center to Charles White, January 18, 1966, reel 3189 microfilm, CWWP.

Edward Biberman is also listed on the organizing committee for the "Negro in the Creative Arts" affair. A book on his work titled *Time and Circumstance: Forty Years of Painting* (1968) was published a year after White's *Images of Dignity* came out, from the same press. During 1967–68 Biberman hosted the television show *Dialogues in Art* on KNBC, Los Angeles, on which White appeared. Frances Barrett White describes socializing with Ed and his brother Herbert in the Hollywood Hills. Through them the Whites befriended Dalton Trumbo, on whose property they would live for several years. Herbert Biberman and Dalton Trumbo were Hollywood professionals who were part of the Hollywood Ten; they were jailed on contempt after coming before the House Committee on Un-American Activities, as well as blacklisted. The Bibermans were great-uncles of Jeremy Strick, who was director of the Los Angeles Museum of Contemporary Art from 1999 to 2008. Christopher Knight, "MOCA Director a Curator to the Core," *Los Angeles Times*, August 6, 1999; White with Scott, *Reaches of the Heart*, 111–12; Edward Biberman and Emily Corey, *Oral History Transcript*, Oral History Program, University of California, Los Angeles, 1977; Stephanie Barron, Sheri Bernstein, and Iliene Susan Fort, *Made in California: Art, Image, and Identity, 1900–2000* (Los Angeles: Los Angeles County Museum of Art, 2000).

26. Art Seidenbaum, "The Racial Picture in Black and White," *Los Angeles Times*, February 3, 1964, C1, C12; Henry J. Seldis, "White's Visual Spirituals," *Los Angeles Times*, February 7, 1964, C6. White has described several racial beatings that he experienced personally. Two occurred in the South, one in New Orleans when he was teaching at Dillard University and the other while he was completing his mural *The Contribution of the Negro to Democracy*, 1943, at Hampton University in Virginia. Another incident occurred in Greenwich Village, when some white toughs accosted him as he picked up his wife Frances, who was white, from the subway station. White also openly discussed the lynching of no less than five family members—two uncles and three cousins—over the years in Mississippi. "Oral History Interview with Charles Wilbert White, 1965 March 9," Archives of American Art, Smithsonian Institution; White with Scott, *Reaches of the Heart*, 85.

27. Detroit native and visiting assistant professor G. Ray Kerciu generated controversy when his painting *America the Beautiful*—of a Confederate flag inscribed with racist slogans shouted at black students integrating the University of Mississippi in 1962—along with others in the series were shown at the Ole Miss Fine Arts Center. Four paintings were censored. Charges were pressed and later dropped by Ole Miss law school senior Charles G. Blackwell (a member in good standing of several white supremacist Citizen Councils) after Kerciu agreed never to show any paintings on the campus again. Lawrence W. Feinberg, "Ole Miss Student Drops Charges against Anti-Segregationist Artist," *Harvard Crimson*, April 23, 1963; "Education: Obscene and Iridescent," *Time*, April 19, 1963.

28. "Education: Obscene and Iridescent."

29. Charles White, "Address to Second Annual Conference of Negro Artists," reel 2041 microfilm, CWWP. Though this document is undated, I would estimate that it is from 1960. The National Conference of Artists, an organization of black artists, educators, and museum workers, was founded in 1959 and held its first conference in Atlanta. White delivered an address that year titled "To the Meetings of Negro Artists, March 1959, Atlanta University," most probably to that group. His second address is probably to the same group the following year, 1960. In 1961 Elizabeth Catlett made the keynote address. For White's 1959 statement see reel 3190 microfilm, CWWP.

30. Linda Nochlin, *Realism* (Harmondsworth, UK: Penguin, 1971), 34, 236.

31. Nochlin, *Realism*, 35, 32.

32. Cordula Grewe, "Re-Enchantment as Artistic Practice: Strategies of Emulation in German Romantic Art and Theory," *New German Critique* 94 (Winter 2005): 43.

33. Cordula Grewe, "Beyond Hegel's End of Art: Schadow's Mignon and the Religious Project of Late Romanticism," *Modern Intellectual History* 1, no. 2 (2004): 190. See also Stephan Bann, *Romanticism and the Rise of History* (New York: Twayne, 1995).

34. Henry J. Seldis, "White's Visual Spirituals," *Los Angeles Times*, February 7, 1964, C6. Romanticism and sentimentality are also issues for the critic Curt Opliger, "Charles White, Heritage Gallery," *Artforum* 2 (April 1964): 49.

35. Art Seidenbaum, "The Racial Picture in Black and White," *Los Angeles Times*, February 3, 1964, C1, C12.

36. Mrs. Ina Brown Scott to Charles White, August 27, 1965, reel 2041 microfilm, CWWP.
37. Andrea D. Barnwell, *Charles White* (San Francisco: Pomegranate, 2002), 77. Carole Robertson, Cynthia Wesley, Denise McNair, and Addie Mae Collins, ages eleven to fourteen, were the four girls killed in the bombing of the Sixteenth Street Baptist Church in Birmingham, Alabama, on September 15, 1963. For more on artists and the civil rights movement see Kellie Jones, "Civil/Rights/Act," in Carbone and Jones, *Witness*, 11–55.
38. *Birmingham Totem* was eventually acquired by the High Museum of Art in Atlanta. It originally traveled there in 1977 as part of a major survey of the artist's work, which brought together forty-two prints, drawings, and paintings. The show was organized by the museum at the behest of Bunny Jackson, wife of Mayor Maynard Jackson, who was known for the cultivation of the arts during his tenure. James Edward Smethurst, "Retraining the Heartworks: Women in Atlanta's Black Arts Movement," in Dayo F. Gore, Jeanne Theoharis, and Komozi Woodard, eds., *Want to Start a Revolution? Radical Women in the Black Freedom Struggle* (New York: New York University Press, 2009), 205–22; Gudmund Vigtel, foreword to *The Work of Charles White: An American Experience* (Atlanta: High Museum of Art, 1976), 5. In White with Scott, *Reaches of the Heart*, 124, 197–99, Francis White points out that *Birmingham Totem* is related to *Paper Shelter*, another work critiquing the fragility of man-made structures of refuge.
39. Barnwell, *Charles White*, 80. For another discussion of the Dreyfus Affair in relation to the work of African American artists see Albert Boime, "Henry Ossawa Tanner's Subversion of Genre," *Art Bulletin* 75 (September 1993): 415–42. For more on anti-Semitism and art in nineteenth-century Europe see Cordula Grewe, *Painting the Sacred in the Age of Romanticism* (Burlington, VT: Ashgate, 2009), chap. 6.
40. Andrew Hemingway, *Artists on the Left: American Artists and the Communist Movement, 1926–1956* (New Haven, CT: Yale University Press, 2002), 260, 262n205. Hemingway has listed the drawing as a portrait of Paul Robeson in *Freedom* 2, no. 1 (February 1952). It is possibly the ink on cardboard work *Preacher (or Paul Robeson)*, 1952, that is in the collection of the Whitney Museum of American Art.
41. Bogle, *Toms, Coons, Mulattoes, Mammies, and Bucks*, 217.
42. See Horowitz, *Images of Dignity*, 117.
43. Apparently White was appointed after pressure by Ed Biberman and Benjamin Horowitz on the school's administration. White with Scott, *Reaches of the Heart*, 115–16; "Safety Savings High School Art at Music Center Major Attraction," *Los Angeles Sentinel*, June 24, 1965, B11.
44. Richard Wyatt Jr., "His Special Gift for Teaching . . . ," in "Charles White: Art and Soul," special issue, *Freedomways* 20, no. 3 (1980): 177–78. On the Tutor/Art Program see Francine R. Carter, "The Golden State Mutual Afro-American Art Collection," *Black Art* 1, no. 2 (Winter 1976): 15–16; Kerry James Marshall, "Notes on Career and Work," in *Kerry James Marshall*, with contributions by Terrie Sultan and Arthur Jafa (New York: Harry N. Abrams, 2000), 115–16.
45. Doyle Lane to Charles White, October 7, 1976, and Larry Walker at University of the Pacific to Charles White, May 3, 1977, both in reel 3190 microfilm, CWWP. Altadena painter and printmaker Yvonne Cole Meo also published an important article on the art of fellow LA artist Houston Conwill. She completed a dissertation in art

history—"A Survey on Traditional Arts of West Africa and Contemporary Black American Art: A Study of Symbolic Parallels and Cultural Transfer"—through the Union for Experimenting Colleges and Universities in 1977. The following year she took steps toward getting it published. Yvonne Cole Meo to Charles White, April 20, 1978, and invite to art sale, September 30 and October 1, 1978, both in reel 3190 microfilm, CWWP; Yvonne Cole Meo, "Ritual as Art: The Work of Houston Conwill," *International Review of African American Art* 3, no. 3 (Fall 1979): 4–13.

46. Marie Johnson (Calloway) to Charles White, May 14, 1970, Marie to Charles undated but with newspaper clippings from the *San Jose News*, and the *San Jose Mercury* both dated April 13, 1971, reel 3189 microfilm, CWWP. For more on Marie Johnson Calloway see Naima J. Keith, "Marie Johnson Calloway," in Kellie Jones, ed., *Now Dig This! Art and Black Los Angeles, 1960–1980* (New York and Los Angeles: Prestel-Delmonico and Hammer Museum, 2011), 262.

47. Margo Humphrey to Charles White, September 30, 1977, reel 3190 microfilm, CWWP. Oakland native Margo Humphrey received an MFA from Stanford University in 1974 and taught at the University of California, Santa Cruz, from 1974 to 1982. See Adrienne L. Childs, *Margo Humphrey* (Petaluma, CA: Pomegranate, 2009).

Gloria Bohanon to Charles White, January 11, 1974, reel 3189 microfilm, CWWP. Bohanon was a painter included in Samella Lewis and Ruth Waddy's *Black Artists on Art* (1969, 1971). She also participated in exhibitions like *The Sapphire Show* (1970) and *Black Mirror* (1973), early feminist framings in Southern California. She was married to jazz trombonist George Bohanon.

Kazuo Higa was a Nisei born in Los Angeles whose experience of Japanese internment (at Heart Mountain, Wyoming) during World War II politicized his understanding of art and life. On his death in 1994, a scholarship to benefit art students was set up in his name. It was administered by his colleague Gloria Bohanon. See Karin Higa, "Black Art in L.A.: Photographs by Robert A. Nakamura," in K. Jones, *Now Dig This!*, 51–55.

Gloria Bohanon to Charles White, undated note regarding her escorting him to the program "A Praise-Song for the Genius of Henry Dumas, Afro-American Writer, 1934–1968," June 8, 1975, Inner City Cultural Center, with a note from Suzanne Jackson, addressed to Mr. and Mrs. Charles White, both in reel 3189 microfilm, CWWP.

48. See letters from Safety Savings and Loan Association to Charles White, March 21, 1961, and February 6, 1963, reel 3189 microfilm, CWWP. A letter from Allied Arts Committee of Compton Chamber of Commerce to Charles White, November 29, 1968, mentions that society's thirty-seven years of existence, reel 2041 microfilm, CWWP.

For engagement with the Los Angeles School District see letters from Susan Miller, Dorsey High School, March 10, 1960, reel 3189 microfilm, and Los Angeles City School Districts, August 10, 1967, and from John Muir High School in Pasadena, April 7, 1963, both in reel 2041 microfilm, CWWP.

On White's connections with Golden State Mutual Life Insurance see letters from Essie to Charlie, February 15, 1961, reel 3189 microfilm, William E. Pajaud and Golden State Mutual Life Insurance Company to Charles White, August 4, 1965, Mrs. Ina Brown Scott to Charles White, August 27, 1965, and invitation to a press reception and student art show at the Golden State Mutual Life Insurance Company Home Office to present the 1968 calendar featuring drawings by Charles White, November 20, [1967], reel 2041 microfilm, CWWP. See also Carter, "The Golden State Mutual Afro-American Art Collection."

For the voluminous correspondence on Brockman Gallery see Subject File, "Brockman Gallery," reel 3190 microfilm, CWWP; see also Mary Jane Hewitt and the Inner City Cultural Center to Charles White, June 21, 1968, reel 3189 microfilm, CWWP.

49. Barnwell, *Charles White*, 31; Patricia Hills, *Painting Harlem Modern: The Art of Jacob Lawrence* (Berkeley: University of California Press, 2009), 262. Frances Barrett White was a counselor at Wo-Chi-Ca for a number of years and has written about the importance of the institution to modeling values of interracial relations and peace; see White with Scott, *Reaches of the Heart*, 41–47. Dancer Pearl Primus also served as a counselor there; see Griffin, *Harlem Nocturne*, 37. See also June Levine and Gene Gordon, *Tales of Wo-Chi-Ca: Blacks, Whites, and Reds at Camp* (San Rafael, CA: Avon Springs, 2002). For archives of the Workers Childrens Camp and other similar programs see Labor and Left Summer Camps and Related Collections at the Tamiment Library, New York University.

On leftist networks in the United States at midcentury see Smethurst, *The Black Arts Movement*; Mary Helen Washington, "Alice Childress, Lorraine Hansberry, and Claudia Jones: Black Women Write the Popular Front," in Bill V. Mullen and James Edward Smethurst, eds., *Left of the Color Line: Race, Radicalism, and Twentieth-Century Literature of the United States* (Chapel Hill: University of North Carolina Press, 2003), 183–204; Robin D. G. Kelley, *Freedom Dreams: The Black Radical Imagination* (Boston: Beacon, 2002); Hemingway, *Artists on the Left*; Gerald Horne, *Fire This Time: The Watts Uprising and the 1960s* (New York: Da Capo, 1997); Griffin, *Harlem Nocturne*; Mary Helen Washington, *The Other Blacklist: The African American Literary and Cultural Left of the 1950s* (New York: Columbia University Press, 2014).

50. Hemingway, *Artists on the Left*, 212. The institution was first called Harlem Workers School; its name changed during the Popular Front period.

51. Other galleries showing American art were Downtown Gallery and American Place, the latter run by Alfred Stieglitz.

52. Aaron Douglas quoted in T. R. Poston, "Murals and Marx: Aaron Douglas Moves to the Left with PWA Decoration," *New York Amsterdam News*, November 24, 1934, 9. See also Aaron Douglas, "The Negro in American Culture," in Matthew Baigell and Julia Williams, eds., *Artists against War and Fascism: Papers of the First American Artists' Congress* (New Brunswick, NJ: Rutgers University Press, 1986), 78–84; Hemingway, *Artists on the Left*, 64, 264. On the commitment to notions of the social realist image in the period and the work of writers such as Ann Petry see Griffin, *Harlem Nocturne*, 114–16, 125. Jacob Lawrence in Hills, *Painting Harlem Modern*, 163.

53. Smethurst, *The Black Arts Movement*, 55. White's relationship with leftist networks did not necessarily begin in New York. In his hometown of Chicago the painter counted among his mentors the radical playwright Theodore Ward of the Negro People's Theater, of which White was also a brief part. Ward was known for his anticapitalist play *Big White Fog*. Hemingway, *Artists on the Left*, 172.

54. Barnwell, *Charles White*, 38–39.

55. Correspondence from Jacob Lawrence to Charles White from 1943 to 1974 can be

found throughout reel 3189 and reel 3190 microfilm, CWWP. Eldzier Cortor and Charles White were classmates at Englewood High School in Chicago. See Eldzier Cortor, "He Was at Home Creatively in Any Locale," in "Charles White: Art and Soul," special issue, *Freedomways* 20, no. 3 (1980): 149–50.

56. Daniel Schulman, introduction to Daniel Schulman and Peter Max Ascoli, eds., *A Force for Change: African American Art and the Julius Rosenwald Fund* (Chicago: Spertus Museum and Northwestern University Press, 2009), 13. Established by Chicago business figure and Sears and Roebuck owner Julius Rosenwald, the Rosenwald Fund operated in the years between 1917 and 1948. Because the majority of African Americans lived in the South in this era, the fund encouraged projects there. Its most famous program was perhaps the construction of more than five thousand rural southern schools for black children.

57. Charles White, Rosenwald Fellowship "Statement of Plan of Work," unpaginated, undated (c. 1941), Fisk University Special Collections/Archives, quoted in Barnwell, *Charles White*, 29.

58. Barnwell, *Charles White*, 27–34. Charles White was beaten on the streets of New Orleans and forced from a streetcar in Hampton, Virginia, at gunpoint.

59. Houston painter John Biggers, a Hampton student at the time, was a model for one of the figures. Catlett was in residence with White as well and taught sculpture.

60. Henry Louis Gates Jr., "New Negroes, Migration, and Cultural Exchange," in Elizabeth Hutton Turner, ed., *Jacob Lawrence: The Migration Series* (Washington, DC: Rappahannock Press, in association with the Phillips Collection, 1993), 21; White with Scott, *Reaches of the Heart*, 77; Kellie Jones, *Energy/Experimentation: Black Artists and Abstraction, 1964–1980* (New York: Studio Museum in Harlem, 2006); Museum of Fine Arts, Houston, *The Quilts of Gee's Bend* (Atlanta: Tinwood Books in association with the Museum of Fine Arts, Houston, 2002). My mother-in-love, Celia Ramsey Wynn, and her sister Marjorie Jones talked to me about decorating their family home in Valdosta, Georgia, in the 1930s. Their dad, who loved western films, would bring movie posters home, and the family members arranged these on the walls to form new relationships and tableaux. They also would adorn the wall with newspaper. Personal communication, August 27, 2011.

61. Guthrie P. Ramsey Jr., *Race Music: Black Cultures from Bebop to Hip-Hop* (Berkeley: University of California Press, 2003), 47; Gates, "New Negroes, Migration, and Cultural Exchange," 17.

62. Ramsey, *Race Music*, 97; Jacqueline Najuma Stewart, *Migrating to the Movies: Cinema and Black Urban Modernity* (Berkeley: University of California Press, 2005), 16–17, 50, 90, 148.

63. White with Scott, *Reaches of the Heart*, 34, 28–29; "Oral History Interview with Charles Wilbert White, 1965 March 9," Archives of American Art, Smithsonian Institution.

64. Barnwell, *Charles White*, 30.

65. Ernestine Rose quoted in Deborah Willis, "The Schomburg Collection: A Rich Resource for Jacob Lawrence," in Turner, *Jacob Lawrence*, 36. Rose was a white librarian who began working at the 135th Street branch of the New York Public Library in 1920. The Schomburg Collection opened on its third floor in 1927.

66. Willis, "The Schomburg Collection," 38.

67. Willis, "The Schomburg Collection," 34. See also Jean Blackwell Hutson, "The Schomburg Collection," *Freedomways* 3 (Summer 1963): 430–35.
68. Stewart, *Migrating to the Movies*, 31.
69. Stewart, *Migrating to the Movies*, 189.
70. African Americans at war was a topic White pursued as part of the renewal of his Rosenwald Fellowship. Barnwell, *Charles White*, 34. White himself served in World War II.
71. Charles White, Rosenwald Fellowship "Statement of Plan of Work," unpaginated, undated (ca. 1941), Fisk University Special Collections/Archives, quoted in Barnwell, *Charles White*, 29.
72. Smethurst, *The Black Arts Movement*, 27–29, 291.
73. Hemingway, *Artists on the Left*, 263. See also Mary Helen Washington's astute reading of White's work from this period, "Charles White: Robeson with a Brush and Pencil," in *The Other Blacklist: The African American Literary and Cultural Left of the 1950s* (New York: Columbia University Press, 2014), 69–122.
74. Neel quoted in Hemingway, *Artists on the Left*, 248; see also chap. 10. See Michael Duncan, *L.A. Raw: Abject Expressionism in Los Angeles, 1945–1980, from Rico Lebrun to Paul McCarthy* (Santa Monica: Foggy Notion Books, 2012), and Shifra M. Goldman, *Contemporary Mexican Painting in a Time of Change* (Austin: University of Texas Press, 1981).
75. Smethurst, *The Black Arts Movement*, 45; Erik S. McDuffie, "'No Small Amount of Change Could Do': Esther Cooper Jackson and the Making of a Black Left Feminism," in Gore, Theoharis, and Woodard, *Want to Start a Revolution?*, 25–46.
76. White with Scott, *Reaches of the Heart*, 55.
77. Other CNA members included Sidney Portier, Ernest Crichlow, and Harry Belafonte. White with Scott, *Reaches of the Heart*, 55–57. White's correspondence with the circle of leftist writers, including John Oliver Killens and Louise Thompson Patterson, some of whom were part of CNA, was voluminous. See reel 3189 microfilm, CWWP.
78. Belafonte's dedication to the presentation of folk music, in tandem with a commitment to his own work that offered contemporary understandings and engagements with this body of material, is exemplary of the updating of these ideas as well as its leftist inheritance. Smethurst, *The Black Arts Movement*, 16–17 and chap. 1; Kelley, *Freedom Dreams*.
79. Smethurst, *The Black Arts Movement*, 59–62, 29.
80. Smethurst also remarks on the influence of the CPUSA-affiliated Civil Rights Congress in the Bay Area. Particularly its campaigns against police brutality were influential on a young Huey Newton in the 1940s. Smethurst notes the lasting visibility of the CPUSA on the West Coast: the connections with Black Panther Party. Smethurst, *The Black Arts Movement*, 249–53.
81. Smethurst, *The Black Arts Movement*, chap. 5.
82. Barnwell, *Charles White*, 88.
83. The *Wanted Poster* series started out as paintings, largely oil wash on board. White also made a group of prints that became part of it. These were created at June Wayne's renowned Tamarind Lithography Workshop. In the 1990s painter Glenn Ligon would revisit this same material culture of slavery. See Huey Copeland, *Bound to Appear: Art, Slavery, and the Site of Blackness in Multicultural America* (Chicago:

University of Chicago Press, 2013), chap. 3, and Judith Tannenbaum, *Glenn Ligon: Unbecoming* (Philadelphia: Institute of Contemporary Art, University of Pennsylvania, 1997).

84. Smethurst, *The Black Arts Movement*, 89–94. See also Margo Natalie Crawford, "Black Light on the Wall of Respect: The Chicago Black Arts Movement," in Lisa Gail Collins and Margo Natalie Crawford, eds., *New Thoughts on the Black Arts Movement* (New Brunswick, NJ: Rutgers University Press, 2006). On the radical graphics tradition, which was also part of a larger Latin American focus, see Chon Noriega and Holly Barnett-Sánchez, eds., *Just Another Poster? Chicano Graphic Arts in California* (Santa Barbara: University Art Museum, University of California, Santa Barbara, 2001), and Russ Davidson and David Craven, *Latin American Posters: Public Aesthetics and Mass Politics* (Santa Fe: Museum of New Mexico Press, 2006).

85. Like other artists of the period, including Jack Whitten and Williams T. Williams, White had a connection to Leonard Bocour, the owner of Bocour Artists Colors Incorporated. The New York–based Bocour, one of the first manufactures of acrylic paint, often supplied artists with free product to get their feedback. See Leonard Bocour to Charles White, January 23, 1963, reel 3189 microfilm, CWWP. On painting experimentation during the period see K. Jones, *Energy/Experimentation*; Katy Siegel, ed., *High Times, Hard Times: New York Painting 1967–1975* (New York: Independent Curators International, 2006); Michael Darling, ed., *Target Practice: Painting under Attack, 1949–1978* (Seattle: Seattle Art Museum, 2009).

86. Copeland, *Bound to Appear*, 7; Salamishah Tillet, *Sites of Slavery: Citizenship and Racial Democracy in the Post–Civil Rights Imagination* (Durham, NC: Duke University Press, 2012), 3.

87. Copeland, *Bound to Appear*, 10.

88. Copeland, *Bound to Appear*, 18–19.

89. Autobiographical Statement, reel 3189 microfilm, CWWP.

90. Mary Cole, "Charles White," *Art Digest* 25 (February 15, 1951): 22; Betty Holliday, "Charles White," *ArtNews* 49, no. 10 (February 1951): 53; Howard Devree, "In a Wide Range," *New York Times*, February 18, 1951, 88. Even into the 1960s critics continued to recognize the heroic in White's images of women. See James H. Beck, "Charles White," *ArtNews* 60, no. 6 (October 1961): 14.

91. Washington, "Alice Childress, Lorraine Hansberry, and Claudia Jones," 185, 193–94; McDuffie, "'No Small Amount of Change Could Do,'" 25–46; Griffin, *Harlem Nocturne*.

92. The phrase "utopian content" comes from Chela Sandoval, "U.S. Third World Feminism: The Theory and Method of Oppositional Consciousness in the Postmodern World," *Genders* 10 (1991): 1–23.

93. Karen Anne Mason, interviews with William Pajaud (1993), Curtis Tann (1995), and Betye Saar (1996, p. 91), *African American Artists of Los Angeles* (Los Angeles: Oral History Program of the University of California, 1992–2000); Jane Hattie Carpenter, "Conjure Woman: Betye Saar and Rituals of Transformation, 1960–1990" (PhD diss., University of Michigan, 2002), 41–42, 46.

94. "Speaking of People," *Ebony* 6, no. 12 (October 1951): 5.

95. Karen Anne Mason, interviews with Betye Saar (1996, pp. 82–83) and Curtis Tann

(1995, pp. 151–52), *African American Artists of Los Angeles*; Carpenter, "Conjure Woman," 49.

96. John Michael Vlach, *By the Work of Their Hands: Studies in Afro-American Folklife* (Charlottesville: University of Virginia Press, 1991); *Winterthur Portfolio* 33, no. 4 (Winter 1998).

97. Judith Wilson, "How the Invisible Woman Got Herself on the Cultural Map: Black Women Artists in California," in Diana Burgess Fuller and Daniela Salvioni, eds., *Art/Women/California, 1950–2000: Parallels and Intersections* (Berkeley: University of California Press, 2002), 201–16; Getty Research Institute, *Pacific Standard Time: Art in L.A., 1945–1980* (Los Angeles: Getty Research Institute and the J. Paul Getty Museum, 2011).

98. Laura Cottingham, "L.A. Womyn: The Feminist Art Movement in California, 1970–1979," in *Sunshine and Noir: Art in L.A. 1960–1997* (Humlebaek, Denmark: Louisiana Museum of Modern Art, 1997), 190.

99. Karen Anne Mason, interview with Alonzo Davis (1994), *African American Artists of Los Angeles*, 106; Carpenter, "Conjure Woman," 38–39, 44.

100. Karen Anne Mason, interview with Betye Saar (1996), *African American Artists of Los Angeles*, 84–85; Carpenter, "Conjure Woman," 50.

101. Karen Anne Mason, interview with Betye Saar (1996), *African American Artists of Los Angeles*, 94.

102. Betye Saar quoted in *Spirit Catcher—The Art of Betye Saar* (dir. Suzanne Bauman; WNET, 1977).

103. Carpenter, "Conjure Woman," 202, 203; both had daughters—Saar three and Ringgold two. Printmaker, ceramicist, and later filmmaker Camille Billops, active in Los Angeles, Cairo, and New York during this time, rejected the role of mother by giving up her daughter for adoption. Her film *Finding Christa* (1992) explores this.

   In the responses of these two women we understand how ideas of femininity, motherhood, and domestic space may have been refracted differently through the prism of histories of race and gender. The home could be a refuge, a place to dream and strategize, to "come back to" oneself, as bell hooks has offered. Here the notion of ministering to one's family under domination may be seen as a radical act, being at home with one's own children a victory, as scholars Angela Davis and Evelyn Brooks Higginbotham, recounting both the antebellum period and its aftermath, have contended. Such things denied to black women in slavery had continuing legacies into the twentieth century. See hooks, *Yearning: Race, Gender, and Cultural Politics* (Boston: South End, 1990), 116; Angela Y. Davis, "Reflections on Black Women's Role in the Community of Slaves," *Black Scholar* 3 (1971): 7. See also Evelyn Brooks Higginbotham, "African-American Women's History and the Metalanguage of Race," *Signs* 17, no. 2 (Winter 1992): 251–74, in particular her discussion of "female loaferism"—how black women who didn't work were characterized as a problem after emancipation. However, on the other hand, modeling late twentieth-century thinking, we have Toni Cade's *The Black Woman: An Anthology* (New York: New American Library, 1970), which explores the tensions and conflicts in domestic roles.

104. Carpenter, "Conjure Woman," 57–58, 61. Saar studied printmaking at California State University, Long Beach, between 1958 and 1962.

105. Carpenter, "Conjure Woman," 36.
106. Karen Anne Mason, interview with Betye Saar (1996), *African American Artists of Los Angeles*, 108–9; Carpenter, "Conjure Woman," 54, 61–62; Mike Davis, *City of Quartz: Excavating the Future in Los Angeles* (London: Verso, 1990), 58–59; Richard Cándida Smith, *Utopia and Dissent: Art, Poetry, and Politics in California* (Berkeley: University of California Press, 1995). It is also interesting to consider Saar's early and even future predilection toward an alternative mysticism and its relationship to an earlier captivation with these traditions in the music of Mary Lou Williams and her *Zodiac Suite* of the 1940s. See Griffin, *Harlem Nocturne*, 162–68.
107. Carolee Schneemann, *Imaging Her Erotics* (Cambridge, MA: MIT Press, 2002). In fact, Saar considers *Anticipation* a self-portrait, claiming to have finished the print in the afternoon and given birth to her third child, Tracye, that evening. Karen Anne Mason, interview with Betye Saar (1996), *African American Artists of Los Angeles*, 101.
108. Betye Saar quoted in Cindy Nemser, "Conversation with Betye Saar," *Feminist Art Journal* 4, no. 4 (Winter 1975–76): 22; "2 Tie for Top Art Awards," *Los Angeles Times*, January 29, 1961, CS5; Henry J. Seldis, "Art Free-for-All: A Most Memorable All City Festival," *Los Angeles Times*, June 28, 1964, T10; "Phelan Competitors Slated at Barnsdale," *Los Angeles Times*, April 18, 1965, M28.
109. In this iconography birds are warnings or enlightenment, dogs are friends, butterflies represent immortality, and cats are harbingers of psychic mysteries. Carpenter, "Conjure Woman," 61–62. See also Arlene Tognetti and Lisa Lenard, *Tarot and Fortune Telling* (New York: Amaranth/Alpha Books, 1999); Ankrum Gallery Records, 1960–1990, Archives of American Art, Smithsonian Institution; Betye Saar, Artist File, Museum of Modern Art, New York.
110. See John Szwed, *Space Is the Place: The Life and Times of Sun Ra* (New York: Da Capo, 1977), cited in Jane H. Carpenter with Betye Saar, *Betye Saar* (San Francisco: Pomegranate, 2003), 18.
111. Lowery Stokes Sims, "Melvin Edwards: An Artist's Life and Philosophy," and Michael Brenson, "Lynch Fragments," both in Lucinda H. Gedeon, ed., *Melvin Edwards Sculpture: A Thirty-Year Retrospective, 1963–1993* (Purchase: Neuberger Museum of Art, State University of New York at Purchase, 1993), 11, 22.
112. Sims, "Melvin Edwards"; Brenson, "Lynch Fragments," 21, 26; Lynne Kenny, "Chronology," in Gedeon, *Melvin Edwards Sculpture*, 129. Edwards and Ron Miyashiro eventually would have studios next to each other on Van Ness Avenue. They would be neighbors in New York when both moved into spaces on Canal Street later in the 1960s. On at least one occasion Edwards organized an exhibition of the work of his friends. *Yes on 10, Los Angeles Images* took place in the fall of 1964 at the Little Gallery of San Bernardino Valley College. It presented a mixed group, both in its array of creative production and in the diversity of its participants. Johnson, Ron Miyashiro, and Edmund Bereal all worked in mixed-media assemblage at the time; Marvin Harden, Edward's buddy from USC, made paintings and drawings that could be categorized as West Coast pop (in the manner of Ed Ruscha, Joe Goode, and Llyn Foulkes); Virginia Jaramillo and Karen Hamre (Edwards's first wife) were abstract painters. The design of the exhibition poster mimicked a paper ballot, perhaps a commentary on one of the greatest political issues for African Americans in 1964, the passage of the Civil Rights Act. However, the concept of the show seems to have

hinged more on local politics. The exhibition opened in November 1964 days after a vote on, among other things, California's Proposition 10, a statute governing the proceeds from the sale of land grants.
113. David Gebhard, "Melvin Edwards, Santa Barbara Museum of Art," *Artforum* 3 (May 1965): 14. On Romare Bearden in this period see Dore Ashton, "Romare Bearden Projections," *Quadrum* 17 (1964): 99–110; Charles Childs, "Bearden: Identification and Identity," *ArtNews* 63 (October 1964): 24–25, 54, 61.
114. Maurice Tuchman, *Five Younger Los Angeles Artists: Tony Berlant, Melvin Edwards, Llyn Foulkes, Lloyd Hamrol, Philip Rich, Contemporary Art Council New Talent Purchase Award Recipients 1963–1965* (Los Angeles: Los Angeles County Museum of Art, 1965), unpaginated. The show was on view November 26–December 26, 1965.
115. Don Factor, "Five Younger Los Angeles Artists," *Artforum* 4 (February 1966): 14.
116. Melvin Edwards quoted in Brenson, "Lynch Fragments," 21, 27; Melvin Edwards interviewed by Maurice Tuchman in Tuchman, *Five Younger Los Angeles Artists*.
117. Brenson, "Lynch Fragments," 28. The *Lynch Fragments* appeared in three phases: 1963–67, while Edwards was still based in Los Angeles; 1973, after he had settled in New York; and from 1978 to the present.
118. In *Afro-Phoenix* we see Afro-American. The mamba is venomous snake that is ubiquitous throughout sub-Saharan Africa. A mojo is an African American charm; the piece also remembers his paternal grandmother, Cora Ann Nickerson, and her home at 1404 Wayne Street in Houston. Known as Coco, she would also be the inspiration for numerous works in the 1970s that Edwards called "rockers." Melvin Edwards, interview with the author, February 2011. For Edwards's ideas on the role of the African Diaspora in his own work see his statement "Notes on Black Art" (1971), reprinted in Studio Museum in Harlem, *Melvin Edwards, Sculptor* (New York: Studio Museum in Harlem, 1978), 20–21.
119. Darlene Clark Hine, personal communication, May 2011; Melvin Edwards interviewed by Maurice Tuchman in Tuchman, *Five Younger Los Angeles Artists*.
120. Melvin Edwards interviewed by Maurice Tuchman in Tuchman, *Five Younger Los Angeles Artists*. Edwards was referring to *Chaino*, 1964, and *Standing Hang-Up #1*, 1965, two pieces in the show.
121. Karen Anne Mason, interview with Marvin Harden (1992), *African American Artists of Los Angeles*, 25; Horne, *Fire This Time*, 181.
122. Melvin Edwards quoted in Brenson, "Lynch Fragments," 27.
123. On the police violence against the mosque see "Muslims Charge Cop Brutality," *Chicago Defender*, April 30, 1962, 1. That year Edwards had also run across citations of lynchings in *Freedomways* magazine, as well as a book by Ralph Ginzburg, *100 Years of Lynchings* (New York: Lancer Books, 1962). Brenson, "Lynch Fragments," 27.
124. Frank Bowling, "Discussion on Black Art—II," *Arts Magazine* 43 (May 1969): 22.
125. Factor, "Five Younger Los Angeles Artists," 14.
126. Melvin Edwards, interview with the author, February 2011; Horne, *Fire This Time*, 123–25; "Both Sides of Near Riot Story Revealed," *Los Angeles Sentinel*, May 3, 1962, A1. *Mamba*, also from 1965, also related to the life of Malcolm X and his legacy. This African snake is one of most lethal of its kind and was linked by Edwards not only to the importance of the activist himself, but also to the power of his ideas. Brenson, "Lynch Fragments," 28.

127. Edwards recalls repairing the Tinguely works in 1966. Tinguely had a solo show at Dwan in 1963. Due to the French artist's popularity in the 1950s and into the 1960s and Virginia Dwan's interest in the work of the New Realists, he probably participated in group shows there into mid-1967, when the Los Angeles Gallery closed. Sims, "Melvin Edwards," 14; Brenson, "Lynch Fragments," 21–22. On the Los Angeles Tower of Protest see Francis Frascina, *Art, Politics, and Dissent: Aspects of the Art Left in Sixties America* (Manchester, UK: Manchester University Press, 1999), chap. 2. See also Pamela M. Lee's illuminating discussion of Tinguely in *Chronophobia: On Time in the Art of the 1960s* (Cambridge, MA: MIT Press, 2004), chap. 2.
128. "Art of Young Sculptor on Bob Hope Theater," *Dispatch* (Moline, IL), c. October 8, 1966, in Melvin Edwards, Artist File, Museum of Modern Art, New York. *Bob Hope Presents the Chrysler Theatre* presented ninety-six episodes between 1963 and 1967. "Crazier Than Cotton" aired October 12, 1966, and was episode 5 of season 4. See the *TV Guide* listing at http://www.tvguide.com/tvshows/bob-hope-presents-the-chrysler-theatre-1966/episode-5-season-4/crazier-than-cotton/200149, accessed December 27, 2011.
129. Among his variety of jobs in Los Angeles, Edwards also worked for the Peterson Company, which specialized in film production. It was owned by the father of painter David Novros, a classmate of Edwards from his days at USC. Sims, "Melvin Edwards," 14; Brenson, "Lynch Fragments," 12.
130. Edwards divorced Karen Hamre in 1968.
131. Raised in Watts, Cortez wrote poetry, studied music, and made art throughout her childhood. During high school music filled her life, whether she was attending dances featuring live performances by Johnny Otis and "Little" Esther Philips or sneaking into jam sessions with emerging players such as Dexter Gordon. Indeed, the life of black cultural Los Angeles found its heart in the music scene of Central Avenue and that of Watts, which saw its heyday from the early part of the century into the 1950s. Cortez's marriage to Ornette Coleman, who lived in Los Angeles between 1953 and 1959, took place in 1954.

    Interestingly, it was through Cortez that Coleman met an early collaborator, Don Cherry, one of the small coterie of musicians that began to form around him, including Ed Blackwell, and Charlie Haden, and who would eventually pioneer "free jazz" in New York. Cherry and Cortez were the same age, grew up in Watts, and ran in the same circles, and both were inspired by the Los Angeles music scene. "Cherry says that he knew her three or four years before he knew Ornette, and that he had first heard of Ornette through her." A. B. Spellman, *Four Lives in the Bebop Business* (London: MacGibbon & Kee, 1967), 108–9. See also John Litweiler, *Ornette Coleman: A Harmolodic Life* (New York: W. Morrow, 1992), 34–40; Jayne Cortez, "Jayne Cortez, in Her Own Words," in *Watts: Art and Social Change in Los Angeles, 1965–2002* (Milwaukee: Haggerty Museum of Art, Marquette University, 2002).
132. Jon Woodson, "Jayne Cortez," in Trudier Harris and Thadious M. Davis, eds., *Afro-American Poets since 1955* (Detroit: Gale Research, 1985), 70. During that time she performed with a number of bands, including those of Curtis Army, Horace Tapscott, and John Carter and his trio.
133. Roberto Tejada, "Los Angeles Snapshots," in K. Jones, *Now Dig This!*, 72.
134. Tejada, "Los Angeles Snapshots," 72.

135. Mary Schmidt Campbell, introduction to Studio Museum in Harlem, *Melvin Edwards, Sculptor* (New York: Studio Museum in Harlem, 1978), 4.
136. Melvin Edwards, "Notes on Black Art," in Studio Museum in Harlem, *Melvin Edwards, Sculptor*, 20.

TWO. CLAIM

1. Harriet Janis and Rudi Blesh identify collages in China in 700 A.D., while Penelope Mason cites similar techniques in Japan in the twelfth century. Harriet Grossman Janis and Rudi Blesh, *Collage: Personalities, Concepts, and Techniques* (Philadelphia: Chilton, 1967), 153; Penelope Mason, *History of Japanese Art* (New York: Harry N. Abrams, 1993). See also Katherine Hoffman, ed., *Collage: Critical Views* (Ann Arbor: UMI Research Press, 1989); Eddie Wolfram, *History of Collage: An Anthology of Collage, Assemblage and Event Structures* (New York: Macmillan, 1975); Christine Poggi, *In Defiance of Painting: Cubism, Futurism, and the Invention of Collage* (New Haven, CT: Yale University Press, 1992); Diane Waldman, *Collage, Assemblage, and the Found Object* (New York: Harry N. Abrams, 1992); Richard Flood, *Unmonumental: The Object in the 21st Century* (New York: New Museum, 2007); Richard Flood, Massimiliano Gioni, and Laura J. Hoptman, *Collage: The Unmonumental Picture* (London: Merrell, 2007).
2. Henry Hopkins, "Recollecting the Beginnings," in Henry Hopkins and Anne Ayres, *Forty Years of California Assemblage: UCLA Art Council Annual Exhibition* (Los Angeles: Wight Art Gallery, 1989), 15.
3. Helen Comsock, "Stieglitz Group in Anniversary Show," *ArtNews* 23 (March 14, 1925): 5. In the wake of World War I the use of materials with associational values pressed a nativist edge. See Francis M. Naumann and Beth Venn, *Making Mischief: Dada Invades New York* (New York: Whitney Museum of American Art, 1996).
4. Harold Rosenberg, "Collage: Philosophy of Put-Togethers," in Hoffman, *Collage*, 59.
5. Pablo Picasso quoted in Poggi, *In Defiance of Painting*, 45.
6. William Chapin Seitz, *The Art of Assemblage* (New York: Museum of Modern Art, 1961), 94.
7. Georges Bataille quoted in Yve-Alain Bois and Rosalind E. Krauss, *Formless: A User's Guide* (New York: Zone Books, 1997), 226.
8. Sallie Bingham, *Passion and Prejudice: A Family Memoir* (1991), quoted in bell hooks, *Black Looks: Race and Representation* (Boston: South End, 1992), 168.
9. Hopkins and Ayres, *Forty Years of California Assemblage*; Rebecca Solnit, *Secret Exhibition: Six California Artists of the Cold War Era* (San Francisco: City Lights Books, 1990).
10. Clement Greenberg, "The Pasted Paper Revolution," *ArtNews* (September 1958): 62; Clement Greenberg, "Modernism with a Vengeance, 1957–1969," in John O'Brien, ed., *Clement Greenberg: The Collected Essays and Criticism* (Chicago: University of Chicago Press, 1986), 4:61–66. This essay was substantially reworked and appears in Greenberg's important essay collection *Art and Culture* (Boston: Beacon, 1961) as "Collage," where the word "intrusion" disappears.
11. Thomas E. Crow, *Modern Art in the Common Culture* (New Haven, CT: Yale University Press, 1996), 8.

12. Solnit, *Secret Exhibition*, ix.
13. From *One to One: Quarterly Report on Aspects of Creativity* (January–March 1967): 8; Noah Purifoy Papers, 1935–1998, Archives of American Art, Smithsonian Institution (hereafter NPP). Although the quote is not attributed in this issue of the magazine, Purifoy does repeat a modified version in a second issue under his own name. See Noah Purifoy, "19 Points and Five Footnotes, or 'What the Artist Should Know!,'" *One to One: Quarterly Report on Aspects of Creativity* (April–June 1967): 4, NPP.
14. From *One to One: Quarterly Report on Aspects of Creativity* (January–March 1967): 1–2, NPP.
15. David Cogswell and Joe Lee, *Existentialism for Beginners* (Hanover, NH: For Beginners, 2008).
16. Sara Ahmed, *Queer Phenomenology: Orientations, Objects, Others* (Durham, NC: Duke University Press, 2006), 2.
17. "Living experience of meaning": Dermot Moran, "Editor's Introduction," in Dermot Moran and Timothy Mooney, eds., *The Phenomenology Reader* (New York: Routledge, 2002), 5; "reachable" and "bodily horizon," Ahmed, *Queer Phenomenology*, 2. For a useful discussion of Freud and Purifoy see Yael Lipschutz, "*66 Signs of Neon* and the Transformative Art of Noah Purifoy," in Connie Rogers Tilton and Lindsay Charlwood, eds., *L.A. Object and David Hammons Body Prints* (New York: Tilton Gallery, 2011), 214–59.
18. Alma Thomas quoted in Eleanor Munro, "The Late Springtime of Alma Thomas," *Washington Post Magazine*, April 15, 1979, 24. W. E. B. Du Bois, then editor of the NAACP's magazine, *The Crisis*, discussed such notions in a symposium he conducted in the publication's pages between February and November 1926 under the title "Criteria of Negro Art." See also Amy Helene Kirschke, *Art in Crisis: W. E. B. Du Bois and the Struggle for African American Identity and Memory* (Bloomington: Indiana University Press, 2007), 118–22.
19. Among the writers Purifoy might have looked to regarding sociology and African American life are E. Franklin Frazier, W. E. B. Du Bois, and Kenneth Clark. See Jonathan Scott Holloway and Ben Keppel, eds., *Black Scholars on the Line: Race, Social Science, and American Thought in the Twentieth Century* (Notre Dame, IN: University of Notre Dame, 2007).
20. Karen Anne Mason, interview with Noah Purifoy (1992), *African American Artists of Los Angeles*, 8, 12. Another source suggests he learned to weld and create in wood in high school in Cleveland, where his family moved when he was twelve. "Noah Purifoy," *College Art Association News* (July 2004): 27.
21. Karen Anne Mason, interview with Noah Purifoy (1992), *African American Artists of Los Angeles*, 8–11. Some documents list the year of Purifoy's graduation from college as 1943 (Biography, Noah Purifoy Foundation, http://www.noahpurifoy.com/CV/cv_biography.html, accessed August 1, 2006). In this scenario it appears as if his work as a high school teacher preceded his college degree. He then appears to have a smooth work history from college to the military to graduate degree. This sleight of hand basically elides the racism that many black college graduates faced prior to the civil rights movement. It is possible that Purifoy organized the résumé himself in such a way and at a certain moment to make himself appear more employable as well as to make such ugly details of his life disappear. Purifoy's college diploma list-

ing 1939 at the graduation date can be found in the NPP. In his 1992 interview with the Oral History Program of the University of California, he does openly discuss his inability to get a job after college: Karen Anne Mason, interview with Noah Purifoy (1992), *African American Artists of Los Angeles*, 8–9.

22. Karen Anne Mason, interview with Noah Purifoy (1992), *African American Artists of Los Angeles*, 33–37, 42, 56. John H. Smith continued in the field of interiors, as evidenced by a highlight of his practice later appearing in the *Los Angeles Times* and featuring art by his former partner Noah Purifoy. "Here's a Lesson in Organization," *Los Angeles Times*, September 3, 1967, 24.

23. Karen Anne Mason, interview with Noah Purifoy (1992), *African American Artists of Los Angeles*, 42.

24. Karen Anne Mason, interview with Noah Purifoy (1992), *African American Artists of Los Angeles*, 42–43.

25. Cecile Whiting, *Pop L.A.: Art and the City in the 1960s* (Berkeley: University of California Press, 2006), chap. 4.

26. Jonathan Harris, "Nationalizing Art: The Community Art Center Programme of the Federal Art Project 1935–1943," *Art History* 14 (June 1991): 250–69.

27. On notions of "uplift" in African American communities see Kevin K. Gaines, *Uplifting the Race: Black Leadership, Politics, and Culture in the Twentieth Century* (Chapel Hill: University of North Carolina Press, 1996).

28. From *One to One: Quarterly Report on Aspects of Creativity* (January–March 1967): 3, NPP.

29. Noah Purifoy, "Art in the Community," transcript of a presentation to a seminar "A Day with Experts in the Arts," October 26, 1974, 7, NPP.

30. Karen Anne Mason, interview with Noah Purifoy (1992), *African American Artists of Los Angeles*, 68–70.

31. These included the Watts Happening Coffee House (later Mafundi Institute), 1967–70, a former furniture showroom made over into a café and performance space after the uprising; Performing Arts Society of Los Angeles, 1966; the Compton Communicative Arts Academy, 1970; Mechicano Art Center, 1969; and Plaza de la Raza, 1970, among others. One model was Karamu House in Cleveland, where Purifoy spent his teenage years. It specialized in theater and had opened in 1915. As he later elaborated, "What happened in the '60s in L.A. is that neighborhood groups, community art centers and support groups usurped the role of the art museums, theaters and concert halls—by taking art out of high places, where it was inaccessible to community people, and placing it in the streets." Noah Purifoy, "Art in the Community," transcript of a presentation to a seminar "A Day with Experts in the Arts," October 26, 1974, 8–9, NPP.

32. Noah Purifoy, "Art in the Community," transcript of a presentation to a seminar "A Day with Experts in the Arts," October 26, 1974, 1, NPP.

33. Karen Anne Mason, interview with Noah Purifoy (1992), *African American Artists of Los Angeles*, 42.

34. Noah Purifoy as told to Ted Michel, "The Art of Communication as Creative Act," in *Junk Art: "66 Signs of Neon"* (Los Angeles: 66 Signs of Neon, c. 1966), unpaginated.

35. Whiting, *Pop L.A.*, 158–59.

36. Karen Anne Mason, interview with Noah Purifoy (1992), *African American Artists of*

Los Angeles, 60; Noah Purifoy, "Art in the Community," transcript of a presentation to a seminar, "A Day with Experts in the Arts," October 26, 1974, 7, NPP.

37. Whiting, *Pop L.A.*, 160.
38. Karen Anne Mason, interview with Noah Purifoy (1992), *African American Artists of Los Angeles*, 124, 126, 97, 19, 27–28. Grey Gundaker has also discussed the use of books, particularly the Bible, as spiritual and therapeutic objects in African American communities. Grey Gundaker, *Signs of Diaspora, Diaspora of Signs: Literacies, Creolization, and Vernacular Practice in African America* (New York: Oxford University Press, 1998). Purifoy's use of art as a tool of psychotherapy, a way to reintegrate the mind and body, mirrors that of Lygia Clark of Brazil, whose object-making led her to a similar practice during roughly the same period. On Lygia Clark see Cornelia Butler, ed., *Lygia Clark: The Abandonment of Art, 1948–1988* (New York: Museum of Modern Art, 2014).
39. In writings during the period, Purifoy ascribed his leaving to this loss of funds. In his 1990 interview with UCLA's oral history program he talks about being let go—replaced when he returned to work after sustaining a broken leg on the job—because the committee wanted a more sophisticated arts program. From *One to One: Quarterly Report on Aspects of Creativity* (January–March 1967): 2, NPP; and Karen Anne Mason, interview with Noah Purifoy (1992), *African American Artists of Los Angeles*, 68–70. Cecile Whiting also speculates about this. Whiting, *Pop L.A.*, chap. 4, 235n74.
40. Noah Purifoy, "'66' Philosophy: Seeing Old Things in New Ways," *One to One: Quarterly Report on Aspects of Creativity* (January–March 1967): 3, NPP.
41. As evidenced by the catalogue, the artists involved in the project were Frank Anthony, Debby Brewer, David Mann, Max Neufeldt, Judson Powell, Noah Purifoy, Leon Saulter, Arthur Secunda, Ruth Saturensky, and Gordon Wagner. There were additional collaborators on the catalogue. Karen Anne Mason, interview with Noah Purifoy (1992), *African American Artists of Los Angeles*, 90–92. Although this is not noted in the catalogue or in Purifoy's recollection in his oral history, John Riddle claims he took part in the exhibition as well. Karen Anne Mason, interview with John Riddle (2000), *African American Artists of Los Angeles*, 117. Riddle is also seen in an article on the second festival in 1967. Though there he is holding a painting, we know Riddle worked with sculpture during that period as well. See Jack Jones, "Watt's 2nd Annual Week-Long Festival of the Arts Opens Today," *Los Angeles Times*, March 19, 1967, DB.
42. Cecile Whiting speculates about this as well. Whiting, *Pop L.A.*, 143, 162.
43. Ahmed, *Queer Phenomenology*, 25.
44. Ahmed, *Queer Phenomenology*, 41.
45. Ahmed, *Queer Phenomenology*, 43. See also Arjun Appadurai, "Introduction: Commodities and the Politics of Value," in Arjun Appadurai, ed., *The Social Life of Things: Commodities in Cultural Perspective* (Cambridge: Cambridge University Press, 1986), and Lipschutz, "*66 Signs of Neon* and the Transformative Art of Noah Purifoy," 214–59.
46. Art Berman, "Junk from First Watts Riot Turned into Works of Art," *Los Angeles Times*, March 28, 1966, 3.
47. Noah Purifoy quoted in Berman, "Junk from First Watts Riot Turned into Works of Art."

48. Gerald Horne, *Fire This Time: The Watts Uprising and the 1960s* (New York: Da Capo, 1997; first published 1995), 339.
49. Sarah Schrank interprets Purifoy as being more interested in aspects of developing personal creativity over any kind of permanent structure, marshalling services for the Watts community, part of most everyone's efforts during this period. However, on two occasions in 1967 and 1968 Purifoy was involved with offering designs for a permanent cultural center in Watts. "Art, Drama Mark Watts Festival," *Los Angeles Sentinel*, March 23, 1967, A1, 8D; Jack Jones, "New Neighborhood Antipoverty Plan Will Begin Jan. 1," *Los Angeles Times*, December 22, 1968, E1–E2; Sarah Schrank, "Picturing the Watts Towers: The Art and Politics of an Urban Landmark," in Stephanie Barron, Sheri Bernstein, and Ilene Susan Fort, eds., *Made in California: Art, Image, and Identity, 1900–2000* (Los Angeles: Los Angeles County Museum of Art; Berkeley: University of California Press, 2000), 380; "Report on Art Festival 1968," NPP. On cultural efforts in the immediate postuprising moment see Art Seidenbaum, "Cultural Approach to Watts," *Los Angeles Times*, December 8, 1965, D1, D14.

    Other artists became drawn to Watts as a place to begin developing projects. This was the case with radical showman Oscar Brown Jr. After performing in Watts during the summer of 1967, he returned in the fall to begin developing his next theatrical musicals. "Watts Area Scene of Talent Search," *Los Angeles Sentinel*, November 16, 1967, D5.
50. The second festival took place March 19–25, 1967, again at Markham Junior High School. Purifoy says that *66 Signs of Neon* traveled to nine sites between 1966 and 1969. Karen Anne Mason, interview with Noah Purifoy (1992), *African American Artists of Los Angeles*, 90.
51. Purifoy reports that during that show's time at Berkeley there was indeed campus unrest. Karen Anne Mason, interview with Noah Purifoy (1992), *African American Artists of Los Angeles*, 90. In one of the artist's scrapbooks he writes that the Berkeley show took place in 1967. However, a review of the show's catalogue lists the exhibition as taking place there in December 1966. This date coincides with activism at Berkeley in late 1966. Jerome A. Donson, "Review of *Junk Art*," *Art Journal* 26, no. 3 (Spring 1967): 318.
52. "Signposts That Point the Way," *Los Angeles Times*, October 9, 1966, 30. Purifoy lists this venue as the Science and Industry Building: see Joined for the Arts scrapbook, NPP.
53. "People in battle": Samella Lewis, *African American Art and Artists* (New York: Harcourt Brace Jovanovich, 1978), 170. See also Lipschutz, "*66 Signs of Neon* and the Transformative Art of Noah Purifoy," 232.
54. Paul Richard, "Art Found in the Ruin of Watts," *Washington Post–Times Herald*, May 26, 1968, K7. Another review in the *Christian Science Monitor* was less interested in this version of the exhibition: Christopher Andreae, "Destruction Art: Sometimes Gentle," *Christian Science Monitor*, June 1, 1968, 6.
55. It seems that Gregory Peck, who early on purchased a piece from *66 Signs of Neon* and worked with the National Endowment for the Arts, assisted in getting funding for the exhibition and helping it get to Washington, DC. Karen Anne Mason, interview with Noah Purifoy (1992), *African American Artists of Los Angeles*, 82. Hopps

was fired from the Pasadena Art Museum in 1967 and made his way to Washington, DC, after that.

56. Hopps's more sustained interaction with African American artists seems to have happened after he left the West Coast. Though Sam Gilliam had made his draped canvases since 1965, it was at the Corcoran in 1969, during Hopps's tenure, that he unveiled *Light Depth*, a canvas that covered a seventy-five-foot expanse of the gallery walls. The curator later included Gilliam in his exhibition for the 1972 Venice Biennale.

    Hopps may have been responsible for bringing the Alma Thomas exhibition from the Whitney Museum to the Corcoran. Calvin Tompkins, "Profile: A Touch for the Now (Walter Hopps)," *New Yorker*, July 29, 1991, 49–50; Franklin Sirmans, "Find the Cave, Hold the Torch: Making Art Shows since Walter Hopps," in Kellie Jones, ed., *Now Dig This! Art and Black Los Angeles, 1960–1980* (New York and Los Angeles: Prestel-Delmonico and Hammer Museum, 2011); Jonathan Binstock, *Sam Gilliam: A Retrospective* (Washington, DC: Corcoran Gallery of Art, 2006); Nicholas Lemann, *The Promised Land: The Great Black Migration and How It Changed America* (New York: Vintage Books, 1992; first published 1991), 159–61.

    As we know, Marcia Tucker, another curatorial luminary during the period, was based at the Whitney between 1969 and 1977. James Monte was her colleague there during much of that period and was involved with many of the same projects she was, including perhaps both the Betye Saar and Alma Thomas exhibitions. Before arriving at the Whitney, Monte was a West Coast–based curator, first at the San Francisco Art Institute and then at the Los Angeles County Museum of Art, where in 1968 he organized *Late Fifties at the Ferus*, a year after the gallery's demise. During the period 1964–69 he was also an associate editor at *Artforum*. It is likely that Monte knew Hopps from those connections and would have been able to collaborate on the Thomas show. The exhibition debuted at the Whitney in spring 1972 and arrived at the Corcoran that fall.

57. Sally Latham, "Watts Art Items at Hunter Gallery," *Chattanooga Post*, April 24, 1969, 14. This may be the only venue for *66 Signs of Neon* in the Deep South. Purifoy mentions that the show might have gone to Alabama, which would make sense, given his connection to the state. Karen Anne Mason, interview with Noah Purifoy (1992), *African American Artists of Los Angeles*, 96–97; Purifoy, "'66' Philosophy," 4. For a wonderful discussion of this exhibition see Lipschutz, "*66 Signs of Neon* and the Transformative Art of Noah Purifoy," 214–59.

58. Moran and Mooney, *The Phenomenology Reader*, 1–26, 57–174.

59. Lipschutz, "*66 Signs of Neon* and the Transformative Art of Noah Purifoy," 214–59.

60. Art Berman, "Watts Easter Week Art Festival Put Riot Debris to Cultural Uses," *Los Angeles Times*, April 8, 1966, A1.

61. Schrank, "Picturing the Watts Towers," 374; "Plans Told for Watts Art Festival," *Los Angeles Sentinel*, December 21, 1965, C13; Art Seidenbaum, "Cultural Approach to Watts," *Los Angeles Times*, December 8, 1965, D1, D14; "Angelenos Exhibit at Whitney Museum," *Los Angeles Times*, December 12, 1965, B44.

62. Ann Petry, *The Street* (1946), quoted in Farah Jasmine Griffin, *Harlem Nocturne: Women Artists and Progressive Politics during World War II* (New York: Basic Books, 2013), 109; Horne, *Fire This Time*, 309–10, 347–48. Tensions would flare again at Jordan High School on March 15, 1966.

63. The *Los Angeles Times* reported three thousand people after four days, while Purifoy counted ten thousand in retrospect. Art Berman, "Watts Easter Week Art Festival Put Riot Debris to Cultural Uses," *Los Angeles Times*, April 8, 1966, A1; Purifoy, "'66' Philosophy," 3; "Art Work of Riot Rubble Ready for Exhibition," *Chicago Daily Defender*, March 29, 1966, 10; "Watts Rubble Becomes Art," *Washington Post-Times Herald*, March 29, 1966, A4.

64. "Watts Group Plans Second Art Festival," *Los Angeles Times*, February 23, 1967, A3; Jack Jones, "Watt's 2nd Annual Week-Long Festival of the Arts Opens Today," *Los Angeles Times*, March 19, 1967, DB; "Watts Festival of the Arts Scheduled at Markham," *Los Angeles Sentinel*, March 16, 1967, A7; "Art, Drama Mark Watts Festival," *Los Angeles Sentinel*, March 23, 1967, A1, 8D.

65. Bruce M. Tyler, "The Rise and Decline of the Watts Summer Festival, 1965 to 1986," *American Studies* 31, no. 2 (Fall 1990): 63.

66. Scot Brown, *Fighting for US: Maulana Karenga, the US Organization, and Black Cultural Nationalism* (New York: New York University Press, 2003), 21.

67. "Watts 'Comeback' Amazes Nation," *Los Angeles Sentinel*, August 17, 1967, A1, D1; Bob Lucas, "Stars Light Up Watts Festival," *Los Angeles Sentinel*, August 10, 1967, A1, D6; "Ken Grumpu," *Los Angeles Sentinel*, October 5, 1967, A8; Leonard Feather, "A Jazz Happening at Watts Festival," *Los Angeles Times*, August 15, 1967, E9.

68. Gary Libman, "Festival Will Mark First Anniversary of Watts Area Riot," *Los Angeles Times*, July 15, 1966, A1; "Support the Watts Summer Festival," *Los Angeles Times*, August 5, 1966, A4.

69. The Rev. H. Hartford Brookins, "Racial Cooperation Cited in Festival," *Los Angeles Sentinel*, August 18, 1966, A7.

70. Betty Pleasant, "Watts Summer Festival Week Proclaimed; Pageant Opens Event," *Los Angeles Sentinel*, August 4, 1966, D5; "Shriver Agrees to Head Watts Parade Sunday," *Los Angeles Times*, August 11, 1966, A1; Ray Rogers, "Gaiety Replaces Terror as Charcoal Alley Glows Anew," *Los Angeles Times*, August 13, 1966, 1; Karen Anne Mason, interview with Noah Purifoy (1992), *African American Artists of Los Angeles*, vi, 98, 143.

71. Other artists included Wilbur Haynie and Herman Bailey. Jane Livingston, a curator at the Los Angeles County Museum of Art, was also a judge of the prize competition. Maggie Savoy, "Watts Art Festival," *Los Angeles Times*, August 6, 1969, D5, D6; William Wilson, "Watts Festival Strives for an Afro-American Art Style," *Los Angeles Times*, August 15, 1969, D9.

72. Noah Purifoy, "Art in the Community," transcript of a presentation to a seminar, "A Day with Experts in the Arts," October 26, 1974, 8–9, NPP.

73. Undated letter to Sue, NPP. Some of the concepts and language mimic the paper cited above. This, as well as some of the events mentioned in the letter, leads me to believe it was written in the winter of 1974, after he returned from the conference mentioned above.

74. Appointed to the council along with Purifoy, by Governor Jerry Brown, were a diverse array of practicing artists, including sculptor Ruth Asawa; theater workers Luis Valdez and Peter Coyote; and poet Gary Snyder. Dancer Bella Lewitsky later served on the council with Purifoy as well. Barbara Isenberg, "State Arts Council Allocates Funds," *Los Angeles Times*, March 18, 1976, E21; Zan Dubin, "Arts Panel: Status Quo

Predicted," *Los Angeles Times*, December 30, 1986, H1, H8; Karen Anne Mason, interview with Noah Purifoy (1992), *African American Artists of Los Angeles*, 123, 127–33.
75. John Outterbridge quoted in Jorge Daniel Veneciano, "A Conversation with John Outterbridge," *Artweek* 24, no. 21 (November 4, 1993): 20.
76. For information on the artist's life see Karen Anne Mason, interview with John Outterbridge (1993), *African American Artists of Los Angeles*; Allen Bassing, "Interview with John Outterbridge," *Archives of American Art*, January 3, 1973; Elton C. Fax, *Black Artists of the New Generation* (New York: Dodd, Mead & Company, 1977), 294–313; *John Outterbridge: A Retrospective* (Los Angeles: California African American Museum, 1993); Barbara Isenberg, *State of the Arts: California Artists Talk about Their Work* (New York: William Morrow, 2000), 117–22.
77. Karen Anne Mason, interview with John Outterbridge (1993), *African American Artists of Los Angeles*, 55.
78. John Outterbridge quoted in Jorge Daniel Veneciano, "A Conversation with John Outterbridge," *Artweek* 24, no. 21 (November 4, 1993): 20–21. John Riddle and cultural worker Claude Booker, like Outterbridge, were veterans of the conflict in Korea.
79. Most of the original music was written by the group's tenor, John Esterridge. The other singers were Sam Bowens, a baritone, and Vera Sanford, whose voice was compared to Sarah Vaughan's. Karen Anne Mason, interview with John Outterbridge (1993), *African American Artists of Los Angeles*, 135–38.
80. The collective included Elliot Hunter (a former student of Leroy Neiman), Moses Rowe, and Jose Williams. Another member, Andy Anderson, made work by dropping pigment from a ladder onto a waiting canvas fifteen feet below, and was as interested in the sonic result as the visual result. Karen Anne Mason, interview with John Outterbridge (1993), *African American Artists of Los Angeles*, 114–17.
81. Gayle Galleries, located on Sixty-Third Street and St. Lawrence Avenue, was run by Edna Gayle. Marion B. Campfield, "Mostly about Women," *Chicago Defender*, July 6, 1957, 15.
82. Bassing, "Interview with John Outterbridge"; Isenberg, *State of the Arts*, 120.
83. Outterbridge noted that many artists were hired there because of the flexible hours. John Outterbridge quoted in Jerry Raynor, "Artist Claims That Art Is Functional, Public," *Daily Reflector* (Greenville, NC), June 30, 1974, B5.
84. Karen Anne Mason, interview with John Outterbridge (1993), *African American Artists of Los Angeles*, 169–76. Melvin Edwards, who by the early 1960s was getting a lot of notice, had a studio in the same building as Hill on Jefferson Boulevard.
85. Karen Anne Mason, interview with John Outterbridge (1993), *African American Artists of Los Angeles*, 303–5. On Vertis Hayes see Greta Berman, "Walls of Harlem," *Arts Magazine* 52 (October 1977): 122–26.
86. Karen Anne Mason, interview with John Outterbridge (1993), *African American Artists of Los Angeles*, 178–89. John Outterbridge quoted in Raynor, "Artist Claims That Art Is Functional, Public," B5; Bassing, "Interview with John Outterbridge."
87. Karen Anne Mason, interview with John Outterbridge (1993), *African American Artists of Los Angeles*, 237–38.
88. Outterbridge quoted in Francine R. Carter, "The Golden State Mutual Afro-American Art Collection," *Black Art* 1, no. 2 (Winter 1976): 15–16.

89. Karen Anne Mason, interview with John Outterbridge (1993), *African American Artists of Los Angeles*, 362.
90. Karen Anne Mason, interview with John Outterbridge (1993), *African American Artists of Los Angeles*, 243.
91. Bassing, "Interview with John Outterbridge."
92. Troy Robinson came to California with the thought of writing movie scores but ended up as a major contributor to CCAA, leading the orchestra, teaching music, and providing music for theater pieces there. Like Outterbridge, in Chicago he was a bus driver with the Chicago Transit Authority. Drummer Thurman Barker remembers Monday jam sessions in the early 1960s with Robinson and other bus drivers as well, bearing out Outterbridge's observation of the profession as one compatible with artistic life. Robinson was known as a prolific composer during his Chicago years; one review notes a piece whose frenetic rhythms were taken from the Southside bus route. John Litweiler, "Chicago's AACM," *Sounds and Fury*, June 1966; George Lewis, *A Power Stronger Than Itself: The AACM and American Experimental Music* (Chicago: University of Chicago Press, 2008), 71–72, 82, 98n60, 133, 188–89.
93. bell hooks, "Homeplace: A Site of Resistance," in *Yearning: Race, Gender, and Cultural Politics* (Boston: South End, 1990), 41–49.
94. David Hammons would draw from similar inspiration for *Delta Spirit*, 1986, a New York shack built on landfill in Battery Park. Kellie Jones, "An Interview with David Hammons," *Reallife*, no. 16 (Autumn 1986).
95. Ayofemi Folayan, "Community Carver: An Interview with Artist and Activist John W. Outterbridge," *High Performance* 15 (Winter 1992): 44; Bassing, "Interview with John Outterbridge"; Karen Anne Mason, interview with John Outterbridge (1993), *African American Artists of Los Angeles*, 376–408, 425, 430–31; Compton Communicative Arts Academy Collection, California State University, Los Angeles.
96. K. Jones, *Now Dig This!*
97. Pierre Picot, "John Outterbridge," *New Art Examiner* 21 (December 1993): 33.
98. Christopher Knight, "Outterbridge: Assembling Stories," *Los Angeles Times*, September 2, 1993, 1.
99. Lizzetta LeFalle-Collins, "Keeper of Traditions," in California African American Museum, *John Outterbridge: A Retrospective* (Los Angeles: California African American Museum, 1993), 7–22.
100. LeFalle-Collins, "Keeper of Traditions."
101. Bassing, "Interview with John Outterbridge"; Isenberg, *State of the Arts*, 120; Karen Anne Mason, interview with John Outterbridge (1993), *African American Artists of Los Angeles*, 200–202; LeFalle-Collins, "Keeper of Traditions." James K. Monte, *Mark di Suvero* (New York: Whitney Museum of American Art, November 13, 1975–February 8, 1976); *Mark di Suvero: Dreambook* (Berkeley: University of California Press, 2008).
102. Henry J. Seldis and William Wilson, "Art Walk: A Critical Guide to the Galleries," *Los Angeles Times*, October 31, 1969, G4.
103. More famously, Wilson was prodded to write this review only after being confronted on a television program by Outterbridge and his fellow artists and gallerists. Karen Anne Mason, interview with John Outterbridge (1993), *African American Artists of Los Angeles*, 244–47. Appearing on the program for NBC-KCET were Bernie Casey,

Alonzo Davis, David Hammons, Samella Lewis, and John Outterbridge, along with William Wilson.

William Wilson was actually the protégé of Henry J. Seldis, the older, more ensconced critic at the *Los Angeles Times* during this period. Interestingly, however, Seldis's criticism of the Los Angeles African American art scene was much more even-handed and less caustic than that of his younger colleague.

104. Information on such works by Sam Gilliam, Al Loving, and Joe Overstreet can be found in Kellie Jones, *Energy/Experimentation: Black Artists and Abstraction, 1964–1980* (New York: Studio Museum in Harlem, 2006).

105. bell hooks, "Choosing the Margin as a Space of Radical Openness," in *Yearning*, 147.

106. Karen Anne Mason, interview with John Outterbridge (1993), *African American Artists of Los Angeles*, 217. Singer and playwright Oscar Brown Jr. recorded a chant in homage to those of the ragman on his debut album during this time: "Rags and Old Iron," on *Sin and Soul . . . and Then Some* (Columbia CL 1577 1960).

107. hooks, "Choosing the Margin as a Space of Radical Openness," 145–53.

108. hooks, "Choosing the Margin as a Space of Radical Openness," 145–53; Huey Copeland, introduction to *Bound to Appear: Art, Slavery, and the Site of Blackness in Multicultural America* (Chicago: University of Chicago Press, 2013).

109. Grey Gundaker and Judith McWillie, *No Space Hidden: The Spirit of African American Yard Work* (Knoxville: University of Tennessee Press, 2005), 27–41.

110. hooks, *Yearning*, 116.

111. Alice Walker, *In Search of Our Mothers' Gardens: Womanist Prose* (New York: Harcourt Brace Jovanovich, 1983), 241.

112. Walker, *In Search of Our Mothers' Gardens*, 242.

113. John Outterbridge quoted in Isenberg, *State of the Arts*, 122.

114. Gundaker and McWillie, *No Space Hidden*, 51.

115. Robert Farris Thompson, "Bighearted Power: Kongo Presence in the Landscape and Art of Black America," in Grey Gundaker and Tynes Cowan, eds., *Keep Your Head to the Sky: Interpreting African American Home Ground* (Charlottesville: University Press of Virginia, 1998), 45; Robert Farris Thompson, *Flash of the Spirit: African and Afro-American Art and Philosophy* (New York: Vintage Books, 1984).

116. Karen Anne Mason, interview with John Outterbridge (1993), *African American Artists of Los Angeles*, 33.

117. Karen Anne Mason, interview with John Outterbridge (1993), *African American Artists of Los Angeles*, 581; Bassing, "Interview with John Outterbridge."

118. Westmacott in Grey Gundaker, "African American History, Cosmology, and the Moral Universe of Edward Houston's Yard," *Journal of Garden History* 14, no. 3 (1994): 200; Grey Gundaker, "Tradition and Innovation in African American Yards," *African Arts* 26, no. 2 (1993): 59.

119. Karen Anne Mason, interview with John Outterbridge (1993), *African American Artists of Los Angeles*, 30–35. See also David Driskell, foreword to Jane H. Carpenter with Betye Saar, *Betye Saar* (San Francisco: Pomegranate, 2003), vii–viii.

120. Karen Anne Mason, interview with John Outterbridge (1993), *African American Artists of Los Angeles*, 98.

121. Gundaker, "Tradition and Innovation in African American Yards," 34, 49, 64; Wyatt MacGaffey, "The Black Loincloth and the Son of Nzambi Mpungu," in Bernth Lind-

fors, ed., *Forms of Folklore in Africa* (Austin: University of Texas Press, 1977): 147; Thompson, *Flash of the Spirit*.

122. John Outterbridge quoted in Jorge Daniel Veneciano, "A Conversation with John Outterbridge," *Artweek* 24, no. 21 (4 November 1993): 20.
123. Betye Saar quoted in Cindy Nemser, "Conversation with Betye Saar," *Feminist Art Journal* 4, no. 4 (Winter 1975–76): 23. "Hoodoo You Love" is the sonic equivalent of "Who Do You Love?," a 1956 hit by Chicago blues guitarist Bo Diddley. The lyrics of the song also suggest that he has the former idea of African American spiritualism and sympathetic magic in mind. Gundaker and McWillie, *No Space Hidden*, 54.
124. Carpenter with Saar, *Betye Saar*, 20. See also Betye Saar quoted in Nemser, "Conversation with Betye Saar"; *Spirit Catcher—The Art of Betye Saar* (dir. Suzanne Bauman; WNET, 1977).
125. Betye Saar quoted in Eleanor C. Munro, "Betye Saar," in *Originals: American Women Artists* (New York: Simon and Schuster, 1979), 358.
126. Michael D. Harris, *Colored Pictures: Race and Visual Representation* (Chapel Hill: University of North Carolina Press, 2003); Kenneth W. Goings, *Mammy and Uncle Mose: Black Collectibles and American Stereotyping* (Bloomington: Indiana University Press, 1994); Patricia A. Turner, *Ceramic Uncles and Celluloid Mammies: Black Images and Their Influence on Culture* (New York: Anchor Books, 1994); Tavia Nyong'o, *The Amalgamation Waltz: Race, Performance, and the Ruses of Memory* (Minneapolis: University of Minnesota Press, 2009); Nicole Fleetwood, *Troubling Vision: Performance, Visuality, and Blackness* (Chicago: University of Chicago Press, 2011).
127. Tavia Nyong'o, "Racial Kitsch and Black Performance," *Yale Journal of Criticism* 15, no. 2 (Fall 2002): 371; Clement Greenberg, "Avant-Garde and Kitsch," in *Art and Culture*.
128. Karen Anne Mason, interview with Betye Saar (1996), *African American Artists of Los Angeles*, 112.
129. Mary Schmidt Campbell, *Tradition and Conflict: Images of a Turbulent Decade* (New York: Studio Museum in Harlem, 1988).
130. Carpenter with Saar, *Betye Saar*, 43.
131. Sylvia Wynter, "Sambos and Minstrels," *Social Text* 1 (Winter 1979): 152.
132. Daphne A. Brooks, introduction to *The Great Escapes: Four Slave Narratives* (New York: Barnes and Noble, 2007); Paul Gilroy, "'. . . To Be Real!': The Dissident Forms of Black Expressive Culture," in Catherine Ugwu, ed., *Let's Get It On: The Politics of Black Performance* (London: Institute of Contemporary Art, 1995), 12–33.
133. Darlene Clark Hine, "Rape and the Inner Lives of Black Women in the Middle West: Preliminary Thoughts on the Culture of Dissemblance," *Signs* 14, no. 4 (Summer 1989): 915. See also Evelyn Brooks Higginbotham, "African-American Women's History and the Metalanguage of Race," *Signs* 17, no. 2 (Winter 1992): 251–74.
134. Carpenter with Saar, *Betye Saar*, 43.
135. Deborah Willis, "Looks and Gazes: Photographic Fragmentation and the Found Objects," in University of Michigan Museum of Art, *Betye Saar: Extending the Frozen Moment* (Ann Arbor and Berkeley: University of Michigan Art Museum and University of California Press, 2005), 25; Karen Anne Mason, interview with Betye Saar (1996), *African American Artists of Los Angeles*, 120–22.
136. Willis, "Looks and Gazes," 25. See also M. D. Harris, *Colored Pictures*, chap. 3. For

more on the collectible and the stereotype see Goings, *Mammy and Uncle Mose*, and Turner, *Ceramic Uncles and Celluloid Mammies*. On the use of these figures as oppositional work see Bridget Cooks, "See Me Now: Visual Depictions of Black Americans," *Camera Obscura* 36 (September 1995): 66–83, and Nyong'o, "Racial Kitsch and Black Performance," 371–91.

137. However, hoodoo is sometimes considered more sympathetic magic rather than full-blown religion, while American voodoo, particularly in the Louisiana area, is considered to have religious tenets and observers. Jeffery E. Anderson, preface to *Conjure in African American Society* (Baton Rouge: Louisiana State University Press, 2005).

138. In Kikongo the word for such root spirits is *funza*. See Wyatt MacGaffey, *Religion and Society in Central Africa: The BaKongo of Lower Zaire* (Chicago: University of Chicago Press, 1986), 14, 79–80; Jeffery E. Anderson, preface to *Conjure in African American Society*, 39; Gundaker and McWillie, *No Space Hidden*.

139. Anderson, *Conjure in African American Society*, 28, 37.

140. See Reed's prose poem "Neo-Hoodoo Manifesto" (1970), in Ishmael Reed, *Conjure: Selected Poems, 1963–1970* (Amherst: University of Massachusetts Press, 1972), 21.

141. "Gliberals," "A Westward Movement," and "Betye Saar, Artist," in Ishmael Reed, *Shrovetide in Old New Orleans* (Garden City, NY: Doubleday, 1978); Ishmael Reed, *A Secretary to the Spirits* (Lagos: Nok, 1978). The poetry book was published in Nigeria by NOK, a company formed in the 1960s in the wake of independence. H. C. Otokenefor and C. O. Nwodo, "The Coming of Age of Book Publishing and Indexing in Nigeria," *Library Review* 39, no. 4 (1990): 33–40.

142. Reed, *Shrovetide in Old New Orleans*, 153; Karen Anne Mason, interview with Betye Saar (1996), *African American Artists of Los Angeles*, 119–20, 136–37.

143. There are also materials for amulet making—pods, bark, bones—contained in hidden compartments in the work. "Betye Saar, Artist," in Reed, *Shrovetide in Old New Orleans*, 150.

144. Wynter, "Sambos and Minstrels," 149.

145. Samella Lewis, introduction to *Betye Saar, Selected Works 1964–1973* (curator: Josine Ianco Starrels), Fine Arts Gallery, California State University, Los Angeles, October 1–October 25, 1973, unpaginated; Karen Anne Mason, interview with Betye Saar (1996), *African American Artists of Los Angeles*, 140.

146. *Betye Saar: Ritual, Recent Assemblages and Collages*, Jan Baum–Iris Silverman Gallery, Los Angeles, October 11–November 12, 1977, invitation card, Betye Saar, Artist File, Museum of Modern Art, New York.

147. While some of the materials left by viewers were culled (crumpled paper, trash, "things that weren't interesting"), some eventually made their way into *Mti* itself, which changed, if slightly, over time. Karen Anne Mason, interview with Betye Saar (1996), *African American Artists of Los Angeles*, 142; Melinda Wortz, "Los Angeles," *ArtNews* 76, no. 10 (December 1977): 108–9; Betye Saar, "Installation as Sculpture," *International Review of African American Art* 6, no. 1 (1984): 44–48; Houston Conwill, "Interview with Betye Saar," *Black Art* 3, no. 1 (1979): 4–15; "Betye Saar; Mojotech, April 24–June 28, 1987," in *19 Projects: Artists-in-Residence at the MIT List Visual Arts Center* (Cambridge, MA: MIT List Visual Arts Center, 1996), 91–100; Arnold Rubin, "Accumulation: Power and Display in African Sculpture," *Artforum* 13 (May 1975): 35–47.

148. Thompson *Flash of the Spirit*, 182.
149. Now most commonly written as Damballah.
150. In 1974 Saar traveled to Haiti, Nigeria, and Mexico.
151. Isenberg, *State of the Arts*, 277.
152. "Betye Saar," in Lynn F. Miller, Sally S. Swenson, Beryl K. Smith, and Joan Arbeiter, *Lives and Works: Talks with Women Artists* (Metuchen, NJ: Scarecrow, 1981), 176–84; Munro, "Betye Saar," 355–63; Nemser, "Conversation with Betye Saar," 19–24. Although Nemser's article appeared the same year as her book, *Art Talk: Conversations with 12 Women Artists* (New York: Charles Scribner's Sons, 1975), it did not make it into her volume. An updated edition twenty years later added Saar as the only African American artist. See Cindy Nemser, *Art Talk: Conversations with 15 Women Artists* (New York: IconEditions, 1995).
153. Lucy R. Lippard, "Introduction: Changing since *Changing*," in *From the Center: Feminist Essays on Women's Art* (New York: Dutton, 1976), 4.
154. Lippard, "Introduction: Changing since *Changing*," 11, emphasis in original. See also Nemser's introduction to *Art Talk: Conversations with 12 Women Artists*.
155. Norma Broude and Mary D. Garrard, "Introduction: Feminism and Art in the Twentieth Century," in Broude and Garrard, eds., *The Power of Feminist Art: The American Movement of the 1970s, History and Impact* (New York: Harry N. Abrams, 1994). See also Linda Nochlin, "Why Have There Been No Great Women Artists," *ArtNews* 69 (January 1971): 22.
156. Betye Saar quoted in Nemser, "Conversation with Betye Saar."
157. "Inextricably linked": Higginbotham, "African-American Women's History and the Metalanguage of Race," 254; "functioning beyond the demands of dominant ideology": Chela Sandoval, "U.S. Third World Feminism: The Theory and Method of Oppositional Consciousness in the Postmodern World," *Genders* 10 (1991): 1–23. See also hooks, "Homeplace," 41–49, and Kum-Kum Bhavnani, ed., *Feminism and "Race"* (New York: Oxford University Press, 2001).
158. Betye Saar quoted in Miller et al., *Lives and Works*, 182–84.
159. Lucy R. Lippard, "Dreams, Demands, and Desires: The Black Antiwar and Women's Movements," in Campbell, *Tradition and Conflict*, 75–81; Moira Roth and Yolanda Lopez, "Social Protest: Racism and Sexism," in *The Power of Feminist Art* (New York: Harry N. Abrams, 1994); Vijay Prashad, *Everybody Was Kung Fu Fighting: Afro-Asian Connections and the Myth of Cultural Purity* (Boston: Beacon, 2001). In New York Kay Brown and others began the collective Where We At Black Women Artists in 1971, while Faith Ringgold and her daughter, writer Michelle Wallace, began the organization Women Students and Artists for Black Art Liberation in 1970. Valerie Smith, "Abundant Evidence: Black Women Artists in the 1960s and 70s," in Cornelia H. Butler and Lisa Gabrielle Mark, eds., WACK! *Art and the Feminist Revolution* (Los Angeles: Museum of Contemporary Art, 2007), 400–413. On women writers from the period see Elizabeth Alexander, *The Black Interior* (Minneapolis: Graywolf, 2004), 61–65; and on political activism in California see Jane Rhodes, "Black Radicalism in 1960s California: Women in the Black Panther Party," in Quintard Taylor and Shirley Ann Wilson Moore, eds., *African American Women Confront the West, 1600–2000* (Norman: University of Oklahoma Press, 2003), 346–62; Faith Ringgold, *We Flew over the Bridge: The Memoirs of Faith Ringgold* (Boston: Little,

Brown, 1995); Howardena Pindell, *The Heart of the Question: The Writings and Paintings of Howardena Pindell* (New York: Midmarch Arts Press, 1997).

160. Lisa Gail Collins, "The Art of Transformation: Parallels in the Black Arts and Feminist Art Movements," in Lisa Gail Collins and Margo Natalie Crawford, eds., *New Thoughts on the Black Arts Movement* (New Brunswick, NJ: Rutgers University Press, 2006), 273, 281.

161. Carpenter with Saar, *Betye Saar*, 213–14; Karen Anne Mason, interview with Suzanne Jackson (1998), *African American Artists of Los Angeles*, 267; Roth and Lopez, "Social Protest"; Harryette Mullen, "'Artistic Expression Was Flowing Everywhere': Alison Mills and Ntozake Shange, Black Bohemian Feminists in the 1970s," *Meridians* 4, no. 2 (2004): 228.

162. William Wilson, "'Women' Exhibition Nicely Balances Art, Femininity," *Los Angeles Times*, March 18, 1968, C14.

163. W. Wilson, "'Women' Exhibition Nicely Balances Art, Femininity"; Lucy R. Lippard, "Judy Chicago Talking to Lucy R. Lippard," in *From the Center*, 214–30; Judy Chicago, *Through the Flower: My Struggle as a Woman Artist* (Garden City, NY: Doubleday, 1975); Laura Meyer and Faith Wilding, eds., *A Studio of Their Own: The Legacy of the Fresno Feminist Experiment* (Fresno: Press at California State University, Fresno, 2009).

164. Josine Ianco-Starrels was born in Bucharest, Romania, in 1926, the same year that Betye Saar was born in Los Angeles. Her father was Marcel Janco, an artist active with Zurich Dada and performance at Cabaret Voltaire in 1916. She fled with her family to Palestine during World War II. She arrived in New York in 1950, studied at the Arts Students League, and eventually made her way to Los Angeles.

165. Jody Jacobs, "Womanspace Art Benefit Slated," *Los Angeles Times*, August 6, 1973, part 4, p. 2; Josine Ianco-Starrels, "Art News," *Los Angeles Times*, September 9, 1973, calendar, 63, 65.

166. Betye Saar, "Black Mirror," *Womanspace Journal* 1, no. 2 (April/May 1973): 22.

167. "Womanspace Calendar of Events for April and May 1973," *Womanspace Journal* 1, no. 2 (April/May 1973): 36–37; "Black Mirror at Womanspace," *Los Angeles Sentinel*, April 12, 1973, B4A; Claudia Chapline, "Reflections on Black Mirror, March 31–April 22," *Womanspace Journal* 1, no. 3 (Summer 1973): 20; Karen Anne Mason, interview with Betye Saar (1996), *African American Artists of Los Angeles*, 184–86.

168. Carol Zeitz, "A Women's Place Revealed," *Neworld* 2 (Fall 1975): 33. This new woman-centered space of pedagogy was named after the structure at the Chicago World's Columbian Exposition of 1893 that housed exhibits honoring women's labor and crafts, and designed by Sophia Hayden, the first female graduate of the Massachusetts Institute of Technology. The Feminist Art Program at Fresno State College continued after Chicago's departure, first under the leadership of Rita Yokoi, and then under Joyce Aiken until her retirement in 1992. Judy Chicago was able to bring her program to California Institute of Arts (CalArts) because Miriam Schapiro's husband, Paul Brach, was dean there. CalArts had also replaced the Chouinard Art Institute, thus the initial site of the Woman's Building in that space also had continuing links to the largesse of CalArts and Schapiro's connection there. Chicago left her role in the Woman's Building in 1974 to work on the monumental piece that would become *The Dinner Party*, 1979. The Woman's Building closed in 1991. Meyer and

Wilding, *A Studio of Their Own*; Terry Wolverton, *Insurgent Muse: Life and Art at the Woman's Building* (San Francisco: City Lights, 2002); Butler, *WACK!*; Broude and Garrard, *The Power of Feminist Art*; Chicago, *Through the Flower*.

169. Sheila de Bretteville created all aspects of the Woman's Building's graphic identity, from the entrance and reception areas to its posters, announcements, and educational materials. She also inaugurated the Women's Graphic Center, a program that offered design services and training in the field. Writings by Sheila de Bretteville, Woman's Building Records, 1970–1992, Box 4, Folder 19, Archives of American Art, Smithsonian Institution.

170. The catalogues included the one for her solo show at the Museum of Contemporary Art, Los Angeles, in 1984 and *Secrets, Dialogues, and Revelations: The Art of Betye and Alison Saar* in 1989 at Wight Art Gallery, UCLA.

171. Marianne Hirsch, "Introduction: Familial Looking," in *The Familial Gaze* (Hanover, NH: University Press of New England, 1999), and Marianne Hirsch, "The Generation of Postmemory," *Poetics Today* 29, no. 1 (Spring 2008): 103–28.

172. Nemser, "Conversation with Betye Saar," 23.

173. Saar quoted in Munro, "Betye Saar," 359.

174. David Bourdon, "Salt Mines Turn to Art, Photographs to Politics," *Village Voice*, May 17, 1976, 111; *Spirit Catcher: The Art of Betye Saar* (dir. Suzanne Bauman; WNET, 1977).

175. Munro, *Originals*, 359. Painter Jack Whitten also made use of Xerox technology through a grant from the company itself during that decade; see K. Jones, *Energy/Experimentation*.

176. Judy Chicago quoted in Josephine Whithers, "Judy Chicago's Dinner Party: A Personal Vision of Women's History," in Norma Broude and Mary D. Garrard, eds., *The Expanding Discourse: Feminism and Art History* (Boulder, CO: Westview, 1992), 460.

177. Karen Anne Mason, interview with Betye Saar (1996), *African American Artists of Los Angeles*, 27.

178. Karen Anne Mason, interview with Betye Saar (1996), *African American Artists of Los Angeles*, 154–55; Munro, *Originals*, 359, 361; Jane Hattie Carpenter, "Conjure Woman: Betye Saar and Rituals of Transformation, 1960–1990" (PhD diss., University of Michigan, 2002), 238–39.

179. Carpenter, "Conjure Woman," 238–39.

180. Gundaker and McWillie, *No Space Hidden*, 12, 36, 38, 80–81; Thompson, *Flash of the Spirit*.

181. Shirley Ann Moore, "Getting There, Being There: African American Migration to Richmond, California, 1910–1945," in Joe William Trotter Jr., ed., *The Great Migration in Historical Perspective: New Dimensions of Race, Class, and Gender* (Bloomington: Indiana University Press, 1991), 117–18, 15.

182. Manthia Diawara, "Afro-Kitsch," in Gina Dent and Michele Wallace, eds., *Black Popular Culture* (Seattle: Bay, 1992), 285–91.

183. Bourdon, "Salt Mines Turn to Art," 111; Larry Rosing, "Betye Saar," *Arts Magazine* 50 (June 1976): 7; Barbara Schwartz, "New York / Sculpture and Craft," *Craft Horizon* 36 (August 1976): 50; Ann-Sargent Wooster, "Betye Saar," *ArtNews* 75 (October 1976): 124–25. For a further discussion of intimacy in the work see Lowery S. Sims, "Betye Saar: A Primer for Installation Work," in *Betye Saar, Resurrection: Site Installations 1977–1987* (February 6–March 6, 1987, Main Art Gallery—Visual Arts Cen-

ter, California State University, Fullerton, organized by Dextra Frankel), 9. See also Lowery S. Sims, "From Frozen Moment to Spectator Participation: Assemblage and Installation in the Oeuvre of Betye Saar," in University of Michigan Museum of Art, *Betye Saar: Extending the Frozen Moment*, 52–61.
184. Susan Larsen, "Ethical Alchemy," in *George Herms—The Secret Archives* (Los Angeles: Los Angeles Municipal Art Gallery, 1992), 49. Saar's daughter Alison Saar has recently confirmed this rarely discussed framing of Saar as a '60s artist, in speaking about the creative freedom that was nurtured in her home environment, and of neighbors like Mama Cass and Frank Zappa, linking them to the hippie environment. See Erin Clark, "Alison Saar," *Artworks Magazine* (Winter 2008), http://artworksmagazine.com/2009/03/alison-saar/, accessed November 20, 2010.
185. "Celebrant of secret mysteries": Edward Leffingwell and George Herms, "A Drug Store for Artie," in *George Herms—The Secret Archives* (Los Angeles: Los Angeles Municipal Art Gallery, 1992), 5; "forgiving cosmology": Larsen, "Ethical Alchemy," 46.
186. Larsen, "Ethical Alchemy," 45.
187. Larsen, "Ethical Alchemy," 45; Paul Karlstrom, "Oral History Interview with George Herms, 1993 December 8, 10, 13–1994 March 10," Archives of American Art, Smithsonian Institution, pp. 5–6.
188. The exhibition at Ferus Gallery was held December 10, 1962–January 5, 1963. The show at Pasadena Art Museum took place December 27, 1966–February 11, 1967.
189. Saar quoted in University of Michigan Museum of Art, *Betye Saar: Extending the Frozen Moment*, 16; Benny Andrews, "Jemimas, Mysticism, and Mojos: The Art of Betye Saar," *Encore American and Worldwide News*, March 17, 1975, 30.
190. Susan Stewart, *On Longing: Narratives of the Miniature, the Gigantic, the Souvenir, the Collection* (Durham, NC: Duke University Press, 1993), 135, 48.
191. Dickran Tashjian, *Joseph Cornell: Gifts of Desire* (Miami Beach: Grassfield, 1992), 18.
192. Stewart, *On Longing*, 93; Jason Edwards, "Coming Out as a Cornellian, Cornell and His World," and Anna Dezeuze, "Unpacking Joseph Cornell: Consumption and Play in the Work of Robert Rauschenberg, Andy Warhol and George Brecht," in Jason Edwards and Stephanie L. Taylor, eds., *Joseph Cornell: Opening the Box* (Bern, Switzerland: Peter Lang, 2007), 37–39, 221–41; Robert Morris, "American Quartet," *Art in America*, December 1981, 92–105.
193. Eve Kosofsky Sedgwick, "Paranoid Reading and Reparative Reading, or You're So Paranoid, You Probably Think This Essay Is about You," in Eve Kosofsky Sedgwick and Adam Frank, *Touching Feeling: Affect, Pedagogy, Performativity* (Durham, NC: Duke University Press, 2003), 149–50. See also J. Edwards, "Coming Out as a Cornellian," 25–46.
194. Larsen, "Ethical Alchemy," 44.
195. Branden Joseph, *Random Order: Robert Rauschenberg and the Neo-Avant-Garde* (Cambridge, MA: MIT Press, 2003), 144.
196. Stewart, *On Longing*, ix.
197. Lowery Stokes Sims, "Modernism and Its Discontents," in *Challenge of the Modern: African American Artists, 1925–1945* (New York: Studio Museum in Harlem, 2003), 13–14.
198. The additional five painters in *New Painting of Common Objects* were Jim Dine,

Robert Dowd, Joe Goode, Phillip Hefferton, and Wayne Thiebaud: *Ferus*, 2nd ed. (New York: Rizzoli and Gagosian Gallery, 2009); Kristine McKenna, *The Ferus Gallery: A Place to Begin* (Göttingen, Germany: Steidl, 2009); Calvin Tompkins, "Profile: A Touch for the Now (Walter Hopps)," *New Yorker*, July 29, 1991, 33–57; Ann Temkin, "One More Once," *Artforum* 44, no. 1 (September 2005): 49–50; Sirmans, "Find the Cave, Hold the Torch."

199. Shirley Neilsen Blum quoted in McKenna, *The Ferus Gallery*, 206. On the machismo of Ferus and Hopps's own relationship to questions of women and feminism see McKenna, *The Ferus Gallery*, 174–76, 277, and Tompkins, "A Touch for the Now," 52.

200. McKenna, *The Ferus Gallery*, 95. For more on Edmund Bereal see K. Jones, introduction to *Now Dig This!*; and Sirmans, "Find the Cave, Hold the Torch."

201. Henry Hopkins and Ed Ruscha in McKenna, *The Ferus Gallery*, 309.

202. Tompkins, "A Touch for the Now," 38; Sirmans, "Find the Cave, Hold the Torch"; "Walter Hopps Hopps Hopps: Hans-Ulrich Obrist Talks with Walter Hopps," *Artforum* 34, no. 6 (February 1996): 60; Temkin, "One More Once." James Newman went on to found the Dilexi Gallery in San Francisco. Opening in 1957, the same year as Ferus, it was known for championing San Francisco abstract painting and the Beat scene. Dilexi Gallery Records, 1957–71, Archives of American Art, Smithsonian Institution; Lisa Phillips, *Beat Culture and the New America, 1950–1965* (New York: Whitney Museum of American Art in association with Flammarion, Paris, 1995).

203. Calvin Reid, "Chasing the Blue Train," *Art in America* 77, no. 9 (1989): 196–97.

204. McKenna, *The Ferus Gallery*, 218. Several standalone objects made by Kienholz at the same time that he was developing his larger voice in tableaux also involve African American figures and subjects. The wall box *It Takes Two to Integrate, Cha, Cha, Cha*, 1961, is a comment on the Freedom Rides in the South, which forced the issue of integration in public transportation and began the same year. By the end of the decade, Kienholz would complete the horrifying *Five Car Stud*, 1969–72, with its focus on black male castration. In later years, he would touch intermittently on emblematic black figures—in *Claude Nigger Claude*, 1988, and *Drawing from Tank*, 1990—as vehicles for explorations of prejudice or inequality.

205. George Lipsitz, "Weeds in a Vacant Lot: The Hidden History of Urban Renewal," in *Footsteps in the Dark: The Hidden Histories of Popular Music* (Minneapolis: University of Minnesota Press, 2007), 110.

206. Guthrie P. Ramsey Jr., *The Amazing Bud Powell: Black Genius, Jazz History, and the Challenge of Bebop* (Berkeley: University of California Press, 2013); Amiri Baraka, *Black Music* (New York: Morrow, 1967); Griffin, *Harlem Nocturne*, 159–62.

207. Mona Lisa Saloy, "Black Beats and Black Issues," and Maurice Berger, "Libraries Full of Tears: The Beats and the Law," in Phillips, *Beat Culture and the New America*, 152–65; Lemann, *The Promised Land*, 199–200. Bruce Conner has talked about the atmosphere of violence he experienced in this regard, "Oral History Interview with Bruce Conner, 1974 March 29," Archives of American Art, Smithsonian Institution.

208. Thomas Crow, "Modernism and Mass Culture in the Visual Arts," in *Modern Art in the Common Culture* (New Haven, CT: Yale University Press, 1996), 36.

209. Lyotard quoted in Bois and Krauss, *Formless*, 108.

210. Joseph, *Random Order*, 168; Katherine McKittrick, *Demonic Grounds: Black Women*

and the Cartographies of Struggle (Minneapolis: University of Minnesota Press, 2006); Toni Morrison, *Playing in the Dark: Whiteness and the Literary Imagination* (Cambridge, MA: Harvard University Press, 1992).

211. Lawrence Alloway, in "The Art of Assemblage: A Symposium (1961)," in Museum of Modern Art, *Essays on Assemblage* (New York: Museum of Modern Art; Distributed by Harry N. Abrams, 1992), 140. Other participants in the symposium included Marcel Duchamp, Richard Huelsenbeck, Robert Rauschenberg, Roger Shattuck, and William C. Seitz. Alloway had coined the term "junk culture" earlier that year to address ideas about assemblage and popular culture. See Lawrence Alloway, "Junk Culture," *Architectural Design* 31, no. 3 (March 1961): 122.
212. Joseph, *Random Order*, chap. 3.
213. Cheryl Finley, "Committed to Memory: The Slave-Ship Icon and the Black-Atlantic Imagination," *Chicago Art Journal* 9 (Spring 1999): 9.
214. Patricia Leighten, "Picasso's Collages and the Threat of War, 1912–13," *Art Bulletin* 67, no. 4 (December 1985): 653–72. For her equally fascinating take on the latent politics in Picasso's use of primitivism see Leighten's "The White Peril and *L'Art negre*: Picasso, Primitivism, and Anticolonialism," *Art Bulletin* 72, no. 4 (December 1990): 609–30.
215. Joseph, *Random Order*, 168.

THREE. ORGANIZE

1. Tony Bennett, "The Exhibitionary Complex," *New Formations* 4 (Spring 1988): 73–102, and Tony Bennett, *The Birth of the Museum: History, Theory, Politics* (London: Routledge, 1995). See also Bridget R. Cooks, *Exhibiting Blackness: African Americans and the American Art Museum* (Amherst: University of Massachusetts Press, 2011); Anne Higonnet, *A Museum of One's Own: Private Collecting, Public Gift* (Pittsburgh: Periscope, 2009); Mabel O. Wilson, *Negro Building: Black Americans in the World of Fairs and Museums* (Berkeley: University of California Press, 2012).
2. Bennett, *The Birth of the Museum*, 35.
3. Wilson, *Negro Building*, 4.
4. Wilson, *Negro Building*, 8.
5. Miriam Matthews interviewed by Eleanor Roberts, March 14, 16, 17, and 22, 1977, in Ruth Edmonds Hill, ed., *The Black Women Oral History Project*, vol. 7 of the Arthur and Elizabeth Schlesinger Library on the History of Women in America, Radcliffe College (Westport, CT: Meckler, 1991), 375, 379, 451–52.
6. Matthews's life and career not surprisingly intersected with Schomburg's and also with Bontemps's. Arriving on New Year's Eve 1939 and in residence through June 1940, Matthews spent an exciting six months in New York, drinking in East Coast culture and traveling the Eastern Seaboard from Washington, DC, to Boston. During this period she worked for the New York Public Library, primarily based at the 135th Street branch, but also in the 145th Street library and with tasks downtown. In the early 1940s she would be one of the finalists considered to head the 135th Street branch—the position Schomburg made legendary, first when the New York Public Library purchased his materials in 1926, and between 1932 and 1938 as the curator of that collection.

   Matthews and Arna Bontemps were of the same generation, and their lives were a clear product of the Great Migration. Born in 1902 in Alexandria, Louisiana, Bontemps moved with his family to Los Angeles at age three. On graduating from Pacific Union College in Northern California Bontemps headed to New York and became part of the Harlem Renaissance. In the 1940s he returned to school for a master's degree. He was awarded an MA in library science from the University of Chicago in 1943; Matthews would attend the same program, getting her MA in 1945. From the 1940s onward Bontemps developed important collections in African American literature and history at Fisk University, the University of Illinois Chicago, and Yale University. Miriam Matthews interviewed by Eleanor Roberts, March 14, 16, 17, and 22, 1977, in Hill, *The Black Women Oral History Project*, 7:372–73, 397–403.

7. Miriam Matthews interviewed by Eleanor Roberts, March 14, 16, 17, and 22, 1977, in Hill, *The Black Women Oral History Project*, 7:372, 394, 436, 441.

8. The Negro Art Exhibit was on view November 14–21, 1937, and demonstrates Woodard and Matthews's connections to the Los Angeles art world of the day. Gallery owner Earl Stendahl had opened his space in 1911 and showed California impressionism, pre-Columbian antiquities, and what was then contemporary art from Europe and Latin America, including the work of Picasso, Matisse, Klee, Rivera, and Siqueiros. Among Stendahl's clients were Mildred and Robert Bliss, whose major pre-Columbian holdings formed the basis of their museum, Dumbarton Oaks, in Washington, DC. Stendahl also cultivated a relationship with Walter and Louise Arensberg, whose exquisite modern collection would, in a few short years, provide curator Walter Hopps with a singular art education as a young man. Miriam Matthews interviewed by Eleanor Roberts, March 14, 16, 17, and 22, 1977, in Hill, *The Black Women Oral History Project*, 7:372, 394, 436, 441; "Art Exhibit Draws Huge Attendance," *California Eagle*, Thursday, December 2, 1937, 5B, quoted in Judith Wilson, "How the Invisible Woman Got Herself on the Cultural Map: Black Women Artists in California," in Diana Burgess Fuller and Daniela Salvioni, eds., *Art/Women/California, 1950–2000* (Berkeley: University of California Press, 2002), 201–16; "Negro Art Group," *Los Angeles Times*, November 14, 1937, C9; Higonnet, *A Museum of One's Own*, 73. Interestingly, the collection museum movement and black populations intersect in the philanthropic sector. Funds from railroad magnate Henry Huntington, for instance, contributed to the development of Tuskegee Institute. Wilson, *Negro Building*, 40–41.

9. "Artists to Open New Art Gallery Sunday," *Los Angeles Sentinel*, May 25, 1950, A2. Along with Woodard, the gallery's members included Alice Taylor Gafford, Artie Parks, Masood Ali Warren, William Pajaud, Nonie Moore, William E. Smith, Curtis Tann, Constance McClendon, William Cobb, Leon Leonard, and P'lla Mills. The only nonblack member was Tyrus Wong, a painter and Disney animator with whom Pajaud would informally study Chinese brushwork. Landscape painter Paul Lauritz, an invited artist in an August 1950 show, had been one of Gafford's instructors when she took classes at Otis Art Institute in the late 1930s. Karen Anne Mason, interview with William Pajaud (1993), *African American Artists of Los Angeles*, 78–80; Karen Anne Mason, interview with Curtis Tann (1995), *African American Artists of Los Angeles*, 115, Miriam Matthews interviewed by Eleanor Roberts, in Hill, *The Black Women Oral History Project*, 7:441; "Art Events," *Los Angeles Times*, July 30, 1950, D5; A. M., "Traffic Theme Marks Warshaw's Exhibition," *Los Angeles Times*, August 6, 1950, D4;

"Art Events," *Los Angeles Times*, September 24, 1950, D5; "Deltas Art Exhibit Sunday at Wilfandel," *Los Angeles Sentinel*, November 16, 1950, C1; Andrea Gyorody, "Tyrus Wong," in Kellie Jones, ed., *Now Dig This! Art and Black Los Angeles, 1960–1980* (New York and Los Angeles: Prestel-Delmonico and Hammer Museum, 2011), 155.

Matthews remembered Eleven Associated gallery as open for two years, while Tann claims it was only open for one. Mentions appeared in the press for about six months in 1950.

10. Gafford also had at least one show at the library's Vernon branch in 1942. Miriam Matthews interviewed by Eleanor Roberts, in Hill, *The Black Women Oral History Project*, 7:443; "Arts League Awards Veteran Artist," *Los Angeles Sentinel*, February 16, 1967, C2; Tessie Mae Brown, "Your Social," *Los Angeles Sentinel*, September 19, 1974, C2; Marsha Mitchell, "Miriam Matthews Preserves Los Angeles' Black Art," *Los Angeles Sentinel*, February 10, 1994, C5; Maria L. La Ganga, "Librarian Miriam Matthews: Chronicler of State's Black History," *Los Angeles Times*, March 2, 1983, F1.

11. Marsha Mitchell, "Miriam Matthews Preserves Los Angeles' Black Art," *Los Angeles Sentinel*, February 10, 1994, C5; Miriam Matthews interviewed by Eleanor Roberts, in Hill, *The Black Women Oral History Project*, 7:443.

12. Mabel Wilson mentions the visibility of the National Negro Insurance Association at the 1940 American Negro Exposition in Chicago. Detroit's Great Lakes Mutual Life Insurance Company was involved in art activities over decades; its owners, Louis C. Blount and Moses L. Walker, were commissioners for the city's Negro Progress Exposition in 1940. Wilson, *Negro Building*, 200–201, 216–17, 272–74.

Miriam Matthews's brother, Charles Hearde Matthews Sr., a lawyer, moved his offices into the Family Savings and Loan building at 3683 Crenshaw Boulevard in 1977; he was also on its board. Prior to that he had offices at Liberty Savings and Loan, at 2510 S. Central Avenue; he was a member of the board of directors there too, while another sister, Ella, was married to its president and was integral to the organization. One of the first places Charles Matthews set up his law practice prior to World War II was also on Central Avenue in the famous Elks Hall, demonstrating again the importance of space, its possession and control. Miriam Matthews interviewed by Eleanor Roberts, in Hill, *The Black Women Oral History Project*, 7:442, 418–20.

However, as Gerald Horne documents, after the Watts Rebellion, some black-owned financial institutions, like their white-owned contemporaries, refused to make loans to potential black clients. This included Safety Savings and Loan. Gerald Horne, *Fire This Time: The Watts Uprising and the 1960s* (New York: Da Capo, 1997; first published 1995), 312–15.

13. The show ran from December 2, 1962, to January 4, 1963. Cole Meo is listed as having studied with Gafford. Gafford herself studied at Otis Art Institute in the late 1930s and received a teaching certificate from UCLA in the early 1950s. She went on to teach children and adults in Val Verde and Newhall, a nearby town. This may be where their paths first crossed. Cole Meo would participate in *The Sapphire Show* at Suzanne Jackson's Gallery 32 in 1970. She wrote "Ritual as Art: The Work of Houston Conwill," *International Review of African American Art* 3, no. 3 (Fall 1979):4–13, a key article on Conwill's practice. "Gov. Brown to Thank Workers at Victory Fete," *Los Angeles Sentinel*, December 6, 1962, A2; "Photo Standalone 17—No Title," *Los*

Angeles Sentinel, December 13, 1962, A14; "Artist Receives Accolades for Her Many Achievements," *Los Angeles Sentinel*, September 5, 1974, C2.
14. "Magazines Feature Art Program," *Los Angeles Sentinel*, May 7, 1964, D5.
15. Some of the artists Waddy worked with through Arts West Associated were Charles White, Daniel Larue Johnson, and Melvin Edwards. Others involved with the group included Gafford; Dale and Alonzo Davis; and Ron Karenga's older brother, Chestyn Everett. Karenga first stayed with Chestyn when he arrived in Los Angeles from rural Maryland in 1958 after graduating from high school. Samella Lewis, "Ruth Waddy: A California Signature," *International Review of African American Art* 9, no. 4 (1991): 52; Scot Brown, "The US Organization, Black Power Vanguard Politics, and the United Front Ideal: Los Angeles and Beyond," *Black Scholar* 31, nos. 3–4 (Fall/Winter 2001): 22; Karen Anne Mason, interview with John Riddle (2000), *African American Artists of Los Angeles*, 15; "Artist Ruth Waddy Dies," *Sun Reporter* (San Francisco), June 26, 2003, 1.

    Norman O. Houston, head of Golden State Mutual Life Insurance, was also enlisted in this effort. Karen Anne Mason, interview with Ruth Waddy (1993), *African American Artists of Los Angeles*, 55–57; Lewis, "Ruth Waddy," 52.
16. Some of the artists showing in the earliest of Art West exhibitions included Dorothy Fleming, Helen Talley, Carol Angel, Ron Griffin, Charles Clavin, Fred R. Wilson, Johnny Otis, and of course Waddy. William (Bill) Smith and Alice Gafford had also been part of Eleven Associated. "Throngs Witness Exhibit," *Los Angeles Sentinel*, February 14, 1963, B2; "Art West Members in Show," *Los Angeles Sentinel*, July 11, 1963, A22; "Art West Members in City Festival," *Los Angeles Sentinel*, August 22, 1963, C5; "Art West Installs Officers," *Los Angeles Sentinel*, August 22, 1963, C4; "Art West Associated Makes Art History," *Los Angeles Sentinel*, January 16, 1964, A21; "Busy Month for Art West Club," *Los Angeles Sentinel*, April 30, 1964, C3; Karen Anne Mason, interview with Ruth Waddy (1993), *African American Artists of Los Angeles*, 50–60, 127–31.
17. "Throngs Witness Exhibit," *Los Angeles Sentinel*, February 14, 1963, B2; "Negro History Week Queen Contest Opens," *Los Angeles Sentinel*, December 21, 1967, C2; "Our Authors Study Club '68 Report," *Los Angeles Sentinel*, February 29, 1968, D3; Jessie Mae Brown, "Your Social Chronicler," *Los Angeles Sentinel*, February 19, 1970, C2; William Wilson, "Survey Profiles Spray Technique," *Los Angeles Times*, May 16, 1971, R48; "History Week Events Listed," *Los Angeles Sentinel*, February 10, 1972, A1; "Club Plans 'All States Tea' after Successful Black History Week," *Los Angeles Sentinel*, April 6, 1972, C5; "Authors' Party Scheduled," *Los Angeles Sentinel*, July 17, 1975, A12.
18. Karen Anne Mason, interview with Ruth Waddy (1993), *African American Artists of Los Angeles*; William Wilson, "Show Features Negroes' Prints from New Book," *Los Angeles Times*, June 27, 1965, N34; Art Seidenbaum, "One Woman's Mission to Moscow," *Los Angeles Times*, July 9, 1966, B1.
19. Johnny Otis, "Let's Talk," *Los Angeles Sentinel*, July 25, 1963, A6; "Origins of Fire at First AME Church Questioned," *Los Angeles Sentinel*, July 13, 1972, A1.
20. Karen Anne Mason, interview with William Pajaud (1993), *African American Artists of Los Angeles*, 111–12; Miriam Matthews interviewed by Eleanor Roberts, in Hill, *The Black Women Oral History Project*, 7:412. Interestingly, Meta Vaux Warrick

Fuller sought similar historical advice from W. E. B. Du Bois in connection with her tableaux for the Jamestown Exposition in 1907. Wilson, *Negro Building*, 130–34.

21. Karen Anne Mason, interview with William Pajaud (1993), *African American Artists of Los Angeles*, 178–87; Miriam Matthews interviewed by Eleanor Roberts, in Hill, *The Black Women Oral History Project*, 7:441–42.

22. Pajaud, who was in charge of purchasing art for the collection, worked wonders with his budget, which eventually reached five thousand dollars per year. The collection was liquidated in 2007. Swann Galleries, *The Golden State Mutual Life Insurance Company African-American Art Collection*, October 4, 2007; Karen Anne Mason, interview with William Pajaud (1993), *African American Artists of Los Angeles*, 191–93, 213–18; "73 Years: Golden State Mutual Life Celebrates Anniversary," *Los Angeles Sentinel*, July 8, 1998, A4.

23. Pajaud also worked with his professional colleague Bill Tara in developing Tutor/Art. Karen Anne Mason, interview with William Pajaud (1993), *African American Artists of Los Angeles*, 129–47. On the Tutor/Art Program see Francine R. Carter, "The Golden State Mutual Afro-American Art Collection," *Black Art* 1, no. 2 (Winter 1976): 15–16. On Norman O. Houston see Horne, *Fire This Time*, 177–79.

24. Horne, *Fire This Time*; Kimberlé Crenshaw and Gary Peller, "Reel Time / Real Justice," in Robert Gooding-Williams, ed., *Reading Rodney King, Reading Urban Uprising* (New York: Routledge, 1993), 56–70.

25. Karen Anne Mason, interview with Alonzo Davis (1994), *African American Artists of Los Angeles*, 133.

26. Karen Anne Mason, interview with Alonzo Davis (1994), *African American Artists of Los Angeles*, 133.

27. Karen Anne Mason, interview with Alonzo Davis (1994), *African American Artists of Los Angeles*, 107; Dale Davis in *Leimert Park: The Story of a Village in South Central Los Angeles* (dir. Jeanette Lindsay; Foster Johnson Studios, 2008).

28. The Davis brothers' maternal grandfather Stephen Moses was a contemporary of Booker T. Washington who opened the first elementary and secondary schools for black people in the town of Anniston, Alabama. Their mother, aunts, and uncles attended Talladega College in Alabama. Their father, Alonzo Davis Sr., was born in Washington, DC, attended Howard University, studied briefly at Yale, and received a PhD from the University of Minnesota in child psychology. Karen Anne Mason, interview with Alonzo Davis (1994), *African American Artists of Los Angeles*, 22–28.

29. Karen Anne Mason, interview with Alonzo Davis (1994), *African American Artists of Los Angeles*, 24–25.

30. Karen Anne Mason, interview with Alonzo Davis (1994), *African American Artists of Los Angeles*, 45, 52–53.

31. Personal communication, Dale Brockman Davis, October 19, 2012.

32. Horne, *Fire This Time*, 294–95. During the 1970s and 1980s numerous African American business owners in South LA would then turn around and sell them to Korean entrepreneurs. See Sumi K. Cho, "Korean Americans vs. African Americans: Conflict and Construction," in Gooding-Williams, *Reading Rodney King*, 196–211.

Leimert Park, one of the first planned communities in Los Angeles, was created by Walter H. Leimert in 1928 and designed by the Olmsted Brothers Company. It boasted a Home Owners Association and was restricted to white residents until the

Los Angeles Westside began changing in the 1950s and 1960s. Gil Robertson, "Inside Leimert Park," *Black Enterprise* 27, no. 11 (June 1997): 336; *Leimert Park* (dir. Lindsay); Karen Anne Mason, interview with Alonzo Davis (1994), *African American Artists of Los Angeles*, 138, 143–45, 148; Kay Lindsay, "Brockman Gallery," *Art Papers*, July–August 1990, 23; Dale Davis, "Brockman Gallery," in Connie Rogers Tilton and Lindsay Charlwood, eds., *L.A. Object and David Hammons Body Prints* (New York: Tilton Gallery, 2011), 76–84; California African American Museum, *Affirming a Visual Heritage: The Collection of Alonzo and Dale Davis* (Los Angeles: California African American Museum, 1996).

33. While early on he thought of pursuing a degree in art therapy, ultimately Alonzo embraced the metaphysical and spiritual through his own art practice. Karen Anne Mason, interview with Alonzo Davis (1994), *African American Artists of Los Angeles*, 71–72, 106, 241–46, 253, 286; Steve Harvey, "Anti-L.A. Zinger: Look Who's Talking," *Los Angeles Times*, November 8, 1983, C1; K. Jones, *Now Dig This!*, 217–31; Andrea Gyorody, "Alonzo Davis," and Connie H. Choi, "Dale Brockman Davis," in K. Jones, *Now Dig This!*, 258, 259.

34. "Brockman Gallery Presents Paintings, Sculpture Drawings and Graphics," September 15–October 8, 1967; "Christmas Come to Brockman Gallery," December 3–24, 1967; "Brockman Gallery Presents Noah Purifoy and David Hammons," February 5–March 2, 1969 (this show was eventually extended); Alonzo Davis, Brockman Gallery, to Mr. Donahue, Los Angeles County Museum of Art, February 27, 1969; Brockman Gallery file, Balch Art Research Library, Los Angeles County Museum of Art.

35. William Wilson, "Art Walk," *Los Angeles Times*, March 26, 1971, F8.

36. Information on *Niggers Ain't Never Ever Gonna Be Nothin'—All They Want to Do Is Drink and Fuck* can be found in Wilson, "Art Walk," F8; Melinda Tarbell, "Los Angeles," *Arts Magazine* 45 (May 1971): 48; and Karen Anne Mason, interview with Noah Purifoy (1992), *African American Artists of Los Angeles*, 47–54.

37. Karen Anne Mason, interview with Noah Purifoy (1992), *African American Artists of Los Angeles*, 51.

38. Michael Omi and Howard Winant, "The Los Angeles 'Race Riot' and Contemporary U.S. Politics," in Gooding-Williams, *Reading Rodney King*, 97–114.

39. Tarbell, "Los Angeles," 48.

40. Karen Anne Mason, interview with Noah Purifoy (1992), *African American Artists of Los Angeles*, 49.

41. Interestingly, this companion piece may have even been inspired by William Wilson's review, one of the few to find redeeming points in the work of an African American artist. Wilson writes: "Purifoy's important effort could only be more effective moved into a dustless La Cienega gallery next to the chic boutiques and Rolls-Royces." William Wilson, "Art Walk," *Los Angeles Times*, March 26, 1971, F8.

42. Jacob Lawrence's exhibition took place in 1981. Elizabeth Catlett's show was supported, in part, by Charles White, her first husband. This was done discreetly due to remaining tensions in their relationship. Karen Anne Mason, interview with Alonzo Davis (1994), *African American Artists of Los Angeles*, 214–15, 151, 169–70, 199–202.

43. Karen Anne Mason, interview with Alonzo Davis (1994), *African American Artists of Los Angeles*, 153, 183–84; K. Jones, *Now Dig This!*, 333.

44. Karen Anne Mason, interview with Alonzo Davis (1994), *African American Artists of Los Angeles*, 202; *Leimert Park* (dir. Lindsay, 2008).
45. At the time Brockman Gallery opened in 1967 Alonzo was a teacher at Crenshaw High School. After leaving that position in 1970 and before being able to work full-time at Brockman in 1976 he taught as an adjunct professor at various colleges and universities, including Mount Saint Antonio College, Pasadena City College, UCLA, California State University at Northridge, and Otis Art Institute. Dale Davis left the day-to-day operations of the gallery business by 1973, eventually helping out with their nonprofit Brockman Gallery Productions. He remained as a high school teacher with the Los Angeles Unified School District for thirty-five years. Alonzo and Dale's mother and aunt also purchased works to help keep the gallery afloat. These later became part of the Brockman Gallery Collection, which has been shown throughout the years. Karen Anne Mason, interview with Alonzo Davis (1994), *African American Artists of Los Angeles*, viii–ix, 204–5. *Affirming a Visual Heritage: The Collection of Alonzo and Dale Davis* (Los Angeles: California African-American Museum, 1996).
46. James Prigoff and Robin J. Dunitz, *Walls of Heritage, Walls of Pride: African American Murals* (San Francisco: Pomegranate, 2000).
47. "County Seeks Walls for Mural Artists," *Los Angeles Times*, December 9, 1973, CS2; "Six Artists Selected for Mural Project," *Los Angeles Times*, January 24, 1974, WS8; Lee Curtis Hampton, "Street Art," *Neworld* 1 (Spring 1975): 24–29; Suzanne Muchnic, "Painting the Town for Fun, Profit and Jobs," *Los Angeles Times*, October 22, 1978, L102; "Professional Artist Employment Program Gets Underway at Brockman Gallery Productions," *Black Art* 2, no. 1 (Fall 1977): 68; Josine Ianco Starrels, "Art News," *Los Angeles Times*, November 6, 1977, O89; K. Jones, *Now Dig This!*, 302.
48. Their congressperson, Yvonne Braithwaite Burke, suggested this approach because as a nonprofit Brockman Gallery Productions was eligible for funds from the National Endowment of the Arts. Its Expansion Arts program (begun in 1971 and headed at that time by Vantile Whitfield, a former Los Angeles theater producer) funded the offsite projects. Karen Anne Mason, interview with Alonzo Davis (1994), *African American Artists of Los Angeles*, 257–65.
49. Richard Wyatt, Kent Twitchell, Judith Baca, Frank Romero, Willie Herron (of the Chicano performance collective Asco), and Roderick Sykes (a founder of St. Elmo Village, a live/work environment established in the 1960s) all participated in Davis's Olympic mural project.
50. Karen Anne Mason, interview with Alonzo Davis (1994), *African American Artists of Los Angeles*, 270–75; Barbara Isenberg, "Freeway Fare: Olympic Murals," *Los Angeles Times*, July 20, 1983, H1; "Art in the Fast Lane," *Los Angeles Times*, September 18, 1983, Z23; "Artists Battle Traffic and Smog," *Washington Post*, February 8, 1984, F15; Suzanne Muchnic, "Freeway Artists Paint in Danger," *Los Angeles Times*, April 15, 1984, X76; Suzanne Muchnic, "Art from the Fast Lane," *Los Angeles Times*, April 15, 1984, X76; Joseph Giovanni, "Murals Deck Freeways Approaching Olympics," *New York Times*, July 17, 1984, C16; Lois Timnick, "A Dash of Art and Color for the 55-Mile-an-Hour Set," *Los Angeles Times*, June 23, 1984, F2; Morgan Gendel, "Black Eye for Mural," *Los Angeles Times*, June 27, 1984, L2; "The Arts," *Los Angeles Times*, August 15, 1984, SE-A4. Other artists connected with the Olympic mural program included Terry Schoonhoven, Glenna Boltuch, and John Wehrle.

51. Alicia Griffin and Debbie Byars were the managers of the Brockman enterprise in the late 1980s. Having completed his MFA at Otis Art Institute in 1973, Alonzo Davis moved around the country following the shuttering of Brockman, in a series of administrative and academic positions: coordinator, Sacramento Metropolitan Arts Commission; vice president and dean of academic affairs, San Antonio Art Institute; and dean of academic affairs, Memphis College of Art. Karen Anne Mason, interview with Alonzo Davis (1994), *African American Artists of Los Angeles*, viii–ix, 311–13.
52. Karen Anne Mason, interview with Suzanne Jackson (1998), *African American Artists of Los Angeles*, 1–34. Jackson's parents were Roy Dedrick Jackson, born in Poplar Bluff, Missouri, and Anne Marie (Butler) Jackson, born in St. Louis, Missouri.
53. Karen Anne Mason, interview with Suzanne Jackson (1998), *African American Artists of Los Angeles*, 39–40, 44, 79, 90.
54. *Fly Blackbird* toured to the West Coast in the early 1960s. There Hatch met Los Angeles artist Camille Billops, his future wife. In the wake of the Watts rebellion, C. Bernard Jackson opened the Inner City Cultural Center, which supported diverse creative cultures and the careers of people like George Takei, Betye Saar, Edward James Olmos, and Beah Richards. Karen Anne Mason, interview with Suzanne Jackson (1998), *African American Artists of Los Angeles*, 74–75.
55. Karen Anne Mason, interview with Suzanne Jackson (1998), *African American Artists of Los Angeles*, 53–61, 89, 93–95.
56. The gallery took its name from the apartment suite number, 32; Jackson was inspired by the precedent of Alfred Stieglitz's modernist gallery, 291. Karen Anne Mason, interview with Suzanne Jackson (1998), *African American Artists of Los Angeles*, 113–17, 253. Mae Tate, "Suzanne Jackson," *Black Art* 4, no. 3 (1980): 13.
57. On Gallery 32 and the development of this gallery scene see Tate, "Suzanne Jackson," 3–21.
58. Karen Anne Mason, interview with Suzanne Jackson (1998), *African American Artists of Los Angeles*, 200.
59. Most probably Jackson knew Stinson from her post office days.
60. In her oral history Suzanne Jackson seems to suggest that Elizabeth Leigh-Taylor is a white artist. However, in a more recent telephone call she told the author that Leigh-Taylor's grandfather or father was a black or colored South African and that her family had come to the United States to escape and fight apartheid. Karen Anne Mason, interview with Suzanne Jackson (1998), *African American Artists of Los Angeles*, 239; personal communication, May 2013.
61. Karen Anne Mason, interview with Suzanne Jackson (1998), *African American Artists of Los Angeles*, 256–57. For more on Gallery 32 and its exhibitions see Carolyn Peter and Damon Willick, *Gallery 32 and Its Circle* (Los Angeles: Laband Art Gallery, Loyola Marymount University, 2009).
62. Karen Anne Mason, interview with Suzanne Jackson (1998), *African American Artists of Los Angeles*, 126.
63. She was harassed on tax issues and even jailed for parking violations. Karen Anne Mason, interview with Suzanne Jackson (1998), *African American Artists of Los Angeles*, 150–53, 124–34. Yvonne Carter, widow of Alprentice Bunchy Carter, the recently assassinated leader of the Los Angeles Panthers, approached Jackson about doing the Emory Douglas show.

64. Suzanne Jackson's turn as an exotic dancer was perhaps the most surprising effort at keeping Gallery 32 afloat. Karen Anne Mason, interview with Suzanne Jackson (1998), *African American Artists of Los Angeles*, 146.

65. Samella Lewis to Mr. and Mrs. Roy D. Jackson, August 17, 1970, in Samella Lewis Papers (collection 1132), Box 2, Folder: Letters & Statements County Museum, item no. 15, Manuscripts, Archives, and Rare Book Library, Emory University (hereafter MARBL); Karen Anne Mason, interview with Suzanne Jackson (1998), *African American Artists of Los Angeles*, 102, 119, 142–43; Peter and Willick, *Gallery 32 and Its Circle*, 6–7. Jackson married Pete M. Mhunzi, né Walter Preston Smith. They later divorced but had one son, Rafiki Casey Dedrick Smith-Mhunzi.

66. On Jackson's appointment to the California Arts Commission see Mary Murphy, "CAC Appointees Practicing Artists," *Los Angeles Times*, February 18, 1975, G7.

   Black Expo '72 was held for four days in September 1972 and dreamed of itself as a celebration of black culture and gathering of black people in the vein of the Woodstock music festival of 1969 featuring a range of producers, from the then-popular films of Gordon Parks and Melvin Van Peebles to the just-emerging. Ray Charles performed, among others. Thulani Davis (then known simply as Thulani) coordinated poetry presentations. The exhibition Jackson put together included almost two hundred artists from the past—such as Edmonia Lewis, who had important, if barely remembered, works at the nearby San Jose Public Library, and Henry O. Tanner—as well as contemporary headliners like Romare Bearden and the young radical Emory Douglas.

   As Jackson recounts, it was Black Expo '72 that inspired work on another exhibition project over the next several years, a show of "black masters." Based on the research she had done for Black Expo '72, rather than produce a four-day show at a convention center in the mode of the grand exposition, she desired a more lasting and well-documented presence of the history of African American artists. With research partner Sherry Ayo, a staff member at Berkeley Art Museum, Jackson recalls they honed the idea over several years, presenting it to the Los Angeles County Museum of Art. The show would eventually come to fruition, but without any further input from them or acknowledgment of their contribution. *Two Centuries of Black American Art*, organized by artist and curator David Driskell, opened at LACMA in 1976. Karen Anne Mason, interview with Suzanne Jackson (1998), *African American Artists of Los Angeles*, 279–89; Suzanne Jackson to Mrs. Ankrum, November 28, 1971, and Suzanne Jackson to Joan Ankrum and William Challee, February 13, 1973, Suzanne Jackson file, Ankrum Gallery Records, 1960–1990, Archives of American Art, Smithsonian Institution (hereafter AGR); "Suzanne Jackson Named Art Coordinator for EXPO '72," *Sun Reporter*, June 24, 1972, 34; Gina Taylor, "Black Expo Runs into Big Hassle," *Sun Reporter*, July 29, 1972, 2; "Black Messages," *Sun Reporter*, July 29, 1972, 32; Earl Caldwell, "New Black Culture, Quietly Evolving in All of the Arts since the 1960's, Comes into Focus at Exposition," *New York Times*, September 24, 1972, 32.

67. Suzanne Jackson quoted in Suzanne Muchnic, "Painting the Town for Fun, Profit and Jobs," *Los Angeles Times*, October 22, 1978, 103. See also Tate, "Suzanne Jackson," 20.

68. On Jackson's show in Stockton see "Black Artist to Exhibit Work in UOP Tower," *Stockton (California) Record*, February 17, 1972, 32; "BSU Presents Black Artist," *The*

Pacifican, February 15, [1972], both in Clippings, Suzanne Jackson file, AGR; Karen Anne Mason, interview with Suzanne Jackson (1998), *African American Artists of Los Angeles*, 183; Josine Ianco-Starrels, "Art News: Gilbert Mosaics on View," *Los Angeles Times*, February 2, 1975, 67. Several years later Larry Walker would host a group show with Jackson, Charles White, and William Pajaud.

On Jackson at Ankrum Gallery see Karen Anne Mason, interview with Suzanne Jackson (1998), *African American Artists of Los Angeles*, 185–86; Joan Ankrum statement, January 5, 1974, and "Suzanne Jackson—Paintings and Drawings," press release, September 1978, and "Invoices," Suzanne Jackson file, AGR; "Greet Artist," *Los Angeles Sentinel*, September 12, 1974; Gordon J. Hazlitt, "Creating Her Own World," *ArtNews* 73 (November 1974): 38. A 1974 solo show was accompanied by a concert by Troy Robinson, a former AACM member and the music director at the Compton Communicative Arts Academy; Robinson's pieces had also appeared in theaters and on television.

On Jackson in New York see Benny Andrews to Suzanne Jackson, August 4, 1973, and Joan Ankrum to Benny Andrews, August 12, 1973, Suzanne Jackson file, AGR; Jackson was included in the exhibition *Black U.S.A.*, curated by Andrews for the New York Cultural Center that year. Thomas W. Leavitt, director, Herbert F. Johnson Museum, Cornell University, to Suzanne Jackson, September 7, 1973, Suzanne Jackson file, AGR; the artist participated in "Directions in Afro-American Art" at the museum in April 1974. Jackson was also featured in Just Above Midtown Gallery's inaugural exhibition *Statements Known and Unknown* of 1974, and the 1977 exhibition *In Recognition*, which featured women artists including Valerie Maynard, Betye Saar, Wendy Wilson, Howardena Pindell, Shelley Farkas, Senga Nengudi, and Barbara Chase-Riboud. See Barbara Cavaliere, "Arts Reviews," *Arts Magazine* 51, no. 7 (March 1977): 27–28; Benny Andrews, "A JAM Session on Madison Avenue," *Encore American and Worldwide News*, March 21, 1977, 34.

69. Karen Anne Mason, interview with Suzanne Jackson (1998), *African American Artists of Los Angeles*, 241–42, 183–85, 80.
70. *What I Love: Paintings, Poetry, and a Drawing*, 1972, was published by Samella Lewis's company Contemporary Crafts, Inc., while Jackson self-published *Animal*, 1978, under her own imprint, Sunflower Seed Productions. For critical reception see Henry J. Seldis, "Art Walk: A Critical Guide to the Galleries," *Los Angeles Times*, September 15, 1972, part 4, p. 4; Henry J. Seldis, "Art Walk: A Critical Guide to the Galleries," *Los Angeles Times*, September 13, 1974, part 4, p. 10; William Wilson, "A Critical Guide to the Galleries," *Los Angeles Times*, September 24, 1976, F11.

For Printed Matter Inc.—the New York–based organization dedicated to artist-generated publications begun in 1976—Jackson's book *Animal* did not fit its concept of a proper artist's book even with Jackson's intricate weaving of text and image and her clear self-publication. In a response to her query about distribution, the organization responded, "Unfortunately we will not be able to distribute it, since we distribute only self referential artists' books, and not books containing reproductions of drawings and paintings conceived of independently." Nancy Princenthal, Printed Matter Inc., to Suzanne Jackson c/o Sunflower Seed Productions, November 15, 1978, Suzanne Jackson, Artist File, Museum of Modern Art, New York.

71. Liz Herron, *Streets of Desire: Women's Fiction in the Twentieth Century City* (London: Virago, 1993), 3, quoted in Linda McDowell, *Gender, Identity, and Place: Understanding Feminist Geographies* (Minneapolis: University of Minnesota Press, 1999), 155.
72. Suzanne Jackson, *What I Love* (Los Angeles: Contemporary Crafts, Inc., 1972), unpaginated. In fact, Jackson first came to attention as an artist in Los Angeles when paintings of white people that she submitted to the Watts Festival sold. Karen Anne Mason, interview with Suzanne Jackson (1998), *African American Artists of Los Angeles*, 107–9, 51, 273–75. See also in this regard a nice comparison of Jackson and writer Pearl Cleage from this time period: Janice Cobb, "The Parallel Evolution of Greatness," *Sun Reporter*, March 24, 1973, 16.
73. Karen Anne Mason, interview with Suzanne Jackson (1998), *African American Artists of Los Angeles*, 88–89.
74. Suzanne Jackson quoted in Tate, "Suzanne Jackson," 16.
75. Karen Anne Mason, interview with Suzanne Jackson (1998), *African American Artists of Los Angeles*, 277–78, 43. In 1996 Jackson moved to Savannah, Georgia, to teach at Savannah College of Art and Design. She has been based there ever since.
76. Marvel Cooke, "Carving for Posterity," *New York Amsterdam News*, November 13, 1937, 12, on Henry "Mike" Bannarn; Terry Adkins, *Nutjuitok (Polar Star) after Matthew Henson*, 2012, a project for the exhibition *Intense Proximity: An Anthology of the Near and the Far*, La Triennale 2012, Palais de Tokyo, curated by Okwui Enwezor. See also Terry Adkins, "Nutjuitok (Polar Star) after Matthew Henson," *Journal de la Triennale* no. 5, (2012): 22–27; Isaac Julien, *True North: Fantome Afrique* (Ostfildern: Hatje Cantz, 2006); Tavares Strachan, *I Belong Here* (Nassau, Bahamas, and Hong Kong: Isolated Labs and Conceptio Unlimited, 2013).
77. Ankrum Gallery had at least two locations: 930 N. La Cienega Boulevard, then 657 N. La Cienega Boulevard. It appears that Joan Ankrum actually owned the latter space, a two-story building appointed with sculpture gardens on its roof and a patio. Michael Leopold, "There Aren't Any Come-Ons at This Elegant Gallery," *Society West* (December 1977): 13, in AGR.
78. Joan Ankrum was inspired to open her gallery by her nephew Morris Broderson, an artist who was also deaf. She represented him throughout the gallery's life. Ankrum's partner and gallery associate was Bill Chalee, a veteran actor who appeared in the film *Five Easy Pieces* (1970). See AGR, and "Oral History Interview with Joan Ankrum, 1997 November 5–1998 February 4," both Archives of American Art, Smithsonian Institution; Ankrum Gallery file, Balch Art Research Library, Los Angeles County Museum of Art.
79. Ceeje—open from 1962 to 1970 and founded by Cecil Hedrick and Jerry Jerome—also exhibited the work of Mexican American artists of the era, including Roberto Chavez and Eduardo Carrillo. It was located down the street from Ankrum Gallery. See Terezita Romo, "Mexican Heritage, American Art: Six Angeleno Artists," in Chon A. Noriega, Terezita Romo, and Pilar Tompkins Rivas, eds., *L.A. Xicano* (Los Angeles: UCLA Chicano Studies Research Center Press, 2011), 22–23, 27n57.
80. Kristine McKenna, *The Ferus Gallery: A Place to Begin* (Göttingen, Germany: Steidl, 2009), 201; Dwan Gallery Records, 1959–82, Archives of American Art; "Oral History Interview with Virginia Dwan, 1984 March 21–June 7," Archives of American

Art, Smithsonian Institution; Hunter Drohojowska-Philp, *Rebels in Paradise: The Los Angeles Art Scene and the 1960s* (New York: Henry Holt, 2011), chap. 8.
81. Jones, introduction, and Franklin Sirmans, "Find the Cave, Hold the Torch: Making Art Shows since Walter Hopps," in K. Jones, *Now Dig This!*, 15–27, 57–67.
82. Henry T. Hopkins, "Third Annual Exhibition of California Painting and Sculpture," *Artforum* 1, no. 9 (March 1963): 47; Donald Factor, "Assemblage," *Artforum* 2 (Summer 1964): 38.
83. For more on the history of the Pasadena Art Museum see Jay Belloli and Karen Jacobson, *Radical Past: Contemporary Art and Music in Pasadena, 1960–1974* (Pasadena: Armory Center for the Arts / Art Center College of Design, 1999). Significantly, during this period the exhibition *Romare Bearden: The Prevalence of Ritual*, curated by Caroll Greene Jr. for the Museum of Modern Art, traveled to the Pasadena Art Museum, where it was on view December 20, 1971–January 30, 1972. Yet it is not listed in the aforementioned institutional history. See William Wilson, "Pasadena Art Museum: Black Artist Exhibits Works," *Los Angeles Times*, January 3, 1972, F12.
84. Among the Los Angeles artists included in *The Negro in American Art* were Ed Bereal, Melvin Edwards, Marvin Harden, Daniel LaRue Johnson, Sargent Johnson, Judson Powell, Noah Purifoy, Betye Saar, Raymond Saunders, Van Slater, Ruth G. Waddy, and Charles White. The exhibition traveled to the University of California, Davis, and the Fine Arts Gallery of San Diego, ending its tour at the Oakland Museum in 1967. Eventually the Dickson Art Center would be renamed Wight Art Gallery in celebration of Frederick Wight's vision for art in a collegiate setting. In 1994 the Wight Art Gallery became the Armand Hammer Museum. Dickson Art Center, *The Negro in American Art* (Los Angeles: UCLA Art Galleries, Dickson Art Center, 1966); "Negro Culture Contribution to Be Shown," *Los Angeles Times*, September 4, 1966, 130; Henry J. Seldis, "Negro in Art—Talent Is Color Blind," *Los Angeles Times*, September 25, 1966, M34; Kimmis Hendrick, "I Am a Negro—That Is What I Am," *Christian Science Monitor*, November 14, 1966, 6.
85. Tony Bennett, *The Birth of the Museum: History, Theory, Politics* (London: Routledge, 1995), 62, 67.
86. The Black Culture Festival was held December 28, 1968. Sharon E. Fay, "Black Culture Festival: Some Firsts at the Museum of Art," *Los Angeles Times*, December 31, 1968, B5; Alex Apostolides, "Black Is Beautiful at County Art Museum," *Los Angeles Free Press*, January 3, 1969; Sculpture of Black Africa / Paul Tishman Collection file, Balch Art Research Library, Los Angeles County Museum of Art. For interesting reviews of the show itself see Jehanne Teilhet, "Unity in Diversity in Black Africa Sculpture," *Los Angeles Times*, October 20, 1968, 11, and Arthur Miller, "Two Large Shows of African Art," *Los Angeles Herald Examiner*, November 10, 1968. See also Roy Sieber and Arnold Rubin, *Sculpture of Black Africa: The Paul Tishman Collection* (Los Angeles: Los Angeles County Museum of Art, 1968).
87. Sharon E. Fay, "Black Culture Festival: Some Firsts at the Museum of Art," *Los Angeles Times*, December 31, 1968, B5.
88. Karen Anne Mason, interview with Cecil Fergerson (1996), *African American Artists of Los Angeles*, 152–53.
89. The show traveled to the Santa Barbara Museum of Art.

90. Ebria Feinblatt, foreword to Joseph E. Young, *Three Graphic Artists: Charles White, David Hammons, Timothy Washington* (Los Angeles: Los Angeles County Museum of Art, 1971), 4.
91. Timothy Washington quoted in Joseph E. Young, "Three Graphic Artists," in Young, *Three Graphic Artists*, 9. Young developed some of his ideas in an earlier review. See Joseph E. Young, "Los Angeles," *Art International* 14 (October 20, 1970): 74.
92. The works purchased were Hammons, *Injustice Case*, 1970; Washington, *One Nation under God*, 1970; and White, *Seed of Love*, 1969. While it has been mentioned that all works were sold by Brockman Gallery, it is more likely that at least White's piece came from Heritage Gallery, which represented him. See Three Graphic Artists file, Balch Art Research Library, Los Angeles County Museum of Art. The exhibition catalogue also lists Washington's piece *Parakeets*, 1970, as a museum purchase: Young, *Three Graphic Artists*, 14.
93. Los Angeles 1972: A Panorama of Black Artists file, Balch Art Research Library, Los Angeles County Museum of Art.
94. MoMA's *Romare Bearden: The Prevalence of Ritual* exhibition eventually traveled to the Pasadena Art Museum, where it was on view December 20, 1971–January 30, 1971, just prior to the opening of LACMA's *Los Angeles, 1972: A Panorama of Black Artists*.
95. Carroll Greene Jr., *Los Angeles 1972: A Panorama of Black Artists* (Los Angeles: Los Angeles County Museum of Art, 1972), unpaginated.
96. *Two Centuries of Black American Art* was also seen at the High Museum of Art, Atlanta, Museum of Fine Arts, Dallas, and the Brooklyn Museum. As a student at Fisk at the time, Terry Adkins also worked on this project with David Driskell.
97. For instance, in 1967 Caroll Greene Jr. and Romare Bearden had organized *The Evolution of Afro-American Artists: 1800–1950* for the City College of New York.
98. The contemporary was brought in, however, through film, music, and lectures. The Broadway department store even hosted demonstrations by Alonzo Davis, Ruth Waddy, and Charles Dickson. "Artists Paid Tribute," *Los Angeles Sentinel*, September 30, 1976, B6; "The Broadway Salutes 'Two Centuries of Black American Art,'" *Los Angeles Times*, October 17, 1976, F20. On other programs see "Black Art Exhibit to Feature Show," *Los Angeles Times*, October 10, 1976, WS4, and "Black Composers' Works at Museum," *Los Angeles Times*, November 2, 1976, E11.
99. LACMA owned several works by Tanner but almost never put them on view.
100. David C. Driskell quoted in C. Gerald Fraser, "'Black Art' Label Disputed by Curator," *New York Times*, June 29, 1977, 63. C. Gerald Fraser was one of the few African American critics at the *New York Times* during this period.
101. David C. Driskell quoted in Fraser, "'Black Art' Label Disputed by Curator."
102. On protest against major American museums during this period see Francis Frascina, *Art, Politics and Dissent: Aspects of the Art Left in Sixties America* (Manchester, UK: Manchester University Press, 1999); Julia Bryan-Wilson, *Art Workers: Radical Practice in the Vietnam War Era* (Berkeley: University of California Press, 2009); Kellie Jones, "'It's Not Enough to Say "Black Is Beautiful"': Abstraction at the Whitney, 1969–1974," in Kobena Mercer, ed., *Discrepant Abstractions* (London: Institute of International Visual Arts, 2006).

103. Karen Anne Mason, interview with Cecil Fergerson (1996), *African American Artists of Los Angeles*, 140.
104. Karen Anne Mason, interview with Cecil Fergerson (1996), *African American Artists of Los Angeles*.
105. Emory Holmes II, "A Pit Bull in the World of Fine Art," *Los Angeles Times Magazine*, February 14, 1999, 33.
106. Kimberlé Crenshaw and Gary Peller, "Reel Time / Real Justice," and Michael Omi and Howard Winant, "The Los Angeles 'Race Riot' and Contemporary U.S. Politics," both in Gooding-Williams, *Reading Rodney King*.
107. Karen Anne Mason, interview with Cecil Fergerson (1996), *African American Artists of Los Angeles*, 290.
108. Karen Anne Mason, interview with Cecil Fergerson (1996), *African American Artists of Los Angeles*, 99–100, 147, 260–61, 472.
109. Emory Holmes II, "A Pit Bull in the World of Fine Art," *Los Angeles Times Magazine*, February 14, 1999, 33–34; Karen Anne Mason, interview with Cecil Fergerson (1996), *African American Artists of Los Angeles*, 261.
110. James Weschler, interview with Edward Kienholz, in *Los Angeles Art Community* (Los Angeles: Oral History Program of the University of California, 1976), 385–87.
111. Some of those who formed a part of the BAC early on were Alonzo Davis, John Outterbridge, John Riddle, Gloria Bohanon, Arenzo Smith, and Dan Concholar. Karen Anne Mason, interview with Cecil Fergerson (1996), *African American Artists of Los Angeles*, 163. Fergerson also gained a lot of respect from the Mexican American community for his work with those artists at LACMA and beyond. See Emory Holmes II, "A Pit Bull in the World of Fine Art," *Los Angeles Times Magazine*, February 14, 1999, 34; Robert Tejada, "Los Angeles Snapshots," in K. Jones, *Now Dig This!*, 69–83.
112. "Museum Group Holds Black Lecture Series," *Los Angeles Sentinel*, August 28, 1969, A12; "Local Black Art Series to Be Held," *Los Angeles Sentinel*, September 18, 1969, A10; "Black Arts Council Hosts Bernie Casey, Dr. Lewis," *Los Angeles Sentinel*, September 25, 1969, A11; "Attendance Mark Set at Black Arts Lecture," *Los Angeles Sentinel*, October 2, 1969, A11; "Charles White, Artist, to Host 2nd Art Lecture," *Los Angeles Sentinel*, October 16, 1969, A12; "Music, Panel Discussion to Highlight Black Art Show," *Los Angeles Sentinel*, December 4, 1969, B6; Karen Anne Mason, interview with Cecil Fergerson (1996), *African American Artists of Los Angeles*, 176–78, 241–42.
113. Karen Anne Mason, interview with Cecil Fergerson (1996), *African American Artists of Los Angeles*, 214–16.
114. Suzanne Jackson to Mrs. Samella Lewis, November 29, 1971, Samella Lewis Papers (collection 1132), Box 36, Folder: Front of Box, item no. 35, MARBL.
115. See Claude Booker, "Critic Criticized," *Los Angeles Times*, February 27, 1972, X4, and William Wilson, "County Museum Showing Work by Local Blacks," *Los Angeles Times*, February 13, 1972, V50. For Cecil Fergerson's take on the *Panorama* show see Karen Anne Mason, interview with Cecil Fergerson (1996), *African American Artists of Los Angeles*, 209–14.
116. "Black Artists Highlighted at County Museum," *Los Angeles Sentinel*, February 10,

1972, B4A, and "Works of Local Black Artists Praised," *Los Angeles Sentinel*, February 24, 1972, B3A.

117. Karen Anne Mason, interview with Cecil Fergerson (1996), *African American Artists of Los Angeles*, 227–30; Rexford A. Stead, "Acknowledgments," in David C. Driskell, *Two Centuries of Black American Art* (Los Angeles: Los Angeles County Museum of Art, 1976), 7. The BAC's role in the exhibition was also acknowledged in the *New York Times*. See C. Gerald Fraser, "'Black Art' Label Disputed by Curator," *New York Times*, June 29, 1977, 63. Claude Booker died suddenly of a heart attack in 1974. He was thirty-six years old.

118. Cooks, *Exhibiting Blackness*, 102. Cooks offers a masterful reading of all these LACMA shows; see Cooks, *Exhibiting Blackness*, chap. 3.

119. Josine Ianco-Starrels, "Exhibit of Black Works Opens Thursday," *Los Angeles Times*, September 26, 1976, N71; and "Black American Art Day Proclaimed by Mayor Bradley," *The Skanner* (Portland, OR), October 14, 1976, 10.

120. The board members were Charles Z. Wilson and Robert Wilson. LACMA's version of this institutional history can be found on its website at http://www.lacma.org/whos-who, accessed July 9, 2016.

121. Karen Anne Mason, interviews with Suzanne Jackson (1998, pp. 253–54) and Cecil Fergerson (1996, pp. 172, 164, 194–98, 340, 346–47, 471–72, 475), *African American Artists of Los Angeles*; William Wilson, "A Serving of Afro-Americana on Tennis Court," *Los Angeles Times*, July 4, 1971, 44; letter from Black Arts Council regarding the Security-Pacific National Bank Traveling Exhibit of Black Artists, Samella Lewis Papers (collection 1132), Box 10, Folder: Black Arts Council, item no. 28, MARBL; K. Jones, *Now Dig This!*, 337.

122. Artists whose works appeared on the show included Noah Purifoy, Bernie Casey, Abdu, and possibly Suzanne Jackson. Claude Booker to Mrs. Paul G. Lewis, January 3, 1973, Samella Lewis Papers (collection 1132), Box 10, Folder: Black Arts Council, item no. 29, MARBL, and Claude Booker to Mrs. Joan Ankrum, Bernie Casey file, in AGR. For more on *Black Omnibus* see also the PBS affiliate Channel Thirteen's website: "Black Omnibus, Hosted by James Earl Jones," Broadcasting While Black, Thirteen, http://www.thirteen.org/broadcastingwhileblack/video/black-omnibus-hosted-by-james-earl-jones/, accessed July 9, 2016.

123. For more on Lewis's early life see Mary Jane Hewitt, *Interview of Samella Lewis: Artist and Influence* (New York: Hatch Billops Collection, 2002); and Samella Lewis interviewed by Richard Cándida Smith, *Image and Belief* (Los Angeles: Getty Research Institute for the Arts and Humanities, 1999); Karen Anne Mason, interview with Samella Lewis (1995), *African American Artists of Los Angeles*.

124. Lewis taught at Morgan State University between 1948 and 1953, and at Florida Agricultural & Mechanical University from 1953 to 1958.

125. Lewis interviewed by Smith, *Image and Belief*, 148–72; Leonard Wise, "Portrait of Samella Lewis," *Essence* 3, no. 10 (February 1973): 80; Hewitt, *Interview of Samella Lewis*, 160.

126. Another important figure pressing for change at LACMA was Dr. J. Alfred Canon. A community leader and psychiatrist based at UCLA, Canon was known for demanding better medical facilities and care for inner cities, with a particular focus on mental health. Two other alliances focusing on change at LACMA with which

Canon may have been involved were the Committee for the Encouragement of Afro-American Art (a group internal to LACMA itself) and Concerned Citizens for Black Art. See Untitled Statement, January 22, 1971, in Samella Lewis Papers (collection 1132), Box 37, Folder: LA Museum Protest, item no. 36, MARBL; Naima J. Keith, "Samella Lewis," in K. Jones, *Now Dig This!*, 261; Lewis interviewed by Smith, *Image and Belief*, 188–89, 321; George Ramos, "Had an Apparent Heart Attack in Zimbabwe: Dr. J. Alfred Canon, Health Crusader," *Los Angeles Times*, March 11, 1988.

127. "Museum Group Holds Black Lecture Series," *Los Angeles Sentinel*, August 28, 1969, A12; "Local Black Art Series to Be Held," *Los Angeles Sentinel*, September 18, 1969, A10; "Black Arts Council Hosts Bernie Casey, Dr. Lewis," *Los Angeles Sentinel*, September 25, 1969, A11; "Attendance Mark Set at Black Arts Lecture," *Los Angeles Sentinel*, October 2, 1969, A11; "Charles White, Artist, to Host 2nd Art Lecture," *Los Angeles Sentinel*, October 16, 1969, A12; "Music, Panel Discussion to Highlight Black Art Show," *Los Angeles Sentinel*, December 4, 1969, B6.

128. Lewis interviewed by Smith, *Image and Belief*, 189–90; Samella Lewis to Mr. Kenneth Donahue, director, Los Angeles County Museum of Art, December 1, 1970, in Samella Lewis Papers (collection 1132), Box 13, Folder: Samella Lewis, item no. 31, MARBL.

129. Samella Lewis kept much of the voluminous correspondence regarding protests in both Los Angeles and New York of this moment. Besides documenting her dealings with LACMA, she also kept in close contact with Benny Andrews and the BECC regarding the situation in New York in 1970–71, and flew to the East Coast to support BECC's protest against the controversial Whitney Museum exhibition *Contemporary Black Artists in America* (April 6–May 16, 1971). On Los Angeles see Concerned Citizens for Black Art to Board of Trustees, Los Angeles County Museum of Art, August 24, 1970, Box 37, Folder: LA Museum Protest, item no. 36; Jacob Lawrence to Mr. and Mrs. Paul Lewis, March 7, 1971, and Suzanne Jackson to Mrs. Samella Lewis, November 29, 1971, both Box 36, Folder: Front of Box, item no. 35; Samella Lewis to Mr. Kenneth Donahue, director, Los Angeles County Museum of Art, December 1, 1970, Box 13, Folder: Samella Lewis, item no. 31, all in Samella Lewis Papers (collection 1132), MARBL. On New York see Samella Lewis Papers (collection 1132), Box 38, Folder: Whitney Museum, MARBL.

130. Mae Tate, "Samella Lewis: Keeping Social Comment Alive, Vigorous in Art," *Progress-Bulletin* (Pomona, CA), January 15, 1972, 2.

131. McDowell, *Gender, Identity, and Place*.

132. University of Michigan Museum of Art, *Betye Saar: Extending the Frozen Moment* (Ann Arbor and Berkeley: University of Michigan Museum of Art and University of California Press, 2005), 161.

133. Lewis's various galleries had independent names but were sometimes also called by the name of her publishing company, Contemporary Crafts, which over the years shared space with the gallery endeavors. Tate, "Samella Lewis"; Leanna Ford, "Dr. Samella Lewis: A Persistent Fighter for Black Art," *Los Angeles Sentinel*, February 8, 1973, A14.

134. Some exhibition highlights include *The Harlem Renaissance* at Gibraltar Savings and Loan, *Arts of Africa and the Diaspora* at Santa Monica College, *The Art of the Poster* at

Angelus Plaza senior residence, and *American Craft Traditions* at San Francisco Airport. For a full listing see *African American Eye: Newsletter of the Museum of African American Art* 1, no. 1 (Winter 1985–86).

135. Pat Russell was only the fourth woman to hold office on the Los Angeles City Council (1969–87) and the first to serve as city council president (1983–87). Augustus F. Hawkins, one of the first African American politicians in California and its first congressman, and Mayor Tom Bradley also threw their support behind the museum. See Mary Jane Hewitt to Warren A. Hollier, commissioner, Board of Public Works, April 15, 1980; Mary Jane Hewitt to Mayor Tom Bradley, May 2, 1980, and June 10, 1980; Mary Jane Hewitt to Councilman Robert Farrell, June 10, 1980, all in Samella Lewis Papers (collection 1132), Box 7, Folder: Museum of African American Art, item no. 23, MARBL. Minutes of Meeting of the Board of Directors of the Museum of African American Art, October 30, 1980, and Phoebe Beasley, president, the Museum of African American Art, to Board of Directors, February 16, 1983, both in Samella Lewis Papers (collection 1132), Box 7, Folder: Museum of African American Art, item no. 24, MARBL.

A significant early gift to the museum was a collection of more than fifty works by modernist painter Palmer Hayden, donated by his widow. See *African American Eye* 1, no. 1 (Winter 1985–86).

136. Evangeline Juliette (E. J.) Montgomery, who had been active in Los Angeles art networks in the 1950s and early 1960s, moved to the Bay Area in 1965. By 1967 she had founded an African American artists' advocacy group there after Waddy's example, calling it Art West Associated North. Paralleling Lewis's hire at LACMA, Montgomery joined the staff of the Oakland Museum in 1968 as an "ethnic art consultant," a position she held through 1974 and under the guise of which she curated eight exhibitions. The Oakland Museum's wonderful collection of works by African American artists of this era is due to her eye and input.

The Oakland Museum's openness to such collecting was part of its institutional culture from the outset. As journalist Carol Kino reports, "The Oakland Museum of California was known as 'the people's museum' even before it opened in 1969, in part because it took pains to consult with and otherwise reach out to its intended audience." A municipal museum, it was "initially conceived as a grand social experiment to rejuvenate the city center by melding the city's history, science and art institutions into a single complex." In a city that was 40 percent black, and home to the Black Panthers, the museum had a governing board that was 100 percent white. In what Kino notes as an early take on public engagement, the museum's initial director, J. S. Holliday, instituted a Community Relations Advisory Committee fifty-one members strong. Learning of this group just weeks before the 1969 opening, an angered governing board fired Holliday. Community protests and picketing ensued, and a version of the advisory committee was reinstated. It would seem that E. J. Montgomery was part of this group. See Carol Kino, "Giving Museumgoers What They Want," *New York Times*, May 16, 2010, AR27, 29; Lewis interviewed by Smith, *Image and Belief*, 199–201, and E. J. Montgomery, interview with the author, May 18, 2003.

137. Remarkably, William Wilson of the *Los Angeles Times* included the first volume of *Black Artists on Art* in a review of "serious art publications [emerging] among the usual bright confetti of holiday art books" during winter 1969. These were tomes that

revealed a new direction for American culture, "devoted to kitsch, pop, earth, post–World War and black art [and sharing] a look at an art world they think needs drastic overhaul." William Wilson, "New Volumes Mirror a Feeling of Uneasiness," *Los Angeles Times*, December 7, 1969, C74.

138. See *African American Eye* 1, no. 1 (Winter 1985–86). Mary Jane Hewitt also worked at the magazine as an editor during the early years, demonstrating the connection between the museum and the magazine. Jeanne Zeidler, "Reflections on Twenty Years of IRAA: A Conversation with Samella Lewis," *International Review of African American Art* 13, no. 2 (Spring 1996): 8; Hewitt, *Interview of Samella Lewis*, 167.

139. Editorial Statement, *Black Art* 1, no. 1 (Fall 1976): 3.

140. The print, *Boys*, [n.d.], was also later offered through mail order. See *Black Art* 1, no. 3 (Spring 1977): 64.

141. Working with prison populations was something that Lewis was committed to. For instance, she and some of her students brought art classes to the Maryland State Penitentiary during the time she taught at Morgan State. Hewitt, *Interview of Samella Lewis*, 157.

142. See *Black Art* 1, no. 2 (Winter 1976): 64, 68, and *Black Art* 1, no. 3 (Spring 1977): 61, 63. In 1992, the magazine's operations shifted to Hampton University. See Zeidler, "Reflections on Twenty Years of IRAA," 4–12, and Juliette Harris, "Samella Lewis: An Art Institution in Her Own Right," *International Review of African American Art* 18, no. 1 (2001): 14–15.

143. *Art: African American* was first published in 1978 by Harcourt, Brace and Jovanovich. A second edition was published by the University of California Press in 1990 under the title *African American Art and Artists*; this version was updated in 2003.

144. Samella Lewis, *Art: African American* (New York: Harcourt, Brace and Jovanovich, 1978), 3.

145. Lewis, *Art*, 3.

146. Hewitt, *Interview of Samella Lewis*.

147. Contemporary Crafts Brochure, c. 1971, in Box 36, Folder: Front of Box, item no. 35; Contemporary Crafts to Louis Baker, April 7, 1978, in Box 7, Folder: Museum of African American Art Exhibits, item no. 26; Sanders Art Media Brochure, c. 1990, in Box 7, Folder: Sanders Art Media, item no. 22, all in Samella Lewis Papers (collection 1132), MARBL. It is not clear how long Mildred Sanders worked with her sister or whether she collaborated on Sanders Art Media.

148. Lewis's other films include *E.C.: The Art of Elizabeth Catlett* (1985), *Decoy Carving: A Bayou Heritage* (1986), and *The Art of Richmond Barthé* (1988). All were distributed under Lewis's Sanders Art Media imprint. In the case of the projects on Catlett and Barthé, books and slide sets were also produced. The article "Wetlands Heritage: The Duck Decoy" by Charles W. Frank Jr., which appeared in Lewis's journal *Black Art* 3, no. 1 (1978), seems to have been the inspiration for the 1986 film.

149. Hewitt, *Interview of Samella Lewis*.

150. Lewis originally applied to the University of Virginia for graduate school. When she was rejected because of her race, the school was forced to pay for her education out of state. This strategy for attending graduate school was suggested to her by one of her mentors at Hampton, Viktor Lowenfield. Hewitt, *Interview of Samella Lewis*, 155–56. Lowenfield was an Austrian Jew who escaped Nazi Germany and ended up

teaching at Hampton Institute for some time, where he encouraged a generation of African American artists, including Lewis, Catlett, and John Biggers. An exhibition of the work of some of his students, *Young Negro Art: Work of Students at Hampton Institute*, was shown at the Museum of Modern Art in 1943. See Sarah Newmeyer, press release of September 30, 1943, MoMA, http://www.moma.org/docs/press_archives/904/releases/MOMA_1943_0056_1943-10-04_431004-53.pdf?2010, accessed October 4, 2013.

151. "Samella Lewis Art at Rainbow Sign," *The Post* (Oakland, CA), March 30, 1972, 6; K. Jones, *Now Dig This!*, 251. See also Keith, "Samella Lewis," 260–61.

152. Lewis interviewed by Smith, *Image and Belief*, 204. In the 1930s, for instance, Paul Stover Wingert introduced non-Western fields of study at Columbia University. One of Samella Lewis's students at Scripps College was the young artist Alison Saar. One can see the imprint of Lewis's interests in Saar's work.

153. As part of what we now call "community engagement," in the mid-1970s, Lewis received a grant to set up an apprenticeship program for CUC students, who worked in her gallery as docents and in administrative capacities. As early as 1970, she curated exhibitions in CUC's various university galleries, like *Benny Bernie Betye Noah & John*, December 1970–February 1971, and *The Renaissance in Harlem*, which opened in November 1971; both were at the Lang Gallery. Later shows were done under the rubric of the budding Museum of African American Art's off-site exhibition program, such as *Arts of Kenya* at the Lang Gallery, and *Icons and Images for Children of All Ages* and *Jacob Lawrence and Gwendolyn Knight—A Retrospective*, both at Clark Humanities Museum. On Scripps College and Claremont University Center's support of Lewis and her projects see Lewis interviewed by Smith, *Image and Belief*, 211; Peter Emmet, director, Public Affairs Office, Claremont University Center, News for Release, March 26, 1974, in Box 36, Folder: S. Lewis / Selected Information, item no. 34; National Endowment for the Arts to Dr. Edward Brooks, provost, Claremont University Center, December 13, 1974, in Box 2, Folder: Contemporary Crafts, item no. 12, both in Samella Lewis Papers (collection 1132), MARBL; *African American Eye* 1, no. 1 (Winter 1985–86): unpaginated. Lewis retired from Scripps College in 1984.

154. We can also include on this list of Hollywood collectors actors Ruby Dee and Ossie Davis, musicians Stevie Wonder and Johnny Mathis, and playwright Lorraine Hansberry.

155. Camille O. Cosby, "Introduction," and William H. Cosby Jr., "Introduction," in David C. Driskell, *The Other Side of Color: African American Art in the Collection of Camille O. and William H. Cosby, Jr.* (San Francisco: Pomegranate, 2001), xiii, xviii.

156. "Black Mirror at Womanspace," *Los Angeles Sentinel*, April 12, 1973, B4A. Some works from Marguerite Ray's collection can be found in K. Jones, *Now Dig This!*, 234, 237, 282.

157. Alain Locke had been the first African American Rhodes Scholar. The novelist John Edgar Wideman also won in 1963.

158. Mary Ann Callan, "2 Rhodes Scholars' Backgrounds Differ," *Los Angeles Times*, December 19, 1962, A1. Sanders's brother Ed Sanders, a boxer, won the Olympic heavyweight championship in 1952. Shortly after turning pro he died of boxing-related injuries, which may have changed Stan's mind about a career in professional sports.

159. Stanley Sanders, "Riot as Weapon: The Language of Watts," *The Nation*, December 20, 1965, 490.

160. "Stan Sanders to Head Watts College Program," *Los Angeles Sentinel*, March 31, 1966, A8; "ACLU to Assist Watts Residents in Police Cases," *Los Angeles Times*, July 13, 1966, 3.

161. Jeff Prugh, "Star Athlete to Lawyer: Stan Sanders: From Watts to Oxford, Yale—and Back," *Los Angeles Times*, July 4, 1972, G1, G3; "Attorney from Watts among Jaycees' Top 10," *New Journal and Guide*, January 20, 1973, 1; Gary Libman, "Festival Will Mark Anniversary of Watts Area Riot," *Los Angeles Times*, July 15, 1966, A1–2; Horne, *Fire This Time*, 50–51.

162. Betty Pleasant, "Watts Summer Festival Surpasses Expectations," *Los Angeles Times*, August 18, 1966, 4E.

163. Kevin West, "Can You Dig It?," *W Magazine*, October 2011, 128; Karen Anne Mason, interview with Cecil Fergerson (1996), *African American Artists of Los Angeles*, 165–67. A work from Sanders's collection can be found in K. Jones, *Now Dig This!*, 186–87.

164. West, "Can You Dig It?," 127–30. Some works from the collections of Leon Banks and Vaughn C. Payne Jr. can be seen in K. Jones, *Now Dig This!*, 146, 161, 171, 207, 232, 235, 236.

165. Wilson, *Negro Building*, 235, 246–48, 265–66.

166. Karen Anne Mason, interview with William Pajaud (1993), *African American Artists of Los Angeles*, 187.

167. Karen Anne Mason, interview with Cecil Fergerson (1996), *African American Artists of Los Angeles*, 365.

168. Horne, *Fire This Time*, 160.

169. Stanley Sanders, "Riot as Weapon: The Language of Watts," *The Nation*, December 20, 1965, 490–93; Stan Sanders, "The New Mood of Watts," *Los Angeles Sentinel*, May 20, 1971, 11; Celeste Durant, "The Watts Rebuilding Dream Is a Dream Deferred," *Los Angeles Times*, March 23, 1975, B3, B7.

170. David C. Driskell quoted in C. Gerald Fraser, "'Black Art' Label Disputed by Curator," *New York Times*, June 29, 1977, 63.

FOUR. IN MOTION

1. Lucy Lippard, "Eccentric Abstraction," *Art International* 10, no. 9 (November 1966), which also appeared as an exhibition at New York's Fischbach Gallery in September–October 1966.

2. Lippard, "Eccentric Abstraction."

3. Lucy Lippard and John Chandler, "The Dematerialization of Art," *Art International* 12, no. 2 (February 1968): 31–36. The term "dematerialization" was first used by Argentine writer Oscar Masotta to describe early conceptual art practice in that country. See Inés Katzenstein, ed., *Listen, Here, Now! Argentine Art of the Sixties: Writings of the Avant-Garde* (New York: Museum of Modern Art; London: Thames & Hudson, 2004), and Claire Bishop, *Artificial Hells: Paticipatory Art and the Politics of Spectatorship* (London: Verso, 2012), chap. 5. See also James K. Monte and Marcia Tucker, *Anti-Illusion: Procedures/Materials* (New York: Whitney Museum of American Art, 1969); Robert Pincus-Witten, *Postminimalism* (New York: Out of London,

1977); Richard Armstrong and Richard Marshall, *The New Sculpture 1965–1975: Between Geometry and Gesture* (New York: Whitney Museum of American Art, 1990); Richard J. Williams, *After Modern Sculpture: Art in the United States and Europe, 1965–1970* (Manchester, UK: Manchester University Press, 2000).

4. Robert Pincus-Witten, "Postminimalism: An Argentine Glance," in Armstrong and Marshall, *The New Sculpture 1965–1975*; Sally Banes, *Terpsichore in Sneakers: Post-Modern Dance* (Middletown, CT: Wesleyan University Press, 1987; first published 1977).

5. Paul Gilroy, *There Ain't No Black in the Union Jack: The Cultural Politics of Race and Nation* (London: Hutchinson, 1987), 178. Gilroy focuses his discussion on music in particular.

6. Farah Jasmine Griffin, *"Who Set You Flowin'?": The African American Migration Narrative* (New York: Oxford University Press, 1995), 16, 46, 120–23. Other important writers Griffin names who think about the ancestral South in this period are Maya Angelou, Ntozake Shange, Toni Cade Bambara, Paule Marshall, Alice Walker, Amiri Baraka, Albert Murray, and Ernest J. Gaines. See also Robert Stepto, *From behind the Veil: A Study of Afro-American Narrative* (Urbana: University of Illinois Press, 1979).

7. Lippard, "Eccentric Abstraction."

8. R. J. Williams, *After Modern Sculpture*, 142–49.

9. Williams here specifically alludes to the exhibition by Harold Seezeman titled *When Attitudes Become Form*, during spring 1969 at the Kunsthalle Bern, Switzerland. R. J. Williams, *After Modern Sculpture*, 154.

10. Pincus-Witten, "Postminimalism: An Argentine Glance," 25. On feminism and postminimal practice see Susan L. Stoops, *More Than Minimal: Feminism and Abstraction in the '70s* (Waltham, MA: Rose Art Museum, Brandeis University, 1996). See also Lucy Lippard, "No Regrets," *Art in America* 95, no. 6 (June/July 2007): 75–79.

11. Peggy Phelan, *Unmarked: The Politics of Performance* (New York: Routledge, 1993), 26. It is interesting to consider Phelan's concept of "other" as ciphers for Western vision in relation to W. J. T. Mitchell's notion of comparing art's "need" to be viewed with subaltern figures' quest for recognition, "What Do Pictures Want?," in *What Do Pictures Want? The Lives and Loves of Images* (Chicago: University of Chicago Press, 2005).

12. Rita Eder, "Razón y sin razón del arte efímero: Algunos ejemplares latinoamericanos," *Plural* 8, no. 90, n.s. (March 1979): 28, translation mine; Rosalind Krauss, "Sculpture in the Expanded Field," *October* 8 (Spring 1979): 30–44.

13. Linda Goode Bryant and Marcy S. Philips, *Contextures* (New York: Just Above Midtown Inc., 1978); the book documented the project "Afro-American Artists in the Abstract Continuum of American Art: 1945–1977," a series of exhibitions held at JAM throughout 1977.

14. Goode Bryant and Philips, *Contextures*, 40.

15. Goode Bryant and Philips, *Contextures*, 40.

16. In reviewing work by Mel Edwards that seemed equally indeterminate, Pincus-Witten's strong negative response to it probably had to do with his difficulty in accepting this type of abstraction from black artists. Robert Pincus-Witten, "Melvin Edwards," *Artforum* 8, no. 9 (May 1970): 77.

17. Senga Nengudi, opening lecture for her solo exhibition *Senga Nengudi: Warp Trance*,

Fabric Workshop and Museum at the Pennsylvania Academy of Fine Arts, Philadelphia, June 8, 2007.
18. Lippard, "Eccentric Abstraction."
19. Amelia Jones, *Body Art: Performing the Subject* (Minneapolis: University of Minnesota Press, 1998), 31.
20. A. Jones, *Body Art*, 18.
21. Stuart Hall, "Minimal Selves," in *Identity: The Real Me*, ICA Documents 6 (London: Institute of Contemporary Art, 1987), 44.
22. W. E. B. Du Bois, *The Souls of Black Folk* (New York: Oxford University Press, 2007; first published 1903).
23. Daphne A. Brooks, *Bodies in Dissent: Spectacular Performances of Race and Freedom, 1850–1910* (Durham, NC: Duke University Press, 2006), 8.
24. Brooks, *Bodies in Dissent*, 4–6. Brooks derives her notion of "stillness" from Hortense J. Spillers, "'Mama's Baby, Papa's Maybe': An American Grammar Book," *Diacritics* 17, no. 2 (Summer 1987): 64–81.
25. Kathy O'Dell, "Toward a Theory of Performance Art: An Investigation of Its Sites" (PhD diss., City University of New York, 1992), cited in A. Jones, *Body Art*, 33.
26. Elizabeth Alexander, "'Can You Be Black and Look at This?': Reading the Rodney King Video(s)," in *The Black Interior* (Minneapolis: Graywolf, 2004). See also Kimberly W. Benston, *Performing Blackness: Enactments of African-American Modernism* (London: Routledge, 2000), 11–14. On notions of hypervisibility/invisibility see Patricia J. Williams, *Seeing a Color-Blind Future: The Paradox of Race* (New York: Noonday, 1998), and E. Patrick Johnson, *Appropriating Blackness: Performance and the Politics of Authenticity* (Durham, NC: Duke University Press, 2003).
27. Phelan, *Unmarked*, 1–2, 11.
28. Houston A. Baker Jr., *Modernism and the Harlem Renaissance* (Chicago: University of Chicago Press, 1987), 76–79. Maroons were self-liberated slaves of the Caribbean and South America. See Richard Price, *Maroon Societies: Rebel Slave Communities in the Americas* (Garden City, NY: Anchor Books, 1973).
29. Paul Gilroy, "'. . . To Be Real!': The Dissident Forms of Black Expressive Culture," in Catherine Ugwu, ed., *Let's Get It On: The Politics of Black Performance* (London: Institute of Contemporary Arts, 1995), 14–15; Katherine McKittrick, *Demonic Grounds: Black Women and the Cartographies of Struggle* (Minneapolis: University of Minnesota Press, 2006), 70–74; Barbara McCaskill, introduction to William Craft and Ellen Craft, *Running a Thousand Miles for Freedom: The Escape of William and Ellen Craft from Slavery* (Athens: University of Georgia Press, 1999); Daphne A. Brooks, introduction to *The Great Escapes: Four Slave Narratives* (New York: Barnes and Nobles Classics, 2007); Saidiya V. Hartman, *Scenes of Subjection: Terror, Slavery, and Self-Making in Nineteenth-Century America* (New York: Oxford University Press, 1997).
30. Nicholas Lemann, *The Promised Land: The Great Black Migration and How It Changed America* (New York: Vintage Books, 1992; first published 1991), 36, 44–45. See also Harryette Mullen, "Reader, I Married Him: An Interview with Alison Mills," *Callaloo* 27, no. 3 (2004): 698–714.
31. Brooks, *Bodies in Dissent*, 8.
32. Brooks, *Bodies in Dissent*, 4–6.

33. David Hammons interviewed by Kellie Jones, *Reallife Magazine*, no. 16 (Autumn 1986): 2.
34. Elois's relatives in Berkeley included Walter Orme, who was among the city's first African American realtors. By leaving Chicago, Elois also escaped from her domineering mother. Senga Nengudi, personal communication, July 22, 2010.
35. For more on *8 Artistes Afro-Américains* see Kellie Jones, "More Than Reverie," in *Senga Nengudi, Alt.* (London: White Cube, 2014).
36. Irons began her college studies in 1961 at Pasadena Community College but transferred after one semester to California State University, Los Angeles. Senga Nengudi (née Sue Irons), telephone interview with the author, June 3, 1996 (hereafter cited as Nengudi interview, June 1996).
37. Nengudi interview, June 1996.
38. Goode Bryant and Philips, *Contextures*, 45. See also Richard A. Long and Joe Nash, *The Black Tradition in American Dance* (New York: Rizzoli, 1989).
39. CETA stood for the Comprehensive Employment and Training Act. In effect from 1974 to 1983, this job-training program used federal block grants for locally targeted programs, which were often aimed at underemployed populations (such as artists). Most programs with creative sections focused on utilizing their artist-employees as "resources," tapping their painting, graphic, writing, and theatrical skills for a broad range of publicly directed activities. Grace A. Franklin and Randall B. Ripley, *C.E.T.A. Politics and Policy 1973–1982* (Knoxville: University of Tennessee Press, 1984); Steven C. Dubin, "Artistic Production and Social Control," *Social Forces* 64, no. 3 (March 1986): 667–88.
40. Nengudi interview, June 1996.
41. Maren Hassinger, telephone interview with the author, May 29, 1996 (hereafter cited as Hassinger interview, May 1996). Performer Frank Parker is also known as Franklin Parker.
42. Hassinger interview, May 1996.
43. Robert Farris Thompson, *African Art in Motion: Icon and Act in the Collection of Katherine Coryton White* (Berkeley: University of California Press, 1974), 13–14, 41.
44. Brenda Dixon Gottschild, *Digging the Africanist Presence in American Performance* (Westport, CT: Greenwood, 1996), 8–9.
45. Dixon Gottschild, *Digging the Africanist Presence in American Performance*, 49.
46. Dixon Gottschild, *Digging the Africanist Presence in American Performance*, 49. Pearl Primus, who was director of Liberia's Performing Arts Center working with the National Dance Company of Liberia in the late 1950s and early 1960s, has also discussed the relationship of earth/land to the African dance body. Pearl Primus, "African Dance," in Kariamu Welsh-Asante, ed., *African Dance: An Artistic, Historical, and Philosophical Inquiry* (Trenton, NJ: Africa World, 1996), 7. For an overview of principles of African dance see Kariamu Welsh-Asante, "Commonalities in African Dance: An Aesthetic Foundation," in Ann Dils and Ann Cooper Albright, eds., *Moving History / Dancing Cultures: A Dance History Reader* (Middletown, CT: Wesleyan University Press, 2001), 144–51.
47. Herbert M. Cole, "Art as a Verb in Igboland," *African Arts* 3, no. 1 (Autumn 1969): 34–41, 88; Thompson, *African Art in Motion*; Sidney Littlefield Kasfir, "Elephant Women, Furious and Majestic: Women's Masquerades in Africa and the Diaspora,"

in "Women's Masquerades in Africa and the Diaspora," special issue, *African Arts* 31, no. 2 (Spring 1998): 18–27, 92.

In an interesting confluence, in 1988 the Maryland Institute College of Art and the Studio Museum in Harlem would host an exhibition, curated by Leslie King-Hammond and Lowery Stokes Sims, titled *Art as a Verb*. It included Senga Nengudi, David Hammons, Adrian Piper, and other African American artists of this generation working with performance. Leslie King-Hammond and Lowery Stokes Sims, *Art as a Verb: The Evolving Continuum: Installations, Performances and Videos by 13 Afro-American Artists* (Baltimore: Maryland Institute College of Art, 1988).

48. Herbert M. Cole, introduction to Herbert M. Cole, ed., *I Am Not Myself: The Art of African Masquerade*, Monograph Series, No. 26 (Los Angeles: Museum of Cultural History, University of California, Los Angeles, 1985), 15.
49. Babatunde Lawal, *The Gẹ̀lẹ̀dé Spectacle: Art, Gender, and Social Harmony in African Culture* (Seattle: University of Washington Press, 1996), xiii.
50. Sidney Littlefield Kasfir, introduction to *West African Masks and Cultural Systems* (Tervuren, Belgium: Musée Royal de L'Afrique Centrale, 1988), 9.
51. Lawal, *The Gẹ̀lẹ̀dé Spectacle*, xiii.
52. Lawal, *The Gẹ̀lẹ̀dé Spectacle*, xiii.
53. Pamela R. Franco, "Dressing Up and Looking Good: Afro-Creole Female Maskers in Trinidad Carnival," in "Women's Masquerades in Africa and the Diaspora," special issue, *African Arts* 31, no. 2 (Spring 1998): 62–63.
54. Yoruba cultures are also found in Benin and Togo.
55. Thompson, *African Art in Motion*, 219.
56. Thompson, *African Art in Motion*, 219, 222. The masking forms differ by area as well as the specific category of Egungun—elder, trickster, child. This last category is known for its elaborate appliqué and is also connected to Yoruba contact with this strong Fon tradition in Benin.
57. Henry John Drewal and Margaret Thompson Drewal, *Gẹ̀lẹ̀dé: Art and Female Power among the Yoruba* (Bloomington: Indiana University Press, 1990; first published 1983), and Lawal, *The Gẹ̀lẹ̀dé Spectacle*.

While Gẹ̀lẹ̀dé and Esu are proper Yoruba spellings, Betye Saar spelled these terms somewhat differently in her early 1970s pieces. See page 113.
58. Senga Nengudi would serve on the Women's Building's performance committee in the early 1980s. Indeed, the presence of artists of color in the organization's activities was minimal until that decade.
59. Rebecca Schneider, *The Explicit Body in Performance* (New York: Routledge, 1997), 6.
60. Franco, "Dressing Up and Looking Good," 62.
61. Judith Bettelheim, "Women and Masquerade and Performance," in "Women's Masquerades in Africa and the Diaspora," special issue, *African Arts* 31, no. 2 (Spring 1998): 70; Franco, "Dressing Up and Looking Good," 64.
62. Gerardo Mosquera, "Eleggúa at the (Post?)Modern Crossroads," in Arturo Lindsay, ed., *Santería Aesthetics in Contemporary Latin American Art* (Washington, DC: Smithsonian Institution Press, 1996), 227.
63. Lawal, *The Gẹ̀lẹ̀dé Spectacle*, 16.
64. Z. S. Strother, *Inventing Masks: Agency and History in the Art of the Central Pende* (Chicago: University of Chicago Press, 1998), 17.

65. Bettelheim, "Women and Masquerade and Performance," 70.
66. Nengudi interview, June 1996.
67. Nengudi interview, June 1996; O. Donald Odita, "The Unseen, Inside Out: The Life and Art of Senga Nengudi," *Nka* 6/7 (Summer/Fall 1997): 25; Moyo Okediji, *The Shattered Gourd: Yoruba Forms in Twentieth Century American Art* (Seattle: University of Washington Press, 2003), 13.
68. Robert Farris Thompson, "The Three Warriors: Atlantic Altars of Esu, Ogun, and Osoosí," in Rowland Abiodun, Henry John Drewal, and John Pemberton III, eds., *The Yoruba Artist: New Theoretical Perspectives on African Arts* (Washington, DC: Smithsonian Institution Press, 1994), 225; Virginia E. Sánchez Korrol, *From Colonia to Community: The History of Puerto Ricans in New York City* (Berkeley: University of California Press, 1994; first published 1983).
69. The term "fets" was short for "fetishes." Like "juju," "fetish" is a word that comes with a lot of baggage, especially when applied to the African context. Within a colonial framework it was used in a disparaging manner to identify African religious articles. Certainly the confluence with psychoanalytic meaning—as an object that elicits erotic desire—is not simply fortuitous.
70. Joseph R. Roach, *Cities of the Dead: Circum-Atlantic Performance* (New York: Columbia University Press, 1996), 27–28.
71. Roach, *Cities of the Dead*, 14, emphasis mine.
72. Roach, *Cities of the Dead*, 27.
73. Pierre Nora, "Between Memory and History: Les Lieux de Mémoire," in Genevieve Fabre and Robert O'Meally, eds., *History and Memory in African-American Culture* (New York: Oxford University Press, 1994), 295.
74. Renato Rosaldo quoted in Roach, *Cities of the Dead*, 29.
75. Josh Sides, *L.A. City Limits: African American Los Angeles from the Great Depression to the Present* (Berkeley: University of California Press, 2003), 124; Eric Avila, *Popular Culture in the Age of White Flight: Fear and Fantasy in Suburban Los Angeles* (Berkeley: University of California Press, 2004), chap. 6.
76. "New archetypes" and "modernity as a circulatory system": Okwui Enwezor, introduction to *Trade Routes: History and Geography*, Second Johannesburg Biennale (Johannesburg: Greater Johannesburg Metropolitan Council, 1997), 9, 7; "diasporic histories": Roach, *Cities of the Dead*, 4.
77. Nengudi remembers seeing the work particularly of the Gutai Art Association mentioned briefly for the first time in a book on the Japanese avant-garde. It is interesting that Allan Kaprow's text *Assemblage, Environments and Happenings* (New York: H. N. Abrams, 1966) includes references to the collective in luscious illustrations but which comprise only a sliver of the book's content. Nengudi may have come in contact with it at the Pasadena Art Museum. It was also published in 1966, the same year Nengudi left for Japan.
78. Bruce Altshuler, *The Avant-Garde in Exhibition: New Art in the 20th Century* (New York: Harry N. Abrams, 1994), 176. Curator Alexandra Monroe translates the word *Gutai* slightly differently, as "concreteness": Alexandra Munroe, "To Challenge the Mid-Summer Sun: The Gutai Group," in *Japanese Art after 1945: Scream against the Sky* (New York: Harry N. Abrams, 1994), 84.
79. In *Challenging Mud*, 1955, Kazuo Shiraga stripped down to his shorts, wrestled with

a pile of the substance for twenty minutes, then presented the resulting articulations of earth as a finished product. Shiraga also created mural-size paintings using his feet as "brushes." For his *Many Screens of Paper*, 1956, Saburo Murakami made "action paintings" by crashing through parallel "canvases" of brown paper; the resulting tears were the markmaking. For discussion of the Gutai Art Association see Altshuler, *The Avant-Garde in Exhibition*, 174–91, 277; Shinichiro Osaki, "Body and Place: Action in Postwar Art in Japan," in Paul Schimmel, ed., *Out of Actions: Between Performance and the Object, 1949–1979* (Los Angeles: Museum of Contemporary Art, 1998), 121–57; Ming Tiampo and Alexandra Munroe, *Gutai: Splendid Playground* (New York: Guggenheim Museum, 2013).

80. Nengudi interview, June 1996.
81. Benito Ortolani, "From Shamanisn to BUTO: Continuity and Innovation in Japanese Theater History," in James R. Brandon and Samuel L. Leiter, eds., *Japanese Theater in the World* (New York: Japan Society, 1997), 17.
82. Gunter Zobel and Goto Hajime, "Snow in a Silver Bowl: No Theater," in Brandon and Leiter, *Japanese Theater in the World*, 49.
83. Zobel and Hajime, "Snow in a Silver Bowl," 50.
84. Kusuhara-Saito Tomoko, "The Past in the Future: Explosion of the Japanese Avant-Garde," in Brandon and Leiter, *Japanese Theater in the World*, 78.
85. Tomoko, "The Past in the Future," 79.
86. Nengudi interview, June 1996. For more on Japan's cultural influence on the West see J. Thomas Rimer, "Japanese Theater in the World," in Brandon and Leiter, *Japanese Theater in the World*, 25–31.
87. Karen Anne Mason, interview with Kinshasha Holman Conwill (1996), *African American Artists of Los Angeles*, 32–33.
88. James Prigoff and Robin J. Dunitz, *Walls of Heritage, Walls of Pride: African American Murals* (San Francisco: Pomegranate, 2000).
89. Jeff Donaldson received his PhD from Northwestern University in 1974. He pioneered the first-ever arts major at the University of Arkansas, Pine Bluff (his home town), receiving his BA in 1954. He went on to finish an MA in 1963 from Illinois Institute of Technology in Chicago, the city he referred to as the place of his "rebirth."
90. Early members of AfriCOBRA were Jeff Donaldson, Jae Jarrell, Wadsworth Jarrell, Barbara J. Jones, Gerald Williams, Napoleon Henderson, Nelson Stevens, Sherman Beck, Omar Lama, Howard Mallory Jr., and Carolyn Lawrence. See Jeff Donaldson, "Ten in Search of a Nation," *Black World* 19, no. 12 (October 1970): 80–89.
91. AfriCOBRA members Frank Smith and Wadsworth Jarrell taught there, James Phillips came later, and Nelson Stevens visited frequently from Massachusetts; all were painters. Another member of the faculty Donaldson hired during this era was Skunder Boghossian, an important modernist from Ethiopia. Most sources place Boghossian at Howard in 1974, arriving there from Atlanta, where he had taught beginning in 1969. However, both Rosalind Jeffries and Kinshasha Holman Conwill place him there earlier in the 1970s, perhaps first as a visiting professor. Rosalind Robinson Jeffries, "Arthur Carraway and Houston Conwill: Ethnicity and Re-Africanization in American Art" (PhD diss., Yale University, 1992), 183–85; Karen Anne Mason, interview with Kinshasha Holman Conwill (1996), *African American Artists of Los Angeles*, 28.

92. Karen Anne Mason, interview with Kinshasha Holman Conwill (1996), *African American Artists of Los Angeles*, 40. Kinshasha Holman Conwill (née Karen Holman) was born in Atlanta, Georgia, into a family of civil rights activists, including her father, poet M. Carl Holman. She attended Mt. Holyoke College briefly before transferring to Howard University, where she received a BFA. While in Los Angeles she completed an MBA at UCLA. When the Conwills moved to New York she landed a job as deputy director of the Studio Museum in Harlem in 1980. She served as the museum's director from 1988 to 1999.
93. Gilliam was a force in the Washington, DC, art world from the 1960s onward. When the art gallery at Howard University presented a solo show of the artist's work in 1973, it was clear that Gilliam's total abstraction—even with its reference to black cultural heroes (including *April 4, 1969*, titled for the one-year anniversary of the assassination of Martin Luther King Jr., and the later *Three Panels for Mr. Robeson*, 1975) and visual and material correlation to African textile traditions—was not enough to consider it part of a canon of Afrocentric or Black Arts Movement–driven aesthetics. The painter Alma Thomas was also an important presence in the nation's capital in the 1960s and 1970s.
94. See Yvonne Cole Meo, "Ritual as Art: The Work of Houston Conwill," *International Review of African American Art* 3, no. 3 (Fall 1979): 4–13.
95. Houston Conwill quoted in Arturo Lindsay, "Performance Art Ritual as Postmodern Thought: An Aesthetic Investigation" (PhD diss., New York University, 1990), 73.
96. Jeffries, "Arthur Carraway and Houston Conwill," 180–92.
97. Cole Meo, "Ritual as Art," 4–13.
98. Bearden's move to collage seemed to have a real impact on painters who were trying to reinvigorate the medium. See Al Loving's comments in Kellie Jones, *Energy/Experimentation: Black Artists and Abstraction 1964–1980* (New York: Studio Museum in Harlem, 2006), 14–34.
99. The artists designed their wedding program in consultation with Kojo Fuso, a Howard faculty member from Ghana. Karen Anne Mason, interview with Kinshasha Holman Conwill (1996), *African American Artists of Los Angeles*, 35; Jeffries, "Arthur Carraway and Houston Conwill," 248; "Howard Students Marry in Capitol," *Chicago Daily Defender*, January 29, 1972, 10.
100. Lindsay, "Performance Art Ritual as Postmodern Thought," 72; Jeffries, "Arthur Carraway and Houston Conwill," 6–7, 72; Okediji, *The Shattered Gourd*, 13; Kamari Maxine Clarke, *Mapping Yorùbá Networks: Power and Agency in the Making of Transnational Communities* (Durham, NC: Duke University Press, 2004).
101. "Howard Students Marry in Capitol," *Chicago Daily Defender*, January 29, 1972, 10; Karen Anne Mason, interview with Kinshasha Holman Conwill (1996), *African American Artists of Los Angeles*, 41, 64.
102. The Louisville Conwills were active Catholics. The artist at one point had studied to become a priest, and his older brother Giles in fact became one. The congregation of Saint Augustine was black, but the priest was a white man, Father Donald Fisher, who invited the artists to complete the project as part of a larger renovation, a way to update the imagery with a "Black Is Beautiful" theme. This was a pattern in Catholic churches throughout the 1960s and 1970s as they struggled to keep and attract black members; a key marker was the canonization of the Afro-Peruvian saint Saint

Martin de Porres in 1962. Conwill relied on a colorful palette and a figurative style in the manner of AfriCOBRA rather than pushing a more abstract agenda. Murals and public art in general would continue to captivate Conwill. His collaborative projects with Kinshasha in college had included a mural for an elementary school, a project that may have been a school assignment. Later in Los Angeles, they would join LA Street Graphics, an organization under the umbrella of Brockman Gallery Productions that created murals along Crenshaw Boulevard and elsewhere and also did similar work with Communicative Arts Academy in Compton.

On reaching his sixteenth birthday Conwill joined Saint Meinrad, the Benedictine Monastery in St. Meinrad, Indiana. Conwill's two older brothers, Giles and William, both went to Verona Fathers Seminary in Cincinnati, Ohio, after eighth grade, and Rosalind Jeffries writes of Conwill's signing up to become a monk as in part acting out a sibling rivalry, going his brothers one better. Conwill's father died in the mid-1950s, leaving his mother with five sons and one daughter. Availing themselves of boarding school opportunities was probably a good solution for a family stretched to its limits. Jeffries, "Arthur Carraway and Houston Conwill," 171.

For images of these murals see *St. Augustine Church* (1976). As Holman Conwill recalls of the Conwills' Louisville project, a portion of the congregation itself initially fought some of their imagery, so used to worshipping white images that they were not convinced that they needed to see their saints or the Virgin Mary as black. This was surely a shock to young artists whose training had emphasized the radical nature of unapologetic black figuration at this moment. Karen Anne Mason, interview with Kinshasha Holman Conwill (1996), *African American Artists of Los Angeles*, 40–60; Tammy L. Kernodle, *Soul on Soul: The Life and Music of Mary Lou Williams* (Boston: Northeastern University Press, 2004), 199–222. Dwight Andrews also reports this push by the Catholic Church in Detroit and Chicago, personal communication, Jazz Studies Group, Columbia University, March 3, 2007.

103. In her review in *Artweek* Suzanne Muchnic refers to the performance by the more generic title *JuJu Ritual*. That the performance remains basically the same from Los Angeles to New York is confirmed by Houston Conwill's later interviews with Arturo Lindsay and Rosalind Jeffries. Lindsay, "Performance Art Ritual as Postmodern Thought," 77; Jeffries, "Arthur Carraway and Houston Conwill," 250; Suzanne Muchnic, "JuJu Ritual—Cycles of Life," *Artweek* 9, no. 8 (February 25, 1978): 4.

Rosalind Jeffries notes at least seven ritual performances at different galleries as well as the Conwill studio in Los Angeles, and locales in New York between 1975 and 1979, as well as others that were undocumented. Jeffries, "Arthur Carraway and Houston Conwill," 249–50. Other significant performances in Los Angeles by Conwill in this period included *Warrior Chants, Love Songs and New Spirituals* (with poets Kamau Daaood, Charles Dickson, and Ojenke), performed at the Watts Towers Art Center in 1979, and *Getup*, written by Senga Nengudi in 1980.

104. Although the term is used throughout West Africa, its origins are often tied to the Hausa word *djudju*, which connotes roughly the same thing. Other sources recognize "juju" as a slang or creole term that comes from the French *jou jou* (meaning "play play") and was used derogatorily to refer to African religious and healing arts. Another contemporary use of the term was applied to popular Nigerian music. Like the Afrobeat sounds of the Nigerian Fela Kuti, "juju music" received growing inter-

national attention in the 1970s and particularly in the early 1980s through touring bands such as King Sunny Ade and His African Beats. Juju music, created in Nigeria in the early part of the twentieth century, was a syncretic mix of Christian, Muslim, and Latin American religious and big band musics (brought to the country by repatriated slaves) and Yoruba forms of polyrhythmic drumming and guitar. These came together in coastal Lagos, mixing with song styles from other West African musicians as well as Yorubas from the interior. The frame drum (called the samba, from Brazil) and tambourine mark this music as modern and Christian, as these instruments were used in the dissemination of Christianity in Nigeria and were employed to distinguish this music from "pagan" indigenous forms. Vocally juju music adopted Yoruba praisesong form, and after World War II the pressure or talking drum was added, which sonically appeared to imitate Yoruba speech patterns and thus act as a counterpoint to juju vocals. This is further evidence of the re-Africanization of African culture, a protest culture of sort as Nigeria, like other countries, moved toward independence. Christopher Alan Waterman, *Jùjú: A Social History and Ethnography of an African Popular Music* (Chicago: University of Chicago Press, 1990).

105. Houston Conwill quoted in Barry Craig, "A Ritual Experience," *Artweek* 6, no. 36 (October 25, 1975): 6. Rosalind Jeffries reports perhaps the earliest use of this sack imagery by Conwill. Rather than large constructed objects, this was an installation in 1974 where 350 small bags were affixed to the walls of a gallery. Filled with tea, they diffused aroma into the space. Jeffries, "Arthur Carraway and Houston Conwill," 244–45.

106. On the juju bags and their construction see Cole Meo, "Ritual as Art," 4, and Judith Wilson, "Creating a Necessary Space: The Art of Houston Conwill, 1975–1983," *International Review of African American Art* 6, no. 1 (1984): 50. Information on *nkisi* can be found in Robert Farris Thompson, *Flash of the Spirit: African and Afro-American Art and Philosophy* (New York: Vintage Books, 1984). On African American folk traditions see Newbell Niles Puckett, *Folk Beliefs of the Southern Negro* (Chapel Hill: University of North Carolina Press, 1926); Jeffery E. Anderson, preface to *Conjure in African American Society* (Baton Rouge: Louisiana State University Press, 2005), 28, 37.

107. Cole Meo, "Ritual as Art," 4.

108. On brands and cicatrisation or scarification see Cole Meo, "Ritual as Art," 8, and Jeffries, "Arthur Carraway and Houston Conwill," 211–12.

109. On the evolution of Conwill's painting process see Wilson, "Creating a Necessary Space," 50, and Jeffries, "Arthur Carraway and Houston Conwill," 208–9, 218. It is interesting to consider this parallel with artists working strictly using nonobjective abstraction on the East Coast, such as Jack Whitten, William T. Williams, and others. But Conwill also represents a further development of their materials of choice, acrylic media, and the introduction of visible rather than occluded narrative. For more on East Coast painters see K. Jones, *Energy/Experimentation*.

110. Wilson, "Creating a Necessary Space," 50.

111. Houston Conwill quoted in Craig, "A Ritual Experience," 7. The author is listed as a professor of African and Oceanic art at the University of Southern California and may have been one of Conwill's professors there.

112. Goode Bryant and Philips, *Contextures*, 64.
113. Goode Bryant and Philips, *Contextures*, 64. Rosalind Jeffries actually describes the gutbucket in the work as rough-hewn, bringing to mind the many tubs and buckets (for his bathers) in Romare Bearden's collages and prints. There is a sense, then, that Conwill has made this mundane ritual illuminated by Bearden both three-dimensional and more holy.
114. Sharon F. Patton, "The Stool and Asante Chieftaincy," *African Arts* 13, no. 1 (November 1979): 74. For more on Akan traditions as well as the functions of seats in African cultures, see Herbert M. Cole and Doran H. Ross, *The Arts of Ghana* (Los Angeles: Museum of Cultural History, University of California, 1977), and Sandro Bocola and Ezio Bassani, eds., *African Seats* (Munich: Prestel, 1995).
115. Lawal, *The Gẹ̀lẹ̀dẹ́ Spectacle*, 7. In the case of the Golden Stool, we also note its literal enthronement on another kind of chair. These are Asipim and Hwedom chairs, modeled after fifteenth- to seventeenth-century European prototypes, which often function as thrones and are also reiterated in sculptures depicting royalty. In each case, what is enthroned are concepts of continuity between the living and their ancestors, the persistence of the family or the state.
116. See Janet Berry Hess, *Art and Architecture in Postcolonial Africa* (Jefferson, NC: McFarland, 2006); Salah Hassan, "The Modernist Experience in African Art: Visual Expressions of the Self and Cross-Cultural Aesthetics," in Okwui Enwezor and Olu Oguibe, eds., *Reading the Contemporary: African Art from Theory to Marketplace* (London: Institute of International Visual Arts; Cambridge, MA: MIT Press, 1999); Olu Oguibe, *The Culture Game* (Minneapolis: University of Minnesota Press, 2004), 36–37; Manthia Diawara, "The 1960s in Bamako: Malick Sidibé and James Brown," in Harry J. Elam Jr. and Kennell A. Jackson, eds., *Black Cultural Traffic: Crossroads in Global Performance and Popular Culture* (Ann Arbor: University of Michigan Press, 2005), 242–65; Manthia Diawara, "Blaxploitation in Africa," in Richard J. Powell, David A. Bailey, and Petrine Archer-Straw, eds., *Back to Black: Art, Cinema, and the Racial Imaginary* (London: Whitechapel Gallery, 2005), 162–65.
117. Cheryl Finley, "Of Golden Anniversaries and Bicentennials: The Convergence of Memory, Tourism, and National History in Ghana," *Journeys* 7, no. 1 (Spring 2007): 15–32.
118. Saidiya Hartman, "The Time of Slavery," *South Atlantic Quarterly* 101, no. 4 (Fall 2002): 757–77; Salamishah Tillet, *Sites of Slavery: Citizenship and Racial Democracy in the Post–Civil Rights Imagination* (Durham, NC: Duke University Press, 2012).
119. Rebecca Schneider, *Performing Remains: Art and War in Times of Theatrical Reenactment* (New York: Routledge, 2011), 2.
120. José Muñoz, "Cruising the Toilet: LeRoi Jones / Amiri Baraka, Radical Black Traditions, and Queer Futurity," *GLQ* 13, nos. 2–3 (2007): 357. In this essay and all of his writing Muñoz gives us so much think about and carry forward. However, I am compelled to point out a significant historical error in this text, one that takes nothing away from its crucial theoretical framings. It appears that Muñoz has confused Diane di Prima with my mother, Hettie Jones, who did have two children with her husband LeRoi Jones: Kellie Jones and Lisa Jones. Diane di Prima did have one child out of wedlock with Jones: Dominque di Prima. See Hettie Jones, *How I Became Hettie Jones* (New York: Penguin Books, 1990).

121. Schneider, *Performing Remains*, 12.
122. Schneider, *Performing Remains*, 27.
123. Gregory P. Pitts was the founder and director of the Pearl C. Wood Gallery, an alternative space in Los Angeles active between 1975 and 1980. Housed in the Triangular Church of Religious Science at Twentieth Street and Western Avenue, the gallery was named for the church's founder, Pitts's maternal grandmother. Mrs. Wood, who arrived in Los Angeles in 1930 and started the church in her home in 1932, fit the profile of many African American women southern migrants of the era. In 1972 Mrs. Wood retired from the ministry and was succeeded by her son-in-law Dr. Philip G. Pitts. In 1998 Gregory P. Pitts replaced his father as senior minister. The church was very active culturally in the 1970s and 1980s. In addition to the gallery where Senga Nengudi and Maren Hassinger also had shows during this period, the church sponsored a jazz series called "Concerts by the Freeway" and began collecting art. Much of this activity can be ascribed to Greg Pitts, a cohort of this younger generation of Los Angeles artists. With a BA from California State University, Long Beach (1974), and an MFA from Otis Art Institute (1981), he was a practicing artist himself as well as a writer and minister. Pitts's writings have appeared in *Neworld* magazine and the *Los Angeles Sentinel*, among other publications. See also Greg Pitts, "Het-Heru: Looking Back Forward at the Emergence of an Amer-I-CAN-A-free-ka-n (Afrikan-American) Aesthetic—An A-free-ka-n Centered Discourse in the Key of G," in Connie Rogers Tilton and Lindsay Charlwood, eds., *L.A. Object and David Hammons Body Prints* (New York: Tilton Gallery, 2011), 62–75, and commemorative program, Triangular Church of Religious Science Seventy-Fifth Anniversary Banquet Celebration, Saturday March 10, 2007.
124. Karen Anne Mason, interview with Kinshasha Holman Conwill (1996), *African American Artists of Los Angeles*, 62–63. However, a book of poetry for which she contributes a printed illustration is released as late as 1978. See Saundra Sharp, *Soft Song* (Los Angeles: Poets Pay Rent, Too, 1978), and an ad announcing its publication, *Black Art: An International Quarterly* 3, no. 1 (1978): 65.
125. Karen Anne Mason, interview with Kinshasha Holman Conwill (1996), *African American Artists of Los Angeles*, 62–63; Muchnic, "JuJu Ritual," 4; Jeffries, "Arthur Carraway and Houston Conwill," 236. See also Thompson, *African Art in Motion*, and Robert Farris Thompson, *Black Gods and Kings: Yoruba Art at UCLA* (Bloomington: Indiana University Press, 1976). The Banyang people of Cameroon, neighbors of the Ejagham, have also adopted the Basinjom masquerade.
126. Octavia Butler, *Kindred* (Garden City, NY: Doubleday, 1979).
127. Elizabeth Freeman, *Time Binds: Queer Temporalities, Queer Histories* (Durham, NC: Duke University Press, 2010), 62, 64.
128. Freeman, *Time Binds*, 62.
129. "Queer desire for history": Carolyn Dinshaw quoted in Elizabeth Freeman, introduction to "Queer Temporalities," special issue, *GLQ* 13, nos. 2–3 (2007): 162; "temporal and historical difference": Freeman, introduction to "Queer Temporalities," 159.
130. Freeman, introduction to "Queer Temporalities," 162.
131. The other two artists were Bob Glover and Diana Hobson.
132. Rosalind Jeffries writes that after the first version of the performance at University of Southern California, the "Africanized stool" replaced the chair. Jeffries, "Arthur

Carraway and Houston Conwill," 241–42. Interestingly, this parallels usage in independence-era Africa, where ceremonial chairs patterned after European prototypes were rejected for ones with more traditionally African structures. Roy Sieber, "African Furniture between Tradition and Colonization," in Bocola and Bassani, *African Seats*, 36.

133. Michael Prestel was on flute, Richard Thompson on congas. Karen Anne Mason, interview with Kinshasha Holman Conwill (1996), *African American Artists of Los Angeles*, 62–63; Muchnic, "JuJu Ritual," 4.

134. Rosalind Jeffries identifies this substance as "ash, chalk, or talcum powder." However, this ethereal dust may allude to or actually be earth from gravesites. In the Kongo tradition (of people from the Congo/Angola area of Africa), where grave is altar, this substance is extremely powerful. In a later work, *Cakewalk*, 1983, in which Conwill became more interested in the "symbolic possibilities of architecture" joined with performance, he created triangular and three-dimensional canvases that were "charged with dust" from cemeteries in four southern cities. Wilson, "Creating a Necessary Space," 54, 60, 64n34; Thompson, *Flash of the Spirit*, 117; Robert Farris Thompson, *Face of the Gods: Art and Altars of Africa and the African Americas* (New York: Museum for African Art and Prestel, 1993); Jeffries, "Arthur Carraway and Houston Conwill," 246.

135. Muchnic, "JuJu Ritual," 4.

136. Karen Anne Mason, interview with Kinshasha Holman Conwill (1996), *African American Artists of Los Angeles*, 62–63; Muchnic, "JuJu Ritual," 4; Cole Meo, "Ritual as Art," 9, 12. For an "Action Format of Most of Conwill's Rituals," see Jeffries, "Arthur Carraway and Houston Conwill," 246–47.

137. Richard J. Powell, "*Notes of a Griot* Demystifies New York," *Neworld* 5, no. 2 (March/April 1979): 12.

138. Hartman, "The Time of Slavery," 762.

139. Freeman, *Time Binds*, 72.

140. José Muñoz, "Cruising the Toilet: LeRoi Jones / Amiri Baraka, Radical Black Traditions, and Queer Futurity," *GLQ* 13, nos. 2–3 (2007): 360.

141. Hartman, "The Time of Slavery," 762; Toni Morrison, "The Site of Memory," in Russell Ferguson, Martha Gever, Trinh T. Minh-ha, and Cornel West, eds., *Out There: Marginalization and Contemporary Cultures* (Cambridge, MA: MIT Press, 1991), 305.

142. Okwui Enwezor, "A Question of Place: Revisions, Reassessments, Diaspora," in Salah Hassan, Iftikhar Dadi, and Leslie A. Adelson, eds., *Unpacking Europe: Towards a Critical Reading* (Rotterdam: Museum Boijmans Van Beuningen, 2001); James Clifford, "Diasporas," *Cultural Anthropology* 9, no. 3 (1994): 302–38; Nicholas Mirzoeff, "The Multiple Viewpoint: Diasporic Visual Cultures," in Nicholas Mirzoeff, ed., *Diaspora and Visual Culture: Representing Africans and Jews* (London: Routledge, 2000); Hartman, "The Time of Slavery."

143. Lawrence Levine, *Black Culture and Black Consciousness* (New York: Oxford University Press, 1970), 30, as cited in Wilson, "Creating a Necessary Space," 53.

144. Mosquera, "Eleggúa at the (Post?)Modern Crossroads," 227.

145. McKittrick, *Demonic Grounds*, 52.

146. Veerle Poupeye, *Caribbean Art* (London: Thames and Hudson, 1998).

147. Thompson, *Face of the Gods*, 20.
148. Richard Price, *Alabi's World* (Baltimore: Johns Hopkins University Press, 1990), 372, quoted in Thompson, *Face of the Gods*, 20.
149. The New Testament, Gospel according to Matthew, 19:20. David L. Smith, paper presented at the Jazz Studies Group, Columbia University, March 3, 2007. Robert Farris Thompson speaks of the same emphemerality in the face of persecution of black religions in twentieth-century Cuba, as recounted by the writer Alejo Carpentier, where European dolls and straw hats became divinely invested substances in a room that magically was transformed into an altar; Thompson, *Face of the Gods*, 21.
150. Judith Wilson notes that even the way the juju bags and other items constructed from the petrigraphs were sewn together had roots in African textile traditions. Wilson, "Creating a Necessary Space," 50.
151. Thompson, *Face of the Gods*, 284.
152. Thompson, *Face of the Gods*, 26.
153. Conwill's Catholicism gave him a tradition that had been used syncretically for centuries, as a mask for fresh configurations of African religiosity in the New World. The murals by Conwill and Kinshasha in Louisville can be seen as an extension of that impulse. His practice also echoed the activities in the 1950s of Catholic jazz pianist Mary Lou Williams, who composed a body of sacred music dedicated initially to healing the jazz community from the ravages of drug culture. See Kernodle, *Soul on Soul*, and Farah Jasmine Griffin, *Harlem Nocturne: Women Artists and Progressive Politics during World War II* (New York: Basic Books, 2013), chap. 3.
154. Muchnic, "JuJu Ritual," 4.
155. Powell, "*Notes of a Griot* Demystifies New York," 12.
156. Powell, "*Notes of a Griot* Demystifies New York," 12.
157. Peter Gorsen, "The Return of Existentialism in Performance Art," in Gregory Battcock and Robert Nickas, eds., *The Art of Performance: A Critical Anthology* (New York: Dutton, 1984), 138.
158. Thomas McEvilley, "Art in the Dark," *Artforum* 21, no. 10 (Summer 1983): 62–71.
159. For Günter Brus, Otto Muehl, Rodolf Schwarzkogler, and Herman Nitsch, such disarticulations of the body and the acting out of ritual suffering were a way to access surrealism's roots, employ the subconscious, and portray the body as avatar of healing in a painful and changing world. These artists were also inspired by certain Austrian branches of philosophy and science that valued the experiential: empiricism could be distilled by artists into "sense-endowing" gestures. Austrian philosopher Vílem Flusser quoted in Hubert Klocker, "Gesture and the Object: Liberation as Aktion: A European Component of Performative Art," in Schimmel, *Out of Actions*, 175. They represented the Viennese body troubled by modernism, with the artist as "an antithetical, indeed, a tragic subject in the center of the work itself." Klocker, "Gesture and the Object," 191.
160. Philip Ursprung, "'Catholic Tastes': Hurting and Healing the Body in Viennese Actionism in the 1960s," in Amelia Jones and Andrew Stephenson, eds., *Performing the Body, Performing the Text* (New York: Routledge, 1999), 138–52.
161. The bag referred to the deaths of Martin Luther King Jr. and Malcolm X as well as Christ's crucifixion. Houston Conwill from an interview in Los Angeles in May 1979 cited in Jeffries, "Arthur Carraway and Houston Conwill," 267n62.

162. In 1970 Saar also created a piece that incorporated a similar window treatment. *Self Window with Reflection*, 1970, offers four portraits of herself. Here she also limits her palette to black, white, and gray, as if this restricted range of tones allows one to focus more clearly on the subject of race. The figure in deep black mirrors that of *Black Girl's Window*. In the later work, however, that persona is covered up by the shade; lifting this element reveals another image of the artist outlined in pencil, which thus allows the figure to read as white.
163. He never actually took this class but saw it as he passed by. David Hammons, personal communication, December 10, 1996. On his switch from Los Angeles Trade Technical College and Otis Art Institute to Chouinard, see Joseph E. Young, *Three Graphic Artists* (Los Angeles: Los Angeles County Museum of Art, 1971), 7.
164. Powell, "*Notes of a Griot* Demystifies New York," 12. In a few instances, Hammons printed others besides himself. Senga Nengudi tells of a fund-raising event in the mid-1970s that involved printing the bodies of Hollywood celebrities. She was Hammons's assistant on that occasion, greasing bodies in preparation for his printing them. The event, which took place in Los Angeles in the summer of 1975, was a fund-raiser for New York's Just Above Midtown Gallery. It was held at Suzanne Jackson's loft with actors such as Roscoe Lee Brown, Bernie Casey, Vonetta McGee, Brock Peters, Denise Nicholas, and Max Julien on hand. Nengudi interview, June 1996. Bill Lane, "Actors Guild in TV 'Brass' Meet," *Tri-State Defender* (Memphis, TN), August 23, 1975, 32. See also Kellie Jones, ed., *Now Dig This! Art and Black Los Angeles, 1960–1980* (Los Angeles and New York: Hammer Museum and DelMonico Prestel, 2011), 278–79, and Tilton and Charlwood, *L.A. Object and David Hammons Body Prints*, 100–101, 113.
165. David Hammons quoted in Samella Lewis and Ruth Waddy, *Black Artists on Art*, vol. 1 (Los Angeles: Contemporary Crafts, 1969), 21.
166. Mary Schmidt Campbell, *Tradition and Conflict: Images of a Turbulent Decade, 1963–1973* (New York: Studio Museum in Harlem, 1985), and Faith Ringgold, *We Flew over the Bridge: The Memoirs of Faith Ringgold* (Boston: Little, Brown, 1995).
167. Although the artist has always been somewhat cryptic about details of the work's creation, *Black Boy's Window*, 1968, and *The Door (Admissions Office)*, 1969, use the same central image—of a boy with raised hands—demonstrating the more extensive use of silkscreen than is often discussed. Linda Goode Bryant and Marcy S. Philips have described these early works, however, as Hammons translating "the body print onto a silkscreen which was then used to transfer the imprint to the final surface." It seems that the earliest works used this transfer technique, but as Hammons discarded more formal processes of artmaking, the silkscreen aspect was left behind and Hammons went solely with a direct transfer of the body. Goode Bryant and Philips, *Contextures*, 40–41.
168. Kristine Stiles, "Survival Ethos and Destruction Art," *Discourse: Journal for Theoretical Studies in Media and Culture* 14, no. 2 (Spring 1992): 74–102.
169. Hartman, "The Time of Slavery," 767.
170. Hartman, "The Time of Slavery," 770.
171. Joseph E. Young, "Los Angeles," *Art International* 14, no. 8 (October 20, 1970): 74.
172. Thomas McEvilley, "I Think Therefore I Art," *Artforum* 23, no. 10 (Summer 1985): 80.
173. David Hammons interviewed by Kellie Jones, *Reallife Magazine*, no. 16 (Autumn 1986): 4. Interestingly, the term "spade" was also used by LA hipsters in the post-

war jazz scene, where Hammons may have heard it. Daniel Widener, "'Perhaps the Japanese Are to Be Thanked?': Asia, Asian Americans, and the Construction of Black California," *positions* 11, no. 1 (Spring 2003): 150. See also Tobias Wofford, "Can You Dig It? Signifying Race in David Hammons' Spade Series," in Tilton and Charlwood, *L.A. Object and David Hammons Body Prints*, 86–134.

174. John Gruen, "Jim Dine and the Life of Objects," *ArtNews* 76, no. 7 (September 1977): 38–42; Graham W. J. Beal, *Jim Dine: Five Themes* (Minneapolis and New York: Walker Art Center and Abbeville Press, 1984); Jean E. Fienberg, *Jim Dine* (New York: Abbeville Press, 1995); Germano Celant and Clare Bell, *Jim Dine: Walking Memory, 1959–69* (New York: Guggenheim Museum, 1999).

175. Goode Bryant and Philips, *Contextures*, 40–41.

176. Jacqueline Denise Goldsby, *A Spectacular Secret: Lynching in American Life and Literature* (Chicago: University of Chicago Press, 2006).

177. Karen Anne Mason, interview with Suzanne Jackson (1998), *African American Artists of Los Angeles*, 153; Calvin Reid, "Mr. Hammons' Neighborhood," in Robert Sill, ed., *David Hammons in the Hood* (Springfield: Illinois State Museum, 1994), 35.

178. Alexander, "'Can You Be Black and Look at This?,'" 181.

179. Alexander, "'Can You Be Black and Look at This?,'" 186.

180. Robert Sill, introduction to *David Hammons in the Hood*, 7.

181. Emphasis added. This was carried out at Till's mother's wishes. *Jet* 8, no. 19 (September 15, 1955): 8, quoted in Alexander, "'Can You Be Black and Look at This?,'" 190.

182. On the Parker incident see Ross Russell, *Bird Lives! The High Life and Hard Times of Charlie (Yardbird) Parker* (London: Quartet Books, 1972), 366–67, cited in Deborah Menaker Rothschild, "Yardbird Suite: Mixing and Matching Crows and Cons," in *Yardbird Suite: Hammons '93* (Williamstown, MA: Williams College Museum of Art, 1994), 37.

183. David Hammons, personal communication, December 10, 1996.

184. Suzanne Lacy's piece was done in collaboration with the students of the Feminist Art Program at California Institute of Arts. For more on the car in art of this period see Cecile Whiting, *Pop L.A.: Art and the City in the 1960s* (Berkeley: University of California Press, 2006), particularly chap. 2.

185. Affectionately known as a "bug," this "people's car" became identified in the United States with a younger generation. It was compact and fuel-efficient and seemed virtually indestructible. However, its German engineering was also identified with the midcentury war industry: the Beetle shape conformed to the helmets of Nazi soldiers. Paul Gilroy, *Against Race: Imagining Political Culture beyond the Color Line* (Cambridge, MA: Belknap Press of Harvard University Press, 2000).

186. Chris Burden quoted in Paul Schimmel, "Just the Facts," in Chris Burden, Anne Ayres, and Paul Schimmel, *Chris Burden: A Twenty-Year Survey* (Newport Beach, CA: Newport Harbor Art Museum, 1988), 17.

187. Frazer Ward, "Gray Zone: Watching Shoot," *October*, no. 95 (Winter 2001): 115–30.

188. Peter Plagens, "He Got Shot—For His Art," *New York Times*, September 2, 1973, 87.

189. Mike Davis would take up this line in *City of Quartz: Excavating the Future in Los Angeles* (London: Verso, 1990) and *Ecology of Fear* (New York: Metropolitan Books, 1998). It was also reinforced in exhibition catalogues about art in LA, including *Chris*

Burden: Beyond the Limits (1996) and Denmark's Louisiana Museum of Art, Sunshine and Noir: Art in L.A., 1960–1997 (1997).

190. Chris Burden, "Dead Man," in Burden, Ayres, and Schimmel, *Chris Burden: A Twenty-Year Survey*, 58.

191. Karen Anne Mason, interview with Suzanne Jackson (1998), *African American Artists of Los Angeles*, 153.

192. Alexander, "'Can You Be Black and Look at This?,'" 201.

193. Goldsby, *A Spectacular Secret*, 6.

194. C. Ondine Chavoya, "Internal Exiles: The Interventionist Public and Performance Art of Asco," in Erika Suderburg, ed., *Space, Site, Intervention: Situating Installation Art* (Minneapolis: University of Minnesota Press, 2000), 193. See also C. Ondine Chavoya, "Orphans of Modernism: The Performance Art of Asco," in Coco Fusco, ed., *Corpus Delecti: Performance Art of the Americas* (New York: Routledge, 2000), 240–63, and C. Ondine Chavoya and Rita Gonzalez, eds., *Asco: Elite of the Obscure, a Retrospective, 1972–1987* (Williamstown, MA: Williams College Museum of Art; Los Angeles: Los Angeles County Museum of Art; and Ostfildern, Germany: Hatje Cantz, 2011).

195. Harry Gamboa Jr., "In the City of Angels, Chameleons, and Phantoms: Asco, a Case Study of Chicano Art in Urban Tones (or, Asco Was a Four-Member Word)," in Richard Griswold del Castillo, Teresa McKenna, and Yvonne Yarbro-Bejarano, *Chicano Art: Resistance and Affirmation* (Los Angeles: Wight Art Gallery, University of California, Los Angeles, 1992), 125, cited in Chavoya, "Internal Exiles," 195.

196. Goldsby, *A Spectacular Secret*, 10.

197. Goode Bryant and Philips, *Contextures*, 41.

198. Paul Gilroy, *The Black Atlantic: Modernity and Double Consciousness* (Cambridge, MA: Harvard University Press, 1993); Goldsby, *A Spectacular Secret*, 35.

199. Michael Rogin, "'Make My Day!': Spectacle as Amnesia in Imperial Politics," *Representations* 29 (Winter 1990): 103, quoted in Goldsby, *A Spectacular Secret*, 27.

200. For a reading of Hammons's spade and labor see David L. Smith, "David Hammons: Spade Worker," in Rothschild, *Yardbird Suite*, 20–39.

201. David Hammons interviewed by Kellie Jones, *Reallife Magazine*, no. 16 (Autumn 1986): 4.

202. The title—*Curtain for William and Peter*—is a dedication to William T. Williams and Peter Bradley, two African American painters who were also working abstractly. See Kellie Jones, "'It's Not Enough to Say "Black Is Beautiful"': Abstraction at the Whitney, 1969–1974," in Kobena Mercer, ed., *Discrepant Abstractions* (London: Institute of International Visual Arts; Cambridge, MA: MIT Press, 2006).

203. Robert Storr, *Dislocations* (New York: Museum of Modern Art, 1991), 20. See also Calvin Reid, "Kinky Black Hair and Barbecue Bones: Street Life, Social History, and David Hammons," *Arts Magazine* 65, no. 8 (April 1991): 59–63.

204. David Hammons, personal communication, December 10, 1996.

205. Hammons was staying at Nengudi's studio at the time. Nengudi interview, June 1996.

206. Nengudi interview, June 1996.

207. On two separate occasions in 1977 and 1978, rebel forces of the Congolese National Liberation Front (FNLC) invaded the province of Shaba, a mineral-rich area whose

mines accounted for 70 percent of Zaire's foreign exchange earnings in 1977. This was just one in a long line of events intended to disrupt Mobutu's government. He was eventually ousted after three decades in 1997; the country is now known as the Democratic Republic of Congo. The conflict in 1977–78 became a stage for Cold War maneuverings as Western allies poured millions of dollars into Zaire to shore up government forces while claiming the USSR and Cuba were backing the Angola-based rebels. Mobuto stoked the flames and was able to once again prop up his flagging regime with fresh infusions of Western cash. *New York Times Index* (1978), vol. 66; *New York Times Index* (1977), vol. 65; and *The Europa World Year Book* (1997), vol. 2, all s.v. "Zaire."

208. Franklin Sirmans, "Searching for Mr. Hammons," in *David Hammons: Selected Works* (New York: Zwirner & Wirth, 2006), unpaginated.

209. Hammons quoted in Marilyn Elias, "American Black Art Class Offered," *Evening Outlook* (Santa Monica), October 11, 1972, in LACMA Clipping File, 1972, Balch Art Research Library, Los Angeles County Museum of Art.

210. Elias, "American Black Art Class Offered," LACMA Clipping file, 1972, Balch Art Research Library, Los Angeles County Museum of Art.

211. Hassinger interview, May 1996.

212. Nengudi interview, June 1996. Maren Hassinger has pointed out that a version of Studio Z performed together until 1986. Between 1982 and 1983 the group met at the studio of Ulysses Jenkins on Vermont Avenue and included Rudy Perez and May Sun. Though the initial place where Studio Z gathered was David Hammons's studio, during that period he was back and forth between New York and Los Angeles and rarely performed with the group. Hassinger interview, May 1996. This was confirmed by David Hammons, personal communication, December 10, 1996. The exhibition is listed in Josine Ianco-Starrels, "Berg to Chair Getty Museum Board," *Los Angeles Times*, August 29, 1976, K79. The artists included are Houston Conwill, Greg Edwards, David Hammons, Sue Irons (aka Senga Nengudi), Monica Peco, Joe Ray, RoHo, Skunder Boghassian, and Timothy Washington.

213. David Hammons interviewed by Kellie Jones, *Reallife Magazine*, no. 16 (Autumn 1986): 2. Hammons has also patterned his self-image as an artist after the example of jazz musicians. See David Hammons interviewed by Deborah Menaker Rothschild, "Reflections of a Long Distance Runner," *Yardbird Suite*, 43–52; and Kellie Jones, "In the Thick of It: David Hammons and Hair Culture in the 1970s," *Third Text* 12, no. 44 (Autumn 1998): 17–24.

214. Reid, "Mr. Hammons' Neighborhood," 34.

215. Calvin Reid, "Chasing the Blue Train," *Art in America* 77, no. 9 (1989): 197.

216. David Hammons from a discussion during August–September 1977 in Goode Bryant and Philips, *Contextures*, 41.

217. Hammons showed much of this work in New York at Just Above Midtown Gallery in solo exhibitions in 1975, 1976, and 1977.

218. David Hammons interviewed by Kellie Jones, *Reallife Magazine*, no. 16 (Autumn 1986): 2.

219. Greg Tate, "Graf Rulers / GrafUnTrained," in Franklin Sirmans and Lydia Yee, eds., *One Planet under a Groove: Hip-Hop and Contemporary Art* (New York: Bronx Museum of the Arts, 2001), 35.

220. David Hammons from a discussion during August–September 1977 in Goode Bryant and Philips, *Contextures*, 41.
221. Hassinger interview, May 1996.
222. Judith Wilson, "Advanced Placement Tests," *Village Voice*, December 24, 1980, 79.
223. Maren Hassinger, interview by Lorraine O'Grady, *Artist and Influence* 12 (March 12, 1993): 28 (hereafter cited as Hassinger interview by O'Grady).
224. *Still Wind* took place not at JAM but at another Tribeca-based space called Stilwende, hence Hassinger's title. The other dancer had, like Hassinger, been a student of the Donald Byrd / The Group dance company in Los Angeles (the company relocated to New York in 1983). Hassinger remembers the dancer's name as Michelle Green (personal communication, April 2011).
225. Maren Hassinger, personal communication, July 22, 2010. For a comprehensive look at Hassinger's career see *Maren Hassinger . . . Dreaming* (Atlanta: Spelman College Museum of Fine Art, 2016).
226. The Summer School of the Dance moved from Bennington to Mills College in Oakland for one year in 1939. In 1948 the program was restarted in New London, Connecticut, at the Connecticut College School of Dance / American Dance Festival. Its base of operations moved to Duke University in 1977. Thomas K. Hagood, *A History of Dance in American Higher Education: Dance and the American University* (Lewiston, NY: Edwin Mellen, 2000); Sali Ann Kriegsman, *Modern Dance in America: The Bennington Years* (Boston: G. K. Hall & Company, 1981).
227. Susan Manning, *Modern Dance, Negro Dance: Race in Motion* (Minneapolis: University of Minnesota Press, 2004), 10.
228. Manning, *Modern Dance, Negro Dance*, 125.
229. Nengudi interview, June 1996; Hassinger interview, May 1996.
230. Bill T. Jones, "You Don't Have to Be Thin to Dance," *New York Times*, July 19, 1997, A19.
231. Alvin Ailey with A. Peter Bailey, *Revelations: The Autobiography of Alvin Ailey* (Secaucus, NJ: Carol, 1995), 51.
232. While one might ascribe this to a lack of a certain type of preparation, the year following her graduation in 1969, Ulysses Dove, a black male dancer, was able to get a degree in dance after Bennington's own move to coeducation. Dove went on to become an important freelance choreographer. A transfer student to Bennington, Dove started out as a medical student at Howard University before switching to dance. From Howard he pursued studies at the University of Wisconsin, another institution that pioneered the training of modern dance as early as the 1920s. Such rigorous training certainly seems to have given Dove the right imprimatur for a BA from Bennington. Thomas F. Defrantz, "Ulysses Dove," *Encyclopedia of African-American Culture and History* (Gale, 2006), Biography in Context, http://ic.galegroup.com/ic/bic1/BiographiesDetailsPage/BiographiesDetailsWindow?failOverType=&query=&prodId=BIC1&windowstate=normal&contentModules=&display-query=&mode=view&displayGroupName=Biographies&limiter=&currPage=&commentary=&disableHighlighting=false&displayGroups=&sortBy=&search_within_results=&p=BIC1&action=e&catId=&activityType=&scanId=&documentId=GALE%7CCK3444700393&source=Bookmark&u=columbiau&jsid=fc18c3dd82b2dd056c15b843f993eeb3, accessed July 24, 2016.

233. Hassinger interview by O'Grady, 23.
234. Charles Harrison, introduction to Clement Greenberg, *Homemade Esthetics: Observations on Art and Taste* (New York: Oxford University Press, 1999), xx; Alice Goldfarb Marquis, *Art Czar: The Rise and Fall of Clement Greenberg* (Boston: MFA, 2006). The 1971 seminars were eventually published in Greenberg, *Homemade Esthetics*. Greenberg's association with Bennington College began as the result of his relationship with Helen Frankenthaler, who was his lover from 1950 to 1955 and whom he met shortly after her graduation from the college in 1949. Greenberg's second wife, Janice Van Horne, was also a Bennington graduate (1955). See Marquis, *Art Czar*.
235. Hassinger interview by O'Grady, 23; Hassinger interview, May 1996.
236. Banes, *Terpsichore in Sneakers*, xvii.
237. Banes, *Terpsichore in Sneakers*, xxiii.
238. Carrie Lambert, "More or Less Minimalism: Six Notes on Performance and Visual Art in the 1960s," in Ann Goldstein, ed., *A Minimal Future? Art as Object 1958–1968* (Los Angeles: Los Angeles Museum of Contemporary Art, 2004), 105. According to Lambert, Simone Forti's *Huddle*, 1961, is a perfect example of a "dance" that "performs" like an object, inviting viewers to circumnavigate a cacophony of bodies tangled together in a solid mass. The pared-down relation to gesture, to dance as task and as object, in Yvonne Rainer's classic *Trio A*, 1966, opened onto the prosaic and routine but also onto minimalism's notion of the serial.
239. Rainer described an intimate substrata lurking beneath form as "the underbelly of High minimalism." Yvonne Rainer quoted in Sid Sachs, *Yvonne Rainer: Radical Juxtapositions, 1961–2002* (Philadelphia: University of the Arts, 2002), 90. For Trisha Brown, the simplified action was an extraction, a reduction of one's own habitual acts, the kinesthetic memory that formed identity but was instead honed down to trace. On one hand, these currents flowed beneath minimalism's solid structures; on the other hand, they soon created a fissure in the armature of primary forms that would eventually erupt into postminimalism. Hendel Teicher, ed., *Trisha Brown: Dance and Art in Dialogue, 1961–2001* (Andover, MA: Addison Gallery of American Art, Philips Academy, 2001).
240. Banes, *Terpsichore in Sneakers*, xx.
241. Banes, *Terpsichore in Sneakers*, xxii. However, these currents had been part of the development of dance modernism in the United States throughout the twentieth century. Consider the early "primitivism" on which modern dance was based, the interpretation and reinterpretation of non-Western tradition that was by the late 1940s and early 1950s suppressed, abstracted, and sublimated (as were the subjects of visual art). In this way, Susan Manning suggests, "whiteness" was redefined through a "mythic abstraction." African, Asian, and Native American subjects simply reasserted themselves in postmodern dance, casting it as generational development rather than postmodern rupture. Manning, *Modern Dance*, xxi, 180.
242. Janice Ross, *Anna Halprin: Experience as Dance* (Berkeley: University of California Press, 2007), 104.
243. Hassinger interview, May 1996.
244. Hassinger interview by O'Grady, 24.
245. William Wilson, "Sculpture with a Poetic Fiber," *Los Angeles Times*, August 16, 1976,

E6; and Sandy Ballatore, "Hassinger and Mahan: Works in Transition," *Artweek* 7, no. 29 (September 4, 1976): 4. For more on ARCO see ARCO Center for Visual Art Records, 1976–1984, Archives of American Art, Smithsonian Institution.
246. *Agnes Martin*, April 3–May 27, 1973 (organized by the Institute of Contemporary Art, University of Pennsylvania, Philadelphia), and *Eva Hesse: A Memorial Exhibition*, September 18–November 11, 1973 (organized by the Guggenheim Museum, New York).
247. Hassinger interview by O'Grady, 24–25.
248. Beryl Wright, *The Appropriate Object* (Buffalo: Albright-Knox Gallery, 1989), 13–14.
249. Maurice Berger, "'The Weeds Smell Like Iron': The Environments of Maren Hassinger," in Hillwood Art Museum, *Maren Hassinger, 1972–1991* (Brookville, NY: Hillwood Art Museum, Long Island University / C. W. Post Campus, 1991), 4.
250. Berger, "'The Weeds Smell Like Iron,'" 5.
251. Interestingly enough, Hassinger's father and stepmother also lived next door to David Hammons and his family during the late 1960s and early 1970s. Hassinger interview, May 1996.
252. Karen Anne Mason, interview with Alonzo Davis (1994), *African American Artists of Los Angeles*, 224–25.
253. Both pieces have been dismantled.
254. In 1982 Hassinger participated in another project involving the California Freeway system, this one part of a more active revolt. *Transitional Use* was a series of street projects by various artists that called attention to areas of a formerly vibrant neighborhood—Lynwood—that had been condemned to make way for Century Freeway (the last to be built). The freeway took more than a decade to complete because of community opposition and was among the ranks of Freeway and expressway revolts during the 1960s and 1970s. Over that time a gash of abandoned homes and communities grew to seventeen miles long and six blocks wide and became a magnet for illegal activity. Hassinger's contribution, *Pink Pathways*—painting abandoned streets and homes with a vibrant color—called attention once again to the sidewalks and alleys—in an area where thirteen hundred people had lived—forcibly abandoned to the encroaching industrial machine. Hassinger also used the color in a piece in New York a year earlier to call attention to waste awaiting cleanup in Central Park (*Pink Trash*, 1981).
255. Maren Hassinger in Gallery Six, *Maren Hassinger: On Dangerous Ground* (brochure) (Los Angeles: Los Angeles County Museum of Art, May 1981).
256. "Maren Hassinger Installation to Be Presented in 'Gallery Six' at Los Angeles County Museum of Art," press release, Los Angeles County Museum of Art, April 28, 1981.
257. Maureen Megerian, "Entwined with Nature: The Sculpture of Maren Hassinger," *Woman's Art Journal* 17, no. 2 (Autumn 1996 / Winter 1997): 23.
258. Hassinger in Gallery Six, *Maren Hassinger*.
259. Maren Hassinger as quoted in Wright, *The Appropriate Object*, 18.
260. This sense of process work as an initiatory practice is raised by Ballatore, "Hassinger and Mahan," 4.
261. Maren Hassinger, "Maren Hassinger," *International Review of African American Art* 6, no. 1 (1984): 40.

262. Hassinger, "Maren Hassinger," 40.
263. Ballatore, "Hassinger and Mahan," 4.
264. Thanks to Maren Hassinger for pointing these works out to me. Hassinger interview, May 1996.
265. Hassinger interview, May 1996.
266. Lawal, *The Gẹlẹdẹ Spectacle*.
267. Margaret Thompson Drewal, "Improvisation as Participatory Performance: Egungun Masked Dancers in the Yoruba Tradition," in Ann Cooper Albright and David Gere, eds., *Taken by Surprise: A Dance Improvisation Reader* (Middletown, CT: Wesleyan University Press, 2003), 122.
268. Drewal, "Improvisation as Participatory Performance," 120–21.
269. April Kingsley, *Afro-American Abstraction* (San Francisco: Art Museum Association, 1982), n.p.
270. Mary Lou Loper, "Jazz and Culture Mix in the Park, Barnsdall Event Honors Afro-American Museums," *Los Angeles Times*, August 18, 1982, F7. *Afro-American Abstraction* traveled between 1982 and 1984 in a somewhat altered configuration, without large and installation-based works by Barbara Chase-Riboud and Hammons.
271. For a while Hammons sublet his LA studio to the artist RoHo, another member of the Studio Z collective, allowing the performance-based practices to continue there. Hassinger interview, May 1996.
272. Hassinger interview, May 1996.
273. I am basing my reading of *Flying* on a review of the piece by D. Francine Farr, "Civilization and Nature," *Artweek* 13, no. 18 (September 4, 1982): 4.
274. Farr, "Civilization and Nature," 4.
275. Farr, "Civilization and Nature," 4.
276. Ann Gibson, "Recasting the Canon: Norman Lewis and Jackson Pollock," *Artforum* 22 (May 1984): 64–70.
277. Benston, *Performing Blackness*, 14. He refers to the work of Brecht, Artaud, and Grotowski here.
278. McKittrick, *Demonic Grounds*; Henri Lefebvre, *The Production of Space* (Oxford, UK: Blackwell, 1991); Miwon Kwon, *One Place after Another: Site-Specific Art and Locational Identity* (Cambridge, MA: MIT Press, 2002), 24–25.
279. Guthrie P. Ramsey Jr., *The Amazing Bud Powell: Black Genius, Jazz History, and the Challenge of Bebop* (Berkeley: University of California Press, 2013), 181.
280. Gylbert Coker, "Human Pegs / Pole Dreams," *Village Voice*, September 28, 1982, 79. For Krista Thompson, on the other hand, glistening and emollient skin does not signal self-love. Instead it reflects continuities with the dynamics of objecthood under economies of transatlantic slavery. See Krista Thompson, *Shine: The Visual Economy of Light in African Diasporic Aesthetic Practice* (Durham, NC: Duke University Press, 2015), chap. 4.
281. Rosalind Krauss, "Robert Morris: Autour du Probleme corps/Esprit," *Art Press* 193 (June 1994): 24–32.
282. José Muñoz, "Cruising the Toilet: LeRoi Jones / Amiri Baraka, Radical Black Traditions, and Queer Futurity," *GLQ* 13, nos. 2–3 (2007): 360.

CONCLUSION

1. Ball's son James Presley Ball Jr. became the editor of Helena's *Colored Citizen* newspaper in the late nineteenth century, along with, it seems, Ball Sr. himself. Deborah Willis, *J. P. Ball, Daguerrean and Studio Photographer* (New York: Garland, 1993); see also Quintard Taylor, *In Search of the Racial Frontier: African Americans in the American West, 1528–1990* (New York: Norton, 1998), 210–12, on black Helena. Honolulu housed a military outpost that was a theater for the Spanish American War; Q. Taylor, *In Search of the Racial Frontier*, chap. 6. On Seattle's black communities see Quintard Taylor, *The Forging of a Black Community: Seattle's Central District from 1870 through the Civil Rights Era* (Seattle: University of Washington Press, 1994).
2. The Nicodemus Historical Society was inaugurated in the 1980s by grandchildren of the town's founders. In the late 1990s, the town was granted national landmark status. Highlighted was the early architecture of the plains, such as sod dugout homes. Cultural celebrations such as Founders Day or storytelling centralizing African American life on the American plains were also featured. La Barbara James Wigfall, "Waiting on the Dawn at Demus," in Craig E. Barton, ed., *Sites of Memory: Perspectives on Architecture and Race* (Princeton, NJ: Princeton Architectural Press, 2001), 146–57. Blackdom, New Mexico, for instance, is now considered a ghost town.
3. Amy Weisser, "Making *Brown v. Board of Education*: Memorializing Separate but Unequal Spaces," in Barton, *Sites of Memory*, 97.
4. "Charles White Park," Department of Parks and Recreation, County of Los Angeles, http://parks.lacounty.gov/wps/portal/dpr/Parks/Charles_White_Park, accessed August 9, 2016.
5. Susan L. Chaney, "Artist Makes Unusual Medium Talk," *Desert Star*, August 19, 1994, C1, C3. See also Franklin Sirmans with Yael Lipschutz, *Noah Purifoy: Junk Dada* (Los Angeles: Los Angeles County Museum of Art, 2015).
6. Terry McMillan, a Purifoy collector, had written the artist into her novel *Waiting to Exhale* (New York: Viking, 1992) when one of the protagonists, Savannah, became an art collector as well. See Sue Welsh, "Noah Purifoy of Joshua Tree," *International Review of African American Art* 10, no. 4 (1993): 6.
7. Julia Chaplin, "Art Blooms in the Desert," *New York Times*, April 21, 2006, F1, F6; Caroline Ryder, "Bloody Bunnies," *LA Weekly*, April 14, 2006, 42.
8. Foundation board members included artists Joe Lewis and Ed Ruscha, and scholars Paul Karlstrom and Richard Cándida Smith. Suzanne Muchnic, "To Protect and Preserve a Desert Legacy," *Los Angeles Times*, January 14, 2001, Calendar, 1.
9. Noah Purifoy, "Joshua Tree: A Celebration of Junk Art," undated statement, Noah Purifoy Papers, 1935–98, Archives of American Art, Smithsonian Institution. Welsh, "Noah Purifoy of Joshua Tree," 6–13.
10. See "125th Street, Houston Conwill, *The Open Secret*, 1986," MTA Arts & Design, MTA, http://web.mta.info/mta/aft/permanentart/permart.html?agency=NYCT&line=6&station=11&artist=1, accessed July 16, 2016.
11. The ring shout is one of the earliest examples of African diasporic spiritual performance in the New World. Found in the Caribbean and the United States, it combines a counterclockwise shuffling movement with singing, rhythmic prayer, and the percussive sounds of clapping hands and stamping feet. Thanks to Guthrie P.

Ramsey Jr. for his ideas on this. See also Samuel A. Floyd Jr., "Ring Shout! Literary Studies, Historical Studies, and Black Music Inquiry," *Black Music Research Journal* 22, no. 1 (Spring 2002).

12. Miwon Kwon, *One Place after Another: Site-Specific Art and Locational Identity* (Cambridge, MA: MIT Press, 2002), 109, 50–51.
13. Nickerson Gardens was completed in 1955 and named for the founder of Golden State Mutual Life Insurance Company, William Nickerson Jr.
14. Kerry James Marshall, Terrie Sultan, and Arthur Jafa, *Kerry James Marshall* (New York: Harry N. Abrams, 2000).
15. Some continued a family tradition of art, such as Alison Saar. Like her mother, Betye, Alison Saar is inspired by found objects, but her carved figures take these traditions toward the monumental. C. Ian White, the keeper of his father's legacy and archive, makes exquisite drawings and funky sculpture in his own right in Altadena's foothills.
16. By 1985 there were no less than seven different galleries, enough for a Leimert Park gallery walk. Though Alonzo and Dale Brockman Davis closed Brockman Gallery in 1990, they sublet its spaces to other artists, a move that maintained the area's profile as a cultural precinct. These sites represented a range of interests including crafts, photographs, and African art; Gallery Tanner was another contemporary-focused space opened by Samella Lewis in the area in 1976. The poet Kamau Daaood and drummer Billy Higgins, for instance, took over Brockman Gallery to create a performance venue called the World Stage. In 2014 Michelle Papillion opened the gallery Papillion at the same site. Michelle Sorey, "7-Gallery Walking Tour of Black Art," *Los Angeles Times*, July 18, 1985, SD-E4; Karen Anne Mason, interview with Alonzo Davis (1994), *African American Artists of Los Angeles*, 311–13; *Leimert Park: The Story of a Village in South Central Los Angeles* (dir. Jeanette Lindsay; Foster Johnson Studios, 2008). Carolina A. Miranda, "Mark Bradford's Art and Practice to Bring Art, Social Services to Leimert," *Los Angeles Times*, December 15, 2014.
17. Other younger LA art stars include Edgar Arceneaux and Brenna Youngblood.
18. Toni Morrison, *Unspeakable Things Unspoken: The Afro-American Presence in American Literature* (Tanner Lecture Library, 2011; first published 1988). As Biggers himself put it, "Particularly for 'minority' artists there is a tendency to be exoticized, and that is something I try to avoid by not being front and center all the time." Sanford Biggers quoted in Tom Butter, "Interview with Sanford Biggers," *Whitehot Magazine*, April 2010.
19. Josh Sides, *L.A. City Limits: African American Los Angeles from the Great Depression to the Present* (Berkeley: University of California Press, 2003), 193.
20. Carol Marie Cropper, "Black Man Fatally Dragged in Possible Racial Killing," *New York Times*, June 10, 1998, A16. In fact, *Bittersweet Fruit* was first shown in Texas in 2002 at the artist's solo exhibition at the Contemporary Arts Museum, Houston, *Sanford Biggers: Afrotemple*, curated by Valerie Cassel. Eugenie Tsai, "A Tree Grows in Brooklyn . . . and Beyond," in Eugenie Tsai, *Sanford Biggers: Sweet Funk—An Introspective* (New York: Brooklyn Museum, 2011), 11. A related work, *Kalimba II*, also from 2002, features an upright piano split by a wall and also accesses the architectural interventions of Gordon Matta-Clark.

    As early as 1989 during his college studies in Atlanta Biggers referenced the history of lynching, responding to a Confederate flag hanging over his apartment complex. That year he made a piece that combined a wall-mounted metal object, highly polished in the manner of minimalism or finish fetish (symbolizing the trajectory of modernism) with a rusted chain, coated with tar and thatch, that hung down from it. Below these items, on the ground, was a sort of package also wrapped in thatch and tar as well as mud. It was the Georgia state flag, which between 1956 and 2001 incorporated the Confederate standard on three-quarters of its surface. Stephanie Cash, "In the Studio with Sanford Biggers," *Art in America* 99, no. 3 (March 2011).

21. While overt lynching imagery by African American artists is not as pervasive as one might imagine, one searing image seems to be in direct conversation with *Bittersweet Fruit*. It is Aaron Douglas's *Idyll of the Deep South*, 1934 (from his mural series *Aspects of Negro Life* at the Schomburg Center for Research in Black Culture), where a pair of feet and a linear rope hang all but hidden among the leafy trees at the upper right.

22. Bottle tree symbolism has of course been used by David Hammons in numerous works from the 1980s, as well as more recently by sculptor Gary Simmons in pieces such as *Wishbone*, 2008.

23. Still, the piece was inspired by Louisiana's Jena 6 case of 2006–7, in which territorial and racial disputes at Jena High School provoked violence as well as the hanging of nooses from a tree. See Gregory Volk, "Blossom (Noun); Blossom (Verb): Five Sections for Sanford Biggers," in Tsai, *Sanford Biggers*, 21–22.

24. Sanford Biggers quoted in Valerie Cassel, *Sanford Biggers: Afrotemple* (Houston: Contemporary Arts Museum, 2002), 8.

25. Volk, "Blossom (Noun); Blossom (Verb)," 24; Grey Gundaker and Judith McWillie, *No Space Hidden: The Spirit of African American Yard Work* (Knoxville: University of Tennessee Press, 2005), 41.

26. Gerald Horne, *Fire This Time: The Watts Uprising and the 1960s* (New York: Da Capo, 1997), 59, 65, 107.

27. Robin D. G. Kelley, *Freedom Dreams: The Black Radical Imagination* (Boston: Beacon, 2002); Christine Y. Kim, *Black Belt* (New York: Studio Museum in Harlem, 2003); Daniel Widener, "'Perhaps the Japanese Are to Be Thanked?': Asia, Asian Americans, and the Construction of Black California," *positions* 11, no. 1 (Spring 2003): 135–81; Vijay Prashad, *Everybody Was Kung Fu Fighting: Afro-Asian Connections and the Myth of Cultural Purity* (Boston: Beacon, 2001); George Lipsitz, *Footsteps in the Dark: The Hidden Histories of Popular Music* (Minneapolis: University of Minnesota Press, 2007), chap. 9. Yet as Muñoz reminds us, we shouldn't forget that "cross-identificatory recognition" is also forged through an at times "brutal choreography." The second half of the twentieth century also witnessed ambivalence and conflict in Afro-Asian relations: the rise of Japanese imperialism marked by World War II; African American soldiers fighting in Asia (first in Japan but extending to Korea, China, Vietnam, Cambodia, and Laos); African Americans along the West Coast inheriting Japanese neighborhoods during the internment years (1942–45); and the conflicts of the second Watts Rebellion in 1992. José Muñoz, "Cruising the Toilet: LeRoi Jones / Amiri Baraka, Radical Black Traditions, and Queer Futurity," *GLQ* 13, nos. 2–3 (2007): 363.

28. Duke Ellington's *The Afro-Eurasian Eclipse (A Suite in Eight Parts)* (1975), with its

own explorations of Asian musical forms, surely was one influence, given both the title and Hammons's fascination with musical cultures.

29. For discussions of American artists' approach to Asia see Alexandra Munroe, *The Third Mind: American Artists Contemplate Asia, 1860–1989* (New York: Guggenheim Museum, 2009), and Cynthia J. Mills, Lee Glazer, and Amelia A. Goerlitz, eds., *East-West Interchanges in American Art: A Long and Tumultuous Relationship* (Washington, DC: Smithsonian Institution Scholarly Press, 2012). On the postwar art of Japan see Ming Tiampo and Alexandra Munroe, *Gutai: Splendid Playground* (New York: Guggenheim Museum, 2013), and Doryun Chong, Michio Hayashi, Kenji Kajiya, and Fumihiko Sumitomo, eds., *From Postwar to Postmodern: Art in Japan 1945–1989* (New York: Museum of Modern Art, 2012). On Asian American art see Margo Machida, *Unsettled Visions: Contemporary Asian American Artists and the Social Imaginary* (Durham, NC: Duke University Press, 2008), and Gordon H. Chang, Mark Dean Johnson, and Paul J. Karlstom, eds., *Asian American Art: A History, 1850–1970* (Stanford, CA: Stanford University Press, 2008). On black and Asian intersectionalities see Hazel M. McFerson, ed., *Blacks and Asians: Crossings, Conflict and Commonality* (Durham, NC: Carolina Academic Press, 2006).

30. The relationship between African American culture, hip-hop stylings, and Japanese context also was explored by Biggers's contemporary Iona Rozeal Brown.

31. Tom Butter, "Interview with Sanford Biggers," *Whitehot Magazine*, April 2010.

32. Jacqueline Tobin and Raymond G. Dobard, *Hidden in Plain View: A Secret Story of Quilts and the Underground Railroad* (New York: Doubleday, 1999). Sanford Biggers is related to the painter John Biggers, who also used the quilt form as an inspiration in many works.

33. Keith Moxey, *Visual Time: The Image in History* (Durham, NC: Duke University Press, 2013), 45.

34. Edward W. Soja, *Thirdspace: Journeys to Los Angeles and Other Real-and-Imagined Places* (Cambridge, MA: Blackwell, 1996), 81, 143. See also bell hooks, "Choosing the Margin as a Space of Radical Openness," in *Yearning: Race, Gender, and Cultural Politics* (Boston: South End, 1990).

35. Sara Ahmed, *Queer Phenomenology: Orientations, Objects, Others* (Durham, NC: Duke University Press, 2006), 116; Edward W. Said, *Orientalism* (New York: Vintage, 1978), as discussed in Ahmed, *Queer Phenomenology*.

36. Homi K. Bhabha, *The Location of Culture* (New York: Routledge, 1990), 211.

37. David Eng, "Transnational Adoption and Queer Diasporas," *Social Text* 21, no. 3 (2003): 4, as cited in Ahmed, *Queer Phenomenology*, 154.

38. Brent Hayes Edwards, *The Practice of Diaspora: Literature, Translation, and the Rise of Black Internationalism* (Cambridge, MA: Harvard University Press, 2003), 237–42. Here Edwards discusses the Paris-based Union Intercoloniale, which around 1924 had members hailing from Algeria, Madagascar, Senegal, Martinique, and Indochina, including figures such as a young Ho Chi Minh.

39. Edwards, *The Practice of Diaspora*, 233.

40. Tom Butter, "Interview with Sanford Biggers," *Whitehot Magazine*, April 2010.

41. Ahmed, *Queer Phenomenology*, 156.

SELECTED BIBLIOGRAPHY

ARCHIVES

Archives of American Art, Smithsonian Institution
    Ankrum Gallery Records, 1960–1990
    ARCO Center for Visual Art Records, 1976–1984
    Dwan Gallery Records, 1959–82
    John Outterbridge Papers, 1953–1997
    Noah Purifoy Papers, 1935–98
    Charles W. White Papers, c. 1930–1982
    Woman's Building Records, 1970–1992

Artists Files, Balch Art Research Library, Los Angeles County Museum of Art

Artists Files, Museum of Modern Art Library, New York

Emory University, Manuscripts, Archives, and Rare Book Library
    Samella Lewis Papers

Getty Research Institute, Research Library, Special Collections and Visual Resources

New York Public Library, Schomburg Center for Research in Black Culture

New York University, Fales Library and Special Collections

University of California, Los Angeles, Department of Special Collections, Charles E. Young Research Library

INTERVIEWS AND ORAL HISTORIES

African American Artists of Los Angeles. Interviews by Karen Anne Mason.
    Los Angeles: Oral History Program of the University of California.
    Kinshasha Holman Conwill, 1996
    Alonzo Davis, 1994
    Cecil Fergerson, 1996
    Marvin Harden, 1992
    Suzanne Jackson, 1998

Samella Lewis, 1995
John Outterbridge, 1993
William Pajaud, 1993
Noah Purifoy, 1992
John Riddle, 2000
Betye Saar, 1996
Curtis Tann, 1995
Ruth Waddy, 1993

Archives of American Art, Smithsonian Institution.
> Bruce Conner: "Oral History Interview with Bruce Conner, 1974 March 29."
> George Herms: Paul Karlstrom, "Oral History Interview with George Herms, 1993 December 8, 10, 13–1994 March 10."
> John Outterbridge: Allen Bassing, "Interview with John Outterbridge, 1973 January 3."
> Charles Wilbert White: "Oral History Interview with Charles Wilbert White, 1965 March 9."

Various
> Maren Hassinger, telephone interview with the author, May 29, 1996.
> *Los Angeles Art Community: Edward Kienholz*, interviewed by James Weschler. Los Angeles: Oral History Program of the University of California, 1976.
> Samella Lewis, interviewed by Richard Cándida Smith. *Samella Lewis: Image and Belief*. Los Angeles: Getty Research Institute for the Arts and Humanities, 1999.
> Miriam Matthews, interviewed by Eleanor Roberts, March 14, 16, 17, and 22, 1977, in Ruth Edmonds Hill, ed., *The Black Women Oral History Project*, vol. 7, The Arthur and Elizabeth Schlesinger Library on the History of Women in America, Radcliffe College. Westport, CT: Meckler, 1991.
> Evangeline Juliette (E. J.) Montgomery, interview with the author, May 18, 2003.
> Senga Nengudi, telephone interview with the author, June 3, 1996.

BOOKS AND ARTICLES

Ahmed, Sara. *Queer Phenomenology: Orientations, Objects, Others*. Durham, NC: Duke University Press, 2006.

Ailey, Alvin, with A. Peter Bailey. *Revelations: The Autobiography of Alvin Ailey*. Secaucus, NJ: Carol, 1995.

Albright, Ann Cooper, and David Gere, eds. *Taken by Surprise: A Dance Improvisation Reader*. Middletown, CT: Wesleyan University Press, 2003.

Alexander, Elizabeth. *The Black Interior*. Minneapolis: Graywolf, 2004.

Altshuler, Bruce. *The Avant-Garde in Exhibition: New Art in the 20th Century*. New York: Harry N. Abrams, 1994.

Anderson, Jeffrey E. *Conjure in African American Society*. Baton Rouge: Louisiana State University Press, 2007.

Appadurai, Arjun. *The Social Life of Things: Commodities in Cultural Perspective*. Cambridge: Cambridge University Press, 1986.

Armstrong, Richard, and Richard Marshall, eds. *The New Sculpture 1965–1975: Between Geometry and Gesture*. New York: Whitney Museum of American Art, 1990.

Avila, Eric. *Popular Culture in the Age of White Flight: Fear and Fantasy in Suburban Los Angeles*. Berkeley: University of California Press, 2004.

Baker, Houston A., Jr. *Modernism and the Harlem Renaissance*. Chicago: University of Chicago Press, 1987.

Baldwin, Davarian L. *Chicago's New Negroes: Modernity, the Great Migration, and Black Urban Life*. Chapel Hill: University of North Carolina Press, 2007.

Ballatore, Sandy. "Hassinger and Mahan: Works in Transition." *Artweek* 7, no. 29 (September 4, 1976): 4.

Banes, Sally. *Terpsichore in Sneakers: Post-Modern Dance*. Middletown, CT: Wesleyan University Press, 1987. First published 1977.

Barnwell, Andrea D. *Charles White*. San Francisco: Pomegranate, 2002.

Barron, Stephanie, Sheri Bernstein, and Ilene Susan Fort. *Made in California: Art, Image and Identity, 1990–2000*. Los Angeles: Los Angeles County Museum of Art; Berkeley: University of California Press, 2000.

Barton, Craig E., ed. *Sites of Memory: Perspectives on Architecture and Race*. Princeton, NJ: Princeton Architectural Press, 2001.

Battcock, Gregory, and Robert Nickas, eds. *The Art of Performance: A Critical Anthology*. New York: Dutton, 1984.

Beardsley, John, et al. *The Quilts of Gee's Bend*. Atlanta, GA: Tinwood Books in association with the Museum of Fine Arts, Houston, 2002.

Belafonte, Harry, and Sidney Portier. "Brothuhs." In "Charles White: Art and Soul," special issue, *Freedomways* 20, no. 3 (1980): 195–96.

Belafonte, Harry, with Michael Shnayerson. *My Song: A Memoir of Art, Race, and Defiance*. New York: Alfred A. Knopf, 2011.

Belloli, Jay, and Karen Jacobson. *Radical Past: Contemporary Art and Music in Pasadena, 1960–1974*. Pasadena: Armory Center for the Arts / Art Center College of Design, 1999.

Bennett, Tony. *The Birth of the Museum: History, Theory, Politics*. London: Routledge, 1995.

———. "The Exhibitionary Complex." *New Formations* 4 (Spring 1988): 73–102.

Benston, Kimberly W. *Performing Blackness: Enactments of African-American Modernism*. London: Routledge, 2000.

Berger, Maurice. "'The Weeds Smell Like Iron': The Environments of Maren Hassinger." In *Maren Hassinger, 1972–1991*, 3–12. Brookville, NY: Hillwood Art Museum, Long Island University / C. W. Post Campus, 1991.

Bernstein, Roberta, and Kirk Varnedoe. *Ferus*. New York: Rizzoli, 2009.

Bettelheim, Judith. "Women and Masquerade and Performance." In "Women's Masquerades in Africa and the Diaspora," special issue, *African Arts* 31, no. 2 (Spring 1998): 68–70, 93–94.

Bhabha, Homi K. *The Location of Culture*. New York: Routledge, 1994.

Bhavnani, Kum-Kum, ed. *Feminism and "Race."* New York: Oxford University Press, 2001.

Bocola, Sandro, and Ezio Bassani, eds. *African Seats*. Munich: Prestel, 1995.

Bogle, Donald. *Toms, Coons, Mulattoes, Mammies, and Bucks*. New exp. ed. New York: Viking, 1991. First published 1973.

Bois, Yve-Alain, and Rosalind E. Krauss. *Formless: A User's Guide*. New York: Zone Books, 1997.

Bontemps, Arna. *God Sends Sunday.* New York: Washington Square Press, 2005. First published 1931.

Brandon, James R., and Samuel L. Leiter, eds. *Japanese Theater in the World.* New York: Japan Foundation, 1997.

Brenson, Michael. "Lynch Fragments." In Lucinda H. Gedeon, ed., *Melvin Edwards Sculpture: A Thirty-Year Retrospective, 1963–1993,* 21–33. Purchase: Neuberger Museum of Art, State University of New York at Purchase, 1993.

Brooks, Daphne A. *Bodies in Dissent: Spectacular Performances of Race and Freedom, 1850–1910.* Durham, NC: Duke University Press, 2006.

———. Introduction to *The Great Escapes: Four Slave Narratives,* xv–lxvii. New York: Barnes & Noble Classics, 2007.

Broude, Norma, Mary D. Garrard, and Judith K. Brodsky. *The Power of Feminist Art: The American Movement of the 1970s, History and Impact.* New York: Harry N. Abrams, 1994.

Brown, Scot. *Fighting for US: Maulana Karenga, the US Organization, and Black Cultural Nationalism.* New York: New York University Press, 2003.

———. "The US Organization, Black Power Vanguard Politics, and the United Front Ideal: Los Angeles and Beyond." *Black Scholar* 31, nos. 3-4 (Fall/Winter 2001): 21–30.

Bryant, Clora, et al. *Central Avenue Sounds: Jazz in Los Angeles.* Berkeley: University of California Press, 1998.

Bryan-Wilson, Julia. *Art Workers: Radical Practice in the Vietnam War Era.* Berkeley: University of California Press, 2009.

Burden, Chris, Anne Ayres, and Paul Schimmel. *Chris Burden: A Twenty-Year Survey.* Newport Beach, CA: Newport Harbor Art Museum, 1988.

Butler, Cornelia H., and Lisa Gabrielle Mark. *WACK! Art and the Feminist Revolution.* Los Angeles: Museum of Contemporary Art, 2007.

Cade, Toni. *The Black Woman.* New York: New American Library, 1970.

California African American Museum. *Affirming a Visual Heritage: The Collection of Alonzo and Dale Davis.* Los Angeles: California African American Museum, 1996.

Campbell, Mary Schmidt. *Tradition and Conflict: Images of a Turbulent Decade, 1963–1973.* New York: Studio Museum in Harlem, 1985.

Cándida Smith, Richard. *Utopia and Dissent: Art, Poetry, and Politics in California.* Berkeley: University of California Press, 1995.

Carbone, Teresa A., and Kellie Jones, eds. *Witness: Art and Civil Rights in the Sixties.* Brooklyn: Monacelli Press and the Brooklyn Museum, 2014.

Carpenter, Jane Hattie. "Conjure Woman: Betye Saar and Rituals of Transformation, 1960–1990." PhD diss., University of Michigan, 2002.

Carpenter, Jane H., with Betye Saar. *Betye Saar.* San Francisco: Pomegranate, 2003.

Carter, Francine R. "The Golden State Mutual Afro-American Art Collection." *Black Art* 1, no. 2 (1976): 15–16.

Cassell, Valerie. *Sanford Biggers: Afrotemple.* Houston: Contemporary Art Center, 2002.

Celant, Germano, and Clare Bell. *Jim Dine: Walking Memory, 1959–69.* New York: Guggenheim Museum, 1999.

Chavoya, C. Ondine. "Internal Exiles: The Interventionist Public Performance Art of Asco." In Erika Suderburg, ed., *Space, Site, Intervention: Situating Installation Art,* 189–208. Minneapolis: University of Minnesota Press, 2000.

―――. "Orphans of Modernism: The Performance Art of Asco." In Coco Fusco, ed., *Corpus Delecti: Performance Art of the Americas*, 240–64. New York: Routledge, 2000.

Chavoya, C. Ondine, and Rita Gonzalez, eds. *Asco: Elite of the Obscure, a Retrospective, 1972–1987*. Williamstown, MA: Williams College Museum of Art; Los Angeles: Los Angeles County Museum of Art; and Ostfildern, Germany: Hatje Cantz, 2011.

Chicago, Judy. *Through the Flower: My Struggle as a Woman Artist*. Garden City, NY: Doubleday, 1975.

Childs, Adrienne L. *Margo Humphrey*. Petaluma, CA: Pomegranate, 2009.

Cho, Sumi K. "Korean Americans vs. African Americans: Conflict and Construction." In Robert Gooding-Williams, ed., *Reading Rodney King, Reading Urban Uprising*, 196–211. New York: Routledge, 1993.

Chong, Doryun, Michio Hayashi, Kenji Kajiya, and Fumihiko Sumitomo, eds. *From Postwar to Postmodern: Art in Japan 1945–1989*. New York: Museum of Modern Art, 2012.

Clarke, Kamari Maxine. *Mapping Yorùbá Networks: Power and Agency in the Making of Transnational Communities*. Durham, NC: Duke University Press, 2004.

Clifford, James. "Diasporas." *Cultural Anthropology* 9, no. 3 (1994): 302–38.

Cogswell, David, and Joe Lee. *Existentialism for Beginners*. Hanover, NH: For Beginners, 2008.

Coker, Gylbert. "Human Pegs / Pole Dreams." *Village Voice*, September 28, 1982, 75–79.

Cole, Herbert M. "Art as a Verb in Igboland." *African Arts* 3, no. 1 (Autumn 1969): 34–41, 88.

Cole, Herbert M., and Doran H. Ross. *The Arts of Ghana*. Los Angeles: Museum of Cultural History, University of California, 1977.

Cole Meo, Yvonne. "Ritual as Art: The Work of Houston Conwill." *International Review of African American Art* 3, no. 3 (Fall 1979): 4–13.

Collier-Thomas, Bettye, and V. P. Franklin, eds. *Sisters in Struggle: African American Women in the Civil Rights and Black Power Movement*. New York: New York University Press, 2001.

Collins, Lisa Gail. "The Art of Transformation: Parallels in the Black Arts and Feminist Art Movement." In Lisa Gail Collins and Margo Natalie Crawford, eds., *New Thoughts on the Black Arts Movement*, 273–96. New Brunswick, NJ: Rutgers University Press, 2006.

Collins, Lisa Gail, and Margo Natalie Crawford, eds. *New Thoughts on the Black Arts Movement*. New Brunswick, NJ: Rutgers University Press, 2006.

Conwill, Houston. "Interview with Betye Saar." *Black Art* 3, no. 1 (1979): 4–15.

Cooks, Bridget R. *Exhibiting Blackness: African Americans and the American Art Museum*. Amherst: University of Massachusetts Press, 2011.

―――. "See Me Now: Visual Depictions of Black Americans." *Camera Obscura* 36 (September 1995): 66–83.

Copeland, Huey. *Bound to Appear: Art, Slavery, and the Site of Blackness in Multicultural America*. Chicago: University of Chicago Press, 2013.

Cortez, Jayne. "Jayne Cortez in Her Own Words." In Jerome Fortier, ed., *Watts: Art and Social Change in Los Angeles, 1965–2002*, 35–37. Milwaukee: Haggerty Museum of Art, Marquette University, 2003.

Cortor, Eldzier. "He Was at Home Creatively in Any Locale." In "Charles White: Art and Soul," special issue, *Freedomways* 20, no. 3 (1980): 149–50.

Craft, Catherine. *Melvin Edwards: Five Decades*. Dallas: Nasher Sculpture Center, 2015.

Crawford, Margo Natalie. "Black Light on the Wall of Respect: The Chicago Black Arts Movement." In Lisa Gail Collins and Margo Natalie Crawford, eds., *New Thoughts on the Black Arts Movement*, 23–42. New Brunswick, NJ: Rutgers University Press, 2006.

Crenshaw, Kimberlé, and Gary Peller. "Reel Time / Real Justice." In Robert Gooding-Williams, ed., *Reading Rodney King, Reading Urban Uprising*, 56–70. New York: Routledge, 1993.

Crow, Thomas E. *Modern Art in the Common Culture*. New Haven, CT: Yale University Press, 1996.

Cuff, Dana. *The Provisional City: Los Angeles Stories of Architecture and Urbanism*. Cambridge, MA: MIT Press, 2000.

Darling, Michael, ed. *Target Practice: Painting under Attack, 1949–1978*. Seattle: Seattle Art Museum, 2009.

Davidson, Russ, and David Craven. *Latin American Posters: Public Aesthetics and Mass Politics*. Santa Fe: Museum of New Mexico Press, 2006.

Davis, Angela Y. "Reflections on the Black Women's Role in the Community of Slaves." *Black Scholar* 3, no. 4 (1971): 2–15.

Davis, Mike. *City of Quartz: Excavating the Future in Los Angeles*. London: Verso, 1990.

de Certeau, Michel. *The Practice of Everyday Life*. Berkeley: University of California Press, 1984.

Dent, Gina, and Michele Wallace, eds. *Black Popular Culture*. Seattle: Bay, 1992.

Diawara, Manthia. "Blaxploitation in Africa." In Richard J. Powell, David A. Bailey, and Petrine Archer-Straw, eds., *Back to Black: Art, Cinema and the Racial Imaginary*, 162–65. London: Whitechapel Gallery, 2005.

———. "The 1960s in Bamako: Malick Sidibé and James Brown." In Harry J. Elam Jr. and Kennell A. Jackson, eds., *Black Cultural Traffic: Crossroads in Global Performance and Popular Culture*, 242–65. Ann Arbor: University of Michigan Press, 2005.

Dickson Art Center. *The Negro in American Art*. Los Angeles: UCLA Art Galleries, Dickson Art Center, 1966.

Dils, Ann, and Ann Cooper Albright, eds. *Moving History / Dancing Cultures: A Dance History Reader*. Middletown, CT: Wesleyan University Press, 2001.

Di Suvero, Mark. *Mark di Suvero: Dreambook*. Berkeley: University of California Press, 2008.

Dixon Gottschild, Brenda. *Digging the Africanist Presence in American Performance: Dance and Other Contexts*. Westport, CT: Greenwood, 1996.

Donaldson, Jeff. "Ten in Search of a Nation." *Black World* 19, no. 12 (1970): 80–89.

Drewal, Henry John, and Margaret Thompson Drewal. *Gẹlẹdẹ́: Art and Female Power among the Yoruba*. Bloomington: Indiana University Press, 1990. First published 1983.

Drewal, Margaret Thompson. "Improvisation as Participatory Performance: Egungun Masked Dancers in the Yoruba Tradition." In Ann Cooper Albright and David Gere, eds., *Taken by Surprise: A Dance Improvisation Reader*. Middletown, CT: Wesleyan University Press, 2003.

Driskell, David C. *The Other Side of Color: African American Art in the Collection of Camille O. and William H. Cosby, Jr.* San Francisco: Pomegranate, 2001.

———. *Two Centuries of Black American Art*. Los Angeles: Los Angeles County Museum of Art, 1976.

Dubin, Steven C. "Artistic Production and Social Control." *Social Forces* 64, no. 3 (March 1986): 667–88.

Duncan, Michael. *L.A. Raw: Abject Expressionism in Los Angeles, 1945–1980, from Rico Lebrun to Paul McCarthy*. Santa Monica: Foggy Notion Books, 2012.

Eder, Rita. "Razón y sin razón del arte efímero: Algunos ejemplares latinoamericanos." *Plural* 8, no. 90, n.s. (March 1979): 28.

Edwards, Brent Hayes. *The Practice of Diaspora: Literature, Translation, and the Rise of Black Internationalism*. Cambridge, MA: Harvard University Press, 2003.

Edwards, Jason, and Stephanie L. Taylor, eds. *Joseph Cornell: Opening the Box*. Bern, Switzerland: Peter Lang, 2007.

Enwezor, Okwui. "A Question of Place: Revisions, Reassessments, Diaspora." In Salah Hassan and Iftikar Dadi, eds., *Unpacking Europe: Towards a Critical Reading*, 234–43. Rotterdam: Museum Boijmans Van Beuningen, 2001.

Fabre, Genevieve, and Robert G. O'Meally, eds. *History and Memory in African-American Culture*. New York: Oxford University Press, 1994.

Farr, D. Francine. "Civilization and Nature." *Artweek* 13, no. 18 (September 4, 1982): 4.

Fax, Elton C. *Black Artists of the New Generation*. New York: Dodd, Mead & Company, 1977.

Finley, Cheryl. "Of Golden Anniversaries and Bicentennials: The Convergence of Memory, Tourism, and National History in Ghana." *Journeys* 7, no. 1 (Spring 2007): 15–32.

Fleetwood, Nicole R. *Troubling Vision: Performance, Visuality, and Blackness*. Chicago: University of Chicago Press, 2011.

Flood, Richard. *Unmonumental: The Object in the 21st Century*. New York: New Museum, 2007.

Flood, Richard, Massimiliano Gioni, and Laura J. Hoptman. *Collage: The Unmonumental Picture*. London: Merrell, 2007.

Fortier, Jerome. *Watts: Art and Social Change in Los Angeles, 1965–2002*. Milwaukee: Haggerty Museum of Art, Marquette University, 2003.

Franco, Pamela. "Dressing Up and Looking Good: Afro-Creole Female Maskers in Trinidad Carnival." In "Women's Masquerades in Africa and the Diaspora," special issue, *African Arts* 31, no. 2 (Spring 1998): 62–67, 91, 95–96.

Frascina, Francis. *Art, Politics, and Dissent: Aspects of the Art Left in Sixties America*. Manchester, UK: Manchester University Press, 1999.

Freeman, Elizabeth. *Time Binds: Queer Temporalities, Queer Histories*. Durham, NC: Duke University Press, 2010.

Gaines, Kevin K. *Uplifting the Race: Black Leadership, Politics, and Culture in the Twentieth Century*. Chapel Hill: University of North Carolina Press, 1996.

Gates, Henry Louis, Jr. "Belafonte's Balancing Act." *New Yorker*, August 26, 1996, 132–43.

———. "New Negroes, Migration, and Cultural Exchange." In Elizabeth Hutton Turner, ed., *Jacob Lawrence: The Migration Series*, 17–22. Washington, DC: Rappahannock Press in association with the Phillips Collection, 1993.

Gedeon, Lucinda H., ed. *Melvin Edwards Sculpture: A Thirty-Year Retrospective, 1963–1993*. Purchase: Neuberger Museum of Art, State University of New York at Purchase, 1993.

Getty Research Institute. *Pacific Standard Time: Art in L.A., 1945–1980*. Los Angeles: Getty Research Institute and the J. Paul Getty Museum, 2011.

Gilroy, Paul. *The Black Atlantic: Modernity and Double Consciousness.* Cambridge, MA: Harvard University Press, 1993.

———. *There Ain't No Black in the Union Jack: The Cultural Politics of Race and Nation.* London: Hutchinson, 1987.

———. "'. . . To Be Real!': The Dissident Forms of Black Expressive Culture." In Catherine Ugwu, ed., *Let's Get It On: The Politics of Black Performance*, 12–33. London: Institute of Contemporary Arts, 1995.

Goings, Kenneth W. *Mammy and Uncle Mose: Black Collectibles and American Stereotyping.* Bloomington: Indiana University Press, 1994.

Goldman, Shifra M. *Contemporary Mexican Painting in a Time of Change.* Austin: University of Texas Press, 1981.

Goldsby, Jacqueline Denise. *A Spectacular Secret: Lynching in American Life and Literature.* Chicago: University of Chicago Press, 2006.

Gomez, Michael A. *Exchanging Our Country Marks: The Transformation of African Identities in the Colonial and Antebellum South.* Chapel Hill: University of North Carolina Press, 1998.

Goode Bryant, Linda, and Marcy S. Philips. *Contextures.* New York: Just Above Midtown, Inc., 1978.

Gooding-Williams, Robert, ed. *Reading Rodney King, Reading Urban Uprising.* New York: Routledge, 1993.

Gore, Dayo F., Jeanne Theoharis, and Komozi Woodard, eds. *Want to Start a Revolution? Radical Women in the Black Freedom Struggle.* New York: New York University Press, 2009.

Green, Adam. *Selling the Race: Culture, Community, and Black Chicago, 1940–1955.* Chicago: University of Chicago Press, 2007.

Greenberg, Clement. *Homemade Esthetics: Observations on Art and Taste.* New York: Oxford University Press, 1999.

Greenberg, Clement, and John O'Brian. *Clement Greenberg: The Collected Essays and Criticism.* Chicago: University of Chicago Press, 1986.

Greene, Carroll, Jr. *Los Angeles 1972: A Panorama of Black Artists.* Los Angeles: Los Angeles County Museum of Art, 1972.

Grenier, Catherine. *Los Angeles 1955–1985: Birth of an Art Capital.* Paris: Centre Pompidou, 2006.

Grewe, Cordula. *Painting the Sacred in the Age of Romanticism.* Burlington, VT: Ashgate, 2009.

Griffin, Farah Jasmine. *Harlem Nocturne: Women Artists and Progressive Politics during World War II.* New York: Basic Books, 2013.

———. *"Who Set You Flowin'?": The African-American Migration Narrative.* New York: Oxford University Press, 1995.

Griswold del Castillo, Richard, Teresa McKenna, and Yvonne Yarbro-Bejarano. *Chicano Art: Resistance and Affirmation.* Los Angeles: Wight Art Gallery, University of California, Los Angeles, 1991.

Grosz, Elizabeth. *Architecture from the Outside: Essays on Virtual and Real Space.* Cambridge, MA: MIT Press, 2001.

Gundaker, Grey. "African American History, Cosmology, and the Moral Universe of Edward Houston's Yard." *Journal of Garden History* 14, no. 3 (1994): 179–205.

———. *Signs of Diaspora, Diaspora of Signs: Literacies, Creolization, and Vernacular Practice in African America*. New York: Oxford University Press, 1998.

———. "Tradition and Innovation in African-American Yards." *African Arts* 26, no. 2 (1993): 58–71, 94–96.

Gundaker, Grey, and Tynes Cowan, eds. *Keep Your Head to the Sky: Interpreting African American Home Ground*. Charlottesville: University Press of Virginia, 1998.

Gundaker, Grey, and Judith McWillie. *No Space Hidden: The Spirit of African American Yard Work*. Knoxville: University of Tennessee Press, 2005.

Hall, Stuart. "Minimal Selves." In *Identity: The Real Me*. ICA Documents 6, 44–46. London: Institute of Contemporary Art, 1987.

Hamilton, Kenneth Marvin. *Black Towns and Profit: Promotion and Development in the Trans-Appalachian West, 1877–1915*. Urbana: University of Illinois Press, 1991.

Hammons, David, and Louise Neri. "No Wonder." *Parkett* 31 (March 1992): 53.

Harris, Juliette. "Samella Lewis: An Art Institution in Her Own Right." *International Review of African American Art* 18, no. 1 (2001): 14–15.

Harris, Michael D. *Colored Pictures: Race and Visual Representation*. Chapel Hill: University of North Carolina Press, 2003.

Harris, Trudier, and Thadious M. Davis, eds. *Afro-American Poets since 1955*. Detroit: Gale Research, 1985.

Hartman, Saidiya V. *Lose Your Mother: A Journey along the Atlantic Slave Route*. New York: Farrar, Straus and Giroux, 2007.

———. "The Time of Slavery." *South Atlantic Quarterly* 101, no. 4 (Fall 2002): 757–77.

Hassan, Salah M., Iftikhar Dadi, and Leslie A. Adelson, eds. *Unpacking Europe: Towards a Critical Reading*. Rotterdam: Museum Boijmans Van Beuningen, 2001.

Hassinger, Maren. "Maren Hassinger." *International Review of African American Art* 6, no. 1 (1984): 34–41.

Hemingway, Andrew. *Artists on the Left: American Artists and the Communist Movement, 1926–1956*. New Haven, CT: Yale University Press, 2002.

Henderson, Cheryl Brown. "Lucinda Todd and the Invisible Petitioners of *Brown v. Board of Education of Topeka, Kansas*." In Quintard Taylor and Shirley Ann Wilson Moore, eds., *African American Women Confront the West, 1600–2000*, 312–27. Norman: University of Oklahoma Press, 2003.

Hess, Janet Berry. *Art and Architecture in Postcolonial Africa*. Jefferson, NC: McFarland, 2006.

Hewitt, Mary Jane. *Interview of Samella Lewis: Artist and Influence*. New York: Hatch Billops Collection, 2002.

Higa, Karin. "Black Art in L.A.: Photographs by Robert A. Nakamura." In Kellie Jones, ed., *Now Dig This! Art and Black Los Angeles, 1960–1980*, 51–55. New York and Los Angeles: Prestel-Delmonico and Hammer Museum, 2011.

Higginbotham, Evelyn Brooks. "African-American Woman's History and the Metalanguage of Race." *Signs* 17, no. 2 (Winter 1992): 251–74.

High Museum of Art. *The Work of Charles White: An American Experience*. Atlanta: High Museum, 1976.

Higonnet, Anne. *A Museum of One's Own: Private Collecting, Public Gift*. Pittsburgh: Periscope, 2009.

Hills, Patricia. *Painting Harlem Modern: The Art of Jacob Lawrence*. Berkeley: University of California Press, 2009.

Hillwood Art Museum. *Maren Hassinger, 1972–1991*. Brookville, NY: Hillwood Art Museum, Long Island University, C. W. Post Campus, 1991.

Hine, Darlene Clark. "Black Migration to the Urban Midwest, the Gender Dimension, 1915–1945." In Joe William Trotter Jr., ed., *The Great Migration in Historical Perspective: New Dimensions of Race, Class, and Gender*, 127–46. Bloomington: Indiana University Press, 1991.

———. *Hine Sight: Black Women and the Re-Construction of American History*. Bloomington: Indiana University Press, 1994.

———. "Rape and the Inner Lives of Black Women in the Middle West: Preliminary Thoughts on the Culture of Dissemblance." *Signs* 14, no. 4 (Summer 1989): 912–20.

Hirsch, Marianne. *The Familial Gaze*. Hanover, NH: University Press of New England, 1999.

Hoffman, Katherine, ed. *Collage: Critical Views*. Ann Arbor: UMI Research Press, 1989.

Hood, Walter J., Jr., and Mellissa Erikson. "Storing Memories in the Yard: Remaking Poplar Street, the Shifting Black Cultural Landscape." In Craig E. Barton, ed., *Sites of Memory: Perspectives on Architecture and Race*, 171–89. Princeton, NJ: Princeton Architectural Press, 2001.

hooks, bell. *Black Looks: Race and Representation*. Boston: South End, 1992.

———. *Yearning: Race, Gender, and Cultural Politics*. Boston: South End, 1990.

Hopkins, Henry, and Anne Ayres. *Forty Years of California Assemblage: UCLA Art Council Annual Exhibition*. Los Angeles: Wight Art Gallery, 1989.

Horne, Gerald. *Fire This Time: The Watts Uprising and the 1960s*. Charlottesville: University Press of Virginia, 1995.

Horowitz, Benjamin. *Images of Dignity: The Drawings of Charles White*. Los Angeles: Ward Ritchie, 1967.

———. "On the Road with Charlie White." In "Charles White: Art and Soul," special issue, *Freedomways* 20, no. 3 (1980): 165–66.

Hudson, Karen E., and Paul R. Williams. *Paul R. Williams, Architect: A Legacy of Style*. New York: Rizzoli, 1993.

Hunt, Darnell M., and Ana-Christina Ramón, eds. *Black Los Angeles: American Dreams and Racial Realities*. New York: New York University Press, 2010.

Hutson, Jean Blackwell. "The Schomburg Collection." *Freedomways* 3 (Summer 1963): 430–35.

Isenberg, Barbara. *State of the Arts: California Artists Talk about Their Work*. New York: W. William Morrow, 2000.

Jackson, Suzanne. *Animal*. Los Angeles: Sunflower Seed, 1978.

———. *What I Love: Paintings, Poetry, and a Drawing*. Los Angeles: Contemporary Crafts, 1972.

Janis, Harriet Grossman, and Rudi Blesh. *Collage: Personalities, Concepts, and Techniques*. Philadelphia: Chilton, 1967.

Japan Society and Museum Villa Stuck. *Japanese Theater in the World*. New York and Munich: Japan Society and Museum Villa Stuck, 1997.

Jeffries, Rosalind Robinson. "Arthur Carraway and Houston Conwill: Ethnicity and Re-Africanization in American Art." PhD diss., Yale University, 1992.

Johnson, E. Patrick. *Appropriating Blackness: Performance and the Politics of Authenticity.* Durham, NC: Duke University Press, 2003.

Jones, Amelia. *Body Art: Performing the Subject.* Minneapolis: University of Minnesota Press, 1998.

Jones, Bill T. "You Don't Have to Be Thin to Dance." *New York Times*, July 19, 1997, A19.

Jones, Kellie. "Black West: Thoughts on Art in Los Angeles." In Lisa Gail Collins and Margo Natalie Crawford, eds., *New Thoughts on the Black Arts Movement*, 43–74. New Brunswick, NJ: Rutgers University Press, 2006.

———, ed. *Energy/Experimentation: Black Artists and Abstraction, 1964–1980.* New York: Studio Museum in Harlem, 2006.

———. "Interview with David Hammons." *Reallife Magazine* 16 (Autumn 1986): 2–9.

———. "In the Thick of It: David Hammons and Hair Culture in the 1970s." *Third Text* 12, no. 44 (Autumn 1998): 17–24.

———. "It's Not Enough to Say 'Black Is Beautiful': Abstraction at the Whitney, 1969–1974." In Kobena Mercer, ed., *Discrepant Abstraction*, 154–81. London: Institute of International Visual Arts; Cambridge, MA: MIT Press, 2006.

———, ed. *Now Dig This! Art and Black Los Angeles, 1960–1980.* New York and Los Angeles: Prestel-Delmonico and Hammer Museum, 2011.

Joseph, Branden. *Random Order: Robert Rauschenberg and the Neo-Avant-Garde.* Cambridge, MA: MIT Press, 2003.

Kasfir, Sidney Littlefield. "Elephant Women, Furious and Majestic: Women's Masquerades in Africa and the Diaspora." In "Women's Masquerades in Africa and the Diaspora," special issue, *African Arts* 31, no. 2 (Spring 1998): 18–27, 92.

———. *West African Masks and Cultural Systems.* Tervuren, Belgique: Musée Royal de l'Afrique Centrale, 1988.

Kelley, Robin D. G. *Freedom Dreams: The Black Radical Imagination.* Boston: Beacon, 2002.

———. *Race Rebels: Culture, Politics, and the Black Working Class.* New York: Free Press, 1994.

Kernodle, Tammy L. *Soul on Soul: The Life and Music of Mary Lou Williams.* Boston: Northeastern University Press, 2004.

Kim, Christine Y. *Black Belt.* New York: Studio Museum in Harlem, 2003.

King-Hammond, Leslie, and Lowery Stokes Sims. *Art as a Verb: The Evolving Continuum: Installations, Performances and Videos by 13 Afro-American Artists.* Baltimore: Maryland Institute College of Art, 1988.

Kingsley, April. *Afro-American Abstraction.* San Francisco: Art Museum Association, 1982.

Kirschke, Amy Helene. *Art in Crisis: W. E. B. Du Bois and the Struggle for African American Identity and Memory.* Bloomington: Indiana University Press, 2007.

Krauss, Rosalind. "Sculpture in the Expanded Field." *October* 8 (Spring 1979): 30–44.

Kwon, Miwon. *One Place after Another: Site-Specific Art and Locational Identity.* Cambridge, MA: MIT Press, 2002.

Lambert, Carrie. "More or Less Minimalism: Six Notes on Performance and Visual Art in the 1960s." In Ann Goldstein, ed., *A Minimal Future? Art as Object 1958–1968.* Los Angeles: Los Angeles Museum of Contemporary Art, 2004.

Lawal, Babatunde. *The Gẹ̀lẹ̀dẹ́ Spectacle: Art, Gender, and Social Harmony in African Culture.* Seattle: University of Washington Press, 1996.

Lee, Pamela M. *Chronophobia: On Time in the Arts of the 1960s.* Cambridge, MA: MIT Press, 2004.

LeFalle-Collins, Lizzetta. *John Outterbridge: A Retrospective.* Los Angeles: California African American Museum, 1993.

———. *Noah Purifoy: Outside and in the Open.* Los Angeles: California African American Museum, 1998.

Lefebvre, Henri. *The Production of Space.* Oxford, UK: Blackwell, 1991.

Lemann, Nicholas. *The Promised Land: The Great Black Migration and How It Changed America.* New York: Vintage Books, 1992. First published 1991.

Lemke-Santangelo, Gretchen. "'Women Make Community': African American Migrant Women and the Cultural Transformation of the San Francisco East Bay Area." In Quintard Taylor and Shirley Ann Wilson Moore, eds., *African American Women Confront the West, 1600–2000,* 254–75. Norman: University of Oklahoma Press, 2003.

Lewis, George. *A Power Stronger Than Itself: The AACM and American Experimental Music.* Chicago: University of Chicago Press, 2008.

Lewis, Samella S. *Art: African American.* New York: Harcourt, Brace and Jovanovich, 1978.

———. *Benny, Bernie, Betye, Noah and John: 5 Black Artists.* Los Angeles: Contemporary Crafts, 1971.

———. "Ruth Waddy: A California Signature." *International Review of African American Art* 9, no. 4 (1991): 49.

Lewis, Samella S., and Ruth G. Waddy. *Black Artists on Art.* 2 vols. Los Angeles: Contemporary Crafts, 1969, 1971.

Lindsay, Arturo. "Performance Art Ritual as Postmodern Thought: An Aesthetic Investigation." PhD diss., New York University, 1990.

———, ed. *Santería Aesthetics in Contemporary Latin American Art.* Washington, DC: Smithsonian Institution Press, 1996.

Lippard, Lucy R. "Eccentric Abstraction." *Art International* 10, no. 9 (November 1966): 28, 34–40.

———. *From the Center: Feminist Essays on Women's Art.* New York: Dutton, 1976.

Lippard, Lucy R., and John Chandler. "The Dematerialization of Art." *Art International* 12, no. 2 (February 1968): 31–36.

Lipsitz, George. *Footsteps in the Dark: The Hidden Histories of Popular Music.* Minneapolis: University of Minnesota Press, 2007.

———. *The Possessive Investment in Whiteness.* Philadelphia: Temple University Press, 1998.

Litweiler, John. *Ornette Coleman: A Harmolodic Life.* New York: W. Morrow, 1992.

Lokko, Lesley Naa Norle. *White Papers, Black Marks: Architecture, Race, Culture.* Minneapolis: University of Minnesota Press, 2000.

Long, Richard A., and Joe Nash. *The Black Tradition in American Dance.* New York: Rizzoli, 1989.

"Los Angeles and the Future of Urban Cultures." Special issue, *American Quarterly* 56, no. 3 (September 2004).

Los Angeles Municipal Art Gallery. *George Herms.* Los Angeles: Los Angeles Municipal Art Gallery, 1992.

Louisiana Museum of Modern Art. *Sunshine and Noir: Art in L.A., 1960–1997*. Humlebaek, Denmark: Louisiana Museum of Modern Art, 1997.

Love, Nat. *The Life and Adventures of Nat Love*. New York: Arno, 1968. First published 1907.

MacGaffey, Wyatt. *Religion and Society in Central Africa: The BaKongo of Lower Zaire*. Chicago: University of Chicago Press, 1986.

Machida, Margo. *Unsettled Visions: Contemporary Asian American Artists and the Social Imaginary*. Durham, NC: Duke University Press, 2008.

Manning, Susan. *Modern Dance, Negro Dance: Race in Motion*. Minneapolis: University of Minnesota Press, 2004.

Marquis, Alice Goldfarb. *Art Czar: The Rise and Fall of Clement Greenberg*. Boston: MFA, 2006.

Marshall, Kerry James, Terrie Sultan, and Arthur Jafa. *Kerry James Marshall*. New York: Harry N. Abrams, 2000.

McDowell, Linda. *Gender, Identity, and Place: Understanding Feminist Geographies*. Minneapolis: University of Minnesota Press, 1999.

McDuffie, Erik S. "'No Small Amount of Change Could Do': Esther Cooper Jackson and the Making of a Black Left Feminism." In Dayo F. Gore, Jeanne Theoharis, and Komozi Woodard, eds., *Want to Start a Revolution? Radical Women in the Black Freedom Struggle*, 25–46. New York: New York University Press, 2009.

McKenna, Kristine. *The Ferus Gallery: A Place to Begin*. Göttingen, Germany: Steidl, 2009.

McKittrick, Katherine. *Demonic Grounds: Black Women and the Cartographies of Struggle*. Minneapolis: University of Minnesota Press, 2006.

Meyer, Laura, and Faith Wilding, eds. *A Studio of Their Own: The Legacy of the Fresno Feminist Art Experiment*. Fresno: Press at California State University, Fresno, 2009.

Miller, Lynn F., Sally S. Swenson, Beryl K. Smith, and Joan Arbeiter. *Lives and Works: Talks with Women Artists*. Metuchen, NJ: Scarecrow, 1981.

Mills, Cynthia J., Lee Glazer, and Amelia A. Goerlitz, eds. *East-West Interchanges in American Art: A Long and Tumultuous Relationship*. Washington, DC: Smithsonian Institution Scholarly Press, 2012.

Mingus, Charles. *Beneath the Underdog*. Edinburgh: Canongate, 1995. First published 1971.

Miranda, Carolina A. "Mark Bradford's Art and Practice to Bring Art, Social Services to Leimert." *Los Angeles Times*, December 15, 2014.

Mirzoeff, Nicholas, ed. *Diaspora and Visual Culture: Representing Africans and Jews*. London: Routledge, 2000.

Mitchell, W. J. T. *What Do Pictures Want? The Lives and Loves of Images*. Chicago: University of Chicago Press, 2005.

Monte, James K., and Marcia Tucker. *Anti-Illusion: Procedures/Materials*. New York: Whitney Museum of American Art, 1969.

Moore, Shirley Anne. "Getting There, Being There: African American Migration to Richmond, California, 1910–1945." In Joe William Trotter Jr., ed., *The Great Migration in Historical Perspective: New Dimensions of Race, Class, and Gender*, 106–26. Bloomington: Indiana University Press, 1991.

Moran, Dermot, and Timothy Mooney, eds. *The Phenomenology Reader*. New York: Routledge, 2002.

Morrison, Toni. *Playing in the Dark: Whiteness and the Literary Imagination*. Cambridge, MA: Harvard University Press, 1992.

Mosquera, Gerardo. "Eleggúa at the (Post?)Modern Crossroads." In Arturo Lindsay, ed., *Santería Aesthetics in Contemporary Latin American Art*, 225–58. Washington, DC: Smithsonian Institution Press, 1996.

Moxey, Keith. *Visual Time: The Image in History*. Durham, NC: Duke University Press, 2013.

Muchnic, Suzanne. "JuJu Ritual—Cycles of Life." *Artweek* 9, no. 8 (February 25, 1978): 4.

———. "To Protect and Preserve a Desert Legacy." *Los Angeles Times*, January 14, 2001, Calendar, 1.

Mullen, Bill V., and James Edward Smethurst, eds. *Left of the Color Line: Race, Radicalism, and Twentieth-Century Literature of the United States*. Chapel Hill: University of North Carolina Press, 2003.

Mullen, Harryette. "'Artistic Expression Was Flowing Everywhere': Alison Mills and Ntozake Shange, Black Bohemian Feminists in the 1970s." *Meridians* 4, no. 2 (2004): 205–35.

———. "Reader, I Married Him: An Interview with Alison Mills." *Callaloo* 27, no. 3 (2004): 698–714.

Muñoz, José Esteban. *Cruising Utopia: The Then and There of Queer Futurity*. New York: New York University Press, 2009.

Munro, Eleanor C. *Originals: American Women Artists*. New York: Simon and Schuster, 1979.

Munroe, Alexandra. *Japanese Art after 1945: Scream against the Sky*. New York: Harry N. Abrams, 1994.

———. *The Third Mind: American Artists Contemplate Asia, 1860–1989*. New York: Guggenheim Museum, 2009.

Naumann, Francis M., and Beth Venn. *Making Mischief: Dada Invades New York*. New York: Whitney Museum of American Art, 1996.

Nelson, Alondra. "Introduction: Future Texts." In "Afrofuturism," special issue, *Social Text* 20, no. 2 (Summer 2002): 1–15.

Nemser, Cindy. "Conversation with Betye Saar." *Feminist Art Journal* 4, no. 4 (Winter 1975–76): 19–24.

Nochlin, Linda. *Realism*. Harmondsworth, UK: Penguin, 1971.

Nora, Pierre. "Between Memory and History: Les Lieux de Mémoire." In Genevieve Fabre and Robert G. O'Meally, eds., *History and Memory in African-American Culture*, 184–300. New York: Oxford University Press, 1994.

Noriega, Chon, and Holly Barnett-Sánchez, eds. *Just Another Poster? Chicano Graphic Arts in California*. Santa Barbara: University Art Museum, University of California, Santa Barbara, 2001.

Noriega, Chon A., Terezita Romo, and Pilar Tompkins Rivas. *L.A. Xicano*. Los Angeles: UCLA Chicano Studies Research Center Press, 2011.

Nyong'o, Tavia. *The Amalgamation Waltz: Race, Performance, and the Ruses of Memory*. Minneapolis: University of Minnesota Press, 2009.

———. "Racial Kitsch and Black Performance." *Yale Journal of Criticism* 15, no. 2 (Fall 2002): 371–91.

Odita, O. Donald. "The Unseen, Inside Out: The Life and Art of Senga Nengudi." *Nka* 6/7 (Summer/Fall 1997): 24–27.

O'Grady, Lorraine. "Interview with Maren Hassinger." *Artist and Influence* 12 (March 12, 1993): 20–32.

Oguibe, Olu. *The Culture Game*. Minneapolis: University of Minnesota Press, 2004.

Oguibe, Olu, and Okwui Enwezor, eds. *Reading the Contemporary: African Art from Theory to the Marketplace*. London: Institute of International Visual Arts; Cambridge, MA: MIT Press, 1999.

Okediji, Moyosore B. *The Shattered Gourd: Yoruba Forms in Twentieth Century American Art*. Seattle: University of Washington Press, 2003.

Omi, Michael, and Howard Winant. "The Los Angeles 'Race Riot' and Contemporary U.S. Politics." In Robert Gooding-Williams, ed., *Reading Rodney King, Reading Urban Uprising*, 97–114. New York: Routledge, 1993.

Osaki, Shinichiro. "Body and Place: Action in Postwar Art in Japan." In Paul Schimmel, ed., *Out of Actions: Between Performance and the Object, 1949–1979*, 121–57. Los Angeles: Museum of Contemporary Art, 1998.

Painter, Nell Irvin. *Exodusters: Black Migration to Kansas after Reconstruction*. New York: W. W. Norton, 1992. First published 1977.

Patterson, Tiffany Ruby, and Robin D. G. Kelley. "Unfinished Migrations: Reflections on the African Diaspora and the Making of the Modern World." *African Studies Review* 43, no. 1 (2000): 11–45.

Patton, Sharon F. "The Stool and Asante Chieftaincy." *African Arts* 13, no. 1 (November 1979): 74–77, 98–99.

Peter, Carolyn, and Damon Willick. *Gallery 32 and Its Circle*. Los Angeles: Laband Art Gallery, Loyola Marymount University, 2009.

Phelan, Peggy. *Unmarked: The Politics of Performance*. London: Routledge, 1993.

Phillips, Lisa. *Beat Culture and the New America, 1950–1965*. New York: Whitney Museum of American Art in association with Flammarion, Paris, 1995.

Pincus-Witten, Robert. *Eye to Eye: Twenty Years of Art Criticism*. Ann Arbor: UMI Research Press, 1984.

———. "Postminimalism: An Argentine Glance." In Richard Armstrong and Richard Marshall, eds., *The New Sculpture 1965–1975*, 21–27. New York: Whitney Museum of American Art, 1990.

Plagens, Peter. "He Got Shot—For His Art." *New York Times*, September 2, 1973, 87.

———. *Sunshine Muse: Art on the West Coast, 1945–1970*. Berkeley: University of California Press, 1999. First published 1974.

Poggi, Christine. *In Defiance of Painting: Cubism, Futurism, and the Invention of Collage*. New Haven, CT: Yale University Press, 1992.

Poitier, Sidney. *This Life*. New York: Knopf, 1980.

Powell, Richard J. "*Notes of a Griot* Demystifies New York." *Neworld* 5, no. 2 (March/April 1979): 12.

Powell, Richard J., David A. Bailey, and Petrine Archer-Straw, eds. *Back to Black: Art, Cinema, and the Racial Imaginary*. London: Whitechapel Gallery, 2005.

Prashad, Vijay. *Everybody Was Kung Fu Fighting: Afro-Asian Connections and the Myth of Cultural Purity*. Boston: Beacon, 2001.

Prigoff, James, and Robin J. Dunitz. *Walls of Heritage, Walls of Pride: African American Murals*. San Francisco: Pomegranate, 2000.

Primus, Pearl. "African Dance." In Kariamu Welsh-Asante, ed., *African Dance: An Artistic, Historical and Philosophical Inquiry*, 3–12. Trenton, NJ: Africa World, 1996.

Puckett, Newbell Niles. *Folk Beliefs of the Southern Negro*. Chapel Hill: University of North Carolina Press, 1926.

Purifoy, Noah, and Ted Michel. *Junk Art: 66 Signs of Neon*. Los Angeles: 66 Signs of Neon, 1966.

"Queer Temporalities." Special issue. GLQ 13, nos. 2–3 (2007).

Ramsey, Guthrie P., Jr. *The Amazing Bud Powell: Black Genius, Jazz History, and the Challenge of Bebop*. Berkeley: University of California Press, 2013.

———. *Race Music: Black Cultures from Bebop to Hip-Hop*. Berkeley: University of California Press, 2003.

Reed, Ishmael. *Conjure: Selected Poems, 1963–1970*. Amherst: University of Massachusetts Press, 1972.

———. *A Secretary to the Spirits*. Lagos: NOK, 1978.

———. *Shrovetide in Old New Orleans*. Garden City, NY: Doubleday, 1978.

Reid, Calvin. "Chasing the Blue Train." *Art in America* 77, no. 9 (1989): 196–97.

———. "Kinky Black Hair and Barbecue Bones: Street Life, Social History, and David Hammons." *Arts Magazine* 65, no. 8 (April 1991): 59–63.

———. "Mr. Hammons' Neighborhood." In Robert Sill, ed., *David Hammons in the Hood*, 30–47. Springfield: Illinois State Museum, 1994.

Ringgold, Faith. *We Flew over the Bridge: The Memoirs of Faith Ringgold*. Boston: Little, Brown, 1995.

Roach, Joseph R. *Cities of the Dead: Circum-Atlantic Performance*. New York: Columbia University Press, 1996.

Romo, Terezita. "Mexican Heritage, American Art: Six Angeleno Artists." In Chon A. Noriega, Terezita Romo, and Pilar Tompkins Rivas, eds., *L.A. Xicano*, 3–27. Los Angeles: UCLA Chicano Studies Research Center Press, 2011.

Ross, Janice. *Anna Halprin: Experience as Dance*. Berkeley: University of California Press, 2007.

Rothschild, Deborah Menaker. *Yardbird Suite: Hammons '93*. Williamstown, MA: Williams College Museum of Art, 1994.

Sánchez Korrol, Virginia E. *From Colonia to Community: The History of Puerto Ricans in New York City*. Berkeley: University of California Press, 1994. First published 1983.

Sanders, Stanley. "Riot as Weapon: The Language of Watts." *The Nation*, December 20, 1965, 490–92.

Sandoval, Chela. "U.S. Third World Feminism: The Theory and Method of Oppositional Consciousness in the Postmodern World." *Genders* 10 (1991): 1–23.

Schimmel, Paul, ed. *Out of Actions: Between Performance and the Object, 1949–1979*. Los Angeles: Museum of Contemporary Art, 1998.

Schneider, Rebecca. *The Explicit Body in Performance*. London: Routledge, 1997.

———. *Performing Remains: Art and War in Times of Theatrical Reenactment*. New York: Routledge, 2011.

Schrank, Sarah. *Art and the City: Civic Imagination and Cultural Authority in Los Angeles*. Philadelphia: University of Pennsylvania Press, 2009.

———. "Picturing the Watts Towers: The Art and Politics of an Urban Landmark." In Stephanie Barron, Sheri Bernstein, and Ilene Susan Fort, eds., *Made in California: Art, Image and Identity, 1990–2000*, 373–86. Los Angeles: Los Angeles County Museum of Art, 2000.

Schulman, Daniel, and Peter Max Ascoli, eds. *A Force for Change: African American Art and the Julius Rosenwald Fund*. Chicago: Spertus Museum and Northwestern University Press, 2009.

Sedgwick, Eve Kosofsky, and Adam Frank. *Touching Feeling: Affect, Pedagogy, Performativity*. Durham, NC: Duke University Press, 2003.

Seitz, William Chapin. *The Art of Assemblage*. New York: Museum of Modern Art, 1961.

Shaw, Arnold. *Belafonte: An Unauthorized Biography*. Philadelphia: Chilton, 1960.

Sides, Josh. *L.A. City Limits: African American Los Angeles from the Great Depression to the Present*. Berkeley: University of California Press, 2003.

Sieber, Roy, and Arnold Rubin. *Sculpture of Black Africa: The Paul Tishman Collection*. Los Angeles: Los Angeles County Museum of Art, 1968.

Sill, Robert, ed. *David Hammons in the Hood*. Springfield: Illinois State Museum, 1994.

Sims, Lowery Stokes. *Challenge of the Modern: African American Artists, 1925–1945*. New York: Studio Museum in Harlem, 2003.

———. "Melvin Edwards: An Artist's Life and Philosophy." In Lucinda H. Gedeon, ed., *Melvin Edwards Sculpture: A Thirty-Year Retrospective, 1963–1993*, 9–19. Purchase: Neuberger Museum of Art, State University of New York at Purchase, 1993.

Sirmans, Franklin. *David Hammons: Selected Works*. New York: Zwirner & Wirth, 2006.

———. "Find the Cave, Hold the Torch: Making Art Shows since Walter Hopps." In Kellie Jones, ed., *Now Dig This! Art and Black Los Angeles, 1960–1980*, 57–67. New York and Los Angeles: Prestel-Delmonico and Hammer Museum, 2011.

Smethurst, James Edward. *The Black Arts Movement: Literary Nationalism in the 1960s and 1970s*. Chapel Hill: University of North Carolina Press, 2005.

Smith, David L. "David Hammons: Spade Worker." In Deborah Menaker Rothschild, ed., *Yardbird Suite, Hammons 93*, 20–39. Williamstown, MA: Williams College Museum of Art, 1994.

Soja, Edward W. *Postmodern Geographies: The Reassertion of Space in Critical Social Theory*. London: Verso, 1989.

———. *Thirdspace: Journeys to Los Angeles and Other Real-and-Imagined Places*. Cambridge, MA: Blackwell, 1996.

Solnit, Rebecca. *Secret Exhibition: Six California Artists of the Cold War Era*. San Francisco: City Lights Books, 1990.

Spellman, A. B. *Four Lives in the Bebop Business*. London: MacGibbon & Kee, 1967.

Spillers, Hortense J. "'Mama's Baby, Papa's Maybe': An American Grammar Book." *Diacritics* 17, no. 2 (Summer 1987): 64–81.

Stewart, Jacqueline Najuma. *Migrating to the Movies: Cinema and Black Urban Modernity*. Berkeley: University of California Press, 2005.

Stewart, Susan. *On Longing: Narratives of the Miniature, the Gigantic, the Souvenir, the Collection*. Durham, NC: Duke University Press, 1993.

Stiles, Kristine. "Survival Ethos and Destruction Art." *Discourse: Journal for Theoretical Studies in Media and Culture* 14, no. 2 (Spring 1992): 74–102.

Storr, Robert. *Dislocations*. New York: Museum of Modern Art, 1991.

Strother, Z. S. *Inventing Masks: Agency and History in the Art of the Central Pende.* Chicago: University of Chicago Press, 1998.

Studio Museum in Harlem. *Melvin Edwards, Sculptor.* New York: Studio Museum in Harlem, 1978.

Suderburg, Erika, ed. *Space, Site, Intervention: Situating Installation Art.* Minneapolis: University of Minnesota Press, 2000.

Tashjian, Dickran. *Joseph Cornell: Gifts of Desire.* Miami Beach: Grassfield, 1992.

Tate, Greg. "Graf Rulers / GrafUnTrained." In Franklin Sirmans and Lydia Yee, eds., *One Planet under a Groove: Hip-Hop and Contemporary Art*, 35–40. New York: Bronx Museum of the Arts, 2001.

Tate, Mae. "Samella Lewis: Keeping Social Comment Alive, Vigorous in Art." *Progress-Bulletin* (Pomona, CA), January 15, 1972, 2.

———. "Suzanne Jackson." *Black Art* 4, no. 3 (1980): 3–21.

Taylor, Quintard. *The Forging of a Black Community: Seattle's Central District from 1870 through the Civil Rights Era.* Seattle: University of Washington Press, 1994.

———. *In Search of the Racial Frontier: African Americans in the American West, 1528–1990.* New York: Norton, 1998.

Taylor, Quintard, and Shirley Ann Wilson Moore, eds. *African American Women Confront the West, 1600–2000.* Norman: University of Oklahoma Press, 2003.

Tejada, Roberto. "Los Angeles Snapshots." In Kellie Jones, ed., *Now Dig This! Art and Black Los Angeles, 1960–1980*, 69–83. New York and Los Angeles: Prestel-Delmonico and Hammer Museum, 2011.

Thompson, Robert Farris. *African Art in Motion: Icon and Act in the Collection of Katherine Coryton White.* Berkeley: University of California Press, 1974.

———. *Black Gods and Kings: Yoruba Art at UCLA.* Bloomington: Indiana University Press, 1976.

———. *Face of the Gods: Art and Altars of Africa and the African Americas.* New York: Museum for African Art and Prestel, 1993.

———. *Flash of the Spirit: African and Afro-American Art and Philosophy.* New York: Vintage Books, 1984. First published 1983.

———. "The Three Warriors: Atlantic Altars of Esu, Ogun, and Osoosí." In Rowland Abiodun, Henry John Drewal, and John Pemberton III, eds., *The Yoruba Artist: New Theoretical Perspectives on African Arts*, 225–40. Washington: Smithsonian Institution Press, 1994.

Tillet, Salamishah. *Sites of Slavery: Citizenship and Racial Democracy in the Post–Civil Rights Imagination.* Durham, NC: Duke University Press, 2012.

Tilton, Connie Rogers, and Lindsay Charlwood, eds. *L.A. Object and David Hammons Body Prints.* New York: Tilton Gallery, 2011.

Tobin, Jacqueline, and Raymond G. Dobard. *Hidden in Plain View: A Secret Story of Quilts and the Underground Railroad.* New York: Doubleday, 1999.

Tompkins, Calvin. "Profile: A Touch for the Now (Walter Hopps)." *New Yorker*, July 29, 1991, 33–57.

Trotter, Joe William, Jr., ed. *The Great Migration in Historical Perspective: New Dimensions of Race, Class, and Gender.* Bloomington: Indiana University Press, 1991.

Tsai, Eugenie. *Sanford Biggers: Sweet Funk—An Introspective.* New York: Brooklyn Museum, 2011.

Tuchman, Maurice. *Five Younger Los Angeles Artists: Tony Berlant, Melvin Edwards, Llyn Foulkes, Lloyd Hamrol, Philip Rich, Contemporary Art Council New Talent Purchase Award Recipients 1963–1965*. Los Angeles: Los Angeles County Museum of Art, 1965.

Turner, Elizabeth Hutton, ed. *Jacob Lawrence: The Migration Series*. Washington, DC: Rappahannock Press, in association with the Phillips Collection, 1993.

Turner, Patricia A. *Ceramic Uncles and Celluloid Mammies: Black Images and Their Influences on Culture*. New York: Anchor Books, 1994.

Tyler, Bruce M. "The Rise and Decline of the Watts Summer Festival, 1965 to 1986." *American Studies* 31, no. 2 (Fall 1990): 61–81.

Uduku, N. Ola. "The Colonial Face of Educational Space." In Lesley Naa Norle Lokko, ed., *White Papers, Black Marks: Architecture, Race, Culture*, 44–65. Minneapolis: University of Minnesota Press, 2000.

Ugwu, Catherine, ed. *Let's Get It On: The Politics of Black Performance*. London: Institute of Contemporary Arts, 1995.

University of Michigan Museum of Art. *Betye Saar: Extending the Frozen Moment*. Ann Arbor and Berkeley: University of Michigan Art Museum and University of California Press, 2005.

Waldman, Diane. *Collage, Assemblage, and the Found Object*. New York: Harry N. Abrams, 1992.

Walker, Alice. *In Search of Our Mothers' Gardens: Womanist Prose*. San Diego: Harcourt Brace Jovanovich, 1983.

Ward, Frazer. "Gray Zone: Watching Shoot." *October*, no. 95 (Winter 2001): 115–30.

Washington, Mary Helen. "Alice Childress, Lorraine Hansberry, and Claudia Jones: Black Women Write the Popular Front." In Bill V. Mullen and James Edward Smethurst, eds., *Left of the Color Line: Race, Radicalism, and Twentieth-Century Literature of the United States*, 183–204. Chapel Hill: University of North Carolina Press, 2003.

———. "Charles White: Robeson with a Brush and Pencil." In *The Other Blacklist: The African American Literary and Cultural Left of the 1950s*, 69–122. New York: Columbia University Press, 2014.

Waterman, Christopher Alan. *Jùjú: A Social History and Ethnography of an African Popular Music*. Chicago: University of Chicago Press, 1990.

Weisser, Amy. "Making *Brown v. Board of Education*: Memorializing Separate but Unequal Spaces." In Craig E. Barton, ed., *Sites of Memory: Perspectives on Architecture and Race*, 97–108. Princeton, NJ: Princeton Architectural Press, 2001.

Welsh, Sue. "Noah Purifoy of Joshua Tree." *International Review of African American Art* 10, no. 4 (1993): 6.

Welsh-Asante, Kariamu, ed. *African Dance: An Artistic, Historical and Philosophical Inquiry*. Trenton, NJ: Africa World, 1996.

West, Kevin. "Can You Dig It?" *W Magazine*, October 2011, 127–30.

White, Frances Barrett, with Anne Scott. *Reaches of the Heart: A Loving Look at the Artist Charles White*. New York: Barricade Books, 1994.

Whiting, Cecile. *Pop L.A.: Art and the City in the 1960s*. Berkeley: University of California Press, 2006.

Widener, Daniel. *Black Arts West: Culture and Struggle in Postwar Los Angeles*. Durham, NC: Duke University Press, 2010.

———. "'Perhaps the Japanese Are to Be Thanked?': Asia, Asian Americans, and the Construction of Black California." *positions* 11, no. 1 (Spring 2003): 135–81.

Wilding, Faith. *By Our Own Hands*. Los Angeles: Double X, 1977.

Wilkerson, Isabel. *The Warmth of Other Suns: The Epic Story of America's Great Migration*. New York: Random House, 2010.

Wilkins, Craig L. *The Aesthetics of Equity: Notes on Race, Space, Architecture, and Music*. Minneapolis: University of Minnesota Press, 2007.

Williams, Richard J. *After Modern Sculpture: Art in the United States and Europe, 1965–70*. Manchester, UK: Manchester University Press, 2000.

Willis, Deborah. *J. P. Ball, Daguerrean and Studio Photographer*. New York: Garland, 1993.

———. "Looks and Gazes: Photographic Fragmentation and the Found Object." In University of Michigan Museum of Art, *Betye Saar: Extending the Frozen Moment*, 20–27. Ann Arbor and Berkeley: University of Michigan Art Museum and University of California Press, 2005.

———. "The Schomburg Collection: A Rich Resource for Jacob Lawrence." In Elizabeth Hutton Turner, ed., *Jacob Lawrence: The Migration Series*, 33–40. Washington, DC: Rappahannock Press, in association with the Phillips Collection, 1993.

Wilson, Judith. "Advanced Placement Tests." *Village Voice*, December 24, 1980, 79.

———. "Creating a Necessary Space: The Art of Houston Conwill, 1975–1983." *International Review of African American Art* 6, no. 1 (1984): 50–63.

———. "How the Invisible Woman Got Herself on the Cultural Map: Black Women Artists in California." In Diana Burgess Fuller and Daniela Salvioni, eds., *Art/Women/California, 1950–2000: Parallels and Intersections*, 201–16. Berkeley: University of California Press, 2002.

Wilson, Mabel O. *Negro Building: Black Americans in the World of Fairs and Museums*. Berkeley: University of California Press, 2012.

Wise, Leonard. "Portrait of Samella Lewis." *Essence* 3, no. 10 (February 1973): 46–47, 80.

Wolfram, Eddie. *History of Collage: An Anthology of Collage, Assemblage and Event Structures*. New York: Macmillan, 1975.

Wolverton, Terry. *Insurgent Muse: Life and Art at the Woman's Building*. San Francisco: City Lights, 2002.

Woodson, Carter G. *A Century of Negro Migration*. Mineola, NY: Dover, 2002. First published 1918.

Wright, Beryl. *The Appropriate Object*. Buffalo: Albright-Knox Gallery, 1989.

Wyatt, Richard, Jr. "His Special Gift for Teaching . . ." In "Charles White: Art and Soul," special issue, *Freedomways* 20, no. 3 (1980): 177–78.

Wynter, Sylvia. "Sambos and Minstrels." *Social Text* 1 (Winter 1979): 149–56.

Young, Joseph E. *Three Graphic Artists: Charles White, David Hammons, Timothy Washington*. Los Angeles: Los Angeles County Museum of Art, 1971.

INDEX

Note: Page numbers in *italics* refer to illustrations.

AACM. *See* Association for the Advancement of Creative Musicians
Abakanowicz, Magdalena, 250
Abdulrashid, Eileen, 154
Abramson, Charles, 206
abstract expressionism, 60
ACA. *See* American Contemporary Artists (ACA) Galleries
Acconci, Vito, 223
Action 1 (Hopps show), 132–33
activism, artistic, 21, 37–38, 60–61, 90, 95, 98, 169, 176–77, 182–83, 186, 261
Adkins, Terry, 160
aerospace industry, 8–9
Africa: dance influences, 201; as haven, 6, 186; influences on African American art, 113–14, 116, 186, 202–5, 207, 213, 257; as mirror, 221
Africa (Saar sculpture), 113
African Art in Motion (exhibition), 205–6, 218
African Commune of Bad Relevant Artists. *See* AfriCOBRA
African independence movements, 28–29
African Studies Center (UCLA), 205
AfriCOBRA, 85–86, 211–12
Afro-American Abstraction (exhibition), 244, 257–58
Afro Asian Eclipse (or Black China) (Hammons assemblage), 273–74

Afro-futurism, 10, 48
Afro-modernism, 40
Afro-Phoenix #2 (Edwards sculpture), 60
AFSC. *See* American Friends Service Committee
Ahmed, Sara, 275
Ailey, Alvin, 248, 250
Aisenman, Leslie, 79, 86
Alexander, Elizabeth, 190, 230–32, 236
Ali, Muhammad, 88
Alice in Wonderland (Carroll), 272
Alloway, Lawrence, 136
Alston, Charles, 38, 143
altars, 114–16, 223, 225
Altoon, John, 182
American Contemporary Artists (ACA) Galleries, 26–27, 38, 49
American Friends Service Committee (AFSC), 29–30
American Negro History Museum, 183
American Negro Theater, 282–83n8
ancestors, 6, 105–6, 125, 202, 216, 220–21
Andre, Carl, 160–61
Angelou, Maya, 35, 250
Ankrum, Joan, 160
Ankrum Gallery, 156, 160
Anna Lucasta (film), 25
Anthropometries (Klein paintings), 226
antiart aesthetics, 210
Arabian Nights #2 (D. Davis ceramic), 148

Arakawa, 161
ARCO Center for Visual Art, 251, 255
Arman, 160–61
art, African American: African influences, 113–14, 116, 186, 202–5, 207, 213, 257; black art, use of term, 166, 187, 189; black collectors, 180–84; black corporate power and, 142–44; black image in, 164; as change, 71–72; craft and, 103, 120, 176; dissemination of, 85–86; high vs. low art, 42; as living art, 175; making a living in, 51–53, 72–73; migration narratives, 20, 39–40, 101, 107, 126–28, 175, 186, 189–90; new formations, 185–91; safe spaces and, 6, 97–98; social value of, 142–43; south of Pico spaces, 15–17; spatial theory and, 17; as weapon, 115; women's/feminist, 108, 116–28. *See also* Black Arts Movement; Los Angeles art scene, African American; performance art; *specific artists and genres*
Art: African American (Lewis), 175–76
Arte Povera, 186
Artforum (journal), 58, 116
Art in America (journal), 267
Artists' Tower of Protest (Edwards/di Suvero sculpture), 63
ArtNews (journal), 267
Art of African Peoples, The (exhibition), 160
Art of Assemblage, The (exhibition), 20, 68
Art of Henry O. Tanner, The (exhibition), 164
"Art on the Beach" program, 244–46
Arts of Ghana (exhibition), 205–6
Arts of Southern California V (exhibition), 29
Art West Associated, 30, 45, 142–43, 166
Asco, 236–38, *237*
Asian American art-making, 97–98
Asian art influences, 208–11, 273–75
assemblage(s)/collage(s), 6; aesthetic of, 95, 125, 133–38, 161; ephemerality of, 60; interior, 214; invention of, 67; linkage/connection in, 71; place and, 134–35; poverty and, 78, 135; racist kitsch in, 108–13, 115; role of, 20–21; urbanness and, 34; use by people of color, 69–70; use of term, 67. *See also* found objects; junk art; *specific artists and works*
Association for the Advancement of Creative Musicians (AACM), 97

Audubon, John James, 170
Audubon, Walter, 170
August the Squared Fire (Edwards sculpture), 62, *63*
Aunt Hattie series (Saar assemblages), 123–26
Aunt Jemima series (Saar assemblages), 110–13, *112*, 115, 118, 123
avant-garde, impact of, 45, 64, 262
Avila, Adam, *21*
Avila, Eric, 8, 11
Awaken from the Unknowing (White drawing), 33
A-Z West, 267

BAC. *See* Black Arts Council
Baker, Houston, 190
Ball, James Presley, 265
Bandung Conference, 273
Banes, Sally, 186, 249
Banks, Leon, 89, 182
Bannarn, Henry, 38, 159–60
Barnwell, Andrea, 33
Barthé, Richmond, 144
Basinjom masquerade, 218
Bataille, Georges, 68
Baum-Silverman Gallery, 115
Beach (Hassinger installation), 241, 244–46, *245*
Bearden, Romare, 40, 58, 146, 164, 213, 214
Beastie Parade, The (Saar etching), 55
Beat Generation, 71
Beavers, George A., Jr., 27, 144
BECC. *See* Black Emergency Cultural Coalition
Beckford, Ruth, 250
Belafonte, Harry, 25, 181
Bell, Larry, 161
Benglis, Linda, 186
Bennett, Tony, 140
Bennington College, 246–49
Benston, Kimberly, 262
Bereal, Edmund, 57, 132, 161
Berger, Maurice, 249, 252
Berlin Industries Fair, 84
Berman, Wallace, 55, 129
Berman Piece (Herms assemblage), 129
Bernie Casey, Black Artist (Lewis film), 179

Betye Saar in her studio (Nakamura photograph), *117*
Bhabha, Homi, 276
Bibb, Leon, 24
Biberman, Edward, 30
Biggers, Sanford, 270–76; on absence, 276; Asian influences, 272–74; background and education, 270; lynching theme, 270–72; on "noshun," 270; quilts, 275; use of trees, 270–71. *See also specific works*
Billops, Camille, 30
Bird (Hammons sculpture), 230, 232
Birmingham Totem (White drawing), 33–35, *34*
Birth of the Cool, The (M. Davis album), 134
Bittersweet (Bessie's Song) (Saar assemblage), 123
Bittersweet Fruit (Biggers video), 270–71
black art. *See* art, African American
Black Art (magazine), 175, *176*, 177
Black Art in L.A. (exhibition), 37
Black Artists, The (Lewis film), 178–79
Black Artists on Art (Lewis/Waddy), 174–75, 178, 227
Black Arts Council (BAC), 95, 155, 166–72, 253–54
Black Arts Movement, 44, 45, 65, 86, 109, 118, 176–77, 180–84, 187–89, 204, 228–29
Black Boy's Window (Hammons assemblage), 226, 227
Black Culture Festival, 163, 168
Black Dialogue (magazine), 44
Black Emergency Cultural Coalition (BECC), 166, 172
Black Expo '72, 156
Black Girl's Window (Saar assemblage), 108–9, *117*, 226
Black Gods and Kings (exhibition), 205–6
Black Heroes (exhibition), 111
Black Is a Color (Saunders), 161
"Black Is Beautiful" theme, 88, 340n102
Black Mirror (exhibition), 120, *121*, 154, 181
black museum movement, 182–84
black nationalism, 64, 86, 88, 114, 186
blackness, 40
Black Omnibus (television series), 172
Black Panther Party, 154, 227–28, 230, 273

Black Power movement, 2, 15, 21, 56, 118, 186, 204
Black Seat Dodge '38 (Kienholz installation), 233
Black World (journal), 28, 212
Blossom (Biggers sculpture), 271
Blue Hole, Flood Waters, Little Miami River (Duncanson panting), 162
Bob Hope Presents the Chrysler Theatre (television show), 63–64
body prints, 226–27, 230
Boghossian, Skunder, 213
Bohanon, Gloria, 36–37, 96–97, 120, 154, 168
Bois, Yve-Alain, 68–69
Bomb (Connor sculpture), 133
Bond, J. Max, 114
Bontemps, Arna, 141
Booker, Claude, 167, 170, 172
Bounce, Rock, Skate, Roll (Biggers sculpture), 274
Bound (Biggers photographic series), 272
Bowling, Frank, 61–62, 100
Boxes (exhibition), 161
Boy with Flag (Hammons body print), 18, 227
Bradford, Mark, 269
Bradley, Tom, 170, *171*
Braque, Georges, 67, 138
Brenson, Michael, 60
Brent, Linda. *See* Jacobs, Harriet
Brewer, Debbie, 76–77, 266
Bride Stripped by Her Bachelors, Even, The (Duchamp artwork), 84
Brill, Gabi, 55
Brill, Klaus, 55
Brockman Gallery, 37, 45, 95, 99, 132, *145*, 145–52, *148*, *149*, 164, 180, 181, 195, 228, 273
Brockman Gallery Productions, 151, 195, 253
Brooks, Daphne, 190, *191*
Brooks, Gwendolyn, 13, 162
Brown, Beatrice Parson, 53, 127–28
Brown, Betye. *See* Saar, Betye
Brown, Grafton Tyler, 159
Brown, Henry Box, 190
Brown, Jefferson Maze, 53, 126–27
Brown, Jerry, 156
Brown, Trisha, 352n239
Brown Berets, 273

INDEX • **381**

Brown v. Board of Education, 11, 92
Bruce's Beach, 8
Bullins, Ed, 44
Burden, Chris, 223, 233–36, 262
Burke, Georgia, 25
Burroughs, Margaret, 92–93, 183
Butler, Octavia, 219
Butoh dance-theater, 210
Byrd, James, 271

CAAM. *See* California African American Museum
Cage, John, 136, 271
California African American Museum (CAAM), 182
California Arts Council, 90, 140, 156, 266
California Funk, 133
California Museum of Afro-American History and Culture, 258
Campbell, Mary Schmidt, 65, 109
Campbell's Soup Cans (Warhol painting), 98
Candomblé, 113, 205
Canon, J. Alfred, 328–29n126
Car Crash (Dine performance piece), 233
Carmichael, Stokely, 83
Caro, Anthony, 61–62
Carpenter, Jane, 56
Carroll, Lewis, 67, 272
Case in Point (Outterbridge sculpture), 101, 107
Casey, Bernie, 156, 160, 168, 173, 179
Catlett, Elizabeth, 27, 38, 39, 43, 49, 150, 175, 179
CCAA. *See* Compton Communicative Arts Academy
Ceeje, 160, 324n79
Centennial International Exhibition, 140
ceramics, 51–52
Ceremony for Freeway Fets (Nengudi performance piece), 195–202, *198–200*, 204, 205, 206–7
Certeau, Michel de, 4, 6–7, 68
C'est l'amour (White drawing), 32
CETA. *See* Comprehensive Education and Training Act
Chaino (Edwards sculpture), 60, 62
Chair, The (Lam painting), 222
Chamberlain, John, 60

Chandler, John, 185
Chave, Anna, 249
Cherry, Don, 296n131
Cheshire (Biggers sculpture), 272
Cheshire (Biggers video), 271–72
Chicago, Judy, 2, 119, 120–21, 124, 203
Chicago art-making, 97–98
Chicago Defender (newspaper), 213
Chicago Eight, 228
Chrysalis (journal), 122
civic estrangement, notion of, 100
Civil Rights Congress, 35
civil rights movement, 10, 15, 21, 56, 70, 71, 92, 95, 118, 135, 146, 152, 204, 266
CNA. *See* Committee for the Negro in the Arts
Coker, Gylbert, 263
Cole, Herbert M., 201, 205–6
Coleman, Floyd, 175
Coleman, Ornette, 64
Cole Meo, Yvonne, 36, 96, 142, 154, 214
Colescott, Robert, 160
collage(s). *See* assemblage(s)/collage(s)
Collins, Lisa Gail, 118
color bath, theory of, 151
Committee for Simon Rodia's Towers, 75–76
Committee for the Negro in the Arts (CNA), 44
Communism, 43–44
Comprehensive Education and Training Act (CETA), 151, 156, 195, 253
Compton Communicative Arts Academy (CCAA), 94, 95–98, *96*, 101
Concert Hall Workshop, 132
Concholar, Dan, 89, 151, 160, 168
Congolese National Liberation Front, 241
Congress of Racial Equality (CORE), 60
Conner, Bruce, 133, 203
Constellation II (Biggers installation), 274–75
Containment series (Outterbridge sculptures), 98–99, 103, 106, 179
Contemporary Crafts, 178
contemptible collectibles, use of term, 108–9
contextural method, 187
Continuous Project Altered Daily (Morris installation), 263
Contribution of the Negro to Democracy in America, The (White mural), 42, 89

382 • INDEX

Conwill, Houston, 6, 21–22, 97, 151, 173–74, 186, 187, 189, 211–24, 262; award, 268; background and education, 211–13, 340–41n102; collaborations, 268–69; exhibitions and performance, 213–24; as griot, 221–22; juju bags, 214, 215, 223, 225; petrigraphs, 214–16, *215*, 220, 223, 268; Studio Z, 243–44, 257; use of stools, 216
Conwill, Kinshasha Holman, 97, 151, 212, 218
Cooke, Marvel, 49
Cooks, Bridget R., 170
Copeland, Huey, 48, 101, 137
Corcoran Gallery of Art, 83
CORE. *See* Congress of Racial Equality
Cornell, Joseph, 67, 129–32
Cortez, Jayne, 44, 64–65
Cortor, Eldzier, 39, 40
Cosby, Bill, 151, 181
Cosby Show, The (television series), 181
Costume Study for Mesh Mirage (Nengudi installation), 194–95, *196*, 197, 203
Cotton Hang-Up (Edwards sculpture), 62
Courbet, Gustave, 32
Creation/Dissipation (Biggers installation), 274
Creative Time, 244
Crenshaw, Kimberlé, 168
Crichlow, Ernest, 146
crisscrossing, use of term, 4
Crow, Thomas, 70, 249
Cuff, Dana, 6, 97
culture: African American practice, 76–78, 87–88, 104–6, 134, 176–77; black nationalism, 186; of dissemblance, 110–11; identity and, 190; safe spaces and, 6
Curtain for William and Peter (Edwards installation), 240
Curtis, Tony, 26
Curtis Amy–George Bohanon Sextet, 168

Dada art movement, 85, 131–32
Damballa (Saar sculpture), 116
dance: African influences, 201; black, 247–50; modern, 246–47; postmodern, 186, 249, 256
Dance Observer (journal), 247
Dangerous Ground (Hassinger installation), 254

Da Vinci Gallery, 37
Davis, Agnes Moses, 147
Davis, Alonzo, Jr., 21, 37, 45, 89, 95, 146–52, *149*, *171*, 253. *See also* Brockman Gallery
Davis, Alonzo, Sr., 147
Davis, Dale Brockman, 21, 37, 45, 95, 146–48, *149*, 253. *See also* Brockman Gallery
Davis, Miles, 134
Davis, Ossie, 44
Davis, Sammy, Jr., 25, 181
Dead Man (Burden performance piece), *235*, 235–36, 238
de Bretteville, Sheila Levrant, 121–22, *122*
décalage, 275–76
Decoy Gang War Victim (Asco performance piece), 236–38, *237*
Dee, Ruby, 44
Deep Down (Hassinger sculpture), 255
DeFeo, Jay, 132
Defiant Ones, The (film), 26
de Lavallade, Yvonne, 250
Delta Spirit (Hammons installation), 246
dematerialization, 17, 18, 107, 185, 193, 240, 242, 262–63
Democratic National Convention riot (1968), 228
dePace, Joseph, 268
DePillars, Murray, 109
desegregation, 12, 32
Diaries (Part 1 of Lives) (Hassinger performance piece), 255–56
diasporic aesthetics, 1, 20, 24, 39–50, 60, 114, 116, 125, 137, 186, 204–5, 207, 241. *See also* migration, African American
Diawara, Manthia, 129
Dickson, Charles, 89, 96
Dickson Art Center, 162, 166
Dillman, Bradford, 64
Dine, Jim, 229–30, 233, 238
Dinner Party (Chicago), 124
Dipple, Gordon, 154
Directions in Collage (exhibition), 161
discrimination, 9, 11, 56, 90, 118–19, 150
dissimulation, 191
di Suvero, Mark, 60, 62–63, 99, 162
Dixon, Ivan, 26, 163
DJ Jahi Sundance, 270
Donaldson, Jeff, 211–12

Door, The (Admissions Office) (Hammons assemblage), 227
Douglas, Emory, 154, *155*
Douglass, Frederick, 27–28, 232
Dove, Arthur, 67
Dove, Ulysses, 351n232
Dover, Cedric, 176
dreamscapes, 6
Drewal, Margaret Thompson, 257
Dreyfus Affair, 35
Driskell, David C., 100, 165–66, 170, *171*, 184
Drough, Irene Maze Estorage Brown, 127–28
Dry/Flow (Hassinger wall sculpture), 252
Du Bois, W. E. B., 143, 189
Dubuffet, Jean, 68
Duchamp, Marcel, 84, 131
Duncanson, Robert Scott, 159, 162, 166
Dunham, Katherine, 247
DuSable Museum of African American History, 183
Dwan, Virginia, 160–61
Dwan Gallery, 31, 62, 99, 160–61

earthworks movement, 253
Ebony (magazine), 28, 51
Eder, Rita, 187
Edwards, Brent Hayes, 275–76
Edwards, Melvin, 20, 23–24, 30, 57–65, *59*, 93, 94, 239–40; activism, 60–61; Asian influences, 274; collaborations, 62–63, 64–65; commissions, 62; critical reception, 58, 59–60, 62; exhibitions, 57–60, 62–65, 162, 257; welding, 59–60. *See also specific works*
Egungun masquerade, 202–3, 205
Ejagham, 218
Electric Dress (Tanaka performance art), 208, *209*
Eleven Associated Gallery, 141, 273
Ellington, Duke, 162
ellipsis, use of term, 4
employment, 8–11
Epting, Marion, 89
Eshu (The Trickster) (Saar sculpture), 113
Esther Bear Gallery, 62
Ethnic Heritage series (Outterbridge sculptures), 101–3

Evers, Medgar, 230
Evers, Myrlie, 88
Executive Order 8802, 9
exhibitionary complex, defined, 140
existentialism, 71
Extreme Object D-E-D (Purifoy sculpture), 150

Fabric Workshop and Museum, 267
Face of the Gods (Thompson), 222–23
Factor, Don, 59–60, 62
Farmer, James, 29
Farr, D. Francine, 260
Feinblatt, Ebria, 163–64
feminism in art, 108, 116–28, 203–4, 262
Feminist Art Program (Fresno State College), 119, 204
Ferguson, Cecil, 163, 166–68, *167*, 171–72, 182
Ferus Gallery, 25, 129, 132–33, 148, 160
FESTAC (Second World Black and African Festival of Arts and Culture), 113
Festivals and Funerals (Cortez), 64
Fetchit, Stepin, 110
fiber arts, 250–51
Field (Lewis painting), 179
Fiesta of the Dead (Saar assemblage), 114
Fine, Elsa Honig, 176
Fine Arts Galleries at California State University, Los Angeles, 115, 119
Finish Fetish style, 133, 179
Finkelpearl, Tom, 268
Finley, Cheryl, 137
Five Car Stud (Kienholz installation), 313n204
Five Great American Negroes (White mural), 42
Five Younger Los Angeles Artists (exhibition), *58*, 58–59
Flaherty, Linda, 86
Fletcher, Ed, 220
Flying (Hassinger/Nengudi performance piece), *258*, 258–61, *259*, 261
folk art, 39, 67, 186, 237
Folk Singer (White drawing), 24, 283n9
Foreman, Doyle, 114
Forest (Hassinger installation), 246
forgetting, motivated, 239

For Hip Hop Ni Sasagu (Biggers musical composition), 274
For Love of Ivy (film), 24, 35
Foulkes, Llyn, 161
found objects, 59, 60, 67–68, 74, 78–79, 129, 134–36, 227, 242. *See also* assemblage(s)/collage(s); junk art; *specific works*
Fourth Circle, The (Edwards sculpture), 59
Foxx, Redd, 181
Frances Parson White (Saar collage), 124
Francis, Sam, 182
Franco, Pamela R., 204
Frederick S. Wight Art Gallery, 205–6, 218
Freedom (magazine), 43
Freedomways (magazine), 43–44
Freeman, Elizabeth, 219
Friedman, Gary, 167
From the Ashes (anthology), 44

Gafford, Alice Taylor, 142
Gallery, The, 95, 172–74, 214, 217–18. *See also* Multi-Cul Gallery
Gallery 32, 95, *153*, 153–60, *155*
Gallery 79, 92
Gallery Tanner, 174
Gamboa, Harry, Jr., 236
gang violence, 237–38
Garbage Is Beautiful (exhibition), 84
García, Rupert, 46
Garden Project series (Marshall paintings), 269
Garvey movement, 273
Gates, Henry Louis, Jr., 40
Gato, El (Saar assemblage), 114
Gayle Galleries, 92
Gechtoff, Sonia, 132
Gelede (Saar sculpture), 113
Gèlèdé masquerade, 203
General Moses (Harriet Tubman) (White photograph), 1–2, 18, 37, 45, 49, 144
genocide of African Americans, 35
Gerowitz, Judy. *See* Chicago, Judy
ghettos, black, 12, 13–14
GI Bill, 139
Gilbert, George, 57
Gilliam, Sam, 40, 100, 162, 211
Gilroy, Paul, 186, 239
Gleaves, Beverly, 56

Golden State Mutual Life Insurance Company, 1, 27, 33, 36, 37, 89, 143–44, 183
Goldsby, Jacqueline, 230, 233, 239
González, Julio, 60
Goode, Joe, 161
Goode Bryant, Linda, 187, 189, 193, 220, 230, 239, 243, 244
Gottschild, Brenda Dixon, 201, 250
Goya, Francisco, 32
Graham, Martha, 247
Grandma Draugh (Saar assemblage), 124, 128
Grandma's Garden (Saar assemblage), 125
Grandma's House (Saar assemblage), 125
Grant, Bradford C., 12
Greasy Bags and Barbecue Bones (Hammons collages), 255
Great Migration, U.S., 4
Green, Renee, 48
Greenberg, Clement, 70, 109, 248
Greene, Carroll, Jr., 164, 170
Gregory bags, 114, 116, 214
Grewe, Cordula, 32
Griffin, Booker, 87
Griffin, Farah Jasmine, 6, 20, 49
Gris-Gris Box (Saar sculpture), 114, 115
Gronk, 236
Grosvenor, Robert, 160–61
Grosz, Elizabeth, 15, 17
Guess Who's Coming to Dinner? (film), 24
Gundaker, Grey, 103–4, 105–6, 108, 125, 272
Gutai Art Association, 208, 211
Guy, Edna, 247

Hair and Wire (Hammons installation), 19
Hall, Stuart, 189
Halprin, Anna, 250
Hammons, David, 2, 18, 21–22, 37, 45, 74, 111, 119, 133, 186, 187, 224–43, *225*; assemblages, 226–28, 263, 271, 273–74; awards, 267–68; body prints, 226–27, 230; in Conwill performance piece, 220, 241; Edwards's influence on, 239–40; exhibitions, 139, 148, 163–64, *225*, 228, 230, 268; on Nengudi, 192, 197–201; in Nengudi performance piece, 139, 241; performance pieces, 229, 233–36, 238, 246; on purpose of art, 243; on ritual, 224–25, 239, 243; Saar and, 225–26; spade motif, 229–30, 232, 232–34,

INDEX • **385**

Hammons, David (*continued*) 235–36, 238–39, 242, 262; on speech, 228–29; street interventions, 240–41; Studio Z, 241–42, 257. *See also specific works*
Hancraft Studios, 178
Hansberry, Lorraine, 44
Harden, Marvin, 57, 60, 160
Harlem Renaissance, 44, 72, 127
Harris, Kira Lynn, 269
Hartman, Saidiya, 217, 221, 228
Hassinger, Maren, 19, *21*, 21–22, 151, 187, 189, 194, *195*, 197, 206, 243–61, *259*, *261*, 267; on African context, 256–57; background and education, 246–49; exhibitions, 241, 244–46, 251–61; on Hesse, 251–52; public works, 253; Studio Z, 243–44, 255, 257; themes, 249; wire rope medium, 250–52, 255, 262. *See also specific works*
Hassinger, Peter, 250
Hayes, Vertis, 93
Haynes, Hattie Parson. *See* Keys, Hattie Parson
Haynie, Wilbur, 29
Heizer, Michael, 186
Heliton, Bob, *153*
Hemingway, Andrew, 43
Henderson, Ethel Mae, 50–51
Henson, Matthew, 159–60
Herbert F. Johnson Museum, 167
Heritage Gallery, 30–32, 160, 164, 181
Herms, George, 55, 129, 130
Herrón, Willie, 236
Hesse, Eva, 186, 251–52
Hewitt, Mary Jane, 174, 258
Hickman, Paul E., 178–79
Higa, Kuzuo, 37
High Desert Test Sites festival, 267
High Noon (Hassinger performance piece), 255
Hill, John Lamar, 27
Hill, Tony, 93
Hine, Darlene Clark, 4, 6, 110–11
hip-hop artists, 274
Hi Red Center, 211
Hirsch, Marianne, 123
History of the Negro Press, A (White mural), 42
Hoffman, Hans, 248

Holiday, Billie, 271
Hollywood, 13; black artists and, 23, 25–27, 28–29, 178, 180–81; choreography, 250; representation of blacks, 39, 43
Holm, Hanya, 247
Homage to My Father and the Spirit (Edwards sculpture), 62
homeplace, 6, 12, 23, 94, 97–98, 100, 104–8, 118, 159
homesteading, 5
Honeywood, Varnette, 181
hoodoo, 113–14, 205
hooks, bell, 97, 100, 101, 104
Hopkins, Henry, 161
Hopkins, Pauline, 190
Hopper, Dennis, 161
Hopps, Walter, 31, 82–84, 131–33, 162
Horn, Shirley, 35
Horne, Gerald, 62, 145, 273
Horowitz, Benjamin, 30–31
Horst, Louis, 247
Horton, Lester, 249–50
House of Tarot (Saar etching), *54*, 54–55
housing, 12–14; kitchenette apartments, 12–13; public, 14; rights, 14; segregation in, 12, 137
Housing Act (1949), 14
Houston, Norman O., 27, 144
Huddleston, Clive, 57
Huddleston, Modie, 57
Hudson River School, 162
Hughes, Langston, 44, 51, 268
humanism, 43
Humphrey, Doris, 247
Humphrey, Margo, 36
Hunter Gallery, 84
Hurston, Zora Neale, 104
Husserl, Edmund, 84
Hutson, Jean Blackwell, 42
Huysman Gallery, 161
hypervisibility/invisibility, 190, 191

Ianco-Starrels, Josine, 119–20
Images of Dignity (White), 25, 28
Imani's Tale (Conwill performance piece). *See Notes of a Griot / Imani's Tale* (Conwill performance piece)
Inaya, Beata, *7*, 29, 30

indeterminacy, 187, 189
Indigo Mercy (Saar sculpture), 116
Ingram, Rex, 25
Injustice Case (Hammons assemblage), 227, 228–29
Inner Cultural Center, 145
integration, 8, 10–11, 31, 139, 153
International Afro-American Museum, 183
International Review of African American Art (magazine), 175. See also *Black Art* (magazine)
invisibility. *See* hypervisibility/invisibility
Irons, Sue. *See* Nengudi, Senga
It Takes Two to Integrate, Cha, Cha, Cha (Kienholz assemblage), 313n204
I've Got Rhythm (Saar assemblage), 110

J'Accuse! (White series), 35
"J'Accuse . . . !" (Zola), 35
Jackson, Al, 220
Jackson, Esther Cooper, 49
Jackson, Roy, 152
Jackson, Suzanne, 21, 45, 95, 120, 151, 152–60, 169; background and education, 152–53; exhibitions, 156, 157, 160; Gallery 32, 153–60; techniques, 157–60
Jacobs, Harriet (Linda Brent), 232
JAM. *See* Just Above Midtown Gallery
Japanese art/performance, 208–11
jazz aesthetic, 70, 132–33, 134, 263, 296n131
Jeffries, Rosalind, 213
Jemison, Jan, 175
Jenkins, Ulysses, 241, 256, 260
Jewel of Ogun, The (Saar sculpture), 116
Jive Ass Bird (Outterbridge sculpture), 101, 102
John Hay Whitney Fellowship, 26
John Outterbridge, Black Artist (Lewis film), 179
John Outterbridge in his studio (Nakamura photograph), 94
Johns, Jasper, 229
Johnson, Alvin, 10
Johnson, Daniel LaRue, 7, 30, 57, 160, 161
Johnson, James Weldon, 104
Johnson, Jeffalyn, 10
Johnson, Nobel, 42
Johnson, Sargent, 148, 211

Johnson Calloway, Marie, 36, 120
John the Conqueror (Saar sculpture), 113–14
Joined for the Arts, 81–82, 85–86, 87
Jones, A. Quincy, 30
Jones, Bill T., 248
Jones, James Earl, 172
Jones, Lois Mailou, 213
Jones, Quincy, 35
Joseph, Branden, 131, 135, 136
juju bags, 214, 215, 223, 224
juju music, 341–42n104
JuJu Ritual (Conwill performance installations), 173–74, 212–13, 216–20, 223, 225, 236, 239
Julien, Isaac, 160
junk art, 78–82, 86, 89, 105–6, 133, 135–36. See also assemblage(s)/collage(s); found objects; *66 Signs of Neon* (Purifoy sculpture)
Just Above Midtown Gallery (JAM), 167, 193, 214, 220, 244

Kabuki theater, 210
Kaneki, Sumie, 274
Kanemitzu, Matsumi, 161
Kara, Juro, 210
Karamu House, 50–51
Karenga, Ron, 44, 87–88, 186
Kaufman, Bob, 44
Kerciu, G. Ray, 31
Kerouac, Jack, 146
KeyChange, 274
Keys, Hattie Parson, 123–28
Keys, Robert, 125, 126
Kienholz, Edward, 55, 78, 84, 132, 133–34, 168, 233, 313n204. *See also specific works*
Kindred (Butler), 219
King, B. B., 35
King, Martin Luther, Jr., 230
King, Rodney, 232
Kingsley, April, 257
kinship, 221
kitchenette apartments, 12–13
Kitt, Eartha, 25
Klein, Yves, 160–61, 226
Kosuth, Joseph, 46
Krasne, Lucille, 76–77
Krauss, Rosalind, 68–69, 187

INDEX • 387

Ku Klux Klan, 13, 172
Kurosawa, Akira, 209
Kwon, Miwon, 16, 17, 262–63

LACMA. *See* Los Angeles County Museum of Art
Lacy, Suzanne, 233
Lam, Wifredo, 222
Lambert, Carrie, 249
LANAA. *See* Los Angeles Negro Art Association
Lane, Doyle, 36
language, imbrication of, 46
Larsen, Susan, 130
Last Dance (Saar assemblage), 123
Lathrop, Welland, 250
Laughing Magic (Hammons sculpture), 230
Lautner, John, 30
Lawal, Babatunde, 202
Lawrence, Jacob, 27, 39–40, 43, 150, 224
Leaning (Hassinger installation), 254
Learning Tree, The (film), 26
Lefalle-Collins, Lizzetta, 98, 267
Lefebvre, Henri, 15
Leigh-Taylor, Elizabeth, 154
Leimert Park, 151
Lemann, Nicholas, 191
Let Me Entertain You (Saar assemblage), 110, *111*, 272
Letters from Home (Saar collages), 125, 126
Let Us Tie Down Loose Ends (Outterbridge sculpture), 107
Lewis, Edmonia, 166
Lewis, Norman, 146, 261
Lewis, Samella Sanders, 21, 95, 100, 168–69, 172–80; background and education, 172–73, 273; curated exhibition with Saar, 120, *121*, 154, 181; exhibitions, 160; filmmaking, 178–79; galleries, 173–74, 214, 217–18, 258; paintings, 179–80; publications, 174–78, 227. *See also specific works*
LeWitt, Sol, 46, 160–61
Liberation of Aunt Jemima, The (Saar assemblage), 110–13, *112*, 115, 118, 123
libraries, artists' use of, 41–42
Lichtenstein, Roy, 132
lieux de mémoire, 207
Lifted X, The (Edwards sculpture), 59–60, 62

Ligon, Glenn, 48
Lincoln, Abbey, 24, 35
Lindhurst Gallery, 214
Lippard, Lucy, 117, 185
Lipschutz, Yael, 84
Lipsitz, George, 13, 134
Loci (Hassinger sculpture), 251
Locke, Alain, 41, 143
Long Beach Museum, 29
Looking for Mr. Goodbar (film), 156
Los Angeles, 1972 (exhibition), *165*, 169
Los Angeles art scene, African American, 17–24; commercial and nonprofit, 160–72; early exhibitions, 140–42; entertainment industry and, 64; group shows, 257; migration to, 2; performance venue integration, 8; print culture in, 44–45; south of Pico Boulevard, 15–17. *See also specific artists*
Los Angeles County Museum of Art (LACMA), 20, 58, 113, 141, 143, 162–65, *165*, 168–72, 173, 206, 237, 253–54
Los Angeles Negro Art Association (LANAA), 141–42
Los Angeles Street Graphics Committee, 151
Loving, Al, 40, 100
Luther, Martin, 270
Lynch Fragments series (Edwards sculptures), 60, 61–62, 65, 239–40, 271
lynching, 61, 230, 270–72
Lytton Center for Visual Arts, 119

Mafundi Institute, 95. *See also* Watts Happening Coffee House
Mahan, William, 251
Mail Art movement, 125
Mama's Flowers (Saar assemblage), 128
Mamba (Edwards sculpture), 60, 148
Mandala of the B-Bodhisattva II (Biggers installation), 274
Manhattan Beach, 8
Manning, Susan, 247, 250
Mao Zedong, 44
Marcuse, Herbert, 83
Mardi Gras Indians, black, 207
Maren Hassinger in front of Twelve Trees (Avila photograph), 21

marginality, 100, 138
maroonage, concept of, 190
Marshall, Kerry James, 269
Marshall, Thurgood, 11
Martin, Agnes, 251
Martin, John, 247
Masakela, Hugh, 88
masking/masquerade, 201–3, 204, 205, 206, 218–19, 257
Mason, Biddy, 1, 122
Mason, John, 52, 148
Masses and Mainstream (monthly), 39
Mathis, Johnny, 156
Matthews, Miriam, 1, 140–42, 143–44, 273
Mayan Theater, 141
May Department Stores Company, 174
Mbulu, Letta, 88
McCullough, Barbara, 225
McDuffie, Erik S., 49
McKittrick, Katherine, 6, 12, 16, 17, 97, 135
McLaughlin, John, 211
McWillie, Judith, 103–4, 105, 106, 108, 125, 272
Measure for Measure (Saar assemblage), 111
Megerian, Maureen, 254
memory/history/community, 207, 261–63
Méndez, Leopoldo, 39
Menken, Adah Isaacs, 190
Menstruation Bathroom (Chicago installation), 204
Mental Space (A. Davis collographs), 148
Meredith, James, 88
Mexican mural painting, 38–39, 236
Mhunzi, Pete, 156
Micheaux, Oscar, 42
Migrants (Lewis painting), 179
migration, African American, 3–4; Asian parallels, 272–73; demographics in Los Angeles, 9; narratives, 20, 39–40, 101, 107, 126–28, 175, 186, 189–90; promised lands, 5–7; remembrance and, 137; thinking space and, 7–12
minimalism: abstraction and, 48, 185; aesthetics, 49, 119, 244, 251, 255; dance asceticism and, 249; Finish Fetish style, 133, 179; New York style, 161; in performance art, 234; West Coast style, 119
Minneapolis Institute of Arts, 65

minstrelsy, 110
misogyny, 118
Miyashiro, Ron, 57, 161
Modern Dance, Negro Dance (Manning), 247
modernism, 40, 52, 68–69, 118, 131–32, 189, 239
Mojo Bag (Saar sculpture), 113–14
Mojo for 1404 (Edwards sculpture), 60, *61*
Mojozo, Estella Conwill, 268
Montañez Ortiz, Raphael, 271
Montgomery, Evangeline Juliette [E. J.], 111, 330n136
Montonaga, Sadasa, 208
Montoya, Malaquias, 46
Moore, Shirley Ann, 4, 126
Morris, Robert, 186, 263
Morrison, Toni, 135, 186, 221, 270
Mosquera, Gerardo, 205, 222
Motley, Archibald, 92
Movimiento Chicano, 236
Moxey, Keith, 275
Mti (Saar altar), 115
Muchnic, Suzanne, 223
Mullen, Harryette, 118
Multi-Cul Gallery, 115, 172. *See also* Gallery, The
Multi-Cultural Productions, 160
Municipal Art Gallery, 257–58
Muñoz, José, 217, 232, 263
Murakami, Saburo, 208
murals, 38–39, 151, 236–37
Murder Mystery (Hammons performance piece), 233, 235, 238
Museum and Laboratories of Ethnic Arts and Technology (UCLA), 205
Museum of African American Art, 174, 258
Museum of Modern Art, 20, 164, 213
Museum of the National Center of Afro-American Artists, 183

NAACP. *See* National Association for the Advancement of Colored People
Nakamura, Robert A., *94*, *117*
Nascimento, Abdias do, 175
Nation, The (journal), 183
National Association for the Advancement of Colored People (NAACP), 11

Nation of Islam, 61, 62, 273
naturalism, seraphic, 43
Nauman, Bruce, 2
Naylor, Gloria, 186
Negro and Creative Arts Exhibit, 7
Negro Art Exhibit, 141
Negro Digest (magazine), 28
Negro in American Art, The (exhibition), 162, 166
Negro in the Creative Arts, The (program), 29–30
Negro Woman, The (Catlett print series), 39
Neilsen, Shirley, 132
Nelson, Alondra, 10
Nengudi, Senga, 19, 21–22, 75–76, 151, 154, 162, 186, *188*, 189, 192–211, *259*, *261*, 267; Asian art influences, 208–11; background and education, 192–93; exhibitions, 193–95, 258–61; feminist art, 203–4; masking, use of, 201–3, 204; performance art, 195–202; Studio Z, 243–44, 257; Yoruba influences, 202–5, 207, 213. *See also specific works*
Neo-Dada art, 31, 130
Neo-Hoodoo aesthetic, 114
Neutra, Richard, 14, 30
New Breed art space, 147
New Dance Group, 247
Newman, Barnett, 248
Newman, James, 132
New Masses (magazine), 38
New Negro, The (Locke), 41
New Negro Movement, 42–43, 72
Neworld (magazine), 223
New Paintings of Common Objects (exhibition), 31, 132
New Realism, 31
New Ring Shout, The (Conwill terrazzo sculpture), 268
New Talent Purchase awards, 59
Newton, Huey, 44
New York Cultural Center, 167
New York Times (newspaper), 166
Nickerson, William, Jr., 144
Nicodemus, Kansas, 265–66
Niggers Ain't Never Ever Gonna Be Nothin' (Purifoy sculpture), 150
Night Letters (Saar collages), 125

nkisi sculptures, 223
Noah Purifoy (retrospective), 267
Noah Purifoy Foundation, 267
Nochlin, Linda, 32
Nocturne (White drawing), 33
Noh performance, 210
Nora, Pierre, 207
Nora Albion (di Suvero sculpture), 99
Norton, Eileen Harris, 269
noshun, use of term, 270
nostalgia, 131
Notes of a Griot / Imani's Tale (Conwill performance piece), 214, 220–21, 223
Nuestra Señora la Reina de Los Angeles de Porciuncula, 3
Nyong'o, Tavia, 109
Nyuumba Ya Sanaa Academy, 206

Oakland Museum, 330n136
OBAC. *See* Organization of Black American Culture
O'Dell, Kathy, 190
O'Higgins, Pablo, 39
Oldenburg, Claus, 101, 203
Oliver L. Brown v. Board of Education of Topeka, Kansas, 11
Olugebefola, Ademola, 206
Omen (Saar assemblage), 113, 128–29
O'Neal, Frederick, 25
One to One (newsletter), 70–71, 81
Ono, Yoko, 211
On the Road (Kerouac), 146
Open Secret (Conwill relief), 268
Operation Teacup (photograph), 75
Opus de Four (jazz group), 92
Organization of Black American Culture (OBAC), 46, 212
Oriental America (exhibition), 151
Orozco, José Clemente, 39
Outterbridge, Beverly McKissick, 93
Outterbridge, John, 6, 9, 11, 21, 74, 89, 91–108, *94*, 130–40, 162, 168; assemblages, 91, 95, 133; background and education, 91–93, 130; on craft, 103; as crossing artistic boundaries, 99–100; exhibitions, 94–103, 148; film on, 179; on homeplace, 6, 94, 97–98, 100, 104–8; in Los Angeles, 93–95; migration narratives, 101, 107;

musical endeavors, 92; sculptures, 93–94, 98–108; themes, 100–103, 133. *See also specific works*
Outterbridge, John Ivery, 91
Outterbridge, Olivia Northern, 91
Overstreet, Joe, 100, 109, 114
Ozu, Yasujirō, 209

Pacific Town Club (PTC), 27
pacquets congo, 223
Paik, Nam June, 271
Pajaud, Harriet Craft, 120
Pajaud, William, 29, 50, 89, 144, 183
PAM. *See* Pasadena Art Museum
Pan-Africanism, 221
Pan Afrikan Peoples Arkestra, 44, 151
Parker, Charlie "Yardbird," 230, 232
Parker, Frank, 197, 198, 336n41
Parks, Gordon, 26
Parson, Beatrice, 126–27
Parson, Emma Kelley, 124
Pasadena Art Museum (PAM), 31, 84–85, 99, 129, 131–32, 161–62, 251
Pas de Deux (Hassinger sculpture), 252, 255
Pashgian, Helen, 119
Paul Tishman Collection, 113, 163, 168, 206
Payne, Vaughn C., Jr., 182
Peace Tower. *See* Artists' Tower of Protest (Edwards/di Suvero sculpture)
Pearl C. Woods Gallery, 194, 214, 217–18
Peller, Gary, 168
Percy, Walker, 252–53, 254
performance art, 162; African dance influences, 201; dematerialization in, 18, 21, 185; fragmentation and layering in, 90; indeterminacy in, 189; Japanese influences, 208–11; street interventions, 240–41, 353n254; survival and, 190–91. *See also specific artists and works*
petriglaphs, 214–16, *215*, 220, 223, 242
Petry, Ann, 87
Pettibone, Richard, 161
phenomenology, 71–72
Philips, Marcy S., 187, 189, 230, 239, 243
Picasso, Pablo, 67, 68, 137–38, 203
Pico, Pío, 15
Pico Boulevard, art/social space, 15–17
Pincus-Witten, Robert, 186, 187–88

Pinkey, Elliott, 96
Pink Jalopy (Lacy performance piece), 233
Piper, Adrian, 223
Pippin, Horace, 40
Pisstained Stairs and the Monkey Man's Wares (Cortez), 64–65
Pitts, Gregory P., 217–18
Plagens, Peter, 234
Plessy v. Ferguson, 11
Plural (journal), 187
Poitier, Sidney, 24, 25, *26*, 35, 181
police brutality, 61, 62, 181, 184
Pollock, Jackson, 248
pop art, 60, 229
Popular Front, 43, 44, 45
Porter, James, 100, 162, 176
Poster for Emory Douglas exhibition at Gallery 32, 155
postminimalism, 100; aesthetics, 119, 185–86, 203, 244, 249, 261, 269; artistic boundaries and, 99–100; deconstruction in, 227; dematerialization in, 240, 242; in performance art, 234
Powell, Earl "Bud," 263
Powell, Judson, 27, 76–79, *77*, 94
Powell, Richard J., 223, 227
Power of Place initiative, 122
PreColumbian (di Suvero sculpture), 99
Pressure (Purifoy sculpture), 84
Prevalence of Ritual, The (Bearden exhibition), 164, 213
Price, Ken, 148, 211
Price, Vincent, 156
Primus, Pearl, 247
process art, 185–86
progressive networks, 38–39
PS 1 Institute for Art and Urban Resources, 244, 257
PTC. *See* Pacific Town Club
Purifoy, Noah, 6, 13, 21, 27, *80*, 107, 130, 139, 166; on art-as-change, 71–72; assemblages, 70–90, 133, 267; background and education, 72–74, 139; exhibitions, 79–87, 148–50, 266–67; existentialist influences, 71; interior design work, *74*; junk art, 78–82, 86, 89, 133; on marginality, 138; outdoor museum, 266–67; on transformation, 69; Watts arts festivals, 79–80, 82,

Purifoy, Noah (*continued*)
86–90; Watts neighborhood and, 74–90. *See also specific works*
Puryear, Martin, 251

queer time, notion of, 219, 263
quilts, 275

racist kitsch, 108–13, 115
Rag Man series (Outterbridge assemblages), 99–101, *102*, 107
Rainbow Sign Cultural Center, 111, 115
Rainer, Yvonne, 352n239
Ramsey, Guthrie P., Jr., 40, 263
Rauschenberg, Robert, 131, 135, 136–37, 160–61, 182, 229
Raven, Arlene, 121
Ray, Marguerite, 156, 181
realism style, 30–32
Record for Hattie (Saar assemblage), 123
Red Guard Party, 273
Reed, Ishmael, 114
Rees, Thomas M., 30
Rejlander, O. G., 67
remains, use of, 187, 189, 243
remembrance, tradition of, 137. *See also* forgetting, motivated; memory/history/community
representation, 68–70; of blacks by Hollywood, 39, 43; controlling, 180, 184; stereotypical, of blacks, 108–13, 190
respatialization, 16
Richard, Paul, 82
Riddle, John, 37, 74, 89, 111, 139, 148, 160, 168
Riddle, Tony, 151
Ringgold, Faith, 54, 101
ritual: African, 116, 220–21; in African American life, 87–88; in dance, 186, 202, 203; healing, 106; of mandala, 274; objects, 206, 207, 242; in performance art, 211–24, 225, 239, 243, 257, 274; shamanic, 210
Rivera, Diego, 39
Rivers (Conwill terrazzo floor), 268
Rivers, Haywood Bill, 40
Rivers, Larry, 160–61
Roach, Joseph, 206–7
Robeson, Paul, 43

Robinson, Troy, 97, 107
Rodia, Simon, 29, 76. *See also* Watts Towers Arts Center
Roelof-Lanner, T. V., 143
Rogin, Michael, 239
RoHo, 197
Rolf Nelson, 160
romantic style, 32
Room No. 5 (Cortor painting), 40
roots tourism, 217
Rosaldo, Renato, 207
Rosenberg, Harold, 78
Rosenwald Fellowship, 26, 39, 41, 280n28
Ross, Doran, 205–6
Roxy's (Kienholz installation), 133–34
R.S.V.P. #X (Nengudi installation), 193–94, *194*
Rubin, Arnold, 116, 163
Rumi, 274
Ruscha, Edward, 2, 132, 135, 161
Russell, Pat, 174

Saar, Betye, 6, 7, 20, 21, 23, 29, 50–56, 52, 89, 117, *122*; African influences, 113–14, 116; altars, 114–16, 225; assemblages/collages, 109–15, 123–28, 133, 225; book illustrations, 114; constructing counterculture, 108–16; on Conwill, *218*; Cornell and, 129–32; curated exhibition with Lewis, 120, *121*, 154, 181; de Bretteville and, 121–22; exhibitions, 51, 55–56, 115, 119–20, 154, 160, 173; father, 53, 126–27; feminism/women's art, 55, 108, 116–28; Hammons and, 225–26; as lecturer, 267; lynching theme, 272; matriarchal roots, 123–28; migration narratives, 126–28; mother, 126–27; on motherhood, 53–54; sculptures, 113–16; souvenirs, 131; spirituality, 54–55, 56; studio cards, 53; use of racist kitsch, 108–13, 115. *See also specific works*
Saar, Richard, 6, 53, 108
Sadhana (Saar sculpture), 114
safe spaces, 6, 12, 23, 154, 186, 242. *See also* homeplace
Safety Savings and Loan, 142
Said, Edward, 275
Saint Phalle, Niki de, 160–61
Samaras, Lucas, 161

Sambo's Banjo (Saar assemblage), 110, 115, 272
Samhadi (Saar sculpture), 114
Sanders, Stan, 87, 181–84
Sanders Art Media, 178
Sanford and Son (television series), 181
Santa Barbara Museum of Art, 20, 58, 62, 162
Santería, 113, 205, 206
Sapphire Show, The (exhibition), 154
Saret, Alan, 186
Saunders, Raymond, 161
Savage, Augusta, 38
Schneemann, Carolee, 55, 223
Schneider, Rebecca, 204, 217, 262
Schomburg, Arturo, 41, 141
Schomburg Center for Research in Black Culture, 268, 283n8
Schrank, Sarah, 86
Schwitters, Kurt, 84, 131, 134
Scott, Ina Brown, 33
Sculpture Magazine, 267
Sculpture of Black Africa (exhibition), 113, 163, 168, 206
Seale, Bobby, 44, 227–28
Secretary to the Spirits (Reed), 114
Sedgwick, Eve K., 130
segregation: of buses, 92, 137; in housing, 12, 137; poverty and, 87, 91; in public schools, 8, 11–12, 126, 137, 281n36; space and, 8, 15, 169
Seidenbaum, Art, 30–31
Seko, Mobutu Sese, 241
Seldis, Henry, 30
Serra, Richard, 129, 186
Seventy-Ninth Street Collective, 92
Shabazz, Betty, 88
Shamanic trance, 208
Shango, 205
Shapiro, Miriam, 121, 204
Shaw, Ann, 29
Shaw, Leslie, 29
Shelley v. Kraemer, 14
Shepard, Harry, 265
shibari, 272
Shiraga, Kazuo, 208
Shoot (Burden performance piece), 234
Shrine: Mti (Saar altar), 115

Shrovetide in Old New Orleans (Reed), 114
Sieber, Roy, 163
Simmons, V. Joy, 182
Simon Rodia Commemorative Watts Renaissance of the Arts Festival, 79–80, 82, 86–90
Simpson, Merton, 146, 175
Sims, Lowery Stokes, 131
Sinaloa province (Mexico), 3
Siqueiros, David Alfaro, 39
Sirmans, Franklin, 241
Sir Watts (Purifoy sculpture), 82, *83*, 86
site, notion of, 16
Situation Theater, 210
Sixteenth Street Baptist Church, bombing of, 33
66 Signs of Neon (exhibition), 79–82, *80*, 84–86, 87, 89
slavery: abolition, 18; as collective past, 219, 221; housing segregation and, 12; narratives, 232; performance art and, 190–91; in poster series, 45–49; as violence against black bodies, 228
Smethurst, James, 38, 43, 44–45
Smith, Arenzo, 168
Smith, David, 60
Smith, Hughie Lee, 144
Smithson, Robert, 129, 262
Smithsonian Institution, 164
SNCC. *See* Student Nonviolent Coordinating Committee
social sculpture, use of term, 241
social space, 15–16
sociospatial, notion of, 16
Solnit, Rebecca, 70, 133
Some Lines for Jim Beckwourth (Puryear wall sculpture), 251
Some Tales (Puryear wall sculpture), 251
Song of Solomon (Morrison), 186
Sonnier, Keith, 186
Soulbook (magazine), 44
South of Pico, use as metaphor, 15
souvenirs, 131
Space Gallery, 214, 219
space(s): African American migration and, 7–12; art, 15–17; educational, 8, 11–12, 126, 137, 281n36; living, 12–14; safe, 6, 12, 23, 154, 186, 242; social, 15–16; utopic, 24, 265

spade motif, 229–30, 232, 233–34, 235–36, 238–39, 242, 262
Spade Mysteries (Hammons performance pieces), 229–30, 232–34, 262
Spaulding, Val, 175
Spiral artist's group, 146
Spiral Jetty (Smithson sculpture), 129
Spraypaint LACMA (or Project Pie in De/Face) (Asco conceptual art), 237
Springfield race riot (1908), 230–32
Standing Hang-Up #1 (Edwards sculpture), 59–60
Stations of the Cross (Asco walking mural), 237
Stendahl Art Galleries, 141
Stewart, Jacqueline, 40, 42
Stewart, Susan, 130
Stiles, Kristine, 228
Still Wind (Hassinger performance piece), 246
Stinson, John, 89, 154
Storr, Robert, 240
Strachan, Tavares, 160
"Strange Fruit" (Holiday song), 271
Student Nonviolent Coordinating Committee (SNCC), 64
Students for a Democratic Society (SDS), 273
Studio Museum in Harlem, 167, 183, 206
Studio Watts, 44, 64, 78, 95
Studio Z, 241–42, 243–44, 255, 257
suburbanization, 10–11
surrealism, 65, 134, 346n159
Swanson, David, 154
Swing Low (Nengudi installation), 188

Tanaka, Atsuko, 208, *209*
tangled temporalities, 217, 232
Tann, Curtis, 30, 50–51, *52*, 53, 89
Tanner, Henry O., 164, 166
Tanzawa, Paul, 79, 86
Tapscott, Horace, 44, 151
Tate, Greg, 242–43
Tejada, Roberto, 64–65
temporal drag, notion of, 219, 232
Ten Minutes (Hassinger performance piece), 255
Ten Mojo Secrets (Saar assemblage), 114
Thigpen, Joyce, 174

Thirty Contemporary Black Artists (exhibition), 65
Thomas, Alma, 72
Thomas, Bedwick Loyola. *See* Olugebefola, Ademola
Thompson, Bob, 211
Thompson, Robert Farris, 98, 100, 105, 201, 205–6, 218, 222–23
Three Graphic Artists (exhibition), 163–64, 169, 173
Three Spades (Hammons body print), 230, *231*
Tidwell, Billy, 87
Till, Emmett, 230
Tillet, Salamishah, 48, 100, 137, 217
Timothy Washington with one of his pieces outside Gallery 32 (Heliton photograph), *153*
Tinguely, Jean, 62
Tishman, Paul, 113, 163, 168, 206
To Catch a Unicorn (Saar etching), 50, 54–55, 56
Tonight with Belafonte (television show), 25, 26, 283n9
Touré, Sékou, 28–29
Tracy, Spencer, 24
Trans-fixed (Burden performance piece), 233
transformation, concept of, 20
Troupe, Quincy, 44
Trowell, Beatrice Parson Brown. *See* Brown, Beatrice Parson
Tubman, Harriet, 1–2, 18, 37, 45, 49, 144, 274–75
Tuchman, Maurice, 58–59, 170
Turner, Patricia A., 108
Twelve Trees (Hassinger installation), *21*, 253
Twelve Trees #2 (Hassinger installation), 253
Twenty-Eighth Street YMCA, 27–28
25 California Women of Art (exhibition), 119–20
Two Brothers I Have Had on Earth (White drawing), 28–29
Two Centuries of Black American Art (exhibition), 164–65, 170, 182, 322n66

UGRR:US2 (Biggers quilt), 275
UGRR:US2.2 (Biggers quilt), 275
Uhuru (White drawing), 31

Uhuru Day (Freedom Day), 87–88
Umbra, 114
Underground Railroad, 1
union membership, 9
United Nations, 35
United States Information Agency (USIA), 84
Unity Works, 178
Untitled (Purifoy), 81
urban(ness): assemblage and, 134–35; murals and, 151; urban removal, 14; urban renewal, 134–35; urban transformation, 6, 74–76; use of term, 4; violence, 237–38
Urge (Gilliam painting), 162
U.S.-Japan Security Treaty, 211
US Organization, 87, 186
utopianism, 186
utopic space, 24, 265
Uzuri, Imani, 274

Valdez, Patssi, 236
Vanguard Gallery, 38, 256
veil, trope of, 189
Veil of Tears (Saar assemblage), 124
Victor's Lament (di Suvero sculpture), 99
Viennese Actionism, 224, 262
Viet Nam War Games (D. Davis ceramic), 148
Viet-Watts, 273
Visual Communications, 98
Volkswagen Beetle, 146, 233
Voting Rights Act (1965), 18
Voudou, 116, 205
Voulkos, Peter, 52, 148

Waddy, Ruth, 9, 30, 45, 89, 142–43, *148*. See also *Black Artists on Art* (Lewis/Waddy)
Walker, Aida Overton, 190
Walker, Alice, 104, 107, 118
Walker, George, 110, 190
Walker, Kara, 36
Walker, Larry, 36, 156
Walker Art Center, 65
Walking, 148 Elements (Hassinger installation), 254, 255–56
walking figures, 6–7
Wall of Respect, The (OBAC mural), 46, 212
Wanted Poster series (White), 45–49, *47*

War Babies (exhibition), 161
Ward, Frazer, 234
Warhol, Andy, 31, 98, 132
Warp Trance (Nengudi video), 267
Washington, Booker T., 27–28, 143
Washington, Mary Helen, 49
Washington, Timothy, 45, *153*, 154, 163–64
Washington Gallery of Modern Art, 82, 83
Water Compositions (Nengudi sculptures), 193, 194, 203, 208
Watts Arts Festival. *See* Simon Rodia Commemorative Watts Renaissance of the Arts Festival
Watts Happening Coffee House, 145. *See also* Mafundi Institute
Watts neighborhood, Los Angeles, 14, *75*, 88
Watts Poets (anthology), 44
Watts Rebellion (1965), 2, 21, 35–36, 62, 78–79, 82, 84, 86–88, 108, 145, 181, 183–84, 273
Watts Remains (Purifoy sculpture), 84, *85*
Watts Repertory Theater Company, 64
Watts Riot (Purifoy painting/relief), 84
Watts Summer Festival, 30, *83*, 83–84, 87–89, 95, 172, 182
Wattstax Festival, 87, 172
Watts Towers Arts Center (WTAC), 27, 29, *75*, 75–81, *77*, 84, 86–90, 95–96, 139, 155, 166, 172
Watts Towers Jazz Festival, 151
way of making, use of term, 67–68
Weidman, Charles, 247
Weisser, Amy, 11
Welsh, Sue, 76–77, 90, 267
West, Kevin, 182
West, U.S., migration to, 5–6, 8
Weston, Randy, 162
Weusi, 85–86
Wharton, Diana, 220
Whirling, 10 Elements in a Circle (Hassinger installation), 254, 256
White, Charles, 1–2, *7*, 17–18, 20, 23, 26, 168; articles on, 27, 28, 30–31; building design, 27–38; commissions, 27–28, 37; cultural activism, 37–38; exhibitions, 26–27, 29, 30–31, 32–33, 163–64; fellowships, 26, 39, 41; in Hollywood, 24–27, 35, 37, 283n9; influence, 40; as leftist, 43–50; on libraries, 41–42; migration narratives, 39–43;

White, Charles (*continued*)
  murals, 42; park named after, 266; as progressive, 38–39; realism, 30–32; teaching career, 35–37, 38; on women, 49–50. *See also specific works*
White, Frances Barrett, 30
White, Frances Parson, 124
Whitey's Way (Saar assemblage), 109
Whiting, Cecile, 76, 78–79, 80
Whitney Museum of American Art, 169, 240
Widener, Daniel, 13
Wiener, Lawrence, 46
Wight, Frederick, 166. *See also* Frederick S. Wight Art Gallery
Wiley, Kehinde, 269
Wilkins, Craig L., 13
William Grant Still Community Arts Center, 172
Williams, Bert, 110, 190
Williams, Charles, 247
Williams, Paul Revere, 14, 27, 143
Williams, Richard J., 186
Williams, Saul, 270
Williams, William T., 40
Willis, Deborah, 41, 111–13
Wilson, Judith, 51–52, 244
Wilson, Mabel, 140, 142, 182–83
Wilson, William, 99, 119, 169–70
Wish You Were Here (Saar assemblage), 125, 126
witnessing, 231–32
woman's movement, 118–19, 250. *See also* feminism in art
Womanspace Gallery, 120

Womanspace Journal, 120
Women of Brewster Place, The (Naylor), 186
women's art. *See* feminism in art
Women's Building, 120, 121, 125
Wong, Tyrus, 273
Woodard, Beulah, 141, 144, 163, 273
Woodruff, Hale, 143, 146
World Wars I and II, migrations during, 4
Wreath (Hassinger sculpture), 252
Wright, Beryl, 252
Wright, Charles, 183
Wright, Richard, 13
WTAC. *See* Watts Towers Arts Center
Wynter, Sylvia, 110, 115

X, Malcolm, 62, 230
X, Marvin, 44

Yardbird Suite (Hammons installation), 232
yard work, use of term, 103–5, 125
Yoruba influences, 113–14, 116, 202–5, 207, 213, 257
Yoshihara, Jiro, 208
Young, Joseph E., 163
Young, Roderick "Quaku," *198–200*
Young Lords, 273
Yutaka, Matsuzawa, 211

Zermeño, Andrew, 46
Zero Dimension, 211
Zittel, Andrea, 267
Zodiac behind Glass series (Herms assemblages), 129
Zola, Emile, 35